1 MONTH OF
FREE
READING

at

www.ForgottenBooks.com

---◆---

By purchasing this book you are eligible for one month membership to ForgottenBooks.com, giving you unlimited access to our entire collection of over 1,000,000 titles via our web site and mobile apps.

To claim your free month visit:
www.forgottenbooks.com/free885310

ISBN 978-0-265-75734-5
PIBN 10885310

THE

HISTORY

OF

HERODOTUS.

A NEW ENGLISH VERSION, EDITED WITH COPIOUS NOTES AND APPENDICES,
ILLUSTRATING THE HISTORY AND GEOGRAPHY OF HERODOTUS, FROM THE
MOST RECENT SOURCES OF INFORMATION; AND EMBODYING
THE CHIEF RESULTS, HISTORICAL AND ETHNOGRAPHICAL,
WHICH HAVE BEEN OBTAINED IN THE PROGRESS
OF CUNEIFORM AND HIEROGLYPHICAL
DISCOVERY.

BY
GEORGE RAWLINSON, M. A.,
LATE FELLOW AND TUTOR OF EXETER COLLEGE, OXFORD.

ASSISTED BY
COL. SIR HENRY RAWLINSON, K.C.B., AND SIR J. G. WILKINSON, F.R.S.

IN FOUR VOLUMES.—VOL. II.

With Maps and Illustrations.

NEW YORK:
D. APPLETON & COMPANY, 443 & 445 BROADWAY
1866.

CONTENTS OF VOL. II.

THE HISTORY OF HERODOTUS.

THE SECOND BOOK, ENTITLED EUTERPÉ.

APPENDIX TO BOOK II.

CHAPTER I.

"THE EGYPTIANS BEFORE THE REIGN OF THEIR KING PSAMMETICHUS BELIEVED THEMSELVES TO BE THE MOST ANCIENT OF MANKIND."—Chap. 2. [G. W.]

CHAPTER II.

"THE EGYPTIANS WERE THE FIRST TO DISCOVER THE SOLAR YEAR."—
Chap. 4. [G. W.]

CHAPTER III.

"THE EGYPTIANS FIRST BROUGHT INTO USE THE NAMES OF THE TWELVE GODS
WHICH THE GREEKS ADOPTED FROM THEM."—Chap. 4. [G. W.]

CHAPTER IV.

"WHEN MŒRIS WAS KING," &c.—Chap. 18. [G. W.]

CHAPTER V.

"THEY HAVE TWO QUITE DIFFERENT KINDS OF WRITING, ONE OF WHICH IS
CALLED SACRED, THE OTHER COMMON."—Chap. 36. [G. W.]

CONTENTS OF VOL. II.

CHAPTER VI.

CHAPTER VII.

CHAPTER VIII.

HISTORY OF HERODOTUS.

THE THIRD BOOK, ENTITLED THALIA.

APPENDIX TO BOOK III.

ESSAY I.

OF THE WORSHIP OF VENUS URANIA THROUGHOUT THE EAST.—[G. W.]

ESSAY II.

ON THE MAGIAN REVOLUTION, AND THE REIGN OF THE PSEUDO-SMERDIS.

ESSAY III.

ON THE PERSIAN SYSTEM OF ADMINISTRATION AND GOVERNMENT.

ESSAY IV.

ON THE TOPOGRAPHY OF BABYLON.

LIST OF MAPS AND ILLUSTRATIONS.

———◆·◆———

BOOK II.

P. 11.

Map of the country about the mouth of the River Achelous.

P. 15, ch. 14, note [1].

(1.) The owner overlooking the ploughing and sowing of the land. A groom holds the horses of his chariot . . . . (*Thebes.*)

(2.) Ploughing scenes. One man drives the oxen, the other holds the plough. Over the latter is the word *hebi*, "plough;" and the other hieroglyphics seem to refer to the "driving" of the oxen. (Comp. the woodcut in p. 18) . . (*Tomb at the Pyramids.*)

P. 16, ch. 14.

(1.) Ploughing and hoeing. A small barrel stands at the end of the furrows, either containing seed, or rather some beverage for the ploughmen, as in Hom. Il. E. 541 . . . . (*Beni Hassan.*)

(2.) Ploughing, and sowing broadcast . . . . . (*Thebes.*)

P. 17, ch. 14.

The main and lateral canals of an estate . . . . (*Thebes.*)

P. 18, ch. 14, note [2].

(1.) Raising water by the "*Shadoof,*" or pole and bucket . . . (*Thebes.*)

(2.) Driving sheep over the land to tread in the grain . . (*Tomb at the Pyramids.*)

P. 19, ch. 14, note [3].

(1.) The *tritura*, or treading out the corn on the threshing-floor . . (*Thebes.*)

(2.) The *tritura*, and winnowing . . . . . . (*Thebes.*)

P. 25, ch. 19, note [5].

Name of the God Nilus, "*Hapi.*"

P. 36, ch. 19, note [9].

The three-headed Lion-God of Meroë.

P. 37, ch. 19, note [1].

Name of the Ethiopian king *Ergamun*, called by the Greeks *Ergamenes.*

P. 38, ch. 30, note [3].

Inscription of the Greek soldiers sent into Ethiopia by Psammetichus, written on the left leg of the Colossus to the S. of the door of the great temple at Aboosimbel.

P. 41, ch. 32, note [8].

View in the Little Oasis, near Zubbo.

APPENDIX TO BOOK II.

BOOK III.

APPENDIX TO BOOK III.

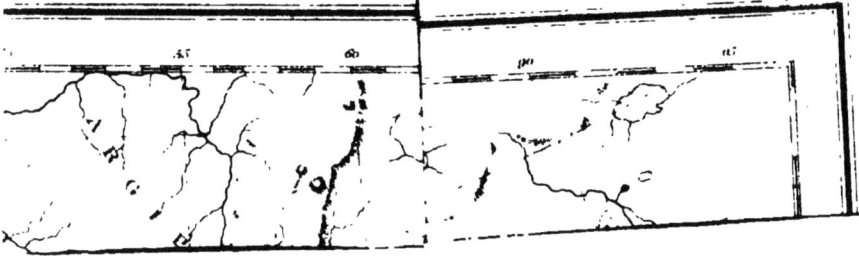

HISTORY OF HERODOTUS.

1. On the death of Cyrus, Cambyses his son by Cassandané daughter of Pharnaspes took the kingdom. Cassandané had died in the lifetime of Cyrus, who had made a great mourning for her at her death, and had commanded all the subjects of his empire to observe the like. Cambyses, the son of this lady and of Cyrus, regarding the Ionian and Æolian Greeks as vassals of his father, took them with him in his expedition against Egypt[1] among the other nations which owned his sway.

2. Now the Egyptians, before the reign of their king Psammetichus, believed themselves to be the most ancient of mankind.[2] Since Psammetichus, however, made an attempt to

---

[1] The date of the expedition of Cambyses against Egypt cannot be fixed with absolute certainty. Manetho, whose authority is of the greatest importance, gave Cambyses, according to Africanus (ap. Syncell. p. 141), a reign of six years in Egypt, which would place his invasion in B.C. 527. Eusebius, however (Chron. Can. Pars I. p. 105), reports Manetho differently, and himself agrees nearly with Diodorus (i. 68), who puts the expedition in the 3rd year of the 63rd Olympiad, or B.C. 525. This date, which is the one ordinarily received, is, on the whole, the most probable.

It is curious that Herodotus, whose principal object, in Books i. to v., is to trace the gradual growth of the Persian power, should say nothing directly of the first four years of Cambyses, omitting thereby so important an event as the subjection of Phœnicia, which was certainly accomplished by him. (See below, iii. 34, and comp. note to Book iii. ch. 19.) This period probably contained, besides the submission of Phœnicia, and of Cyprus, the reduction or submission of Cilicia, which lay in the same quarter. Cilicia, which was independent of the great Lydian kingdom (supra, i. 28), and which was not reduced, so far as appears, by either Cyrus or Harpagus, —for the contrary statement of Xenophon (Cyrop. I. i. § 4), who ascribes to Cyrus the conquest of Cilicia, Cyprus, Phœnicia, and Egypt (!) deserves no credit—must have been added to the empire either by Cambyses or by Darius, and is most probably a conquest of the former. These events would serve to occupy Cambyses during his first four years, and explain the reason why he deferred the Egyptian expedition, already designed by Cyrus (i. 153) till his fifth.

[2] This affectation of extreme antiquity is strongly put by Plato in his Timæus (p. 22, B), where the Greek nation is taxed by the Egyptians with being in its infancy as compared with them. According to the account which Herodotus gives below

discover who were actually the primitive race,[2] they have been of opinion that while they surpass all other nations, the Phrygians surpass them in antiquity. This king, finding it impossible to make out by dint of inquiry what men were the most ancient, contrived the following method of discovery :—He took two children of the common sort, and gave them over to a herdsman to bring up at his folds, strictly charging him to let no one utter a word in their presence, but to keep them in a sequestered cottage, and from time to time introduce goats to their apartment, see that they got their fill of milk, and in all other respects look after them. His object herein was to know, after the indistinct babblings of infancy were over, what word they would first articulate. It happened as he had anticipated. The herdsman obeyed his orders for two years, and at the end of that time, on his one day opening the door of their room and going in, the children both ran up to him with outstretched arms, and distinctly said "Becos." When this first happened the herdsman took no notice ; but afterwards when he observed, on coming often to see after them, that the word was constantly in their mouths, he informed his lord, and by his command brought the children into his presence. Psammetichus then himself heard them say the word, upon which he proceeded to make inquiry what people there was who called anything "becos," and hereupon he learnt that "becos" was the Phrygian name for bread.[4] In consideration of this circumstance the Egyptians

(ch. 142), the priests in some places would seem to have pretended, in their discussions with foreigners, to an antiquity of above 11,000 years for their nation. The entire number of years, however, assigned by Manetho to his 30 dynasties of kings did not greatly exceed 5000, and Syncellus reports Manetho as claiming for the monarchy no longer actual duration than 3555 years before the conquest by Alexander. (See Müller's Fr. Hist. Gr., vol. ii. p. 534.) Even this view, however, seems to be extravagant, for it places the accession of Menes in B.C. 3883, which is considerably before the Deluge, according to the highest computation. Still the Egyptian numbers are moderate compared with those of some other nations. The Babylonians counted 468,000 years from their first king Alorus to the conquest by Cyrus (Beros. ap. Euseb. Chron. Can. i. p. 5–18 ; compare Brandis, Rerum Ass. Temp. Emendata, pp. 16–17) ; and the Indians and Chinese trace their history for a still longer period.

The Egyptian claims to a high *relative* antiquity had, no doubt, a solid basis of truth. It is probable that a settled monarchy was established in Egypt earlier than in any other country. Babylonian *history* does not go back beyond B.C. 2234. Egyptian begins nearly 500 years earlier.

[3] The disposition on the part of Psammetichus towards scientific enquiry is noticed again in ch. 28. Perhaps the contact with the Greeks, which began in his reign (ch. 154), caused the development of the Egyptian mind in this direction.

[4] The word βέκος has been thought to connect with the German "backen" and our "bake." Lassen, however, throws doubt on this connexion, and suggests a formation from the Sanscrit root *pac*, which becomes (he says) in Greek πέκ-ω, Latin *coq*-uo, German *coch-en*, our "cook," Servian *pec-en*, &c. (See his Essay 'Ueber die Lykischen Inschriften, und die Alten Sprachen Klein Asiens,' p. 369.)

yielded their claims, and admitted the greater antiquity of the Phrygians.

3. That these were the real facts I learnt at Memphis from the priests of Vulcan. The Greeks, among other foolish tales, relate that Psammetichus had the children brought up by women whose tongues he had previously cut out; but the priests said their bringing up was such as I have stated above. I got much other information also from conversation with these priests while I was at Memphis, and I even went to Heliopolis and to Thebes,[5] expressly to try whether the priests of those places would agree in their accounts with the priests at Memphis. The Heliopolitans have the reputation of being the best skilled in history of all the Egyptians.[6] What they told me concerning their religion it is not my intention to repeat, except the names of their deities, which I believe all men know equally. If I relate anything else concerning these matters, it will only be when compelled to do so by the course of my narrative.[7]

4. Now with regard to mere human matters, the accounts which they gave, and in which all agreed, were the following. The Egyptians, they said, were the first to discover the solar year, and to portion out its course into twelve parts. They obtained this knowledge from the stars. (To my mind they contrive their year much more cleverly than the Greeks, for these last every other year intercalate a whole month,[8] but the Egyptians, dividing the year into twelve months of thirty days each, add every year a space of five days besides, whereby the

But this connexion, which may be allowed, does not prevent the other from being also real. See on this point, and on the general subject of the Phrygian language, the Essays appended to Book i. Essay xi., " On the Ethnic Affinities of the Nations of Western Asia," § 12. If the story has any truth in it, the children probably (as Larcher observes) were imitating the bleating of the goats. (See note in Appendix to this Book, CH. i. § 1.)

[5] The name of Thebes is almost always written in the plural by the Greeks and Romans—Θῆβαι, Thebæ—but Pliny writes, " Thebe portarum centum nobilis fama." The Egyptian name of Thebes was Ap, or A'pé, the " head," or " capital." This, with the feminine article, became Tápé, and in the Memphitic dialect Thapé, pronounced, as by the Copts, Thaba, whence Θῆβαι in Ionic Greek. The oldest known monuments in Western Thebes were of Amun-m-he I. at Karnak, and of his successor Osirtasen I., who ruled immediately after the sixth dynasty ended at Memphis, about B. C. 2080.—[G. W.]

[6] Heliopolis was the great seat of learning, and the university of Egypt ; and that it was one of the oldest cities is proved by the obelisk of Osirtasen I. of the 12th dynasty. See below note [7] on ch. 8.—[G. W.]

[7] For instances of the reserve which Herodotus here promises, see chapters 45, 46, 47, 48, 61, 62, 65, 81, 132, 170, and 171. The secrecy in matters of religion, which was no doubt enjoined upon Herodotus by the Egyptian priests, did not seem strange to a Greek, who was accustomed to it in the "mysteries" of his own countrymen.

[8] Vide supra, i. 32, and see note ad loc.

circuit of the seasons is made to return with uniformity.[9]) The Egyptians, they went on to affirm, first brought into use the names of the twelve gods,[10] which the Greeks adopted from them ; and first erected altars, images, and temples to the gods ; and also first engraved upon stone the figures of animals. In most of these cases they proved to me that what they said was true. And they told me that the first man[1] who ruled over Egypt was Mên,[2] and that in his time all Egypt, except the Thebaic canton, was a marsh,[3] none of the land below lake

[9] This at once proves they intercalated the quarter day, making their year to consist of 365¼ days, without which the seasons could not return to the same periods. The fact of Herodotus not understanding their method of intercalation does not argue (as Goguet seems to think) that the Egyptians were ignorant of it. Their having fixed the Sothic period in 1322 B. C., and ascertained that 1460 Sothic were equal to 1461 vulgar or "vague" years, as well as the statements of ancient authors, decide the question. But for the date of a king's reign they used the old year of 360 days ; and the months were not reckoned from his accession, but were part of the current year. Thus, if he came to the throne on the 10th of the last month of the year, or Mesóré, he would date in the 1st year, the 12th month, the 10th day ; and his second year would be in the following month Thoth, or 25 days after his accession. The Jews appear to have done the same. (See the Appendix to this Book, CH. ii.)—[G. W.]

[10] Some suppose these to be the twelve gods of Olympus, the same as the Consentes of the Romans, given by Varro,

"Juno, Vesta, Minerva, Ceres, Diana, Venus, Mars,
Mercurius, Jovi, Neptunus, Vulcanus, Apollo,"

and that they do not refer to any arrangement of the Egyptian Pantheon ; but in ch. 145 Herodotus distinctly mentions the three orders of Egyptian gods, the first two consisting of eight and twelve, and the third "born of the twelve." He also shows how much older some were considered in Egypt than in Greece ; Pan being one of the eight oldest, and Hercules of the twelve ; and says (ii. 43) that Neptune was a "god quite unknown to the Egyptians." Again in ch. 4 he distinctly states they had twelve gods. The Etruscans had twelve great gods ; the Romans probably derived that number from them.—(See note in Appendix, CH. iii. § 1.)—[G. W.]

[1] According to the chronological tables of the Egyptians the gods were represented to have reigned first, and after them Menes the Thinite ; and the same is found recorded in the Turin Papyrus of Kings, as well as in Manetho and other writers. Manetho gives them in this order:—1. Vulcan (Pthah) ; 2. Helios (Re), the Sun ; 3. Agathodæmon (Hor-Hat, or possibly Noum) ; 4. Chronos (Seb) ; 5. Osiris ; 6. Typhon (properly Seth) ; and 7. Horus. In the Papyrus there remain only Seb, Osiris, Seth, Horus, Thoth, Thmei (or Mei "Truth "), and apparently Horus (the Younger), who was "the last god who reigned in Egypt." (See n. [5] ch. 43, n. [5] ch. 99, and Tn. P. W., p. 7–11. Menes (Menai) is represented by some to have been a conqueror ; not that the Egyptians then obtained possession of the valley of the Nile for the first time ; for he was from This, and their early immigration from Asia happened long before. But the establishment of royalty introduced luxury into Egypt, and Tnephachthus (Technatis of Plut. de Is. 8), the father of Bocchoris of the 24th dynasty, put up a curse "against Meinis" (Menes) in a temple at Thebes for having led the Egyptians from their previous simple and frugal habits. Diodorus (i. 45) says also that Menas was the first who introduced the worship of the gods, and sacrifices, the use of letters, couches, and rich carpets. Cp. Cicero, Tusc. Disp. v. 35 on Frugal Repasts. See App. CH. viii.—[G. W.]

[2] Herodotus does not call this king Menes, or Menas (as Diodorus, i. 45), but Mên. The Egyptian form is M'na according to Bunsen and Lepsius.

[3] Note, besides the improbability of such a change, the fact that Menes was the

Mœris then showing itself above the surface of the water.   This is a distance of seven days' sail from the sea up the river.

5. What they said of their country seemed to me very reasonable. For any one who sees Egypt, without having heard a word about it before, must perceive, if he has only common powers of observation, that the Egypt to which the Greeks go in their ships is an acquired country, the gift of the river.[4]   The same is true of the land above the lake, to the distance of three days' voyage, concerning which the Egyptians say nothing, but which is exactly the same kind of country.

The following is the general character of the region.   In the first place, on approaching it by sea, when you are still a day's sail from the land, if you let down a sounding-line you will bring up mud, and find yourself in eleven fathoms' water, which shows that the soil washed down by the stream extends to that distance.[5]

reputed founder of Memphis, which is far to the north of this lake; and that Busiris, near the coast, the reputed burial-place of Osiris, Buto, Pelusium, and other towns of the Delta, were admitted by the Egyptians to be of the earliest date.—[G. W.]

[4] Vide infrà, ch. 10, and note ad loc. The theory had been started by Hecatæus, who made use of the same expression. (See Arrian. Exp. Al. v. 6.)

[Herodotus observes that the same might be said of the country above for three days' sail; and exactly the same appearance might have struck him throughout the whole valley of the Nile. But though the depth of the soil has greatly increased, and is still increasing, in various ratios in different parts of the valley, the first deposit did not take place after man existed in Egypt; and as marine productions have not been met with in boring to the depth of 40 feet in the Delta, it is evident that its soil was deposited from the very first on a space already above the level of the Mediterranean.   The formation of the Delta of Egypt is not like that of some other rivers, where the land has been protruded far into the sea; on the contrary, the Nile, after pursuing its course through the alluvial soil, enters the sea at the same distance north of the Lake Mœris as it did in the age of the early kings of Egypt. The sites of the oldest cities are as near the sea-shore as when they were inhabited of old; and yet the period now elapsed since some of them were built is nearly double that between Menes and Herodotus. I have already in another work explained the mistake respecting the Pharos I. having once been distant from Egypt (At. Eg. W. vol. i. p. 7), owing to the name Αἴγυπτος in Homer signifying (not the country, but) the "Nile;" and the Pharos I. and the coast of Alexandria being both *rock*, the distance between them has always been the same. Another great reason for the Delta not encroaching on the sea is that the land is always sinking along the north coast of Egypt (while it rises at the head of the Red Sea); and there is evidence to show that the Mediterranean has encroached, and that the Delta has lost instead of gaining, along the whole of its extent from Canopus to Pelusium. —G. W.]

[5] The distance you see the Mediterranean discoloured by the Nile during the inundation is very great, and the same takes place in a minor degree at the mouths of rivers on the Syrian coast, but without forming any deltas; nor is the shallow sea off the coast of Egypt more a part of the Delta of the Nile now than when sounded in Herodotus' time, about 2300 years ago ; and 11 orgyies (or fathoms) at a day's sail from the coast would alarm a sailor even at the present day. For you only come into 11 fathoms water at about 12 or 13 miles off the coast, about Abookir; and at 25 or 30 miles you have 60, 70, 80, and 90 fathoms, with sand and mud. At 5 or 6 miles from the mouth of the Nile the water on the surface is nearly fresh, and the bottom

6. The length of the country along shore, according to the bounds that we assign to Egypt, namely from the Plinthinétic gulf[6] to lake Serbônis, which extends along the base of Mount Casius, is sixty schœnes.[7] The nations whose territories are scanty measure them by the fathom ; those whose bounds are less confined, by the furlong ; those who have an ample territory, by the parasang ; but if men have a country which is very vast, they measure it by the schœne.[8] Now the length of the parasang is thirty furlongs,[9] but the schœne, which is an Egyptian measure, is sixty furlongs.[1] Thus the coast-line of Egypt would extend a length of three thousand six hundred furlongs.

7. From the coast inland as far as Heliopolis the breadth of Egypt is considerable, the country is flat, without springs, and full of swamps.[2] The length of the route from the sea up to

mostly a stiff mud. The longest day's sail, according to Herodotus (iv. 86), is 700 stadia, about 79½ Eng. m., or (infra, ch. 9) 540 stadia, about 61 miles, where the soundings would be at least the same number of fathoms.—[G. W.]

[6] Plinthiné was a town near the Lake Mareotis (Strabo, xvii. p. 1138 ; Ptol. iv. c. 5 ; Scylax. Perip. 105). From it the lake, as well as the bay, was sometimes called "Plinthinetan." The name "Arapotes," given in Pliny (v. 10) to this lake is evidently a false reading. It should be Racotis, and applies to Alexandria. —[G. W.]

[7] The schœne, an Egyptian measure, varied from 30 and 32 to 40 stadia, according to Pliny (v. 10, xii. 14) ; and Strabo distinctly says (xvii. p. 1140) it was of various lengths in different parts of Egypt. Herodotus says it was equal to 60 stadia, making the length of the coast 3600 stadia, which, at 600 feet to the stadium, would be more than 400 Eng. m. The real length of the coast from the Bay of Plinthiné at Taposiris, or at Plinthiné, even to the *eastern* end of the Lake Serbonis, is by the shore little more than 300 Eng. m. Diodorus estimates the breadth of Egypt by the coast at 2000 stadia ; and Strabo gives only 1770 stadia from the Temple of Jupiter Casius at the Serbonic Lake to Pharos, which, added to 200 stadia to Taposiris, make 1970 stadia. The real distance from Casius to Pharos is about 1944 stadia, and from Pharos to Taposiris or to Plinthiné, nearly 260, being a total of about 2204 stadia.—[G. W.]

[8] Some might imagine this to be confirmed by modern custom ; the English measuring by miles, the French by leagues, the Germans by the "meile," of more than four times our mile in length ; but this will not hold good generally, and the Russian werst is only about two-thirds of an English mile, or 1167 yards.— [G. W.]

[9] See note on Book v. ch. 53.

[1] This would be more than 36,000 English feet, or nearly 7 miles. The Greek σχοῖνος, "rope," is the same word which signifies rush, of which ropes are still made in Egypt and in other countries, and it has been singularly transferred to the skein of our modern measure for thread and silk.—[G. W.]

[2] Heliopolis stood on the edge of the desert, about 4¼ miles to the E. of the apex of the Delta ; but the alluvial land of the Delta extended 5 miles farther to the eastward of that city, to what is now the Birket-el-Hag. The mountains to the S. of Heliopolis closing in to the westward towards the Nile make the valley narrow in that part, and throughout the rest of its course from the S. The southern point of the Delta appears formerly to have extended further up the river (*i. e.* south) than at present, and to have been nearly opposite the modern village of Shoobra (see M. Eg. W. vol. i. p. 401). At the time and long after Cairo was founded, the Nile ran more to the eastward, as Mr. Lane has shown, under its western walls.

PLAN OF HELIOPOLIS

Sarony, Major & Knapp Lith. N.Y.

Pub'd by D. Appleton & Co N.Y.

Heliopolis is almost exactly the same as that of the road which runs from the altar of the twelve gods at Athens[3] to the temple

The accumulation of alluvial soil at the base of the obelisk of Osirtasen at Heliopolis, as around the sitting Colossi in the plain at Thebes, has been often appealed to for determining the rise of the alluvial soil within a certain period, but as there is no possibility of ascertaining how far it stood above the reach of the inundation when first put up, we have *no base for any calculation.* The water of the inundation having been for ages kept out, according to Egyptian custom, from the enclosure in which the temple stood, the accumulation of deposit there was the more rapid when in after times the water was admitted, which readily accounts for " so great a thickness of one kind of sediment without any sign of successive deposition," which seems to have presented a difficulty to Mr. Horner.

I have supposed the deposit to have been raised at Elephantiné about 9 feet in 1700 years, and at Thebes about 7; but this is very uncertain. The increase is of course much less the farther you descend the valley, and at the mouth of the Nile it is very small; for it is there lessened far more than in the same decreasing ratio as between Elephantiné and Heliopolis, owing to the greater extent of land, east and west, over which the inundation spreads, so that in a section representing the accumulated soil and the level of the low Nile, the angle of inclination would be much smaller from the apex of the Delta to the sea, than from Thebes to the Delta. "Thus," as Mr. Horner says, "while the rise of the river at the island of Roda is 24 feet, near Ramanyeh, about 65 miles in a direct line N. of the apex of the Delta, the difference between the highest and the lowest water is about 13 feet, and at Rosetta and Damietta not more than 42 inches." The Nile at Asouan is said to be 300 feet above its level at Cairo, and 365 above the Mediterranean. The distance from the Rosetta mouth to Cairo is 154 miles, from Cairo to Asouan 578, following all the bends of the river, which give a total of 732 miles from the sea to the First Cataract.

According to M. Linant, the volume of water poured during 24 hours into the Mediterranean by the Nile, when low, is—

		Cubic mètres.
By the Rosetta branch	. . . . .	79,582,551,728
By the Damietta branch	. . . . .	71,083,840,640
Cubic mètres	. .	150,566,892,368
When high	. . . .	478,317,838,960
" "	. . . .	227,196,828,480
		705,514,667,440

At Sioôt, which is about half-way from Asouan to Teráneh, the French engineers found that in every second of time the mass of water that passes any one point is 678 cubic mètres at low Nile, and 10,247 at high Nile; and, according to M. Linant, at Cairo 414 cubic mètres at low, and 9440 at high, Nile. (See Mr. Horner's Memoir in Trans. R. Society, vol. 145, p. 101–138.)

The average fall of the river between Asouan and Cairo is " little more than half a foot in a mile, viz. 0·54 feet, and from the foot of the First Cataract to the sea is 0·524 feet in a mile;" but from Cairo to the Damietta mouth, according to the same authority (ib. p. 114), "the average fall is only 3¼ inches in a mile."— [G. W.]

[3] The altar of the twelve gods at Athens stood in the Forum, and seems from this passage and from one or two inscriptions (Rose, Tab. xxxii. p. 251; cf. Boeckh, Corp. Ins. i. i. p. 82) to have served, like the gilt pillar (*milliarium aureum*) in the Forum at Rome, as a central point from which to measure distances. It was originally erected by Pisistratus, the son of the tyrant Hippias, but was afterwards enlarged and beautified by the Athenian people. (Thucyd. vi. 54.) Adjacent to this altar was the enclosure where votes for ostracism were taken. (Leake's Athens, p. 168, note ᵇ.)

of Olympian Jove at Pisa.⁴ If a person made a calculation he would find but a very little difference between the two routes, not more than about fifteen furlongs ; for the road from Athens to Pisa falls short of fifteen hundred furlongs by exactly fifteen,⁵ whereas the distance of Heliopolis from the sea is just the round number.⁶

8. As one proceeds beyond Heliopolis⁷ up the country, Egypt

⁴ This mention of Pisa is curious, considering that it had been destroyed so long before (B. C. 572) by the Eleans (Pausan. VI. xxii. § 2), and that it had certainly not been rebuilt by the close of the Peloponnesian war (Xen. Hell. III. ii. § 31, comp. VII. iv. § 28). Probably Herodotus intends Olympia itself rather than the ancient town, which was six stades distant (Schol. ad Pind. Ol. x. 55) in the direction of Harpinna (Paus. VI. xxi.–xxii.), and therefore doubtless in the vicinity of the modern village of *Mirâka* (see Leake's Morea, ii. p. 211), with which some are inclined to identify it. (Müller's Dorians, ii. p. 463, E. T. Kiepert, Blatt. vii.)

⁵ The correctness of this measurement, as compared with others in Herodotus, or indeed in the Greek writers generally, has been noticed by Col. Leake (Journal of Geograph. Soc. vol. ix. part i. p. 11). There is no reason to believe that the road was actually measured, but it was so frequently traversed that the distance came to be estimated very nearly at its true length.

⁶ Fifteen hundred furlongs (stades) are about equal to 173 English miles. [The real distance of Heliopolis from the sea, at the old Sebennytic mouth, is about 110 miles, or 100 in a direct line.—G. W.]

⁷ The site of Heliopolis is still marked by the massive walls that surrounded it, and by a granite obelisk bearing the name of Osirtasen I. of the 12th dynasty, dating about 3900 years ago. It was one of two that stood before the entrance to the temple of the Sun, at the inner end of an avenue of sphinxes ; and the apex, like some of those at Thebes, was once covered with bronze (doubtless gilt), as is shown by the stone having been cut to receive the metal casing, and by the testimony of Arab history. Tradition also speaks of the other obelisk of Heliopolis, and of the bronze taken from its apex. Pliny (36, 8) supposes that Mitres, the first king who erected an obelisk, held his court at Heliopolis, and that those monuments were dedicated to the Sun ; but that depended upon what god the temple belonged to, the obelisks at Thebes being erected to Amun, and in other places to other deities. The name of Heliopolis was éi-n'-re, "the abode of the Sun," from which the Hebrew On or Aôn corrupted into Aven (Ezek. xxx. 17) was taken, and which was translated Beth-Shemesh, "the house of the Sun" (Jerem. xliii. 13). The Arabs called it Ain Shems, "fountain of the Sun," from the spring there, which the credulous Christians believed to have been salt until the Virgin's visit to Egypt. The Arabic name of the neighbouring village, *Matareéh*, was supposed to signify "fresh water," and to refer to the fountain ; but this is an error, as the masculine word Ma, "water," would require the name to be *Ma-taree*. (See.M. Eg. W., vol. i. p. 295; and on the balsam of Heliopolis see my n. on ch. 107, B. iii.) In later times the artificial Amnis Trajanus ran a short distance to the northward of Heliopolis; and on that side of the city were lakes supplied with water from the neighbouring canal. The large and lofty crude brick walls of Heliopolis enclosed an irregular area measuring 3750 feet by 2870, having the houses on the north side covering a space of 575,000 square feet, to the south of which stood the temple of the Sun. This occupied a large portion of a separate enclosure, or *temenos*, at one side of the town ; and a long avenue of sphinxes, described by Strabo, led to the two obelisks before the temple (*see plan*). Some of the sphinxes may still be traced, as well as the ruins of the houses, which, like those of Bubastis, stood on a higher level than the temenos, owing to their foundations having been raised from time to time, while the temple re mained in its original site. In Strabo's time the houses were shown where Plato and Eudoxus lived while studying under the priests of Heliopolis; but the city

becomes narrow, the Arabian range of hills, which has a direction from north to south, shutting it in upon the one side, and the Libyan range upon the other.   The former ridge runs on without a break, and stretches away to the sea called the Erythræan ; it contains the quarries[8] whence the stone was cut for the pyramids of Memphis : and this is the point where it ceases its first direction, and bends away in the manner above indicated.[9]   In its greatest length from east to west, it is, as I have been informed, a distance of two months' journey ; towards the extreme east its skirts produce frankincense.   Such are the chief features of this range.   On the Libyan side, the other ridge whereon the pyramids stand, is rocky and covered with sand ; its direction is the same as that of the Arabian ridge in the first part of its course.   Above Heliopolis, then, there is no great breadth of territory for such a country as Egypt, but during four days' sail Egypt is narrow ;[1] the valley between the two ranges is a level

which had for ages been the seat of learning, lost its importance after the accession of the Ptolemies, and the schools of Alexandria took the place of the ancient colleges of Heliopolis (see Strab. xvii.).   The walls are in some places double, but throughout of great strength ; and here and there the positions of the gates may still be traced.   From one of these on the S.E. side a large road ran through the desert to the Red Sea, and a smaller one led across the Mokuttum hills (behind Cairo) by what is called the " petrified forest," and rejoined the valley of the Nile near the quarries of " the Trojan hill."   A stone gateway has lately been found at Heliopolis, with the name of Thothmes III.—[G. W.]

[8] The quarries from which the stone for the casing of the pyramids was taken are in that part of the modern El-Mokuttum range of hills called by Strabo the "Trojan mountain" (Τρωικὸν ὄρος. xvii. p. 1147), and now Gebel Mâsarah or Toora Mâsarah, from the two villages below them on the Nile.   Toora, though signifying in Ar. a " canal," is evidently the Troja of Strabo, which stood in this neighbourhood, and which he pretends was built by and named after the Trojan captives of Menelaus.   But the probability is that some Egyptian name was converted by the Greeks into Troja, and by the Arabs into Toora ; and we may perhaps ascribe to it the same origin as the " Tyrian camp " at Memphis mentioned by Herodotus (see note [8] on ch. 112).   The employment of the stone in the pyramids, and the names of the early kings found there, show that these quarries were already used by the ancient Egyptians from the time of the 4th to the 18th dynasty (as well as after that period), and consequently during the Shepherd occupation of Memphis.   On one tablet was the representation of a large stone on a sledge drawn by oxen, having the name of Amosis (Ames), the first king of the 18th dynasty : and on others the date of the 42nd year of Amun-m-he (3rd of the 12th dynasty) and the names of later kings.   The quarries are still worked by the modern Egyptians, and this even-grained magnesian limestone is used for floors of rooms and for other building purposes.—[G. W.]

[9] That is, towards the Erythræan Sea, or Arabian Gulf.   [The bend of the mountain is really where Cairo now stands, whence it runs towards the Red Sea. The notion of Herodotus respecting its extent to the E. was vague, and he evidently confounds, or connects, it with the peninsula of Arabia, the country of incense ; though he speaks of the mountain-range on the E. of the Nile extending southwards along the Red Sea.   Its breadth from the Nile to the Red Sea direct is 82 miles in lat. 30°, increasing to 175 in lat. 24°.—G. W.]

[1] That is, from Heliopolis southward ; and he says it becomes broader again beyond that point.   His 200 stadia are about 22½ to 23 miles.   The whole breadth

plain, and seemed to me to be, at the narrowest point, not more than two hundred furlongs across from the Arabian to the Libyan hills.   Above this point Egypt again widens.[2]

9. From Heliopolis to Thebes is nine days' sail up the river ; the distance is eighty-one schœnes, or 4860 furlongs.[3]   If we now put together the several measurements of the country we shall find that the distance along shore is, as I stated above, 3600 furlongs, and the distance from the sea inland to Thebes 6120 furlongs.   Further, it is a distance of eighteen hundred furlongs from Thebes to the place called Elephantiné.

10. The greater portion of the country above described seemed to me to be, as the priests declared, a tract gained by the inhabitants.   For the whole region above Memphis, lying between the two ranges of hills that have been spoken of, appeared evidently to have formed at one time a gulf of the sea.[4]   It resembles (to compare small things with great) the parts about Ilium and Teuthrania, Ephesus, and the plain of the Mæander.[5]   In all these regions the land has been formed by rivers, whereof the greatest is not to compare for size with any one of the five

of the valley from the Eastern to the Western hills is only from 12 to 16 m.   This must have appeared a very great change after leaving the spacious Delta, a level plain, without any mountains being seen to the E. or W.   The four days, reckoning, as he does, 540 stadia to a day, would be about 245 Eng. m., or to about the vicinity of Sioót; but it cannot be the spot, where he thinks the valley "becomes broader," according to his calculation of nine days to Thebes, which would require it to be less than half-way, or about Gebel-aboofaydeh, and this would agree still less with his description of the increasing breadth of the valley, which is there only 7 miles from the Eastern to the Western hills.—[G. W.]

[2] Compare the description of Scylax (Peripl. p. 103), who says that Egypt is shaped like a double-headed battle-axe (πελέκυς or bipennis), the neck which joins the two heads being in the vicinity of Memphis.

[3] The nine days' sail, which Herodotus reckons at 4860 stadia, would give about 552 Eng. miles ; but the distance is only about 421, even following the course of the river.   From the sea to Thebes he reckons 6120 stadia, at the least computation —about 700 miles—but the distance is by modern measurement only 566 miles ; and his distance of 1800 stadia from Thebes to Elephantine, at least 206 miles, exceeds the truth by above 700 stadia, being really 124 miles.—[G. W.]

[4] See above, notes on ch. 5.   Herodotus says, most of the country is "acquired by the Egyptians," and "a gift of the river;" but as the same deposit continues throughout the whole valley, these remarks can only apply to the *original* formation of the land; the soil since the time that Egypt was first inhabited being only deeper, and more extended E. and W. towards the mountains; and whatever form the valley may have had in the early ages of the world, it could not have been a gulf of the sea since Egypt was inhabited.—[G. W.]

[5] In some of these places the gain of the land upon the sea has been very great. This is particularly the case at the mouth of the Mæander, where the alluvial plain has advanced in the historic times a distance of 12 or 13 miles.   (See note to Book i. ch. 142.)   At Ephesus there is now a plain of three miles between the temple and the sea (Leake's Asia Minor, p. 259, note), which has been entirely created since the days of Herodotus.   At the mouths of the Scamander and the Caïcus (which drained Teuthrania, Strab. xiii. p. 883, Plin. H. N. v. 30), the advance of the land, though less, is still very perceptible.

mouths of the Nile.[6]   I could mention other rivers also, far inferior to the Nile in magnitude, that have effected very great changes. Among these not the least is the Acheloüs, which, after passing through Acarnania, empties itself into the sea opposite the islands called Echinades,[7] and has already joined one half of them to the continent.[8]

[6] This signifies the natural branches of the Nile; and when seven are reckoned, they include the two artificial ones, the Bolbitine' and Bucolic or Phatmetic, which Herodotus says were the work of man. See note [1] on ch. 17.—[G. W.]

[7] These islands, which still bear the same name among the educated Greeks, consist of two clusters, linked together by the barren and rugged *Petald*. The northern cluster contains 15 or 16 islands, the principal of which is *Dhragondra*. The southern contains only five or six: the most important are *Oxiá*, *Makrí*, and *Vrómona*. They are British dependencies, being included in the Ionian islands. Except *Oxiá*, they all lie north of the present mouth of the Acheloüs (*Aspro*). See Leake's Northern Greece, vol. iii. pp. 30–1.

[8] That the Acheloüs in ancient times formed fresh land at its mouth with very

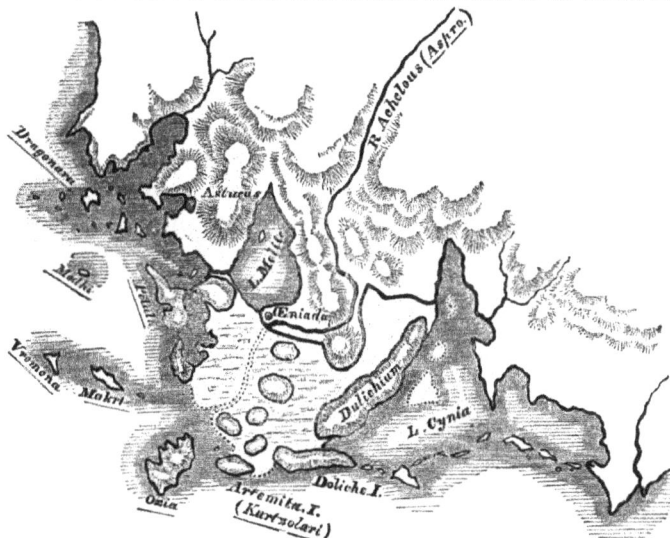

Map of the country about the mouth of the River Acheloüs, chiefly after Kiepert.
N.B. The dark lines mark the ancient coast and islands.

great rapidity is certain, from the testimony of various writers besides Herodotus. Thucydides (ii. 102), Scylax (Peripl. p. 81), and Strabo (i. p. 87), all speak in equally strong terms on the subject. Thucydides even conjectures that in a short space of time all the Echinades would become portions of the continent. This prediction has failed; and at present, owing probably to the projection of the coast and the sweep of the current round it, the advance of the land is very slow and gradual. (Leake, iii. p. 570.) So far as appears, no island has been added to the shore since the time of Strabo. Col. Leake indeed says that he could only find two heights in this vicinity which seemed to him to have once been islands, viz., the peninsula of *Kurtzolari* (Strabo's Artemita), and a small hill opposite *Petald;* but it may be questioned whether the representation of Kiepert (Blatt. xiii.) does not give a truer idea of the actual growth of the land.

11. In Arabia, not far from Egypt, there is a long and narrow gulf running inland from the sea called the Erythræan,[2] of which I will here set down the dimensions. Starting from its innermost recess, and using a row-boat, you take forty days to reach the open main, while you may cross the gulf at its widest part in the space of half a day. In this sea there is an ebb and flow of the tide every day.[1] My opinion is, that Egypt was formerly very much such a gulf as this—one gulf penetrated from the sea that washes Egypt on the north,[2] and extended itself towards Ethiopia ; another entered from the southern ocean, and stretched towards Syria ; the two gulfs ran into the land so as almost to meet each other, and left between them only a very narrow tract of country. Now if the Nile should choose to divert his waters from their present bed into this Arabian gulf, what is there to hinder it from being filled up by the stream within, at the utmost, twenty thousand years ? For my part, I think it would be filled in half the time. How then should not a gulf, even of much greater size, have been filled up in the ages that passed before I was born, by a river that is at once so large and so given to working changes ?

12. Thus I give credit to those from whom I received this account of Egypt, and am myself, moreover, strongly of the same opinion, since I remarked that the country projects into the sea further than the neighbouring shores, and I observed that there were shells upon the hills,[3] and that salt exuded from the soil

---

[2] The Greeks generally did not give the name Erythræan, or Red Sea, to the Arabian Gulf, but to all that part of the Indian Ocean reaching from the Persian Gulf to India (as in ii. 102; and iv. 39). It was also applied to the Persian Gulf (i. 1, 180, 189), and Herodotus sometimes gives it to the Arabian Gulf, and even the western branch between Mount Sinai and Egypt (ii. 158). Even Taprobané (now Ceylon) was placed in the Erythræan Sea, towards the Golden Chersonesus. Agatharcides is careful in distinguishing the "Red Sea" from the Arabian Gulf. Herodotus reckons the length of this gulf at 40 days' passage in a rowing boat, and its breadth at half a day in the broadest part; but in this last he probably had in view the upper part of the Suez Gulf. The real length of the Red Sea, or Arabian Gulf, from the straits of Bab-el-Mandeb to Suez is 1400 Eng. m., and its greatest breadth, in lat. 18°, is 175 ; and the broadest part of the Suez Gulf is 25 miles.— [G. W.]

[1] Herodotus is perfectly right in speaking of the tide in this gulf. At Suez it is from 5 to 6 feet, but much less to the southward.—[G. W.]

[2] The Mediterranean, called by the Arabs "the White Sea" as well as "the North Sea."—[G. W.]

[3] The shells imbedded in rocks have led to much absurd reasoning till a very late time ; and the accuracy of Strabo's judgment is the more surprising since his mode of accounting for the upheavings and subsidings of the land, and the retirement and encroachments of the sea, as well as the gradual changes always going on from subterraneous agencies, accord with our most recent discoveries. "The reason," he says, "that one is raised, and the other subsides, or that the sea inundates some places, and recedes from others, is not from some being lower and others higher, but because the same ground is raised or depressed . . . The cause must

to such an extent as even to injure the pyramids ; and I noticed
also that there is but a single hill in all Egypt where sand is
found,[4] namely, the hill above Memphis ; and further, I found
the country to bear no resemblance either to its border-land
Arabia, or to Libya[5]—nay, nor even to Syria, which forms the
seaboard of Arabia ; but whereas the soil of Libya is, we know,
sandy and of a reddish hue, and that of Arabia and Syria inclines
to stone and clay, Egypt has a soil that is black and crumbly,
as being alluvial and formed of the deposits brought down by
the river from Ethiopia.

13. One fact which I learnt of the priests is to me a strong
evidence of the origin of the country. They said that when
Mœris was king, the Nile overflowed all Egypt below Memphis,
as soon as it rose so little as eight cubits. Now Mœris had not
been dead 900 years at the time when I heard this of the
priests ;[6] yet at the present day, unless the river rise sixteen,

therefore be ascribed either to the ground under the sea, or to that inundated by
it, but rather to that below it . . . and we ought to draw our conclusions from things
that are evident, and in some degree of daily occurrence, as deluges, earthquakes,
and (volcanic) eruptions, and sudden risings of the land under the sea . . . and not
only islands but continents are raised up, and large and small tracts subside, some
being swallowed up by earthquakes." (Strabo, i. p. 74 et seqq.) On Volcanos, see
Lyell's Princ. of Geol. vol. i. c. 2 to 5.—[G. W.]

[4] The only mountain where sand abounds is certainly the African range, and
though there are some lofty drifts in one place on the opposite side, just below the
modern Suez road, the eastern part of the valley of the Nile is generally free from
it. It does not, however, encroach on the W. to the extent that some have imagined ; and if downs of sand have been raised here and there along the edge of the
cultivated land, the general encroachment is greatly in favour of the alluvial deposit.
In Ethiopia the sand has invaded the W. bank, but this is owing to the fall in the
level of the Nile, mentioned in n. [1], ch. iii. and App. ch. iv. 4.—[G. W.]

[5] It is perfectly true that neither in soil nor climate is Egypt like any other
country. The soil is, as Herodotus says, "black and crumbly." The deposit of the
Nile, when left on a rock and dried by the sun, resembles pottery in its appearance
and by its fracture, from the silica it contains ; but as long as it retains its moisture it has the appearance of clay, from its slimy and tenacious quality. It varies
according to circumstances, sometimes being mixed with sand, but it is generally of
a black colour, and Egypt is said to have been called hence " black," from the prevailing character of its soil. The analysis given by Regnault in the Description de
l'Egypte is—

11 ·	water.
9 ·	carbon.
6 ·	oxide of iron.
4 ·	silica.
4 ·	carbonate of magnesia.
18 ·	carbonate of lime.
48 ·	alumen.
100	

That the soil of Libya is red and sandy is true, and the abundance of iron, especially
at the Little Oasis, makes it in some parts like that of Devonshire.—[G. W.]

[6] This would make the date of Mœris about 1355 B. c. ; but it neither agrees
with the age of Amun-m-he III. of the Labyrinth, nor of Thothmes III., whom
some have supposed to be Mœris, nor of Maire, or Papi (Apappus) of the 6th

or, at the very least, fifteen cubits, it does not overflow the lands.
It seems to me, therefore, that if the land goes on rising and
growing at this rate, the Egyptians who dwell below lake Mœris,
in the Delta (as it is called) and elsewhere, will one day, by the
stoppage of the inundations, suffer permanently the fate which
they told me they expected would some time or other befall the
Greeks. On hearing that the whole land of Greece is watered
by rain from heaven, and not, like their own, inundated by rivers,
they observed—"Some day the Greeks will be disappointed of
their grand hope, and then they will be wretchedly hungry;"
which was as much as to say, "If God shall some day see fit
not to grant the Greeks rain, but shall afflict them with a long
drought, the Greeks will be swept away by a famine, since they
have nothing to rely on but rain from Jove, and have no other
resource for water." [7]

14. And certes, in thus speaking of the Greeks the Egyptians say nothing but what is true. But now let me tell the
Egyptians how the case stands with themselves. If, as I said
before, the country below Memphis, [8] which is the land that is
always rising, continues to increase in height at the rate at
which it has risen in times gone by, how will it be possible for
the inhabitants of that region to avoid hunger, when they will
certainly have no rain, [9] and the river will not be able to over-

dynasty. The Mœris, however, *from whom these dates are calculated*, appears to
have been Menophres, whose æra was so remarkable, and was fixed as the Sothic
period, B. C. 1322, which happened about 900 years before Herodotus' visit, only
falling short of that sum by 33 years. It is reasonable to suppose that by Mœris
he would refer to that king who was so remarkable for his attention to the levels of
the Nile, shown by his making the lake called after him; and who, from the records
at Semneh, and from his name being again found in the Labyrinth (by Dr. Lepsius),
is shown to have been Amun-m-he III.; but if his date is to be taken from Herodotus, it will not accord with this king of the 12th dynasty, who lived about 1500
years before the historian; and the Egyptians were not in the habit of diminishing antiquity, nor of curtailing dates. Herodotus perhaps confounded two or more kings,
to whom the name of Mœris had been given by the Greeks; as the statue of Amunoph, and a palace and a tomb of two Remeses, were ascribed to Memnon. See note
[5] on ch. 100, note [6] on ch. 142, and note [2] on ch. 148.—[G. W.]

[7] This resembles the common remark of the Egyptians at the present day regarding those countries which depend for water on rain.—[G. W.]

[8] This with the Delta Herodotus seems to consider the only part raised by the
annual deposit (αὕτη γάρ ἐστι ἡ αὐξανομένη), which is of course erroneous, as the al-
luvium is left throughout the valley from Abyssinia to the sea.—[G. W.]

[9] Pomponius Mela calls Egypt "terra expers imbrium," and Proclus says if
showers fell in Lower Egypt they were confined to that district, and heavy rain was
a prodigy in the Thebaïd. Herodotus indeed affirms (iii. 10) that rain at Thebes
portended some great calamity, and the conquest of Egypt by the Persians was
thought to have been foretold by this unusual phenomenon at that place. In Upper Egypt showers only occur about five or six times in the year, but every fifteen
or twenty years heavy rain falls there, which will account for the deep ravines cut
in the valleys of the Theban hills, about the Tombs of the Kings; in Lower Egypt

flow their corn-lands ? At present, it must be confessed, they obtain the fruits of the field with less trouble than any other people in the world, the rest of the Egyptians included, since they have no need to break up the ground with the plough, nor to use the hoe, nor to do any of the work which the rest of mankind find necessary if they are to get a crop ; [1] but the hus-

rain is more frequent; and in Alexandria it is as abundant in winter as in the south of Europe. These ravines, and the precautions taken to protect the roofs of the temples at Thebes against rain, show that it fell there of old as now; but a continuation of heavy rain in Upper Egypt, or even at Cairo, for two or three days would be considered a great wonder, and would cause many houses to fall down, as in 1823. (Cp. Exod. ix. 18, where the hailstorm is not said to have been the only one, but such as was unlike any before it in Egypt.) The Eastern desert, between the Nile and the Red Sea, where the mountains are higher, is frequently visited by heavy rain and thunderstorms in the winter, though the climate is drier than the valley of the Nile; and every four or five years the torrents run down to the Red Sea on one side and to the Nile on the other. In less than a month's time after this the beds of those torrents are covered with green herbs and numerous small flowers, and the Arabs take their flocks to graze there till the Khamseen winds and the hot sun of May have dried them up, and nothing remains except a few acacia-trees and the usual hardy shrubs of those arid districts. There are scarcely any springs in the valley of the Nile, and the few found there are probably caused by the filtration of the Nile-water through the soil.—[G. W.]

[1] That the labour for growing corn was less in Egypt than in other countries is certainly true; and in the low lands of the Delta, to which Herodotus here alludes,

as well as in the hollows away from the river, near the edge of the desert, where the level of the land is the lowest, they probably dispensed with the plough, as at the present day, and simply dragged the mud with bushes after the seed had been thrown upon it, driving in a number of sheep, goats, or pigs, to tread in the grain;

but for other crops considerable labour was required in raising water to irrigate the land; and during the summer and autumn few soils require more attention than in the dry climate of Egypt. Though the fields were occasionally sown, as now, by casting the seed into the mud on the retiring of the waters, this was not the uni

bandman waits till the river has of its own accord spread itself
over the fields and withdrawn again to its bed, and then sows

versal custom among the Egyptians, and the plough is always represented in the
agricultural scenes, both in Upper Egypt and on the monuments about Memphis.

his plot of ground, and after sowing turns his swine into it—
the swine tread in the corn [2]—after which he has only to await

The furrows were not deep; and Diodorus and Columella say that they were contented to " trace slight furrows with a light plough on the surface of the land," a
mode of tillage resembling the *scarificatio* of the Romans, continued in Egypt at the
present day. After the plough followed the hoe to break the clods; and the land
having been prepared, the sower was sent in, who threw the seed broadcast over
the field. The land was all open, having no hedge-rows, but merely simple land-
marks to define the boundaries of a farm or field, as with the Jews (Deut. xix. 14),
and sometimes an estate was separated from its neighbour by a large canal, from
which smaller channels distributed the water in proper directions through the fields.

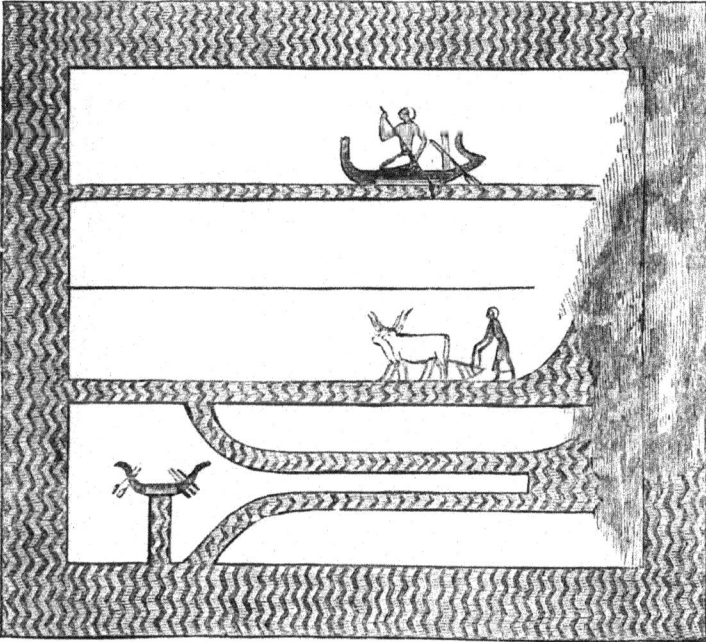

When the Nile was low, the water was raised by the pole and bucket, the *shadoof*
of modern Egypt, and by other means; and this attention to artificial irrigation,
instead of depending for it on rain, is alluded to in Deuteronomy xi. 10. There is
one instance, and one only, of *men* drawing the plough in Egypt. The painting,
which is from a tomb at Thebes, is preserved in the Louvre. Two men are at the
end of the pole, and two others pull a rope attached to the base where the handle,
pole, and share unite; another holds the plough as usual, and the rest of the scene
is like that in other agricultural scenes, with the hoeing, sowing broadcast, and the
harvest operations.—[G. W.]
   [2] Plutarch, Ælian (Nat. Animal. x. 16, on the authority of Eudoxus), and Pliny,
mention this custom of treading in the grain " with pigs " in Egypt; but no instance occurs of it in the tombs, though goats are sometimes so represented in the
paintings. It is indeed more probable that pigs were turned in upon the land to
eat up the weeds and roots; and a painting at Thebes, where pigs are introduced
with water-plants, seems to point to this fact; their habits were ill suited to benefit
the farmer after the seed had been sown; and to muzzle each pig, when goats or

the harvest.   The swine serve him also to thrash the grain,[2] which is then carried to the garner.

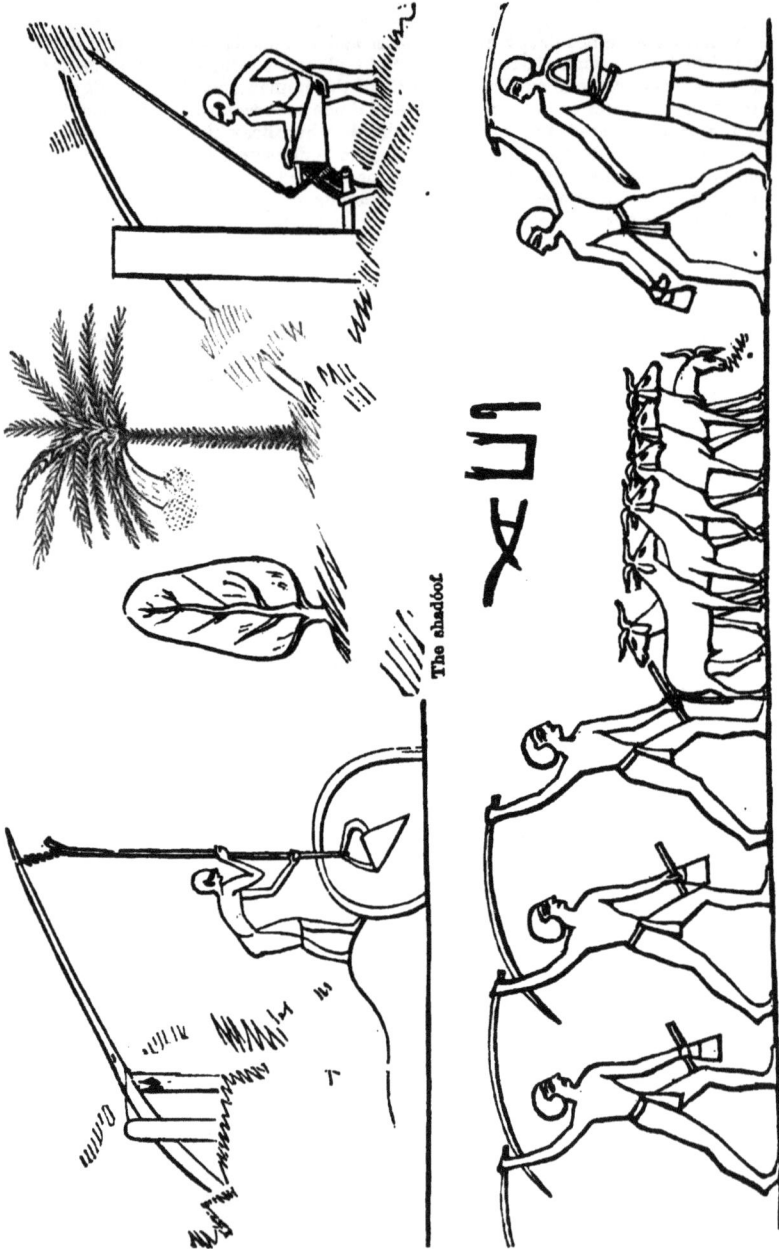

other animals abounded, would have been lost labour.   In the district of Gower, in South Wales, corn is trodden in by sheep to this day.—[G. W.]

[2] The paintings show that oxen were commonly used to tread out the grain from

15. If then we choose to adopt the views of the Ionians concerning Egypt, we must come to the conclusion that the

the ear at harvest-time, and occasionally, though rarely, asses were so employed; but pigs not being sufficiently heavy for the purpose, are not likely to have been substituted for oxen. This process was performed, as it is still in Italy, Spain, and other countries, by driving the oxen (horses or mules) over the corn strewed upon the ground, or upon a paved area near the field; and the Jews, who also adopted it, were forbidden to muzzle the

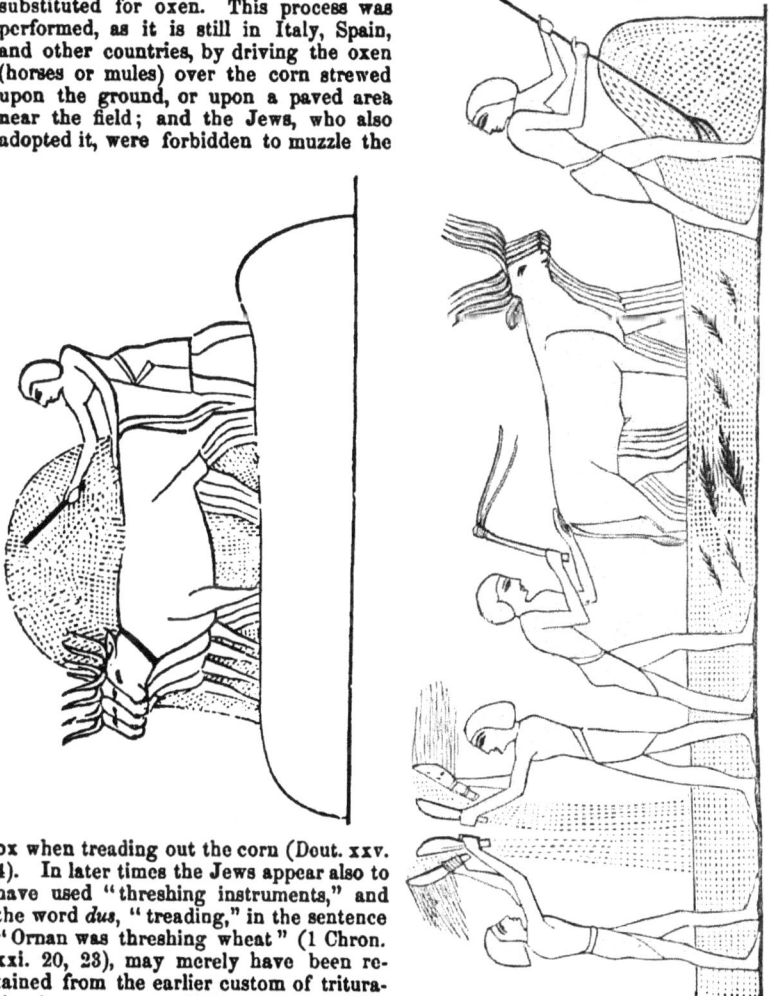

ox when treading out the corn (Deut. xxv. 4). In later times the Jews appear also to have used "threshing instruments," and the word *dus*, "treading," in the sentence "Ornan was threshing wheat" (1 Chron. xxi. 20, 23), may merely have been retained from the earlier custom of triturating by oxen. Another more distinct mention of a "new sharp threshing instrument having teeth" is found in Isaiah (xli. 15), which calls to mind the *Nóreg*, or corn-drag, of modern Egypt, a name closely resembling the Hebrew *Moreg*, applied to the threshing instruments of Ornan (as in Isaiah), and the oxen he offered to David were doubtless those that had been yoked to it. The modern Egyptian *Nóreg* is drawn by two oxen, and consists of a wooden frame, with three axles, on which are fixed circular iron plates, the first and last having each four, the centre one three plates; and these not only force out the grain but chop the straw as the machine is dragged over it. It appears to be very similar to the *tribulum* of the Romans mentioned by Varro (de Re rusticâ, i. 52), who describes it as "a frame

Egyptians had formerly no country at all.   For the Ionians [4] say that nothing is really Egypt [5] but the Delta, which extends along shore from the Watch-tower of Perseus, [6] as it is called, to the Pelusiac Salt-pans, [7] a distance of forty schœnes, and stretches

made rough by stones, or pieces of iron, on which the driver or a weight was placed, and this being drawn by beasts yoked to it pressed out the grain." The "plostemum Pœnicum" was doubtless introduced into Spain by the Phœnicians.—[G. W.]

[4] Under the general expression of "Ionians" in this passage, Herodotus has been thought to mean principally, if not solely, Hecatæus. (Müller ad Hecat. Fragm. Fr. 295 and 296.)   Col. Mure shows satisfactorily (Literature of Greece, vol. iv. p. 148, note [1]) that this is not the case, since the persons here spoken of divided the world into three parts (infrà, ch. 16), Hecatæus into two. (See the map, note to Book iv. ch. 36.)   Perhaps the allusion is to Anaximander, who as a geographer had preceded Hecatæus. (Strab. i. p. 10; Agathemer. i. 1.)

[5] There is no appearance of the name "Egypt" on the ancient monuments, where the country is called "Chemi," represented in hieroglyphics by the tail of a crocodile.   Chemi, "the black land," "the land of Ham," or of Khem (the Egyptian god Pan, or the Generative principle of Nature) is said by Plutarch to have been so called from the "blackness of the soil."   Khem is singularly like the Greek χαμαί.   Ham (Kham), the Hebrew name of the patriarch, signifies also "soot," and is like the Arabic hem, hami, "hot;" and the Hebrew hôm (or khôm), signifying brown (or black), as in Gen. xxx. 32, 40, is also "burnt up."   Ægyptus was in old times the name of the Nile, which was so called by Homer (Odys. iv. 477; xiv. 257); and Strabo (xvii. p. 691) says the same was the opinion of Nearchus.   Manetho pretends that the country received the name from Ægyptus, a surname of King Sethos (or Sethi).   Aristotle thinks that "Ægypt was formerly called Thebes," and Herodotus states, in opposition to the opinion of the "Ionians," that "Thebes (i. e. the Thebaïd) had of old the name of Egypt."   And if this is not confirmed by the monuments, the word "Egypt" was at all events connected with Coptos, a city of the Thebaïd.   From Kebt, Koft, or Coptos the modern inhabitants have been called Copts: its ancient name in hieroglyphics was Kebt-hor; and Mr. Poole is evidently right in supposing this to be the same as the Biblical Caphtor.   He thinks the name to be composed of Αἶα, "land," and Γύπτος; and to be traced in the Ai-Caphtor, "land (or coast) of Caphtor," in Jeremiah (xlvii. 4).   The word Coptitic is found in a Gnostic papyrus, supposed to be of the second century (see note [3] on ch. 83).   Egypt is said to have been called originally Aetia, and the Nile Aetos and Siris.   Upper Egypt, or the Thebaïd, has even been confounded with, and called, Ethiopia; perhaps too by Pliny (vi. 35; see note [6] on ch. 110); Nahum (iii. 9) calls Ethiopia and Egypt the strength of No (Thebes); and Strabo says (i. p. 57) that Menelaus' journey to Ethiopia really meant to Thebes.   The modern name Musr or Misr is the same as the Biblical Mizraim, i. e. "the two Misrs" applied to Egypt, which corresponds to "the two regions" of the sculptures; but the word Misr does not occur on the monuments.   Mr. Poole notices the meaning of the Arabic Misr, "red mud," and the name Rahab, "the proud," given to Egypt in the Bible. Of Caphtor, see Deut. ii. 23; Amos ix. 7.   See note [6] on ch. 106.—[G. W.]

[6] This tower stood to the W. of the Canopic mouth; and, as Rennell supposes, on the point of Aboukír, not, as Strabo thinks, on a sandy point at the Bolbitine mouth.   The Canopic was by some called the Heracleotic mouth, from the city of Hercules (see n. [1] ch. 113).   The name Canopus, written more correctly by Herodotus Κάνωβος, said to signify χρύσεον ἔδαφος, has been derived from kahi noub, "golden land."   The term "Canopic," applied to sepulchral vases with a human head, is quite arbitrary.—[G. W.]

[7] The Greek, like the modern, name of Pelusium, is thought to have been derived from the mud that surrounded it, πηλὸς in Greek, and Teen in Arabic, signifying "mud."   It is now called Teeneh.   It is, however, very probably taken from the old Egyptian name, and not Greek.   Larcher considers the ταριχείαι to be called from the embalmed mummies preserved there, but the name evidently applies to the

inland as far as the city of Cercasôrus,[s] where the Nile divides
into the two streams which reach the sea at Pelusium and
Canôbus respectively. The rest of what is accounted Egypt
belongs, they say, either to Arabia or Libya. But the Delta,
as the Egyptians affirm, and as I myself am persuaded, is formed of the deposits of the river, and has only recently, if I may use
the expression, come to light. If then they had formerly no
territory at all, how came they to be so extravagant as to fancy
themselves the most ancient race in the world ? Surely there
was no need of their making the experiment with the children
to see what language they would first speak. But in truth I
do not believe that the Egyptians came into being at the same
time with the Delta, as the Ionians call it ; I think they have
always existed ever since the human race began ; as the land
went on increasing, part of the population came down into the
new country, part remained in their old settlements. In ancient
times the Thebaïs bore the name of Egypt, a district of which
the entire circumference is but 6120 furlongs.

16. If then my judgment on these matters be right, the
Ionians are mistaken in what they say of Egypt. If, on the
contrary, it is they who are right, then I undertake to show that
neither the Ionians nor any of the other Greeks know how to
count. For they all say that the earth is divided into three
parts, Europe, Asia, and Libya, whereas they ought to add a
fourth part, the Delta of Egypt, since they do not include it
either in Asia or Libya.[9] For is it not their theory that the

---

salt-pans, as in ch. 113, where Herodotus mentions others near the Canopic mouth.
—[G. W.] Lepsius suggests that Pelusium means "Philistine-town" (Chronologie
der Ægypter. vol. i. p. 341), and regards it as so called because it was the last town
held by the Hyksos, whom he believes to have been Philistines, before their final
expulsion from Egypt.
    [s] Or Cercasôrum. It is impossible to say which form Herodotus intended.
    [9] Though Egypt really belongs to the continent of Africa, the inhabitants were
certainly of Asiatic origin ; and the whole of the valley of the Nile has been peopled by the primeval immigration of a Caucasian race. This seems to be indicated
also by the Bible history, where the grandsons of Noah are made the inhabitants of
Ethiopia, Egypt, Libya, and Canaan ; and Juba, according to Pliny, affirms with
reason that the people of the banks of the Nile from Syene to Meroe, were not
Ethiopians (blacks) but Arabs. Till a later time half Egypt was ascribed to Africa,
"which extended to the sources of the Nile" (Strabo, ii. p. 170), and "the Tanais
and Nile were the limits of Asia" (Plin. iii. Proœm.) ; but more reasonable people,
says Strabo (i. p. 51), think the Arabian Gulf the proper separation of the two continents rather than the Nile. Ptolemy gives both banks of the Nile to Africa (iv. 5).
Herodotus justly blames the inconsistency of making Egypt belong to neither continent, and of considering the country and its people a new creation. In Book iv.
chs. 39 and 41, Herodotus does not mean to exclude Egypt both from Asia and
from Libya, as he shows by mentioning the ships of Neco sailing from the Arabian
Gulf round Libya to the Mediterranean coasts of Egypt (ch. 42) ; he treats Libya as
a distinct region, lying W. of Egypt, and makes Egypt itself the division between it

Nile separates Asia from Libya ?   As the Nile therefore splits
in two at the apex of the Delta, the Delta itself must be a separate country, not contained in either Asia or Libya.

17. Here I take my leave of the opinions of the Ionians, and
proceed to deliver my own sentiments on these subjects. I consider Egypt to be the whole country inhabited by the Egyptians,
just as Cilicia is the tract occupied by the Cilicians, and Assyria
that possessed by the Assyrians. And I regard the only proper
boundary-line between Libya and Asia to be that which is
marked out by the Egyptian frontier. For if we take the boundary-line commonly received by the Greeks,[10] we must regard
Egypt as divided, along its whole length from Elephantiné and
the Cataracts to Cercasôrus, into two parts, each belonging to a
different portion of the world, one to Asia, the other to Libya ;
since the Nile divides Egypt in two from the Cataracts to the
sea, running as far as the city of Cercasôrus[1] in a single stream,

and Asia. But in a geographical point of view his description is very unsatisfactory.
Diodorus seems to think that Herodotus made the Nile the boundary of Libya.
—[G. W.]

[10] That is, the course of the Nile ; which is made the boundary by Strabo (ii. p.
170), Mela (i. 1, 2, and 4), Dionysius Periegetes (l. 230), and, in one place, by Agathemer (i. 1). Scylax (Peripl. p. 105) and Pliny (H. N. v. 9) agree with Herodotus
in assigning the whole of Egypt to Asia. Ptolemy (Geog. i. 1) is the first extant
geographer who formally assigns the Red Sea and the Isthmus of Suez as the true
boundary. In this he is followed by the Armenian geography (§ 16), and, in his
description of the three continents, by Agathemer (ii. 6, 7).

[1] Strabo calls it Cercesura, others Cercasorum. It is noticed again in chs. 15
and 97. Strabo shows it to have been in the same parallel as Heliopolis, and Herodotus considers the Delta to end at Heliopolis (ii. 7), which brings the point of the
Delta nearly opposite the present *Shoobra*. Here the river separated into three
branches, the Pelusiac or Bubastite to the E., the Canopic or Heracleotic to the W.,
and the Sebennytic which ran between them, continuing in the same general line of
direction northward which the Nile had up to this point, and piercing the Delta
through its centre. The Tanitic, which ran out of the Sebennytic, was at first the
same as the Busiritic, but afterwards received the name of Tanitic, from the city of
Tanis (now *San*), which stood on its eastern bank ; and between the Tanitic and
Pelusiac branches was the isle of Myecphoris, which Herodotus says was opposite
Bubastis (ii. 166). The Mendesian, which also ran eastward from the Sebennytic,
passed by the modern town of *Mansoorah*, and thence running by Mondes (from
which it was called) entered the sea to the W. of the Tanitic. The Bolbitine mouth
was that of the modern Rosetta branch, as the Bucolic or Phatmetic was that of
Damietta, and the lower parts of both these branches were artificial, or made by the
hand of man ; on which account, though Herodotus mentions seven, he confines the
number of the mouths of the Nile to five. These two artificial outlets of the Nile are
the only ones now remaining, the others having either disappeared, or being dry in
most places during the summer ; and this fact seems to confirm an otherwise inex-
plicable prophecy of Isaiah (xi. 15), thought by some to apply to the Euphrates—
(He) "shall smite it in its seven streams, and make men go over dry-shod." Most
ancient writers agree in reckoning seven mouths, the order of which, beginning from
the E., was—1. the Pelusiac or Bubastite ; 2. the Saltic or Tanitic ; 3. the Mendesian ;
4. the Bucolic or Phatmetic (now of Damietta) ; 5. the Sebennytic ; 6. the Bolbitine (now
of Rosetta) ; 7. the Canopic or Heracleotic ; but eleven are mentioned by Pliny, to
which he adds four others called "false mouths." Most of these false mouths are

but at that point separating into three branches, whereof the
one which bends eastward is called the Pelusiac mouth,[2] and
that which slants to the west, the Canobic.　Meanwhile the
straight course of the stream, which comes down from the upper
country, and meets the apex of the Delta, continues on, dividing
the Delta down the middle, and empties itself into the sea by a
mouth, which is as celebrated, and carries as large a body of
water, as most of the others, the mouth called the Sebennytic.
Besides these there are two other mouths which run out of the
Sebennytic called respectively the Saitic and the Mendesian.
The Bolbitine mouth, and the Bucolic, are not natural branches,
but channels made by excavation.

18. My judgment as to the extent of Egypt is confirmed by
an oracle delivered at the shrine of Ammon, of which I had no
knowledge at all until after I had formed my opinion.　It hap
pened that the people of the cities Marea[3] and Apis, who live
in the part of Egypt that borders on Libya, took a dislike to the
religious usages of the country concerning sacrificial animals,
and wished no longer to be restricted from eating the flesh of
cows.[4]　So, as they believed themselves to be Libyans and not

described by Strabo as very shallow, being probably dry in summer, and there is
reason to believe that the three great mouths were the Pelusiac, the Sebennytic, and
the Canopic, which last was originally the only one (Herod. ii. 179) which strangers
were allowed to enter.　See note [b] on ch. 178.—[G. W.]

[2] From the Greek word for "mouth," στόμα, or from the Latin ostium, the Arabs
have given the name ostoóm or oshtoóm to each of the mouths of the Nile, with its
regular plural ashateém.　The o is prefixed from the repugnance of Arabic to words
beginning with s followed by another consonant.　Thus too the French has étable,
école, état, the Spanish ispejo, and even the Italian places lo instead of il before
specchio.—[G. W.]

[3] The town of Marea stood near the lake to which it gave the name Mareotis
(see note [a] ch. 6.)　It was celebrated for the wine produced in its vicinity, which
appears to be included in the "wine of the Northern country," so often mentioned
in the lists of offerings in the Egyptian tombs.　Strabo says in this district is the
greatest abundance of wine, which is confirmed by Athenæus, πολλὴ δὲ ἡ περὶ τὴν
γῆν ταύτην ἄμπελος.　Virgil (Georg. ii. 91) says, "Sunt Thasiæ vites, sunt et Mare-
otides albæ;" and the expression of Horace, "lymphatam Mareotico," meaning
"Egyptian wine," points it out as the most noted of that country.　Athenæus says
"its colour is white, its quality excellent, and it is sweet and light, with a fragrant
bouquet, by no means astringent, nor affecting the head;" and Strabo gives it the
additional merit of keeping to a great age.　Athenæus, however, considers it inferior
to the Teniotic, and that of Anthylla appears to have been preferred to it
and to all others.　See below, n. [b] on ch. 37, n. [b] on ch. 60, and n. [1] on ch. 77.—
[G. W.]

[4] Though oxen were lawful food to the Egyptians, cows and heifers were forbidden to be killed, either for the altar or the table, being consecrated (not as Herodotus states, ch. 41, to Isis, but as Strabo says) to Athor, who was represented
under the form of a spotted cow, and to whose temple at Atarbechis, "the city of
Athor," as Herodotus afterwards shows, the bodies of those that died were carried
(ch. 41).　It is, however, very excusable in him to confound the two goddesses, as
they often assume each other's attributes, and it is then difficult to distinguish them

Egyptians, they sent to the shrine to say that, having nothing in common with the Egyptians, neither inhabiting the Delta nor using the Egyptian tongue, they claimed to be allowed to eat whatever they pleased. Their request, however, was refused by the god, who declared in reply that Egypt was the entire tract of country which the Nile overspreads and irrigates, and the Egyptians were the people who lived below Elephantiné,[5] and drank the waters of that river.

19. So said the oracle. Now the Nile, when it overflows, floods not only the Delta, but also the tracts of country on both sides the stream which are thought to belong to Libya and Arabia,[6] in some places reaching to the extent of two days' journey from its banks, in some even exceeding that distance, but in others falling short of it.

Concerning the nature of the river, I was not able to gain any information either from the priests or from others. I was particularly anxious to learn from them why the Nile, at the commencement of the summer solstice, begins to rise,[7] and continues to increase for a hundred days—and why, as soon as that

without the hieroglyphic legends. See note [8] on ch. 40, and note [9] on ch. 41.—[G. W.]

[5] Syene and Elephantiné were the real frontier of Egypt on the S.; Egypt extending "from the tower (Migdol) of Syene" to the sea (Ezek. xxix. 10). When the frontier was extended southward by the conquests of the Pharaohs, lower Ethiopia to the second cataract (the modern Nubia) was still considered out of Egypt, though part of its dominions; and the places there are often designated as "foreign."—[G. W.]

[6] By the "tracts thought to belong to Libya and Arabia," Herodotus means the lands about the lake Mareotis, and those on the canal which communicated with the Red Sea, as well as on the E. bank of the Pelusiac branch.—[G. W.]

[7] Herodotus was surprised that the Nile should rise in the summer solstice and become low in winter. In the latitude of Memphis it begins to rise at the end of June, about the 10th of August it attains to the height requisite for cutting the canals and admitting it into the interior of the plain; and it is generally at its highest about the end of September. This makes from 92 to 100 days, as Herodotus states. At the Cataracts the first rise is perceived some time sooner, about the end of May or the beginning of June, which led Seneca to say that "the first increase of the Nile was observable about the islands of Philæ." But in proportion as you go higher into Ethiopia, the inundation is earlier, and at Khartoom it begins about the 2nd of May, or, according to some, "early in April." But it sometimes happens that it rises a little and then falls again before the regular inundation sets in, which is owing to partial rains in the upper part of its course. In Egypt the first change from the previous clearness of the stream in May is observed in its red and turbid colour, and it soon afterwards assumes a green appearance, when the water is no longer considered wholesome. For this reason a supply previously laid up in jars was then used by the ancient Egyptians until it re-assumed a turbid but wholesome red colour; which explains a remark of Aristides (Orat. Egypt. vol. ii.) that the Egyptians are the only people who preserve water in jars, and calculate its age as others do that of wine. It was not long before the water of the river became wholesome again, and the latter part of his assertion, respecting its improvement by age when preserved in *jars*, is only one of those antitheses in which the Greeks delighted. In large *reservoirs* it may be kept two or three years, as in some houses of Cairo, but

number is past, it forthwith retires and contracts its stream, continuing low during the whole of the winter until the summer solstice comes round again. On none of these points could I obtain any explanation from the inhabitants,[2] though I made

not improved like wine. Though very wholesome, the water of the Nile sometimes disagrees for a few days with strangers, or with persons who have sojourned for a few months in the desert; which accounts for the Persians having brought water into Egypt from Asia, and agrees with the remark of Athenæus (Deipn. ii. p. 41), who attributes it to the nitre it contains. On the supposed causes of the inundation, *see* Eur. Hel. i. 3; Athen. ii. p. 278 seq. ed. Bip.; and Palmerius n. in Oudendorp's Lucan, b. x. 215 seq.—[G. W.]

[2] The cause of the inundation is the water that falls during the rainy season in Abyssinia; and the range of the tropical rains extends even as far N. as latitude 17° 43'. Homer was therefore right in giving to the Nile the epithet of διιπετέος ποταμοῖο, and the passages quoted from the Koran relating to "the water sent by God from Heaven," inscribed on the Nilometer of the isle of Roda, show that the Arabs were at a very early time correctly informed respecting the cause of the inundation. In the highlands of Abyssinia the rains continue from the middle of June to the middle of September, but at the sources of the White river the rains seem to set in about the middle of March, and also to last three months. The Bahr-el-Azrek, together with the more northerly Atbara, and their tributary streams, continue their supply of water from Abyssinia until the end of the inundation. The two main branches of the Southern Nile are the Bahr-el-A'biad and the Bahr-el-Azrek, which unite at the modern Khartoom, a new town on the point of land, about 160 miles to the N. of Sennár; but though the latter is the smaller of the two, it is the one which possesses the real characteristics of the Nile, having the same black alluvial deposit, and the same beneficent properties when it inundates the land. The White river, on the contrary, has a totally different character, and its waters possess none of those fertilizing qualities for which the Nile is celebrated; and this is probably the reason why the source of the Abyssinian branch has been so often looked upon as the real "fountain of the Nile." The names (Bahr el) *Abiad* and *Azrek* appear to signify the "white" and "black" rather than the "white" and "blue" (river). For though *Aswed* is commonly put in opposition to *Abiad* (as "black" and "white"), *Azrek*, which is properly "blue," is also used for what we call "jet black;" and *Hossán Azrek* is a "dark black," not a "blue horse." It is true that "blue" is applied to rivers, as *Nil ab*, "blue water" (or "river") to the Indus, and the Sutlej is still the "blue river;" but the name *Azrek* seems to be given to the Abyssinian branch to distinguish it from the Western or White Nile. Neel, or Nil, itself signifies "blue," and indigo is therefore "Neeleh;" but the word is Indian not Arabic, Nila in Sanscrit being "blue." Though the Greeks called the river "Nile," as the Arabs do, that name is not found in the hieroglyphics, where the god Nilus and the river are both called "Hapi." The Hindoo Puranas also call the Nile "*Nila*," but it was not an old Egyptian name, and those writings are of late date. It is called in Coptic *iaro*, "river," or *iom*, "sea" (cp. 'Ωκεανός), analogous to the modern Arabic name *bahr*, "river," properly "sea" (see note [1] on ch. 111). Nahum (iii. 3) speaks of "populous No (Thebes) whose rampart was the *sea*." The resemblance of the name Hapi, "Nilus," and the bull-god Hapi or Apis (see ch. 28, B. iii.) recalls the Greek representation of a river under the form of a bull, like the Acheloüs and others (see Ælian. Var. Hist. ii. 33). Nilus is not taken from Nahr or Nahl, "river;" but Nahr, "river," is applied to the Euphrates, and Nahl to a ravine or torrent-bed, as (in 2 Kings xxiv. 7) to the "*torrens Ægypti*." Nahl is not a "river," but, like Nullah, a "ravine," in India. Cp. Nahr, Nar, Naro, and other names of rivers, the Nereïds, &c. (See n. [2] on ch. 50). For *black* applied to water, cp. μέλαν ὕδωρ of Homer. The Nile was said to have received its name from King Nilus, but this is doubtless a fable; and Homer calls it Ægyptus. The sources of the White Nile are still unknown; and recent discoveries seem to as-

every inquiry, wishing to know what was commonly reported—they could neither tell me what special virtue the Nile has which makes it so opposite in its nature to all other streams, nor why, unlike every other river, it gives forth no breezes[*] from its surface.

20. Some of the Greeks, however, wishing to get a reputation for cleverness, have offered explanations of the phenomena of the river, for which they have accounted in three different ways. Two of these I do not think it worth while to speak of, further than simply to mention what they are. One pretends that the Etesian winds[1] cause the rise of the river by preventing the Nile-water from running off into the sea. But in the first place it has often happened, when the Etesian winds did not blow, that the Nile has risen according to its usual wont ; and further, if the Etesian winds produced the effect, the other rivers which flow in a direction opposite to those winds ought to present the same phenomena as the Nile, and the more so as they are all smaller streams, and have a weaker current. But these rivers, of which there are many both in Syria[2] and Libya, are entirely unlike the Nile in this respect.

sign a different position from that conjectured by the explorers sent by Mohammed Ali, who brought it from the eastward, at the back or S. of the Galla mountains ; as did a very intelligent native of the Jimma country I met at Cairo, who affirmed that he had crossed the White river in going from his native land to Adderay or Hurrur and the Somáuli district, on his way to the port of Berbera. Seneca's description of the Upper Nile, " magnas solitudines pervagatus, et in paludes diffusus, gentibus sparsus," might suit the character of the White Nile, though he is wrong in supposing it only assumed a new one by forming a single stream " about Philæ." See Nat. Quæst. b. iv. s. 2 ; cp. Plin. vi. 30.—[G. W.]

[*] If this signifies that breezes are not generated by, and do not rise from, the Nile, it is true ; but not if it means that a current of air does not blow up the valley. Diodorus (i. 38) is wrong in stating that " the Nile has no clouds about it, does not engender cold winds, and has no fogs." The fogs are often very thick, though they disappear before midday.—[G. W.]

[1] The annual N.W. winds blow from the Mediterranean during the inundation ; but they are not the *cause* of the rise of the Nile, though they help in a small degree to impede its course northwards. For the navigation of the river they are invaluable, as well as for the health of the inhabitants ; and a very large boat could scarcely ascend the river during the inundation unless aided by them. Nor can they be said to cause the inundation by driving the clouds to Abyssinia, as the rise of the Nile begins before they set in, though they may add to the water by later showers.—[G. W.]

[2] It is possible to justify this statement, which at first sight seems untrue, by considering that the direction of the Etesian winds was *north-westerly* rather than north. (Arist. Meteor. ii. 6 ; Diod. Sic. i. 39.) This was natural, as they are caused by the rush of the air from the Mediterranean and Egean, to fill up the vacuum caused by the rarefaction of the atmosphere over the desert lands in the neighbourhood of the sea, which desert lands lie as much in Syria and Arabia on the east, as in Africa on the south. Though Syria therefore has only a torrent-bed generally dry (the *Wady el Arish*, or River of Egypt) which faces the north, it has many rivers which the Etesian winds might affect—all those, namely, which face the west.

21. The second opinion is even more unscientific than the one just mentioned, and also, if I may so say, more marvellous. It is that the Nile acts so strangely, because it flows from the ocean, and that the ocean flows all round the earth.[3]

22. The third explanation, which is very much more plausible than either of the others, is positively the furthest from the truth ; for there is really nothing in what it says, any more than in the other theories. It is, that the inundation of the Nile is caused by the melting of snows.[4] Now, as the Nile flows out of Libya,[5] through Ethiopia, into Egypt, how is it possible that it can be formed of melted snow, running, as it does, from the hottest regions of the world into cooler countries? Many are the proofs whereby any one capable of reasoning on the subject may be convinced that it is most unlikely this should be the case. The first and strongest argument is furnished by the winds, which always blow hot from these regions. The second is, that rain and frost are unknown there.[6] Now, whenever

---

[3] That the Nile flowed from the ocean, and that the ocean flowed all round the earth, were certainly opinions of Hecatæus (Fr. 278). It is probable, therefore, that his account of the inundation is here intended.

[4] This was the opinion of Anaxagoras, as well as of his pupil Euripides and others (Diodor. i. 38 ; Euripid. Helena, beg[s]. ; Seneca, Nat. Quæst. iv. 2 ; Ptol. Geog. iv. 9.) Herodotus and Diodorus are wrong in supposing snow could not be found on mountains in the hot climate of Africa ; perpetual snow is not confined to certain latitudes ; and ancient and modern discoveries prove that it is found in the ranges S. of Abyssinia. Nor is the heat always there what Herodotus imagines, and the cold of winter is often sensibly felt in the plains of Ethiopia about Gebel Birkel, far distant from high mountains, though the thermometer does not range below freezing. "The lower limit of perpetual snow is not a mere function of geographical latitude, or of mean annual temperature ; nor is it at the equator, or even within the tropics, that the snow-line reaches its greatest elevation above the level of the sea." (Humboldt, Cosmos, i. p. 328.) At the equator, on the Andes of Quito, the limit is at 15,790 feet above the sea ; on the southern declivity of the Himalaya it lies at 12,982 feet, and on the northern declivity at 16,630 ; and the volcano of Aconcagua in lat. 32° 30', which was found "to be more than 1400 ft. higher than Chimborazo, was once seen free from snow" (p. 329). See also Lyell's Pr. of Geology, c. vii.—[G. W.]

[5] That is from Central Africa, which was and still is the opinion of some geographers. There appears more reason to place the source of the "White Nile" to the S. of the Abyssinian ranges, between lat. 7° and 8° N. ; though a branch does come from the W., called Adda or Jengeh, which seem to be two names of the same stream.—[G. W.]

[6] Herodotus was not aware of the rainy season in Sennár and the S.S.W. of Abyssinia, nor did he know of the Abyssinian snow which is mentioned in the inscription of Ptolemy Philadelphus at Adulis, on the mountains beyond the Nile, "to the depth of a man's knee." (See Plin. vi. 34, and Vincent's Periplus.) The tropical rains do not extend as far N. as the Dar Shegéëh (Shaikéëh) and the great bend of the Nile, where showers and storms only occur occasionally, generally about the beginning of the inundation, and where a whole year sometimes passes without rain. The tropical rains begin about the end of March or beginning of April on the White Nile in lat. 4° N., and both the White and Blue Niles begin to rise at Khartoom the first week in May. The climate there is then very unhealthy, even for the natives.

snow falls, it must of necessity rain within five days ;[7] so that, .if there were snow, there must be rain also in those parts. Thirdly, it is certain that the natives of the country are black with the heat, that the kites and the swallows remain there the whole year, and that the cranes, when they fly from the rigours of a Scythian winter, flock thither to pass the cold season.[8] If then, in the country whence the Nile has its source, or in that through which it flows, there fell ever so little snow, it is absolutely impossible that any of these circumstances could take place.

The rain falls for many hours, but with intervals of clear weather and a strong sun, raising a vapour that causes a bad fever. The vegetation is very rapid and luxurious. That part of the valley immediately to the N. of the range of the rains is then infested with clouds of flies—a perfect plague—but they do not extend into the desert. Philostratus (Vit. Apoll. Tyan. ii. 9) says he does "not mean to gainsay the snows of the Ethiopians, or the hills of the Catadupi;" but he evidently disbelieves the accounts given of them. The cause of the two branches rising at the same time at Khartoom is the rain that falls at no great distance from that spot. The effect of the more southerly rains is felt afterwards. Calisthenes, the pupil of Aristotle, and afterwards Agatharcides and Strabo attributed the inundation to the rainy season in Ethiopia; and correctly, for it is *caused* by this, and not by the melting of snow. See Athenæus, Epit. ii. 89; Diod. i. 41; Strabo, xvii. p. 1121.— [G. W.]

[7] I have found nothing in any writer, ancient or modern, to confirm, or so much as to explain, this assertion. Aulus Gellius seems to have noticed it as an instance of "over rapid generalisation" (Epitom. lib. viii. c. 3); but his remarks on the subject are lost. It does not appear that at present, either in Asia Minor or in Southern Italy, rain necessarily follows snow within a certain number of days. But the meteorology of the countries bordering on the Mediterranean has no doubt undergone great changes since the time of Herodotus. In some parts of England there is a saying, that "three days of white frost are sure to bring rain."

[8] Cranes, and other wading birds are found, in the winter, in Upper Egypt, but far more in Ethiopia, and in spring immense flights of storks (*Ciconia alba*) collect together, which after soaring round in circles at a great height, return for the summer to the N. From the migration of cranes to Ethiopia arose the fable of the Cranes and Pygmies. The Ardea cinerea and garzetta, the platalea or spoonbill, the pelican, and some others remain the whole year in Egypt. The Grus cinerea winters in Ethiopia about Gebel Berkel. This last has been strangely mistaken for an ostrich at Beni Hassan, and is probably the Grus undetermined by Pickering (p. 169). The Ibis is rarely seen except near the Lake Menzaleh, where ducks, coots, and numerous water-fowl abound. The avocet was a native of Egypt as early as the 12th dynasty. The Numidian demoiselle (*Anthropoides Virgo*) is found, but not common, in Upper Egypt. Kites remain all the winter, and swallows also, though in small numbers, even at Thebes. The swallow was always the harbinger of spring, as in Greece and the rest of Europe; and the subject is represented on Greek vases, where a youth exclaims "Behold the swallow!" and another answers "Then it is now spring." (See Panofka's Bilder ant. Lebens, pl. xvii. fig. 6.) Boys (as Mr. Cumby observes) went about in Rhodes to collect gifts on the return of the swallow, as for the "grotto" at the beginning of our oyster season, though with greater pretensions, as Athenæus, quoting Theognis, shows (viii. p. 360), since they sometimes threatened to carry off what was not granted to their request :—" We will go away if you give us something; if not, we will never let you alone. We will either carry off the door, or the lintel, or the woman who sits within; she is small, and we can easily lift her. If you give any gift, let it be large. Open, open the door to the swallow, for we are not old men, but boys."—[G. W.]

23. As for the writer who attributes the phenomenon to the ocean,[*] his account is involved in such obscurity, that it is impossible to disprove it by argument. For my part I know of no river called Ocean, and I think that Homer, or one of the earlier poets, invented the name, and introduced it into his poetry.

24. Perhaps, after censuring all the opinions that have been put forward on this obscure subject, one ought to propose some theory of one's own. I will therefore proceed to explain what I think to be the reason of the Nile's swelling in the summer time. During the winter, the sun is driven out of his usual course by the storms, and removes to the upper parts of Libya. This is the whole secret in the fewest possible words ; for it stands to reason that the country to which the Sun-god approaches the nearest, and which he passes most directly over, will be scantest of water, and that there the streams which feed the rivers will shrink the most.

25. To explain, however, more at length, the case is this. The sun, in his passage across the upper parts of Libya, affects them in the following way. As the air in those regions is constantly clear, and the country warm through the absence of cold winds, the sun in his passage across them acts upon them exactly as he is wont to act elsewhere in summer, when his path is in the middle of heaven—that is, he attracts the water.[1] After attracting it, he again repels it into the upper regions, where the winds lay hold of it, scatter it, and reduce it to a vapour, whence it naturally enough comes to pass that the winds which blow from this quarter—the south and south-west—are

---

[*] The person to whom Herodotus alludes is Hecatæus. He mentions it also as an opinion of the Greeks of Pontus, that the ocean flowed round the whole earth (B. iv. ch. 8). That the Nile flowed from the ocean was maintained by Hecatæus, and by Euthymenes of Marseilles (Plut. de Pl. Phil. iv. 1), who related that, "having sailed round Africa, he found, as long as the Etesian winds blew, the water forced into the Nile caused it to overflow, and that, when they ceased, the Nile, no longer receiving that impulse, subsided again. The taste of the water of the sea was also sweet, and the animals similar to those in the Nile." This mistake was owing to another river on the coast of Africa having been found to produce crocodiles and hippopotami. The name "Ocean" having been given by the Egyptians to the Nile does not appear to be connected with the remark of Herodotus, as it is not noticed by him but by Diodorus (i. 96), and Herodotus says he "never knew of a river being called Ocean." We see from Plut. Plac. Ph. iv. 1, that Eudoxus knew that the summer and winter seasons were different in the N. and S. hemispheres.—[G. W.]

[1] Herodotus does not here allude to the old notion of the sun being "fed by water," but to the moisture it attracts which is carried by the winds to the S., and then returned in the form of rain by the southerly winds. Compare Aristot. Meteor. ii. 2: Anacreon, Od. xix. πίνει . . . ὁ δ᾽ ἥλιος θάλασσαν. Cic. Nat. Deor. b. ii.—[G. W.]

of all winds the most rainy. And my own opinion is that the sun does not get rid of all the water which he draws year by year from the Nile, but retains some about him. When the winter begins to soften, the sun goes back again to his old place in the middle of the heaven, and proceeds to attract water equally from all countries. Till then the other rivers run big, from the quantity of rain-water which they bring down from countries where so much moisture falls that all the land is cut into gullies ; but in summer, when the showers fail, and the sun attracts their water, they become low. The Nile, on the contrary, not deriving any of its bulk from rains, and being in winter subject to the attraction of the sun, naturally runs at that season, unlike all other streams, with a less burthen of water than in the summer time. For in summer it is exposed to attraction equally with all other rivers, but in winter it suffers alone. The sun, therefore, I regard as the sole cause of the phenomenon.

26. It is the sun also, in my opinion, which, by heating the space through which it passes, makes the air in Egypt so dry. There is thus perpetual summer in the upper parts of Libya. Were the position of the heavenly regions reversed, so that the place where now the north wind and the winter have their dwelling became the station of the south wind and of the noon-day, while, on the other hand, the station of the south wind became that of the north, the consequence would be that the sun, driven from the mid-heaven by the winter and the northern gales, would betake himself to the upper parts of Europe, as he now does to those of Libya, and then I believe his passage across Europe would affect the Ister exactly as the Nile is affected at the present day.

27. And with respect to the fact that no breeze blows from the Nile, I am of opinion that no wind is likely to arise in very hot countries, for breezes love to blow from some cold quarter.

28. Let us leave these things, however, to their natural course, to continue as they are and have been from the beginning. With regard to the *sources* of the Nile,[2] I have found no one among

---

[2] The sources of the great eastern branch of the Nile have long been discovered. They were first visited by the Portuguese Jesuit, Father Lobo, and afterwards by Bruce; those of the White river are still unknown (see above n. [8] on ch. 19). Herodotus affirms that of all the persons he had consulted, none pretended to give him any information about the sources, except a scribe of the sacred treasury of Minerva at Saïs, who said it rose from a certain abyss beneath two pointed hills between Syene and Elephantine. This is an important passage in his narrative, as it involves the question of his having visited the Thebaïd. He soon afterwards (ch. 29) asserts that "as far as Elephantine he was an eye-witness" of what he describes; and yet, though so much interested about this great question, and persuaded that the hierogrammat of Saïs was joking, he did not when at Elephantine look or inquire whether

all those with whom I have conversed, whether Egyptians, Libyans, or Greeks,[3] who professed to have any knowledge, except
a single person.   He was the scribe[4] who kept the register
of the sacred treasures of Minerva in the city of Saïs, and he
did not seem to me to be in earnest when he said that he knew
them perfectly well.   His story was as follows :—" Between
Syêné, a city of the Thebaïs, and Elephantiné, there are " (he

the Nile actually rose beneath the peaked hills of Crophi and Mophi, nor detect the
fallacy of the story about the river flowing from the same source northwards into
Egypt and southwards into Ethiopia. Its course was as well known in his day at
Elephantine as now. This, and the fact of his making so much of the Labyrinth,
when the monuments of Thebes would have excited his admiration in a far greater
degree, have been thought to argue against his having been at Thebes and Elephantine ; and any one on visiting Elephantine would be expected to speak of it as an
island rather than as a "city." It is, however, possible that his omitting to describe
the monuments of Thebes, which to this day excite the wonder of all who see them,
may have been owing to their having been fully described by Hecatæus. The
names Crophi and Mophi are like the unmeaning words used in joke, in the nursery, by Orientals, at the present day ; the second repeating the sound of the first,
and always beginning with m, as "fersh mersh," "salta malta," &c. Crophi and
Mophi do not, as has been supposed, signify "bad" and "good."—[G. W.]

Colonel Mure (Lit. of Greece, vol. iv. p. 387) compares the Crophi and Mophi of
the Saitic tribe to the Gog and Magog "*of our own nursery mythology*," apparently
forgetting that the words Gog and Magog come to us from Scripture (Ezek. xxxviii.
2 ; Rev. xx. 8). The formation of unmeaning or absurd words by means of a rhym-
ing repetition, together with a change of the initial letter, is common in our own
language. With us the second word begins ordinarily, not with m, but with the
labial nearest to m, viz. b, or with its cognate tenuis, p. Examples of this usage are
—*hurly-burly, hocus-pocus, higgledy-piggledy, hubbub, niminy-piminy, namby-pamby,*
&c. In *hugger-mugger* and *pell-mell,* we keep to the Oriental usage, and employ the
m. In *helter-skelter, hum-drum,* and perhaps a few other words, we adopt an entirely
different sound.

[3] This was one of the great problems of antiquity, as of later times ; and Cæsar
is even reported to have said :—

"—— spes sit mihi certa videndi
Niliacos fontes, bellum civile relinquam."

—Luc. Phars. x. 191. Cp. Hor. iv. Od. xiv. 45 :—

"Fontium qui celat origines
Nilus."

See above, note [9], ch. 19.—[G. W.]

[4] The scribes had different offices and grades. The sacred scribes held a high
post in the priesthood ; and the royal scribes were the king's sons and military men
of rank. There were also ordinary scribes or notaries, who were conveyancers,
wrote letters on business, settled accounts, and performed different offices in the
market. The sacred scribes, or hierogrammats, had also various duties. Some, as
the one here mentioned, were scribes of the treasury, others of the granaries, others
of the documents belonging to the temple, &c. The scribes always had with them
a bag, or case having wooden sides, ornamented with coloured devices generally on
leather, and a pendent leather mouth tied by a thong to hold the ink-palette with
its reed-pens, the papyrus-rolls, and other things they required, which was carried
by an attendant slung at his back ; but in the house a box was sometimes used in
its stead. Lucian says (Macrob. s. 4) they were remarkable for longevity, like the
Brachmanes (Brahmins) of India, and others, owing to their mode of life. (Of
their dress and duties, see note [1] ch. 37, figs. 8, 9, and woodcut note [8] ch. 177.)
—[G. W.]

said) "two hills with sharp conical tops ; the name of the one is Crophi, of the other, Mophi. Midway between them are the fountains of the Nile, fountains which it is impossible to fathom. Half the water runs northward into Egypt, half to the south towards Ethiopia." The fountains were known to be unfathomable, he declared, because Psammetichus, an Egyptian king, had made trial of them. He had caused a rope to be made, many thousand fathoms in length, and had sounded the fountain with it, but could find no bottom. By this the scribe gave me to understand, if there was any truth at all in what he said, that in this fountain there are certain strong eddies, and a regurgitation, owing to the force wherewith the water dashes against the mountains, and hence a sounding-line cannot be got to reach the bottom of the spring.

29. No other information on this head could I obtain from any quarter. All that I succeeded in learning further of the more distant portions of the Nile, by ascending myself as high as Elephantiné, and making inquiries concerning the parts beyond, was the following :—As one advances beyond Elephantiné, the land rises.[5] Hence it is necessary in this part of the river to attach a rope to the boat on each side, as men harness an ox, and so proceed on the journey. If the rope snaps, the vessel is borne away down stream by the force of the current. The navigation continues the same for four days, the river winding greatly, like the Mæander,[6] and the distance traversed amount-

[5] This fact should have convinced Herodotus of the improbability of the story of the river flowing southwards into Ethiopia. That boats are obliged to be dragged by ropes in order to pass the rapids is true ; and in performing this arduous duty great skill and agility are required, the men being often obliged to swim from rock to rock to secure the ropes and alter the direction of the draft. After passing the first cataract at Asouan (the ancient Syene), which is done in about five hours, the boat sails unimpeded to the second cataract, a distance of 232 miles ; a rocky bed of the river called Batn-el-Hadjar, "belly of stone," continues thence about 45 m. to Semneh, after which it is navigable here and there, with occasional rapids, as far as the third cataract of Hannek, below Tombos, about lat. 19° 40'. Beyond this is an unimpeded sail of 200 m. (passing the modern Ordee and Old Dongola) to the fourth cataract, about 18 m. above Gebel Berkel. From thence to the N. end of the isle of Meroë is a sail of about 240 m., the river being open some way further to the S., beyond the site of the city of Meroë and the modern Shendy. Between Meroë and Dongola is the great bend or "elbow" of the Nile, where the course of the river changes from a northerly to a southerly direction, as described by Strabo (b. xvii. beg[s].) Part of the route from Asouan to Meroë may be performed by land, leaving the Nile at Korosko, below Derr the capital of Nubia, from which point is a caravan round to the great bend at Aboo-Hamed, above Gebel Berkel, a journey of eight days with camels.—[G. W.]

[6] The windings of the Mæander are perhaps at the present day still more remarkable than they were anciently, owing to the growth of the alluvial plain through which it flows. Chandler observes : "The river runs from the mouth of the lake *with many windings*, through groves of tamarisk, toward Miletus, proceeding by the right wing of the theatre *in mazes* to the sea, which is in view, and distant, as we

ing to twelve schœnes. Here you come upon a smooth and level plain, where the Nile flows in two branches, round an island called Tachompso.[7] The country above Elephantiné is

computed, about eight miles." (Travels, i. ch. 53.) A good representation of these sinuosities will be found in the Ionian Antiquities (vol. i. ch. iii. plate 1). By the age of Augustus the word "Mæander" had come to be used in its modern generic sense (Strab. xii. p. 835; Virg. Æn. v. 251).

[7] The distances given by Herodotus are 4 days through the district of Dodeca-schœnus to Tachompso Isle, then 40 days by land, then 12 days by boat to Meroë, altogether 56 days. The Nile, however, is not tortuous like the Mæander, nor is there any great bend before that near Korosko, and his isle of Tachompso is uncertain; but as he speaks of its being inhabited partly by Egyptians, partly by Ethiopians, it is possible that he may have confounded it with Philæ, which Strabo calls "an abode common to" those two people. Ptolemy places *Metacompso* opposite Pselcis, where a large Egyptian fortress of very early date still remains, and which must have continued to be a strong post in the time of the Romans. It was at Pselcis that Petronius defeated the generals of Candace, before he advanced to Napata, and the island mentioned by Strabo, to which the routed enemy swam for protection, was perhaps the Tachompso of Herodotus. If so, that island has since been carried away. The large *lake*, said to have been in its vicinity, was merely the open Nile (a reach being probably called, as it now is, a "lake" or *birkeh*); and from thence was a march of 40 days by land to that part where the Nile was again navigable (at the island now called Tombos, on the frontier of Dongola). From this was a sail of 12 days more to Meroë. The omission of all mention of Napata, the old capital of Ethiopia, by the informant of Herodotus, might at first sight lead us to suppose the land-journey was through the desert (to Aboo-Hamed); but the distance of 12 days thence to Meroë is far too much; and Herodotus evidently speaks of the journey by the river-side to the spot where the Nile was again navigable. Gebel Berkel is apparently the "sacred mountain" mentioned by Strabo (xvi.), and it is always so called in the hieroglyphics. The distances from Syene to Napata, and from this to Meroë, do not agree with the position of Gebel Berkel, and if Napata was placed lower down at old Dongola, that position would agree better with the ancient measurements. They are—

	M.P.	Eng. miles.				Eng. miles.
Syene to Napata	. .	514 nearly 474	Asouan to Old Dongola	. . . .		484
Napata to Meroë	. .	360 above 331¼	Dongola to Gebel Berkel 80 } Dongola to }			337
			G. Berkel to Meroë Island 257 } Meroë Island }			
		874 about 804¼		Total . . .		821

The Roman mile may be reckoned at 4860 feet; for though I found 4785 to be its length, by measuring two, marked by milestones on the coast of Syria, and other authorities give it 4842 and 4828, or 4820 feet, Caval° Canina has shown it to be 4861 English feet, or mètres 1487·730. The great remains at Gebel Berkel, and the many pyramids near it, argue that it was the capital, unless indeed it was merely the "holy hill," like that of Sarábat el Khádem in the peninsula of Mount Sinai, chosen by the Egyptians as early as the reign of Osirtasen I. If "the small city of Napata" stood at old Dongola (formerly called Dankala), which was evidently the site of an ancient town, and has long been the capital of that part of Ethiopia, this might account for Meroë having a similar name, "Dunkalah." On the other hand, the distance, 80 Roman miles, from Tergedum to Napata, agrees well with that from old Dongola to Gebel Berkel; and the large island (now Tangol or Tangos) just above old Dongola might answer to the I. of Gagaudes. On the whole, there is good reason for placing Napata at Gebel Berkel; and it is one of the greatest errors to suppose the ancients must always be right in their distances, or in any other information. The name fi-ape-t seems to signify " of Ape-t " or " Tape," as if it were derived from or an offset " of Thebes " (in Harris's Standards); and it was not unusual to give the names of Egyptian cities to those of Ethiopia, as was often done in Nubia.

inhabited by the Ethiopians, who possess one half of this island, the Egyptians occupying the other. Above the island there is

The Itinerary of Antoninus gives these names of places in Lower Ethiopia (or Nubia):

			M.P.
Contra-Syene to	Parembole (*Dabôd*)	. .	12
" "	Tzitzi	. . .	2
" "	Taphis (Téfi, Táyfee)	. .	14
" "	Talmis (Kalabshee)	. .	8
" "	Tutzis (Gerf Hossayn)	. .	20
" "	Pselcis (Dakkeh) .	. .	12
" "	Corte (Kórtee)	. .	4
" "	Heirasycaminon (Maharraka)	.	4
			—
			80

(About 73³/₄ English miles; the real distance being about 71¼ by land, and by water about 84.)

On the opposite bank:—

		M.P.
Heirasycaminon to	Contra-Pselcis	11
"	Contra-Talmis . .	24
"	Contra-Taphis . .	10
"	Philæ	24
"	Syene	3
		—
		72

(About 66¼ English miles.)

Pliny (b. xxix.) mentions the towns taken by Petronius on his way to Napata:—

Pselcis.
Primis.
Abocois.
Phthuris.
Cambusis.
Attena.
Stadysis, remarkable for its cataract.
Napata, plundered by him; and he went 870 M.P. above Syene.

The distances given by Pliny are—

			M.P.
From Syene to	Heirasycaminon		54
" "	Tama	.	75
" "	the Ethiopian district of Euonymiton	.	120
" "	Acina	.	54
" "	Pitara	.	25
" "	Tergedum (between which two is the island Gagaudes)		106
" "	Napata, a small city		80
			—
			514
Then to Meroë island, the city being 60 M.P. from the beginning of the island			360
			—
			874

(About 804¼ English miles.)

Ptolemy (Geog. iv. 5, 7 & 8) omits the names of towns between Syene and Pselcis; but opposite Pselcis he places *Metacompso;* and then "after *Pselcis* and the great cataract (of Wadee Halfeh) he mentions Tasitia, Boüm (Bóων), Autoba, Phthuri, Pierê, Ptemythis (Πτεμυθίς), *Abuncis, Cambysis ærarium,* Erchoas, Satachtha, Mori (Μόρου), Nacis, and Tathis, on the W. bank; and on the opposite side Pnups, Berêthis, Gerbô, Patæta, Ponteris, *Primis-parva*, Arabis, *Napata*, Sacolê, Sandacê, Orbadari, Primis-magna, and then the island forming the district of Meroë, lying between the Nile which flows to the W. of it, and the Astaboras which is to the E., beyond which is Sacolchê, Esêr, Dororum (Δόρων) Vicus, and then the junction of the Nile and Astapus. But his adding "and then the junction of the Astaboras and the Astapus" tends to mislead; and he probably meant " of the Astasobas and the Astapus."—[G. W.]

a great lake, the shores of which are inhabited by Ethiopian nomads ; after passing it, you come again to the stream of the Nile, which runs into the lake.   Here you land, and travel for forty days along the banks of the river, since it is impossible to proceed further in a boat on account of the sharp peaks which jut out from the water, and the sunken rocks which abound in that part of the stream.   When you have passed this portion of the river in the space of forty days, you go on board another boat, and proceed by water for twelve days more, at the end of which time you reach a great city called Meroë, which is said to be the capital of the other Ethiopians.[3]   The only gods wor-

[3] This is in contradistinction to the νομάδες, which in this instance may have been merely a corruption of "Nobatæ," since an agricultural people could not have been nomade.   For though late writers pretend that the Nobatæ were a Libyan people, introduced into the valley of the Nile under the Roman Empire, it is evident that the name was of early date and Ethiopian, having been taken from the ram-headed deity principally worshipped there, Noub, Noum, or Nou, who was the great god of Ethiopia from the most remote periods (see next note, and App. CH. iii. § 2). Αἰθίοψ was evidently a corruption of the Egyptian name for southern Ethiopia or Nubia, "Ethaush" or "Ethosh," the ps being substituted for sh, a sound the Greeks could neither write nor pronounce.   The Greeks (like the Arabs) often adopted a word having some signification in their own language, if it resembled a foreign one, and the Greek derivation of Αἰθίοψ is on a par with that of Isis, from εἶσις, "knowledge" (Plut. de Is. s. 2), and many others.   The isle of Meroë, formed by three rivers, as Strabo and Josephus state, contained between the main branch of the Nile on the west; the Astapus or the modern Abáwee Nile, or Bahr-el-Azrek, with its tributary the Rahad (probably the Astasobas) on the south ; and the Astaboras, now the A'tbara, on the east; and according to Strabo (xvi. and xvii. pp. 1095, 1162) it had the form of an oblong shield, measuring 3000 stadia (at least 341 miles) and 1000 stadia (about 113¾ miles) in breadth (see Plin. vi. 29).   The city of Meroë stood near the modern Dankalah, remarkable for its numerous pyramids, 27 m. N.E. of the modern Shendy. Napata was also the capital of Ethiopia, and that too at a very remote period ; and Meroë was probably the seat of an independent kingdom.   The appearance of the pyramids of Dankalah indeed show it to have been very ancient, and after the Egyptian kings of the 12th and 18th dynasties had established themselves at Napata, Meroë became the sole capital of the Ethiopian kings; and though Napata was the royal seat in the time of the Sabacos and Tirhaka, Meroë was still the metropolis of Southern Ethiopia, as it was in the days of Herodotus and of the Ptolemies ; but it had lost all its importance in the time of the Roman Empire.   The pyramids of Noori doubtless belonged also to Napata, the neighbouring ones at Gebel Berkel (Napata) itself being of a rather more recent date ; and though the pyramids of Dankalah have so great an appearance of age, the tropical rains have had an effect on them to which those of Noori were not subject, and no ruins of temples exist at Meroë of an antiquity at all comparable to that of the oldest ones at Gebel Berkel.   The notion of Diodorus and Strabo that Meroë was built by Cambyses is too extravagant to be noticed.   There are some curiously fortified lines on the hills about five or six miles below Gebel Berkel, commanding the approaches to that place, by the river and on the shore, apparently of Ethiopian time.   I believe they have not been noticed ; and I was led to examine them by perceiving their stone walls upon the irregularly indented cliffs they cover.   They extend about half-a-mile inland from the river, and from their following every projecting corner of the hills, the total number of feet of wall is nearly 10,000; but there are no vestiges of houses or other buildings within the area they enclose.—[G. W.]

Meroë is frequently mentioned under the name of Mirukh in the Assyrian inscriptions.

shipped by the inhabitants are Jupiter and Bacchus ;[*] to whom great honours are paid. There is an oracle of Jupiter in the city, which directs the warlike expeditions of the Ethiopians ; when it commands they go to war,[1] and in whatever direction it bids them march, thither straightway they carry their arms.

[*] Amun and Osiris answered to Jupiter and Bacchus; and both the Amun of Thebes and the ram-headed Nou (Noum, Noub, or Kneph) were worshipped in Ethiopia. But it is this last deity to whom Herodotus alludes; for he says "the Egyptians call Jupiter Ammon," and in later times the ram-headed god was also supposed to answer to Jupiter. This is shown by inscriptions at the Oasis and at Syene, where he was worshipped under the name of Jupiter-Ammon-Cenubis, in company with Sate (Juno) and Anouké (Vesta), who formed the triad of the cataracts. (See note [*] ch. 42.) Osiris, the god of the dead, was worshipped in Ethiopia, as throughout Egypt, the religious rites of that country having been borrowed from the Egyptians; but it cannot be said that these two were the only gods of Ethiopia. Strabo mentions the worship of Hercules, Pan, and Isis, as well as a barbaric god, at Meroë (xvii. 565); and in the temples of that country, whether erected by Ethiopians or by Egyptian monarchs who ruled there, many other gods shared in the worship paid to the principal deity of the sanctuary. Besides many of the usual Egyptian deities are some of uncommon form peculiar to Ethiopia; and at Wady Owatayb is one with three lion's heads and four arms, more like an Indian than an Egyptian god, though he wears a head-dress common to gods and Kings, especially in Ptolemaic and Roman times. He was perhaps the barbaric god mentioned by Strabo. The whole character of the temple is copied from Egypt, and the Amun of Thebes and the ram-headed Noum or Noub hold the most conspicuous places there. Indeed the ram-headed god was the chief deity throughout Ethiopia; and though a lion-headed god is found at Amâra, as well as at Wady Owatayb, there is no appearance of his having been of the same early age as Noum, and the king whose name occurs on both temples is of late time. It is to these two, Jupiter and Osiris, that Strabo alludes when he says "the Ethiopians acknowledge two gods, one immortal, the cause of all things, the other mortal, who has no name," or more properly whose name was not uttered, the mysterious Osiris, who had lived on earth, and, dying, had become the judge of men in a future state. He also mentions other inferior gods.—[G. W.]

[1] The influence of the priests at Meroë, through the belief that they spoke the commands of the Deity, is more fully shown by Strabo and Diodorus, who say it was their custom to send to the king, when it pleased them, and order him to put an end to himself, in obedience to the will of the oracle imparted to them; and to such a degree had they contrived to enslave the understanding of those princes by superstitious fears, that they were obeyed without opposition. At length a king, called Ergamenes, a contemporary of Ptolemy Philadelphus, dared to disobey their orders, and having entered "the golden chapel" with his soldiers, caused them to

30. On leaving this city, and again mounting the stream, in the same space of time which it took you to reach the capital from Elephantiné, you come to the Deserters,[2] who bear the name of Asmach. This word, translated into our language, means "the men who stand on the left hand of the king."[3]

be put to death in his stead, and abolished the custom (Diod. iii. 6; Strabo, xvii. p. 1163). Ergamenes had "studied the philosophy of Greece," and had the sense to distinguish between priestly rule and religion, knowing that blind obedience to the priests did not signify obedience to the divine will; but these vested rights on man's credulity seem to have been afterwards revived among the Ethiopians, and the expedition sent by Mohammed Ali up the White Nile learnt that the same custom of ordering the king to die now exists among some of their barbarous descendants. The name of Ergamenes is found in the temple of Dakkeh, in Nubia.— [G. W.]

[3] The descendants of the 240,000 deserters from Psammetichus lived, according to Herodotus, 4 months' journey above Elephantine (ch. 31), from which Meroë stood half-way. He reckons (ch. 29) 56 days from Elephantine to Meroë, the double of which would be·112, instead of 120 days; and Meroë being half-way would require the country of the Automoli to be in the modern Abyssinia. They were called 'Ασμάχ, in allusion to their original post on the "left," not of the king, but of the Egyptian army, the cause of their desertion (see following note). This word may be traced in the *shemal*, "left," of the Arabic; and Esar, a city mentioned by Pliny, 17 days from Meroë, where the Egyptian deserters lived 300 years, is remarkable from having the same signification in Arabic, *yesár* being also "the left." Some have derived the name of Axum in Abyssinia from 'Ασμάχ. According to Strabo (xvii. p. 541) they were called Sembrites, or Sebritæ, meaning "strangers," which may either be compounded of the Egyptian *shemmo*, "stranger," and *beri* (or *mberi*), "new;" or be taken from the name of the country they inhabited, *Saba*; for "Sembrites" is the same as "Sebrites," *mb* being often pronounced simply *b*. It is remarkable that Strabo places the country they inhabited, called Tenesis, inland from the port of Saba (xvii. p. 530). They lived in an island above that of Meroë, and in his time they were subject to one of the many queens who at various periods ruled Ethiopia: for there was a queen Candace in the time of Petronius; and this title, rather than name, passed, according to Pliny (vi. 29) from one queen to another for many years. The monuments of Gebel Berkel, and other places, also show that queens frequently held the sceptre in Ethiopia; but the queen of Sheba in Solomon's time, claimed by the Abyssinians, was evidently not from that country, for Sheba was probably in the southern part of Arabia, and the Arabians, like the Ethiopians, were frequently governed by queens. (See note to Book iii. ch. 107). The name Saba may point out a connexion with the country where the *lion*-god was worshipped (*saba* meaning "lion"); and Josephus (Antiq. ii. 5) says that Saba was a name of Meroë. The withdrawal of the Egyptian troops to Ethiopia is readily accounted for by the intercourse that had so long subsisted between the two countries, the royal family of Ethiopia being often related by marriage to that of Egypt, which accounts for some princes of Cush having the title "royal son" in the Theban sculptures (though these are mostly Egyptian viceroys, and sons of Pharaohs); and the fact of the royal succession having been maintained in the female line explains the reason of so many queens having ruled in Ethiopia. This too gave the Ethiopians a claim on the throne of Egypt when the direct line failed, and accounts for the Sabacos and others occasionally obtaining the crown of Egypt by right and not by conquest. —[G. W.]

[3] Diodorus says that the reason of the Egyptian troops deserting from Psammetichus was his having placed them in the *left* wing, while the right was given to the strangers in his army, which is not only more probable than the reason assigned by Herodotus, but is strongly confirmed by the discovery of an inscription at Aboosim-

These Deserters are Egyptians of the warrior cast, who, to the number of two hundred and forty thousand, went over to the Ethiopians in the reign of king Psammetichus. The cause of their desertion was the following :—Three garrisons were maintained in Egypt at that time,[4] one in the city of Elephantiné

bel in Nubia, written apparently by the Greeks who accompanied Psammetichus when in pursuit of the deserters. These Greeks were the Ionians and Carians taken into his pay, in order, as Herodotus was told (ch. 152), to aid in dethroning his colleagues, though in reality from the advantage of employing the Greeks against the increasing power of his Asiatic neighbours (see note [5] on ch. 152). The first Greeks known to the Egyptians being Ionians led to the name Ionian being afterwards used by them for all Greeks, as we find in the Rosetta stone, and other documents. The Asiatics, for a similar reason, called the Greeks "Ionians," "the race of Javan." Ionia in the Nakhshi-Rustam Inscription is "Yavaná," or Yuná, and the ancient Greeks are still known in Arabic as the "Yunáni," or "Iunáni." The inscription states that Psammetichus himself went as far as Elephantine, the Greeks being sent forward with some of his adherents into Ethiopia; and the point where they had a parley with the deserters was apparently, from the inscription, near Kerkis, some distance above Aboosimbel, where on their return they left this record of their journey. It is also curious from its style; and from the early indication of the long vowels H and Ω (the latter apparently an O with a dot in the centre), which—as well as other arguments—proves that they came gradually into use, and long before the time of Simonides, who was not born till 556 B.C. The reign of Psammetichus dates in the middle of the 7th century B.C. The inscription, of which the following is a transcript, is thus translated by Colonel Leake :—"King Psam-

metichus having come to Elephantine, those who were with Psammetichus, the son of Theocles, wrote this. They sailed, and came to above Kerkis, to where the river rises (?) . . . . . the Egyptian Amasis. The writer is Damearchon the son of Amœbichus, and Pelephus (?) the son of Udamus" (?). (This Ph looks rather like the old K or Q.) In the same place are several other inscriptions, some of the same style and time, and others written by Phœnicians in their language, the date of which is unknown. If this was the 3rd, instead of the 1st Psammetichus, "the Egyptian Amasis" may have been the general, afterwards king of Egypt; for Herodotus, who only mentions one Psammetichus, may have been wrong in supposing the desertion of the troops took place under the son of Neco. This would bring the date of the inscription within 600 B.C. (See note [5] on ch. 161, and hist. notice App. ch. viii. § 3¾.) There is a coin of Thrace of date about 550 B.C. which has the Ω (in Millingen), though many much later have not the long vowels. Coins and vases are no authorities against their use, as the archaic style was imitated to a late time. Some inscriptions, as that of Potidea in the British Museum, as late as 432, have no H nor Ω. The Ξ is ΧΣ, and the Ψ is ΦΣ; and it has been supposed that there was no Ω in public inscriptions till the archonship of Euclid, B.C. 403. But the long vowels were used earlier by the Greeks of Asia Minor. The Ω and Σ were changed to ω and C in the age of the later Ptolemies, and were re-introduced in the reign of Adrian.—[G. W.]

[4] It was always the custom of the Egyptians to have a garrison stationed, as

against the Ethiopians, another in the Pelusiac Daphnæ,[5] against the Syrians and Arabians, and a third, against the Libyans, in Marea. (The very same posts are to this day occupied by the Persians, whose forces are in garrison both in Daphnæ and in Elephantiné.) Now it happened, that on one occasion the garrisons were not relieved during the space of three years; the soldiers, therefore, at the end of that time, consulted together, and having determined by common consent to revolt, marched away towards Ethiopia. Psammetichus, informed of the movement, set out in pursuit, and coming up with them, besought them with many words not to desert the gods of their country, nor abandon their wives and children. "Nay, but," said one of the deserters with an unseemly gesture, "wherever we go, we are sure enough of finding wives and children." Arrived in Ethiopia, they placed themselves at the disposal of the king. In return, he made them a present of a tract of land which belonged to certain Ethiopians with whom he was at feud, bidding them expel the inhabitants and take possession of their territory. From the time that this settlement was formed, their acquaintance with Egyptian manners has tended to civilise the Ethiopians.[6]

31. Thus the course of the Nile is known, not only throughout Egypt, but to the extent of four months' journey either by land or water above the Egyptian boundary; for on calculation it will be found that it takes that length of time to travel from Elephantiné to the country of the Deserters. There the direc-

---

Herodotus states, on the frontier, at Elephantine, at Daphnæ of Pelusium, and at Marea; but in the time of the victorious kings of the 18th dynasty others were stationed at Semneh, above the second cataract, and also farther south in Upper Ethiopia, as well as in various parts of Asia where they had extended their conquests, which last were only finally taken from them in the time of Neco II., the son and successor of this Psammetichus.—[G. W.]

[5] Daphnæ, Daphné, or Daphnes was 16 Roman miles from Pelusium, according to the Itinerary of Antoninus. It was the Tahpanhes of Scripture. See Jer. xliii. 8; Ezek. xxx. 18.—[G. W.]

[6] This would be a strong argument, if required, against the notion of civilisation having come from the Ethiopians to Egypt; but the monuments prove beyond all question that the Ethiopians borrowed from Egypt their religion and their habits of civilisation. They even adopted the Egyptian as the language of religion and of the court, which it continued to be till the power of the Pharaohs had fallen, and their dominion was again confined to the frontier of Ethiopia. It was through Egypt too that Christianity passed into Ethiopia, even in the age of the Apostles (Acts viii. 27), as is shown by the eunuch of queen Candace (see note [2] on this chapter). Other proofs of their early conversion are also found, as in the inscriptions at Farras, above Aboosimbel, one of which has the date of Diocletian, though the Nobatæ are said not to have become Christians till the reign of Justinian. The erroneous notion of Egypt having borrowed from Ethiopia may perhaps have been derived from the return of the Egyptian court to Egypt after it had retired to Ethiopia on the invasion of the Shepherds.—[G. W.]

tion of the river is from west to east.[7]   Beyond, no one has any
certain knowledge of its course, since the country is uninhabited
by reason of the excessive heat.

32. I did hear, indeed, what I will now relate, from certain
natives of Cyrênê.   Once upon a time, they said, they were on
a visit to the oracular shrine of Ammon,[8] when it chanced that
in the course of conversation with Etearchus, the Ammonian
king, the talk fell upon the Nile, how that its sources were unknown to all men.   Etearchus upon this mentioned that some
Nasamonians[9] had once come to his court, and when asked if
they could give any information concerning the uninhabited parts
of Libya, had told the following tale.   (The Nasamonians are a
Libyan race who occupy the Syrtis, and a tract of no great size
towards the east.[1])   They said there had grown up among them
some wild young men, the sons of certain chiefs, who, when they
came to man's estate, indulged in all manner of extravagancies,
and among other things drew lots for five of their number to go

[7] This only applies to the white river, or western branch of the Nile.—[G. W.]

[8] This was in the modern Oasis of See-wah (Siwah), where remains of the temple
are still seen. The oracle long continued in great repute, and though in Strabo's time
it began to lose its importance (the mode of divination learnt from Etruria having
superseded the consultation of the distant Ammon), still its answers were sought in
the solution of difficult questions in the days of Juvenal, "after the cessation of the
Delphic oracle."   In consulting the god at the Oasis of Ammon, it was customary,
says Quintus Curtius, "for the priests to carry the figure of the god in a gilded
boat, ornamented with numerous silver pateræ hanging from it on both sides, behind
which followed a train of matrons and virgins singing a certain uncouth hymn, in
the manner of the country, with a view to propitiate the deity, and induce him to
return a satisfactory answer."   See the boat or ark of Nou (Nef) in the temple of
Elephantine in Pl. 56, 57 of Dr. Young and the Egyptian Society.   Of the appearance of the god he says, "id quod pro Deo colitur, non eandem effigiem habet,
quam vulgo Diis artifices accommodaverunt, umbriculo maxime similis est habitus,
smaragdis et gemmis coagmentatus:" but the word umbriculo has perplexed all commentators.
All the cultivable spots, abounding with springs, in that desert, are called Wah;
the chief of which are the See-wah, the Little Oasis, the Wah surnamed e' Dakhleh,
i. e., "the inner," or western, and the Wah el Khargeh, "the outer Oasis," to the
east of it, which is the great Oasis. The others, of El Hayz, Faráfreh, and the Oases
of the Blacks, in the interior, to the westward, are small, and some of them only
temporarily inhabited; but those above mentioned are productive, and abound in
palms, fruit-trees, rice, barley, and various productions.   They are not, as often
supposed, cultivated spots in the midst of an endless level tract of sand, but abrupt
depressions in the high table-land, portions of which are irrigated by running
streams, and, being surrounded by cliffs more or less precipitous, are in appearance
not unlike a portion of the valley of the Nile, with its palm-trees, villages, and gardens, transported to the desert, without its river, and bordered by a sandy plain
reaching to the hills that surround it, in which stunted tamarisk bushes, coarse
grasses, and desert plants struggle to keep themselves above the drifted sand that
collects around them.—[G. W.]

[9] This word seems to be "Nahsi Amun," or "Negroes of Ammonitis," or Northern Libya; Nahsi being the Egyptian name for the Negroes of Africa. See my
note on ch. 182, Book iv.—[G. W.]

[1] Vide infra, iv. 172–3.

The Little Oasis.

and explore the desert parts of Libya, and try if they could not penetrate further than any had done previously. (The coast of Libya along the sea which washes it to the north, throughout its entire length from Egypt to Cape Soloeis,[2] which is its furthest point, is inhabited by Libyans of many distinct tribes, who possess the whole tract except certain portions which belong to the Phœnicians and the Greeks.[3] Above the coast-line and the country inhabited by the maritime tribes, Libya is full of wild beasts ; while beyond the wild beast region there is a tract

[2] This is supposed by Rennell to be Cape *Cantin*, near Mogador, on the W. coast of Africa ; but, with great deference to so high an authority, I am inclined to think it Cape *Spartel*, near Tangier, as the Persian Sataspes, condemned by Xerxes to undertake the voyage round Africa, is said, after sailing through the Straits of Gibraltar (Pillars of Hercules) and doubling the Libyan promontory called Soloeis, to have steered southwards, for here the southerly course evidently begins (see Book iv. ch. 42). Herodotus, too, measures the breadth of Libya from Egypt to the extreme end of the northern coast, not to the most westerly headland to the south of it, which too he is not likely to have known ; and Aristotle (De Mundo, 3) shows the Greeks measured the extent of Africa E. and W., only along the northern coast, by saying "it extends to the Pillars of Hercules."—[G. W.]

[3] That is, the Cyrenaica, and the possessions of the Phœnicians and Carthaginians, or more properly the Pœni, on the N. and W. coasts. Pœni, Punici, and Phœnices were the same name of the race, *oi*, or *œ*, or *u* having the same sound in Greek. Carthaginian signified properly the people of Carthage, as Tyrians did the "Phœnicians of Tyre ; " for the Phœnicians called themselves from the name of their towns, Tyrians, Sidonians, &c. Cartha, the "city," was first applied to Tyre, from which Hercules obtained the title of Melcarthus, or Melek-Kartha, "Lord of the City," corrupted into Melicertes or Melicartus, "who," Sanconiatho says, "was Hercules," and who in a Phœnician inscription at Malta is called Adonin Melkarth Baal Tzura, אדנן מלקרת בעל צרא, "our Lord Melkarth, Baal of Tyre."

Carthagena (Carthagina, Carthage) was Kartha Yena, the "new city" (καινὴ πόλις), in opposition to the parent Tyre, or to Utica, *i. e.* Atika, the "old" (city), which was founded before by the Phœnicians on the African coast about B. C. 1520, or, according to Velleius Paterculus (i. 2), at the same time as Megara, B. C. 1131. Utica was probably not so called till after the building of Carthage (as Musr-el-Atika received that name after the foundation of the new Musr, or Cairo). The "new town," Carthagena, was the "nova Carthago" of Dido (Ovid, Ep. Dido to Æn. ; Virg. Æn. i. 366) ; but it was founded B. C. 1259, long before Dido's supposed time. Some think it was built more than two centuries after Gades and Tartessus in Spain, and Velleius Paterculus says Gades was a few years older than Utica. He dates the building of Carthage by Elissa, or Dido, 60 years before Rome, or 813 B. C. (i. 6) ; but his authority is of no weight. (Cp. Justin. xviii. 5.) Cartha is the same as Kiriath, common in Hebrew names. Some object to the above derivation of Cartha-jena, because *jena* or *yena*, "new," is not a Semitic, but a Turk or Tartar word, and is properly *yengi* or *yeki ;* and they prefer the Greek Carchedo as the name of the city, deriving it from Caer or Car, and hedo, "new." But whether *jena* is admissible or no, Cartha is the word used, as in Melkarth, or Melek Kartha, "Lord of the City," applied to Hercules in Phœnician inscriptions, and found in Carteia and Kiriath. The resemblance of the name of its citadel Byrsa (said to have been called from the hide) to those of Borsippa, or Birs-Nimroud, and the Arab Boursa, near Babylon, is singular.

A record seems still to be preserved of the Phœnician trade on the western coast of Africa in the peculiar glass-beads found there, which are known to be ancient, and are now highly prized. The Venetians send out a modern imperfect imitation of them to Africa. They are also said to have been found in Cornwall and in Ireland.—[G. W.]

which is wholly sand, very scant of water, and utterly and entirely a desert.[4])   The young men therefore, despatched on this errand by their comrades with a plentiful supply of water and provisions, travelled at first through the inhabited region, passing which they came to the wild beast tract, whence they finally entered upon the desert, which they proceeded to cross in a direction from east to west.   After journeying for many days over a wide extent of sand, they came at last to a plain where they observed trees growing; approaching them, and seeing fruit on them, they proceeded to gather it.   While they were thus engaged, there came upon them some dwarfish men,[5] under the middle height, who seized them and carried them off. The Nasamonians could not understand a word of their language, nor had they any acquaintance with the language of the Nasamonians.   They were led across extensive marshes, and finally came to a town, where all the men were of the height of their conductors, and black-complexioned.   A great river flowed by the town,[6] running from west to east, and containing crocodiles.

33. Here let me dismiss Etearchus[7] the Ammonian, and his story, only adding that (according to the Cyrenæans) he declared that the Nasamonians got safe back to their country, and that the men whose city they had reached were a nation of sorcerers.   With respect to the river which ran by their town, Etearchus conjectured it to be the Nile;[8] and reason favours

[4] Vide infrà, iv. 181, for the division of Africa into three regions; and for the true character of the desert, see note on iv. 185.

[5] Men of diminutive size really exist in Africa, but the Nasamones probably only knew of some by report.   Those to the S.W. of Abyssinia are called Dokos. They are not Negroes.   (See Ethnological Journal, No. 1, p. 43, and No. 2.)   Some have thought the Simia Sylvanus of Africa gave rise to the story, agreeing as it does with their description by Photius (Cod. iii. Bibl. p. 8): "ὑπὸ δὲ τριχῶν δεδασυμένους διὰ παντὸς τοῦ σώματος." The pygmies are mentioned by Homer (Il. iii. 6) and others, and often represented on Greek vases.   Homer and Aristotle (Hist. An. viii. 12) place them near the sources of the Nile, which might agree with the Dokos. Pliny (vi. 19), Philostratus (Vit. Apoll. Ty. iii. 47), and others, place them in India (see Ctesias Ind. § 11).   Strabo (i. p. 50) says the fable was invented by Homer, who represented them living by the sources of the Nile, whither the cranes retiring from the winter and snows of the north brought slaughter and death on the Pygmæan race.   He thinks that certain little men of Ethiopia were the origin of the fable (xvii. p. 1162), as Aristotle does (H. An. viii. 12), who calls them Troglodytæ.   Pomp. Mela (iii. 8) places them very far south, and speaks of their fighting with the cranes, "pro satis frugibus."   (Cp. Strabo i. p. 53; xvii. p. 1162.)   Ælian (Hist. An. xv. 29) has a fable of Juno turning their queen "Gerana" into a crane.—[G. W.]

[6] It seems not improbable that we have here a mention of the river Niger, and of the ancient representative of the modern city of Timbuctoo.   See Blakesley ad loc.

[7] If Etearchus was not a corruption of a native name, he must have been a Greek, probably from that Oasis having been conquered by the Cyrenæans.— [G. W.]

[8] This large river, which traversed the centre of Africa, and abounded in croc-

that view. For the Nile certainly flows out of Libya, dividing it down the middle, and as I conceive, judging the unknown from the known, rises at the same distance from its mouth as the Ister.[*] This latter river has its source in the country of the Celts near the city Pyrêné, and runs through the middle of Europe, dividing it into two portions. The Celts live beyond the pillars of Hercules, and border on the Cynesians,[1] who dwell at the extreme west of Europe. Thus the Ister flows through the whole of Europe before it finally empties itself into the Euxine at Istria,[2] one of the colonies of the Milesians.[3]

odiles (ch. 22), probably represented more than one of the rivers which run to the Atlantic from Central Africa; and the marsh or lake it traversed was in like manner not confined to the Tchad, or any particular one of those regions. One of Strabo's lakes, from which the Nile comes in the East (xvii. p. 1116), as well as his large lake Psebôa, above Meroë, was evidently the modern Dembea of Abyssinia, the Coloe Palus of Ptolemy's Astapus, through which the Blue (or Black) Nile runs. See Plin. viii. 21, "Lake Nigris," and v. 9; and compare Strabo, xvii. p. 1162.— [G. W.]

[*] The meaning of this passage has been much disputed, but Schweighæuser's final decision upon it (Lex. Herod. ad voc. μέτρον), which is here followed, may be accepted as fairly satisfactory. Herodotus does not intend any such exact correspondency between the Nile and the Danube as Larcher (note ad loc.), much less such as Niebuhr (Scythia, p. 40, Engl. Trans.) and Dahlmann (Life, p. 65) imagined. He is only speaking of the comparative length of the two streams, and conjectures that they are equal in this respect. * Herein no doubt he exhibits his over-love of symmetry (see note to Book iv. ch. 181); but it is quite unnecessary to suppose, with Niebuhr, that he considered the two streams to correspond in all points, and because the Nile made an angle in its course above the country of the Deserters (ch. 31), regarded the Danube as making a similar angle in the upper parts of Thrace. There is absolutely no indication of his having entertained any such notion. His placing the sources of the Danube in the country of the Celts, near the city Pyrêné, implies no doubt a considerable error as to the region from which that river flows, but it is interesting as exhibiting a dim acquaintance with the name and position of the Pyrenean range, of which not only Hecatæus, but even Scylax (Peripl. pp. 3–4), seems to have been ignorant; and which is (I believe) first mentioned by Polybius (III. xxxix. § 4, &c.).

[1] The Cynesians are mentioned again in iv. 49 as Cynêtes. They are a nation of whom nothing is known but their abode from very ancient times at the extreme S.W. of Europe. Herodôrus of Heracléa, a coutemporary of Socrates, who appears to have possessed a fair knowledge of the Spanish peninsula, spoke of them (Fr. 20) as dwelling the furthest to the W. of all the Spanish nations, and said they were bordered upon towards the N. by the Gletes. (Γλῆτες, query? Γαλάται, Celts.) By the later geographers (Strabo, Pliny, Ptolemy) they are ignored altogether, yet curiously enough they re-appear in Avienus, a writer of the fifth century after Christ, nearly in their old settlements, on the banks of the Anas or Guadiana. (Ora Maritim. 202–223).

[3] If the Danube in the time of Herodotus entered the Euxine at Istria, it must have changed its course very greatly since he wrote. Istria, Ister, or Istriopolis (as we find it variously called) was situated near the modern Kostendje, 60 miles below the most southerly of the Danube's present mouths. The name undoubtedly remains in the modern Wisteri, on the road from Kostendje to Babadagh, but the ancient town must have been nearer the coast—perhaps at Karaglak. (See Strab, vii. p. 461–2; Anon. Peripl. Pont. Eux. p. 157; Ptolem. iii. 10; Itin. Ant. p. 14, &c.). It is perhaps conceivable that the Danube may once have thrown out a branch from the angle in its course near Rassova to the Black Sea near Kostendje, in the line of the projected ship-canal; but if so, great alterations in the height of

34. Now as this river flows through regions that are inhabited, its course is perfectly well known ; but of the sources of the Nile no one can give any account, since Libya, the country through which it passes, is desert and without inhabitants. As far as it was possible to get information by inquiry, I have given a description of the stream. It enters Egypt from the parts beyond. Egypt lies almost exactly opposite the mountainous portion of Cilicia,[4] whence a lightly-equipped traveller may reach Sinôpé on the Euxine in five days by the direct route.[5] Sinôpé lies opposite the place where the Ister falls into the sea.[6] My opinion therefore is that the Nile, as it traverses the whole of Libya, is of equal length with the Ister. And here I take my leave of this subject.

35. Concerning Egypt itself I shall extend my remarks to a great length, because there is no country that possesses so many wonders,[7] nor any that has such a number of works which

the land must have taken place within the historic period, since at present the Black Sea is separated from the valley of the Danube by a range of hills, whose elevation is at the lowest point 200 or 300 feet.

[3] According to Scymnus Chius (Fr. 21) Istria was founded about the time of the Scythian invasion of Asia (B. C. 633). Pliny calls it a most beautiful city ("urbs pulcherrima," H. N. iv. 11).

[4] Cilicia was divided into two portions, the eastern, or "Cilicia campestris," and the western, or "Cilicia aspera." (Strab. xiv. p. 954.) Egypt does not really lie "opposite"—that is, in the same longitude with—the latter region. It rather faces Pamphylia, but Herodotus gives all Africa, as far as the Lesser Syrtis, too easterly a position. (Vide infrà, iv. 179, note.)

[5] Suprà, i. 72, sub fin.

[6] This of course is neither true, nor near the truth ; and it is difficult to make out in what sense Herodotus meant to assert it. Perhaps he attached no very distinct geographical meaning to the word "opposite."

[7] By this statement Herodotus prepares his readers for what he is about to relate ; but the desire to tell of the wonders in which it differed from all other countries led Herodotus to indulge in his love of antithesis, so that in some cases he confines to one sex what was done by both (a singular instance being noted down by him as an invariable custom), and in others he has indulged in the marvellous at a sacrifice of truth. If, however, Herodotus had told us that the Egyptian women enjoyed greater liberty, confidence, and consideration than under the *hareem* system of the Greeks and Persians (Book i. ch. 136), he would have been fully justified, for the treatment of women in Egypt was far better than in Greece. The assertion of Nymphodorus that Sesostris, fearing the people, who had become very numerous, might revolt against him, obliged the men to adopt the occupations of women (in order to enervate the whole race during his reign), is too ridiculous to be worth contradicting. In many cases where Herodotus tells improbable tales, they are on the authority of others, or mere hearsay reports, for which he at once declares himself not responsible, and he justly pleads that his history was not only a relation of facts, but the result of an "ἱστορία," or "inquiry," in which all he heard was inserted. We must, however, sometimes regret that he did not use his own judgment, and discard what must have shown itself unworthy of credit and of mention. For we gladly allow that when he does offer his own reflections they are sound ; and too much credit cannot be given him for being so far above prejudice, and superior to many of the Greeks, who were too apt to claim the honour of originating things they borrowed from others, or to derive from Greece what was of older date than them-

defy description.   Not only is the climate different from that of
the rest of the world, and the rivers unlike any other rivers, but
the people also, in most of their manners and customs, exactly
reverse the common practice of mankind.   The women attend
the markets[a] and trade, while the men sit at home at the loom ;[1]
and here, while the rest of the world works the woof up the
warp,[2] the Egyptians work it down ; the women likewise carry

selves ; as, for instance, Thoth (Mercury) having gone from Arcadia " to Egypt, and
given laws and learning to the Egyptians" (Cic. Nat. Deor. iii.) ; and Actinus, the
son of Sol, being an astronomer who went from Greece to Egypt, where he founded
the city of Heliopolis. Herodotus also shows more fairness and judgment than those
who claim for the Greeks many inventions and ideas evidently borrowed from the
country they visited for instruction, and who forget to attribute to the Greeks
some of their great merits:—as the emancipation of the human mind from the
trammels of fixed and unvarying rules, which cramped genius and prevented improvement; the invention of real history; the establishment of taste in arts and
literature; and that development of the mind for which modern nations are so much
beholden to them. In art too Greece was unrivalled, and was indebted for it to her
own genius ; nor from the occasional adoption of some hints in architecture and ornamental designs, as well as certain branches of knowledge, at an early period, can
the origin of Greek *taste* be ascribed to Egypt or any other country.—[G. W.]

[a] The market-place was originally outside the walls, generally in an open space,
beneath what was afterwards the citadel or the acropolis; as we see in the old sites
of Greek and also Roman towns, as at Rome itself, whence perhaps called Forum.
The same is still the case in some countries at the present day, as at Cattaro in
Dalmatia.

This first antithesis is an instance of Herodotus confining to one sex what applies
to both; and the sculptures show that sedentary occupations were *more* followed by
women than by men.—[G. W.]

[1] This is one of the
passages in our author,
where his words so
closely resemble those
of Sophocles, as to raise
suspicion of plagiarism
on the one side or the
other. (See note [a] B. i.
ch. 32; and vide infrà,
iii. 119.) The ancients
generally seem to have
believed the charge of
effeminacy brought by
Herodotus against the
Egyptians.   Various
writers repeat it, and
one (Nymphodorus) de-
clares its origin. (See
the Scholiast on Soph.
Œd. Col. 337 ; and com-
pare the advice said to
have been given by
Crœsus to Cyrus, suprà,
i. 155.)

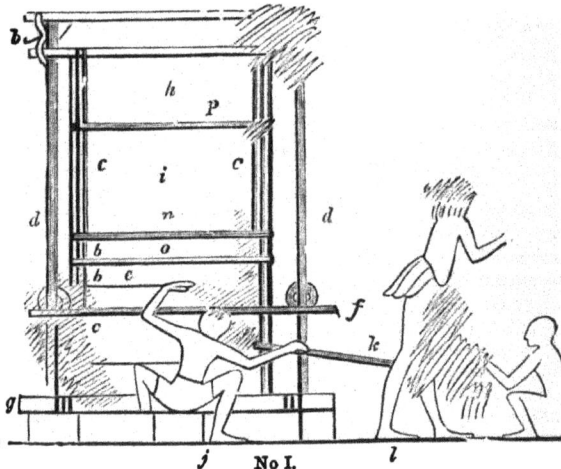

No I.

[2] The foregoing remark, that a general conclusion is drawn from particular and rare
cases, applies also to this, as the Egyptians sometimes pushed the woof upwards,
sometimes down ; and also to their mode of carrying burthens, for men almost always

burthens upon their shoulders, while the men carry them upon their heads.   They eat their food out of doors in the streets,[3]

[3] carried them on their shoulders, or on a yoke, like that now in use in Europe (see woodcut fig. 4 in note [1] on ch. 136), and rarely on their heads, except bakers, as in other countries; while very few instances occur of a woman bearing a burthen on her shoulders.—[G. W.]

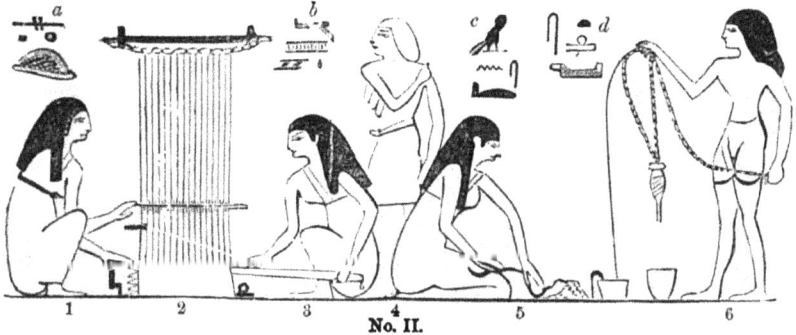

No. II.

[3] That they sometimes ate in the street is not to be doubted; but this was only the poorer class, as in other parts of ancient and modern Europe, and could not be mentioned in contradistinction to a Greek custom.   The Egyptians generally dined at a small round table, having one leg (similar to the monopodium or orbis), at which one or more persons sat, and they ate with their fingers like the Greeks and the modern Arabs.   Several dishes were placed upon the table, and before eating it was their custom to say grace. (Joseph. Antiq. xii. 2. 12 ; see At. Eg. W. vol. ii. p. 392 to 415.)   Athenæus (Deipn. iv. p. 150) speaks of the sumptuousness of an Egyptian feast, and says they had one kind of dinner or supper " at which there was no table, the dishes being brought round."—[G. W.]

[4] Though men held the priesthood in Egypt, as in other countries, women were not excluded from certain important duties in the temples, as Herodotus also shows (chs. 54, 56); the queens made offerings with the kings; and the monuments, as well as Diodorus, show that an order of women, chosen from the principal families, were employed in the service of the gods.   It is of these that Diodorus, and even Herodotus (i. 182), have told stories, the absurdity of which is sufficiently evident when we consider that queens and women of the highest rank held the office in the temple of Amun ; and it is probable that these were members of a sacred college, into which they entered on the death of their husbands, in order to devote themselves to religious duties. It was perhaps then that they received the title of "divine wife," or "god's wife;" which from the following formula— "the royal daughter, the royal wife, the divine (god's) wife, the god's mother," would refer to her relationship to a king; as no office could make any one the mother of Amun.

No. I.

but retire for private purposes to their houses, giving as a reason
that what is unseemly, but necessary, ought to be done in secret,
but what has nothing unseemly about it, should be done openly.
A woman cannot serve the priestly office,⁴ either for god or god-

The widow of Ames, however, seems to be called " Goddess wife of Amun ; " which
would show them to be spouses of the deity.   They were also styled " god's hand,"
and " god's (the divine) star."   Their chief office in the religious ceremonies was
to sing the praises of the deity, playing on various instruments ; in the temple the
highest of their order, as queens and princesses, held the sistra ; and at Thebes they
were called the minstrels and chiefs of the women of Amun.   (On the Pallacides,
see At. Eg. W. vol. iv. p. 203.)   A sort of monastic institution seems to have ori-

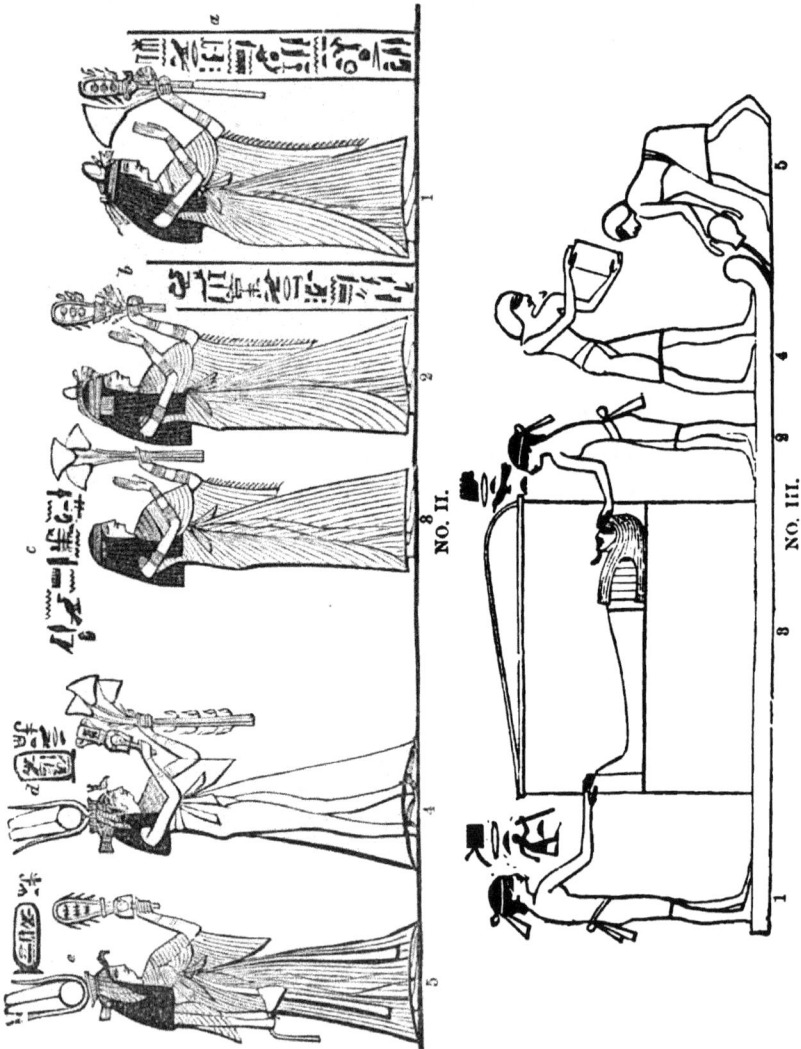

dess, but men are priests to both; sons need not support their parents unless they choose, but daughters must, whether they choose or no.[5]

36. In other countries the priests have long hair, in Egypt their heads are shaven;[6] elsewhere it is customary, in mourning, for near relations to cut their hair close; the Egyptians, who wear no hair at any other time, when they lose a relative, let

ginated in Egypt at an early time, and to have been imitated afterwards when the real conventual system was set on foot by the Christians in the same country. Cp. the Vestal virgins at Rome. (See woodcut No. II. opp. page.)

Herodotus (ii. 54) speaks of two women, belonging to the Temple of Jupiter at Thebes, who founded the oracles of Ammon and Dodona; and priestesses are mentioned on the Rosetta stone, and in the papyrus of D'Anastasy. (See At. Eg. W. vol. i. p. 261.) Nor can this be ascribed to innovations, among a people so jealous as the Egyptians of the interference of foreigners in their religion. It must, however, be observed that no woman, except the queen, attended in the grand processions of a king's coronation, or on similar occasions; and there is no ceremony in which women took the part they did at the Panathenaic festival of Athens. The monuments, however, show they did attend in processions in honour of Athor, as well as of Bubastis (infra, ch. 60); and in the funeral pageants women performed a great part, being the mourners for the dead, independently of those hired, as at the present day. Two, indeed, held an important office on that occasion. (Woodcut No. III. figs. 1, 2.)

There was also a ceremony performed by a woman and a man, each holding the end of a rope tied in a knot round a wooden pillar, the pointed end of which they struck against the ground; and this appears also to have been of a religious character connected with the dead. (No. IV.) Women were not therefore excluded from the service of religion; and the fact of queens holding the sceptre suffices to prove it, every monarch being privileged, and obliged, to become a member of the hierarchy, and to be initiated in the mysteries. Diodorus also describes Athyrtis, the daughter of Sesostris, so well versed in divination that she foretold to her father the future success of his arms.—[G. W.]

[5] Of the daughters being forced to support their parents instead of the sons, it is difficult to decide; but the improbability of the custom is glaring; and it is the son on whom the duty fell of providing for the services in honour of his deceased parent; and the law of debt mentioned by Herodotus (in ch. 136) contradicts his assertion here.—[G. W.]

[6] The custom of shaving the head as well as beard was not confined to the priests in Egypt, it was general among all classes; and all the men wore wigs or caps fitting close to their heads, except some of the poorest class. In this the Egyptians were unlike the "κυρηκομόωντας Ἀχαίους:" but the custom of allowing the hair to grow in mourning was not confined to Egypt; and Plutarch (Op. Mor. p. 267) says that in misfortune the Greek women cut off their hair, and the men let it grow, contrary to their ordinary custom. He probably means *long* and *negligently;* for in most states the Greeks wore their hair moderately long; young men and athletes short. Beards began first to be shaved in Greece in the time of Alexander. (Plut. Lysand. 1.) The habit of making a baldness between the eyes for the dead (Deut. xiv. 1), which was forbidden by the Mosaic law, was not Egyptian, but Syrian.—[G. W.]

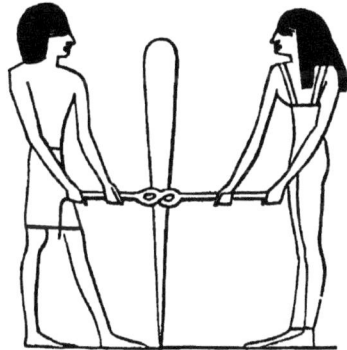

No. IV.

their beards and the hair of their heads grow long. All other men pass their lives separate from animals, the Egyptians have animals always living with them ;[7] others make barley and wheat their food, it is a disgrace to do so in Egypt,[8] where the grain they live on is spelt, which some call *zea.* Dough they knead with their feet,[9] but they mix mud, and even take up dirt, with their hands. They are the only people in the world—

[7] Their living with animals not only contradicts a previous assertion of their eating in the streets, but is contrary to fact; and if Herodotus really associated with any who were so badly lodged, he must have kept very bad company during his stay in Egypt.—[G. W.]

[8] Their considering it a "*disgrace*" to live on wheat and barley is equally extravagant; and though they also cultivated the *holcus sorghum* (or doora), and poor people may have used it, as at the present day, when they could not afford wheaten bread, it does not follow that the custom was obligatory, or ever adopted by an Egyptian of rank, and the assertion of Herodotus is much on a par with Dr. Johnson's definition of "oats."

It is not known what the olyra really was; Pliny shows it was not rice, nor the same as zea, as Herodotus supposed, and it was probably the *doora* of modern Egypt, which is the only grain besides wheat and barley *represented* in the sculptures (though *this* has been thought to be "flax"). (See At. Eg. W. vol. ii. p. 397.)

Pliny (xviii. 7) says, "far in Ægypto ex olyrâ conficitur," but not of course to the exclusion of other grain, as he notices wheat and barley there, and adds (xviii. 8), "Ægyptus similaginem conficit e tritico suo." Both wheat and barley are noticed in Lower Egypt long before Herodotus' time (Exod. ix. 31, 32), and the paintings of the Thebaïd prove that they were grown extensively in that part of the country; they were among the offerings in the temples ; and the king, at his coronation, cutting some ears of wheat afterwards offered to the gods as the staple production of Egypt, shows how great a value was set on a

No. I.

grain which Herodotus would lead us to suppose was held in abhorrence. It is remarkable that though oats are unknown in Egypt, the. wild oat grows there.—[G. W.]

[9] That they trod the dough with their feet is true, fashioning it afterwards with the hand into cakes; but the mud was also mixed with the feet, after having been broken up with the hoe, as we see in the representation of the brickmakers at

they at least, and such as have learnt the practice from them[1]
—who use circumcision. Their men wear two garments apiece,
their women but one.[2] They put on the rings and fasten the
ropes to sails inside,[3] others put them outside. When they
write[4] or calculate,[5] instead of going, like the Greeks, from left
to right, they move their hand from right to left; and they insist, notwithstanding, that it is they who go to the right, and

Thebes. See woodcut, figs. 11, 13, in note
[1] on ch. 136.—[G. W.]

[1] Vide infrà, ch. 104.

[2] The men having two dresses and the
women one gives an erroneous impression.
The usual dress of men was a long upper
robe and a short kilt beneath it, the former being laid aside when at work; while
women had only the long robe. When an
extra upper garment was worn over these
the men had three, the women two; so
that, instead of limiting the latter to one,
he should have given to men always one
more garment than the women. See woodcuts in notes on chs. 35, 37, and 81.—
[G. W.]

[3] The Greek κάλοι generally corresponded to our "stays" of the mast, ὑπέραι
to "braces," πόδες to "sheets," and κεροῦ-
χοι to "halliards;" but Herodotus only
speaks of "the ropes and rings of the

No. II.

sails;" and the ancient custom of fastening the braces and sheets of the sails to rings
within the gunwale fully agrees with that still adopted in the Nile boats.—See notes
[1], [2], ch. 96.—[G. W.]

[4] The Egyptians wrote from right to left in hieratic and demotic (or enchorial),
which are the two modes of *writing* here mentioned. The Greeks also in old times
wrote from right to left, like the Phœnicians, from whom they borrowed their alphabet. This seems the natural mode of writing; for though we have always been accustomed to write from left to right, we invariably use our pencil, in shading a drawing, from right to left, in spite of all our previous habit; and even our down-strokes
in writing are all from right to left. The Arabs say "it is more reasonable to see
where the pen is coming, than not to see where it is going." It was continued by
the Etruscans, the early imitators of the Greeks, to a very late period. Dr. Brugsch
very ingeniously observes (Gram. Demot. pp. 15, 16), that though in Demotic the
general direction of the writing was from right to left, each individual letter was
formed from left to right, as is evident in the unfinished ends of horizontal letters
when the ink failed in the pen.—[G. W.]

[5] In writing numbers in Hieratic and Enchorial they placed the
units to the left, that is last, according to their mode of writing from
right to left. Thus 1851 would stand 1581. In 18 they would first
come to the ten, and in 13,432 they would begin with the thousands.
The same mode of beginning with the largest number is followed in
hieroglyphics, whether written from right to left, or from
left to right. This is like our arrangement of the thousand
first and the unit last, in our writing from left to right.
The Arabs, from whom we borrowed this, think we ought
to have changed the arrangement, as we write in an opposite direction. But they borrowed their numerals from
India (hence called by them "Hindee," "Indian"), and
there the arrangement is as in our own, 133 being

the Greeks who go to the left. They have two quite different kinds of writing,[6] one of which is called sacred, the other common.

37. They are religious to excess, far beyond any other race of men,[7] and use the following ceremonies :—They drink out of brazen cups,[8] which they scour every day : there is no exception to this practice. They wear linen garments, which they are

Indian, 188.

which are singularly like the ordinal numbers of the Hieratic in Egypt—

Hieratic, 188d.

Both these resemble the Chinese, and the origin of the three numbers was evidently from simple lines,

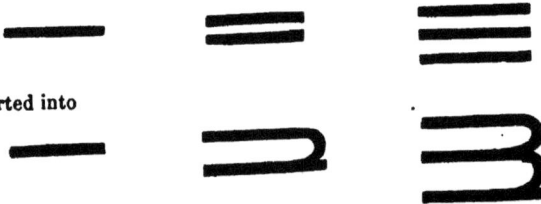

converted into

Tippoo Sultan, seeing the inconsistency of following the arrangement used in a language read from left to right, altered it on some of his late coins, and placed the unit to the right. There is no representation on Egyptian monuments of an abacus for calculating, like that of the Greeks.—[G. W.]

[6] See note in Appendix, CH. V.

[7] The extreme religious views of the Egyptians became at length a gross superstition, and were naturally a subject for ridicule and contempt. Lucian makes Momus express his surprise that so many persons were allowed to share divine honours, but is indignant at the Egyptian crew of apes, ibiscs, bulls, and other ridiculous creatures who intruded themselves into heaven, and wonders how Jupiter can allow himself to be caricatured with rams' horns. Jupiter gives an answer worthy of an Egyptian priest, that they were mysteries not to be derided by the uninitiated (Deor. Concil. s. 10). Juvenal and others take advantage of the same opening for ridicule.—[G. W.]

[8] This, he says, is the universal custom, without exception; but we not only know that Joseph had a silver drinking-cup (Gen. xliv. 2, 5), but the sculptures show the wealthy Egyptians used glass, porcelain, and gold, sometimes inlaid with a coloured composition resembling enamel, or with precious stones. That persons who could not afford cups of more costly materials should have been contented with those of bronze is very probable; and Hellanicus (quoted by Ath. Deipn. xi. p. 470 D) mentions the phialé (dish), cyas (upright handled cup), and ethanion (strainer), in Egypt of bronze; but, as in Etruria, Greece, and Rome, many drinking cups were also of other materials. The bronze is often gilt, and long ladles (simpula) and other utensils are often found with the gilding still visible ; and fragments of glass, porcelain, and other cups are common in Egypt as in Italy. The custom then was not universal either in the time of Herodotus, or before, or afterwards. See note on ch. 151.—[G. W.]

specially careful to have always fresh washed.[*] They practise circumcision for the sake of cleanliness, considering it better to be cleanly than comely. The priests shave their whole body every other day, that no lice or other impure thing may adhere to them when they are engaged in the service of the gods. Their dress is entirely of linen,[1] and their shoes of the papyrus

[*] Their attention to cleanliness was very remarkable, as is shown by their shaving the head and beard, and removing the hair from the whole body, by their frequent ablutions, and by the strict rules instituted to ensure it. Herodotus soon afterwards says the priests washed themselves twice every day and twice every night in cold water; and Porphyry (de Abstin. iv. 7), besides three ablutions every day, and an occasional one at night, mentions a grand ceremony of purification previous to their fasts, many of which lasted forty-two days, or even longer, during which time they abstained entirely from animal food, from herbs, and vegetables, and, above all, from the indulgence of the passions. The same motive of cleanliness led them to practise circumcision, which Herodotus afterwards mentions. Nor was this confined to the priests, as we learn from the mummies and from the sculptures, where it is made a distinctive mark between the Egyptians and their enemies; and in later times, when Egypt contained many foreign settlers, it was looked upon as a distinctive sign between the orthodox Egyptian and the stranger, or the non-conformist. None therefore were allowed to study all the secrets of Egyptian knowledge unless they had submitted to this rite; and this probably led to the notion that the priests alone were circumcised. Its institution in Egypt reaches to the most remote antiquity: we find it existing at the earliest period of which any monuments remain, more than 2400 years before our era, and there is no reason to doubt that it dated still earlier.—[G. W.]

[1] The dress of the priests consisted, as Herodotus states, of linen (ch. 81); but

No. I.

plant :² it is not lawful for them to wear either dress or shoes of any other material. They bathe twice every day in cold water, and

he does not say they were confined (as some have supposed) to a single robe; and whether walking abroad, or officiating in the temple, they were permitted to have more than one garment. The high-priest styled *Sem* always wore a leopard-skin placed over the linen dress as his costume of office. (No. II.) Plutarch (de Is. s. 4) agrees with Herodotus in stating that their dress was of linen and not of wool; for, he adds, it would be inconsistent in men, who take so much pains to remove the hair from their body, to wear clothes made of the wool or hair of animals; and no Egyptian was allowed to enter a temple without taking off his outer woollen cloak (Her. ii. 81), nor could he be buried in cloths of that material. But though their under-garment was of linen, it did not prevent their wearing an upper one of cotton. Pliny (xix. 1) affirms that cotton dresses were particularly agreeable to the priests; and the Rosetta stone states that "cotton garments" were supplied by the government for the use of the temple. But these were probably the sacred robes for the statues of the gods (Plut. de Is. s. 78); and the priests may only have been forbidden to wear cotton garments while in the temple. The votaries of Isis at Rome were subject to the same prohibition, and linen dresses were adopted by those who had been initiated into the mysteries (Plut. de Is. s. 3; Apul. Metam. lib. xi.). The Egyptian and Jewish priests were the only ones (except perhaps those

No. II.

of India) whose dresses were ordered to be of linen. That worn by the former was of the finest texture, and the long robe with full sleeves, which covered the body and descended to the ankles, was perfectly transparent, and placed over a short kilt of thicker quality reaching to the knees. Some wore a long robe of linen, extending from the neck to the ankles, of the same thick substance, and some officiated in the short kilt alone, the arms and legs being bare. Some again had a long thin dress, like a loose shirt, with full sleeves, reaching to the ankles, over which a wrapper of fine linen was bound, covering the lower part of the body, and falling in front below the knees; the hieraphoros, while bearing the sacred emblems, frequently wore a long full apron, tied in front with long bands, and a strap, also of linen, passed

No. III.

over the shoulder to support it; and some priests wore a long smock reaching from below the arms to the feet, and supported over the neck by straps. (No. I. fig. 4.) Their head was frequently bare, sometimes covered with a wig or a tight cap; but in all cases the head was closely shaved. They had a particular mode of gouffreying their linen dresses (also adopted in Greece, to judge from the ancient statues and the vases, as well as in Etruria), which impressed upon them the waving lines represented in the paintings, and this was done by means of a wooden instrument, divided into segmental partitions 1¼ inch broad on its upper face,

twice each night. Besides which they observe, so to speak, thousands of ceremonies. They enjoy, however, not a few ad-

which was held by the hand while the linen was pressed upon it. One of them is in the Museum of Florence (fig. 2 gives the real size of the divisions).

The fine texture of the Egyptian linen is fully proved by its transparency, as represented in the paintings, and by the statements of ancient writers, sacred (Gen. xli. 42 ; and 2 Chron. i. 16) as well as profane, and by the wonderful texture of a piece found near Memphis, part of which is in my possession. In general quality it is equal to the finest now made ; and for the evenness of the threads, without knot or break, it is far superior to any of modern manufacture. It has in the inch 540 threads, or 270 double threads in the warp, and 110 in the woof—a disparity which, as Mr. Thompson observes, belonged to the Egyptian "system of manufacture." (See At. Eg. W. vol. iii. p. 120, &c.) Pliny mentions four kinds of linen particularly noted in Egypt, the Tanitic, the Pelusiac, the Butine and the Tentyritic ; and the same fineness of texture was ex-

No. IV.

tended to the nets of Egypt, which were so delicate that they could pass through a man's ring, and a single person could carry a sufficient number of them to surround a whole wood. (Plin. xix. 1. On the Byssus, see note * ch. 86.)   The transparent

No. V.

fineness of the linen dresses of men and women in the Egyptian paintings recalls the remark of Seneca (de Benef. vii. 9) on "sericas vestes," so thin that a woman appeared as if naked.—[G. W.]

    * Their sandals were made of the papyrus, or of other kinds of Cyperus ; an inferior quality being of matted palm-leaves ; and they either slept on a simple skin stretched on the ground (Eust. in Homer. Il. xvi. 235), or on a wicker bed, made of palm-branches, which Porphyry very justly says were called *bai* (de Abstin. iv. 7). On this bedstead, which was similar to the *caffas* of modern Egypt, made of the same materials, a mat or a skin was spread for a mattress, and their head was supported by a half cylinder of wood in lieu of a pillow. These pillows are frequently found in the tombs, made of acacia, sycamore, or tamarisk wood, or sometimes of alabaster ; and they are represented among the furniture of an Egyptian mansion, in the Tombs of the Kings, together with the richest sofas and fauteuils. They are still used in Ethiopia, and also in places distant from the Nile, in

vantages.[3]   They consume none of their own property, and are at no expense for anything ;[4] but every day bread is baked for them of the sacred corn, and a plentiful supply of beef and of goose's flesh is assigned to each, and also a portion of wine[5] made

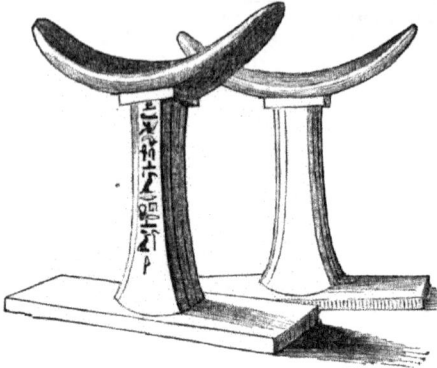

Japan, China, the Western Coast of Africa, in Otaheite (Tahiti), and other places. But soft pillows and lofty couches were also adopted in Egypt, to which last they mounted by steps.   Cp. 2 Kings i. 4; Ps. cxxxii. 3; Prov. vii. 16.—[G. W.]

[3] The greatest of these was the paramount influence they exercised over the spiritual, and consequently over the temporal, concerns of the whole community, which was secured to them through their superior knowledge, by the dependence of all classes on them for the instruction they chose to impart, and by their exclusive right of possessing all the secrets of religion which were thought to place them far above the rest of mankind.   Nor did their power over an individual cease with his life; it would even reach him after death; and their veto could prevent his being buried in his tomb, and consign his name to lasting infamy.   They thus usurped the power and place of the gods, whose will they affected to be commissioned to pronounce; and they acted as though the community had been made for their rule, and not their own office for the benefit of the community.   Priestcraft indeed is always odious, but especially when people are taught to believe what the priests themselves know to be mere fable; and the remark of Cato, "It appears strange that one priest can refrain from laughing when he looks at another," might well apply to those of Egypt.   (Cic. de Nat. Deor. i. 26; de Div. ii.)   It must however be admitted that they did not make a show of great sanctity, nor set themselves above the customs of society, in order to increase their power over it ; they were good husbands and fathers, and they showed the highest regard for all social duties.   Mankind too had not then been enlightened by Christianity; and the Egyptian hierarchy had the merit of having enjoined, practised, and ensured morality, and contributed greatly to the welfare of the people they so long governed.—[G. W.]

[4] They were exempt from taxes, and were provided with a daily allowance of meat, corn, and wine ; and when Pharaoh, by the advice of Joseph, took all the land of the Egyptians in lieu of corn (Gen. xlvii. 20, 22), the land of the priests was exempt, and the tax of the fifth part of the produce was not levied upon it. Diodorus (i. 72) says the land was divided into three portions, one of which belonged to the king, another to the priests, and the third to the military caste.—[G. W.]

[5] Herodotus is quite right in saying they were allowed to drink wine, and the assertion of Plutarch (de Is. s. 6) that the kings (who were also of the priestly caste), were not permitted to drink it before the reign of Psammetichus is contradicted by the authority of the Bible (Gen. xl. 10, 13) and the sculptures; and if on some oc-

from the grape.   Fish they are not allowed to eat ;⁶ and beans,
—which none of the Egyptians ever sow, or eat, if they come
up of their own accord, either raw or boiled⁷—the priests will
not even endure to look on, since they consider it an unclean
kind of pulse.   Instead of a single priest, each god has the attendance of a college, at the head of which is a chief priest ;⁸
when one of these dies, his son is appointed in his room.

casions it really was not admitted into the temple of Heliopolis, it was not excluded
from other temples, and wine was among the usual offerings made to the gods. Herodotus tells us (ch. 39) that they began their sacrifices by a libation of wine; and it
is evident from the sculptures that it was also admitted into the temples of the Sun,
or at least at his altar in other temples. And though Hecataeus asserts that the
kings were allowed a stated quantity, according to the regulations in the sacred
books (Plut. de Is. s. 6), they were reported by the Egyptians to have exceeded
those limits, as in the case of Mycerinus and Amasis. (Her. ii. 133, 174.) Of the
kings and the laws respecting them, see At. Eg. W. vol. i. p. 219-255, and compare
notes on chs. 18, 60, 63, 77.—[G. W.]

⁶ Though fish were so generally eaten by the rest of the Egyptians, they were
forbidden to the priests, and when on the 9th day of the 1st month (Thoth), when
a religious ceremony obliged all the people to eat a fried fish before the door of their
houses, the priests were not even then expected to conform to the general custom,
but were contented to burn theirs at the appointed time (Plut. de Is. s. 7.) The
principal food of the priests, as Diodorus justly states, was beef and goose, and the
gazelle, ibex, oryx, and wild-fowl were not forbidden; but they "abstained from
most sorts of pulse, from mutton, and swine's flesh, and in their more solemn purifi-
cations they even excluded salt from their meals" (Plut. de Is. s. 5). Garlick,
leeks, onions, lentils, peas, and above all beans, are said to have been excluded
from the tables of the priests. See Diod. Sic. i. 81, 89; Plut. de Is. s. 8; Juv. Sat.
xv. 9.—[G. W.]

⁷ Diodorus (i. 89) is more correct when he says that some only of the Egyptians
abstained from beans, and it may be doubted if they grew in Egypt without being
sown. The custom of forbidding beans to the priests was borrowed from Egypt by
Pythagoras. Cicero (de Div. i. 30) thinks it was from their disturbing the mind
during sleep. In like manner the prohibition against eating swine's flesh and fish
was doubtless from the desire to abstain from food which was apt to engender cuta-
neous disorders in persons of sedentary habits, while the active life of other classes
(having the "dura messorum ilia") enabled them to eat the same things without
endangering their health. This will not, however, account for mutton being forbidden in the Thebaid, which is the most wholesome meat in Egypt; and we can
only suppose it was owing to sheep having been few in number at the time the law
was first made ; when they were anxious to encourage the breed for the sake of the
wool, and feared to lessen their number, as was the case with the cow both in Egypt
and India. The name κύαμος was also applied to the seeds of the Nelumbium or
Indian Lotus. See note ⁹ on ch. 92.—[G. W.]

⁸ This is fully confirmed by the sculptures. They were not, however, always replaced at their death by their sons; and though this was often the case, a son might
become a priest of another deity, and have a higher or lower grade than his father.
He could also be a priest during his father's lifetime, and numerous sons could not
expect the same office as their father. The son of a priest was generally a priest
also ; and when an elder son succeeded to the same office held before by his father,
it is very possible that he inherited the same dress of investiture, which was also
the custom of the Jews (Exod. xxix. 29); but a priest's son might be a military
man.

The priests had various grades. The chief priests held the first posts, and one
of them had an office of great importance, which was usually fulfilled by the king

38. Male kine are reckoned to belong to Epaphus,[*] and are therefore tested in the following manner :—One of the priests

himself. He was the prophet and officiating high-priest, and had the title of "*Sem*,"

in addition to that of chief priest, and he was distinguished by wearing a leopard's skin over his ordinary robes. (See n. [1] ch. 37, woodcut No. II. He does not appear to have ranked above chief-priests, being mentioned after them on the Rosetta stone, but to have been one of them in a particular capacity. He might also be a chief-priest of one god, and *Sem* of another ; and one in a tomb at Thebes is called "chief-priest of Amun, *Sem* in the temple of Pthah, superior of the priests of the upper and lower country ;" and his father was chief-priest without the additional office of *Sem*. The prophets were particularly versed in all matters relating to the ceremonies, the worship of the gods, the laws, and the discipline of the whole order, and they not only presided over the temple and the sacred rites, but directed the management of the sacred revenues. (Clem. Alex. Strom. vi. p. 758). In the solemn processions they had a conspicuous part ; they bore the holy *hydria* or vase, which was frequently carried by the king on similar occasions, and they with the chief-priests were the first whose opinion was consulted respecting the introduction of any new measure connected with religion, as we find in the decree of the Rosetta stone, which was "established by the chief-priests and prophets, and those who have access to the adytum to clothe the gods, and the pterophoræ, and the sacred scribes, and all the other priests .... assembled in the temple of Memphis." Some of the principal functionaries "in the solemn processions" are thus mentioned by Clemens (Strom. vi. p. 757): "The singer usually goes first, bearing the symbols of music, whose duty is said to be to carry two of the books of Hermes .... he is followed by the Horoscopus, bearing in his hand the measure of time (hourglass), and the palm (branch), the symbols of astrology (astronomy) .... next comes the Hierogrammat (sacred scribe) having feathers on his head (see woodcut fig. 9, note [1] on ch. 37), and in his hands a book (papyrus) with a ruler (palette) in which is ink and a reed for writing (fig. 1), then the stolistes, bearing the cubit of justice (fig. 2),

and the cup of libation (fig. 3) ... and lastly the Prophet, the president of the temple, who carries in his bosom a water-jar, followed by persons bearing loaves of bread." See procession in pl. 76 of At. Eg. W. vol. vi. ; and below, note [*] on ch. 58.—[G. W.]

[*] Epaphus, Herodotus says (in ch. 153), is the Greek name of Apis, of which it is probably only a corruption (see also B. iii. chs. 27, 28). In examining a bull for sacrifice, he adds, they admitted none but those which were free from black hairs ; and Maimonides states that "if only two white or black hairs were found lying upon each other, the animal was considered unfit for sacrifice" (Maim. de Vaccâ rufâ, c. 1). This calls to mind the law of the Israelites, commanding them to "bring a red heifer without spot, wherein was no blemish" (Numb. xix. 2). But the sculptures show that bulls with black, and red, or white spots, were commonly killed both for the altar and the table, and the only prohibition seems to have been against killing heifers ; and to ensure a regard for them they were held sacred (see below, n. [1] ch. 41). It was on this account that Moses proposed to go three days in the desert, lest the anger of the Egyptians should be raised on seeing the Israelites

appointed for the purpose searches to see if there is a single black hair on the whole body, since in that case the beast is unclean. He examines him all over, standing on his legs, and again laid upon his back ; after which he takes the tongue out of his mouth, to see if it be clean in respect of the prescribed marks (what they are I will mention elsewhere[1]); he also inspects the hairs of the tail, to observe if they grow naturally. If the animal is pronounced clean in all these various points, the priest marks him by twisting a piece of papyrus round his horns, and attaching thereto some sealing-clay, which he then stamps with his own signet-ring.[2] After this the beast is led away ; and it is forbidden, under the penalty of death, to sacrifice an animal which has not been marked in this way.

39. The following is their manner of sacrifice :—They lead the victim, marked with their signet, to the altar where they are about to offer it, and setting the wood alight, pour a libation of wine upon the altar in front of the victim, and at the same time invoke the god. Then they slay the animal,[3] and cutting

sacrifice a heifer (Exod. viii. 26) ; and by this very opposite choice of a victim they were made unequivocally to denounce, and to separate themselves from, the rites of Egypt.—[G. W.]

[1] It is not at all clear that the reference is to iii. 28, as the commentators generally suppose (see Larcher, Bähr, and Blakesley ad loc.): for Herodotus is there describing, not the animal which might be offered to Apis, but the animal which was regarded as an incarnation of Apis. Perhaps we have here, as in vii. 213, a promise that is unfulfilled.

[2] The sanction given for sacrificing a bull was by a papyrus band tied by the priest round the horns, which he stamped with his signet on sealing-clay. Documents sealed with fine clay and impressed with a signet are very common; but the exact symbols impressed on it by the priest on this occasion are not known. Castor says they consisted of a man kneeling with his hands tied behind him, and a sword pointed to his throat, which was probably this (of woodcut), though it has not been found on a seal. The clay used in closing and sealing papyri is of very fine quality. A similar kind was employed for official seals by the Greeks and Assyrians. On signet-rings see my note on B. iii. ch. 41.—[G. W.]

[3] We learn from the sculptures that the victim, having its feet tied together, was thrown on the ground ; and the priest having placed his hand on its head (as in Levit. i. 4 ; iii. 8), or holding it by the horn, cut its throat, apparently from ear to ear, as is the custom of the Moslems at the present day. The skin was then re-

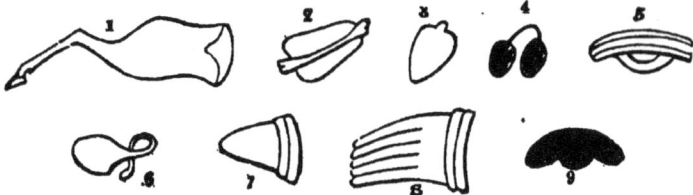

No. I.

off his head, proceed to flay the body.⁴   Next they take the
head, and heaping imprecations on it, if there is a market-place
and a body of Greek traders in the city, they carry it there and
sell it instantly ; if, however, there are no Greeks among them,
they throw the head into the river.   The imprecation is to this
effect :—They pray that if any evil is impending either over
those who sacrifice, or over universal Egypt, it may be made to
fall upon that head.   These practices, the imprecations upon
the heads, and the libations of wine, prevail all over Egypt, and
extend to victims of all sorts ; and hence the Egyptians will
never eat the head of any animal.

40. The disembowelling and burning are however different
in different sacrifices.   I will mention the mode in use with

moved, and after the head had been taken away, the foreleg or shoulder, generally
the right (as in Levit. viii. 26), was the first joint cut off.   This was considered, and
called, the chosen part (*Sapt*), and was the first offered on the altar.   (Cp. 1 Sam.
ix. 24 ; Levit. vii. 33 ; viii. 25.)   The other parts were afterwards cut up ; and the
shoulder, the thigh, the head, the ribs, the rump, the heart, and the kidneys, were
the principal ones placed on the altar.   The head, which Herodotus says was either
taken to the market and sold to strangers, or thrown into the river, is as common

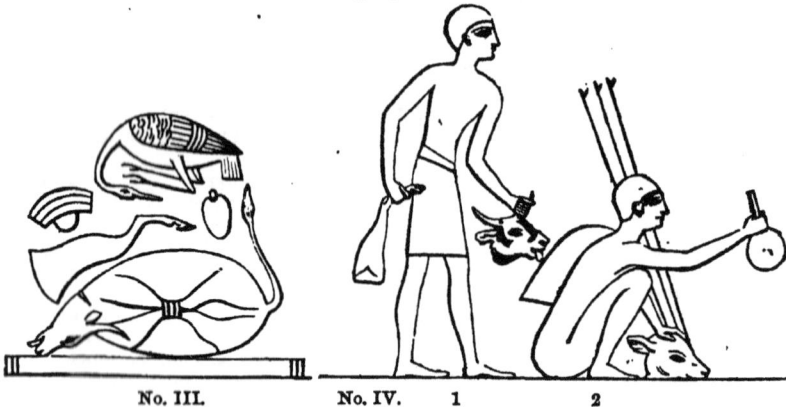

No. III.   No. IV.   1   2

on the altars as any other joint, and an instance sometimes occurs of the whole animal being placed upon it.   We may therefore conclude that the imprecations he
says were called down upon the head were confined to certain occasions and to one
particular victim, as in the case of the scapegoat of the Jews (Levit. xvi. 8, 10, 21),
and it was of that particular animal that no Egyptian would eat the head.   It may
not have been a favourite joint, since we find it given to a poor man for holding the
walking-sticks of the guests at a party ; but he was an Egyptian, not a foreigner,
and this is in the paintings of a tomb at Thebes, of the early time of the 18th dynasty (woodcut No. IV.)—[G. W.]
⁴ Homer's description of the mode of slaughtering an animal (Il. i. 459–466) is
very similar : "They drew back the head and killed it, and after skinning it they
cut off the legs (μηροὺς), which being wrapped up in the fat (caul) folded double,
they placed portions of raw meat thereon ; an old man then burnt it on split wood,

respect to the goddess whom they regard as the greatest,[5] and honour with the chiefest festival.   When they have flayed their

No. II.

and poured black wine on it, while the young men beside him held five-pronged spits. . When the legs (thighs and shoulders) were burnt, and they had tasted the 'inward parts,' they cut the rest into small pieces, and put them on skewers (spits), roasting them cleverly, and took all off again."—[G. W.]

[5] Herodotus here evidently alludes to Isis, as he shows in chs. 59, 61, where he speaks of her fête at Busiris; but he afterwards confounds her with Athor (ch. 41). This is very excusable in the historian, since the attributes of those two goddesses are often so closely connected that it is difficult to distinguish them in the sculptures, unless their names are directly specified.   It was however more so in late than in early times, and at Dendera Athor has very nearly the same appearance as Isis,

steer they pray, and when their prayer is ended they take the paunch of the animal out entire, leaving the intestines and the fat inside the body; they then cut off the legs, the end of the loins, the shoulders, and the neck; and having so done, they fill the body of the steer with clean bread, honey, raisins, figs, frankincense, myrrh, and other aromatics.[6] Thus filled, they burn the body, pouring over it great quantities of oil. Before offering the sacrifice they fast, and while the bodies of the victims are being consumed they beat themselves. Afterwards, when they have concluded this part of the ceremony, they have the other parts of the victim served up to them for a repast.

41. The male kine, therefore, if clean, and the male calves, are used for sacrifice by the Egyptians universally; but the female they are not allowed to sacrifice,[7] since they are sacred to Isis. The statue of this goddess has the form of a woman but with horns like a cow, resembling thus the Greek representations of Io;[8] and the Egyptians, one and all, venerate cows

though still a distinct goddess, as is shown by each of them having a temple at that place. Herodotus (in ch. 41) says that cows were sacred to Isis, whose statues had the head of that animal; but it was to Athor, the Venus of Egypt, that they were sacred; and it is only when one adopts the attributes of the other, that Isis has the head of the spotted cow of Athor, or that this goddess takes the name of Isis. Plutarch says Isis was called Muth, Athyri, and Methuer (de Is. s. 56). That Herodotus was really describing Athor and not Isis is shown by the city where the cattle were sent being Atarbechis. (See below note[8] on ch. 41.) The Roman poets made a double error in confounding Isis with Athor, and even with Juno, whence "niveâ Saturnia vaccâ." Great honours were also paid to the Cow of Athor at Momemphis, where Venus was particularly worshipped; and wherever she had a temple a sacred Cow was kept, as Strabo says was the case at Momemphis as well as other places in the Delta; and at Chusæ, a small village in the Hermopolite nome where Venus was worshipped under the title of Urania.—[G. W.]

[6] The custom of filling the body with cakes and various things, and then burning it all, calls to mind the Jewish burnt offering (Levit. viii. 25, 26).—[G. W.]

[7] In order to prevent the breed of cattle from being diminished; but some mysterious reason being assigned for it, the people were led to respect an ordonnance which might not otherwise have been attended to. This was the general system, and the reason of many things being held sacred may be attributed to a necessary precaution. It is indeed distinctly stated by Porphyry (de Abstin. ii. s. 11), who says "the Egyptians and Phœnicians would rather eat human flesh than that of cows, on account of the value of the animal, though they both sacrifice and eat bulls;" and the same was doubtless the origin of a similar superstition in India. In another place Porphyry (iv. 7) says the same thing, and adds "that certain bulls were held in the same veneration, while others were preserved for labour." Some years ago no one was allowed to kill a calf in Egypt, and a permission from the government was required for the slaughter of a bull; but this soon degenerated into a mere tax, and cows and calves were permitted to be killed on the payment of a duty. In India and Thibet the veneration for the cow is as remarkable as in Egypt. Jerome also remarks, "In Ægypto et Palæstinâ propter boum raritatem nemo vaccam comedit" (ii. adv. Jovin. 7). Porphyry (de Abstin.) says the first who sacrificed did not offer animals, but herbs and flowers; and (de Sacrif. ii.) flour, honey, and fruits.—[G. W.]

[8] This name is evidently connected with *Ehe*, "the Cow," of the Egyptians,

much more highly than any other animal. This is the reason why no native of Egypt, whether man or woman, will give a Greek a kiss,[2] or use the knife of a Greek, or his spit, or his cauldron, or taste the flesh of an ox, known to be pure, if it has been cut with a Greek knife. When kine die, the following is the manner of their sepulture :—The females are thrown into the river ; the males are buried in the suburbs of the towns, with one or both of their horns appearing above the surface of the ground to mark the place. When the bodies are decayed, a boat comes, at an appointed time, from the island called Prosô-pitis,[1]—which is a portion of the Delta, nine schœnes in circum-

which was given to one of their goddesses; but the remark of Eustathius that "Io, in the language of the Argives, is the moon," is explained by its being the Egyptian name *Ioh*, " the moon," which, though quite distinct from *Ehe*, agrees well with Io being looked upon by the Greeks as the moon, and with the supposed relationship of the Egyptians and the Argives, who were said to have been a colony taken by Danaus from the Nile. Io is reported to have visited Egypt in her wanderings, and to have been changed into Isis, in the city of Coptos, where she was worshipped under that name. (See Diod. i. 24; and comp. Ovid Met. i. 588, 747; Propert. ii. Elog. 28. 17; and At. Eg. W. vol. iv. p. 382, 388, 390; vol. v. p. 195.) The story of her having given birth to Epaphus (the Apis of Egypt) was probably a later addition: but her wandering to the Nile, like the fable related by Herodotus (Book i. ch. 5), points to the connection between Egypt and Argos. The name Ioh, or Aah, written Iho, or Aha, is an instance of the medial vowel at the end of a word in hieroglyphics. (See below, n.[2], and App. ch. v. § 16.)—[G. W.]

[2] The Egyptians considered all foreigners unclean, with whom they would not eat, and particularly the Greeks. " The Egyptians might not eat bread with the Hebrews, for that is an abomination unto the Egyptians " (Gen. xliii. 32); and the same prejudice is continued by the Hindoos, and by many of the Moslems, to the present day. But the last have gradations, like the ancient Egyptians, who looked with greater horror on those who did not cut the throat from ear to ear of all animals used for food.—[G. W.]

[1] Some suppose the town of Prosôpitis to have been also called Nicium. The island was between the Canopic and Sebennytic branches, at the fork, and on the west side of the apex of the Delta. It was there that the Athenians, who came to assist the Egyptians against the Persians, were besieged, B.C. 460–458. (Thucyd. i. 109.) It is not to be supposed that *all* the bulls that died in Egypt were carried to Atarbechis to be buried; and much less that all the bodies of heifers were thrown into the river. Like other animals they were embalmed and buried in the place where they died, and their mummies are consequently found at Thebes and in other

ference,—and calls at the several cities in turn to collect the bones of the oxen. Prosôpitis is a district containing several cities; the name of that from which the boats come is Atarbè-chis.[2] Venus has a temple there of much sanctity. Great numbers of men go forth from this city and proceed to the other towns, where they dig up the bones, which they take away with them and bury together in one place. The same practice pre-vails with respect to the interment of all other cattle—the law so determining; they do not slaughter any of them.

42. Such Egyptians as possess a temple of the Theban Jove, or live in the Thebaïc canton,[3] offer no sheep in sacrifice,[4] but

parts of the country. The Egyptians were particular in preventing anything re-maining above ground, which by putrefaction could taint the air; and this was the reason of their obliging every town to embalm whatever died there. It is probable that villages *near* Atarbechis sent the carcases of bulls to that city, which led He-rodotus to suppose that all places did so; as other animals were sent from different villages in the *neighbourhood* to the chief city, where they were sacred. To pollute the Nile with dead carcases would have been in the highest degree inconsistent in a people so particular on this point; and the notion of Herodotus can only be ex-plained by their *sometimes* feeding the crocodiles with them. The prejudice in fa-vour of the river still remains in Egypt, and even the Moslems swear "by that pure stream."—[G. W.]

[2] Athor being the Venus of Egypt, Atarbechis was translated Aphroditopolis. It was composed of *atar* or *athor*, and *bechi* or *bek*, "city," which occurs again in Baalbek, the city of Baal, or the Sun (Heliopolis); Rabek, the Assyrian name of the Egyptian Heliopolis, from the Egyptian Re or Ra, "the sun." This Aphroditopolis is supposed to have been at the modern *Shibbeen*, in the Isle of Prosôpitis, between the Canopic and Sebennytic branches of the Nile, on an offset of the latter, called Thermuthiac, which formed the western, as the Sebennytic did the eastern, boundary of the Isle of Natho. There were other towns called Aphroditopolis in Upper Egypt. Athor signifies, as Plutarch says, "Horus' habitation," Thy-hor, or Téihor, THI-ϨOP, the origin of the name Thueris, who, however, was made into another person (Plut. de Is. s. 56, and 19). As the morning-star she issued from the moun-tain of Thebes under the form of a spotted cow, and as the evening-star she retired behind it at night. She also represented Night, and in this capacity received the sun at his setting into her arms as he retired behind the western mountain of Thebes. It was from this that the western part of the city was called Pathyris, "belonging to Athor," who presided over the west. (On Athor see At. Eg. W. vol. iv. 386 to 394.) Her great importance is shown by the many cities dedicated to her in Upper and Lower Egypt, as well as temples in other places, from the earliest times to the Ptolemies and Cæsars; and Venus was the great goddess of Phœnicia and other countries.—[G. W.]

[3] On the cantons or nomes of Egypt see note [7] on ch. 164. It has erroneously been supposed that each nome "was kept distinct from the others by the difference of religion and rites." It is true there was a chief god of the nome; but cities of different nomes were often dedicated to the same deity; and even a city might have a chief god who was not the one of the nome, as Eileithyia was in her city within the nome of Apollinopolis. The numerous divinities worshipped throughout Egypt were also admitted as contemplar gods in any part of the country. See note [a] on this chapter.—[G. W.]

[4] Sheep are never represented on the altar, or slaughtered for the table, at Thebes, though they were kept there for their wool; and Plutarch says "none of the Egyptians eat sheep, except the Lycopolites" (de Isid. s. 72). Goats were killed, but the Theban gentry seem to have preferred the ibex or wild goat, the oryx, the gazelle, and other game. These, however, were confined to the wealthier classes;

only goats; for the Egyptians do not all worship the same gods,[5] excepting Isis and Osiris, the latter of whom they say is the Grecian Bacchus.[6]　Those, on the contrary, who possess a tem-

others lived principally on beef, Nile geese, and other wild fowl; and some were satisfied with fish, either fresh or salted, with an occasional goose or a joint of meat; and the numerous vegetables Egypt produced appeared in profusion on every table. Lentil porridge was, as at present, a great article of food for the poor, as well as the *raphanus* (*figl*) (Herod. ii. 125), " cucumbers (or gourds), melons, and leeks, onions, and garlick" (Num. xi. 5), of which the gourd (*kus*, Arabic *kúz*), melon (*abtikh*, Arabic *batikh*), onion (*busl*, Arabic *busl*), and garlick (*tóm*, Arabic *tóm*) retain their names in Egypt to the present day. They had also fruits and roots of various kinds; and Diodorus (i. 80) says that children had merely " a little meal of the coarsest kind, the pith of the papyrus, baked under the ashes, and the roots and stalks of marsh-weeds." Beef and goose, ibex, gazelle, oryx, and wild fowl were also presented to

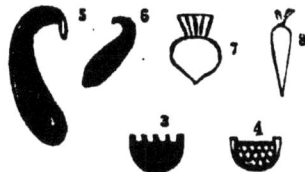

the gods; and onions, though forbidden to the priests, always held a prominent place on their altar, with the *figl* (raphanus, figs. 7, 8), and gourds (figs. 5, 6), grapes, figs (especially of the sycamore, figs. 3, 4), corn, and various flowers. (See ch. 39, woodcut No. II.)　Wine, milk, beer, and a profusion of cakes and bread, also formed part of the offerings, and incense was presented at every great sacrifice.— [G. W.]

[5] Though each city had its presiding deity, many others of neighbouring and of distant towns were also admitted to its temples as contemplar gods, and none were positively excluded except some local divinities, and certain animals, whose sanctity was confined to particular places. In one city Amun was the chief deity, as at Thebes; in another Pthah, as at Memphis; in another Re (the sun), as at Heliopolis; and some cities which were consecrated to the same deity were distinguished by the affix "the great," "the lesser," as Aphroditopolis, and Diospolis, Magna, and Parva. Many again bore a name not taken from the chief god of the place; but every city and every sanctuary had its presiding deity, with contemplar gods, who were members of the general Pantheon—those of a neighbouring town generally holding a conspicuous post in the temple, after the chief deity of the place. Each town had also a triad composed of the great god of the place and two other members. Many local deities scarcely went beyond their own city or nome; and some animals, sacred in one province, were held in abhorrence in another. Thus, the inhabitants of Ombos, Athribis, and the Northern Crocodilopolis (afterwards called Arsinoë), near the Lake Mœris, honoured the crocodile; those of Tentyris, Heracleopolis, and Apollinopolis Magna were its avowed enemies; and as the Ombites fought with the Tentyrites in the cause of their sacred animal, so a war was waged between the Oxyrhinchites and Cynopolites in consequence of the former having eaten a dog, to avenge an affront offered by the Cynopolites, who had brought to table the sacred fish of Oxyrhinchus. (Plut. de Isid. v. 44.) The reason of these local honours was not originally connected with religion; and the sanctity of the crocodile, and of certain fish, at Crycodilopolis, Oxyrhinchus, and other places distant from the Nile, was instituted in order to induce the inhabitants to keep up the canals. All, it is true, worshipped Osiris, as well as his sister Isis, for as he was judge of the dead, all were equally amenable to his tribunal; but it cannot be said that he and Isis were the only deities worshipped throughout Egypt, since Amun, Pthah, and the other great gods, and many also of the second, as well as of the third order, were universally venerated.—[G. W.]

[6] See below, note [6] on ch. 48. " Osiris," says Diodorus, " has been considered the same as Sarapis, Bacchus, Pluto, or Ammon; others have thought him Jupiter; many Pan:" and he endeavours to identify him with the sun, and Isis with the moon. But these notions were owing to similarities being traced in the attributes of certain gods of the Greek and Egyptian Pantheons,

ple dedicated to Mendes,[7] or belong to the Mendesian canton, abstain from offering goats, and sacrifice sheep instead. The Thebans, and such as imitate them in their practice, give the following account of the origin of the custom :—" Hercules," they say, " wished of all things to see Jove, but Jove did not choose to be seen of him.[8] At length, when Hercules persisted, Jove hit on a device—to flay a ram, and, cutting off his head, hold the head before him, and cover himself with the fleece. In this guise he showed himself to Hercules." Therefore the Egyptians give their statues of Jupiter the face of a ram ;[9] and from them the practice has passed to the Ammo-

and one often possessed some that belonged to several. Thus the principal character of Osiris was that of Pluto, because he was Judge of the dead, and ruler of Amenti or Hades; and he was supposed to be Bacchus, when he lived on earth, and taught man to till the land.—[G. W.]

[7] The mounds of *Ashmoun*, on the canal leading to *Ménzaleh*, mark the site of Mendes. The Greeks considered Pan to be both Mendes and Khem; they called Chemmis in Upper Egypt Panopolis, and gave the capital of the Mendesian nome to Pan, who was said by Herodotus (ch. 46) to have been figured with the head and legs of a goat. Unfortunately no monument remains at *Ashmoun* to give the name and form of the god of Mendes; but it is certain that he was not Khem, the " Pan of Thebes" (Πὰν Θήβων), who had the attributes of Priapus, and was one of the great gods. Mandoo again (or Munt), whose name appears to be related to Mendes, had the head of a hawk: and no god of the Egyptian Pantheon is represented with the head and legs of a goat. The notion is Greek; and Jablonski is quite right in saying that Mendes did not signify a "goat." There is a tablet in the British Museum (No. 356) with a goat represented much in the same manner as an Apis; but the legend over it contains no reference to Mendes. Khem, like the Greek Pan, was "universal nature;" and as he presided over everything generated, he was the god of vegetable as well as animal life; and though the god of gardens had with the Greeks another name, he was really the same deity under his phallic form. —[G. W.]

[8] This fable accords with the supposed meaning of the name of Amun, which Manetho says was " concealment;" but the reason of the god having the head of an animal would apply to so many others, that it ceases to do so to any one in particular. Hecatæus derived Amun from a word signifying "come," in allusion to his being invoked (Plut. de Isid. 5. 9); and Iamblichus says it implies that which brings to light, or is manifested. *Amoni* means " envelope," and *amoine* is " come." —[G. W.]

[9] See above, notes [8], [9], on ch. 29. The god Noum (Nou, Noub, or Nef), with a ram's head, answered to Jupiter, and he was the first member of the Triad of the Cataracts, composed of Noum, Sate, and Anouké (Jupiter, Juno, and Vesta). Amun again was also considered the same as Jupiter, because he was the King of the gods; and it was from his worship that Thebes received the name of Diospolis, " the city of Jove," answering to No-Amun or Amûn-na of the Bible (Jer. xlvi. 25; Ezek. xxx. 14, 15, 16), the Amun-êi ("abode of Amun "), or Amun-êi Na ("the great abode of Amun," or " Amun-êi" only?) of the sculptures. Amun and Noum, having both some of the attributes of Jupiter, naturally became confounded by the Greeks; and the custom of one god occasionally receiving the attributes of another doubtless led them into error. The greatest interchange, however, was between Amun and Khem; but as this was only at Thebes, and little known to the Greeks, the same misapprehension did not take place, and Khem by the Greeks was only considered to be Pan. Yet Pan again was supposed by them to be Mendes; and the two names of Amun and Amunre, given

nians, who are a joint colony of Egyptians and Ethiopians, speaking a language between the two ; hence also, in my opinion, the latter people took their name of Ammonians, since the Egyptian name for Jupiter is Amun.   Such then is the reason why the Thebans do not sacrifice rams, but consider them sacred animals.   Upon one day in the year, however, at the festival of Jupiter, they slay a single ram, and stripping off the fleece, cover with it the statue of that god, as he once covered himself, and then bring up to the statue of Jove an image of Hercules. When this has been done, the whole assembly beat their breasts in mourning for the ram, and afterwards bury him in a holy sepulchre.

43. The account which I received of this Hercules makes him one of the twelve gods.[1]   Of the other Hercules, with whom the Greeks are familiar, I could hear nothing in any part of Egypt.   That the Greeks, however (those I mean who gave the son of Amphitryon that name), took the name[2] from the Egyp-

to the same god, would probably have perplexed the Greeks, if they had happened to perceive that additional title of Amun.   It is, however, only right to say that the Ethiopians frequently gave the name of Amun to the ram-headed Noum, and, being their greatest god, was to them what Jupiter was to the Greeks.   See my note on Book iv. ch. 181.—[G. W.]

[1] Here again the same confusion occurs, from the claims of two gods to the character of Hercules—*Khons*, the third member of the Theban Triad, and Moui, who is called "Son of the Sun."   The latter was the god of Sebennytus, where he was known under the name of Gem, Sem, or Gemnouti, whence the Coptic appellation of that city Gemnouti.   There was another Heracleopolis, the capital of a nome of the same name, which is now marked by the mounds of Anásieh, the Hnês of the Copts, a little to the south of the entrance to the Fyóom.   Moui appears to be the splendour or force of the sun, and hence the god of power, a divine attribute —the Greek Hercules being strength, a gift to man.   The Egyptian Hercules was the *abstract idea* of divine power, and it is not therefore surprising that Herodotus could learn nothing of the Greek Hercules, who was a hero unknown in Egypt.   The connexion between strength and heat may be traced even in the Greek appellation of Hercules.   Alcides, his patronymic (taken from his grandfather Alcæus), and the name of his mother Alcmæna, were derived from ἀλκή, "strength ;" and Hercules may even be related to the Semitic *har, harh*, "heat," or "burning" (analogous to the Teutonic *kar*, "fire"), and perhaps to *aor*, "light," in Hebrew, or to the Hor (Horus) of Egypt.   The Etruscans called him Herkle, or Ercle.   In the Hebrew, "Samson" recalls the name of Sem, the Egyptian Hercules.   Hercules being the sun, the twelve labours of the later hero may have been derived from the twelve signs of the zodiac.   Hercules, as Herodotus, Macrobius, and others state, was particularly worshipped at Tyre ; "but," adds Macrobius, "the Egyptians venerate him with the most sacred and august rites, and look upon the period when his worship was first adopted by them as beyond the reach of all memorials.   He is believed to have killed the Giants, when in the *character* of the valour of the gods he fought in defence of Heaven ;" which accords with the title of a work called "Semnuthis," written by Apollonides or Horapius (in Theophil. Antioch. ad Autolyc. 2. 6), describing the wars of the gods against the Giants, and recalls the Egyptian title of the god of Sebennytus.   Cicero mentions one Hercules who was "Nilogenitus ;" but Hercules was derived by the Greeks from the Phœnicians rather than from Egypt. See note [1] on ch. 44, and note [3] ch. 171.—[G. W.]

[2] Herodotus, who derived his knowledge of the Egyptian religion from the pro-

tians, and not the Egyptians from the Greeks,[3] is I think clearly proved, among other arguments, by the fact that both the parents of Hercules, Amphitryon as well as Alcmêna, were of Egyptian origin.[4] Again, the Egyptians disclaim all knowledge of the names of Neptune and the Dioscûri,[5] and do not include them in the number of their gods ; but had they adopted the name of any god from the Greeks, these would have been the likeliest to obtain notice, since the Egyptians, as I am well convinced, practised navigation at that time, and the Greeks also were some of them mariners, so that they would have been more likely to know the names of these gods than that of Hercules. But the Egyptian Hercules is one of their ancient gods. Seventeen thousand years before the reign of Amasis, the twelve gods were, they affirm, produced from the eight :[6] and of these twelve, Hercules is one.

44. In the wish to get the best information that I could on these matters, I made a voyage to Tyre in Phœnicia, hearing

fessional interpreters, seems to have regarded the *word* "Hercules " as Egyptian. It is scarcely necessary to say that no Egyptian god has a name from which that of Hercules can by any possibility have been formed. The word ('Ηρακλῆς) seems to be pure Greek, and has been reasonably enough derived from ʿΗρα, "the goddess Juno," and κλέος " glory " (see Scott and Liddell's Lexicon, p. 597).

[3] See the last note but one. The tendency of the Greeks to claim an indigenous origin for the deities they borrowed from strangers, and to substitute physical for abstract beings, readily led them to invent the story of Hercules, and every *dignus vindice nodus* was cut by the interposition of his marvellous strength. Even the Arabs call forth some hero to account for natural phenomena, or whatever wonderful action they think right to attribute to man ; and the opening of the Straits of Gibraltar is declared by Edrisi to have been the work of Alexander the Great ; any stupendous building is ascribed to Antar ; and Solomon (like Melampus in Greek fable) is supposed to have explained the language of animals and birds—a science said by Philostratus to have been learnt from the Arabs by Apollonius Tyanæus (i. 14). In order to account for the discrepancies in the time when Hercules was supposed to have lived, the Greeks made out three, the oldest being the Egyptian, and the son of Jove, another of Crete, and the youngest was the hero, also a son of Jove. Some Latin writers (as Varro) increased the number to forty-three. The Cretan Hercules was also related to the god of Egypt ; and the latter, as Moui, was intimately connected with the funeral rites, and was generally painted black in the tombs of Thebes.—[G. W.]

[4] The parentage of the former was Alcæus, Perseus, Jupiter and Danaë, Acrisius, Abas, Lynceus (who married a daughter of Danaus), Ægyptus, the twin-brother of Danaus, the son of *Belus.* Alcmena was daughter of Electryon, the son of Perseus. This accords with what Herodotus mentions (ch. 91) of Perseus, Danaus, and Lynceus having been natives of Chemmis, and connects them all with the sun.— [G. W.]

[5] Herodotus is quite right in saying that these gods were not in the Egyptian Pantheon. See note [2] on ch. 50, and note [8] ch. 91.—[G. W.]

[6] This is the supposed period from Hercules to Amasis ; and 15,000 were reckoned from Bacchus to Amasis (ch. 145). According to Manetho, the Egyptians believed that the gods reigned on earth before men. The first were Vulcan, the Sun, Agathodæmon, Chronos (Saturn), Osiris, Typhon (or Seth), Horus (which four last

there was a temple of Hercules at that place,[7] very highly venerated.   I visited the temple, and found it richly adorned with
a number of offerings, among which were two pillars, one of pure

are found also in this order in the Turin Papyrus).   The royal authority then continued through a long succession to Bytis (or Bites), occupying

	Years.	Years.
18,900 years	. . .	18,900
Then after the gods reigned Heroes	1255	
Other kings	1817	
30 *other* (?) Memphite kings	1790	
10 Thinites	350	
Manes and demigods	5813	
Sum . .	11,000, or really	11,025
Total		24,925

which agrees very nearly with the sum given by Eusebius, from Manetho, of 24,-
900, from the beginning of the reign of Vulcan to Mences.
    Syncellus, again, on the authority of Manetho, gives the reigns of the gods
thus :—

	Reigned years.		Reduced from
1. Vulcan . . .	727¾		9000
2. Helios . .	80¹/₆		992
3. Agathodæmon .	56⁷/₁₂		700
4. Chronos . .	40½		501
5. Osiris and Isis .	35		433
6. Typhon . .	29		359
7. Horus the demigod	25		309
	994 reduced from .		12,294

		Years.
8. Mars the demigod		23
9. Anubis id.		17
10. Hercules id.		15
11. Apollo id.		25
12. Ammon id.		30
13. Tithoês id.		27
14. Zôsos id.		32
15. Jupiter id.		20
Years reduced to . . .		189
from about 2338.		

    In this list the relative positions of Osiris (Bacchus) and Hercules do not agree
with the statement of Herodotus; and in deducting the sums of 12,294 + 680 (to
the end of Hercules' reign) = 12,974 from the total rule of the gods, or 24,925, we
have 11,951 years; and this added to the 2799 of Manetho's lists, from Menes to
the end of Amasis, gives 14,750 years, from Hercules, or 15,418 years from Osiris
to the end of Amasis. But it sufficiently appears from the names in the above list
that it is not even certain the Egyptians calculated in this manner; and the Turin
Papyrus gives, after Horus, Thoth (who seems to have reigned 7226 years), and
Thmei, and apparently Horus (the younger); after whom seems to come the first
King Menes; or a summation of demi-gods, followed by the name of Menes.   It is
however possible that Herodotus was told of some list similar to the one above. See
Tn. P. K. W., p. 7 to 11.—[G. W.]
    [7] The temple of Hercules at Tyre was very ancient, and, according to Herodotus,
as old as the city itself, or 2300 years before his time, *i. e.* about 2755 B.C.   Hercules presided over it under the title of Melkarth, or Melek-Kartha, "king" (lord) of
the city. (See note ⁴ on ch. 32.) Diodorus also (i. 24) speaks of the antiquity of Hercules; and his antiquity is fully established, in spite of the doubts of Plutarch. (De
Herod. Mal.) The Phœnicians settled at the Isle of Thasos, on account of its gold
mines, which they first discovered there (Herod. vi. 46, 47 ; Apollodor. iii. 1), as

gold, the other of emerald,[s] shining with great brilliancy at night. In a conversation which I held with the priests, I inquired how

they were the first to visit Britain for its tin. Pausanias says the Thasians being of Phœnician origin, coming with Agenor and other Phœnicians from Tyre, dedicated a temple to Hercules at Olympia. They worshipped the same Hercules as the Tyrians (Pausan. v. xxv. § 7), and Apollodorus (iii. 1) states that Thasos, son of Poseidon (Neptune), or, according to Pherecydes, of Cilix, going in quest of Europa, founded the Thracian Thasus. Phœnix went to Phœnicia, Cilix to Cilicia, Cadmus and Telephus to Thrace. The Melcarthus mentioned by Plutarch (de Is. s. 15) as a king of Byblos, and his queen Astarté, were the Hercules and Astarté (Venus) of Syria; the latter called also Saosis and Nemanoun, answering to the Greek name Athenaïs. The Temple of Hercules is supposed to have stood on the hill close to the aqueduct, about 1½ mile east of the modern town, which last occupies part of insular Tyre taken by Alexander. The temple marks the site of the early city. As the Temple of Hercules at Tyre was the oldest of that deity in Syria, so that of Venus Urania, or Astarté, at Askalon, was the oldest of that goddess.

In 2 Maccabees iv. 18, 20, mention is made of a great game every fifth year, kept at Tyre, with sacrifices to Hercules. The absurdity of connecting the name Melicertes with "honey," as in the Gnostic Papyrus, is obvious. (See note [s] on ch. 83.) The sea deity, Melicertes of Corinth, afterwards called Palæmon, was only an adaptation of a foreign god. The Tyrian Hercules was originally the sun, and the same as Baal, "the lord," which, like Melkarth, was only a title. Hercules and Venus (Astarté) were really nature deified, one representing the generating, or vivifying, and the other the producing principle; hence the mother goddess. The sun was chosen as the emblem of the first, and the earth of the second, or sometimes the moon, being looked upon as the companion of the sun. This nature system will explain the reason of so many gods having been connected with the sun in Egypt and elsewhere; as Adonis (Adonai, "our Lord") was the sun in the winter solstice.—[G. W.]

[s] This pillar is mentioned by Theophrastus (Lap. 23), and Pliny (H. N. xxxvii. 5). The former expresses an opinion that it was false.

[It was probably of glass, which is known to have been made in Egypt at least 3800 years ago, having been found bearing the name of a Pharaoh of the 18th dynasty. The monuments also of the 4th dynasty show the same glass bottles (see

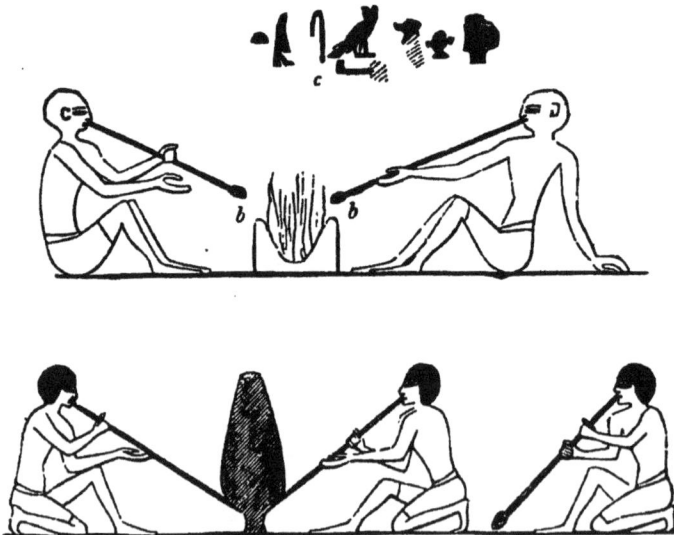

long their temple had been built, and found by their answer that they too differed from the Greeks. They said that the temple was built at the same time that the city was founded, and that the foundation of the city took place two thousand three hundred years ago. In Tyre I remarked another temple where the same god was worshipped as the Thasian Hercules. So I went on to Thasos,[2] where I found a temple of Hercules which had been built by the Phœnicians who colonised that island when they sailed in search of Europa.[1]   Even this was five gen-

---

woodcut, n. [7], ch. 77) were used then as in later times, and glass-blowing is represented in the paintings from the 12th to the 26th dynasty, and also in those of the 4th at the tombs near the Pyramids. Various hues were given to glass by the Egyptians, and this invention became in after times a great favourite at Rome, where it was much sought for ornamental purposes, for bottles and other common utensils, and even for windows, one of which was discovered at Pompeii. (Comp. Seneca. Ep. 90; de Benef. vii. 0; and de VII. lii. 40.) The manufacture appears to have been introduced under the Empire. They also cut, ground, and engraved glass, and had even the art of introducing gold between two surfaces of the substance; specimens of all which I have, as well as of false pearls from Thebes, scarcely to be distinguished from real ones, if buried the same number of years. Pliny even speaks of glass being malleable. The glass of Egypt was long famous (Athen. xi. p. 784 c), and continued so to the time of the Empire. Strabo (xvi. p. 1077) mentions its many colours, and one very perfect kind which could only be made with a particular vitreous earth found in that country; and the ruins of glass furnaces are still seen at the Natron Lakes. Of all stones, says Pliny, the emerald was the most easily imitated (xxvii. 12); and the colossus of Sarapis in the Egyptian Labyrinth, 9 cubits (between 13 and 14 feet) high, and others mentioned by Pliny (xxxvii. 5) were doubtless of glass; like the λίθινα χυτὰ of Herodotus (infra, ch. 69. See At. Eg. W. vol. iii. p. 88 to 107.) There seems every probability that glass was first invented in Egypt; and fires lighted frequently on the sand in a country producing natron, or subcarbonate of soda, would be more likely to disclose the secret than the solitary accident of sailors using blocks of natron for supporting their saucepans on the sea-shore of Syria, as stated by Pliny (xxxvi. 65). Pliny's nitrum is "natron," and the natron district was called Nitriotis.—G. W.]

[2] Thasos, which still retains its name, is a small island off the Thracian coast, opposite to the mouth of the Nestus (*Karasu*). It seems to have been a very early Phœnician settlement (infra, vi. 46—7).

[1] This signifies exploring the "western lands," Europa being Ereb (the Arabic *gharb*), "the west." It is the same word as Erebus, or "darkness;" and Europa is said to be χώρα τῆς δύσεως, ἡ σκοτεινή—Εὐρωπόν, σκοτεινόν. (Hesych. comp. Eur. Iph. in Taur. v. 626.) The same word occurs in Hebrew, where ברע signifies "mixed," or "grey colour," and is applied to the evening, and sun-setting, to the raven and to the Arabs;—"the mingled people (Arabs) that dwell in the desert." (Jerem. xxv. 20, 24.) The story of Europa was really Phœnician colonisation, represented as a princess, carried to Crete, their first and nearest colony, by Jupiter, under the form of a bull, where she became the mother of Minos. Hence Europa is called by Homer (Il. xiv. 321) a daughter of Phœnix, whom some consider her brother; and his voyage to *Africa* in search of Europa ("the west") points to Phœnician colonisation there also. There can be no doubt that the name of the "Arabs" was also given from their living at the *westernmost* part of Asia; and their own word *Gharb*, the "West," is another form of the original Semitic name Arab. The Arabs write the two غرب *Gharb*, عرب *Arab*; and their *ghoráb*, "crow," answers to the Hebrew אֹרֵב "raven;" which last is called by them *ghoráb Nooh*, "Noah's crow."

crations earlier than the time when Hercules, son of Amphitryon, was born in Greece. These researches show plainly that
there is an ancient god Hercules ; and my own opinion is, that
those Greeks act most wisely who build and maintain two temples of Hercules,[2] in the one of which the Hercules worshipped
is known by the name of Olympian, and has sacrifice offered to
him as an immortal, while in the other the honours paid are
such as are due to a hero.

45. The Greeks tell many tales without due investigation,
and among them the following silly fable respecting Hercules :
—"Hercules," they say, "went once to Egypt, and there the
inhabitants took him, and putting a chaplet on his head, led
him out in solemn procession, intending to offer him a sacrifice
to Jupiter. For a while he submitted quietly ; but when they
led him up to the altar, and began the ceremonies, he put forth
his strength and slew them all." Now to me it seems that such
a story proves the Greeks to be utterly ignorant of the character
and customs of the people. The Egyptians do not think it al-
lowable even to sacrifice cattle, excepting sheep, and the male
kine and calves, provided they be pure, and also geese. How
then can it be believed that they would sacrifice men ?[3] And

---

The name *Arab*, "western," may either have been given them by a Semitic people
who lived more to the East, or even by themselves. The Arabs call the north
"*Shemâl*," or "the left," i. e. looking towards sunrise. The Portuguese title, "Prince
of the Algarves," is from *al Gharb*, "the West." The Egyptians called Hades
"*Amenti*;" and the name for the "West," *Ement*, shows the same relationship as
between Erebus and the West. Again, "Hesperia," the Greek name for Italy, was
the "West," like the fabled gardens of the Hesperides ; and the Phœnicians, Greeks,
and others, talked of "the *West*" as we do of "the *East*." The name of Cadmus,
the Phœnician who gave letters to Greece, is of similar import ; and he is a mythical, not a real, personage. His name *Kadm* signifies the "East," as in Job i. 3,
where *Beni Kudm* are "sons of the East," and Cadmus was therefore reputed to be
a brother of Europa. Kadm, or Kudéem, also signifies "old" in Hebrew, as in
Arabic ; and the name in this sense too might apply to Cadmus. In Semitic languages *the East, old, before, to present, to go forward, a foot*, &c., are all related.—
[G. W.]

[2] Later writers made three (Diod. Sic. iv. 39), six (Cic. de Nat. Deor. iii. 16),
and even a greater number of Herculeses. In Greece, however, temples seem to
have been erected only to two. (See Pausan. v. xiv. § 7 ; IX. xxvii. § 5, &c.)

[3] Herodotus here denies, with reason, the possibility of a people with laws, and
a character like those of the Egyptians, having human sacrifices. This very aptly
refutes the idle tales of some ancient authors, which, to our surprise, have even
been repeated in modern times. The absurdity of Amosis having been the first to
abolish them is glaring, since the Egyptians had ages before been sufficiently civilised to lay aside their arms, and to have institutions incompatible with the tolera-
tion of a human sacrifice. The figures of captives on the façades of the temples
slain by the king, often hastily supposed to be human sacrifices, are merely emblematic representations of his conquests, which therefore occur also on the monuments
of the Ptolemies. It is possible that in their earliest days they may have had human sacrifices, like the Greeks and others ; and the symbolic group meaning a

again, how would it have been possible for Hercules alone, and, as they confess, a mere mortal, to destroy so many thousands? In saying thus much concerning these matters, may I incur no displeasure either of god or hero!

46. I mentioned above that some of the Egyptians abstain from sacrificing goats, either male or female. The reason is the following :—These Egyptians, who are the Mendesians, consider Pan to be one of the eight gods who existed before the twelve, and Pan is represented in Egypt by the painters and the sculptors, just as he is in Greece, with the face and legs of a goat.[4] They do not, however, believe this to be his shape, or consider him in any respect unlike the other gods ; but they represent him thus for a reason which I prefer not to relate. The Mendesians hold all goats in veneration, but the male more than the female, giving the goatherds of the males especial honour. One is venerated more highly than all the rest, and when he dies there is a great mourning throughout all the Mendesian canton. In Egyptian, the goat and Pan are both called Mendes.

47. The pig is regarded among them as an unclean animal, so much so that if a man in passing accidentally touch a pig, he instantly hurries to the river, and plunges in with all his clothes on. Hence too the swineherds, notwithstanding that they are of pure Egyptian blood, are forbidden to enter into any of the temples, which are open to all other Egyptians ; and further, no one will give his daughter in marriage to a swineherd, or take a wife from among them, so that the swineherds are forced to intermarry among themselves. They do not offer swine[5] in sacrifice to any of their gods, excepting Bacchus and

"Victim" (supra, n.[2] on ch. 38) may have been derived from that custom. Some notion may be had of the antiquity of Egyptian civilisation, if we recollect the period when the Greeks first went about the city unarmed, and how far they had advanced before that took place. The Athenians were the first Greeks who did this ; and some wore arms even in the time of Thucydides. (Thucyd. i. 5.) It is not long since modern Europe discontinued the custom, and the Dalmatian peasants are still armed. If Herodotus had submitted every story of Greek ciceroni to his own judgment, and had rejected those that were inadmissible, he would have avoided giving many false impressions respecting the Egyptians (as in chaps. 46, 121, 126, 131, and other places). On human sacrifices in old times, see note[9] on ch. 119.—[G. W.]

[4] In the original, "with the face of a goat, and the legs of a he-goat,"—which seems to be a distinction without a difference. No Egyptian god is really represented in this way (At. Eg. W. i. p. 260); but the goat, according to some Egyptologers, was the symbol and representative of Khem, the Pan of the Egyptians. (See Bunsen's Egypt, vol. i. p. 374, and compare notes[7],[9], on ch. 42.)

[5] The pig is rarely represented in the sculptures of Thebes. The flesh was forbidden to the priests, and to all initiated in the mysteries, and it seems only to have

the Moon, whom they honour in this way at the same time, sacrificing pigs to both of them at the same full moon, and afterwards eating of the flesh. There is a reason alleged by them for their detestation of swine at all other seasons, and their use of them at this festival, with which I am well acquainted, but which I do not think it proper to mention. The following is the mode in which they sacrifice the swine to the Moon: —As soon as the victim is slain, the tip of the tail, the spleen, and the caul are put together, and having been covered with all the fat that has been found in the animal's belly, are straightway burnt. The remainder of the flesh is eaten on the same day that the sacrifice is offered, which is the day of the full moon: at any other time they would not so much as taste it.

been allowed to others once a year at the fête of the full moon, when it was sacrificed to the Moon. The Moon and Bacchus (supposed to be Isis and Osiris) were the only deities to whom it was sacrificed, if we may believe Plutarch, who pretends that this ceremony commemorated the finding of the body of Osiris by Typhon, when he was hunting by the light of the moon. (De Is. s. 18.) The reason of the meat not being eaten was its unwholesomeness, on which account it was forbidden to the Jews and Moslems; and the prejudice naturally extended from the animal to those who kept it, as at present in India and other parts of the East, where a Hindoo or a Moslem is, like an ancient Egyptian, defiled by the touch of a pig, and looks with horror on those who tend it and eat its flesh. On this point a remarkable difference existed between the Egyptians and Greeks; and most people would scruple to give to a swineherd the title "divine" (as Homer does), even though they might not feel the same amount of prejudice as the Egyptians. Pigs are not found in the Egyptian sculptures before the time of the 18th dynasty; but this is no proof that they were not known in Egypt before that time.—[G. W.]

⁶ Plutarch (de Is. ss. 12 and 36), in speaking of the Paamylia, attributes to Osiris what really belongs to the god Khem—the generative principle; and Herodotus also evidently alludes to Osiris on this occasion. The reason of this may be that the attributes of various gods were not very distinctly explained to foreigners, who were taught nothing but what was said to relate to Isis and Osiris, in whose mysteries several myths were combined, and others added which tended to mystify rather than to explain them: for it is evident that the Greeks did not understand the nature of the Egyptian gods, and many of the events related by them in the history of Osiris are at variance with the monuments of Egypt. Bacchus is certainly the god of the Greeks who corresponds to Osiris, and his dying and rising again, his being put into a chest and thrown into the sea, and the instructions he gave to mankind, are evidently derived from the story of Osiris; and the "histories on

The poorer sort, who cannot afford live pigs, form pigs of dough, which they bake and offer in sacrifice.

48. To Bacchus, on the eve of his feast, every Egyptian sacrifices a hog before the door of his house, which is then given back to the swineherd by whom it was furnished, and by him carried away. In other respects the festival is celebrated almost exactly as Bacchic festivals are in Greece,[a] excepting that the

which the most solemn feasts of Bacchus, the Titania and Nuktelia, are founded, exactly correspond (as Plutarch says, de Is. s. 35) with what are related of the cutting to pieces of Osiris, of his rising again, and of his new life."

Wreaths and festoons of ivy, or rather of the wild convolvulus, or of the *periploca secamone*, often appear at Egyptian fêtes. For ivy is not a plant of the Nile, though Plutarch says it was there called chenosiris, or " plant of Osiris " (de Is. s. 37; Diod. i. 17), and the leaves being sometimes represented hairy, are in favour of its being the *secamone* (fig. 4). It may have been chosen from some quality attributed to its milky juice, like the soma of India, a juice extracted from the *asclepias acida*, which plays a divine part in the Vedas, and is in the Zend-Avesta of Persia. (See Jour. Americ. Or. Soc. vol. iii. No. 2, p. 299.)

The thyrsus is shown by Plutarch to be the staff (fig. 1), often bound by a fillet, to which the spotted skin of a leopard is suspended near the figure of Osiris; for it is

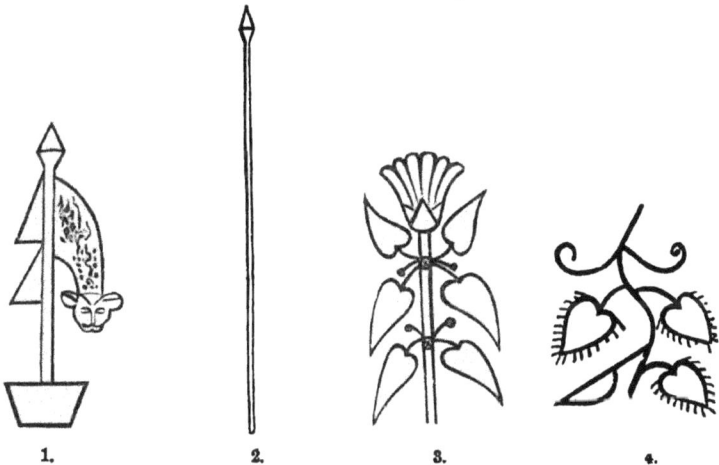

1.　　　　　　2.　　　　　　3.　　　　　　4.

the same that the high priest, clad in the leopard skin dress, carries in the processions (Plut. de Is. s. 35). Another form of it is the head of a water-plant (similar to that in fig. 3), to which Athenæus (Deipn. v. p. 196) evidently alludes when he speaks of some columns having the form of palm-trees, and others of the *thyrsus*.

The adoption of the pine-cone to head the spear of Bacchus originated in the use of the resinous matter put into wine-skins, and afterwards into amphoræ; but the thyrsus was also represented as a spear having its point " concealed in ivy leaves: " " Pampineis agitat velatam frondibus hastam." (Ovid, Met. iii. 667; comp. xi. 27, &c. Diodor. iii. 64. Athen. Deipn. xiv. 631 A.) Thus the poets generally describe it, as well as the paintings on Greek vases; and if the pine-cone was preferred for *statues* of Bacchus, that was probably from its being better suited to

Egyptians have no choral dances.[7] They also use instead of phalli another invention, consisting of images a cubit high, pulled by strings, which the women carry round to the villages. A piper goes in front,[8] and the women follow, singing hymns

sculpture. The resemblance of the *nebris*, and the Semitic name of the leopard, *nimr*, is striking, the car of Bacchus being drawn by leopards; and Bochart points to the analogy between Nebrodes, a title of Bacchus and Nimrod, who is called by Philo-Judæus "Nebrôd." The pine-cone was adopted by the Arabs as an ornament in architecture at an early time, and passed thence to Cashmire shawls and embroidery.—[G. W.]

[7] The reading χορῶν here is preferable to χοίρων, for the Greeks did sacrifice a pig at the festivals of Bacchus, as their authors and sculptures show. The τριττύα consisted of an ox, a sheep, and a pig, like the Roman *suovetaurilia;* and Eustathius on Hom. Od. xx. 156, says the Ithacans sacrificed three pigs at the feast of the new moon.—[G. W.]

[8] The instrument used was probably the double-pipe; but some consider it the flute (properly the πλαγίαυλος, or *obliqua tibia*), which was also an Egyptian instrument. It was played by men (fig. 8; and woodcut in n. [1], ch. 58, figs. 3, 5), but the double-pipe more frequently by women (see woodcut No. III. fig. 3.) The latter was a very common instrument with the Greeks, and its noisy and droning tones are still kept up in the *Zumára* of modern Egypt. The flute, however, was a common instrument in Egypt on sacred occasions (see woodcut in n. [1], ch. 58), and one or more musical instruments were present at every Egyptian procession. The clapping of hands and the *crotala*, the tambourine, and the harp, were also commonly introduced on festive occasions, as well as the voice, which sometimes accompanied two harps, a single pipe, and a flute; and when soldiers attended, they had the trumpet and drum (woodcut No. II. figs. 1, 2). A greater variety of instruments

No. II.

was admitted to private parties; the harp of four, six, seven, to twenty-two strings, the guitar of three; the lyre of five, seven, ten, and eighteen strings; the double pipe, the flute, the square and the round tambourine, the crotala or wooden clappers, were very common there; but cymbals appear to have been mostly used by the minstrels of certain deities. The lyres were of very varied sharp tone, and they may be supposed to answer to the nabl, sambuc, and "ten"-stringed ashur

in honour of Bacchus. They give a religious reason for the peculiarities of the image.

of the Jews. The varieties of lyres in Nos.
IV., V., and VI. may serve to illustrate
some of the numerous instruments mentioned by Julius Pollux (iv. 9), Athenæus (iv.
25), and other ancient writers. The sis-

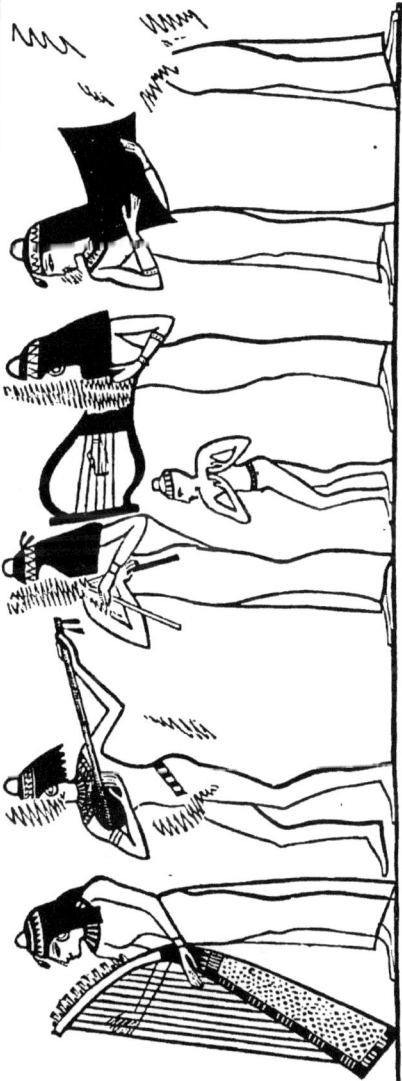

trum was peculiarly a sacred instrument,
and it was to the queen and princesses
that its use was entrusted, or to other la-
dies of rank who held the important of

49. Melampus,[9] the son of Amytheon, cannot (I think) have been ignorant of this ceremony—nay, he must, I should conceive,

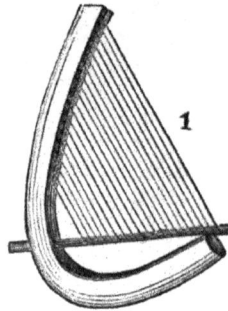

No. IV.

No. V.

fice of accompanying the king or the high priest, while making libations to the gods. See above, note [4] on ch. 35, and At. Eg. W. vol. ii. p. 222 to 327 on the music and instruments of the Egyptians.—[G. W.]

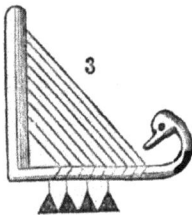

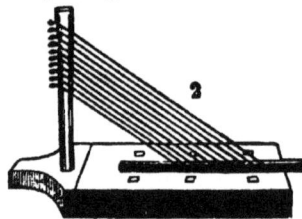

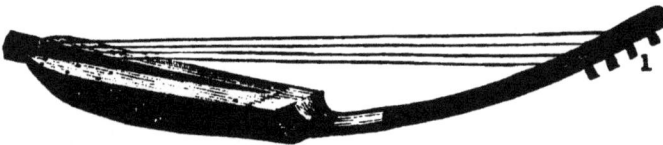

No. VI.

[9] Either Melampus, as some maintain, really existed, and travelling into Egypt, brought back certain ceremonies into Greece, or he was an imaginary personage;

have been well acquainted with it.   He it was who introduced
into Greece the name of Bacchus, the ceremonial of his worship,
and the procession of the phallus.   He did not, however, so completely apprehend the whole doctrine as to be able to commu-
nicate it entirely, but various sages since his time have carried
out his teaching to greater perfection.   Still it is certain that
Melampus introduced the phallus, and that the Greeks learnt
from him the ceremonies which they now practise.   I therefore
maintain that Melampus, who was a wise man, and had acquired the art of divination, having become acquainted with the
worship of Bacchus through knowledge derived from Egypt, introduced it into Greece, with a few slight changes, at the same
time that he brought in various other practices.   For I can by
no means allow that it is by mere coincidence that the Bacchic
ceremonies in Greece are so nearly the same as the Egyptian—
they would then have been more Greek in their character, and
less recent in their origin.   Much less can I admit that the
Egyptians borrowed these customs, or any other, from the
Greeks.   My belief is that Melampus got his knowledge of them
from Cadmus the Tyrian, and the followers whom he brought
from Phœnicia into the country which is now called Bœotia.[1]

and the fable was intended to show that the Greeks borrowed some of their religious ceremonies from Egypt. This name "blackfoot" would then have been invented to show their origin. The name of Egypt, *Chemi*, signified "black."—
[G. W.]
   [1] The settlement of a body of Phœnicians in the country called afterwards
Bœotia, is regarded by Herodotus as an undoubted fact. (See, besides the present
passage, v. 57-8, where the Gephyræans are referred to this migration.) He does
not, however, seem to have had a very distinct notion as to the course by which
the strangers reached Greece (compare ii. 44, with iv. 147). Some moderns, as C.
O. Müller (Orchom. ch. iv. pp. 113–122), Welcker (Ueber eine Kretische Colonie in
Theben), and Wachsmuth (Antiq. i. 1. § 11), entirely discredit the whole story of a
Phœnician settlement, which they regard as the invention of a late era. Others, as
Mr. Grote (Hist. of Greece, vol. ii. p. 357), profess their inability to determine the
question. But the weight of modern authority is in favour of the truth of the tradition. (See Niebuhr's Lectures on Ancient History, vol. i. p. 80; Thirlwall's Hist.
of Greece, vol. i. ch. 3, pp. 68–9; Kenrick's Phœnicia, pp. 98-100; Bähr, note on
Herod. v. 57, &c.) The principal arguments on this side are the following:—1. The
unanimous tradition. 2. The fact that there was a race called Cadmeians at Thebes
from very early times, claiming a Phœnician descent, combined with the further
fact, that "Cadmeian" would bear in the Phœnician tongue a meaning unintelligible
to mere Greeks, but which in the early legend it was certainly intended to have,—
Cadmus coming in search of Europa being clearly קֶדֶם *Kedem*, "the East," seeking
to discover עֶרֶב *Ereb*, "the West." 3. The fact that the early worship at Thebes
was that of Phœnician deities, as the Cabiri (see note[e] on ch. 51), and Minerva
Onca (Cf. Pausan. IX. xii. § 2, and xxv. § 6; Æschyl. S. c. Th. 153 and 496; Euphorion ap. Steph. Byz. ad voc. 'Ογκαῖαι; Hesych. ad voc. Ὄγγα, &c.). And, 4. The
occurrence of a number of Semitic words in the provincial dialect of Bœotia, as
Ελιεὺς for Ζεὺς or the Supreme God (compare Heb. אֱלֹהִי "God"); βάννα, "woman"
or "girl" (Heb. בַּת "woman" or "daughter"); ἀχάνη (compare the אָצַת of the

50. Almost all the names of the gods came into Greece from Egypt.[2] My inquiries prove that they were all derived from a foreign source, and my opinion is that Egypt furnished the greater number. For with the exception of Neptune and the Dioscûri,[3] whom I mentioned above, and Juno, Vesta, Themis, the Graces, and the Nereids, the other gods have been known from time immemorial in Egypt. This I assert on the authority of the Egyptians themselves. The gods, with whose names they profess themselves unacquainted, the Greeks received, I believe, from the Pelasgi, except Neptune. Of him they got their knowledge from the Libyans,[4] by whom he has been always honoured, and who were anciently the only people that had a god of the name. The Egyptians differ from the Greeks also in paying no divine honours to heroes.[5]

Talmud), a measure of capacity which the Persians and Bœotians seem both to have adopted from the Phœnicians (cf. Aristoph. Acharn. 108, Hesych. ad voce. ἀχάνη and ἀχάνας, Pollux. x. 164), σίδα "a pomegranate" (comp. Arabic *sidra*), &c. The name Thebes itself is also tolerably near to צבן *Thebez* (Judg. ix. 50), a Canaanite town, which the LXX. call Θήβης, though this resemblance may be accidental. Bochart, however, identifies the two names, and regards Thebes as so called from its "mud," בֹץ, since it was situated in a marsh. (See his Geograph. Sac. Part. II. book i. ch. 16.) The cumulative force of these arguments must be allowed to be very great.

[2] See below, note[5] on ch. 51. There is no doubt that the Greeks borrowed sometimes the names, sometimes the attributes, of their deities from Egypt; but when Herodotus says the *names* of the Greek gods were always known in Egypt, it is evident that he does not mean they were the *same* as the Greek, since he gives in other places (chaps. 42, 59, 138, 144, 156) the Egyptian name to which those very gods agree, whom he mentions in Egypt. Neptune, the Dioscuri, the Graces, and Nereids, were certainly not Egyptian deities; but Juno was Sátè, Vesta Anouké, and Themis was not only an Egyptian goddess, but her name was taken from Thmei, the Egyptian goddess of "Justice" or "Truth;" from which the Hebrew derived the word Thummim, translated in the Septuagint by ἀλήθεια. The name Nereids was evidently borrowed from the idea of "water;" and though the word is only traced in ὑηρὸς, "moist," in Nereus, the Nereids, ναρὸς, "liquid," and some other words in ancient Greek, it has been retained to the present day, through some old provincialism, and νερόν, or νερρὸ, still signifies "water" in the Romaic of modern Greece. Comp. the Indian name for "water," and the divine spirit, *Narayan* (a), *i. e.* "floating on the waters" at the beginning of time in Hindoo mythology; also the *Nerbudda*, &c., and *nahr*, "river," in Arabic. One of the Greek Vulcans mentioned by Cicero (de Nat. Deor. iii. 22) "was the Egyptian Phthas;" one sun was the god of Heliopolis (ibid. 21), and other deities were from the same Pantheon. —[G. W.]

[3] Comp. the two deities *Açvin*, having no particular names, but called simply *Açvinau,* "the two horsemen," found in the Vedas of India and in the Zend-Avesta. (Jour. Americ. Or. Soc. vol. iii. No. 2, p. 322.)—[G. W.]

[4] Cf. iv. 188.

[5] Herodotus is quite correct in saying the Egyptians paid no divine honours to heroes, and their creed would not accord with all the second and third lines of the Golden Verses of Pythagoras:

Ἀθανάτους μὲν πρῶτα θεοὺς νόμῳ ὡς διάκεινται
Τίμα· καὶ σέβου ὅρκον· ἔπειτ' Ἥρωας ἀγαυοὺς,
Τούς τε καταχθονίους σέβε δαίμονας, ἔννομα ῥέζων.

51. Besides these which have been here mentioned, there are many other practices whereof I shall speak hereafter, which the Greeks have borrowed from Egypt.⁴ The peculiarity, how-

No Egyptian god was supposed to have lived on earth as a mere man afterwards deified (infra, n.⁹, ch. 143); and the tradition of Osiris having lived on earth implied that he was a manifestation or *Avatar* of the Deity—not a real being, but the abstract idea of goodness (like the Indian Booddha). The religion of the Egyptians was the worship of the Deity in all his attributes, and in those things which were thought to partake of his essence; but they did not transfer a mortal man to his place, though they allowed a king to pay divine honours to a deceased predecessor, or even to himself, his human doing homage to his divine nature. The divine being was like the Divus Imperator of the Romans; and a respect was felt for him when good, which made them sacrifice all their dearest interests for his service: he was far above all mortals, as the head of the religion and the state; and his funeral was celebrated with unusual ceremonies. (Diodor. i. 71, 72). But this was not divine worship. They did however commit the error of assigning to emblems a degree of veneration, as representatives of deities, which led to gross superstition, as types and relics have often done; and though the Moslems forbid all "partnership" with the Deity in adoration, even they cannot always prevent a bigoted veneration for a saint, or for the supposed footstep of "the Prophet."—[G. W.]

⁴ We cannot too much admire the candour of Herodotus in admitting that the Greeks borrowed from the Egyptians, and others who preceded them; for, as Bacon justly observes, "the writings that relate these fables, being not delivered as inventions of the writers, but as things before believed and received, appear like a soft whisper from the traditions of more ancient nations, conveyed through the flutes of the Grecians."

Diodorus (i. 96) makes the same remark, and affirms that "Orpheus introduced from Egypt the greatest part of his mythical ceremonies, the orgies that celebrate the wanderings of Ceres, and the whole fable of the shades below. The rites of Osiris and Bacchus were the same; the punishment of the wicked, the Elysian Fields, and all the common fictions, were copied from the Egyptian funerals;" and he says the same of the Acherusian lake, Charon, Styx, and "many other things mentioned in fable." Herodotus expressly gives it as his opinion that nearly all the names of the gods were derived from Egypt, and shows that their ceremonies (chaps. 81, 82) and science come from the same source. This is also stated by many ancient writers. Lucian (de Deâ Syr.) says "the Egyptians are reputed the first men who had a notion of the gods and a knowledge of sacred affairs, . . . and sacred names." The same is mentioned by the oracle of Apollo quoted by Eusebius. Comp. Iamblichus (de Myst. s. 7, ch. v.), and others. Aristotle (de Cœlo, ii. 12) shows the obligations of the Greeks to the Egyptians and Babylonians for information respecting all the heavenly bodies; and these two people are mentioned by Cicero (de Div. i. 42), Pliny (vii. 56), and others as the great and earliest astronomers. Herodotus (supra, ch. 4) ascribes to the Egyptians the invention of the year, as well as geometry; and Macrobius says that Cæsar was indebted to Egypt for his correction of the calendar: "Nam Julius Cæsar . . . . siderum motus . . . . ab Ægyptiis disciplinis hausit." (Saturn. i. 18.) Strabo (xvi. p. 1076; xvii. p. 1118) ascribes astronomy and arithmetic to the Sidonians, and the origin of them to night sailing and reckonings at sea, as geology to the Egyptians, from which two people they went to Greece; and Pliny (v. 12) says the Phœnicians invented letters, astronomy, and naval and warlike arts. (Comp. Pomp. Mela, i. 12.) Diodorus (i. 98) states "that Pythagoras learnt holy lore, geometry, the science of numbers, and the transmigration of souls into animals from Egypt . . . and Œnopides derived the obliquity of the sun's path from the priests and astronomers there." (Comp. Plut. Pl. Ph. iii. 13. See note on ch. 109, in App. CH. vii.) Diodorus (i. 81, and 28) even thinks "the Chaldæans obtained their knowledge of astrology (astronomy) from the priests of Egypt;" but, on the other hand, Josephus states that "it went from the Chaldæans to Egypt, whence it proceeded to Greece." (See n.⁹, ch. 123, and App. CH. vii.)—[G. W.]

ever, which they observe in their statues of Mercury they did not derive from the Egyptians, but from the Pelasgi ; from them the Athenians first adopted it, and afterwards it passed from the Athenians to the other Greeks. For just at the time when the Athenians were entering into the Hellenic body,[7] the Pelasgi came to live with them in their country,[8] whence it was that the latter came first to be regarded as Greeks. Whoever has been initiated into the mysteries of the Cabiri[9] will understand what I mean. The Samothracians received these mysteries from the Pelasgi, who, before they went to live in Attica, were dwellers in Samothrace, and imparted their religious ceremonies to the inhabitants. The Athenians, then, who were the first of all

---

[7] Vide supra, i. 57, and 58, note[8].

[8] The Pelasgi here intended are the Tyrrhenian Pelasgi, who are mentioned again, iv. 145, and vi. 138. (See Thucyd. iv. 109 ; and cp. Ap. to B. vi.)

[9] Nothing is known for certain respecting the Cabiri. Most authorities agree that they varied in number, and that their worship, which was very ancient in Samothrace and in Phrygia, was carried to Greece from the former by the Pelasgi. Some believe them to have been Ceres, Proserpine, and Pluto ; and others add a fourth, supposed to be Hermes ; while others suppose them to have been Jupiter, Pallas, and Hermes. They were also worshipped at an early time in Lemnos and Imbros. Some think they were an inferior order of gods, but were probably in the same manner as the third order of gods in Egypt, who in one capacity ranked even above the great gods. The name Cabiri was doubtless derived from the Semitic word *kabir*, "great," a title applied to Astarte (Venus), who was also worshipped in Samothrace, together with Pothos and Phæton, in the most holy ceremonies, as Pliny says (xxxvi. 5). The eight great gods of the Phœnicians, the offspring of one great father, Sydik, the "just," were called Cabiri, of whom Esmoun was the youngest, or the eighth (as his name implies), the *shmoun*, "eight," of Coptic, and the "*theman*" or "*saman*" ثمان of Arabic, and שְׁמֹנֶה of Hebrew. This Esmoun was also called Æsculapius. Damascius says, Ὅτι ὁ ἐν Βηρυτῷ φησὶν Ἀσκληπιὸς οὐκ ἔστιν Ἕλλην οὐδὲ Αἰγύπτιος ἀλλά τις ἐπιχώριος Φοῖνιξ. Σαδύκῳ γὰρ ἐγένοντο παῖδες οὓς Διοσκούρους ἑρμηνεύουσι καὶ Καβείρους. Οὗτος κάλλιστος ὢν θέαν καὶ νεανίας ἰδεῖν ἀξιάγαστος, ἐρώμενος γέγονεν, ὥς φησιν ὁ μῦθος, Ἀστρονόης θεοῦ Φοινίσσης, μητρὸς θεῶν. Εἰωθώς τε κυνηγετεῖν ἐν ταῖσδε ταῖς νάπαις ἐπειδὴ ἐθεάσατο τὴν θεὸν αὐτὸν ἐκκυνηγετοῦσαν καὶ φεύγοντα ἐπιδιώκουσαν καὶ ἤδη καταληψομένην, ἀποτέμνει πελέκει τὴν αὐτὸς αὐτοῦ παιδοσπόρον φύσιν. Ἡ δὲ τῷ πάθει περιαλγήσασα καὶ Παιῶνα καλέσασα τὸν νεανίσκον τῇ τε ζωογόνῳ θέρμῃ ἀναζωπυρήσασα θεὸν ἐποίησεν, Ἐσμουνον ὑπὸ Φοινίκων ὠνομασμένον ἐπὶ τῇ θέρμῃ τῆς ζωῆς. Οἱ δὲ τὸν Ἐσμουνον ὄγδοον ἀξιοῦσιν ἑρμηνεύειν, ὅτι ὄγδοος ἦν τῷ Σαδύκῳ παῖς. Damascii Vit. Isidori (à Photio Excerpt.), 302. This mention of Esmoun with Palestine reminds us of the account in the Bible that the Philistines came of an Egyptian stock. Ashmoun would thus be made a son of Mizraim (comp. Sanchoniatho), as in Arab tradition. Herodotus mentions the Egyptian Cabiri at Memphis (iii. 37), whose temple no one was permitted to enter except the priest alone : they were said to be sons of Vulcan or Phtha (as the Egyptian Asclepius called *Emeph*, or Aimothph, also was), and, like that god in one of his characters, were represented as pygmy figures. It is not impossible that the Cabiri in Egypt were figured as the god Phtha-Sokar-Osiris, who was a deity of Hades ; and the three names he had agree with the supposed number of the Cabiri of Samothrace. The number 8 might also be thought to accord with that of the eight great gods of Egypt. (See my note on B. iii. ch. 87.) *Oshmounayn*, the Coptic and modern name of Hermopolis in Egypt, signifying the "two eights," was connected with the title of Thoth or Hermes, "lord of the eight regions."— [G. W.]

the Greeks to make their statues of Mercury in this way, learnt the practice from the Pelasgians ; and by this people a religious account of the matter is given, which is explained in the Samothracian mysteries.

52. In early times the Pelasgi, as I know by information which I got at Dodôna, offered sacrifices of all kinds, and prayed to the gods, but had no distinct names or appellations for them, since they had never heard of any. They called them gods (θεοί, disposers), because they had disposed and arranged all things in such a beautiful order.[1] After a long lapse of time the names of the gods came to Greece from Egypt, and the Pelasgi learnt them, only as yet they knew nothing of Bacchus, of whom they first heard at a much later date. Not long after the arrival of the names they sent to consult the oracle at Dodôna about them. This is the most ancient oracle in Greece, and at that time there was no other. To their question, "Whether they should adopt the names that had been imported from the foreigners?" the oracle replied by recommending their use. Thenceforth in their sacrifices the Pelasgi made use of the names of the gods, and from them the names passed afterwards to the Greeks.

53. Whence the gods severally sprang, whether or no they had all existed from eternity, what forms they bore—these are questions of which the Greeks knew nothing until the other day, so to speak. For Homer and Hesiod were the first to compose Theogonies, and give the gods their epithets, to allot them their

[1] The same derivation is given by Eustathius (ad Hom. Il. p. 1148-51), and by Clement of Alexandria (Strom. i. 29, p. 427), but the more general belief of the Greeks derived the word θεός from θεῖν, "currere," because the gods first worshipped were the sun, moon, and stars. (See Plat. Cratyl. p. 397, C. D. Etym. Magn. ad voc. θεός, Clemens. Alex. Cohort. ad Gent. p. 22, Strom. iv. 23, p. 633.) Both these derivations are purely fanciful, having reference to the Greek language only, whereas θεός is a form of a very ancient word common to a number of the Indo-European tongues, and not to be explained from any one of them singly. The earliest form of the word would seem to be the Doric and Æolic Ζδεύς, afterwards written Ζεύς. This, by omission of the σ, became Sans. Dyaus and deva, Gk. Δεύς, Διός, and δῖος, Lat. Deus and divus, Lithuanian diewas, &c. θεός is a mere softened form of Δεύς or deus, analogous to ψεύδος, ψύδος; θάω, Sanscr. dhê; δάρσω, dare; δέρω, dry; θύρα, door; &c. With the words Ζεύς and θεός we may connect the old German god Zio, or Tius, whose name under the latter of the forms appears in our word Tuesday. Sanscrit scholars trace these many modifications of a single word to an old root div, which they tell us means "to shine," and Dyaus, the first substantive formed from this verb, meant "light," or "the shining sun," one of the earliest objects of worship in most countries. Deva is a later formation from div, and has a more abstract sense than dyaus, being "bright, brilliant, divine," and thence passing on to the mere idea of God. θεός in Greek, and Deus in Latin, are the exact equivalents of this term. (See Professor Max Müller's article on Comparative Philology in the Edinburgh Review, No. 192, Art. 1. pp. 334-8.)

The statement of Herodotus that the Pelasgi "called the gods θεοί, because they had disposed and arranged all things in such a beautiful order," shows that he considered them to have spoken a language nearly akin to the Greek.

several offices and occupations, and describe their forms ; and they lived but four hundred years before my time,[2] as I believe. As for the poets, who are thought by some to be earlier than these,[3] they are, in my judgment, decidedly later writers. In these matters I have the authority of the priestesses of Dodôna for the former portion of my statements ; what I have said of Homer and Hesiod is my own opinion.

54. The following tale is commonly told in Egypt concerning the oracle of Dodôna in Greece, and that of Ammon in Libya. My informants on the point were the priests of Jupiter at Thebes. They said "that two of the sacred women were once carried off from Thebes by the Phœnicians,[4] and that the story went that one of them was sold into Libya, and the other into Greece, and these women were the first founders of the oracles in the two countries." On my inquiring how they came to know so exactly what became of the women, they answered, "that diligent search had been made after them at the time, but that it had not been found possible to discover where they were ; afterwards, however, they received the information which they had given me."

55. This was what I heard from the priests at Thebes ; at Dodôna, however, the women who deliver the oracles relate the matter as follows :—"Two black doves flew away from Egyptian

---

[2] The date of Homer has been variously stated. It is plain from the expressions which Herodotus here uses that in his time the general belief assigned to Homer an earlier date than that which he considered the true one. His date would place the poet about B. C. 880–830, which is very nearly the mean between the earliest and the latest epochs that are assigned to him. The earliest date that can be exactly determined, is that of the author of the life of Homer usually published with the works of Herodotus, who places the birth of the poet 622 years before the invasion of Xerxes, or B. C. 1102. The latest is that of Theopompus and Euphorion, which makes him contemporary with Gyges—therefore B. C. 724–686. (For further particulars, see Clinton's F. H. vol. i. pp. 145–7 , and Ap. p. 359.) Probability is on the whole in favour of a date considerably earlier than that assigned by our author.

The time of Hesiod is even more doubtful, if possible, than that of his brother-poet. He was made before Homer, after him, and contemporary with him. Internal evidence and the weight of authority are in favour of the view which assigns him a comparatively late date. (See Clinton, i. p. 359, n. *.) He is probably to be placed at least 200 or 300 years after Homer.

[3] The "poets thought by some to be earlier than Homer and Hesiod" are probably the mystic writers, Olen, Linus, Orpheus, Musæus, Pamphos, Olympus, &c., who were generally accounted by the Greeks anterior to Homer (Clinton, i. pp. 341–4), but seem really to have belonged to a later age. (See Grote, vol. ii. p. 161.)

[4] See the next note. This carrying off priestesses from Thebes is of course a fable. It may refer to the sending out and establishing an oracle in the newly-discovered West (Europe) through the Phœnicians, the merchants and explorers of those days, who were in alliance with Egypt, supplied it with many of the productions it required from other countries, and enabled it to export its manufactures in their ships.—[G. W.]

Thebes, and while one directed its flight to Libya, the other came to them.[5] She alighted on an oak, and sitting there began to speak with a human voice, and told them that on the spot where she was, there should thenceforth be an oracle of Jove. They understood the announcement to be from heaven, so they set to work at once and erected the shrine. The dove which flew to Libya bade the Libyans to establish there the oracle of Ammon." This likewise is an oracle of Jupiter. The persons from whom I received these particulars were three priestesses of the Dodonæans,[6] the eldest Promeneia, the next Timareté, and the youngest Nicandra—what they said was confirmed by the other Dodonæans who dwell around the temple.[7]

56. My own opinion of these matters is as follows :—I think that, if it be true that the Phœnicians carried off the holy women, and sold them for slaves,[8] the one into Libya and the other into Greece, or Pelasgia (as it was then called), this last must have been sold to the Thesprotians. Afterwards, while undergoing servitude in those parts, she built under a real oak a temple to Jupiter, her thoughts in her new abode reverting—as it was likely they would do, if she had been an attendant in a temple

---

[5] The two doves appear to connect this tradition with the Phœnician Astarté, who appears to be the Baaltis or Dioné of Byblus. If the rites of Dodona were from Egypt, they were not necessarily introduced by any individual from that country. The idea of women giving out oracles is Greek, not Egyptian.—[G. W.]

[6] Were it not for the tradition of the priestesses that Dodona was indebted to Egypt for its oracle, we should at once discredit what appears so very improbable ; but the Greeks would scarcely have attributed its origin to a foreigner, unless there had been some foundation for the story ; and Herodotus maintains that there was a resemblance between the oracles of Thebes and Dodona. It is not necessary that the stamp of a foreign character should have been strongly impressed at Dodona ; and the influence of the oracle would have been equally great without the employment of a written language, or any reference to particular religious doctrines with which those who consulted the oracles of Amun, Delphi, and other places did not occupy themselves.—[G. W.]

[7] The Temple of Dodona was destroyed B.C. 219 by Dorimachus when, being chosen general of the Ætolians, he ravaged Epirus. (Polyb. iv. 67.) No remains of it now exist. It stood at the base of Mount Tomarus, or Tmarus (Strabo, vii. p. 476 ; Plin. ii. 103), on the borders of Thesprotia, and was said to have been founded by Deucalion. The name Timareté is here given by Herodotus to one of the priestesses. Strabo says the oracles were given out by a class of priests, called Selli (the Helli, according to Pindar), who were remarkable for their austere mode of life, and thought to honour the Deity by a bigoted affectation of discomfort, and by abjuring cleanliness ; whence Homer says, Il. xvi. 233—

Ζεῦ ἄνα, Δωδωναῖε, Πελασγικέ, τηλόθι ναίων
Δωδώνης μεδέων δυσχειμέρου· ἀμφὶ δὲ Σελλοὶ
Σοὶ ναίουσ' ὑποφῆται ἀνιπτόποδες, χαμαιεῦναι.

—in which impure piety they were very unlike the cleanly priests of Egypt. The sacred oaks of Dodona call to mind those of the Druids. The φηγὸς is not the beech, but an oak, so called from its acorn, which was eaten.—[G. W.]

[8] Comp. Joel iii. 6, where the Tyrians are said to have sold Jewish children " to the Grecians." (Beni-Ionim.)—[G. W.]

of Jupiter at Thebes—to that particular god. Then, having acquired a knowledge of the Greek tongue, she set up an oracle. She also mentioned that her sister had been sold for a slave into Libya by the same persons as herself.

57. The Dodonæans called the women doves because they were foreigners, and seemed to them to make a noise like birds. After a while the dove spoke with a human voice, because the woman, whose foreign talk had previously sounded to them like the chattering of a bird, acquired the power of speaking what they could understand. For how can it be conceived possible that a dove should really speak with the voice of a man? Lastly, by calling the dove black the Dodonæans indicated that the woman was an Egyptian. And certainly the character of the oracles at Thebes and Dodôna is very similar. Besides this form of divination, the Greeks learnt also divination by means of victims from the Egyptians.

58. The Egyptians were also the first to introduce solemn assemblies,* processions, and litanies[l] to the gods; of all which

---

* "Solemn assemblies" were numerous in Egypt, and were of various kinds. The grand assemblies, or great panegyries, were held in the large halls of the principal temples, and the king presided at them in person. Their celebration was apparently yearly, regulated by the Sothic, or by the vague year; and others at the new moons, when they were continued for several successive days, and again at the full moon. There were inferior panegyries in honour of different deities every day during certain months. Some great panegyries seem to have been held after very long periods. Many other ceremonies also took place, at which the king presided;

No. 1.

the greatest of which was the procession of shrines of the gods, which is mentioned in the Rosetta Stone, and is often represented in the sculptures. These shrines were of two kinds: one was an ark, or sacred boat, which may be called the great shrine, the other a sort of canopy. They were attended by the chief priest, or prophet, clad in the leopard skin; they were borne on the shoulders of several priests, by means of staves sometimes passing through metal rings at the side, and being taken into the temple, were placed on a table or stand prepared for the purpose. The same mode of carrying the ark was adopted by the Jews (Joshua iii. 12; 1 Chron. xv. 2, and 15; 2 Sam. xv. 24; 1 Esdr. i. 4); and the gods of Babylon, as well as of Egypt, were borne and "set in their place" in a similar manner. (Is. xlvi. 7;

the Greeks were taught the use by them. It seems to me a sufficient proof of this, that in Egypt these practices have been established from remote antiquity, while in Greece they are only recently known.

59. The Egyptians do not hold a single solemn assembly, but several in the course of the year.   Of these the chief, which

Baruch, vi. 4, and 26.) Apuleius (Met. xi. 250) describes the sacred boat and the high priest holding in his hand a lighted torch, an egg, and sulphur, after which the (sacred) scribe read from a papyrus certain prayers, in presence of the assembled *pastophori*, or members of the Sacred College ; which agrees well with the ceremony described on the monuments.

Some of the sacred boats or arks contained the emblems of life and stability, which, when the veil was drawn aside, were partially seen ; and others contained the sacred beetle of the sun, overshadowed by the wings of two figures of the goddess Thmei, or " Truth," which call to mind the cherubim (kerubim) of the Jews. The

shrines of some deities differed from those of others, though most of them had a ram's head at the prow and stern of the boat ; and that of Pthah-Sokar-Osiris was marked by its singular form, the centre having the head of the hawk, his emblem, rising from it in a shroud, and the prow terminating in that of an oryx. It was carried in the same manner by several priests. The god Horus, the origin of the Greek Charon, is the steersman par excellence of the sacred boats, as Vishnu is of the Indian ark. (See my note on Pthah-Sokar-Osiris, in B. iii. ch. 37, and on the ark of Isis, see note [6] on ch. 61.)

The Niloa, or Festival of the inundation ; the harvest ; the fêtes in honour of the gods ; the

NO. II.

royal birthdays ; and other annual as well as monthly festivals, were celebrated with great splendour ; and the procession to the temples, when the dedicatory offerings were presented by the king, or by the high priest, the public holidays, the new moons, and numerous occasional fêtes, kept throughout the year, as well as the many assemblies successively held in different cities throughout the country, fully justified the remark that the Egyptians paid greater attention to divine matters than any other people. And these, as Herodotus observes, had been already established long before any similar custom existed in Greece.—[G. W.]

    [1] The mode of approaching the deity and the ceremonies performed in the solemn processions varied in Egypt, as in Greece (Procl. Chrestomath. p. 381, Gd.), where persons sometimes sang hymns to the sound of the lyre, sometimes to the flute, and with dances. These last were the προσόδια, which, as well as the former

is better attended than any other, is held at the city of Bubastis[2] in honour of Diana.[3]   The next in importance is that which

(see woodcut 1 in ch. 48), are represented on the monuments of Egypt. Sometimes
the harp, guitar, and flutes, were played while the high priest offered incense to
the gods. The song of the Egyptian priests was called in their language Pæan

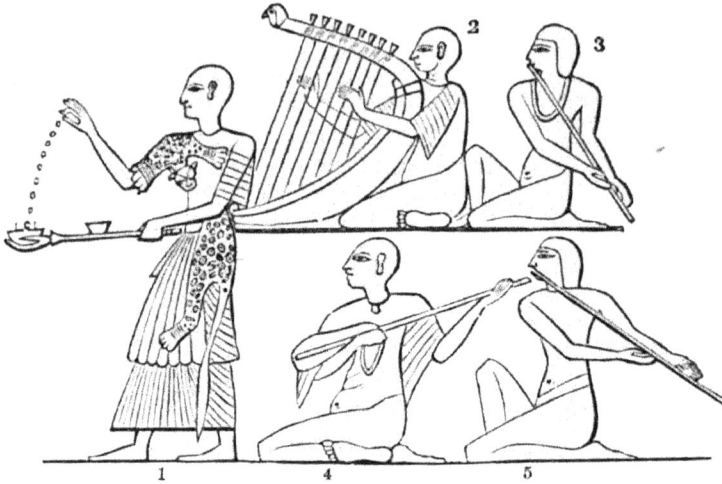

(Clem. Pædagog. iii. 2), which is evidently an Egyptian word, having the article
Pi prefixed.—[G. W.]
   [3] Bubastis, or Pasht, corresponded to the Greek Diana. At the Speos

Artemidos (near Beni Hassan) she is represented as a lioness with her

name "Psht, the lady of the cave." At Thebes she has also the head of a

lioness, with the name Pasht, thus written

At Bubastis the name of the chief goddess whose figure remains appears to read
Buto, and is thus written ; and here she may have the character of Buto or
Latona. They both have the same head, though it is difficult to distinguish between
that of the lioness and the cat. It is indeed probable that both these animals were
sacred to and emblems of Pasht. The notion of the cat being an emblem of the
moon was doubtless owing to the Greeks supposing Bubastis the same as Diana,
but the moon in Egypt was a male deity, the Ibis-headed Thoth ; and another mistake was their considering the Egyptian Diana the sister of Apollo. Remains of
the temple and city of Bubastis, the "Pibeseth" (Pi-basth) of Ezekiel, xxx. 17, are
still seen at Tel Basta, "the mounds of Pasht," so called from its lofty mounds.
(See below, n. [6], ch. 138.) At the Speos Artemidos numerous cat mummies were
buried, from their being sacred to the Egyptian Diana.—[G. W.]
   [3] Herodotus (infra, ch. 156) supposes her the daughter of Bacchus (Osiris) and

takes place at Busiris, a city situated in the very middle of the Delta ; it is in honour of Isis, who is called in the Greek tongue Demêter (Ceres).   There is a third great festival in Saïs to Minerva, a fourth in Heliopolis to the Sun, a fifth in Buto⁴ to Latona, and a sixth in Paprèmis to Mars.

60. The following are the proceedings on occasion of the assembly at Bubastis :—Men and women come sailing all together, vast numbers in each boat, many of the women with castanets, which they strike, while some of the men pipe during the whole time of the voyage ; the remainder of the voyagers, male and female, sing the while, and make a clapping with their hands.   When they arrive opposite any of the towns upon the banks of the stream, they approach the shore, and, while some of the women continue to play and sing, others call aloud to the females of the place and load them with abuse, while a certain number dance, and some standing up uncover themselves. After proceeding in this way all along the river-course, they reach Bubastis, where they celebrate the feast with abundant sacrifices. More grape-wine⁵ is consumed at this festival than in all the rest of the year besides.   The number of those who attend, counting only the men and women and omitting the children,

Isis, which is, of course, an error, as Osiris had no daughter, and the only mode of accounting for it is by supposing Horus, the son of Osiris, to have been mistaken for the sun, the Apollo of the Greeks, whose sister Diana was reputed to be.   The goddess Bubastis, or Pasht, is called on the monuments "beloved of Pthah," whom she generally accompanies, and she is the second member of the great triad of Memphis.   Bubastis, the city, was only the Egyptian name Pasht, with the article ΠΙ prefixed, as in the Hebrew Pi-basth ; and the change of P into B was owing to the former being pronounced B, as in modern Coptic.—[G. W.]

⁴ Vide infra, note ⁵ on ch. 155.   The goddess mentioned at Bubastis should be Buto ; as her name occurs there, and so frequently about the pyramids, which were in the neighbourhood of Letopolis, another city of Buto, or Latona.   The city of Buto Herodotus here speaks of stood between the Sebennytic and Bolbitine branches, near the Lake of Buto, now Lake *Boorlos*.   The Sebennytic branch appears here to have been divided into several channels, as one of them passed, according to Herodotus and Ptolemy, near to Buto, which was at no great distance from the Canopic branch, where it separated from the Bolbitine.   (See Rennell, ii. p. 168.)—[G. W.]

⁵ This is to be distinguished from beer, οἶνος κρίθινος, "barley-wine," both of which were made in great quantities in Egypt.   The most noted were those of Mareotis, Anthylla, Plinthine, Coptos, and the Teniotic, Sebennytic, and Alexandrian ; and many were noticed in the offerings made in the tombs and temples of Egypt.   Among them wine of the "Northern Country" is mentioned, and that long before the Greeks carried wine to Egypt.   In later times, when the prejudices of the Egyptians had begun to relax, a trade was established with the Greeks, and Egypt received wine from Greece and Phœnicia twice every year (Herod. iii. 6), and many Greeks carried it direct to Naucratis.   (See note ⁸ on ch. 18 and note ⁴ on 37 ; and on beer, n. ¹, ch. 77.   On the wines of Egypt, see At. Eg. W. vol. ii. p. 158 to 170.)   The wine-presses and offerings of wine in the tombs at the Pyramids show wine was made in Egypt at least as early as the 4th dynasty.—[G. W.]

amounts, according to the native reports, to seven hundred thousand.

61. The ceremonies at the feast of Isis in the city of Busiris[*]

[*] There were several places called Busiris in Egypt (Diod. i. 17; i. 88; Plin. v. 10; and xxxvi. 12.) It signifies the burial-place of Osiris, and therefore corresponds in meaning to Taposiris, a Greek name given to another town on the sea-coast to the W. of Alexandria. Many places claim the honour of having the body of Osiris, the chief of which were Memphis, Busiris, Philæ, Taposiris, and Abydus (Plut. de Is. s. 21). The Busiris mentioned by Herodotus stood a little to the S. of Sebennytus and the modern *Abooseer*, the Coptic *Busiri*, of which nothing now remains but some granite blocks since used as the thresholds of doors, and a few stones, one of which is of very early time. This is a sepulchral monument, probably of the time of the 4th dynasty, which has the funereal eye on each side. There was also a Busiris near the pyramids, which gave its name to the modern *Aboosir*, near which the burial-place of Apis, called Apis-Osiris, has lately been discovered. The city of Isis was lower down the river, and it is more probable that the fête of Isis was held there than at Busiris. It is now called *Bebâyt*, and its site is marked by the ruins of a granite temple, the only one, except that at Bubastis, entirely built of that beautiful and costly material, which was doubtless thought worthy to succeed "the very large temple to Isis" mentioned by Herodotus—for it was built during the reign of the Ptolemies. It was formerly called Iseum, and by the ancient Egyptians *Hebai*, or *Hebait*, of which Isis is always called in the sculptures "the Mistress." *Hebai* signified a "panegyry," or assembly, and this was the real meaning of the name of the place. Osiris is also sometimes called in the legends there, "Lord of the land of Hebai." There was another ancient town, in Middle Egypt, apparently consecrated to Isis, the ruins of which are now called *Haybee*. On a wall at *Bebâyt*, probably once part of the Sékos, is a remarkable bas-relief of the ark of Isis, in the centre of which the goddess sits on a lotus-flower, a female standing on either side with outstretched wings; below the same three are kneeling, and under this are the goddess or Genius Mert or Milt, with the usual four kneeling figures (one with the head of a man and three with jackals'-heads) beating themselves, illustrating what Herodotus says in ch. 40. This was done in honour of Osiris, whose death was lamented, as that of Adonis (Adoni; cp. Judg. i. 5; Josh. x. 1) by the Syrians, alluded to in Ezekiel (viii. 14):—"There sat women weeping for Tammûz." This last name, meaning, "concealed," may be related to the Atmoo of Egypt, who answers to "Sol Inferus;" and the mention (in Ezek. viii. 16) of men worshipping "the Sun" (though it should have been the West, rather than towards "the East") seems to confirm this. (See notes [7] and [3] on chaps. 85 and 171.) The temple of Bebâyt is now so completely destroyed that it is difficult to ascertain its exact plan; the stones are thrown together in the greatest confusion, and a man can go down beneath them to the depth of 12 to 15 feet. None seem to be in their original places, though some of the doorways can be traced; and fragments of cornices, and ceilings with the usual white stars on a blue ground, lie in a mass heaped one on the other. The force and labour employed in its destruction must have been very great. All the remaining sculptures are of the time of Ptolemy Philadelphus, and it is probable that the temple was rebuilt in his reign of those unusual materials, which would have justified the remark applied by Herodotus to that of Bubastis, that many temples were larger but few so beautiful, and which prove that the Egyptians then, as before the time of Herodotus, sought to honour Isis with monuments worthy of her importance. The sculptures in relief on the granite show the immense labour bestowed upon them, and some of the hieroglyphics on the architraves are 14 inches long. On the cornices are the names of Ptolemy alternating with three feather ornaments forming an Egyptian triglyph, and one of them has the heads of Isis alternating with kings' names. The large columns were surmounted by heads of Isis, like those of Dendera, but with the remarkable difference that they were of granite; and on the bases of the walls was the not unusual row of figures of the god Nilus.

have been already spoken of. It is there that the whole multitude, both of men and women, many thousands in number, beat themselves at the close of the sacrifice, in honour of a god, whose name a religious scruple forbids me to mention.[7] The Carian dwellers in Egypt proceed on this occasion to still greater lengths, even cutting their faces with their knives,[8] whereby they let it be seen that they are not Egyptians but foreigners.

62. At Saïs,[9] when the assembly takes place for the sacri-

bearing vases and emblems. The sculptures mostly represent offerings made to Isis (frequently with the emblem of Athor), to Osiris, Anubis, and the crocodile-headed god; and the hawk-headed Hor-Hat is figured in one place leading up the King to the presence of Isis, who is styled " defender of her brother (Osiris)." A crude brick wall surrounded the *temenos* or sacred enclosure, in which the temple stood, and which had as usual stone gateways.—[G. W.]

[7] This was Osiris, and men are often represented doing this in the paintings of the tombs. See the preceding note, and n. [1], ch. 05.—[G. W.]

[8] The custom of cutting themselves was not Egyptian; and it is therefore evident that the command in Leviticus (xix. 28 ; xxi. 5) against making " any cuttings in their flesh " was not directed against a custom derived from Egypt, but from Syria, where the worshippers of Baal " cut themselves after their manner with knives and lancets" (darts), 1 Kings xviii. 28.—[G. W.]

[9] The site of Saïs is marked by lofty mounds, enclosing a space of great extent. (See n. [5], ch. 169, and n. [9], ch. 170.) Its modern name *Sa*, or *Sa-el-Hagar*, " Sa of the stone," from the ruins formerly there, shows it was derived from the ancient *Ssa*, or *Sais*, of which Neith (Minerva) is said in the legends to be the " Mistress ; " showing that Plato is right in calling Neith the Minerva of Saïs (Timæus, p. 22, A.). She is sometimes called Neit-Ank, or Onk, in which we recognise Onka, the name given to the Bœotian Minerva, according to Plutarch, and confirmed by Æschylus, who calls her Onka Pallas, and speaks of a gate at Thebes, called Oncæan after her (Sept. c. Theb. 487). It is also called Oncæan by Apollodorus ; but Euripides, Pausanias, and Statius call it Ogygian. The scholiast on Æschylus says Cadmus founded a temple there to the Egyptian Minerva, who was called Oncæa. This temple and name are also mentioned by the Schol. Pind. Ol. ii. 44, who says the name is Phœnician. Pausanias also calls it Phœnician (ix. 12, 2), and uses it as an argument to prove Cadmus was a Phœnician and not an Egyptian, as some supposed (see Gale and Selden). But Onk is the name of the Egyptian Vesta, made into Anouké by the Greeks, who is shown to be a character of Neith or Minerva by the hieroglyphic legends. Anouké was a very ancient goddess, and the third person of the triad at the first cataract. Nepthys, Neb-t-ei (" the lady of the house ") has even the title Ank in a legend at Dendera ; she was also a character of Vesta, with whom she agrees as daughter of Saturn and Rhea (Seb and Netpe), and was protectress of the hearth ; one of many proofs how much the deities of different orders have in common with each other ; Nepthys being connected with Neith, as Isis, the mother of the child, is with *Maut*, " the *mother*" goddess. Plutarch (de Is. s. 9) mentions an inscription in the temple of Minerva—"I am everything which has been, which is, and which will be, and no mortal has yet lifted my veil ; " but he is wrong in considering the still unveiled or the unmarried goddess the same as Isis, and in saying the latter was called by the *Egyptians* "*Athena*," signifying "I proceeded from myself" (de Is. s. 62). Nor did the Egyptians attribute the gift of the olive to Minerva, but to Mercury (Diodor. i. 16). Still less is *Zeth*, " olive," of the Hebrew (the Arabic *Zit* " oil," *Zitoun* " olive ") related to the name of Saïs. Neith is often represented with a bow and arrows, being, as Proclus says (in Tim.), goddess of war as well as of philosophy ; and her holding the sceptre of the male deities is consistent with her being " ἀρσενόθηλυς." Pliny says Minerva was armed to show that both male and

fices, there is one night on which the inhabitants all burn a
multitude of lights in the open air round their houses. They
use lamps, which are flat saucers filled with a mixture of oil and
salt,[1] on the top of which the wick floats. These burn the whole
night, and give to the festival the name of the Feast of Lamps.
The Egyptians who are absent from the festival observe the
night of the sacrifice, no less than the rest, by a general lighting
of lamps ; so that the illumination is not confined to the city of
Saïs but extends over the whole of Egypt. And there is a religious reason assigned for the special honour paid to this night,
as well as for the illumination which accompanies it.

63. At Heliopolis[2] and Buto[3] the assemblies are merely for
the purpose of sacrifice ; but at Paprèmis,[4] besides the sacrifices
and other rites which are performed there as elsewhere, the following custom is observed. When the sun is getting low, a few
only of the priests continue occupied about the image of the god,
while the greater number, armed with wooden clubs, take their
station at the portal of the temple. Opposite to them is drawn
up a body of men, in number above a thousand, armed, like the
others, with clubs, consisting of persons engaged in the performance of their vows. The image of the god, which is kept in a

female natures can pursue every virtue. Some think 'Aθηνᾶ a transposition of the
Egyptian Nηϑ.—[G. W.]
    [1] The oil floated on water mixed with salt. This fête of lamps calls to mind a
Chinese as well as an Indian custom. It is remarkable that Homer mentions no
one but Minerva with an oil-lamp (Odys. xix. 34) ; and her figure is sometimes attached to the upright terra-cotta lamps of the Etruscans. (See Batrachom. 179, Strab.
ix. 396, Plut. Sympos. viii. 716 E, Pausan. i. 26. 7.) There was a festival or race of
torches at Athens (Aristoph. Wasps 1203, Frogs 131, 1087, 1098, and Sch.), but
this was quite different from the fête of lamps at Saïs. Strabo (ix. p. 574) speaks of
the old temple of Minerva Polias in the Acropolis of Athens, in which a lamp was
always kept burning. The Minerva and Vulcan of Athens were supposed to have
been from Egypt.—[G. W.]
    [2] Plutarch asserts that when the sacrifices were offered at Heliopolis, no wine
was allowed to be taken into the temple of the sun ; but this may only signify that
they were forbidden to drink it in the temple, "it being indecent to do so under the
eyes of their lord and king" (de Is. s. 6). See note [5] on ch. 37.—[G. W.]
    [3] See n. [2] on ch. 59 and n. [3] on ch. 155.
    [4] Papremis is not known in the sculptures as the name of the Egyptian Mars ;
and it may only have been that of the city, the capital of a nome (ch. 165) which
stood between the modern *Menzaleh* and *Damietta* in the Delta. It was here that
Inaros routed the Persians (infra, iii. 12) ; and it is remarkable that in this very isl-
and, formed by the old Mendesian and the modern Damietta branches, the Crusaders
were defeated in 1220, and again in 1249, when Louis IX. was taken prisoner. The
deity who seems to have borne the most resemblance to Mars was Mandoo ; Ranpo
(supposed to be Remphan) and Anta being the god and goddess of war. Honurius,
a name of Mars, which is also unknown in the sculptures, may be a corruption of
Horus. The hippopotamus was sacred to Mars, and is said to have been worshipped
at Papremis (ch. 71). Macrobius considers Mars the sun, which agrees with the
character of Mandoo or Mandoo-Re (Saturn. i. 19). Some suppose the fortified town
of *Ibreem* (Primis-parva) to have been called from him.—[G. W.]

small wooden shrine covered with plates of gold, is conveyed from the temple into a second sacred building the day before the festival begins. The few priests still in attendance upon the image place it, together with the shrine containing it, on a four-wheeled car,[5] and begin to drag it along ; the others, stationed at the gateway of the temple, oppose its admission. Then the votaries come forward to espouse the quarrel of the god, and set upon the opponents, who are sure to offer resistance. A sharp fight with clubs ensues, in which heads are commonly broken on both sides. Many, I am convinced, die of the wounds that they receive, though the Egyptians insist that no one is ever killed.

64. The natives give the subjoined account of this festival. They say that the mother of the god Mars once dwelt in the temple. Brought up at a distance from his parent, when he grew to man's estate he conceived a wish to visit her. Accordingly he came, but the attendants, who had never seen him before, refused him entrance, and succeeded in keeping him out. So he went to another city and collected a body of men, with whose aid he handled the attendants very roughly, and forced his way in to his mother. Hence they say arose the custom of a fight with sticks in honour of Mars at this festival.

The Egyptians first made it a point of religion to have no

[5] This was of unusual occurrence in the Egyptian sculptures; but a representation of a car, bearing a small shrine in a boat, found on the bandages of a mummy be-

longing to Signor d'Athanasi, seems to be similar to the one mentioned by Herodotus, with this difference, that the figure representing the deceased is recumbent instead of being the standing image of a deity. Four-wheeled cars were common in many countries. The Latin name petoritum is derived, as Festus says, from *petor*, "four" in Oscan, and *rit* (rota) "wheel." *Petôr* is another form of *quatuor*, the Gothic *fidvôr*, Æolic *Pisures*, Sanscrit *Chatûr*.—[G. W.]

converse with women in the sacred places, and not to enter them without washing, after such converse. Almost all other nations, except the Greeks and the Egyptians, act differently, regarding man as in this matter under no other law than the brutes. Many animals, they say, and various kinds of birds may be seen to couple in the temples and the sacred precincts, which would certainly not happen if the gods were displeased at it. Such are the arguments by which they defend their practice, but I nevertheless can by no means approve of it. In these points the Egyptians are specially careful, as they are indeed in every thing which concerns their sacred edifices.

65. Egypt, though it borders upon Libya, is not a region abounding in wild animals.[6] The animals that do exist in the country, whether domesticated or otherwise, are all regarded as sacred. If I were to explain why they are consecrated to the several gods, I should be led to speak of religious matters, which I particularly shrink from mentioning ; the points whereon I have touched slightly hitherto have all been introduced from sheer necessity. Their custom with respect to animals is as follows. For every kind there are appointed certain guardians, some male, some female,[7] whose business it is to look after them ; and this honour[8] is made to descend from father to son. The

[6] This was thought to be extraordinary, because Africa abounded in wild animals (infra, iv. 191-2); but it was on the west and south, and not on the confines of Egypt that they were numerous. Though Herodotus abstains from saying why the Egyptians held some animals sacred, he explains it in some degree by observing that Egypt did not abound in animals. It was therefore found necessary to ensure the preservation of some, as in the case of cows and sheep; others were sacred in consequence of their being unwholesome food, as swine, and certain fish; and others from their utility in destroying noxious reptiles, as the cat, ichneumon, ibis, vulture, and falcon tribe: or for some particular purpose, as the crocodile was sacred in places distant from the Nile, where the canals required keeping up. The same is stated by Porphyry (de Sacrificiis) and Cicero (Nat. Deor. i. 36), who says that the custom of "representing the gods with the heads of oxen, birds, and other creatures, was introduced in order that the people might abstain from eating them, or for some other mysterious reason." In this they observed certain gradations. All that are said to have been worshipped did not really receive that honour. Some were in themselves sacred, being looked upon, as Strabo and Porphyry say, "really to be gods," as the bull Apis, and others; some were only representations of certain deities, and many were mere emblems. Diodorus and Cicero also attribute their worship to their utility to man ; but the same satisfactory reason is not to be found in all cases. See above, note [8] on ch. 42.—[G. W.]

[7] Women were probably employed to give the food to many of the animals; but the curators appear to have been men, of the sacerdotal class. Diodorus speaks of certain revenues for the support of the sacred animals, besides the donations of the devout ; and he describes their feeding the hawks by throwing up the meat cut into small pieces; the cats and ichneumons being fed with bread soaked in milk, or with fish cut up for them. Even in the present day cats are fed at the Kadi's court and at the Nahasin (copper-market) of the Khan Khaleel, in Cairo, from funds left for the purpose. See At. Eg. W. vol. v. p. 165.—[G. W.]

[8] Herodotus and Diodorus agree in representing the office of feeding the sacred

inhabitants of the various cities, when they have made a vow to any god, pay it to his animals in the way which I will now explain.   At the time of making the vow they shave the head of the child,' cutting off all the hair, or else half, or sometimes a third part, which they then weigh in a balance against a sum of silver ; and whatever sum the hair weighs is presented to the guardian of the animals, who thereupon cuts up some fish, and gives it to them for food—such being the stuff whereon they are fed.   When a man has killed one of the sacred animals, if he

animals as an honourable one ; " and so far," says Diodorus, " are they from declining or feeling ashamed openly to fulfil this office, that they pride themselves upon it, going in procession through the towns and country, with the distinguishing marks of their occupation, as if they were partakers of the highest honours of the gods. And being known by a peculiar emblem belonging to each, the people perceive, on their approach, of what animal they have the care, and show them respect by bowing to the ground, and by other marks of honour" (i. 83).   The expense incurred for the maintenance of these animals was often very great, and their funerals were sometimes performed in so sumptuous a manner, that they cost the curators more than they had the means of paying ; and when in foreign countries, the Egyptian army was never known to leave behind it the cats and hawks, even though they had a difficulty in obtaining the means of transport ; and they were always brought back to Egypt, to be buried in holy ground.   In consequence of various reasons for the respect or the hostility felt towards a particular animal in different parts of Egypt, many quarrels took place in later times between towns and districts (Juven. Sat. xv. 36, see above n. ' on ch. 42).   But these were not likely to have been permitted during the age of the Pharaohs, when the law was strong, the real object better understood, and the priests were more interested in maintaining their authority, and in preventing an exposure of their system ; and no opinion can be formed of the Egyptians or their customs when in the degraded state to which they had fallen under the Romans.   For, as De Pauw observes, "there is no more reason to believe such excesses were committed in old times, than to expect the modern towns of Europe to make war on each other, in order to maintain the pre-eminence of their saints and patrons" (Rech. sur les Eg. et Chinois, i. 145).   But whatever may have been the original motive, there is no doubt that the effect of this sanctity of animals was only what might have been foreseen, and like the division of the deity into various forms and attributes, or the adoration of any but the Supreme Being, could not possibly end in anything but superstition and error.   And though Plutarch (de Is. s. 8) thinks that "the religious rites and ceremonies of the Egyptians were never instituted on irrational grounds, or built on mere fable," he feels obliged to allow that, by adoring the animals themselves, and reverencing them as gods, the Egyptians, at least the greater part of them, have not only filled their religious worship with many contemptible and ridiculous rites, but have given occasion to notions of the most dangerous consequence, driving the weak and simple-minded into all the extravagance of superstition.   See At. Eg. W. vol. v. p. 91–114 ; and compare n. ' on ch. 37.—[G. W.]

' Though Egyptian men shaved their heads, boys had several tufts of hair left, as in modern Egypt and China.   Princes also wore a long plaited lock, falling from near the top of the head, behind the ear, to the neck.   This was the sign of childhood, and was given to the infant Harpocrates.   To it Lucian alludes when he says (Navig. 3), " It is a sign of nobility in Egypt, for all freeborn youths to plait their hair until the age of puberty," though in Greece "the hair twisted back and plaited is a sign of one not being free."   The lock worn by princes was not always real hair, but a false one appended to the wig they wore, sometimes plaited to resemble hair, some-

did it with malice prepense, he is punished with death ;[1] if un-
wittingly, he has to pay such a fine as the priests choose to im-
pose. When an ibis, however, or a hawk is killed, whether it
was done by accident or on purpose, the man must needs die.

66. The number of domestic animals in Egypt is very great,
and would be still greater were it not for what befalls the cats.
As the females, when they have kittened, no longer seek the
company of the males, these last, to obtain once more their com-
panionship, practise a curious artifice. They seize the kittens,
carry them off, and kill them, but do not eat them afterwards.
Upon this the females, being deprived of their young, and longing to supply their place, seek the males once more, since they
are particularly fond of their offspring. On every occasion of a
fire in Egypt the strangest prodigy occurs with the cats. The
inhabitants allow the fire to rage as it pleases, while they stand
about at intervals and watch these animals, which, slipping by
the men or else leaping over them, rush headlong into the flames.[2]

times within a covering fastened to the side of the head-dress. One of these, worn
by a Prince Remeses, was highly ornamented.—[G. W.]

[1] The law was, as Herodotus says, against a person killing them on purpose, but
the prejudiced populace in after times did not always keep within the law; and
Diodorus declares that if any person killed an ibis, or a cat, even unintentionally, it
infallibly cost him his life, the multitude collecting and tearing him to pieces; for
fear of which calamity, if any body found one of them dead, he stood at a distance,
and calling with a loud voice made every demonstration of grief, and protested that
it was found lifeless. And to such an extent did they carry this, that they could
not be deterred by any representation from their own magistrates from killing a
Roman who had accidentally caused the death of a cat (Diod. i. 83). This confirms
the statement in a previous note (ch. 65, note [8]) of the change since the time of the
Pharaohs. A similar prejudice exists in India in favour of their sacred animals.
Cicero says it was a capital offence in Egypt to kill " an ibis, an asp, a cat, a dog, or
a crocodile " (Tusc. Disp. v. 27); but the crocodile was not sacred throughout the
country. Plutarch mentions the ibis, hawk, cynocephalus, and the apis, as the
animals in universal estimation throughout Egypt, to which the cat, dog, cow, vulture, and asp, should have been added. Great respect was also paid to the jackal,
as the emblem of Anubis; but many others merely enjoyed local honours.—[G. W.]
[2] The very measures adopted by the Egyptians to prevent the cats being burnt

When this happens, the Egyptians are in deep affliction. If a cat dies in a private house by a natural death, all the inmates of the house shave their eyebrows ; on the death of a dog they shave the head and the whole of the body.

67. The cats on their decease are taken to the city of Bubastis,[3] where they are embalmed, after which they are buried in certain sacred repositories. The dogs are interred in the cities to which they belong, also in sacred burial-places. The same practice obtains with respect to the ichneumons ;[4] the hawks and shrew-mice, on the contrary, are conveyed to the city of Buto for burial, and the ibises[5] to Hermopolis. The bears,

frightened them (as Larcher supposes), and made them rush into the danger.—[G. W.]

[3] Cats were embalmed and buried where they died, except perhaps in the neighbourhood of Bubastis; for we find their mummies at Thebes and other Egyptian towns, and the same may be said of hawks and ibises. At Thebes numerous ibis mummies are found, as well as in the well known ibis-mummy pit of Sakkara ; and cows, dogs, hawks, mice, and other animals are found embalmed and buried at Thebes. They did not therefore carry all the cats to Bubastis ; the shrew mice and hawks to Buto ; or the ibis to Hermopolis. But it is very possible that persons whose religious scruples were very strong or who wished to show greater honour to one of those animals, sent them to be buried at the city of the god to whom they were sacred, as individuals sometimes preferred having their bodies interred at Abydus, because it was the holy burial-place of Osiris. This explains the statement of Herodotus, as well as the fact of a great number of cat mummies being found at the Speos Artemidos, and the number of dog mummies in the Cynopolite nome, and of wolf mummies at Lycopolis. In some places the mummies of oxen, sheep, dogs, cats, serpents, and fishes, were buried in a common repository ; but wherever particular animals were sacred, small tombs, or cavities in the rock, were made for their reception, and sepulchres were set apart for certain animals in the cemeteries of other towns.—[G. W.]

[4] The *viverra* ichneumon is still very common in Egypt, particularly on the western bank, from the modern Geezeh to the Fyóom. It was supposed to be sacred to Lucina and Latona. Heracleopolis was the city where it was principally honoured ; and its hostility to the crocodile, in destroying its eggs, was the cause of the ill-will that subsisted between the Heracleopolites and the people of the neighbouring nome of Crocodilopolis (the modern *Fyóom*). Its habit of destroying eggs is well known, and this is frequently represented in the paintings of Thebes, Beni-Hassan, and Sakkara. It is now called *nims*, or *Got, i. e. (Kot) Pharaóon,* "Pharaoh's cat," probably from the reverence it formerly received in Egypt. This was from its hostility to cats; and above all for its antipathy to serpents, which it certainly has a remarkable facility of destroying. Ælian, and other ancient writers, have overloaded the truth with so many idle tales, that the feats of the ichneumon appear altogether fabulous ; the destruction of the crocodile's eggs having been converted into a direct attack on the crocodile itself, and a cuirass of mud against a snake having been thought necessary to account for what is really done by its extreme quickness. See At. Eg. W. vol. ii. p. 81, and vol. v. p. 149 to 157.—[G. W.]

[5] These birds were sacred to Thoth, the god of letters and the moon, who corresponded to Mercury, being the intermediate agent between the gods and man. He was particularly worshipped at Hermopolis Magna, now *Oshmoonayn*, in Coptic *Shmoun* B, or the "two Eights," in allusion to his title of "Lord of the eight

which are scarce in Egypt,⁴ and the wolves, which are not much
bigger than foxes,⁷ they bury wherever they happen to find them
lying.

68. The following are the peculiarities of the crocodile:—
During the four winter months they eat nothing;⁸ they are four-

regions," common in the hieroglyphic legends. On the edge of the desert, west of
that place, are many pits where the sacred ibises were buried. Hermopolis parva
now *Damanhour* in the Delta, was also a city named after this god. Another,
called Ibeum, nearly opposite Acôris, was either sacred to, or was the burial-place
of, the ibis; and Champollion supposed it received the name of Nibis from Ma-n-
hip, or n-hip "the place (city) of the ibis," which in Egypt was called *Hip*. (See
below note ⁹ on ch. 76.) The Cynocephalus ape was also sacred to Thoth.—[G. W.]

⁶ It is very evident that bears were not natives of Egypt; they are not represented among the animals of the country; and no instance occurs of a bear in the
sculptures except as a curiosity brought by foreigners. These people are the Rot-
n-no (divided by the Egyptians into "upper and lower") who lived by Mesopotamia;
and the coming of the bear from the neighbourhood of the Euphrates accords well
with the present *habitat* of the small light-coloured *Ursus Syriacus*.—[G. W.]

⁷ Herodotus is quite correct in saying that wolves in Egypt were scarcely larger
than foxes. It is singular that he omits all mention of the hyæna, which is so common in the country, and which is represented in the sculptures of Upper and Lower
Egypt. The wolf is an animal of Upper and Lower Egypt. Its Egyptian name was
" *Ouónsh*."—[G. W.]

⁸ If the crocodile rarely comes out of the river in the cold weather, because it
finds the water warmer than the external air at that season, there is no reason to
believe it remains torpid all that time, though, like all the lizard tribe, it can exist a
long time without eating, and I have known them live in a house for three months
without food, sleeping most of the time; indeed, when the weather is warm, even
in winter, it frequently comes out of the water to bask on the sand-banks, and
there during the great heats of summer it sleeps with its mouth wide open towards
the wind. In Herodotus' time crocodiles frequented the lower part of the Nile more
than at present, and may have remained longer under water in that latitude. Indeed
for many months they have little opportunity of being seen, owing to the inundation
covering their favourite sand-banks. They do not now frequent the Nile below
Beni Hassan, and they are seldom seen north of the latitude of Manfaloot. Their
eggs, as Herodotus says, are laid in the sand often under the bank, and hatched by
the heat of the sun; and the great disparity between the animal when full-grown,
and its original size in the egg is remarkable, since the latter only measures three
inches in length and two inches in breadth (or diameter), being less than that of
the goose which measures 3⁸/₉ by 2⅖. The two ends are exactly alike. When formed,
the young crocodile lies within with its tail turned round to its head; and
when full-grown it becomes nearly 70 times longer than the egg, the crocodile of
Egypt attaining to the size of 20 to 22 feet. In Ethiopia it is larger; and Herodotus
gives it 17 cubits (=25¼ feet, or 29, if by the cubit of the Nilometer) in Egypt, or even
more. Its small eyes are long, which makes Herodotus compare them to those of
a pig, and they are covered by a thin pellucid (nictitating) membrane, mentioned
by Plutarch (de Is. s. 75), which passes over them from the outer corner, and continues there while it sleeps. It is perfectly true that it has no tongue, and the
throat is closed by a thick membrane which is only opened when it swallows; but
the story of its moving its upper jaw is owing to its throwing *up* its whole head
when it seizes its prey, at the same time that it really moves its lower jaw *downwards*.
The strength of its skin, particularly on the back, where it is covered with scales,
has made it useful for shields (as Pliny says of the Hippopotamus, " Tergoris ad
scuta galeasque impenetrabilis "), which are still made of it in Ethiopia. Though
the scales serve to indicate the two species known in the Nile, they differ very little
in their position; and the black and green colour of the two crocodiles is a more
evident distinction. The notion of this animal, which catches fish, not being able

footed, and live indifferently on land or in the water. The female lays and hatches her eggs ashore, passing the greater portion of the day on dry land, but at night retiring to the river, the water of which is warmer than the night-air and the dew. Of all known animals this is the one which from the smallest size grows to be the greatest: for the egg of the crocodile is but little bigger than that of the goose, and the young crocodile is in proportion to the egg; yet when it is full grown, the animal measures frequently seventeen cubits and even more. It has the eyes of a pig, teeth large and tusk-like, of a size proportioned to its frame; unlike any other animal, it is without a tongue; it cannot move its under-jaw, and in this respect too it is singular, being the only animal in the world which moves the upper-jaw but not the under. It has strong claws and a scaly skin, impenetrable upon the back. In the water it is blind, but on land it is very keen of sight. As it lives chiefly in the river, it has the inside of its mouth constantly covered with leeches; hence it happens that, while all the other birds and beasts avoid it, with the trochilus it lives at peace, since it owes much to that bird: for the crocodile, when he leaves the water and comes out upon the land, is in the habit of lying with his mouth wide open, facing the western breeze: at such times the trochilus goes into his mouth and devours the leeches. This benefits the crocodile, who is pleased, and takes care not to hurt the trochilus.

69. The crocodile is esteemed sacred by some of the Egyptians, by others he is treated as an enemy.[9] Those who live near

to see under water, is contrary to all reason, as is the annoyance to which Herodotus supposes it subject, of having its mouth invaded by leeches. The story of the friendly offices of the Trochilus appears to be derived from that bird's uttering a shrill note as it flies away on the approach of man, and (quite unintentionally) warning the crocodile of danger. In its range of long tusks the two end ones of the lower jaw pass through corresponding holes in the upper jaw, near the nose, when the mouth is closed. These are formed by the teeth growing long, there being as yet no such holes while the animal is young.—[G. W.]

[9] See above, note [8] on ch. 42. Strabo speaks of a sacred crocodile kept at Crocodilopolis (afterwards called Arsinoe) called *Suchus*, which was 'fed by the priests with the bread, meat, and wine contributed by strangers. This name was evidently taken from *Savak*, the crocodile-headed god—and that mentioned by Herodotus, "Champsee," was the Egyptian *msah*, or *emsóh*, which may be traced in the Arabic *temsah*. The Greeks prefixed the χ as they now change the *h* of Arabic into a hard *k*, as "*kagi*" for "*hagi*," &c. At Crocodilopolis, and at another town of the same name above Hermopolis, at Ombos, Coptos, Athribis, (called also Crocodilopolis,) and even at Thebes, and some other places, the crocodile was greatly honoured; and Ælian (x. 24) says that their numbers increased so much that it was not safe for any one to wash his feet, or draw water at the river, near those towns; and no one could walk by the stream at Ombos, Coptos, or Arsinoe, without great caution. Herodotus says the sacred crocodiles of the Crocodilopolite nome were buried in the lower chambers of the Labyrinth (infra, ch. 148). The Tentyrites, and the people of Apollinopolis, Heracleopolis, and the Island of Elephan-

Thebes, and those who dwell around Lake Mœris, regard them with especial veneration. In each of these places they keep one crocodile in particular, who is taught to be tame and tractable. They adorn his ears[1] with ear-rings of molten stone[2] or gold, and put bracelets on his fore-paws, giving him daily a set portion of bread, with a certain number of victims; and, after having thus treated him with the greatest possible attention while alive, they embalm him when he dies and bury him in a sacred repository. The people of Elephantiné, on the other hand, are so far from considering these animals as sacred that they even eat their flesh. In the Egyptian language they are not called crocodiles, but Champsæ. The name of crocodiles was given them by the Ionians, who remarked their resemblance to the lizards, which in Ionia live in the walls, and are called crocodiles.[3]

70. The modes of catching the crocodile[4] are many and various. I shall only describe the one which seems to me most

tine, looked upon them with particular aversion, and the same hatred was shown to them whenever they were considered types of the Evil Being. The skill of the Tentyrites in destroying them was well known, and their facility in overpowering them in the water is attributed by Pliny (viii. 25) and Seneca (Nat. Quæst. iv. 2) to their courage, as well as to their dexterity, the crocodile being "timid before the bold, and most ready to attack those who were afraid of it." The truth of the skill of the Tentyrites was even tested at Rome; and Strabo says they went after them into a tank of water prepared for the purpose, and entangling them in a net dragged them to its shelving edge and back again into the water, in the presence of numerous spectators. Mummies of crocodiles have been found at Thebes and other places, but principally at the large natural cave near Maábdeh (opposite Manfaloot), near which it is probable that some town formerly stood where they were particularly honoured.—[G. W.]

[1] The crocodile's ears are merely small openings without any flesh projecting beyond the head.—[G. W.]

[2] By molten stone seems to be meant glass, which was well known to the Egyptians (see note [8] on ch. 44), as it was also to the Assyrians (Layard's Nineveh and Babylon, 196–7, &c.) and Babylonians (ibid. p. 503).

[3] Κροκόδειλος was the term given by the Ionians to lizards, as the Portuguese al legato "the lizard" is the origin of our alligator. The Ionians are here the descendants of the Ionian soldiers of Psammetichus. The crocodile is not the Leviathan of Job xli. as some have supposed. Isaiah xxvii. 1, calls "Leviathan the piercing serpent," and "that crooked serpent," corresponding to the Aphophis or "great serpent" of Egypt, the emblem of sin.—[G. W.]

[4] One, which is now adopted, is to fasten a little puppy on a log of wood, to the middle of which a strong rope is tied, protected to a certain distance by iron wire, and this when swallowed by the crocodile turns, on being pulled across its throat. It is then dragged ashore, and soon killed by blows on the head from poles and hatchets. They have another mode of catching it. A man swims, having his head covered by a gourd with two holes for his eyes, to a sandbank where the crocodile is sleeping; and when he has reached it, he rises from the water with a shout, and throws a spear into its side, or armpit if possible, when feeling itself wounded, it rushes into the water. The head of the barbed spear having a rope attached to it, the crocodile is thereby pulled in, and wounded again by the man (and his companions who join him) until it is exhausted and killed; and the same method is adopted for catching the hippopotamus in Ethiopia.—[G. W.]

worthy of mention.   They bait a hook with a chine of pork and let the meat be carried out into the middle of the stream, while the hunter upon the bank holds a living pig, which he belabours. The crocodile hears its cries and, making for the sound, encounters the pork, which he instantly swallows down.   The men on the shore haul, and when they have got him to land, the first thing the hunter does is to plaster his eyes with mud.   This once accomplished, the animal is despatched with ease, otherwise he gives great trouble.

71. The hippopotamus,[5] in the canton of Paprèmis, is a sacred animal, but not in any other part of Egypt.   It may be thus described :—It is a quadruped, cloven-footed, with hoofs like an ox, and a flat nose.   It has the mane and tail of a horse, huge tusks which are very conspicuous, and a voice like a horse's neigh.   In size it equals the biggest oxen, and its skin is so tough that when dried it is made into javelins.[6]

---

[5] This animal was formerly common in Egypt, but is now rarely seen as low as the second cataract.   The chase of the hippopotamus was a favourite amusement. It was entangled by a running noose, and then struck by a spear, to the barbed blade of which a strong line was fastened.   On striking it the shaft left the blade, the line running on a reel was let out, and it was then dragged back again to receive other spear-wounds till it was exhausted, when the ropes of the various blades were used to secure it. (Cp. Diodor. i. 35 ; see pl. xv. At. Eg. W. vol. iii. p. 71.)   The description of the hippopotamus by Herodotus is far from correct.   Its feet are divided into four short toes, not like the hoof of a bull ; the teeth certainly project, but it has no mane, and its tail, almost trilateral at the end, is very unlike that of a horse ; nor does it neigh, the noise being between lowing and grunting.   Its size far exceeds that of the largest bull, being, when full grown, from 14 to 18 ft. long. Shafts of javelins (cp. i. 52) may possibly have been made of the hide, but it is better suited for whips (now called corbâg) and shields, both which were made of it in ancient as in modern times.   Pliny justly says, "ad scuta galeasque impenetrabilis" (viii. 25).   Its Egyptian name was opt, with the article p-opt.   It is said to have been sacred to Mars (ch. 63), probably the pygmy deity armed with sword and shield (At. Eg. pl. xli. pt. 1).   It was a Typhonian animal, and "a hippopotamus bound" was stamped on the cakes used in the sacrifices of the festival for the return of Isis from Phœnicia, on the 11th of Tybi (Plut. de Is. s. 50). It was probably the behemôth of Job (xl. 15), that "eateth grass like an ox," and "lieth . . . in the covert of the reed and fens."   See Gesenius' Heb. Lex., where the word is thought to be Egyptian, p-ehe-môut, "the water-ox."   Shields are still made of its hide by the Ethiopians and Blacks of Africa as of old, as well as of the crocodile, giraffe, and bull's hide.—[G. W.]

[6] According to Porphyry (ap. Euseb. Præp. Ev. X. iii. p. 166 B.)   Herodotus transferred his accounts of the phœnix, the hippopotamus, and the mode of catching the crocodile bodily from Hecatæus, making only a few verbal alterations.   It is possible that the statement may be true as regards the two quadrupeds, though one would think that Herodotus might have had equal means of personal observation with the earlier writer.   In the case of the phœnix, Porphyry's account cannot be received, for it is evident that Herodotus drew directly from the Egyptian pictures. He says, moreover (infra, ch. 99), that all his account of Egypt is the result of his own ideas and observations.   This however, may be an exaggeration.

72. Otters[7] also are found in the Nile, and are considered
sacred.   Only two sorts of fish are venerated,[8] that called the

[7] The name ἐνύδριες is indefinite, and the otter is unknown in Egypt; but Ammianus Marcellinus (xxii. 14, p. 336) explains it by showing that the " hydrus was
a kind of ichneumon ; " and though Herodotus was aware of the existence of the
ichneumon, he may easily have mistaken it for the otter, as modern travellers are
known to do, on seeing it coming out of the river.—[G. W.]

[8] The fish particularly sacred were the Oxyrhinchus, the Lepidotus, and the
Phagrus or eel; and the Latus was sacred at Latopolis, as the Mæotes at Elephantine.   The Oxyrhinchus, which gave its name to the city where it was particularly
honoured, had, as its name shows, a "pointed nose," and was the same as the modern
Mizdeh, the Mormyrus Oxyrhinchus.   It is often found in bronze.   So highly was

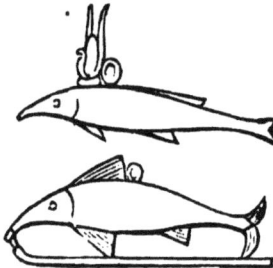
No. I.

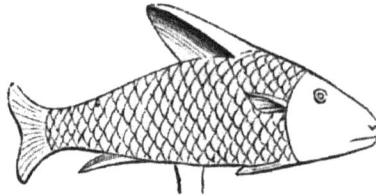
No. II.

it revered at Oxyrhinchus that a quarrel took place between that city and the people
of Cynopolis, in consequence of their having eaten one ; and no Oxyrhinchite would
eat any other fish taken by a hook, lest it should have been defiled by having at

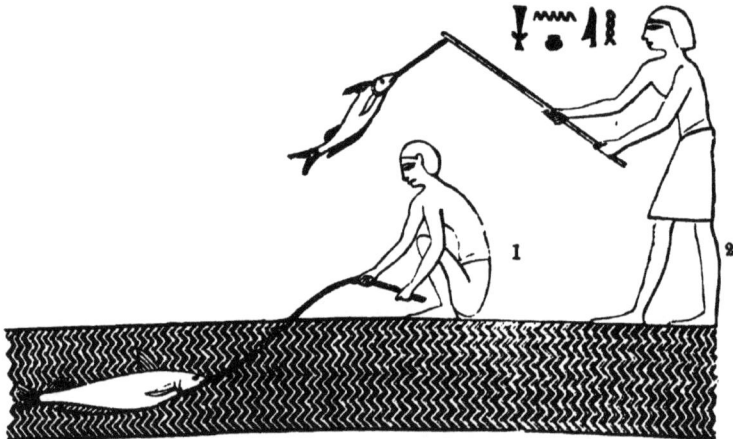
No. III.

any time wounded one of their sacred fish (Plut. de Is. vii. 18, 22).   The Lepidotus
was a scaly fish, but it is uncertain whether it was the Kelb-el-Bahr (Salmo dentex),
the Kisher (or Gisher), a name signifying " scaly," the Perca Nilotica, or the Benny
(Cyprinus Lepidotus); and the bronze representations do not clear up the question,
though they favour the claims of the last of the three (see Plut. de Is. s. 18).   The

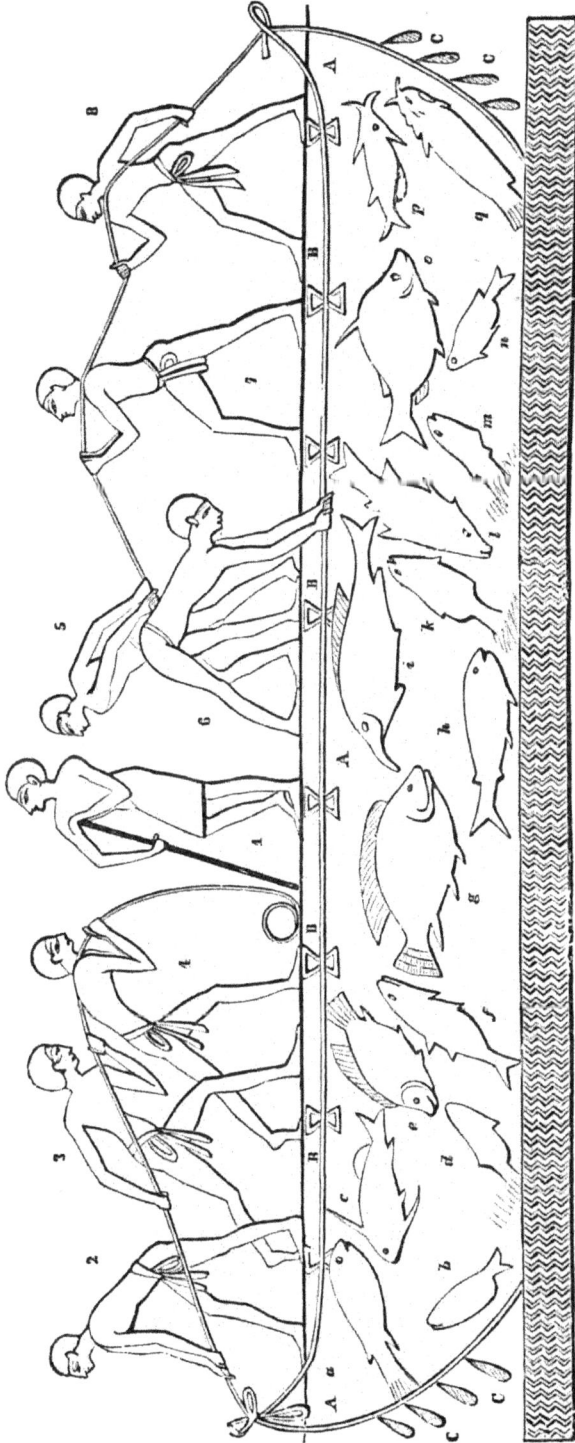

No. IV.

lepidôtus and the eel.   These are regarded as sacred to the Nile, as likewise among birds is the vulpanser, or fox-goose.'

Phagrus or eel was sacred at Syene and at Phagroriopolis, and the reason of its being sacred at this last place was evidently in order to induce the people to keep up the canal. Of the habits of some fish of Egypt, see Strabo xv. p. 486. It is uncertain what species the Latus and Mæotes were, and Ælian thinks the Phagrus and Mæotes were the same fish (see At. Eg. W. vol. v. p. 253). But all people did not regard these fish with the same feelings, and all kinds are represented as caught and eaten in different parts of Egypt. The people, not priests, ate them both fresh and salted, and fishing with the hook, the bident (At. Eg. W. vol. iii. p. 41), and the net, are among the most common representations in the paintings of Thebes and other places, and an amusement of the rich as well as an occupation of the poor. Several fish have been found embalmed in the tombs; but it has been difficult to ascertain their species; though this would not prove their sanctity, as everything found dead was embalmed and buried, to prevent its tainting the air.— [G. W.]

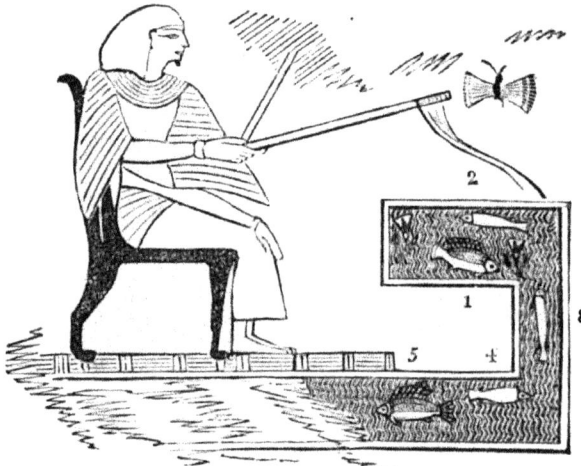

No. V.

' This goose of the Nile was an emblem of the god Seb, the father of Osiris; but it was not a sacred bird. It signified in hieroglyphics a "son," and occurs over the nomens of Pharaohs with the Sun, signifying "son of the sun." Horapollo pretends that it was so used because of its affection for its young, but though it does display great courage and cunning in protecting them, it was not adopted on that account, but from the phonetic initial of its name, s, with a line being se, "son." As an emblem of Seb it was connected with the great Mundane Egg, in which form the chaotic mass of the world was produced. Part of the 26th chapter of the funereal ritual translated by Dr. Hincks contains this dogma, alluded to in the Orphic Cosmogony: "I am the Egg of the Great Cackler. I have protected the Great Egg laid by Seb in the world: I grow, it grows in turn: I live, it lives in turn: I breathe, it breathes in turn." This Mr. Birch shows to be used on coffins of the period about the 12th dynasty. (See Gliddon's Otia Eg. p. 83). On the Orphic Cosmogony and the connexion between the Egg and Chronus (Saturn, the Seb of Egypt), see Damascius in Cory's Fragments, p. 313; Aristophanes, (Birds, 700) mentions the egg produced by "black-winged night." (Cory, p. 293,

73. They have also another sacred bird called the phœnix,[1] which I myself have never seen, except in pictures. Indeed it is a great rarity even in Egypt, only coming there (according to the accounts of the people of Heliopolis) once in five hundred years, when the old phœnix dies. Its size and appearance, if it is like the pictures, are as follows :—The plumage is partly red, partly golden, while the general make and size are almost exactly that of the eagle. They tell a story of what this bird does, which does not seem to me to be credible : that he comes all the way from Arabia, and brings the parent bird, all plastered over with myrrh, to the temple of the Sun, and there buries the body. In order to bring him, they say, he first forms a ball of myrrh as big as he finds that he can carry ; then he hollows out the ball, and puts his parent inside, after which he covers over the opening with fresh myrrh, and the ball is then of exactly the same weight as at first ; so he brings it to Egypt, plastered over as I have said, and deposits it in the temple of the Sun. Such is the story they tell of the doings of this bird.

74. In the neighbourhood of Thebes there are some sacred serpents[2] which are perfectly harmless. They are of small size,

and see Orphic Hymn to Protogonus, p. 294.) As Seb and Netpe answered to Saturn and Rhea, their children Osiris and Isis, being brother and sister, answered to Jupiter and Juno, though they did not really bear any other resemblance to them. Seb and Netpe were the Earth and the Heaven above.—[G. W.]

[1] This bird I formerly supposed to be the one represented on the monuments with human hands, and often with a man's head and legs, in an attitude of prayer (figs. 1, 2), but it is evident that Mr. Stuart Poole is right in considering the Benno (the bird of Osiris) the true Phœnix (fig. 3); and the former appears to be the "pure soul" of the king. Herodotus, Tacitus, and Pomp. Mela fix its return at 500 years, which is evidently an astronomical period; but Tacitus says some give it 1461 years, which points to the coincidence of the 1460 intercalated with the 1461 vague years : and this is confirmed by its being placed at an equal distance of time between each Sothic period (or 730 years before and after the dogstar), on the ceiling of the Memnonium.—[G. W.]

Fig. 1.   2.   8.

[2] The horned snake, *vipera cerastes*, is common in Upper Egypt, and throughout the deserts. It is very poisonous, and its habit of burying itself in the sand renders it particularly dangerous. Pliny (N. H. viii. 23) notices this habit. Herodotus is correct in describing it of small size, but the harmless snakes he mentions had doubtless been made so ; and Diodorus very properly classes them among venomous reptiles. There is no authority from the sculptures for its being sacred, even at Thebes,

and have two horns' growing out of the top of the head. These snakes, when they die, are buried in the temple of Jupiter, the god to whom they are sacred.

75. I went once to a certain place in Arabia, almost exactly opposite the city of Buto,⁴ to make inquiries concerning the winged serpents.⁵ On my arrival I saw the back-bones and ribs

though the asp is shown to have been a sacred snake. The frequent repetition of the cerastes in the hieroglyphics is owing to its occurring so often in "he," "him," "his," and for the letter *f* in other words. It is found embalmed at Thebes, like other reptiles and animals which have no claim to sanctity, and in ordinary tombs, but not in the temple of Amun. Diodorus even thinks the hawk was honoured on account of its hostility to these, as well as other, noxious reptiles; and as Herodotus does not notice the asp, it is possible that he may have attributed to the cerastes the honour that really belonged to that sacred snake. The asp or *Naia* was the emblem of the goddess Ranno, and was chosen to preside over gardens, from its destroying rats and other vermin. Altars and offerings were placed before it, as before dragons in Etruria and Rome. It was also the snake of Neph or Nou, and apparently the representative of Agathodæmon. In hieroglyphics it signified "goddess;" it was attached to the head-dresses of gods and Kings, and a circle of those snakes composed the "asp-formed crowns" mentioned in the Rosetta stone. Being the sign of royalty, it was called βασιλίσκος (basilisk), "royal," equivalent to its Egyptian name *uræus*, from *ouro*, "king." It is still common in gardens, and called in Arabic *Násher*. In length it varies from 3 to 4½ feet, and the largest I have found was 5 ft. 11 in. It is very venomous. It resembles the Indian cobra (*Naia tripudians*) in its mode of raising itself, and expanding its breast; but it has no "spectacles" on its head. If Cleopatra's death had been caused by any serpent, the small viper would rather have been chosen than the large asp; but the story is disproved by her having decked herself in " the royal ornaments," and being found dead "without any mark of suspicion of poison on her body." Death from a serpent's bite could not have been mistaken; and her vanity would not have allowed her to choose one which would have disfigured her in so frightful a manner. Other poisons were well understood and easy of access, and no boy would have ventured to carry an asp in a basket of figs, some of which he even offered to the guards as he passed, and Plutarch (Vit. Anton.) shows that the story of the asp was doubted. Nor is the statue carried in Augustus' triumph which had an asp upon it any proof of his belief in it, since that snake was the emblem of Egyptian royalty : the statue (or the crown) of Cleopatra could not have been without one, and this was probably the origin of the whole story.—[G. W.]

⁸ The bite of the cerastes or horned snake is deadly; but of the many serpents in Egypt, three only are poisonous—the cerastes, the asp or naia, and the common viper. Strabo (xv. p. 1004) mentions large vipers in Egypt, nearly 9 cubits long, but the longest asp does not exceed 6 feet, and that is very unusual.—[G. W.]

⁴ This city of Buto was different from that in the Delta. Some think it was at *Belbáys* (Bubastis Agria), or at *Abbaséh*.—[G. W.]

⁵ The winged serpents of Herodotus have puzzled many persons from the time of Pausanias to the present day. Isaiah (xxx. 60) mentions the " fiery flying serpent." The Egyptian sculptures represent some emblematic snakes with bird's wings and human legs. The *Draco volans* of Linnæus has wings, which might answer to the description given by Herodotus, but it does not frequent Egypt. The only flying creature the ibis could be expected to attack, on its flight into Egypt, and for which it would have been looked upon as a particular benefactor to Egypt, was the locust; and the swarms of these large destructive insects do come from the east. In Syria I have seen them just hatched in the spring still unable to fly; and some idea of the size and destructiveness of a flight of locusts may be derived from the fact of a swarm settling and covering the ground for a distance of 4½ miles. It is singular that Herodotus should not have mentioned locusts, flights of which

of serpents in such numbers as it is impossible to describe : of
the ribs there were a multitude of heaps, some great, some small,
some middle-sized.   The place where the bones lie is at the entrance of a narrow gorge between steep mountains, which there
open upon a spacious plain communicating with the great plain
of Egypt.   The story goes, that with the spring the winged
snakes come flying from Arabia towards Egypt, but are met in
this gorge by the birds called ibises, who forbid their entrance
and destroy them all.   The Arabians assert, and the Egyptians
also admit, that it is on account of the service thus rendered
that the Egyptians hold the ibis in so much reverence.

76. The ibis is a bird of a deep-black colour, with legs like a
crane ; its beak is strongly hooked, and its size is about that of
the landrail.   This is a description of the black ibis which con-
tends with the serpents.   The commoner sort, for there are two
quite distinct species,⁶ has the head and the whole throat bare
of feathers ; its general plumage is white, but the head and
neck are jet black, as also are the tips of the wings and the extremity of the tail ; in its beak and legs it resembles the other
species.   The winged serpent is shaped like the water-snake.

are seen in winter, spring, and summer; and among the many monsters, real animals, and birds represented in the Egyptian paintings, so extraordinary a serpent
could not be unnoticed.   The locusts and the real existence of a *Draco volans* may
have led to the story; and, as Cuvier remarks, all that can be said is that Herodotus saw a heap of bones without having ascertained, beyond report, how they
came there.   Pausanias seems to have convinced himself of their existence by believing in a still stranger reptile, a scorpion with wings like a bat's, brought by a
Phrygian (ix. c. 21).   There is, however, no doubt that the ibis destroyed snakes;
and Cuvier found the skin of one partly digested in the intestines of one of those
mummied birds.   Its food also consisted of beetles, which have been found in another
specimen.   See Herodotus, B. iii. ch. 108, where he describes the winged serpents
of Arabia.—[G. W.]

⁶ The first described by Herodotus as all black, was the one which fought against
the (winged) serpents.   It is the *Ibis Falcinellus* (Temm.) or glossy ibis.   The
colour is a reddish-brown shot with dark-green and purple; the size 1 foot from the
breast to the end of the tail.   The other is the "*Numenius Ibis*," or "*Ibis religiosa*"
of modern naturalists, the *Aboo Hannes* of Bruce, which is white with black pinions
and tail ; the head and part of the back being without feathers, as described by
Herodotus.   This is the one so frequently found embalmed in Egypt.   Its body
measures 12 inches in length, and 4½ in diameter, and the beak 6 inches.   The leg
from the knee to the plant of the foot is about 4½ inches.   (See Cuvier's Theory of
the Earth, Jameson, p. 300.)   Both species have a curved beak.   The great services the ibis rendered by destroying snakes and noxious insects were the cause of
its being in such esteem in Egypt.   The stork was honoured for the same reason in
Thessaly ; and even now the Turks look upon it with such good-will that it would
be considered a sin to kill one ; on which account it feels so secure that, in Asia
Minor, it builds its nests on the walls and houses within reach of man; and to the
credit of the Turks it must be said that they treat animals in general much more
kindly than Europeans.   A similar regard is paid to storks in Holland.
   The ibis was sacred to Thoth, the Egyptian Hermes.   See above, note ⁸, on ch.
67.—[G.W.]

Its wings are not feathered, but resemble very closely those of ·the bat. And thus I conclude the subject of the sacred animals.

77. With respect to the Egyptians themselves, it is to be remarked that those who live in the corn country,[7] devoting themselves, as they do, far more than any other people in the world, to the preservation of the memory of past actions, are the best skilled in history of any men that I have ever met. The following is the mode of life habitual to them :—For three successive days in each month they purge the body by means of emetics and clysters, which is done out of a regard for their health, since they have a persuasion that every disease to which men are liable is occasioned by the substances whereon they feed. Apart from any such precautions, they are, I believe, next to

[7] This is in contradistinction to the marsh-lands; and signifies Upper Egypt, as it includes the city of Chemmis; but when he says they have no vines in the country and only drink beer, his statement is opposed to fact, and to the ordinary habits of the Egyptians. In the neighbourhood of Memphis, at Thebes, and the places between those two cities, as well as at Eileithyias, all corn-growing districts, they ate wheaten bread and cultivated the vine. Herodotus may, therefore, have had in view the corn-country, in the interior of the broad Delta, where the alluvial soil was not well suited to the vine, and where Sebennytus alone was noted for its wine. Most of the other vineyards were at Marea, and in places similarly situated near the edge of the desert, where the light soil was better suited to them; though grapes for the table were produced in all parts of the country. Wine was universally used by the rich throughout Egypt, and beer supplied its place at the tables of the poor, not because "they had no vines in their country," but because it was cheaper; and the same was their reason for eating bread made of the *Holcus sorghum* (or *Doora*) like the peasants of modern Egypt, and not because it was "the greatest disgrace to eat wheaten bread." (See above, note [8] on ch. 36.) And that wine was known in Lower as well as Upper Egypt is shown by the Israelites mentioning the desert as a place which had "no figs, or *vines*, or pomegranates" in contradistinction to Egypt (Gen. xl. 10; Numb. xx. 5). Wines of various kinds were offered at the temples; and being very generally placed by the altar in glass bottles of a particular shape, these came to represent in hieroglyphics what they contained, and to signify "wine," without the word itself "erp" being mentioned. It is remarkable that this word "erpis" is introduced by Athenæus (Deipn. ii. 39 A), quoting Sappho, as the name of "wine:"—

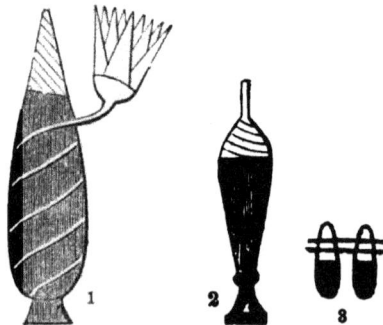

'Αμβροσίας μὲν κρατὴρ ἐκέκρατο
'Ερμᾶς δ' ἑλὼν ἔρπιν θεοῖς οἰνοχόησεν,

unless indeed he uses it for ὅλπιν, "a ladle," or "small jug," which the sense seems to require and which is in X., 425 D. (See note on chs. 18, 37, and 60.) Another reading has ἔρπεν ... οἰνοχοήσων. Athenæus (i. p. 33 E) describes the Egyptians as much addicted to wine, on his own and on the authority of Dio; and says (i. p. 34 A) that Hellanicus fancies the vine was first *discovered* at Plinthinè, a city of Egypt.—[G. W.]

the Libyans,[5] the healthiest people in the world—an effect of their climate, in my opinion, which has no sudden changes. Diseases almost always attack men when they are exposed to a change, and never more than during changes of the weather. They live on bread made of spelt, which they form into loaves called in their own tongue *cyllêstis.*[9] Their drink is a wine which they obtain from barley,[1] as they have no vines in their country. Many kinds of fish they eat raw, either salted or dried in the sun.[2] Quails[3] also, and ducks and small birds, they eat

[5] Their health was attributable to their living in the dry atmosphere of the desert, where sickness is rarely known, as the Arabs show who now live there. See note [6] on ch. 84.—[G. W.]

[9] Athenæus (X. p. 418 x) says the Egyptians were great eaters of bread, and had a kind called Cyllêstia. This he affirms on the authority of Hecatæus. He also speaks of a "subacid bread of the Egyptians called Cyllastia, mentioned by Aristophanes in the Danaids;" and adds, "Nicander mentions it as made of barley" (iii. p. 114). Hesychius says, κύλλαστις ἄρτος τις ἐν Αἰγύπτῳ ὑπὸ ῥιζῶν ἐξ ὀλύρας.—[G. W.]

[1] This is the οἶνος κρίθινος of Xenophon. Diodorus (i. 34) mentions it as "a beverage from barley called by the Egyptians *zythus,*" which he thinks "not much inferior to wine." Athenæus (i. p. 84 A; X. p. 418 x) calls it "macerated barley;" and says Aristotle supposes that men drunk with wine lie on their faces, but those with beer on their backs. He cites Hecatæus respecting the use of beer in Egypt, whose words are, τὰς κριθὰς εἰς τὸ πόμα καταλέουσι. I have found the residue of some malt at Thebes, once used for making beer. Xenophon (Anab. iv. 5) speaks *25* of a sort of fermity of beer in Armenia drunk through reeds having no joints.—[G. W.]

[2] The custom of drying fish is frequently represented in the sculptures of Upper and Lower Egypt. (On the fisheries, see n. [6] ch. 149). Fishing was a favourite amusement of the Egyptians; and the skill of sportsmen was shown by spearing fish with the bident. The fishermen by trade caught them in long drag-nets, the

line being confined to poor people, and to those who "cast angle" for amusement; and a large double-handled landing-net was employed for shoals of small fry. It is also probable that when the inundation retired, they used the wicker trap of modern Egypt and India. It is a basket about 2¼ feet high, entirely open at the bottom, where it is about 2 feet wide, and with a smaller opening at the top about 8 inches in diameter; and being put down into shallow water, whatever fish is enclosed within it is taken out by the man who thrusts his arm through the upper orifice. See At. Eg. W. vol. iii. p. 41 and 53-68.—[G. W.]

[3] Quails were caught, both in Upper and Lower Egypt, like other birds, in large

uncooked, merely first salting them. All other birds and fishes, excepting those which are set apart as sacred, are eaten either roasted or boiled.

78. In social meetings among the rich, when the banquet is

clap-nets and in traps (woodcuts I. and II.), and at Rhinocolura, on the edge of the Syrian desert, the culprits, banished by Actisanes to that spot, caught them in long

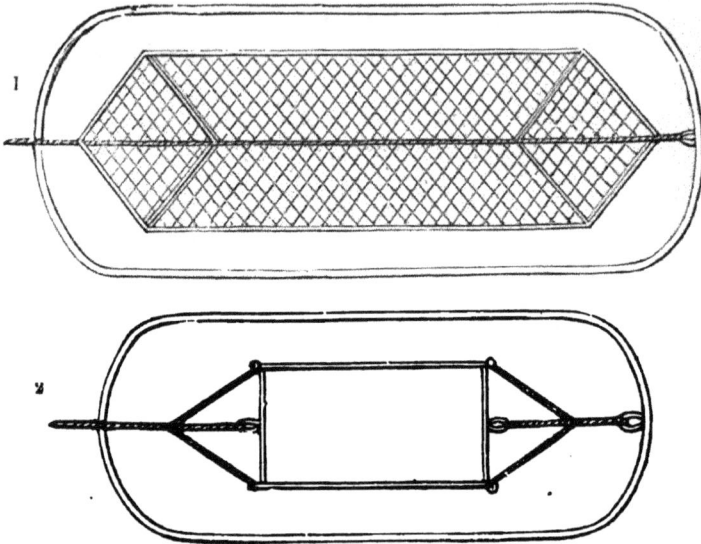

No. I.—Note 3.

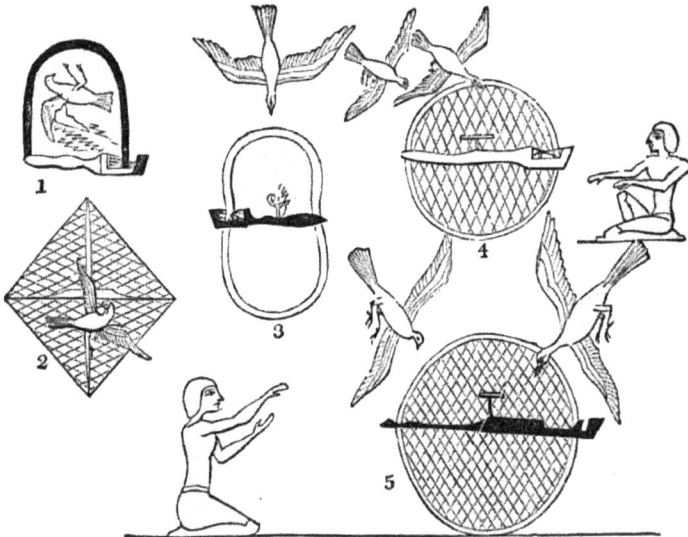

No. II.—Note 3.

ended, a servant carries round to the several guests a coffin, in
which there is a wooden image of a corpse,[4] carved and painted
to resemble nature as nearly as possible, about a cubit or two
cubits in length.   As he shows it to each guest in turn, the servant says, "Gaze here, and drink and be merry; for when you
die, such will you be."

79. The Egyptians adhere to their own national customs,

nets made of split reeds (Diod. i. 60).   The catching, drying, and salting of birds
are frequently represented in the sculptures.   (Woodcut III.)—[G. W.]

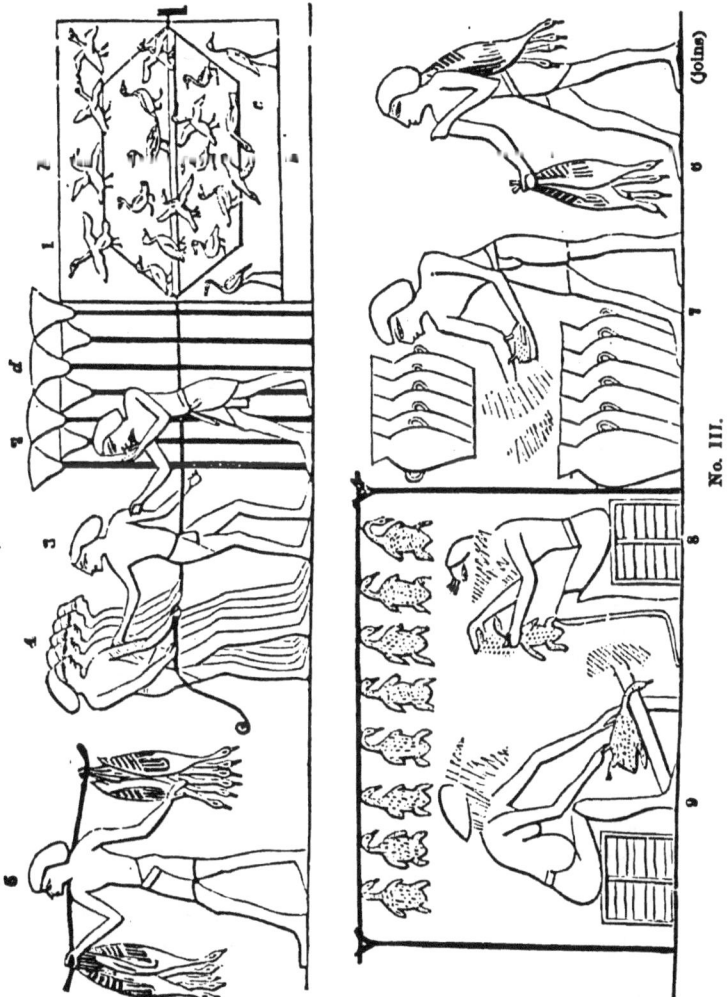

[4] The figure introduced at supper was of a mummy in the usual form of Osiris,
either standing, or lying on a bier, intended to warn the guests of their mortality;

and adopt no foreign usages. Many of these customs are worthy of note : among others their song, the Linus,[5] which is sung under various names not only in Egypt but in Phœnicia, in Cyprus, and in other places ; and which seems to be exactly the same as that in use among the Greeks, and by them called Linus. There were very many things in Egypt which filled me with astonishment, and this was one of them. Whence could the Egyptians have got the Linus ? It appears to have been sung

and the same is described at the feast of Trimalchio (Petron. Satyric. c. 34). The original object of the custom was doubtless with a view to teach men "to love one another, and to avoid those evils which tend to make them consider life too long, when in reality it is too short" (see Plut. de Is. s. 15; and Sept. Sap. Conviv. p. 148 A); but the salutary advice was often disregarded, and the sense of it perverted by many who copied the custom ; as the "ungodly" in Judæa used it to urge men to enjoy the good things of this life, and banish the thoughts of all beyond the present. (Book of Wisdom, ii. 1, &c. ; Is. xxii. 3; lvi. 12; Eccles. ii. 24; Luke xii. 19; and Corinth. xv. 32. Cp. Anac. Od. iv. and Hor. 2 Od. iii. 13.) Some have supposed this custom proved the Egyptians to be of a serious character, though it would rather be a necessary hint for a too lively people. But their view of death was not a gloomy one, connected as it was with the prospect of a happy union with Osiris.—[G. W.]

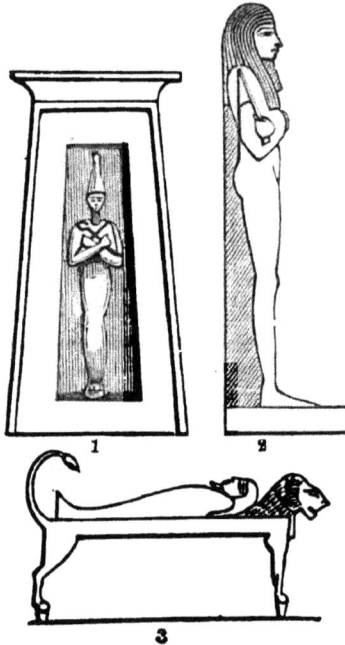

1   2

3

[5] This song had different names in Egypt, in Phœnicia, in Cyprus, and other places. In Greece it was called Linus, in Egypt Maneros. The stories told of Linus, the inventor of melody, and of his death, are mere fables ; and it is highly improbable that the death of Maneros, the son of the first king of Egypt, should have been recorded in the songs of Syria. Julius Pollux (iv. 7) says the song of Maneros was sung by the Egyptian peasants, and that this fabulous personage was the inventor of husbandry, an honour always given to Osiris—γεωργίας εὑρετής, Μουσῶν μαθητής. Some think the "son of the first king" means Horus, the son of Osiris; and the name might be Man-Hor. Indeed there appears in the hieroglyphics to be this legend, "Men-Re, the maker of hymns," which would apply to Re, the sun. Plutarch (de Is. s. 17) states that the song was suited to festivities and the pleasures of the table; and adds that Maneros was not a name, but a complimentary mode of greeting, and a wish "that what they were engaged in might turn out fortunately." Pausanias (ix. 29) says that "Linus and Adonis were sung together by Sappho, and thinks that Homer mentions him (II. xviii. 570); though others refer λίνον to the flaxen cords of the lyre (on the shield of Achilles) :—

τοῖσιν δ' ἐν μέσσοισι παῖς φόρμιγγι λιγείη
ἱμερόεν κιθάριζε · λίνον δ' ὑπὸ καλὸν ἄειδε
λεπταλέη φωνῇ ·

by them from the very earliest times.⁶ For the Linus in Egyptian is called Manerôs ; and they told me that Manerôs was the only son of their first king, and that on his untimely death he was honoured by the Egyptians with these dirgelike strains, and in this way they got their first and only melody.

80. There is another custom in which the Egyptians resemble a particular Greek people, namely the Lacedæmonians. Their young men, when they meet their elders in the streets, give way to them and step aside ;⁷ and if an elder come in where young men are present, these latter rise from their seats. In a third point they differ entirely from all the nations of Greece.

when having gathered the grapes, they danced to the air. Athenæus (Dcipn. xiv. p. 620 A) says, "Nymphis speaks of a youth having gone to fetch water for the reapers, who never returned, and was lamented by different people. In Egypt he was called Maneros." The name Linus was related to αἴλινον, an expression of grief (αἴλινά μοι στοναχεῖτε, Mosch. Id. 1), partly compounded of the usual exclamation *al*, and some think to the Hebrew *lun*, "to complain" or "murmur." (Cp. Exod. xv. 24; and *melinim*, "murmurings;" Numbers xiv. 27.) But the song of Linus, like that of Maneros, was not necessarily of grief; and Euripides (cited by Athenæus, xiv. p. 619 c) says Linus and Ailinus were suited to joy also. Linus and Maneros were probably the genius or impersonation of song. The Egyptians now use "*ya laylee! ya layl!*" as a chorus for lively songs, meaning "O my joy! O night!" alluding to the wedding-night; "*ya laylee, doos, ya laylee!*" "O my joy, step, O my joy!" alluding to the dance. Cp. Hebr. *Hallel*, "singing, praising," whence *hallelu-iah.*—[G. W.]

⁶ The Egyptian songs and hymns were of the earliest date, and, like their knowledge of painting and sculpture, were *said* to be 10,000 years old; but Porphyry hints at the reason of their origin being attributed to Isis, for it was in order to ensure respect for them that "they were preserved through successive ages as the actual poems of that goddess." (Plato's Laws, book ii. p. 790.) Some have supposed their songs were of a mournful kind, and the character of the Egyptians to be the same; but the term "magis mœstiores" applied to them by Ammianus Marcellinus is not consistent with their habits of buffoonery, love of caricature, and natural quickness, nor with the opinion of Xenophon, confirmed by Polybius (v. 81), who says, of all people they were the most addicted to raillery. (Cp. Her. ii. 60, 121. See At. Eg. W. ii. p. 264, 442.) This is inherited by their successors; as well as "gratitude for favours conferred on them," which Diodorus (i. 90) says was most remarkable in the Egyptians.—[G. W.]

⁷ A similar respect is paid to age by the Chinese and Japanese, and even by the modern Egyptians. In this the Greeks, except the Lacedæmonians, were wanting, and the well-known instance at the theatre, mentioned by Plutarch, agrees with what Herodotus says of them. The Jews were commanded to "rise up before the hoary head and honour the face of the old man" (Levit. xix. 32). The mode of bowing with their hand extended towards the knee agrees with the sculptures: one hand was then placed on the other shoulder or on the heart, or on the mouth, to keep the breath from the face of a superior. (See woodcut in note ⁵ to ch. 177.) Some even prostrated themselves on the ground before great personages, "in obeisance bowing themselves to the earth" (Gen. xlii. 26, 28), and knelt or "bowed the knee" before them, as the people were ordered to do before Joseph (Gen. xli. 43). And it is worthy of remark that the word "*abrek*" or "*berek*" is the name applied in Arabic to the kneeling of a camel to the present day. (Cp. *rŭkbeh*, "knee," *bŭraka*, a "blessing," from kneeling in prayer.) Before a king, or the statue of a god, they often held up both arms, and uttered an exclamation, probably resembling the Io triumphe, and Io Bacche, of later times.—[G. W.]

Instead of speaking to each other when they meet in the streets, they make an obeisance, sinking the hand to the knee.

81. They wear a linen tunic fringed about the legs,[s] and

[s] The great use of linen has been noticed above (see n. [1] ch. 37). The fringes were the ends of the threads (see woodcut No. 1, figs. 7, 9, in ch. 37). In some women's dresses the fringes were also left, but these were also more frequently hemmed. A shirt, given by Professor Rosellini (below, No. I. fig. 1), has the fringes. The same custom was adopted by the Israelites (Num. xv. 38), who were ordered to sew a blue riband on the fringe of the border; which calls to mind the blue border dyed with indigo found on some Egyptian linen, though that of the Israelites was intended to prevent its tearing. The woollen upper garment was only worn in cold weather (see At. Eg. W. vol. iii. p. 344 to 351), and the prejudice against its use in sacred places is

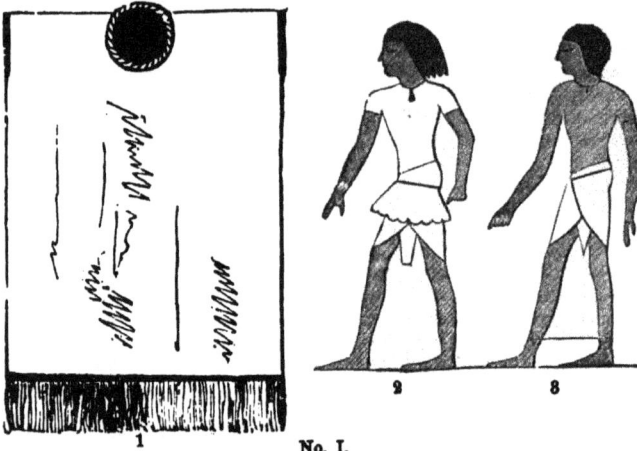

No. I.

perhaps the reason of its not being represented in the paintings. The name Calasiris is supposed to be *Klashr* (κλασρ). The most usual dresses of men are these:—

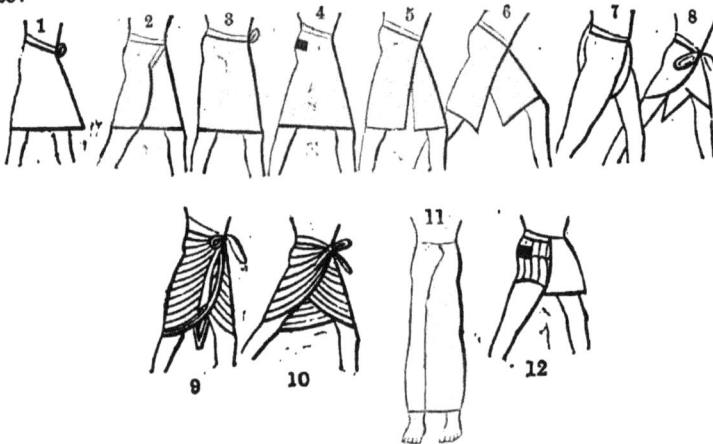

No. II.

called *calasiris ;* over this they have a white woollen garment
thrown on afterwards. Nothing of woollen, however, is taken
into their temples or buried with them, as their religion forbids
it. Here their practice resembles the rites called Orphic and
Bacchic, but which are in reality Egyptian and Pythagorean ; [9]
for no one initiated in these mysteries can be buried in a woollen shroud, a religious reason being assigned for the observance.

82. The Egyptians likewise discovered to which of the gods
each month and day is sacred ; [1] and found out from the day of

For those of the priesthood, see above n. [1] ch. 37. The "white" sandal (φαικας),
said to be worn by the Egyptian (and Athenian) priests, is perhaps of late time.—
[G. W.]

[9] The fact of these, the Bacchic, and the Pythagorean being the same as the
Egyptian, sufficiently proves whence they were derived. See above, note [6] on ch.
51.—[G. W.]

[1] This may partly be traced in the names of some of the months, as Thoth,
Athor, and Pachons; and on a ceiling of the Memnonium at Thebes, and on another
at Edfoo, each has a god to which it belongs. Some suppose they indicate the
festivals of the gods; but this would limit the festivals to twelve in the year. It is,
however, singular that the months are not called by those names, but are designated,
as usual, as the 1st, 2nd, 3rd, and 4th months of the three seasons. (See n. on ch.
4 in the Ap., ch. ii.) The Romans also made their twelve gods preside over the
months; and the days of the week, when introduced in late times, received the
names of the sun and moon and five planets, which have been retained to the present day. The names of gods were also affixed to each day in the Egyptian alma-
nacs, according to Cheræmon, in the same manner as those of saints in the modern
calendar. The Egyptians divided the year into 12 months of 30 days, from the
earliest times of which we have any re-
cord; and the fabulous reign of Osiris, 28
years, appears to have been taken from the
7 days of 4 weeks, or 4 weeks of years,
as the period of Triacontaeterides, of 30
years, was from the month of 30 days.
Dion Cassius (xxxvii. 18), too, distinctly
states that "the practice of referring the
days of the week to the 7 planets began
among the Egyptians." The week of 7
days (sheba, שבע) is mentioned at the period of the Creation, and it continued to
be used in the time of patriarchs (Gen.
vii. 4; xxix. 27). It was probably of very
early use among the Egyptians also, judging from the 7 days' fête of Apis and other
hebdomadal divisions; but they generally
make mention of decades or tens of days,
which are still in use among the Chinese.
(On the use of 7 days in Egypt, see n.
on ch. 109 in Ap. ch. vii.) The Egyptians
had 12 hours of night and 12 of day, and
each had its peculiar genius or goddess,
represented with a star on her head, called
Nau, "hour." Night was considered older
than day, as darkness preceded light, and
"the evening and the morning were the
first day." The expression "night and
day," is still used in the East, and our

Fig. 1. Of day.   Fig. 2. Of night.

a man's birth, what he will meet with in the course of his life,[2] and how he will end his days, and what sort of man he will be —discoveries whereof the Greeks engaged in poetry have made a use. The Egyptians have also discovered more prognostics than all the rest of mankind besides. Whenever a prodigy takes place, they watch and record the result ; then, if anything similar ever happens again, they expect the same consequences.

83. With respect to divination, they hold that it is a gift which no mortal possesses, but only certain of the gods ;[3] thus they have an oracle of Hercules, one of Apollo, of Minerva, of Diana, of Mars, and of Jupiter. Besides these, there is the oracle of Latona at Buto, which is held in much higher repute than any of the rest. The mode of delivering the oracles is not uniform, but varies at the different shrines.

"fortnight" points to an old custom of counting nights instead of days. The notion that the Egyptians had not the 12 hours of day and of night in the time of Herodotus is erroneous, as they occur in a tomb of the time of Psammetichus II., and in the tombs of the 20th Dynasty at Thebes. The word "hour" is said to be found as early as the 5th Dynasty (see Lepsius, Band iii. Abth. ii. Bl. 72, 76), and with the name of King Assa.—[G. W.]

[2] Horoscopes were of very early use in Egypt (Iambl. 8. 4), as well as the interpretation of dreams; and Cicero (De Div. i. 1) speaks of the Egyptians and Chaldees predicting future events, as well as a man's destiny at his birth, by their observations of the stars. This was done by them, as the monuments show, by observing the constellations that appeared on the eastern horizon at the moment of his birth, or any event they wished to decide about, took place. The fallacy of predicting a particular death from the "ascendant" at the time of any one's birth has been well exposed by Cicero, who asks, "Were all those who fell at Cannæ born under the same constellation, for they had all one and the same death?" (De Div. ii. 47.) Interpreters of dreams were often resorted to in Egypt (Exod. xli. 8); and Diodorus (i. 25) says the prayers of the devout were rewarded in a dream by an indication of the remedies an illness required. Cicero (De Fato, 6) speaks of the belief that "any one born at the rising of the Dogstar could not be drowned in the sea."—[G. W.]

[3] Yet the Egyptians sought "to the idols, and to the charmers, and to them that had familiar spirits, and to the wizards" (Is. xix. 8). Herodotus probably means that none but oracles gave the real answer of the deity; and this would not prevent the "prophets" and "magicians" pretending to this art, like the μάντεις of Greece. To the Israelites it was particularly forbidden "to use divination, to be an observer of times, or an enchanter, or a witch, or a charmer, or a consulter with familiar spirits, or a wizard, or a necromancer." (Deut. xviii. 10, 11.) It is singular that the Hebrew word nahash, "to use enchantments," is the same as the Arabic for "serpent." A Gnostic Papyrus in the British Museum, supposed to be of the 2nd century, and found in Egypt, mentions divination "through a boy with a lamp, a bowl, and a pit," very like what is now practised in Egypt and Barbary; and the employment of boys of old is mentioned by Origen and others. It also contains spells for obtaining power over spirits, for discovering a thief, for commanding another man's actions, for obtaining any wish, for preventing anything, &c. Others in the Leyden Museum contain recipes for good fortune, for procuring dreams, for making a ring to bring good fortune and success in every enterprise, for causing separation between man and wife, giving restless nights, for making oneself loved, &c. Magical tricks were practised of old also (Exod. vii. 11), and they probably became more general in later corrupt times. (See Publ. Cambridge Ant. Soc. 8vo. No. 2.) Apuleius also mentions the magic of Egypt.—[G. W.]

84. Medicine is practised among them[4] on a plan of separation ; each physician treats a single disorder, and no

[4] Not only was the study of medicine of very early date in Egypt, but medical men there were in such repute that they were sent for at various times from other countries. Their knowledge of medicine is celebrated by Homer (Od. iv. 229), who describes Polydamna, the wife of Thonis, as giving medicinal plants " to Helen, in Egypt, a country producing an infinite number of drugs . . . . . where each physician possesses knowledge above all other men." "O virgin daughter of Egypt," says Jeremiah (lxvi. 11), "in vain shalt thou use many medicines." Cyrus and Darius both sent to Egypt for medical men (Her. iii. 132) ; and Pliny (xix. 5) says *post mortem* examinations were made in order to discover the nature of maladies. Doctors received their salaries from the treasury ; but they were obliged to conform in the treatment of a patient to the rules laid down in their books, his death being a capital crime, if he was found to have been treated in any other way. But deviations from, and approved additions to, the sacred prescriptions were occasionally made ; and the prohibition was only to prevent the experiments of young practitioners, whom Pliny considers the only persons privileged to kill a man with impunity. Aristotle indeed says "the Egyptian physicians were allowed after the third day to alter the treatment prescribed by authority, and even before, taking upon themselves the responsibility" (Polit. iii. 11). Experience gradually taught them many new remedies ; and that they had adopted a method (of no very old standing in modern practice) of stopping teeth with gold is proved by some mummies found at Thebes.

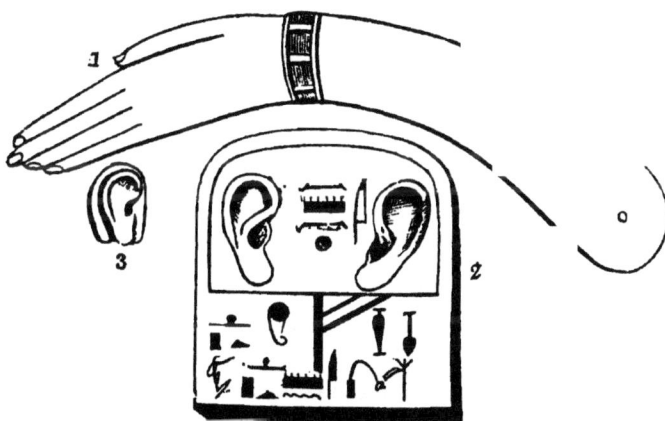

In Fig. 2 is a dedication "to Amun-ra."

Besides the protection of society from the pretensions of quacks, the Egyptians provided that doctors should not demand fees on a foreign journey or on military service, when patients were treated free of expense (Diod. i. 82) ; and we may conclude that they were obliged to treat the poor gratis, on consideration of the allowance paid them as a body by government. This has again become the custom in (Modern) Egypt. Herodotus (ii. 77) and Diodorus (i. 82) mention some methods of treatment ; but poor and superstitious people sometimes had recourse to dreams, to wizards, to donations to sacred animals, and to *exvotos* to the gods ; and the model of an arm, a leg, an eye, or an ear, often recorded the accidental cure and the evident credulity of an individual, as in some countries at the present day. Charms were also written for the credulous, some of which have been found on small pieces of papyrus, which were rolled up and worn as by the modern Egyptians.

Accoucheurs were women ; which we learn from Exodus i. 15, and from the sculptures, as in modern Egypt. The Bedouins of the desert still retain a know-more :[5] thus the country swarms with medical practitioners, some undertaking to cure diseases of the eye, others of the head, others again of the teeth, others of the intestines, and some those which are not local.[6]

85. The following is the way in which they conduct their mournings[7] and their funerals :—On the death in any house of a man of consequence, forthwith the women of the family beplaster their heads, and sometimes even their faces, with mud ; and then, leaving the body indoors, sally forth and wander through the city, with their dress fastened by a band, and their bosoms bare, beating themselves as they walk. All the female relations join them and do the same. The men too, similarly begirt, beat their breasts separately. When these ceremonies are over, the body is carried away to be embalmed.

86. There are a set of men in Egypt who practise the art of

ledge of the properties of the medicinal plants that grew there, with some of which they supply the druggists of the towns. It is to the Arabs, who derived it from Egypt and India, that Europe is indebted for its first acquaintance with the science of medicine, which grew up in the school of Salerno ; and a slight memento of it is still retained in the Arab symbols used by our chemists. Pliny (vii. 56) says, "the study of medicine was claimed as an Egyptian in ention ; by others attributed to *Arabas*, the son of Babylon and Apollo."—[G. W.] v

[6] The medical profession being so divided (as is the custom in modern Europe), indicates a great advancement of civilisation, as well as of medicinal knowledge. The Egyptian doctors were of the sacerdotal order, like the embalmers, who are called (in Genesis l. 2) "Physicians," and were "commanded by Joseph to embalm his father." They were of the class called Pastophori, who, according to Clemens (Strom. lib. 6) being physicians, were expected to know about all things relating to the body, and diseases, and remedies, contained in the six last sacred books of Hermes. Manetho tells us that Athothes, the second king of Egypt, who was a physician, wrote the *anatomical* books ; and his name, translated Hermogenes, may have been the origin of the tradition that ascribed them to Hermes, the Egyptian Thoth. Or the fable may mean that they were the result of intellect personified by Thoth, or Hermes. It is difficult to understand how their having "physicians for particular members of the body, and for particular diseases, affords another proof how rigidly the subdivisions of the *castes were kept separate*," as Heeren imagines, for they were of the same class ; and our modern custom does not certainly lead to such an inference. In the Hermaic books a whole chapter was devoted to diseases of the eye.—[G. W.]

[6] Pliny thinks the Egyptians were subject to numerous diseases (xxvi. 1); but in this he differs from Herodotus (ii. 77). Luxury, and disregard to the regimen they followed of old, may have caused a change in later times, when leprosy, elephantiasis, and other diseases became common in Egypt ;

    "Est Elephas morbus, qui propter flumina Nili
    Gignitur Ægypto in mediâ, neque præterea usquam."—Lucret. vi. 560.

for Herodotus (ch. 77) shows how careful they were of health, and Diodorus (i. 82) says, " θεραπεύουσι τὰ σώματα κλυσμοῖς, καὶ νηστείαις, καὶ ἐμέτοις," as well as by abstinence ; being persuaded that the majority of disorders proceed from indigestion and excess in eating.—[G. W.]

[7] The custom of weeping, and throwing dust on their heads, is often represented on the monuments ; when the men and women have their dresses fastened by a

embalming, and make it their proper business. These persons, when a body is brought to them, show the bearers various models of corpses,[8] made in wood, and painted so as to resemble nature

No. I.

band round the waist, the breast being bare, as described by Herodotus. For seventy days (Gen. l. 3), or, according to some, seventy-two days, the family mourned at home, singing the funeral dirge, very much as it is now done in Egypt; and during this time they abstained from the bath, wine, delicacies of the table, and rich clothing (Diod. i. 91); and even after the body had been removed to the tomb it was not unusual for the near relations to exhibit tokens of grief, when the liturgies, or services for the dead, were performed by the priests, by beating themselves on the breast in presence of the mummy. "Smiting themselves on the breast" was a common token of grief in the East (Luke xxiii. 48) which continues to

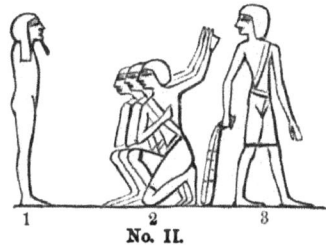

No. II.

the present day. (See woodcut above, and in n. [9] ch. 58; and comp. At. Eg. W. vol. v. p. 259.) The Egyptians did not "cut themselves" in mourning; this was a Syrian custom, and forbidden to the Jews.—[G. W.]

[8] These were in the form of Osiris, and not only those of the best kind, but all the mummies were put up in the same position, representing the deceased as a figure of Osiris, those only excepted which were of the very poor people, and which were merely wrapped up in mats, or some other common covering. Even the small earthenware and other figures of the dead were in the same form of that deity, whose name Herodotus, as usual, had scruples about mentioning, from having been admitted to a participation of the secrets of the lesser Mysteries. Diodorus says (i. 91), "The most expensive mode cost a talent of silver (nearly 250l.), the second twenty-two minæ (90l.), and the third was very cheap. When the price had been agreed upon, and the body given to the embalmers, the scribe marked on the left side of the body the extent of the incision to be made, and then the 'paraschistes' (dissector) cut open as much of the flesh as the law permitted with an Ethiopian stone (flint), and immediately ran away, pursued by those present with bitter execrations, who pelted him with stones. One then introduced his hand, and took out all the viscera, except the kidneys and heart; another cleansed them with palm wine, and aromatic preparations, and lastly, after having applied oil of cedar, and

The most perfect is said to be after the manner of him whom I do not think it religious to name in connexion with such a matter ; the second sort is inferior to the first, and less costly ; the third is the cheapest of all.   All this the embalmers explain, and then ask in which way it is wished that the corpse should be prepared.   The bearers tell them, and having concluded their bargain, take their departure, while the embalmers, left to themselves, proceed to their task.   The mode of embalming, according to the most perfect process, is the following :—They take first a crooked piece of iron,' and with it draw out the brain through

other things to the whole body for upwards of thirty days, they added myrrh, cinnamon, and various drugs for preserving the body, and it was restored to the friends, so well preserved that every feature might be recognised." On this it may be observed, 1st, that the opening in the left side is perfectly correct; and over it the sacred eye represented on a flat piece of lead, or wax, was placed ; and through it the viscera were returned. Four wax figures, of the four genii of Amenti, were also put in with them, when the viscera were not deposited in the vases, which are so often found in the tombs. Of these four vases one had a lid representing the head of a man, another had that of a Cynocephalus, another of a jackal, and the fourth of a hawk; and in these the viscera of first-class mummies were generally deposited. The first held the stomach and large intestines ; the second the small intestines ; the third the lungs and heart (showing Diodorus to be in error); and the fourth the gall-bladder and liver. 2nd. Herodotus and Diodorus are not justified in confining the modes of embalming to three, since the mummies show a far greater variety, and the prices must have varied in like manner. 3rd. The execrations against the "paraschistes" could only have been a form, if really uttered, which seems very doubtful. 4th. The features could not be recognised, being covered with numerous folds of cloth, and the only face seen was that of the painted mummy case. The statement of Porphyry that the intestines were thrown into the river, after an invocation to the sun, is unworthy of belief. Everything belonging to the body was buried, and apparently even the sawdust, used for absorbing the water that washed the intestines, which was put up into small linen bags, and deposited in earthenware jars.—[G. W.]

' The mummies afford ample evidence of the brain having been extracted through the nostrils; and the "drugs" were employed to clear out what the instrument could not touch.   There can be no doubt that iron was used in Egypt, though it is not preserved there, nor in any other country, beyond a certain time. The blue colour of swords, and other weapons in the painted tombs of Thebes, shows that the Egyptians used iron, or steel, as well as bronze; and this last was also employed by the Romans and Etruscans, long after iron implements and arms were common.   Iron was known in the days of Job (xxviii. 2); Moses mentions Tubal Cain the instructor of every artificer in brass and iron (Gen. iv. 22), and compares Egypt to the "iron furnace" (Deut. iv. 20); Og King of Bashan, who lived about 1450 B.C., had a bedstead of iron (Deut. iii. 11); and Homer shows the quenching of iron to caseharden it was well known when he adopts it as a simile, and compares the hissing noise produced by piercing the eye of Polyphemus to the effect of plunging the heated metal in water. (Od. ix. 391.) Thrasyllus (Clem. Strom. i.) agrees with the Arundelian marbles in supposing that iron was known long before the Trojan war ; and it would be inconsistent to suppose that the most civilised nation of those days could have been ignorant of it even if the paintings of Thebes did not prove its use.   We even see butchers sharpening their knives on a steel fastened to their apron; and weapons of that blue-coloured metal were represented in common use long before the Trojan war.   In metallurgy the Egyptians possessed some secrets scarcely known to us; for they had the means of enabling copper to cut stone without hardening it by an alloy, and of giving to bronze blades the elasticity of

the nostrils, thus getting rid of a portion, while the skull is cleared of the rest by rinsing with drugs ; next they make a cut along the flank with a sharp Ethiopian stone,[1] and take out the whole contents of the abdomen, which they then cleanse, washing it thoroughly with palm-wine,[2] and again frequently with an

steel, with great hardness and sharpness of edge. In Asia the Chalybes were noted for their iron works, by which they obtained great profits (Xenoph. Anab. s. v.),

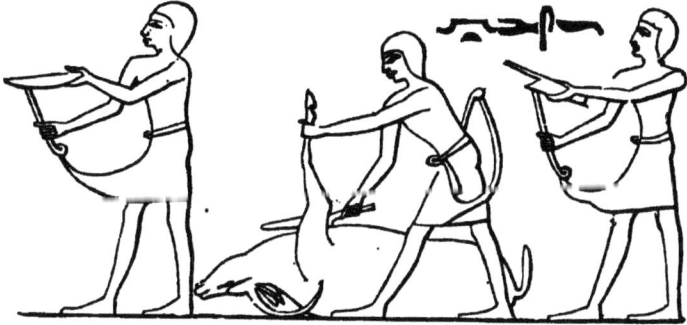

and Pliny (vii. 56) ascribes the invention of steel to the Idæi Dactyli of Crete.—[G. W.]

[1] Ethiopian stone either is *black* flint, or an Ethiopian agate, the use of which was the remnant of a very primitive custom. Flints were often employed in Egypt for tipping arrows, in lieu of metal heads. Stone knives have been found in Egypt, which many people had, as the Britons and others, and even the Romans (Liv. i. 24.) The Ethiopians (Her. vii. 69) had reed arrows tipped with agate, or pebbles, "on which seals were cut," and which, known to us as "Egyptian pebbles," are in great abundance in Dongola and other districts. (See my n. on B. vii. ch. 69.) The knife used in Egypt for sacrificing was generally of tempered iron, exactly like that of the Romans (so often represented on their altars), one of which, in my possession, is 11¼ inches long, by 2 in the broadest part. (Fig. 4.)—[G. W.]

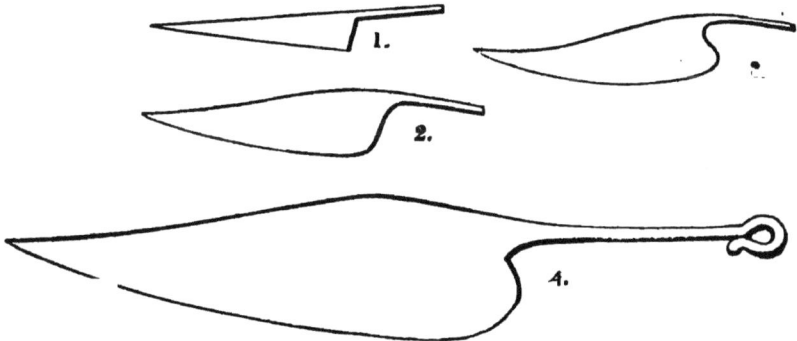

[2] The wine and pith (*jumár*, or *kulb*, "heart," in Arabic) are mentioned by Xenophon. (Anab. ii. 3.) He is right in saying that when taken from it the tree withers. In the Oasis they still make this wine, which they call *lówbgeh*. They

infusion of pounded aromatics. After this they fill the cavity with the purest bruised myrrh, with cassia, and every other sort of spicery³ except frankincense, and sew up the opening. Then the body is placed in natrum⁴ for seventy days,⁵ and covered entirely over. After the expiration of that space of time, which must not be exceeded, the body is washed, and wrapped round, from head to foot, with bandages of fine linen cloth,⁶ smeared over with gum, which is used generally by the Egyptians in the

merely tap the centre of the date tree, where the branches grow, and the juice runs off into a vase fastened there to receive it.—[G. W.]

³ The "spicery, and balm, and myrrh," carried by the Ishmaelites (or Arabs) to Egypt were principally for the embalmers, who were doubtless supplied regularly with them. (Gen. xxxvii. 25.) Other caravans, like the Medianite merchantmen (Gen. xxxvii. 28), visited Egypt for the purposes of trade; and "the spice merchants" are noticed (1 Kings x. 15) in Solomon's time. See my n. B. iii. ch. 107. —[G. W.]

⁴ Not nitre, but the subcarbonate of soda, which abounds at the natron lakes in the Libyan desert, and at El Hegs in Upper Egypt. This completed the usual mode of embalming; but some few appear to have been prepared with wax and tanning, by which the limbs were less rigid, and retained great flexibility. Dr. Granville has made some interesting experiments on preserving bodies by that process, in imitation of one brought from Egypt, probably of late time; for a description of which I refer to his work. Mr. Pettigrew also (p. 73) mentions a child preserved with wax.—[G. W.]

⁵ This included the whole period of mourning. The embalming only occupied forty days (Gen. l. 3); Diodorus says "upwards of thirty." Both seventy and seventy-two days are mentioned as the full number, the first being ten weeks of seven days, or seven decads; the other 12×6=72, the duodecimal calculation being also used in Egypt.

The name mummy is supposed to be an Arabic word, *moomia*, from *múm*, "wax." In Egyptian it is called *sah;* the bier λ, *Gol.*

The origin of embalming has been ingeniously derived from their first merely burying in the sand, impregnated with natron and other salts, which dried and preserved the body; which natural process they afterwards imitated—drugs, and subsequently bitumen, being later improvements. Bitumen does not appear to have been generally used before the 18th Dynasty. The dried body of the supposed Mycerinus, however, will be no evidence that the simple salting process was retained till his time, unless the body and woollen dress are proved to be ancient Egyptian. (See Gliddon's Horæ Ægyptiacæ and M. Eg. W. vol. i. p. 348.) On bitumen, see n. ⁹ on B. i. ch. 179.—[G. W.]

⁶ Not cotton. The microscope has decided (what no one ever doubted in Egypt) that the mummy-cloths are linen. The question arose in consequence of the use of the word *byssus.* Pausanias unequivocally describes it as cotton, and growing in Elis. On the other hand, the Hebrew *shash* is translated Byssus in the Septuagint version, and in our own "fine linen" (Ex. xxiv. 4). Many consider it linen, and Julius Pollux calls it a sort of Indian flax. Herodotus again speaks of the (linen) mummy-cloths as "byssine sindon," and both he and J. Pollux call cotton "tree wool." Some indeed think this last was silk; but Pliny (xix. 1) shows that the ξύλον of Herodotus was cotton,—"Superior pars Ægypti in Arabiam vergens gignit fruticem quem aliqui gossipion vocant, plures xylon; et ideo lina inde facta xylina." The confusion appears to have arisen partly from the conventional use of the names of the various *cloths.* Sindon was the *general* term for every *fine* stuff; so that it was even applied to woollen fabrics. Josephus speaks of sindon made of hair, and the ark had one covering of linen, and another of sindon made of goat's hair (Antiq. 3, 6, 4). Sindon was therefore any stuff of a very fine texture (and might be applied to modern Cashmere and Jerbee shawls, as well as to muslin and cambric). Byssus in its real sense was cotton, but it was also a *general* term (like

place of glue, and in this state it is given back to the relations, who enclose it in a wooden case which they have had made for the purpose, shaped into the figure of a man.   Then fastening the case, they place it in a sepulchral chamber,[7] upright against the wall.   Such is the most costly way of embalming the dead.

our word "linen"), and Josephus speaks of byssine sindon made of linen, *i.e.* "fine cotton linen." With Pliny, on the contrary, linen (linteum or linum) is the *general* term for all stuffs, including cotton (xix.1), and he even calls asbestus " linen." "Komash," properly " linen," is used in the same way by the Arabs for all stuffs. It is also reasonable to suppose that ancient, like modern people, may have been mistaken sometimes about the exact quality of the stuffs used, since the microscope was required to set us right. Sindon may possibly be taken from " India," or from the Egyptian "*shent*" (see n. [1] on ch. 105). Clemens thinks byssine garments were invented in the time of Semiramis, king of *Egypt* (Strom. i. p. 307). The Egyptians employed gum for the bands, or mummy-cloths, but not for other purposes where glue was required. They also stained them with carthamus or safflower. The custom of swathing the body with bandages was common also to the Jews, as well as the process of embalming it with spices (Luke xxiii. 56 ; John xix. 40). Their mode of bandaging the dead body is shown in the case of Lazarus (John xi. 44); and the early Italian masters have represented it more correctly than many of later time. The legs, however, were bandaged separately, as in the Græco-Egyptian mummies, since he "came forth" out of the tomb.— [G. W.]

[7] This was not in their own houses, but, as Herodotus says, in a room made for the purpose, which was attached to the tomb. In the floor of this room the pit was sunk, often to the depth of more than 40 feet, where, after certain services had been performed by a priest before the mummy, it was finally deposited. In the meantime it was kept (as he says, upright) in a moveable closet, and occasionally taken out to receive those priestly benedictions ; or stood within an open canopy for the same purpose, the relations weeping before it. A less expensive kind of tomb had not the chamber, but only the pit, which was properly the place of sepulture, though the name " tomb " is always applied to the apartment above. The coffin or mummy-case was placed at the bottom, or in a lateral chamber or recess, at "the side of the pit." Those who were

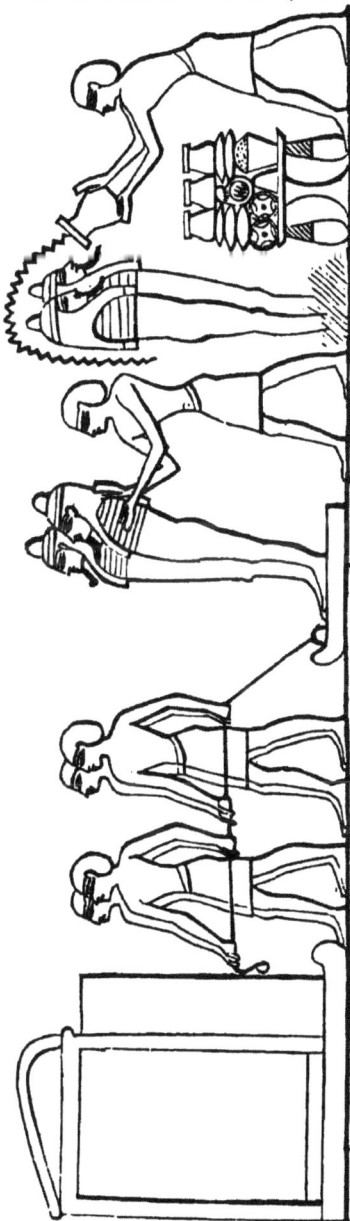

No. I.

87. If persons wish to avoid expense, and choose the second process, the following is the method pursued :—Syringes are filled with oil made from the cedar-tree, which is then, without any incision[8] or disembowelling, injected into the abdomen. The passage by which it might be likely to return is stopped, and the body laid in natrum the prescribed number of days. At the end of the time the cedar-oil is allowed to make its escape ; and such is its power that it brings with it the whole stomach and intestines in a liquid state. The natrum meanwhile has dissolved the flesh, and so nothing is left of the dead body but the skin and the bones. It is returned in this condition to the relatives, without any further trouble being bestowed upon it.

88. The third method of embalming,[9] which is practised in the case of the poorer classes, is to clear out the intestines with a clyster,[1] and let the body lie in natrum the seventy days,

considered worthy were buried in the tomb they had made, or purchased, at a very high price ; but wicked people were forbidden the privilege, as if undeserving of burial in consecrated ground.—[G. W.]

No. II.

[8] Second-class mummies without any incision are found in the tombs ; but the opening in the side was made in many of them, and occasionally even in those of an inferior quality ; so that it was not exclusively confined to mummies of the first class. There were, in fact, many gradations in each class. The mummies of Greeks may generally be distinguished by the limbs being each bandaged separately. On Embalming, see Rouger's Notice sur les Embaumemens des Anciens Egyptiens ; Pettigrew's History of the Egyptian Mummies ; and At. Eg. W. vol. v. p. 451 to the end. —[G. W.]

[9] Of these, as of the others, there were several kinds, the two principal ones being " 1. Those salted and filled with bituminous matter less pure than the others ; 2. Those simply salted." Others, indeed, were prepared in more simple ways ; some were so loosely put up in bad cloths that they are scarcely to be separated from the stones and earth in which they are buried, and others were more carefully enveloped in bandages, and arranged one over the other in one common tomb, often to the number of several hundred.—[G. W.]

[1] The word used here ($\sigma\upsilon\rho\mu\alpha\iota\eta$) is the name of the modern figl, or raphanus

after which it is at once given to those who come to fetch it away.

89. The wives of men of rank are not given to be embalmed immediately after death, nor indeed are any of the more beautiful and valued women. It is not till they have been dead three or four days that they are carried to the embalmers. This is done to prevent indignities from being offered them. It is said that once a case of this kind occurred : the man was detected by the information of his fellow-workman.

90. Whensoever any one, Egyptian or foreigner, has lost his life by falling a prey to a crocodile, or by drowning in the river, the law compels the inhabitants of the city near which the body is cast up to have it embalmed, and to bury it in one of the sacred repositories with all possible magnificence.[2] No one may touch the corpse, not even any of the friends or relatives, but only the priests of the Nile,[3] who prepare it for burial with their own hands—regarding it as something more than the mere body of a man—and themselves lay it in the tomb.

91. The Egyptians are averse to adopt Greek customs, or, in a word, those of any other nation. This feeling is almost universal among them. At Chemmis,[4] however, which is a large

sativus (var. edulis) of Linnæus (see n. [5] on ch. 125); but the liquid here mentioned seems rather to be a powerful cleansing preparation.—[G. W.]

[2] The law which obliged the people to embalm the body of any one found dead, and to bury it in the most expensive manner, was a police, as well as a sanatory, regulation. It was a fine on the people for allowing a violent death, even by accident, to occur in their district; and with the same object of protecting life, they made it a crime to witness an attempt to murder, or even a personal attack of any kind, without endeavouring to prevent it, or at least laying an information and prosecuting the offender. It was not "because the body was something more than human;" but to ensure the proper mode of embalming, by having the money paid at once to the priests, and to prevent any evasion of the expense.—[G. W.]

[3] Herodotus would lead us to infer that every city had its priests of the Nile; but this was probably only when situated near its banks, as we do not find any of these Nile temples.

The city of Nilopolis, where the god Nilus was greatly worshipped, was in middle Egypt, in the province of Heptanomis (afterwards called Arcadia, from the son of Theodosius). At Silsilis, too, Nilus (or Hapi-moou) was greatly honoured. Silsilis is remarkable for its large quarries of sandstone, which was used to build nearly all the temples of Egypt, and for having been the place where the Nile burst the barrier of rock, and lowered its level throughout its course southward of that spot. (See n. on ch. 13, in App. ch. iv.) The Niloa, according to Heliodorus (Æthiop. lib. ix.), was one of the principal festivals of Egypt. It was celebrated about the winter solstice, when the Nile began to rise; and Libanius pretends that the rites were thought of so much importance, that unless performed properly, the river would not rise to the proper height. It was celebrated by men and women in the capital of each nome; which seems to argue, like the statement of Herodotus, that the god Nilus had a temple in every large city; and a wooden statue of the river god was carried in procession through the villages on that occasion.—[G. W.]

[4] Khem, the god of Chemmis, or Khemmo, being supposed to answer to Pan, this city was called Panopolis by the Greeks and Romans. The lion-headed goddess

city in the Thebaïc canton, near Neapolis,[5] there is a square enclosure sacred to Perseus, son of Danaë. Palm trees grow all round the place, which has a gateway of stone of an unusual size, surmounted by two colossal statues,[6] also in stone. Inside

Thriphis shared the honours of the sanctuary with Khem, and is mentioned in a Greek inscription there of the 12th year of Trajan, when the restored or newly-built temple was finished (συνετελέσθη). Khem was the generative principle, or universal nature. His name resembles that of "Egypt," which Plutarch tells us was called Chemi, "from the blackness of the soil," and was the same word applied to the "black" or pupil "of the eye." (See n. [5] on ch. 15.) This is confirmed by the hieroglyph-

ics; Khem, Chemi, or Khemo

signifying "Egypt," and corresponding to the "land of Ham," or Khem. It is singular that this town should have had the old name of the country, and another, Coptos, have had that of *Egypt*, which is Koft, or Gypt, with the "*Ai*" prefixed. "Egypt" is not found in hieroglyphics as the name of the country; nor "Nile" as that of the river. The ancient Chemmis (or Khemi) is retained in the modern *Ekhmim*, the inhabitants of which were famed of old as linen manufacturers and workers in stone. Chemi, "Egypt," was the origin of the word alchemy (the *black* art) and of chemistry. The white bull accompanies Khem, as in the procession at Medeenet Haboo, and this accords with the representation of the Indian god who presides over generation mounted on a white bull. (Sir W. Jones, vol. i. p. 256.)—[G. W.]

[5] The "*neighbouring* Neapolis" is at least ninety miles further up the river, and sixty in a direct line. It has been succeeded by the modern *Keneh*, a name taken from the Greek καινὴ πόλις, the "Newtown" of those days. All the Egyptians had an aversion for the customs of the Greeks, as of all strangers; and it is difficult to understand how the people of Chemmis should have had a different feeling towards them. The stories of the Greek Perseus having visited Egypt on his way to Libya, and of his having instituted games at Chemmis, are fables, as is that in Book vii. ch. 61, of his having given his name to the Persians. But there may have been an Egyptian god, a character of the sun, whom the Greeks supposed to be their hero; and the monster Medusa, whose head Perseus cut off, evidently derived its form from the common Typhonian figure of Egypt. (Cp. Diodorus, iii. 69.) The record of a colony having gone to Greece from Egypt ("Khemi") may have led to the story about the people of Chemmis having a friendly feeling towards the Greeks; as that of Perseus having married Astarté, the daughter of Belus, may point to some intercourse with Syria. "Perseus, according to the Persians, was an Assyrian." There is a curious connexion between Perseus and Pharas (faras), "the horse;"— the Pegasus sprang forth from Medusa when killed by Perseus, as represented on one of the metopes of Selinus; and Neptune, who introduced the horse into Greece, and Medusa, are both Libyan. *Farras* signifies the "mare," and *fares* the "horseman," or the "Persian," in Arabic. In the story of Perseus and Andromeda, as of St. George and the Dragon, the scene is placed in Syria; the former at Jaffa, the latter near Beiroot.—[G. W.]

[6] Statues on the large stone propyla, or towers of the Propylæa, would be an anomaly in Egyptian architecture. The enclosure is the usual *temenos*, surrounded by a wall generally of crude brick, within which the temple stood. Cp. the Welsh "*Llan*." The palm-trees constituted the grove round the temple, which was usually planted with other trees. Clemens therefore calls it ἄλσος, and gives the name ὀργὰς to the temenos. The courts surrounded by columns are his αἰλαί. (See n. on ch. 155, and the woodcut there.) The court planted with trees seems to be the "grove" mentioned in the Bible; *ashreh* (1 Kings xv. 13), *ashireh* (Deut. vii. 5), plural *asheróth* (2 Chron. xxxiii. 3: Judg. iii. 7); a word not related, as some

this precinct is a temple, and in the temple an image of Perseus. The people of Chemmis say that Perseus often appears to them, sometimes within the sacred enclosure, sometimes in the open country : one of the sandals which he has worn is frequently found[7]—two cubits in length, as they affirm—and then all Egypt flourishes greatly.   In the worship of Perseus Greek ceremonies are used ; gymnastic games are celebrated in his honour, comprising every kind of contest, with prizes of cattle, cloaks, and skins.   I made inquiries of the Chemmites why it was that Perseus appeared to them and not elsewhere in Egypt, and how they came to celebrate gymnastic contests[8] unlike the rest of the Egyptians : to which they answered, " that Perseus belonged to their city by descent.   Danaüs and Lynceus were Chemmites before they set sail for Greece, and from them Perseus was descended," they said, tracing the genealogy ; " and he, when he came to Egypt for the purpose" (which the Greeks also assign) "of bringing away from Libya the Gorgon's head, paid them a visit, and acknowledged them for his kinsmen—he had heard the name of their city from his mother before he left Greece— he bade them institute a gymnastic contest in his honour, and that was the reason why they observed the practice."

92. The customs hitherto described are those of the Egyptians who live above the marsh-country.   The inhabitants of the marshes have the same customs as the rest, as well in those matters which have been mentioned above as in respect of marriage, each Egyptian taking to himself, like the Greeks, a single wife ;[9] but for greater cheapness of living the marsh-men prac-

think, to *Ashteroth*, nor to *asher*, "ten" (both which begin with *ain*, not *aleph*). The grove brought out from the house of the Lord (2 Kings xxiii. 6 and 7) appears to be like the emblematic grove, or table surmounted by trees, carried in procession behind the Egyptian god Khem.
     The word "highplace," "bemeh," במה (1 Sam. ix. 12; 2 Kings xxiii. 15) is singularly, though accidentally, like the Greek βῆμα.—[G. W.]
     [7] The modern Egyptians show the footstep of their prophet, in default of his sandal, and an impression in stone—a petrified miracle.   The darvishes at Old Cairo have the shoe of their founder, which might almost vie for size with the sandal of Perseus.—[G. W.]
     [8] See Note in Appendix, CH. vi.
     [9] There is no instance on the monuments of Egypt of a man having more than one wife at a time ; nor does Herodotus say, as has sometimes been supposed, that this was the custom of the other Egyptians who lived above the marsh country. Rather he implies the contrary.   From the superior treatment of women throughout Egypt, from what we see of their social habits, and from the queens being allowed to ascend the throne, it is very improbable that any man had more than one wife.   Diodorus (i. 80) says the priests were only allowed one, while the rest might have any number; but this is at variance with his account of the marriage contract, allowing a woman the control over her husband (i. 27); and, if permitted by law, we may be certain that few took advantage of it, since it was forbidden to the rich aristocracy, and the poor could not afford to enjoy the privilege.— [G. W.]

tise certain peculiar customs, such as these following. They gather the blossoms of a certain water-lily, which grows in great abundance all over the flat country at the time when the Nile rises and floods the regions along its banks—the Egyptians call it the lotus[10]—they gather, I say, the blossoms of this plant and dry them in the sun, after which they extract from the centre of each blossom a substance like the head of a poppy, which they crush and make into bread. The root of the lotus is like-

[10] This Nymphæa Lotus grows in ponds and small channels in the Delta during the inundation, which are dry during the rest of the year; but it is not found in the Nile itself. It is nearly the same as our white water-lily. Its Arabic name is *nufâr*, or *nilófer*, or *beshnín ;* the last being the ancient " pi-sshnn," or pi-shneen, of the hieroglyphics. There are two varieties—the white, and that with a bluish tinge, or the Nymphæa Cœrulea. The Buddhists of Tibet and others call it *nentuphar*. Though the favourite flower of Egypt, there is no evidence of its having been sacred; but the god Nofr-Atmoo bore it on his head; and the name *nufar* is probably related to *nofr*, "good," and connected with his title. It was thought to be a flower of Hades, or Amenti; and on it also Harpocrates is often seated. He was the Egyptian Aurora, or day-spring; not the god of Silence, as the Greeks supposed, but figured with his finger in his mouth, to show one of the habits of childhood, of which he was the emblem. Hence he represented the beginning of day, or the rise and infancy of the sun, which was typically portrayed rising every morning from that flower, or from the water; and this may have given rise to the notion of Proclus that the lotus flower was typical of the sun. Eratosthenes also says this son of Isis was the " god of Day." The Egyptian mode of indicating silence was by plac-

ing " the hand on the mouth." (Cp. Job xxix. 9.) The frog was also an emblem "of man as yet in embryo," as Horapollo and the Egyptian monuments show. The lotus flower was always presented to guests at an Egyptian party ; and garlands were put round their heads and necks;—the "multæque in fronte coronæ." (Cp. Hor. Od. i. 26 and 38; ii. 7; iii. 10; iv. 11. Athenæus, xv. Ovid. Fast. v. Anacreon, ode iv.) It is evident that the lotus was not borrowed from India, as it was the favourite plant of Egypt before the Hindoos had established their religion there.

Besides the seeds of the lotus, poor people doubtless used those of other plants for making bread, like the modern Egyptians, who used to collect the small grains of the *Mesembrianthemum nodiflorum* for this purpose; and Diodorus (i. 80) says the roots and stalks of water-plants were a great article of food among the lower classes of Egyptians.—[G. W.]

wise eatable, and has a pleasant sweet taste : it is round, and about the size of an apple.　There is also another species of the lily in Egypt,[1] which grows, like the lotus, in the river, and resembles the rose.　The fruit springs up side by side with the blossom, on a separate stalk, and has almost exactly the look of the comb made by wasps.　It contains a number of seeds, about the size of an olive-stone, which are good to eat : and these are eaten both green and dried.　The byblus[2] (papyrus),

[1] Perhaps the *Nymphæa Nelumbo*, or *Nelumbium*, which is common in India, but which grows no longer in Egypt.　And the care taken in planting it formerly seems to show it was not indigenous in Egypt.　Crocodiles and the Nelumbium are represented, with the Nile god, on the large statue in the Vatican at Rome, and in many Roman-Egyptian sculptures (see woodcut); but it is remarkable that no rep-

resentation of the Nelumbium occurs in the sculptures of ancient Egypt, though the common Nymphæa Lotus occurs so often.　Pliny calls it Colocasia, as well as Cyanon (xxi. 15).　Of the plants of Egypt, too numerous to mention here, see At. Eg. W. vol. iv. p 52 to 85, and Dr. Pickering's Phys. Hist. of Man, p. 368, &c.— [G. W.]

[2] This is the *Cyperus Papyrus*, which, like the Nelumbium, is no longer a native of Egypt.　It now only grows in the Anapus, near Syracuse, and it is said to have been found in a stream on the coast of Syria, as in Pliny's time (xiii. 11).　Herodotus is wrong in calling it an annual plant.　The use of the pith of its triangular stalk for paper made it a very valuable plant; and the right of growing the best quality, and of selling the papyrus made from it, belonged to the Government.　It was particularly cultivated in the Sebennytic nome, and various qualities of the paper were made.　It is evident that other *Cyperi*, and particularly the *Cyperus dives*, were sometimes confounded with the *Papyrus*, or *Byblus hieraticus* of Strabo; and when we read of its being used for mats, sails, baskets, sandals, and other common purposes, we may conclude that this was an inferior kind mentioned by Strabo; and sometimes a common Cyperus, which grew wild, as many still do, was thus employed in its stead.　It is, however, evident that a variety of the Papyrus was so used; men being represented on the monuments making small boats of it (see n. [1] ch. 96); and we may conclude this was a coarser and smaller kind not adapted for paper.　The best was grown with great care.　Pliny says the papyrus was not found about Alexandria, because it was not *cultivated* there; and the necessity of this is shown by Isaiah's mention of "the paper reeds by the brooks . . . and every thing *sown* by the brooks."　(Is. xix. 7.)　This prophecy is still more remarkable from its de-

which grows year after year in the marshes, they pull up, and, cutting the plant in two, reserve the upper portion for other purposes, but take the lower, which is about a cubit long, and either eat it or else sell it. Such as wish to enjoy the byblus in full perfection bake it first in a closed vessel, heated to a glow. Some of these folk, however, live entirely on fish, which are gutted as soon as caught, and then hung up in the sun: when dry, they are used as food.

93. Gregarious fish are not found in any numbers in the rivers; they frequent the lagunes, whence, at the season of breeding, they proceed in shoals towards the sea. The males lead the way, and drop their milt as they go, while the females, following close behind, eagerly swallow it down. From this they conceive,[3] and when, after passing some time in the sea, they begin to be in spawn, the whole shoal sets off on its return to its ancient haunts. Now, however, it is no longer the males, but the females, who take the lead: they swim in front in a body, and do exactly as the males did before, dropping, little by little, their grains of spawn as they go, while the males in the rear devour the grains, each one of which is a fish.[4] A portion of the spawn escapes and is not swallowed by the males, and hence come the fishes which grow afterwards to maturity. When any of this sort of fish are taken on their passage to the sea, they are found to have the left side of the head scarred and bruised; while if taken on their return, the marks appear on the right. The reason is, that as they swim down the Nile seaward, they keep close to the bank of the river upon their left, and returning again up stream they still cling to the same side hugging it and brushing in against it constantly, to be sure that they miss not their road through the great force of the current. When the Nile begins to rise, the hollows in the land and the marshy spots near the river are flooded before any other

---

claring that the papyrus shall no longer grow in the country, that it "shall wither, and be driven away, and be no more." Theophrastus is correct in saying it grew in shallow water; or in marshes, according to Pliny; and this is represented on the monuments, where it is placed at the side of a stream, or in irrigated lands (see woodcut, No. III. fig. 2, ch. 77, note 3; and the end of ch. v. of the App.). Pliny describes the mode of making the paper (xiii. 11), by cutting thin slices of the pith and laying them in rows, and these being crossed with other slices, the whole was made to adhere by great pressure.—[G. W.]

[3] Aristotle (de Gen. Anim. iii. 5) shows the absurdity of this statement, quoting Herodotus by name, and giving his exact words. C. Müller has strangely seen in the passage a fragment of *Herodorus!* (See Fr. Hist. Gr. ii. p. 32, Fr. 11.)

[4] The male fish deposits the milt *after* the female has deposited the spawn, and thus renders it prolific. The swallowing of the spawn is simply the act of any hungry fish, male or female, who happens to find it. The bruised heads are a fable. —[G. W.]

places by the percolation of the water though the river banks ;[5] and these, almost as soon as they become pools, are found to be full of numbers of little fishes. I think that I understand how it is this comes to pass. On the subsidence of the Nile the year before, though the fish retired with the retreating waters, they had first deposited their spawn in the mud upon the banks ; and so, when at the usual season the water returns, small fry are rapidly engendered out of the spawn of the preceding year. So much concerning the fish.

94. The Egyptians who live in the marshes[6] use for the anointing of their bodies an oil made from the fruit of the sillicyprium,[7] which is known among them by the name of "kiki." To obtain this they plant the sillicyprium (which grows wild in Greece) along the banks of the rivers and by the sides of the lakes, where it produces fruit in great abundance, but with a very disagreeable smell. This fruit is gathered, and then bruised and

[5] Percolation supplies the wells in the alluvial soil, even at the edge of the desert ; but wherever there are any hollows and dry ponds, these are filled, as of old, by canals cut for the purpose of conveying the water of the inundation inland. The water would reach the hollows and ponds by percolation, if no canals were made ; we know, however, that these were much more numerous in ancient than in modern Egypt.

The sudden appearance of the young fish in the ponds was simply owing to these being supplied by the canals from the river, or by its overflowing its banks (which it only did in some few places, long after the canals had been opened), and the fish naturally went in *at the same time* with the water.—[G. W.]

[6] The intimate acquaintance of Herodotus with the inhabitants of the marsh-region is probably owing to the important position occupied by that region in the revolt of Inaros, which the Athenians, whom Herodotus accompanied, went to assist. While Inaros the Libyan attacked the Persians in the field, and with the help of the Athenians made himself master of the greater part of Memphis, Amyrtæus the Egyptian, his co-conspirator, established his authority over the marsh-district, the inhabitants of which were reputed the most warlike of the Egyptians. Here he maintained himself even after the defeat of Inaros and his Athenian allies, who seem to have made their last stand in the immediate vicinity of the marsh-country. (See Thucyd. i. 109–110. Herod. ii. 140; iii. 15, &c.) Herodotus, if he accompanied the expedition, would thus have been brought into close contact with the marsh-men.

[7] This was the *Ricinus communis*, the castor-oil plant, or the Palma-Christi, in Arabic *Kharweh*. It was known by the names of Croton, Trixis, wild or tree-Sesamum, Ricinus, and (according to Diodorus) of σέσελι κύπριον, which was doubtless the same as the σιλλικύπριον of Herodotus. It grew abundantly, according to Pliny, as it still does, in Egypt. The oil was extracted either by pressing the seeds, as at the present day, when required for lamps, or by boiling them and skimming off the oil that floated on the surface, which was thought better for medicinal purposes. Pliny was not singular in his taste when he says (xv. 7)), "Cibis fœdum, lucernis utile." It was the plant that gave shade to Jonah (iv. 6)—Kíkíon, mistranslated "gourd." The Egyptians had many other plants that produced oil, the principal of which were the Carthamus tinctorius (or safflower), the Sesamum orientale (or *Simsim*), flax, lettuce, *Selgam* or coleseed (Brassica oleifera), and the Raphanus oleifer (the *Seemga* of modern Nubia), and even the olive; though this tree seldom produced fruit in Egypt, except about the Lake Mœris, and in the gardens of Alexandria. (Plin. xv. 3 ; Strabo, xvii. p. 1147.)—[G. W.]

pressed, or else boiled down after roasting: the liquid which comes from it is collected and is found to be unctuous, and as well suited as olive-oil for lamps, only that it gives out an unpleasant odour.

95. The contrivances which they use against gnats, wherewith the country swarms, are the following. In the parts of Egypt above the marshes the inhabitants pass the night upon lofty towers,[8] which are of great service, as the gnats are unable to fly to any height on account of the winds. In the marsh-country, where there are no towers, each man possesses a net instead. By day it serves him to catch fish, while at night he spreads it over the bed in which he is to rest, and creeping in, goes to sleep underneath. The gnats, which, if he rolls himself up in his dress or in a piece of muslin, are sure to bite through the covering, do not so much as attempt to pass the net.

96. The vessels used in Egypt for the transport of merchandise are made of the Acantha (Thorn),[9] a tree which in its growth is very like the Cyrenaïc lotus, and from which there exudes a gum. They cut a quantity of planks about two cubits in length from this tree, and then proceed to their ship-building, arranging the planks[1] like bricks, and attaching them by ties to a number .

---

[8] A similar practice is found in the valley of the Indus. Sir Alexander Burnes, in his memoir on that river (Geograph. Journ. vol. iii. p. 113, et seqq.), says:— "The people bordering on this part of the Indus—between *Bukker* and *Mittun Kote*— live during the swell in houses elevated eight or ten feet from the ground, to avoid the damp and insects which it occasions. . . . These bungalows are entered by a ladder" (p. 137).

[The custom of sleeping on the flat roofs of their houses is still common in Egypt; and the small tower rising above the roof is found in the representations of some ancient houses in the sculptures. The common fishing-net would be a very inefficient protection against the gnats of modern Egypt, though a net doubled will often exclude flies.—G. W.] ' ~·   *S. I. on Antiq. 9t. Ed., 3. 3.~*

[9] This was Pliny's "Spina Ægyptia," called by Athenæus "Acantha," and described by him (xv. p. 680) with a round fruit on small stalks. It is the modern *Sont*, or Mimosa (Acacia) Nilotica; groves of which are still found in Egypt, as according to Strabo, Athenæus, and others, of old. Gum-arabic is produced from it, as from other mimosas or acacias of Egypt and Ethiopia, particularly the (*Seäleh* or) Acacia Séál, and the (*Tulh* or) A. gummifera, of the desert. The Acacia Farnesiana (or *Fitneh*), and the A. lebbek (*lebbekh*) grow in the valley of the Nile; the small *Gilgil* (with pods like oak apples and seeds like those of the seäleh), perhaps the A. heterocarpa, is found in the Oasis; the *Hárraz* (A. albida), *Sellem*, and *Sunr*, mostly in the Ababdeh desert, and a few of the two first at Thebes; a small one, called *Ombóod*, is found about Belbays; and a sensitive acacia (the A. asperata?) grows in Ethiopia on the banks of the Nile; perhaps the one mentioned by Pliny (xiii. 10) about Memphis. By "Abylus," Athenæus means Abydus. The Shittim wood of Exodus was doubtless Acacia Séál (*Sáyál*) of the desert. "The Cyrenaïc lotus" here mentioned by Herodotus is probably the *Tulh*, not that of the Lotophagi, and is different from that of Pliny (xiii. 17, 19). See my note on Book iv. ch. 177.—[G. W.]

[1] The boats of the Nile are still built with planks of the *sont*. The planks, ar-

of long stakes or poles till the hull is complete, when they lay the cross-planks on the top from side to side. They give the boats no ribs, but caulk the seams with papyrus on the inside.

ranged as Herodotus states, like bricks, appear to have been tied to several long stakes, fastened to them internally (No. I.) Something of the kind is still done, when they raise an extra bulwark above the gunwale. In the large boats of bur-

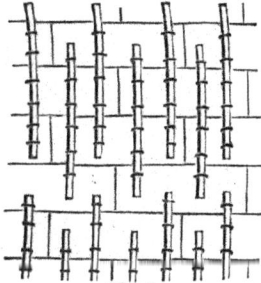

No. I.

then the planks were secured by nails and bolts, which men are represented in the paintings driving into holes, previously drilled for them. There was also a small kind of punt or canoe, made entirely of the papyrus, bound together with bands of the same plant (No. II.)—the " vessels of bulrushes " mentioned in Isaiah xviii. 2 (see Plin. vi. 22; vii. 16; xiii. 11; Theophrast. iv. 9; Plut. de Is. s. 18; Lucan, iv, 186); but these were not capable of carrying large cargoes; and still less would papyrus ships cross the sea to the Isle of Taprobane (Ceylon), as Pliny supposes (vi. 22). This mistake may have originated in some sails and ropes having been made of the papyrus, but these were rarely used, even on the Nile. In one of the paintings at Kom el Ahmar one is represented with a sail, which might be made of the papyrus rind, and which appears to fold up like those of the Chinese (No. III.), and the mast is double, which was usual

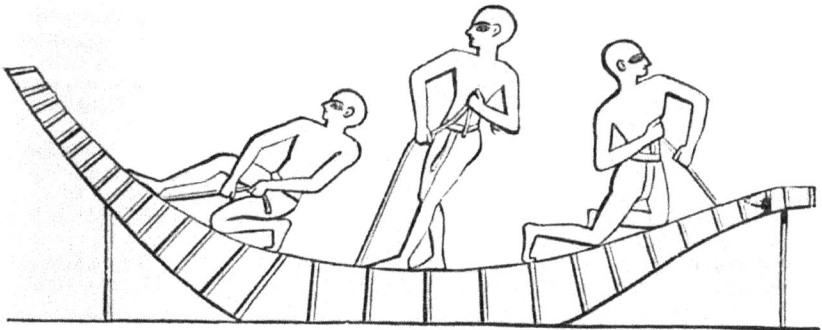

No. II.

in large boats in the time of the 4th and other early dynasties. That cloth sails, occasionally with coloured devices worked or painted on them, should be found on the monuments at least as early as the 18th and 19th dynasties, is not surprising, since the Egyptians were noted at a very remote period for the manufacture of linen and other cloths, and exported sail-cloth to Phœnicia. (Ezek. xxvii. 7.) Hempen (Herodot. vii. 25) and palm ropes are also shown by the monuments to have been adopted for all the tackling of boats. The process of making them is found at Beni Hassan and at Thebes; and ropes made from the strong fibre of the palm-tree are frequently found in the tombs. This last was probably the kind most generally used in Egypt, and is still very common there, as the cocoa-nut ropes are in India.— [G. W.]

Each has a single rudder,[2] which is driven straight through the keel. The mast is a piece of acantha-wood, and the sails are made of papyrus. These boats cannot make way against the current unless there is a brisk breeze; they are, therefore,

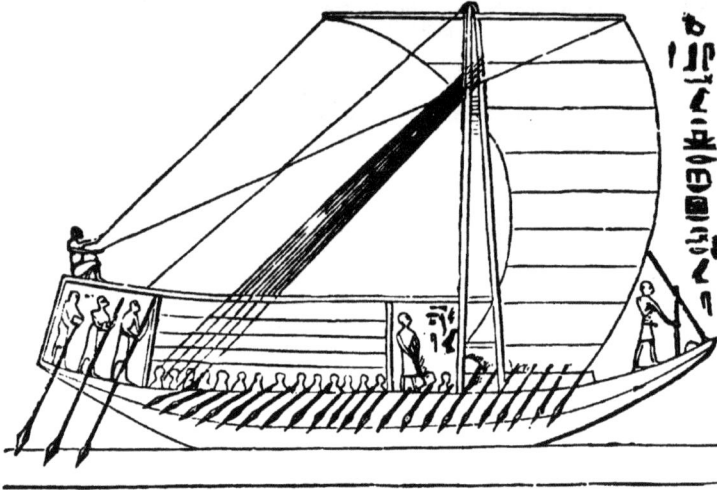

No. IIL.

[2] The large boats had generally a single rudder, which resembled a long oar, and traversed on a beam at the stern, instances of which occur in many countries at the present day; but many had two rudders, one at each side, near the stern, suspended at the gunwale (see cut No. I. in n. [b], ch. 96) or slung from a post, as a pivot, on which it turned. The small-sized boats of burthen were mostly fitted with two rudders; and one instance occurs of three on the same side. On the rudder, as on the bows of the boat, was painted the eye (a custom still retained in the Mediterranean, and in China), but the Egyptians seem to have confined it to the funeral *baris*. The boats always had one mast at the time Herodotus was in Egypt; but it may be doubted if it was of the heavy acantha wood, which could with difficulty have been found sufficiently long and straight for the purpose; and fir-wood was too well known in Egypt not to be employed for masts. Woods of various rare kinds were imported into Egypt from very distant countries as early as the time of the

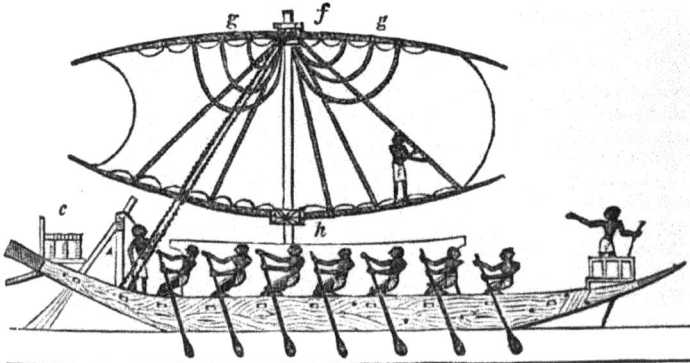

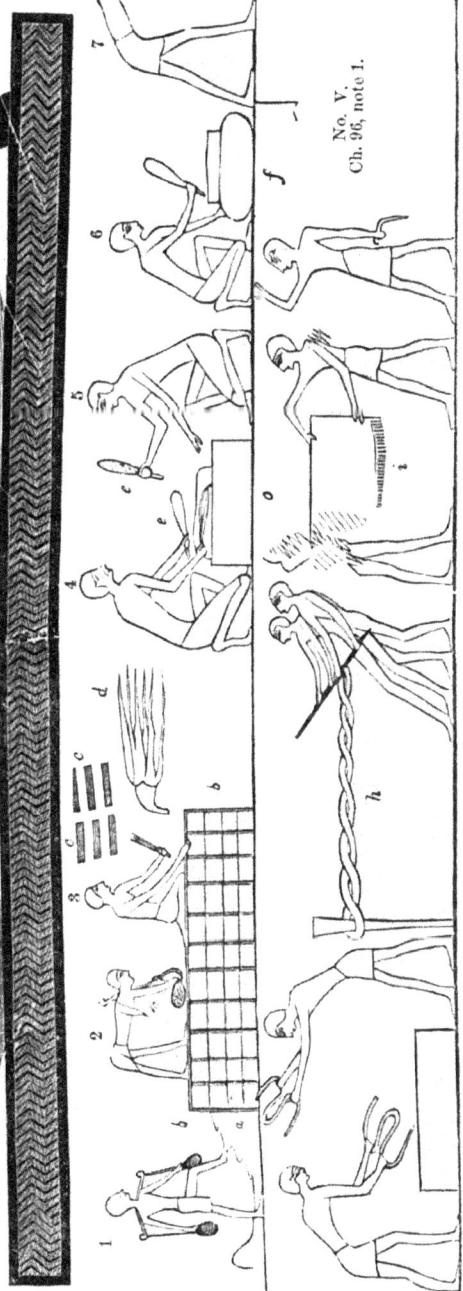

No. IV.
Ch. 96, note 1.

No. V.
Ch. 96, note 1.

towed up-stream from the shore :[3] down-stream they are managed as follows.   There is a raft belonging to each, made of
the wood of the tamarisk, fastened together with a wattling
of reeds ; and also a stone bored through the middle about
two talents in weight.   The raft is fastened to the vessel by a
rope, and allowed to float down the stream in front, while the
stone is attached by another rope astern.[4]   The result is, that
the raft, hurried forward by the current, goes rapidly down the
river, and drags the "baris" (for so they call this sort of boat)[5]

18th dynasty; and deal was then used for all common purposes, as well as the native sycamore. The hulls of boats were even sometimes made of deal; and it would
have been strange if they had not discovered how much more it was adapted for
the masts. In the time of the 4th, 6th, and other early dynasties the mast was
double; but this was given up as cumbrous, and was not used after the accession ot
the 18th, or even of the 12th dynasty.—[G. W.]
   [3] The custom of towing up the stream is the same at present in Egypt; but the
modern boatmen make use of the stone in coming down the stream, to impede the
boat, which is done by suspending it from the stern, while the tamarisk raft before
the head is dispensed with. The contrivance Herodotus mentions was not so much
to increase the speed as to keep the boat straight, by offering a large and buoyant
object to the stream. When the rowers are tired, and boats are allowed to float
down, they turn broadside to the stream ; and it was to prevent this that the stone
and tamarisk raft were applied.—[G. W.]
   [4] A practice almost entirely similar is described by Col. Chesney as prevailing to
this day on the Euphrates. Speaking of the *kufah*, or round river-boat (of which
a representation was given, vol. i. p. 260), he says :—" These boats in descending the
river have a bundle of hurdles attached, which float in advance, and a stone of the
weight of two talents drags along the bottom to guide them." (vol. ii. p. 640.)
   [5] Æschylus had used this word before Herodotus as the proper term for an
Egyptian boat. Cf. Suppl. 815 and 858. He had also poetically extended it to the
whole fleet of Xerxes (Pers. 555). Euripides used it as a *foreign* term. (Cf. Iph.
in Aulid. 297. βαρβάρους βάριδας.) Afterwards it came to be a mere variant for
πλοῖον. (See Blomfield's note on Æschyl. Pers. 559.)
   [I had supposed Baris to mean "Boat of the Sun." (At. Eg. vol. v. p. 413, note.)
Baris has erroneously been derived from Bai, a "palm branch," which had certainly this meaning (and which is even used in John xii. 13, τὰ βαΐα τῶν φοινίκων,
"palm branches"), but *Oua*, or *Ua*, a "boat," is a different word, though a Greek
would write it with a β, or veta. The name Baris is used by Plutarch (de Is. s. 18,

Iamblichus de Myst. s.
6, ch. v.), and others.
There was an Egyptian
boat with a cabin, called
by Strabo thalamegus, or
thalamiferus (xvii. pp.
1134–5), used by the gov-
ernors of provinces for
visiting Upper Egypt ;
and a similar one was em-
ployed in the funeral
processions on the sacred
Lake of the Dead (No. I.).
There was also a small
kind of boat, with a cabin
or awning, in which gen-
tlemen were towed by
their servants upon the

No. I.

after it ; while the stone, which is pulled along in the wake of the vessel, and lies deep in the water, keeps the boat straight.

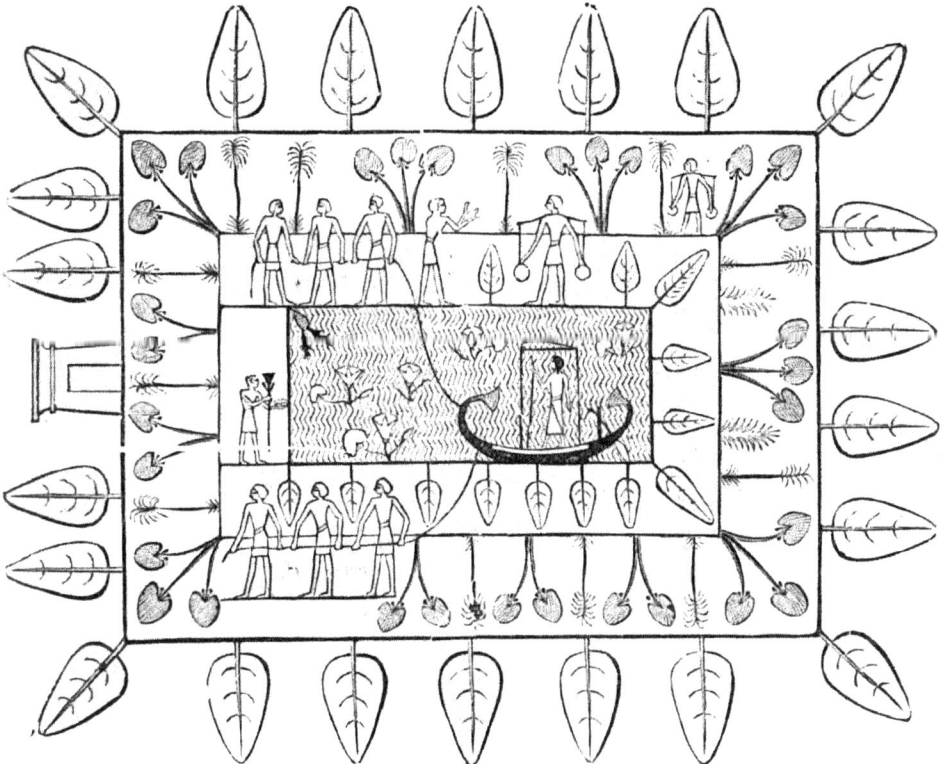

No. II.

lakes in their pleasure grounds (No. II.). But all their large boats had cabins, often of great height and size, and even common market boats were furnished with them, and sufficiently roomy to hold cattle and various goods (No. IV.).—[G. W.]

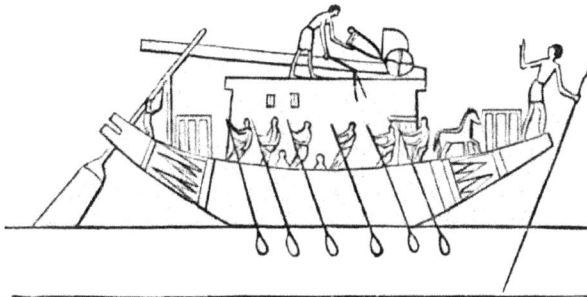

No. III.

There are a vast number of these vessels in Egypt, and some of them are of many thousand talents' burthen.[6]

97. When the Nile overflows, the country is converted into a sea, and nothing appears but the cities, which look like the islands in the Ægean.[7] At this season boats no longer keep the course of the river, but sail right across the plain. On the voyage from Naucratis to Memphis at this season, you pass close

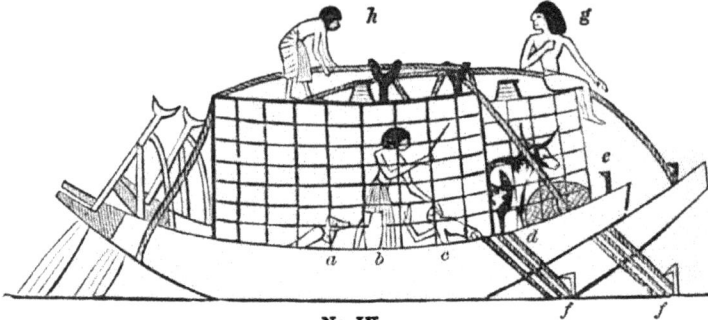

No. IV.

[6] The size of boats on the Nile varies now as of old; and some used for carrying corn, which can only navigate the Nile during the inundation, are rated at from 2000 to 4800 ardebs, or about 10,000 to 24,000 bushels burthen. The ships of war of the ancient Egyptians were not generally of great size, at least in the early times of the 18th and 19th dynasties, when they had a single row of from 20 to 44, or 50 oars, and were similar to the "long ships" and πεντηκόντεροι of the Greeks, and the galleys of the Mediterranean during the middle ages. Some were of much larger dimensions. Diodorus mentions one of cedar, dedicated by Sesostris to the god of Thebes, measuring 280 cubits (from 420 to 478 feet) in length ; and in later times they were remarkable both for length and height ; one built by Ptolemy Philopator having 40 banks of oars, and measuring 280 cubits (about 478 feet) in length, 38 in breadth, and 48 cubits (about 83 feet in height, or 53 from the keel to the top of the poop, which carried 400 sailors, besides 4000 rowers, and near 3000 soldiers. (Plut. Vit. Demet. Athen. Deipn. v. p. 204 ; Pliny, vii. 56, who mentions one of 40, and another of 50 banks of oars.) Athenæus says Philopator built another, used on the Nile, half a stadium (about 300 feet) long, upwards of 30 cubits broad, and nearly 40 high: and "the number belonging to Ptolemy Philadelphus exceeded those of any other king (v. p. 203), he having two of 30 banks, one of 20, four of 14, two of 12, fourteen of 11, thirty of 9, thirty-seven of 7, five of 6, seventeen quinqueremes, and more than twice that number of quadriremes, triremes," &c. He also describes Hiero's ship of 20 banks, sent as a present to Ptolemy (v. pp. 206, 207). It is singular that no Egyptian, Assyrian, Greek, or Roman monument represents a galley of more than one, or at most two tiers of oars, except a Roman painting found in the Orti Farnesiani, which gives one with three, though triremes and quinqueremes were the most generally employed.—[G. W.]

[7] This is perfectly true ; and it still happens in those years when the inundation is very high. Though Savary and others suppose the water no longer rises as in the days of Herodotus, and foretell the gradual decrease of the inundation, it has been satisfactory to see the villages as described by the historian as late as A. D. 1848. Seneca says, "Majorque lætitia gentibus, quo minus terrarum suarum vident."

to the pyramids,* whereas the usual course is by the apex of the Delta, and the city of Cercasôrus.* You can sail also from the maritime town of Canôbus across the flat to Naucratis, passing by the cities of Anthylla[1] and Archandropolis.

98. The former of these cities, which is a place of note, is assigned expressly to the wife of the ruler of Egypt for the time being,[2] to keep her in shoes. Such has been the custom ever

No. I.

(Nat. Quæst. iv. 2.) It is during these high inundations that we see the peasants rescuing their cattle from the flooded lands, as described in the old paintings.— [G. W.]

No. II.

* When the Nile is at that height, boats can go across country, as Herodotus states, without keeping to the stream. As Herodotus says that in sailing to Naucratis from the Canopic mouth you pass by Anthylla and Archandropolis, it is clear that these towns stood to the west of the Canopic branch.—[G. W.]

* See above, note [1], ch. 17.

[1] The neighbourhood of Anthylla was celebrated for its wine, probably from the soil being light. It stood to the west of the Canopic branch, not at Gynæcopolis, as Larcher supposes, but further inland. On the wines of Egypt, see notes on chs. 18, 37, and 60.—[G. W.]

[2] Athenæus (i. p. 33 F) says "to find her in *girdles*" (or dress). Plato uses the same expression when he says "a territory in Persia was set apart for and called the Queen's *girdle*, another for her veil, and others for the rest of her apparel." The

since Egypt fell under the Persian yoke The other city seems to me to have got its name of Archandropolis from Archander the Phthian, son of Achæus,[3] and son-in-law of Danaus. There might certainly have been another Archander ; but, any rate, the name is not Egyptian.[4]

99. Thus far I have spoken of Egypt from my own observation, relating what I myself saw, the ideas that I formed, and the results of my own researches. What follows rests on the accounts given me by the Egyptians, which I shall now repeat, adding thereto some particulars which fell under my own notice.

The priests said that Mèn was the first king of Egypt,[5] and that it was he who raised the dyke which protects Memphis from the inundations of the Nile. Before his time the river flowed entirely along the sandy range of hills which skirts Egypt on the side of Libya. He, however, by banking up the river at the bend which it forms about a hundred furlongs south of Memphis,[6] laid the ancient channel dry, while he dug a new

revenues of the Lake Mœris, which were settled on the queens of Egypt for the purchase of ointments, jewels, and other objects connected with the toilette, amounted, as Diodorus says (i. 52), to a talent every day (see note [9] on ch. 149) ; which, added to those of Anthylla, would be a handsome allowance for "*pin-money*." But a talent could not have been raised daily from that one fishery, and it would more probably include all those in Egypt, if it were necessary to believe that such a sum was allowed to the queens. It was the custom of the Persian kings to assign the revenues of towns as pin-money to the queens (Xenoph. Anab. i. 4, 9 ; Plato, Alcibiad. I. p. 123. C.), and they readily transferred those of the Egyptians to their own ; but Herodotus seems to say it was only after the Persian conquest that the revenues of Anthylla were so applied. See Cic. Verr. iii. 38, and compare Corn. Nep. Vit. Themist. 10.—[G. W.]

[3] It would perhaps be more natural to render this passage, "Archander, the son of Phthius, and grandson of Achæus ;" but as Pausanias makes Archander the son of Achæus and a Phthian, since he brings him from Phthiôtis to the Peloponnese (Achaic. i. § 3), and as the words of Herodotus will bear the meaning given in the text, it seems best to translate him in this way. According to Pausanias (l. s. c.) Archander married Scæa, the daughter of Danaus, and had a son whom he called Metanastes, in memory of his change of country.

[4] This remark of Herodotus is very just, and Archander was doubtless corrupted by the Greeks from some Egyptian name.—[G. W.]

[5] Manetho, Eratosthenes, and other writers, agree with Herodotus that Mèn or Menes (the Mna, or Mænai, of the monuments) was the first Egyptian king ; and this is confirmed by the lists of the Memnonium, or Remeseum, at Thebes, and by the Turin papyrus. The gods were said to have reigned before Menes, which some explain by supposing them the colleges of priests of those deities. Menes is called by Manetho a "Thinite." After his reign the kingdom appears to have been divided, and the remaining kings of the 1st and 2nd dynasties reigned in Upper Egypt, while the 3rd and 4th ruled at Memphis ; as Dr. Hincks and Mr. Stuart Poole have suggested. See Hist. Not. App. ch. viii. and Tn. P. K. W. pp. 29, 31, and 58.—[G. W.]

[6] The dyke of Menes was probably near the modern *Kafr el Iyât*, 14 miles south of *Mitrahenny*, where the Nile takes a considerable bend, and from which point it would

course for the stream half-way between the two lines of hills.
To this day, the elbow which the Nile forms at the point where
it is forced aside into the new channel is guarded with the
greatest care by the Persians, and strengthened every year; for
if the river were to burst out at this place, and pour over the
mound, there would be danger of Memphis being completely
overwhelmed by the flood. Mên, the first king, having thus,
by turning the river, made the tract where it used to run, dry
land, proceeded in the first place to build the city now called
Memphis,[7] which lies in the narrow part of Egypt; after which
he further excavated a lake outside the town, to the north and
west, communicating with the river, which was itself the eastern
boundary. Besides these works[8] he also, the priests said, built
the temple of Vulcan which stands within the city, a vast edifice,
very worthy of mention.

100. Next, they read me from a papyrus, the names of
three hundred and thirty monarchs,[9] who (they said) were his

(if the previous direction of its course continued) run immediately below the Libyan
mountains, and over the site of Memphis. Calculating from the outside of Memphis,
this bend agrees exactly with the hundred stadia, or nearly 11¼ English miles,
Mitrahenny being about the centre of the old city. No traces of these dykes are
now seen.—[G. W.]

[7] The early foundation of Memphis is proved by the names of the kings of the
oldest dynasties being found there; and the precedence of the upper country may
have been owing to Menes being from This, a city of the Thebaid near Abydus, to
which Thebes succeeded as the capital of Upper Egypt. Pthah, or Vulcan, was
the god of Memphis, to whom the great temple was erected by Menes. The lake
was the one on which the funeral ceremonies were performed, and which the dead
crossed on the way to the tombs, as at Thebes; and this, as Diodorus says (i. 92,
96), was the origin of the Acherusian Lake of the Greeks, which he seems to think
was called Acherusia at Memphis. The name of Memphis was Manofre, or Men-
nofr, "the place (or haven) of good men," according to Plutarch (s. 21), or "the
abode of the good one," meaning Osiris; and this has been retained in the Coptic
Mefi, Memfi, Menofre, and Panouf, and in the modern Manouf of the Delta. It was
also called the "land of the pyramid" and "of the white wall," or "building." See
note on B. iii. ch. 13.—[G. W.]

[8] Neither Menes nor his immediate successors have left any monuments. His
name is only mentioned on those of a much later date. The names of the kings of
the 4th dynasty are at the pyramids, and of the 6th mostly in Lower and Middle
Egypt; the 3rd, 4th and 6th being Memphites. Those of the Enentefs (or Nten-
tefs), and others of the 9th Heracleopolite dynasty, are found at Thebes and elsewhere; particularly at Hermonthis. The 9th was contemporary with part of the
5th, the 6th, 11th and 12th; and the monuments of the kings of the two last are
found at Thebes. Osirtasen I., the leader of the 12th, ruled the whole of Egypt,
and it was while this Diospolite dynasty ruled that the Shepherds came into Egypt
and obtained possession of Memphis. During the reign of the 13th they extended
their conquests into the Thebaid, when the Egyptian kings took refuge in Ethiopia,
where their names are found; and it was not till the accession of the 18th that
Amosis, the leader of that dynasty, expelled the Shepherds from Egypt, and
made the whole country into one kingdom. (See Hist. Not. in App. CH. viii.)—
[G. W.]

[9] That is from Menes to Mœris, who had *not* been dead 900 years, when Herodotus was in Egypt about B.C. 455 (supra, ch. 13). This would make the date of

successors upon the throne. In this number of generations
there were eighteen Ethiopian kings,[1] and one queen who was a
native : all the rest were kings and Egyptians. The queen bore
the same name as the Babylonian princess, namely, Nitocris.[2]

Mœris less than 1350 B. C., and might correspond with the era of Menophres B. C.
1322, who seems to be the king he here calls Mœris, the Mendes of Diodorus (i. 61
and 97). The name Mœris was evidently attributed to several kings (see note on
ch. 16). The Mœris here mentioned could not have lived before the founders of
the Pyramids and the first Sesostris ; the 330 kings should therefore include all the
kings of the Egyptian dynasties to the time of Menophres, and this being the great
Egyptian era will account for the reign of that king being mentioned so often as
one from which they dated events. The number of 330 kings, which appears also
to be given by the Turin papyrus, was evidently taken from the sum of all the
reigns to the end of the 18th dynasty, or to the accession of Remeses II. Eusebius
indeed gives little more than 300 kings from Menes to the end of the 18th dynasty,
though his numbers are very uncertain, and his summation comes within four of
Africanus. At all events it is evident that the 330 kings cannot be calculated from
Menes to Amun-m̄-he III. (the Mœris of the Labyrinth, and the Lamaris of Manetho).
As there are only 204 kings from Menes to Lamaris, the 4th king of the 12th dynasty, and far less if contemporaneousness be allowed for, and though Amun-m̄-he III.
was the real Mœris of the Labyrinth, these *calculations of time* were not made to
him, but to a much later reign,—the fixed chronological period of Menophres, who
by mistake has been confounded with Mœris. (See notes on chs. 13 and 124.)
The Sesostris who came "after them" could not be Sesostris of the 12th dynasty,
as he reigned before Amun-m̄-he III. (the real Mœris); and this must refer to the
later (supposed) Sesostris or Sethos, whose exploits, together with those of his son
Remeses II., have been attributed to one king, under the name of Sesostris. See
note [7] on ch. 102.—[G. W.]

[1] The intermarriages of the Egyptian and Ethiopian royal families may be inferred from the sculptures. "The royal son of Kush" (Cush, or Ethiopia) is also
often mentioned, sometimes holding the office of flabellum-bearer on the right of a
Pharaoh ; though this title of "royal son" probably belonged to Egyptian princes
who were viceroys of Ethiopia ; foreign princes being merely styled "chiefs." But
the Ethiopians who sat on the throne of Egypt may have claimed their right either
as descendants of those princes, or through intermarriages with daughters of the
Pharaohs. The eighteen Ethiopian kings were probably the early Sabacos of the
13th dynasty, one of whose names is found on a statue in the Isle of Argo, and another at Semneh, in Ethiopia, who ruled there while the Shepherds were in Egypt.
It was this right of the female members of the royal family to the throne that led so
many foreigners who had married Egyptian princesses to assert their claims, some
of which were successful.—[G. W.]

[2] The fact of Nitocris having been an early
Egyptian queen is proved in her name, Neitakri,
occurring in the Turin Papyrus, and as the last
sovereign of Manetho's 6th dynasty. There was
another Nitocris of the 26th dynasty written
Neitakri, with the usual name of the goddess
Neith. Eratosthenes translates Nitocris "Minerva
Victrix." It is remarkable that Nitocris of the
26th dynasty lived about the same time as the
Babylonian queen. The name is perfectly Egyptian. The queen of Psammetichus III., a daughter of his predecessor, had the same name as the
(supposed) wife of Nebuchadnezzar; and it is not
impossible that the famous Nitocris may have
been another of the same name and family, demanded in marriage by the king of
Babylon on his invasion of Egypt. See note on ch. 177, and historical notice in the
Appendix.—[G. W.]

They said that she succeeded her brother ;[3] he had been king
of Egypt, and was put to death by his subjects, who then
placed her upon the throne.   Bent on avenging his death, she
devised a cunning scheme by which she destroyed a vast number of Egyptians.   She constructed a spacious underground
chamber, and, on pretence of inaugurating it, contrived the following :—Inviting to a banquet those of the Egyptians whom
she knew to have had the chief share in the murder of her brother, she suddenly, as they were feasting, let the river in upon
them, by means of a secret duct of large size.   This, and this
only, did they tell me of her, except that, when she had done
as I have said, she threw herself into an apartment full of ashes,
that she might escape the vengeance whereto she would otherwise have been exposed.

101. The other kings, they said, were personages of no note
or distinction,[4] and left no monuments of any account, with the
exception of the last, who was named Mœris.[5] He left several
memorials of his reign—the northern gateway of the temple of
Vulcan, the lake excavated by his orders, whose dimensions I
shall give presently,[6] and the pyramids built by him in the lake,
the size of which will be stated when I describe the lake itself

[3] This would seem to be Menthesoyphis II., the fifth king of Manetho's 6th dynasty, who reigned only a year.
[4] Their obscurity was owing to Egypt being part of the time under the dominion of the Shepherds, who finding Egypt divided into several kingdoms, or prin-
cipalities, invaded the country, and succeeded at length in dispossessing the Memphite kings of their territories. Their invasion seems to have originated in some
claim to the throne, probably through previous marriages. This would account for
their being sometimes in alliance with the kings of the rest of the country ; for
their conquest having been made "without a battle," as Manetho says ; and for its
not having weakened the power of Egypt, which that of a foreign enemy would have
done. They came into Egypt about the beginning of the 12th dynasty, but did not
extend their dominion beyond Lower Egypt till the end of that dynasty. They then
ruled contemporaneously with the 7th, 8th, 10th, 13th, and 14th dynasties, till at
length the whole of the Egyptian power becoming invested in one native king Ames
(called Amosis and Tethmosis by Manetho and Josephus), who was the first of the
18th dynasty, the Shepherds were driven out of the country, and the Theban or
Diospolite kings ruled the whole of Egypt. It is still uncertain of what race the
Shepherds were. Some are called by Manetho Phœnicians. (See Historical Notice
in the App.) Eusebius (Chron. p. 27) says Phœnix and Cadmus going from Egyptian Thebes reigned over Tyre and Sidon, which might apply to the expulsion of
the "Phœnician Shepherds" from Egypt, and the relationship of Egypt and Phœnicia is pointed out by a pedigree in Apollodorus (Bibl. ii. 1, 4) ; who adds that, ac-

Neptune = Libya.

| Agenor, King of Phœnicia. | | Belus = Anchinoe, daughter of Nilus. | |
| Ægyptus. | | | Danaus. |

cording to Euripides, Cepheus and Phineus were also sons of Belus and Anchinoe.
—[G. W.]
[5] See note [6] on ch. 13, and note [3] on ch. 100.   [6] Infra, ch 149.

wherein they stand. Such were his works: the other kings left absolutely nothing.

102. Passing over these monarchs, therefore, I shall speak of the king who reigned next, whose name was Sesostris.[7] He, the priests said, first of all proceeded in a fleet of ships of war from the Arabian gulf along the shores of the Erythræan sea, subduing the nations as he went, until he finally reached a sea which could not be navigated by reason of the shoals.[8] Hence

[7] The original Sesostris was the first king of the 12th dynasty, Osirtasen, or Sesortasen I., who was the first great Egyptian conqueror; but when Osirei or Sethi (Sethos), and his son Remeses II. surpassed the exploits of their predecessor, the name of Sesostris became confounded with Sethos, and the conquests of that king, and his still greater son, were ascribed to the original Sesostris. This explains the assertion of Dicæarchus that Sesostris was the successor of Horus, mistaken for the god, but really the last king of the 18th dynasty. For those two kings did succeed Horus (the reign of Remeses I., the father of Sethi, being so short as to be over-looked), and their union under one name Sesostris is accounted for by Remeses II. having ruled conjointly with his father during the early and principal part of his reign. Mr. Poole very properly suggests that Manetho's "Σέσως ὁ καὶ Ῥεμέσσης" should be "Σ . . καὶ Ρ . ." This is required also by the length of their reigns (that of the 2nd Remeses being from 63 to 66 years); and by the age of Remeses; and the sculptures at Karnak show that he accompanied his father in his early campaigns. It seems too that in the first Sesostris two kings, Osirtasen I. and III., were comprehended; as several were under the name of Mœris. Strabo (xv. p. 978) makes Sesostris and even Tearkon (Tirhaka) both go into Europe. The great victories over the Scythians could not be attributed to the early Sesostris, though some ruins near old Kossayr (see n. ch. 158) prove that in the reign of Amun-m-he II., who reigned for a short time contemporaneously with Osirtasen I., the Egyptians had already (in his 28th year) extended their conquests out of Egypt, having defeated the people of Pount, with whom the kings of the 18th and 19th dynasties were afterwards at war. The people of Pount were a northern race, being placed at Soleb and elsewhere with the Asiatic tribes. They appear to have lived in Arabia; probably in the Southern, as well as Northern part; and their tribute at Thebes, in the time of Thothmes III., consisted of ivory, ebony, apes, and other southern productions; partly perhaps obtained by commerce. Elephants and brown bears were also brought by the northern race of Rot-ñ-n, or Rot-ñ-no, who come next to Mesopotamia in the list of conquered countries. Osirtasen I. possessed the peninsula of Mount Sinai, already conquered in the age of the 4th dynasty, and extended his arms far into Ethiopia, where his monuments are found; and this may be the expedition alluded to by Diodorus as the beginning of his exploits, unless he had in view the conquests of Sethi and Remeses II., which reached still farther south, continuing those of Amenoph III. in Ethiopia and the Soudán. Some think Osirtasen III. was Sesostris, because he is treated with divine honours on the monuments of Thothmes III.; but this may have been from some rights to the throne being derived from him, or from his having established the frontier on the Ethiopian side at this spot; though it seems also to accord with Manetho's account of Sesostris being considered as "the first (or greatest) after Osiris." But neither the conquests nor the monuments of the third Osirtasen show him to have equalled the first; and if he fixed on Semneh as the frontier of Egypt, it was within the limits of his predecessor's conquests. That it was the frontier defence against the Ethiopians is shown by an inscription there, and by the water-gate in both fortresses being on the Egyptian side of the works. The monuments of Osirtasen I. are found from the Delta into Ethiopia. (See Hist. Notice in App. ch. viii.)—[G. W.]

[8] This is perhaps an indication that the Egyptians in the time of Herodotus were aware of the difficulties of the navigation towards the mouths of the Indus. The waters of this river in the flood-time discolour the sea for three miles, and deposit

he returned to Egypt, where, they told me, he collected a vast armament, and made a progress by land across the continent, conquering every people which fell in his way. In the countries where the natives withstood his attack, and fought gallantly for their liberties, he erected pillars,[9] on which he inscribed his own name and country, and how that he had here reduced the inhabitants to subjection by the might of his arms : where, on the contrary, they submitted readily and without a struggle, he inscribed on the pillars, in addition to these particulars, an emblem to mark that they were a nation of women, that is, unwarlike and effeminate.

103. In this way he traversed the whole continent of Asia, whence he passed on into Europe, and made himself master of Scythia and of Thrace, beyond which countries I do not think that his army extended its march. For thus far the pillars which he erected are still visible,[1] but in the remoter regions they are no longer found. Returning to Egypt from Thrace, he came, on his way, to the banks of the river Phasis. Here I cannot say with any certainty what took place. Either he of his own accord detached a body of troops from his main army and left them to colonise the country, or else a certain number of his soldiers, wearied with their long wanderings, deserted, and established themselves on the banks of this stream.[2]

vast quantities of mud, forming an ever-shifting series of shoals and shallows very dangerous to vessels. (See Geograph. Journ. vol. iii. p. 120.) The voyage of Scylax down the Indus from Caspatyrus to the ocean, and thence along shore to Suez (infra, iv. 44) would have brought the knowledge of these facts to the Egyptians, if they did not possess it before. The conquests of Sesostris in this direction seem to be pure fables.

[9] These memorials, which belong to Remeses II., are found in Syria, on the rocks above the mouth of the Lycus (now *Nahr el Kelb*). Strabo says a stela on the Red Sea records his conquests over the Troglodytæ (b. xvi. p. 1093). The honour paid by Sesostris to those who resisted his arms, and fought courageously, is one of many proofs of the civilised habits of the Egyptians; and these sentiments contrast strongly with the cruelties practised by the Asiatic conquerors, who flayed alive and tortured those who opposed them, as the Turks have done in more recent times. (See Layard's drawings, and the Nineveh sculptures in the British Museum.) The victories of Remeses II. are represented on the monuments of Thebes; and it is worthy of notice that when Germanicus visited them no mention was made of Sesostris, as the great conqueror, but of Rhamses, the real king whose sculptures he was shown by the priests (Tacit. Ann. ii. 60). The mistake is therefore not Egyptian.—[G. W.]

[1] Kiepert (as quoted by M. Texier, Asie Mineure, ii. p. 306) concludes from this, that Herodotus had seen the Thracian stelæ. But Herodotus does not say so, and such a point is certainly not to be assumed without distinct warrant from his words. It is to the last degree improbable that Sesostris or any other Egyptian conqueror ever penetrated through Scythia into Thrace. The Egyptian priests did not even advance such a claim when they conversed with Germanicus (Tacit. Ann. ii. 60). The Caucasus is the furthest limit that can possibly be assigned to the Ramesside conquests, and the Scythians subdued must have dwelt within that boundary.

[2] If it be really true that Sesostris left a colony on the Phasis, his object may be

104. There can be no doubt that the Colchians are an Egyptian race.[3] Before I heard any mention of the fact from others, I had remarked it myself. After the thought had struck me, I made inquiries on the subject both in Colchis and in Egypt, and I found that the Colchians had a more distinct recollection of the Egyptians, than the Egyptians had of them. Still the Egyptians said that they believed the Colchians to be descended from the army of Sesostris. My own conjectures were founded, first, on the fact that they are black skinned and have woolly hair ;[4] which certainly amounts to but little, since several

explained in the same manner as that of the Argonautic expedition; both being to obtain a share of that lucrative trade, which long continued to flow in that direction, and was the object of the Genoese settlements on the Black Sea from the thirteenth to the fifteenth century. The trade from India and Arabia took various channels at different periods. In Solomon's time, the Phœnicians had already brought it through the Red Sea, and his offering them a more convenient road thence through the Valley of Petra, enabled him to enter into an advantageous treaty with, and to obtain a share of the trade from, that jealous merchant people. It was frequently diverted into different channels; as under the Egyptian Caliphs, and at other times. But it also passed at the same periods by an overland route, to which in the earliest ages it was probably confined; and if Colchis was the place to which the former was directed, this would account for the endeavour of the Egyptian conqueror to establish a colony there, and secure possession of that important point. The trade of Colchis may, however, like its golden fleece, simply relate to the gold brought to it from the interior.—[G. W.] Compare Essay x. § 7, sub fin.

[3] According to Agathias (ii. p. 55) the Lazis of the country about Trebizond are the legitimate descendants of the ancient Colchians. The language of this race is Turanian, and bears no particular resemblance to that of ancient Egypt. (See Müller's Languages of the Seat of War, pp. 113–5.)

[4] Herodotus also alludes in ch. 57 to the black colour of the Egyptians; but not only do the paintings pointedly distinguish the Egyptians from the blacks of Africa, and even from the copper-coloured Ethiopians, both of whom are shown to have been of the same hue as their descendants: but the mummies prove that the Egyptians were *neither black nor woolly-haired*, and the formation of the head at once decides that they are of Asiatic, and not of African, origin. It is evident they could not have changed in colour, as Larcher supposes, from the time of Herodotus to that of Ammianus Marcellinus, who after all only says they are "mostly dusky and dark" (xxii. 16), but not "black;" for though the Ethiopians have for more than 3000 years intermarried with black women from the Soudan, who form great part of their *hareems*, they still retain their copper-colour, without becoming negroes; and indeed this may serve as a negative datum for those who speculate on change of colour in the human race. That the Egyptians were dark and their hair coarse, to European eyes, is true; but it is difficult to explain the broad assertion of Herodotus, especially as he uses the superlative of the same word "most woolly," in speaking of the hair of the Ethiopians of the West, or the

other nations are so too ; but further and more especially, on the circumstance that the Colchians, the Egyptians, and the Ethiopians, are the only nations who have practised circumcision from the earliest times.   The Phœnicians and the Syrians of Palestine[5] themselves confess that they learnt the custom of the Egyptians ; and the Syrians who dwell about the rivers Thermôdon and Parthenius,[6] as well as their neighbours the Macronians,[7] say that they have recently adopted it from the

blacks of Africa (B. vii. ch. 70). The hair he had no opportunity of seeing, as the Egyptians shaved their heads and beards; and blackness of colour is, and always was, a very conventional term; for the Hebrews even called the Arabs "black," *kedar*, the "cedrei" of Pliny; though קדר may only mean of a dark, or sunburnt hue (Plin. v. 11: see note on Book iii. ch. 101). The negroes of Africa, in the paintings of Thebes, cannot be mistaken; and the Egyptians did not fail to heighten the caricature of that marked race by giving to their scanty dress of hide the ridiculous addition of a tail. Egypt was called Chemi, "black," from the colour of the rich soil, not from that of the people (see note [6] on ch. 15). Our "blacks and "Indians" are equally indefinite with the blacks or Ethiopians of old. The fact of the Egyptians representing their women yellow and the men red suffices to show a gradation of hue, whereas if a black race the women would have been black also.— [G. W.]

[5] Herodotus apparently alludes to the Jews. Palestin and Philistin are the same name. He may be excused for supposing that the Jews borrowed circumcision from the Egyptians, since they did not practise it as a regular and universal custom until after they left Egypt, which is proved by the new generation in the wilderness not being circumcised till their arrival on the plains of Jericho (Joshua v. 5, 7), though it had been adopted by the Patriarchs and their families from the time of Abraham. Even (in John vii. 22) our Saviour says, "Moses gave you circumcision (not because it is of Moses, but of the fathers);" and any writer of antiquity might naturally suppose that the Jews borrowed from Egypt a rite long established there ; for it was already common at least as early as the 4th dynasty, and probably earlier, long before the birth of Abraham, or b. c. 1996. Herodotus is justified in calling the Jews Syrians, as they were comprehended geographically under that name ; and they were ordered to "speak and say before the Lord God : A *Syrian* ready to perish was my father, and he went down into Egypt, and sojourned there with a few, and became there a nation . . ." (Deut. xxvi. 5). Pausanias (i. 5) speaks of the "Hebrews who are above the Syrians," ὑπὲρ Σύρων. Syria comprehended the whole country from the passes of Cilicia (now *Adana*) to Egypt, though parts of it were separate and distinct provinces. See n. on Book vii. ch. 72.—[G. W.]

[6] The Syrians here intended are undoubtedly the Cappadocians (supra, i. 72, 76), in whose country the river Thermôdon is commonly placed. (Scylax. Peripl. p. 80; Strab. xii. p. 792; Plin. H. N. vi. 3; Ptol. v. 6.) It is curious, however, to find in such a connexion a mention of the Parthenius, which is the modern *Chati Su*, or river of *Bartan*, a stream considerably to the W. of the Halys, ascribed by the geographers either to Paphlagonia (Scylax. p. 81; Strab. xii. p. 787; Plin. H. N. vi. 2) or to Bithynia (Ptol. v. 1). Herodotus elsewhere (i. 72) distinctly states that Cappadocia lay entirely to the E. of the Halys, and that the region to the W. was Paphlagonia. The limits of the countries, no doubt, vary greatly in ancient writers (cp. Xen. Anab. V. v.–vi., with Scyl. Peripl. l. s. c.); but with so distinct an expression of his views on the part of Herodotus in one place, it seems impossible that in another he can have intended to extend Cappadocia *three degrees farther* to the W. I should therefore incline to think, either that the name is corrupted, or that a different Parthenius is meant—the name being one which would be likely to be given by the Greeks to any stream in the country of the Amazons.

[7] The Macronians are mentioned by Xenophon (Anab. IV. viii. § 1) as situated inland at no great distance from Trapezus (*Trebizond*). Strabo (xii. p. 795) agrees

Colchians. Now these are the only nations who use circumcision, and it is plain that they all imitate herein the Egyptians.[6] With respect to the Ethiopians, indeed, I cannot decide whether they learnt the practice of the Egyptians, or the Egyptians of them[9]—it is undoubtedly of very ancient date in Ethiopia—but that the others derived their knowledge of it from Egypt is clear to me, from the fact that the Phœnicians, when they come to have commerce with the Greeks, cease to follow the Egyptians in this custom, and allow their children to remain uncircumcised.

105. I will add a further proof of the identity of the Egyptians and the Colchians. These two nations weave their linen in exactly the same way, and this is a way entirely unknown to the rest of the world ; . they also in their whole mode of life and in their language resemble one another. The Colchian linen[1] is called by the Greeks Sardinian, while that which comes from Egypt is known as Egyptian.

106. The pillars which Sesostris erected in the conquered countries, have for the most part disappeared, but in the part of Syria called Palestine, I myself saw them still standing,[2] with

with this, and informs us that they were afterwards called Sanni. They occur again, iii. 94, and vii. 78.

[6] Circumcision was not practised by the Philistines (1 Sam. xiv. 6; xvii. 26; xviii. 27; 2 Sam. i. 20; 1 Chron. x. 4), nor by the generality of the Phœnicians; for while it is said of Pharaoh (Ezek. xxxi. 18; xxxii. 32) that he should "lie in the *midst* of the uncircumcised," and Edom (xxxii. 29) "with the uncircumcised," Elam, Meshech, Tubal, and the Zidonians (xxxii. 24, 30) "go down uncircumcised." Josephus (Antiq. viii. 20. 3) maintains that no others in Syria were circumcised but the Jews. The Abyssinians still retain the rite, though they are Christians of the Copt Church.—[G. W.]

[9] It has been already shown that the Ethiopians borrowed their religious institutions from Egypt. See notes [9] on ch. 29, and [6] on ch. 30.—[G. W.]

[1] Colchis was famous for its linen. It was taken to Sardis, and being thence imported received the name of Sardian. Σαρδονικὸν "Sardinian," may be a mistake for Σαρδιανόν. The best linen nets for hunting purposes are said by J. Pollux to have come from Egypt, Colchis, Carthage, or Sardis (Onom. 5. 4. 26). It is possible that the linen of Colchis may have had the Egyptian name Sindon, or *shent*, and that this may have been converted into Sardon. (See note [9] on ch. 86.) Sindon was also used sometimes to signify "Indian." (Plin. vi. 20.)—[G. W.]

[2] The stolæ seen by Herodotus in Syria were doubtless those on the rock near Berytus (*Beyroot*), at the mouth of the Lycus (*Nahr el Kelb*), engraved by Remeses II.: one is dedicated to Amun, another to Pthah, and a third to Re, the gods of Thebes, Memphis, and Heliopolis, the three principal cities on his march through Egypt. Almost the only hieroglyphics now traceable are on the jambs of the tablets, which have one of the usual formulas—"the good god," or "Phrah (Pharaoh) the powerful . . . king of kings, Remeses, to whom life has been given like the sun;" but the lines below the figure of the king, who slays the foreign chiefs before the god, and which should contain the mention of his victories, are too much defaced to be legible. The doubts of M. de Saulcy respecting the genuineness of these stelæ are extraordinary in these days.

Close to them are stelæ of an Assyrian king, who is now found to be Sennacherib, who built the great palace at Koyunjik.

Mr. Layard (Nineveh and Babylon, p. 355, note) mentions colossal figures of an Egyptian sphinx and two priests carved on a rock above the city of Antioch.—[G. W.]

the writing above mentioned, and the emblem distinctly visible.[3]
In Ionia also, there are two representations of this prince engraved upon rocks,[4] one on the road from Ephesus to Phocæa,

[3] According to the record seen by Herodotus, Sesostris considered the people
of Palestine a cowardly race. To the power of Egypt they must have been insigni-
ficant; and though the *numbers* of the Philistines made them troublesome to the
Israelites, they are not represented as the same *valiant* people as the Anakim (Num.
xiii. 28, 33; Deut. ii. 21; ix. 2), who being far less numerous were conquered by
Joshua (Josh. xi. 21, 23), a remnant only remaining in Gaza, Gath, and Ashdod
(Azotus). In Amos (ix. 7) the Philistines are said to have come from Caphtor.
(See Hist. Not. App. ch. viii. § 17.)

Josephus (Antiq. viii. 10. 2) applies this bad compliment to the Jews, and supposes it was recorded by Shishak, to whom Rehoboam gave up Jerusalem without
resistance. He thinks Herodotus has applied his actions to Sesostris.—[G. W.]

[4] A figure, which seems certainly to be one of the two here mentioned by Her-

Rock-Sculpture at Ninfi, near Smyrna.

the other between Sardis and Smyrna. In each case the figure is that of a man, four cubits and a span high, with a spear in his right hand and a bow in his left,[5] the rest of his costume

odotus, has been discovered at *Ninfi*, on what appears to have been the ancient road from Sardis to Smyrna. It was first noticed, I believe, by the Rev. J. C. Renouard. The height, as measured by M. Texier (Asie Mineure, ii. p. 304), is two French mètres and a half, which corresponds within a small fraction with the measurement of our author. Its general character is decidedly Egyptian, strongly recalling the Egyptian sculptures at the mouth of the Nahr el Kelb; yet there are points of detail, as the shape of the shoes, in which it is peculiar, and non-Egyptian. No figure has been found in Egypt with shoes of which the points have a tendency to turn up. Again the *clashr* or "calasiris" (supra, ch. 81, note [9]) of an Egyptian is never striped or striated, in the way that that of the *Ninfi* sculpture is. The hat or helmet too, though perhaps it bears a greater resemblance to the ordinary Egyptian head-dress of the kings and gods than to any other known form, yet wants a leading feature of that head-dress—the curious curve projecting in front. (See ch. 35, note [4].) Thus the supposed figure of Sesostris clearly differs from all purely Egyptian types. It bears a bow and a spear exactly as described, only that the former is in the right and the latter in the left hand; but this difference may only indicate a defect of memory in our author. There are not now any traces of hieroglyphics upon the breast of the figure, but as this portion of the rock is much weather-worn, they may have disappeared in the lapse of ages. Some faintly-marked characters, including a figure of a bird, intervene between the spear-head and the face, in which M. Ampère is said to trace some of the titles of Remeses the Great. Rosellini and Kiepert have questioned whether the sculpture is really Egyptian, but there seems to be at any rate no doubt that it is one of the figures seen by Herodotus, and believed by him to represent Sesostris. (See the remarks of M. Texier, Asie Mineure, vol. ii. pp. 305–6.)

[5] Herodotus evidently supposes that one of these is an Egyptian, the other an Ethiopian weapon. Both were used by the two people, but the bow was considered

particularly Ethiopian, as well as Libyan, and "Tosh,"

the Coptic Ethaush, was a name given to Northern Ethiopia. The land of the nine

bows was a term applied to Libya,

which was also called Phit, the "bow,"

Naphtuhim, the son of Mizraim, in Gen. x. 13, is the same as the Egyptian plural Niphaiat, "the bows."

Phut and Lubim are placed together with Ethiopia and Egypt as the helpers of "populous No," Thebes, in Nahum (iii. 9); and in Ezekiel (xxx. 5)," "Ethiopia (Kûsh), and Libya (Phût), and Lydia (Lûd), and all the (Arab) mingled people, and Chub (Kûb), and the men of the land which is in league," are to fall with Egypt and Ethiopia. Lûd is not Lydia in Asia Minor. Phut, or Phit, may have been the Libyan side of the Nile throughout Egypt and Nubia. It is remarkable that the Ethiopian bow is unstrung, that of Libya strung. (See note on Book iii. ch. 21.) The expression in hieroglyphics "Phut Ethosh" appears to be the western bank of Ethiopia. The bow *carried* by the Ethiopians in battle is like that of Egypt; that in the *name* of Northern Ethiopia ("*Tosh*") resembles the bow now used in India. This last is even seen in the hand of one of Sheshonk's (Shishak's) prisoners. —[G. W.].

being likewise half Egyptian, half Ethiopian. There is an inscription across the breast from shoulder to shoulder,[6] in the sacred character of Egypt, which says, "With my own shoulders[7] I conquered this land." The conqueror does not tell who he is, or whence he comes, though elsewhere Sesostris records these facts. Hence it has been imagined by some of those who have seen these forms, that they are figures of Memnon ;[8] but such as think so err very widely from the truth.

107. This Sesostris, the priests went on to say, upon his return home accompanied by vast multitudes of the people whose countries he had subdued,[9] was received by his broth-

---

[6] This is not an Egyptian custom, though Assyrian figures are found with arrowheaded inscriptions engraved across them, and over the drapery as well as the body; and the Assyrian figures close to those of Remeses at the *Nahr el Kelb* may possibly have led to this mistake.—[G. W.]

[7] The idea of strength was often conveyed by this expression, instead of "by the force of my arm" (cp. "os *humerosque* deo similis").—[G. W.]

[8] Herodotus shows his discrimination in rejecting the notion of his being Memnon, which had already become prevalent among the Greeks, who saw Memnon everywhere in Egypt merely because he was mentioned in Homer. A similar error is made at the present day in expecting to find a reference to Jewish history on the monuments, though it is obviously not the custom of any people to record their misfortunes to posterity in painting or sculpture. (See note [1] on ch. 136, and Appendix, CH. v.) The Egyptians seem to have taken advantage of Greek credulity in persuading visitors that the most remarkable statue, tomb, and temple at Thebes, or Abydus, were made by the prince they usually inquired about, and with whose history they fancied themselves acquainted; though Memnon, if he ever existed, was not after all an Egyptian, nor even from any part of the valley of the Nile. According to Diodorus (ii. 22) he was sent by Teutamus, the 21st king of Assyria after Semiramis, with a force of 10,000 Ethiopians and the same number of Susans, and 200 chariots, to assist Priam (the brother of his father Tithonus), when being killed in an ambuscade by the Thessalians, his body was recovered and *burnt* by the Ethiopians. These were Ethiopians of Asia, and those of Africa did not burn their dead. Herodotus also speaks of the palace of Memnon, and calls Susa a Memnonian city (v. 53, 54, and vii. 151). Strabo and Pausanias agree with Herodotus and Diodorus in making Susa the city of Memnon. It is not impossible that the eastern Cushites, or Ethiopians, were the original colonisers of the African Cush, from the Arabian gulf, and that the Ethiopians mentioned by Eusebius from Manetho, "who migrated from the river Indus and settled near to Egypt," at the close of the 18th dynasty, were of the same race. (See Historical Notice in the Appendix.) The resemblance of the name of Miamun may have confirmed the mistake respecting the stelæ of Amunmai- (or Mi-amun) Remeses, on the Lycus, as well as the temples built by him at Thebes and Abydus, attributed to Memnon ; but the vocal statue at Thebes was of Amunoph III. The supposed tomb of Memnon at Thebes was of Remeses V., who had also the title of Mi-amun. Strabo (xvii. p. 1152) says some think Memnon the same as Ismandes, the reputed builder of the Labyrinth, according to Diodorus (i. 61), who calls him Mendes, or Marrus. This name Ismandes seems to be retained in that of the modern village of Isment, near the entrance to the Fyôom, called *Isment s' Gebel* ("of the hill "), to distinguish it from *Isment el Bahr* ("of the river"), which is on the Nile near Benisoof. Ismandes and Osymandyas are the same name. One of the sons of Remeses II. was called Semandoo, or Se-munt. The mistake of Memnon cannot well have arisen from the word *mennu*, "buildings" or "palaces," as it would be applied to all others, and not to an excavated tomb.—[G. W.]

[9] It was the custom of the Egyptian kings to bring their prisoners to Egypt, and

er,[1] whom he had made viceroy of Egypt on his departure, at
Daphnæ near Pelusium, and invited by him to a banquet, which
he attended, together with his sons. Then his brother piled a
quantity of wood all round the building, and having so done set
it alight. Sesostris, discovering what had happened, took counsel instantly with his wife, who had accompanied him to the
feast, and was advised by her to lay two of their six sons upon
the fire, and so make a bridge across the flames, whereby the
rest might effect their escape. Sesostris did as she recommended, and thus while two of his sons were burnt to death, he
himself and his other children were saved.

108. The king then returned to his own land and took vengeance upon his brother, after which he proceeded to make use
of the multitudes whom he had brought with him from the
conquered countries, partly to drag the huge masses of stone
which were moved in the course of his reign to the temple of
Vulcan—partly, to dig the numerous canals with which the
whole of Egypt is intersected. By these forced labours the

to employ them in public works, as the sculptures abundantly prove, and as Herodotus states (ch. 108). The Jews were employed in the same way: for though at
first they obtained grazing-lands for their cattle in the land of Goshen (Gen. xlvi.
34), or the Bucolia, where they tended the king's herds (Gen. xlvii. 6, 27), they were
afterwards forced to perform various services, like ordinary prisoners of war; when
their lives were made " bitter with hard bondage, in mortar, and in brick, and in all
manner of service in the field" (Exod. i. 14), in building treasure-cities (i. 11), in
brickmaking (v. 8), and pottery (Ps. lxxxi. 6); in canals, and embankments, and
public buildings; though these did not include pyramids, as Josephus supposes.
To hew and drag stones from the quarries was also a common employment of captives; inscriptions there in late times state that the writers had furnished so many
stones for a certain temple, as "We have dragged 100 stones for the work of Isis
in Philæ." And the great statue at El Bersheh is represented dragged by numerous
companies of foreigners (as well as of Egyptians), in the early time of the first
Osirtasen, in the 21st century before our æra.—[G. W.]

[1] This at once shows that the conqueror here mentioned, is not the early Sesostris of the 12th dynasty, but the great king of the 19th dynasty; since Manetho
gives the same account of his brother having been left as his viceroy in Egypt, and
having rebelled against his authority. Manetho calls his name Armaïs, and the
king Sethosis, or Rameses (which are the father's and son's names assigned to one
person), and places him in the 18th dynasty, though the names of Sethos and Ram-
pses are repeated again at the beginning of the 19th. He also says that Armaïs was
called by the Greeks Danaus, that he fled to Greece and reigned at Argos, and that
Rameses was called Ægyptus. The monuments have enabled us to correct the
error respecting Sethos and Rameses, who are shown to be two different kings,
father and son, and the 19th dynasty began with a different family, Rameses I.,
Sethos (Sethi, or Osirei I.), and Rameses II.; Horus being the last of the 18th.
The flight of Armaïs was perhaps confounded with that of the "Stranger Kings,"
who ruled about the close of the 18th dynasty. Their expulsion appears to agree
with the story of Danaus leading a colony to Argos, which Armaïs, flying from his
brother, could not have done; and one of the last of their kings was Toônh. The
account given by Diodorus (i. 57) of Armaïs endeavouring to set fire to his brother's
tent at night, is more probable than that of the two children related by Herodotus.
See note 4 on ch. 101, and note 4 on ch. 182.—[G. W.]

entire face of the country was changed ; for whereas Egypt had formerly been a region suited both for horses and carriages, henceforth it became entirely unfit for either.[2]   Though a flat country throughout its whole extent, it is now unfit for either horse or carriage, being cut up by the canals, which are extremely numerous and run in all directions.   The king's object was to supply Nile water to the inhabitants of the towns situated in the mid-country, and not lying upon the river ; for pre-

---

[2] It is very possible that the number of canals may have increased in the time of Rameses II. : and this, like the rest of Herodotus' account, shows that this king is the Sesostris whose actions he is describing.   And here again, in his mention of the increased number of canals, Herodotus evidently reported the deeds of another king, Amun-m-he III. (Mœris of the Lake), who is also considered a claimant to the name of Sesostris ; though the use of chariots will not accord with his reign.   For it is evident that in the time of the Osirtasens, horses and chariots were not known in Egypt ; and there is no notice of a horse or chariot, or any monument, before or during the reigns of those kings, though the customs of Egypt are so fully portrayed in the paintings at Beni Hassan, and sufficiently so in the tombs at the pyramids for this omission not to have been accidental.   The first horses and chariots are represented at Eileithyias of the time of Ames or Amosis, about 1510 B.C.   Horses are therefore supposed not to have been known in Egypt before the 18th dynasty (see Dr. Pickering's 'Races of Man,' p. 373); unless indeed the Shepherd-kings introduced them.   They doubtless came from Asia into Egypt ; and though the Egyptians called a horse *Hthor* (*Htar*), they used for the "mare" the Semitic name *sûs*, and even *susim* (with the female sign "t") for "mares," the same as the plural of the Hebrew word סוס *sûs*.   The Jews applied it to a chariot-horse, the horse for riding being *Pharas* (*Faras*), פָּרָשׁ (1 Kings v. 6 ; Ezek. xxvii. 14): and the same as the modern Arabic word for "mare."   *Fáres* is "horseman" in Arabic and in Hebrew (2 Sam. i. 6).

The chariot again (called *Djolte* in hieroglyphics—the Coptic *asholte*) is "*Merkebat*" in Hieratic, a Semitic word agreeing with the *Merkebeth* מֶרְכָּבָה of Hebrew, which, like *Rekeb*, רָכַב, is derived from the Semitic *rekeb*, *erkeb* (to) "ride," either on a horse, a camel, or a car.   *Merkeb* in Arabic answers to "*monture*" in French, and is applied to a boat as well as a camel ; not that a camel, as often supposed, is called the "ship of the desert," but the name is rather transferred to ships from camels, which were known to Arabs long before ships.   Horses seem to have come originally from Asia, whence they were introduced into Greece ; but the Greeks *may* have obtained them first from Libya.   Mesopotamia sent horses as part of the tribute to Thothmes III. of the 18th dynasty, as well as the neighbouring people of Upper and Lower Rot-n̄-n, or Rot-n̄-no ; the Babylonians bred them for the Persians ; and in Solomon's time Egypt was noted for its horses (2 Chron. i. 16, 37 ; 1 Kings x. 29).   The Arabs in the army of Xerxes rode on camels ; but they were not the people of Arabia, and it is uncertain whether the famous Arab breed of horses was introduced, or was indigenous in that country.   The *Shaso* mentioned on the monuments are either an Arab race in N. Arabia, or *Southern* Syria, and they are placed in the lists of captives with the Pount, who appear to be a people of Arabia (see note [7] on ch. 102).   The Shaso are probably the Shos, the name given to the Shepherds, or "(Hyk)sos," "(reges) pastores ;" and as Rameses II. fell in with them on his expedition against "Atesh," or "Kadesh," they should be a people who lived in, or near, Palestine.   It is singular that the title Hyk "ruler" (which was also given to the Pharaohs), should from the crook apply doubly to the Shepherd-kings.   The horse was known in India at least as early as 1200 B.C., being mentioned in the Vedas, with chariots, but not for riding.—[G. W.]

viously they had been obliged, after the subsidence of the floods, to drink a brackish water which they obtained from the wells.[3]

109. Sesostris also, they declared, made a division of the soil of Egypt among the inhabitants, assigning square plots of ground of equal size to all, and obtaining his chief revenue from the rent which the holders were required to pay him every year. If the river carried away any portion of a man's lot, he appeared before the king, and related what had happened ; upon which the king sent persons to examine, and determine by measurement the exact extent of the loss ; and thenceforth only such a rent was demanded of him as was proportionate to the reduced size of his land. From this practice, I think, geometry first came to be known in Egypt,[4] whence it passed into Greece. The sun-dial, however, and the gnomon,[5] with the division of the day into twelve parts, were received by the Greeks from the Babylonians.

110. Sesostris was king not only of Egypt, but also of Ethiopia. He was the only Egyptian monarch who ever ruled over the latter country.[6] He left, as memorials of his reign, the

---

[3] The water filtrates through the alluvial soil to the inland wells, where it is sweet, though sometimes hard ; and a stone reservoir of perfectly sweet water has lately been found, belonging to the temple of Medeenet Haboo, at Thebes ; but in the desert beyond the alluvial deposit it is brackish, and often salt. See above, n. on ch. 93.—[G. W.]

[4] See Ap. CH. vii. and n. on ch. 51.

[5] The gnomon was of course part of every dial. Herodotus, however, is correct in making a difference between the γνώμων and the πόλος. The former, called also στοιχεῖον, was a perpendicular rod, whose shadow indicated noon, and also by its length a particular part of the day, being longest at sunrise and sunset. The πόλος was an improvement, and a real dial, on which the division of the day was set off by lines, and indicated by the shadow of its gnomon. See Appendix, CH. vii.—[G. W.]

[6] This cannot apply to any one Egyptian king in particular, as many ruled in Ethiopia ; and though Osirtasen I. (the original Sesostris) may have been the *first*, the monuments show that his successors of the 12th dynasty, and others, ruled and erected buildings in Ethiopia. Nor is it certain that Rameses II. was the first who obtained possession of Napata ; and though the lions of Amunoph III., brought by the Duke of Northumberland from Gebel Berkel, were taken from Soleb (the ancient name of this place being in the hieroglyphics upon them), it does not prove that the Egyptian arms extended no farther than Soleb in Amunoph's time ; and the name of a Thothmes was found at Gebel Berkel, by the Duke of Northumberland and Colonel Felix. That of Osirtasen I., on the substructions of the Great Temple, may have been a later addition, not being in the sculptures. (See n. [7] on ch. 102.) Pliny says (vi. 29), "Ægyptiorum bellis attrita est Æthiopia ; vicissim imperitando, serviendoque. Clara et potens etiam usque ad Trojana bella, Memnone regnante, et Syriæ imperitasse (eam) . . . patet." He has made a mistake about Memnon ; but the conquests are either those of Tirhaka, or of the Kings of Thebes (sometimes improperly included in Ethiopia).

The Egyptians evidently overran all Ethiopia, and part of the interior of Africa, in the time of the 18th and 19th dynasties, and had long before, under the Osirtasens and Amun-m-hes, conquered Negro tribes. Thothmes I. recorded other victories over Negroes, on a rock opposite Tombos, as Amunoph III. did at Soleb, over many

stone statues which stand in front of the temple of Vulcan, two of which, representing himself and his wife, are thirty cubits in height,[7] while the remaining four, which represent his sons, are twenty cubits. These are the statues, in front of which the priest of Vulcan, very many years afterwards, would not allow Darius the Persian[8] to place a statue of himself; " because," he said, " Darius had not equalled the achievements of Sesostris the Egyptian : for while Sesostris had subdued to the full as many nations as ever Darius had brought under, he had likewise conquered the Scythians,[9] whom Darius had failed to

southern districts of Africa; many of which are called "*Dar*," as at the present day. Rameses II., who built part of the Great Temple at Gebel Berkel, extended his arms further than Amunoph; and the first Osirtasen overran a great portion of Ethiopia more than six centuries before. Even Osirtasen III. obtained victories over Negroes which are recorded at Semneh; though he appears to be the first who made that place the frontier; and to this the beginning of actual *rule* in Ethiopia may have been applied; for he also has a claim to the name of Sesostris. The Ptolemies continued to have some possessions on the eastern coast of Abyssinia; and the kings of Ethiopia were in alliance with, or perhaps tributary to, them; but the nominal frontier was generally confined to Nubia. The Romans merely extended their arms south, to prevent the depredations of the half-savage Ethiopians; for in the time of Augustus, Petronius only ravaged the country to Napata, and return ed without making any permanent conquests. A fort, however, in the Dar Shaikeëh, of Roman construction, shows that later emperors extended their rule beyond the second cataract, and kept garrisons there. Tacitus says not in his time. —[G. W.]

[7] As the cubits found in Egypt are 1 ft. 8¼ in., if Herodotus reckoned by them he would make the statues more than 51 ft. high. A Colossus is lying at Memphis of Rameses II., which is supposed to be one of the two large ones here mentioned, and its height, when entire, would be about 42 ft. 8 in., without the plinth, or pedestal. Of the other four, 20 cubits (above 34 ft.) high, one seems to have been found by Hekekyan Bey; which if entire would be about 34½ feet. All these point to the site of the temple of Pthah.—[G. W.]

[8] The name of Darius occurs in the sculptures, and great part of the principal Temple of El Khargeh, in the Great Oasis, was built by him, his name being the oldest there.

He seems to have treated the Egyptians with far more uniform lenity than the other Persian kings; and though the names of Cambyses, Xerxes, and Artaxerxes, occur on stelæ, statues, or vases, they are mostly records of persons who lived during their reigns, and are not on any monuments erected by them in Egypt. This accords with his indulgent treatment of the priests mentioned by Herodotus; and the remark of Diodorus, that "he obtained while living the appellation of Divus," is justified by his having received on the monuments the same honours as the old kings. The reply of Darius to the Egyptian priest is said by Diodorus (i. 58) to have been, "that he hoped not to be inferior to Sesostris, if he lived as long." But his mild government did not prevent the Egyptians from rebelling against him; and their impatience of Persian rule had before been the reason of Cambyses' forsaking the lenient line of conduct he first adopted when he conquered the country. See below, Book iii. ch. 15.—[G. W.]

[9] (See Justin. ii. c. 3.) The conquest of the Scythians by Sesostris is a question still undecided. The monuments represent a people defeated by Rameses whose name Sheta (or Khita) bears a strong resemblance to the Scythians, but it is evident they lived in the vicinity of Mesopotamia, and not in the distant Scythia. It is not impossible that they were the same race, established there. (See note [6] on ch. 112.) A further examination of the monuments shows that I was wrong in the extent I

'master. It was not fair, therefore, that he should erect his statue in front of the offerings of a king, whose deeds he had been unable to surpass." Darius, they say, pardoned the freedom of this speech.

111. On the death of Sesostris, his son Pheron,[1] the priests said, mounted the throne. He undertook no warlike expeditions; being struck with blindness, owing to the following circumstance. The river had swollen to the unusual height of eighteen cubits, and had overflowed all the fields, when, a sudden wind arising, the water rose in great waves. Then the king, in a spirit of impious violence, seized his spear, and hurled it into the strong eddies of the stream. Instantly he was smitten with disease of the eyes, from which after a little while he became blind,[2] continuing without the power of vision for ten years. At last, in the eleventh year, an oracular announcement reached him from the city of Buto, to the effect, that "the time of his punishment had run out, and he should recover his sight by washing his eyes with urine. He must find a woman who had been faithful to her husband, and had never preferred to him another man." The king, therefore, first of all made trial of

have given (At. Eg. W. vol. i. p. 83) to the conquests of the Egyptians; but Diodorus extends their conquests still further, and speaks of the Bactrians revolting from the rule of Osymandyas. (Diod. i. 47.) Strabo (xv. p. 978) says that "Sesostris and Tearcon (Tirhaka) actually went into Europe."—[G. W.]

[1] This name does not agree with the son or successor, either of Osirtasen I., of Sethos, or of Remeses. Diodorus (i. 59) calls him Sesoosis II., Pliny Nuncoreus. Pheron has been supposed to be merely a corruption of Phouro, "the king" (whence uræus, see note [2] on ch. 74), or of Pharaoh, properly Phrah, i. e. "the Sun," one of the royal titles. Some suppose Pheron to be Phiaro, "the river," retained in the modern Arabic, Bahr, "the ocean," (comp. 'Ωκεανός, an ancient name of the Nile); and Phiaro is connected with the King Phuron, or Nilus, and with the Ægyptus of Manetho, "the Nile being formerly called Ægyptus." (See n. [7], [8], on ch. 19.)

If the Phuron of Eratosthenes was really one of the early kings of the 13th dynasty, it is possible that the sudden breaking down of the barrier of the Nile at Silsilis, and the momentary submersion of the lands by the sudden flow of the water into Egypt, may be the destructive inundation mentioned by Herodotus.—[G. W.]

Lepsius regards this king as Amenophis or Menephthah III., the Pharaoh of the Exodus. (Joseph. c. Ap. b. i. sub fin.) He finds his name in the Nuncoreus or Nencoreus of Pliny (H. N. xxxvi. 11), which he thinks that writer misread in his authority, mistaking ΜΕΝΕΦΘΗϹ for ΝΕΝϹºΡΕΤϹ. He supposes Herodotus to have received his account of the king from a Semitic informant, who called him Phero, because he was the great Pharaoh of the Jews. (Chronologie der Ægypter, p. 289.) In this case the impiety and blindness of the monarch become traits of peculiar significance.

[2] This is one of the Greek ciceroni tales. A Greek poet might make a graceful story of Achilles and a Trojan stream, but the prosaic Egyptians would never represent one of their kings performing a feat so opposed to his habits, and to all their religious notions. The story about the woman is equally un-Egyptian; but the mention of a remedy which is still used in Egypt for ophthalmia, shows that some simple fact has been converted into a wholly improbable tale.—[G. W.]

his wife, but to no purpose—he continued as blind as before. So he made the experiment with other women, until at length he succeeded, and in this way recovered his sight. Hereupon he assembled all the women, except the last, and bringing them to the city which now bears the name of Erythrabôlus (Red-soil), he there burnt them all, together with the place itself. The woman to whom he owed his cure, he married, and after his recovery was complete, he presented offerings to all the temples of any note, among which the best worthy of mention are the two stone obelisks which he gave to the temple of the Sun.[3] These are magnificent works; each is made of a single stone, eight cubits broad, and a hundred cubits in height.

112. Pheron, they said, was succeeded by a man of Memphis, whose name, in the language of the Greeks, was Proteus.[4] There is a sacred precinct of this king in Memphis, which is very beautiful, and richly adorned, situated south of the great temple of Vulcan. Phœnicians from the city of Tyre dwell all round this precinct, and the whole place is known by the name of the camp of the Tyrians.[5] Within the enclosure stands a temple, which is called that of Venus the Stranger.[6] I con-

---

[3] They were therefore most probably at Heliopolis. The height of 100 cubits, at least 150 feet, far exceeds that of any found in Egypt, the highest being less than 100 feet. The mode of raising an obelisk seems to have been by tilting it from an inclined plane into a pit, at the bottom of which the pedestal was placed to receive it, a wheel or roller of wood being fastened on each side to the end of the obelisk, which enabled it to run down the wall opposite the inclined plane to its proper position. During this operation it was dragged by ropes up the inclined plane, and then gradually lowered into the pit as soon as it had been tilted. (See the representation of the mode of raising an obelisk on the pedestal of that at Constantinople.) The name obelisk is not Egyptian but Greek, from obelos, a "spit" (infra, ch. 135). The Arabs call it *messelleh*, a "packing needle."—[G. W.]

[4] This is evidently a Greek story. Diodorus (i. 62) says "the Egyptians called this king Cetes," which is also a Greek name. Herodotus has apparently transformed the god of the precinct (who seems to have been Dagon, the Phœnician Fish god, often worshipped together with Astarte) into a king who dedicated the precinct.—[G. W.]

[5] Many places in Egypt were called "camps," where foreigners lived apart from the Egyptians, as the "camps" of the Ionians and Carians (ch. 154); of the Babylonians, afterwards occupied by a Roman legion (Strabo xvii. p. 1144); of the Jews (Josephus, Ant. Jud. l. xiv. c. 8, s. 2). The "*Trojan*" camp or village near the quarries of the Eastern hills (Strabo xvii. p. 1147) should probably have been the "*Tyrian*," called from the same people—the Phœnicians of Tyre mentioned by Herodotus; and there is more reason to suppose that the Egyptians had granted to that commercial people the privilege of residing in a quarter of Memphis than that they were a remnant of Manetho's "Phœnician Shepherds," who were expelled from Egypt after occupying the Memphite throne. The Egyptians seem also to have changed the name of Sôr into Tur. (See note [4], ch. 116). The above mistake of *Trojan* for *Tyrian* is confirmed by the name of the place being written in those quarries "the land of the Phœnix" or Phœnicians. "Tros Tyriusque" (Virg. Æn. i. 574) were not always kept distinct.—[G. W.]

[6] This was evidently Astarté, the Venus of the Phœnicians and Syrians. Herodotus is correct in saying that nowhere else had she a temple dedicated to her

jecture the building to have been erected to Helen, the daughter
of Tyndarus ; first, because she, as I have heard say, passed
some time at the court of Proteus ; and secondly, because the
temple is dedicated to Venus *the Stranger;* for among all the
many temples of Venus there is no other where the goddess bears
this title.

113. The priests, in answer to my inquiries on the subject
of Helen,[7] informed me of the following particulars. When
Alexander had carried off Helen from Sparta, he took ship and
sailed homewards. On his way across the Ægean a gale arose,[8]
which drove him from his course and took him down to the sea
of Egypt ; hence, as the wind did not abate, he was carried on
to the coast, when he went ashore, landing at the Salt-Pans,[9]
in that mouth of the Nile which is now called the Canobic.[1]
At this place there stood upon the shore a temple, which still

under that name, and an intercourse with the Phœnicians may have led to her worship at Memphis. The notion of her being Helen arose from the Greek habit of
seeing Homeric personages everywhere. (See note [8] on ch. 106.) The Venus Urania
of Chusæ was Athor of Egypt. (See n. [3], ch. 40 ; and n. [8], ch. 41.) Astarté is mentioned on the monuments as a goddess of the Sheta or Khita. It is now generally
supposed that this people were the Hittites, whose country extended to the Euphrates.
Joshua (i. 4) indeed shows that it reached to that river, when he says "from the
wilderness and this Lebanon even unto the great river, the river Euphrates, all the
land of the Hittites" (Khitím); and "the kings of the Hittites and the kings of the
Egyptians" are spoken of (2 Kings vii. 6) as the terror of the Syrians in the time of
Elisha. On the monuments the Khita (or Sheta) are placed next to Naharayn in
the lists of Eastern nations, enemies of the Egyptians, and defeated by them. At
the Memnonium they are represented routed by Rameses II., and flying across a
river, on which stands the fort of Atesh or Ketesh, the same that is mentioned in
the large inscription at Aboosimbel recording the defeat of the Khita (or Sheta) in
the 5th year of the same Pharaoh. There too their country is called a region of
Nahri or Naharayn (Mesopotamia). Carchemish is supposed to have belonged to
them. It is very probable (as Mr. Stuart Poole also supposes) that the Khita or
Hittites were a tribe of Scythians who had advanced to and settled on the Euphrates.
It is remarkable that the Hittites and Syrians bought Egyptian chariots imported
by Solomon's merchants (1 Kings x. 29) at a later period of Egyptian history.
—[G. W.]
    [7] The eagerness of the Greeks to "inquire" after events mentioned by Homer,
and the readiness of the Egyptians to take advantage of it, are shown in this story
related to Herodotus. The fact of Homer having believed that Helen went to
Egypt, only proves that the story was not invented in Herodotus' time, but was
current long before.—[G. W.]
    [8] Storms on that coast are not unusual now. Ammianus (xxvi. 10) mentions
some very violent winds at Alexandria.—[G. W.]
    [9] There were several of these salt-pans on the Mediterranean coast of Egypt.
Those near Pelusium are mentioned in ch. 15.—[G. W.]
    Cf. Stephen of Byzantium ad voc. Ταριχέαι.
    [1] This branch of the Nile entered the sea a little to the E. of the town of Cano-
pus, close to Heracleum, which some suppose to be the same as Thonis. It is still
traced near the W. end of the Lake Etko, and near it are ruins supposed to be the
site of the city of Hercules, where the temple stood. This temple still existed in
the time of Strabo. It may have been dedicated to the Tyrian Hercules.—
[G. W.]

exists, dedicated to Hercules. If a slave runs away from his master, and taking sanctuary at this shrine gives himself up to the god, and receives certain sacred marks upon his person,[2] whosoever his master may be, he cannot lay hand on him. This law still remained unchanged to my time. Hearing, therefore, of the custom of the place, the attendants of Alexander deserted him, and fled to the temple where they sat as suppliants. While there, wishing to damage their master, they accused him to the Egyptians, narrating all the circumstances of the rape of Helen and the wrong done to Menelaus. These charges they brought, not only before the priests, but also before the warden of that mouth of the river, whose name was Thônis.[3]

114. As soon as he received the intelligence, Thônis sent a message to Proteus, who was at Memphis, to this effect: " A stranger is arrived from Greece ; he is by race a Teucrian, and has done a wicked deed in the country from which he is come. Having beguiled the wife of the man whose guest he was, he carried her away with him, and much treasure also. Compelled by stress of weather, he has now put in here. Are we to let him depart as he came, or shall we seize what he has brought ?" Proteus replied, " Seize the man, be he who he may, that has dealt thus wickedly with his friend, and bring him before me, that I may hear what he will say for himself."

115. Thônis, on receiving these orders, arrested Alexander, and stopped the departure of his ships ; then, taking with him Alexander, Helen, the treasures, and also the fugitive slaves, he went up to Memphis. When all were arrived, Proteus asked Alexander, " who he was, and whence he had come ?" Alexander replied by giving his descent, the name of his country, and a true account of his late voyage. Then Proteus questioned him as to how he got possession of Helen. In his reply Alexander became confused, and diverged from the truth, whereon the slaves interposed, confuted his statements, and told the whole history of the crime. Finally, Proteus delivered judgment as follows : " Did I not regard it as a matter of the utmost consequence that no stranger driven to my country by adverse winds should ever be put to death, I would certainly have

---

[2] Showing they were dedicated to the service of the Deity. To set a mark on any one as a protection was a very ancient custom. Cp. Gen. iv. 15 ; Ezek. ix. 6 ; and Revelation. The word " mark " in Ezekiel is *tau*, תו , the Egyptian sign of life. —[G. W.]

The custom seems to be referred to by St. Paul (Gal. vi. 17).

[3] Thônis, or Thôn, called by Herodotus governor of the Canopic mouth of the Nile, is said by others to have been the name of a town on the Canopic branch. See note [1] on ch. 113.—[G. W.]

avenged the Greek by slaying thee. Thou basest of men,—after accepting hospitality, to do so wicked a deed! First, thou didst seduce the wife of thy own host—then, not content therewith, thou must violently excite her mind, and steal her away from her husband. Nay, even so thou wert not satisfied, but on leaving, thou must plunder the house in which thou hadst been a guest. Now then, as I think it of the greatest importance to put no stranger to death, I suffer thee to depart; but the woman and the treasures I shall not permit to be carried away. Here they must stay, till the Greek stranger comes in person and takes them back with him. For thyself and thy companions, I command thee to begone from my land within the space of three days—and I warn you, that otherwise at the end of that time you will be treated as enemies."

116. Such was the tale told me by the priests concerning the arrival of Helen at the court of Proteus. It seems to me that Homer was acquainted with this story, and while discarding it, because he thought it less adapted for epic poetry than the version which he followed, showed that it was not unknown to him. This is evident from the travels which he assigns to Alexander in the Iliad—and let it be borne in mind that he has nowhere else contradicted himself—making him be carried out of his course on his return with Helen, and after divers wanderings come at last to Sidon[4] in Phœnicia. The passage is in the Bravery of Diomed,[5] and the words are as follows :—

> "There were the robes, many-coloured, the work of Sidonian women:
> They from Sidon had come, what time god-shaped Alexander
> Over the broad sea brought, that way, the high-born Helen."

[4] Sidon, now Sayda, signifies "fishing place," and Sayd in Arabic is applied to "fish" or "game." The first letter, S, Ts, or Tz, is the same in Hebrew as that of Tyre, Sûr, or Tzur, and these towns are now called Sur (Soor) and Sayda. See n. on B. vii. ch. 72. The termination of Sidon signified "great." In Joshua xi. 8, and xix. 28, "great Zidon" is a doubtful reading. Herodotus very properly ranks the Sidonians before the Tyrians (viii. 67), and Isaiah calls Tyre daughter of Sidon (xxiii. 12), having been founded by the Sidonians. Sidon is in Genesis (x. 19), but no Tyre; and Homer only mentions Sidon and not "Tyre" as Strabo observes. It may be "doubtful which was the metropolis of Phœnicia," in later times; Sidon, however, appears to be the older city (xvi. p. 1075). Plutarch might doubt the great antiquity of Tyre, not being noticed by Homer and "other old and wise men;" but it is mentioned by Joshua (xix. 29). Q. Curtius (iv. 4) considers that both it and Sidon were founded by Agenor. The modern Sidon is small, not half a mile in length, and a quarter in breadth.—[G. W.]

[5] Il. vi. 290-2. It has been questioned whether this reference to a portion of the Iliad as "The Bravery of Diomed" can have come from the hand of Herodotus. (Valcknaer ad loc. Heyne ad Hom. Il. vol. viii. p. 787.) But there seems to be no sufficient reason for doubting a passage which is in all the MSS., and has no appearance of being an interpolation. As early as Plato's time portions of the Iliad and Odyssey were certainly distinguished by special titles (see Plat. Cratyl. p. 428,

In the Odyssey also the same fact is alluded to, in these words :[6]—

"Such, so wisely prepared, were the drugs that her stores afforded,
    Excellent; gift which once Polydamna, partner of Thônis,
    Gave her in Egypt, where many the simples that grow in the meadows,
    Potent to cure in part, in part as potent to injure."

Menelaus too, in the same poem, thus addresses Telemachus :[7]—

"Much did I long to return, but the gods still kept me in Egypt—
    Angry because I had failed to pay them their hecatombs duly."

In these places Homer shows himself acquainted with the voyage of Alexander to Egypt, for Syria borders on Egypt, and the Phœnicians, to whom Sidon belongs, dwell in Syria.

117. From these various passages, and from that about Sidon especially, it is clear that Homer did not write the Cypria.[8]   For there it is said that Alexander arrived at Ilium with Helen on the third day after he left Sparta, the wind having been favourable, and the sea smooth; whereas in the Iliad, the poet makes him wander before he brings her home. Enough, however, for the present of Homer and the Cypria.

118. I made inquiry of the priests, whether the story which the Greeks tell about Ilium is a fable, or no.   In reply they related the following particulars, of which they declared that Menelaus had himself informed them.   After the rape of Helen, a vast army of Greeks, wishing to render help to Menelaus, set sail for the Teucrian territory; on their arrival they disembarked, and formed their camp, after which they sent ambassadors to Ilium, of whom Menelaus was one.   The embassy was received within the walls, and demanded the restoration of Helen with the treasures which Alexander had carried off, and likewise required satisfaction for the wrong done.   The Teucrians gave at once the answer in which they persisted ever afterwards, backing their assertions sometimes even with oaths, to wit, that

---

C.; Minos. p. 319, D.), and it is probable that the practice of so distinguishing them began with the early Rhapsodists.   The objection that the passage quoted is from Il. vi., and not Il. v., which now bears the title of "Diomed's Bravery," is of no importance, for our present division of the books dates from Aristarchus, and in the time of Herodotus a portion of the sixth book may have been included under the heading confined afterwards to the fifth.

[6] Odyss. iv. 227–230.
[7] Ib. iv. 351–2.
[8] The criticism here is better than the argument.   There can be no doubt that Homer was not the author of the rambling epic called 'The Cypria.' (Cf. Arist. Poet. 23; Procl. 471–6, ed. Gaisf.)   It was probably written by Stasinus. (Athen. viii. p. 384; Schol. Il. i. 5; Tzetzes Chil. ii. 710.)

neither Helen, nor the treasures claimed, were in their possession,—both the one and the other had remained, they said, in
Egypt ; and it was not just to come upon them for what Proteus, king of Egypt, was detaining. The Greeks, imagining
that the Teucrians were merely laughing at them, laid siege to
the town, and never rested until they finally took it. As, however, no Helen was found, and they were still told the same
story, they at length believed in its truth, and despatched Menelaus to the court of Proteus.

119. So Menelaus travelled to Egypt, and on his arrival
sailed up the river as far as Memphis, and related all that had
happened. He met with the utmost hospitality, received Helen
back unharmed, and recovered all his treasures. After this
friendly treatment Menelaus, they said, behaved most unjustly
towards the Egyptians ; for as it happened that at the time
when he wanted to take his departure, he was detained by the
wind being contrary, and as he found this obstruction continue,
he had recourse to a most wicked expedient. He seized, they
said, two children of the people of the country, and offered them
up in sacrifice.* When this became known, the indignation of
the people was stirred, and they went in pursuit of Menelaus,
who, however, escaped with his ships to Libya, after which the
Egyptians could not say whither he went. The rest they knew
full well, partly by the inquiries which they had made, and
partly from the circumstances having taken place in their own
land, and therefore not admitting of doubt.

120. Such is the account given by the Egyptian priests, and
I am myself inclined to regard as true all that they say of Helen
from the following considerations :—If Helen had been at Troy,
the inhabitants would, I think, have given her up to the Greeks,
whether Alexander consented to it or no. For surely neither
Priam, nor his family, could have been so infatuated as to en-
danger their own persons, their children, and their city, merely
that Alexander might possess Helen. At any rate, if they determined to refuse at first, yet afterwards when so many of the
Trojans fell on every encounter with the Greeks, and Priam too
in each battle lost a son, or sometimes two, or three, or even
more, if we may credit the epic poets, I do not believe that even

* This story recalls the "Sanguine placâstis ventos, et virgine cæsâ," Virg. Æn.
ii. 116, and Herodotus actually records human sacrifices in Achaia, or Phthiotis
(vii. 197). Some have attributed human sacrifices to the Egyptians; and Virgil
says "Quis illaudati nescit Busiridis aras" (Georg. iii. 5); but it must be quite
evident that such a custom was inconsistent with the habits of the civilised Egyptians, and Herodotus has disproved the probability of human sacrifices in Egypt by
his judicious remarks in ch. 45. (See note ⁹ ad loc.)—[G. W.]

if Priam himself had been married to her he would have declined
to deliver her up, with the view of bringing the series of calamities to a close.   Nor was it as if Alexander had been heir to
the crown, in which case he might have had the chief management of affairs, since Priam was already old.   Hector, who was
his elder brother, and a far braver man, stood before him, and
was the heir to the kingdom on the death of their father Priam.
And it could not be Hector's interest to uphold his brother in
his wrong, when it brought such dire calamities upon himself
and the other Trojans.   But the fact was that they had no
Helen to deliver, and so they told the Greeks, but the Greeks
would not believe what they said—Divine Providence, as I
think, so willing, that by their utter destruction it might be
made evident to all men that when great wrongs are done, the
gods will surely visit them with great punishments. Such, at
least, is my view of the matter.

121. (1.) When Proteus died, Rhampsinitus,[1] the priests
informed me, succeeded to the throne.   His monuments were,
the western gateway of the temple of Vulcan, and the two
statues which stand in front of this gateway, called by the
Egyptians, the one Summer, the other Winter, each twenty-five
cubits in height.   The statue of Summer, which is the northernmost of the two, is worshipped by the natives, and has offerings
made to it ; that of Winter, which stands towards the south, is
treated in exactly the contrary way.   King Rhampsinitus was
possessed, they said, of great riches in silver,—indeed to such
an amount, that none of the princes, his successors, surpassed or
even equalled his wealth.   For the better custody of this
money, he proposed to build a vast chamber of hewn stone, one
side of which was to form a part of the outer wall of his palace.
The builder, therefore, having designs upon the treasures, contrived, as he was making the building, to insert in this wall a
stone,[2] which could easily be removed from its place by two

---

[1] This is evidently the name of a Remeses, and not of a king of an early dynasty.
The first individual called Remeses mentioned on the monuments was a person of
the family of Amosis, the first king of the 18th dynasty. Some chambers in the
great temple at Medeenet Haboo, built by Remeses III., where the gold and silver
vases and other precious things are portrayed in the sculptures, recall the treasury
of Rhampsinitus ; and it is not improbable (as suggested in At. Eg. vols. i. p. 85, ii.
358, and in Mater. Hiera. p. 96) that these were the same king. Diodorus calls him
Rhamphis. Herodotus says he erected the great Propylæa on the West of the temple
of Phtha (Vulcan), at Memphis, which would also prove him to have reigned after the
founders of the pyramids, and at least as late as the 18th or 19th dynasty, as those
pyramidal towers (called Propylæa by Herodotus) were not added to temples till the
accession of the 18th dynasty. See below, ch. 155, note [4].—[G. W.]

[2] This story has been repeated in the Pecorone of Ser Giovanni, a Florentine of

men, or even by one. So the chamber was finished, and the king's money stored away in it. Time passed, and the builder fell sick, when finding his end approaching, he called for his two sons, and related to them the contrivance he had made in the king's treasure-chamber, telling them it was for their sakes he had done it, that so they might always live in affluence. Then he gave them clear directions concerning the mode of removing the stone, and communicated the measurements, bidding them carefully keep the secret, whereby they would be Comptrollers of the Royal Exchequer so long as they lived. Then the father died, and the sons were not slow in setting to work; they went by night to the palace, found the stone in the wall of the building, and having removed it with ease, plundered the treasury of a round sum.

(2.) When the king next paid a visit to the apartment, he was astonished to see that the money was sunk in some of the vessels wherein it was stored away. Whom to accuse, however, he knew not, as the seals were all perfect, and the fastenings of the room secure. Still each time that he repeated his visits, he found that more money was gone. The thieves in truth never stopped, but plundered the treasury ever more and more. At last the king determined to have some traps[1] made, and set near the vessels which contained his wealth. This was done, and when the thieves came, as usual, to the treasure-chamber, and one of them entering through the aperture, made straight for the jars, suddenly he found himself caught in one of the traps. Perceiving that he was lost, he instantly called his brother, and telling him what had happened, entreated him to enter as quickly as possible and cut off his head, that when his body should be discovered it might not be recognised, which would have the effect of bringing ruin upon both. The other thief thought the advice good, and was persuaded to follow it; —then, fitting the stone into its place, he went home, taking with him his brother's head.

(3.) When day dawned, the king came into the room, and marvelled greatly to see the body of the thief in the trap without a head, while the building was still whole, and neither entrance nor exit was to be seen anywhere. In this perplexity he com-

the fourteenth century, who substitutes a doge of Venice for the king. Also in other tales. (See Dunlop's Hist. of Fiction, vol. ii. p. 382.) A secret entrance by a moveable stone is a favourite notion of the Arabs, owing to many hidden passages in Egyptian temples having been closed by the same means.—[G. W.]

[1] Traps for birds and hyænas are often represented in the paintings (see above, note ', ch. 77); but one which the robber and his brother were unable to open would require to be very ingeniously contrived.—[G. W.]

manded the body of the dead man to be hung up outside the
palace wall, and set a guard to watch it, with orders that if any
persons were seen weeping or lamenting near the place, they
should be seized and brought before him. When the mother
heard of this exposure of the corpse of her son, she took it sorely
to heart, and spoke to her surviving child, bidding him devise
some plan or other to get back the body, and threatening, that
if he did not exert himself, she would go herself to the king,
and denounce him as the robber.

(4.) The son said all he could to persuade her to let the
matter rest, but in vain : she still continued to trouble him,
until at last he yielded to her importunity, and contrived as
follows :—Filling some skins with wine, he loaded them on
donkeys, which he drove before him till he came to the place
where the guards were watching the dead body, when pulling
two or three of the skins towards him, he untied some of the
necks which dangled by the asses' sides. The wine poured
freely out, whereupon he began to beat his head, and shout with
all his might, seeming not to know which of the donkeys he
should turn to first. When the guards saw the wine running,
delighted to profit by the occasion, they rushed one and all into
the road, each with some vessel or other, and caught the liquor
as it was spilling. The driver pretended anger, and loaded
them with abuse ; whereon they did their best to pacify him,
until at last he appeared to soften, and recover his good humour,
drove his asses aside out of the road, and set to work to re-
arrange their burthens ; meanwhile, as he talked and chatted
with the guards, one of them began to rally him, and make him
laugh, whereupon he gave them one of the skins as a gift.
They now made up their minds to sit down and have a drinking-
bout where they were, so they begged him to remain and drink
with them. Then the man let himself be persuaded, and stayed.
As the drinking went on, they grew very friendly together, so
presently he gave them another skin, upon which they drank so
copiously that they were all overcome with the liquor, and
growing drowsy lay down, and fell asleep on the spot. The
thief waited till it was the dead of the night, and then took
down the body of his brother ; after which, in mockery, he
shaved off the right side of all the soldiers' beards,[4] and so left

<hr/>

[4] This is a curious mistake for any one to make who had been in Egypt, since
the soldiers had no beards, and it was the custom of all classes to shave. This we
know from ancient authors, and, above all, from the sculptures, where the only persons who have beards are foreigners. Herodotus even allows that the Egyptians
shaved their heads and beards (ch. 36 ; cp. Gen. xli. 4). Joseph when sent for

them. Laying his brother's body upon the asses, he carried it home to his mother, having thus accomplished the thing that she had required of him.

(5.) When it came to the king's ears that the thief's body was stolen away, he was sorely vexed. Wishing therefore, whatever it might cost, to catch the man who had contrived the trick, he had recourse (the priests said) to an expedient, which I can scarcely credit. He sent his own daughter[*] to the common stews, with orders to admit all comers, but to require every man to tell her what was the cleverest and wickedest thing he had done in the whole course of his life. If any one in reply told her the story of the thief, she was to lay hold of him, and not allow him to get way. The daughter did as her father willed, whereon the thief, who was well aware of the king's motive, felt a desire to outdo him in craft and cunning. Accordingly he contrived the following plan :—He procured the corpse of a man lately dead, and cutting off one of the arms at the shoulder, put it under his dress, and so went to the king's daughter. When she put the question to him as she had done to all the rest, he replied, that the wickedest thing he had ever done was cutting off the head of his brother when he was caught in a trap in the king's treasury, and the cleverest was making the guards drunk and carrying off the body. As he spoke, the princess caught at him, but the thief took advantage of the darkness to hold out to her the hand of the corpse. Imagining it to be his own hand, she seized and held it fast ; while the thief, leaving it in her grasp, made his escape by the door.

(6.) The king, when word was brought him of this fresh success, amazed at the sagacity and boldness of the man, sent messengers to all the towns in his dominions to proclaim a free pardon for the thief, and to promise him a rich reward, if he came and made himself known. The thief took the king at his word, and came boldly into his presence ; whereupon Rhamp-

from prison by Pharaoh, "shaved himself and changed his raiment." Herodotus could not have learnt this story from the Egyptians, and it is evidently from a Greek source. The robber would have been too intent on his object to lose time or run the risk of waking the guards. The disgrace of shaving men's beards in the East is certainly very great, but they *have* them there, the Egyptians had not.—[G. W.]

  [*] This in a country where social ties were so much regarded, and where the distinction of royal and noble classes was more rigidly maintained than in the most exclusive community of modern Europe, shows that the story was of foreign origin. The arm of a dead man would have been difficult to obtain; but the marriage of an Egyptian king's daughter with a man of low family and a robber was a gross fabrication even for a Greek *cicerone*. This and the stories of the daughter of Cheops, and of Mycerinus, are as illustrative of Greek, as those in the Decameron of Boccaccio are of Italian, ideas ; and the pleasure it gave the Greeks to repeat such tales about kings and their daughters made them overlook the improbability.—[G. W.]

sinitus, greatly admiring him, and looking on him as the most knowing of men, gave him his daughter in marriage. "The Egyptians," he said, "excelled all the rest of the world in wisdom, and this man excelled all other Egyptians."

122. The same king, I was also informed by the priests, afterwards descended alive into the region which the Greeks call Hades,[6] and there played at dice with Ceres, sometimes winning and sometimes suffering defeat. After a while he returned to earth, and brought with him a golden napkin, a gift which he had received from the goddess. From this descent of Rhampsinitus into Hades, and return to earth again, the Egyptians, I was told, instituted a festival, which they certainly celebrated in my day. On what occasion it was that they instituted it, whether upon this or upon any other, I cannot determine. The following are the ceremonies:—On a certain day in the year the priests weave a mantle, and binding the eyes of one of their number with a fillet, they put the mantle upon him, and take him with them into the roadway conducting to the temple of Ceres, when they depart and leave him to himself. Then the priest, thus blindfolded, is led (they say) by two wolves[7] to the temple of Ceres, distant twenty furlongs from the city, where he stays awhile, after which he is brought back from the temple by the wolves, and left upon the spot where they first joined him.

123. Such as think the tales told by the Egyptians credible are free to accept them for history. For my own part, I propose to myself throughout my whole work faithfully to record the traditions of the several nations. The Egyptians maintain that Ceres and Bacchus[8] preside in the realms below. They were also the first to broach the opinion, that the soul of man is immortal,[9] and that, when the body dies, it enters into the form

---

[6] Hades was called in Egyptian Ament or Amenti, over which Osiris presided as judge of the dead. Plutarch (de Isid. s. 29) supposes it to mean the "receiver and giver." It corresponded, like Erebus, to the West, called Ement by the Egyptians, the place of darkness, where the sun set (see note [1] on ch. 44). By Ceres Herodotus means Isis, to whom she was supposed to correspond. He seems to doubt that the festival commemorated that fabulous descent of the king; and with good reason, as it is very un-Egyptian.—[G. W.]

[7] Wolves are not uncommon in Egypt. They are not gregarious, as in other countries, but generally prowl about singly or by twos. The animal, however, represented in Amenti is not a wolf; it is a jackal, the emblem of Anubis, and painted black, in token of its abode there. The wolf, fox, and dog, were all sacred to Anubis; and were treated alike, being of the same genus. See above, ch. 67, note [3]. —[G. W.]

[8] Answering to Isis and Osiris, who were the principal deities of Amenti.— [G. W.]

[9] This was the great doctrine of the Egyptians, and their belief in it is every-

of an animal[1] which is born at the moment, thence passing on from one animal into another, until it has circled through the

where proclaimed in the paintings of the tombs. (See At. Eg. W. pl. 88.) But the souls of wicked men alone appear to have suffered the disgrace of entering the body of an animal, when, "weighed in the balance" before the tribunal of Osiris, they were pronounced unworthy to enter the abode of the blessed. The soul was then sent back in the body of a pig (Ib. pl. 87), and the communication between him and the place he has left is shown to be cut off by a figure hewing away the ground with an axe. Cicero (Tusc. Disp. i. 16) says the immortality of the soul was first taught by Pherecydes of Syros, the preceptor of Pythagoras, "which was chiefly followed out by his disciple;" but this could only allude to its introduction into Greece, since it had been the universal belief in Egypt at least as early as the 3rd and 4th dynasty, more than 1500 years before. Old, too, in Egypt were the Pythagorean notions that nothing is annihilated; that it only changes its form; and that death is reproduction into life, typified by the figure of an infant at the extremity of an Egyptian tomb, beyond the sarcophagus of the dead. (See Ovid. Met. xv. 165, 249, 254, 455.) The same is a tenet of "the Vedantes of India, and of the Sophis of Persia;" and the destroyer *Siva* or *Mahadeva* is also the god of Generation. (Sir W. Jones, vol. i. p. 256). Cp. Lucret. i. 266:—

> "Res . . . . . non posse creari
> De nihilo, neque item genitas ad nil revocari."

Plato and Pythagoras, says Plutarch (de Pl. Phil. iv. 7), "agree that the soul is imperishable . . . . the animal part alone dies." See note[*], ch. 51, and two following notes.—[G. W.]

[1] The doctrine of the Metempsychosis or Metensomatosis was borrowed from Egypt by Pythagoras. (See foregoing and following note.) It was also termed by the Greeks κύκλος ἀνάγκης, "circle (orbit) of necessity;" and besides the notion of the soul passing through different bodies till it returned again to that of a man, some imagined that after a certain period all events happened again in the same manner as before—an idea described in these lines by Virgil, Eclog. iv. 34:

> "Alter erit tum Tiphys, et altera quae vehat Argo
> Delectos Heroas, erunt etiam altera bella,
> Atque iterum ad Trojam magnus mittetur Achilles."

Pythagoras even pretended to recollect the shield of Euphorbus, whose body his soul had before occupied at the Trojan war. (Hor. i. Od. xxiii. 10; Ovid. Metam. xv. 160, 163; Philost. Vit. Apollon. Tyan. i. 1.) The transmigration of souls is also an ancient belief in India, and the Chinese Budhists represent men entering the bodies of various animals, who in the most grotesque manner endeavour to make their limbs conform to the shape of their new abode. It was even a doctrine of the Pharisees according to Josephus (Bell. Jud. ii. 8, 14); and of the Druids, though these confined the habitation of the soul to human bodies (Cæsar. Comm. B. Gall. vi. 13; Tacit. Ann. xiv. 30; Hist. iv. 54; Diodor. v. 31; Strabo, iv. 197.) Plato says (in Phædro), "no souls will return to their pristine condition till the expiration of 10,000 years, unless they be of such as have philosophised sincerely. These in the period of 1000 years, if they have thrice chosen this mode of life in succession . . : shall in the 3000th year fly away to their pristine abode, but other souls being arrived at the end of their first life shall be judged. And of those who are judged, some proceeding to a subterranean place shall there receive the punishments they have deserved; and others being judged favourably shall be elevated to a celestial place . . . . and in the 1000th year each returning to the election of a second life, shall receive one agreeable to his desire. . . . Here also the soul shall pass into a beast, and again into a man, if it has first been the soul of a man." This notion, like that mentioned by Herodotus, appears to have grown out of, rather than to have represented, the exact doctrine of the Egyptians; and there is every indication in the Egyptian sculptures of the souls of *good* men being admitted at once, after a favourable judgment had been passed on them, into the presence of Osiris, whose mysterious name they were permitted to assume. Men and women were then both

forms of all the creatures which tenant the earth, the water, and the air, after which it enters again into a human frame, and is born anew. The whole period of the transmigration is (they say) three thousand years. There are Greek writers, some of an earlier, some of a later date,[2] who have borrowed this doctrine from the Egyptians, and put it forward as their own. I could mention their names, but I abstain from doing so.

124. Till the death of Rhampsinitus, the priests said, Egypt was excellently governed, and flourished greatly ; but after him Cheops succeeded to the throne,[3] and plunged into all manner

called Osiris, who was the abstract idea of "goodness," and there was no distinction of sex or rank when a soul had obtained that privilege. All the Egyptians were then "equally noble;" but not, as Diodorus (i. 92) seems to suppose, during life-time ; unless it alludes to their being a privileged race compared to foreign people. In their doctrine of transmigration, the Egyptian priests may in later times have converted what was at first a simple speculation into a complicated piece of super-stition to suit their own purposes; and one proof of a change is seen in the fact of the name of "Osiris" having in the earliest times only been given to deceased kings; and not to other persons.—[G. W.]

[2] Pythagoras is supposed to be included among the later writers. Herodotus, with more judgment and fairness, and on better information, than some modern writers, allows that the Greeks borrowed their early lessons of philosophy and science from Egypt. Clemens says repeatedly that "the Greeks stole their philo-sophy from the Barbarian" (Strom. i. p. 308 ; ii. p. 358 ; vi. p. 612, and elsewhere); and observes that Plato does not deny its origin (Strom. i. p. 355). The same is stated by Diodorus, Plutarch (de Is. s. 10), Philo, and many other ancient writers, some of whom censure the Greeks for their vanity and disregard of truth; and the candour of Herodotus on this subject is highly creditable to him. It was not agree-able to the Greeks to admit their obligations to "barbarians," and their vanity led them to attribute everything, even the words of foreign languages, to a Greek origin. So too in religion; and Iamblichus says (De Myst. vii. 5), "the search after the truth is too troublesome for the Greeks."—[G. W.]

[3] It is evident that Herodotus had the names of two sets of kings mentioned to him ; the first coming down to the Theban Remeses (Rhampsinitus), the other con-taining the Memphite dynasties, in which were Cheops and the other builders of the pyramids, who were in fact older even than the Sesostris of the 12th dynasty. The 330 kings were mentioned to him as the whole number ; and the Theban and Memphite lists were a separate and detailed account of the succession. Of these two lists he gives merely these names :—

Thinites and Thebans.	*Memphites.*
Menes.	Cheops.
Mœris.	Cephren.
Sesostris.	Mycerinus.
Pheron.	Asychis.
Rhampsinitus.	Anysis.

Those who follow, Sabaco and others, are of later dynasties. But even Mœris is confounded with a later king, and the exploits of Sesostris belong principally to Sethos and his son Remeses—the first kings of the 19th dynasty, who as well as Pheron and Rhampsinitus were Theban princes. It is necessary to mention this, to account for the apparent anachronism ; but other questions respecting the succession of these Memphite kings will be unnecessary here; and I shall only notice their order as given by Herodotus. The name of Cheops, perhaps, more properly *Shefo*, or *Shufu*, translated by Eratosthenes κομάστης, has been ingeniously explained by Professor Rosellini as "the long-haired," which the Egyptian *shofo* or *shufu* signifies (from *fo*, "hair"). Cheops is written more correctly by Manetho "Suphis." Diodorus

of wickedness. He closed the temples, and forbade the Egyptians to offer sacrifice, compelling them instead to labour, one and all, in his service. Some were required to drag blocks of stone down to the Nile from the quarries in the Arabian range of hills ;[4] others received the blocks after they had been conveyed in boats across the river, and drew them to the range of hills called the Libyan.[5] A hundred thousand men laboured constantly, and were relieved every three months by a fresh lot. It took ten years' oppression of the people to make the causeway[6] for the conveyance of the stones, a work not much inferior, in

calls him Chemmis or Chembes, and places seven kings between him and Rhampsinitus or Rhemphis (i. 63 ; see note [1] on ch. 127). The wickedness related of Cheops by Herodotus agrees with Manetho's account, "that he was arrogant towards the gods ; but, repenting, he wrote the Sacred Book."—[G. W.]

[4] The quarries are still worked in the mountain on the E. of the Nile behind Toora and Masarah ; and hieroglyphic inscriptions are found there of early kings. Ptolemy calls the mountain Τρωϊκοῦ λίθου ὄρος, from the neighbouring village of Troja. The blocks used in building the pyramids were partly from those quarries, and partly from the nummulite rock of the Libyan hills, but the outer layers or coating were of the more even-grained stone of the Eastern range (see note [*] on ch. 8). The pyramids and the tombs about them prove that squared stone and even granite had long been employed before the 4th dynasty ; and from the skill they had arrived at in carving granite, we may conclude that hewn stone must have been used even before the reign of Tosorthrus, second king of the 3rd dynasty, who was evidently the same as Athothis, the son of Menes. The pick, stone-saw, wedge, chisel, and other tools were already in use when the pyramids were built.—[G. W.]

[5] The western hills being specially appropriated to tombs in all the places where pyramids were built will account for these monuments being on that side of the Nile. The abode of the dead was supposed to be the West, the land of darkness where the sun ended his course ; and the analogy was kept up by the names *Ement*, the "west," and *Amenti*, the "lower regions of Hades" (see note [*] on ch. 122). Some tombs were in the Eastern hills, but this was because they happened to be near the river, and the Libyan hills were too distant ; and the principal places of burial, as at Thebes and Memphis, were on the W. The only pyramids on the E. bank are in Upper Ethiopia. Tombs of Egyptians being seldom found in Nubia may be owing to their considering it "a foreign land," and being therefore buried in the holy ground of Egypt. In like manner many preferred the sacred Abydus to their own towns as a place of sepulture, in order to be near to Osiris.—[G. W.]

[6] The remains of two causeways still exist—the northern one, which is the largest, corresponding with the great pyramid, as the other does with the third. The outer stones have fallen or been pulled down, so that no traces remain of "the figures of animals," or hieroglyphics. Its length of 5 stadia, 3000 or 3050 feet, has been reduced to about 1424, though in Pococke's time it measured 1000 yards, which very nearly corresponded with the measurement of Herodotus. It is now only 32 feet broad, little more than half the 10 orgyies (or fathoms) of Herodotus, but the height of 85 feet exceeds his 8 orgyies. And as the causeway must necessarily have been as high as the hill or plateau to which the stones were conveyed, and as Herodotus gives 100 feet for the height of the hill, which is from 80 to 85 English feet where the causeway joins it, his 8 orgyies or 48 feet must be an oversight of the historian, or of his copyists. This causeway served for both the great pyramids. Some, however, attribute it to the Caliphs, because Diodorus says it had disappeared in his time, owing to the sandy base on which it stood ; but the ground is not of so sandy a nature as to cause its fall, and the other causeway, leading to the third pyramid, which the Caliphs could have had no object in constructing, is of the same kind of masonry. It is probable the Caliphs repaired the northern one, when the

my judgment, to the pyramid[7] itself. This causeway is five furlongs in length, ten fathoms wide, and in height, at the highest part, eight fathoms. It is built of polished stone, and is covered with carvings of animals. To make it took ten years, as I said—or rather to make the causeway, the works on the

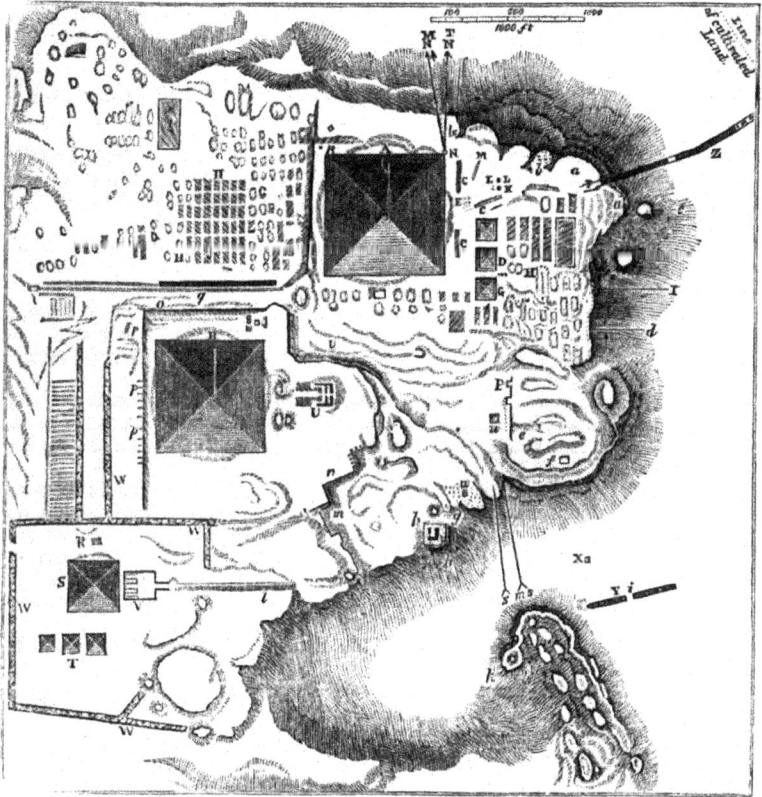

stones of the pyramids were removed to erect mosks, walls, and other buildings in Cairo. An opening, covered over by a single block, was left for persons to pass through, who travelled by land during the inundation, which still remains in the southern causeway.—[G. W.]

[7] The name of pyramid in Egyptian appears to be *br-br;* but Mr. Kenrick, in a note on ch. 136, judiciously observes that "pyramid" is probably Greek on the following authority:—"Etym. M. voc. Πυραμίς, ἡ ἐκ πυρῶν καὶ μέλιτος, ὥσπερ σεσαμίς, ἡ ἐκ σεσάμων καὶ μέλιτος." Πυραμοῦς (he adds) was another name for the same kind of cake ... the σησαμὶς was σφαιροειδής (Athen. p. 646); the πυραμὶς, which was pointed and used in the Bacchic rites, may be seen on the table at the reception of Bacchus by Icarus, and Hope's Costumes, vol. ii. pl. 224. That the name of the mathematical solid was derived from an object of common life, and not *vice versâ,* may be argued from analogy: σφαῖρα was a *hand-ball;* κύβος, a *die* for gaming; κῶνος, a *boy's top;* κύλινδρος, a *husbandman's or gardener's roller.* The Arabic *ahram* or *háram* seems to be taken from the Greek name.—[G. W.]

mound' where the pyramid stands, and the underground chambers, which Cheops intended as vaults for his own use : these
last were built on a sort of island, surrounded by water introduced from the Nile by a canal.' The pyramid itself was
twenty years in building. It is a square, eight hundred feet
each way,¹ and the height the same, built entirely of polished
stone, fitted together with the utmost care. The stones of
which it is composed are none of them less than thirty feet in
length.²

125. The pyramid was built in steps,³ battlement-wise, as it

⁶ This was levelling the top of the hill to form a platform. A piece of rock
was also left in the centre as a nucleus on which the pyramid was built, and which
may still be seen within it to the height of 72 feet above the level of the ground.—
[G. W.]

⁹ There is no trace of a canal, nor is there any probability of its having existed,
from the appearance of the rock, or from the position of the pyramid, standing as it
does upwards of 100 feet above the level of the highest inundation.—[G. W.]

¹ The dimensions of the great pyramid were—each face, 756 ft., now reduced
to 732 ft.; original height when entire, 480 ft. 9 in., now 460 ft. 9 in.; angles at
the base, 51° 50'; angle at the apex, 76° 20'; it covered an area of 571,536 square
feet, now 535,824 square feet.

Herodotus' measurement of eight plethra, or 800 ft., for each face, is not very
far from the truth as a round number; but the height, which he says was the same,
is far from correct, and would require a very different angle from 51° 50' for the
slope of the faces.—[G. W.]

Perhaps Herodotus does not intend vertical height, which he would have no
means of measuring, but the height of the sloping side, which he may even have
measured (infra, ch. 127) from one of the *angles* at the base to the apex. In this
case his estimate would not be so very wrong, for the length of the line from the
apex to the ground at one of the angles of the base would have exceeded 700 feet.

⁹ The size of the stones varies. Herodotus alludes to those of the outer surface, which are now gone; but it may be doubted if all, even at the lower part,
were 30 feet in length. On the subject of the pyramids see M. Eg. W. p. 319 to
371.—[G. W.]

⁸ These steps, or successive stages, had their faces nearly perpendicular, or at
an angle of about 75°, and the triangular space, formed by each projecting considerably beyond the one immediately above it, was afterwards filled in, thus completing the general form of the pyramid. This was first suggested by Mr. Wild,
who observed that "if he had to build a pyramid he should proceed in that manner;" for I had supposed it confined to the Third Pyramid, instead of being a general system of construction. (M. Eg. W.
i. 349.) On each of these stages the machines Herodotus mentions were placed,
which drew up the stones from one to the
other. Two explanations of "the upper
portion of the pyramid being finished
first"—may be given—one that it was adding the pyramidal apex, and filling up the
triangular spaces as they worked downwards; the other that (after the triangular
spaces had been filled in) it referred to
their cutting away the projecting angles of
the stones, and bringing the whole mass to a smooth level surface, which could only be done "as they *descended*, the step immediately below serving as a resting-
place, in lieu of scaffolding, on which the men worked" (as mentioned in M. Eg. W.

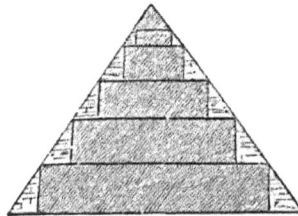

is called, or, according to others, altar-wise. After laying the stones for the base, they raised the remaining stones to their places by means of machines[4] formed of short wooden planks. The first machine raised them from the ground to the top of the first step. On this there was another machine, which received the stone upon its arrival, and conveyed it to the second step, whence a third machine advanced it still higher. Either they had as many machines as there were steps in the pyramid, or possibly they had but a single machine, which, being easily moved, was transferred from tier to tier as the stone rose—both accounts are given, and therefore I mention both. The upper portion of the pyramid was finished first, then the middle, and finally the part which was lowest and nearest the ground. There is an inscription in Egyptian characters[5] on the pyramid which

i. 340). Dr. Lepsius thinks that the size of a pyramid shows the duration of the king's reign who built it ; as additions could be made to the upright sides of the stages at any time before the triangular spaces were filled in ; but though a large pyramid might require and prove a long reign, we cannot infer a short one from a small pyramid. Nor could the small pyramids be the *nuclei* of larger ones, which kings did not live to finish ; and the Plan will show that want of space would effectually prevent their builders hoping for such an extension of their monuments. Any one of those before the First (or the Third) Pyramid would interfere with it, and with their smaller neighbours.

It is a curious question if the Egyptians brought with them the idea of the pyramid, or sepulchral mound, when they migrated into the valley of the Nile, and if it originated in the same idea as the tower, built also in stages, of Assyria, and the pagoda of India.—[G. W.]

[4] The notion of Diodorus that machines were not yet invented is sufficiently disproved by common sense and by the assertion of Herodotus. It is certainly singular that the Egyptians, who have left behind them so many records of their customs, should have omitted every explanation of their mode of raising the enormous blocks they used. Some have imagined inclined planes, without recollecting what their extent would be when of such a height and length of base ; and though the inclined plane may have been employed for some purposes, as it was in sieges by the Assyrians and others, as a "bank" (2 Kings xix. 32 ; 2 Sam. xx. 15), for running up the moveable towers against a perpendicular wall, it would be difficult to adapt it to the sloping faces of a pyramid, or to introduce it into the interior of a large temple. The position of these pyramids is very remarkable in being placed so exactly facing the four cardinal points that the variation of the compass may be ascertained from them. This accuracy would imply some astronomical knowledge and careful observations at that time.—[G. W.]

[5] This must have been in hieroglyphics, the monumental character. The outer stones being gone, it is impossible to verify, or disprove, the assertion of Herodotus, which, however, would have nothing improbable in it, provided it was not confined to the simple inscription he gives. That hieroglyphics were already used long before the pyramids were built is certain, as they were found by Colonel Howard Vyse in the upper chambers he opened, written on the blocks before they were built in, and containing the name of Shofo, or Shufu (Suphis). The cursive style of these hieroglyphics shows that they had been in use a long time before. The names of the two Shufus on those blocks seem to prove that the Great Pyramid was the work of two kings ; and this may explain its having two chambers. (See n. [1], ch. 127.)—[G. W.]

records the quantity of radishes,[6] onions, and garlick[7] consumed by the labourers who constructed it; and I perfectly well remember that the interpreter who read the writing to me said that the money expended in this way was 1600 talents of silver. If this then is a true record, what a vast sum must have been spent on the iron tools[8] used in the work, and on the feeding and clothing of the labourers, considering the length of time the work lasted, which has already been stated, and the additional time— no small space, I imagine—which must have been occupied by the quarrying of the stones, their conveyance, and the formation of the underground apartments.

126. The wickedness of Cheops reached to such a pitch that, when he had spent all his treasures and wanted more, he sent his daughter to the stews, with orders to procure him a certain sum—how much I cannot say, for I was not told; she procured it, however, and at the same time, bent on leaving a monument which should perpetuate her own memory, she required each man to make her a present of a stone towards the works which she contemplated. With these stones she built the pyramid which stands midmost of the three that are in front of the great pyramid, measuring along each side a hundred and fifty feet.[9]

127. Cheops reigned, the Egyptians said, fifty years, and was succeeded at his demise by Chephren, his brother.[1]

---

[6] This is the *Raphanus sativus var. edulis* of Linnæus, the *figl* of modern Egypt, so much eaten by the modern as well as the ancient peasants. It has been called "horse-radish," which would have been pungent food for the Egyptians. But that root does not grow in the country. Strabo mentions lentils, which doubtless constituted their chief food of old, as at present; and it is not probable that they were limited to the three roots mentioned by Herodotus. The notion of the geographer that the rock contains lentils, the petrified residue of the food of the workmen, is derived from the small fossils contained in that nummulite limestone. Their appearance misled him.—[G. W.]

[7] Though garlick grows in Egypt, that brought from Syria is most esteemed. Till the name "Syrian" was tabooed in Cairo, during the war, those who sold it in the streets cried "*Tôm shámee*," "Syrian garlick;" it was then changed to "*infa e' tom*," "garlick is useful."—[G. W.]

[8] Iron was known in Egypt at a very early time. The piece of iron found by Colonel Howard Vyse, imbedded between two stones of the great pyramid, may have been placed there when the pyramid was built, or have been forced between them when the Arabs were removing the blocks; and there is other better evidence of the use of iron by the ancient Egyptians. See above, note [8] on ch. 86.—[G. W.]

[9] In this pyramid the name of king Mencheres (or Mycerinus?) is painted on the flat roof of its chamber, but his sarcophagus was found in the Third Pyramid. (See n. [4], ch. 129.) The story of the daughter of Cheops is on a par with that of the daughter of Rhampsinitus; and we may be certain that Herodotus never received it from "the priests," whose language he did not understand, but from some of the Greek "Interpreters," by whom he was so often misled.—[G. W.]

[1] Manetho mentions Suphis II., or Sen-Suphis, *i. e.* "brother of Suphis." It is evident that two brothers could not have reigned successively 50 and 56 years, or 63 and 66, according to Manetho; nor have built two such immense monuments,

Chephren imitated the conduct of his predecessor, and, like him, built a pyramid, which did not, however, equal the dimensions of his brother's. Of this I am certain, for I measured them both myself. It has no subterraneous apartments, nor any canal from the Nile to supply it with water as the other pyramid has. In that, the Nile water, introduced through an artificial duct, surrounds an island, where the body of Cheops is said to lie. Chephren built his pyramid close to the great pyramid of Cheops, and of the same dimensions, except that he lowered the height forty feet. For the basement he employed the many-coloured stone of Ethiopia.[2] These two pyramids stand both on the same

each requiring a long reign. These two Suphises are the Shofo, or Shufu,

and Nou, or Noum-Shufu,

of the monuments. They appear to have ruled together during the greater part of their reign, and Nou-Shufu or Suphis II., having survived his brother, was considered his successor. Another king has been thought by some to be Cephren;

his name reads Shafre,

and as he is called "of the little pyramid," he has been thought to be the builder of the second, before it was enlarged. The name of Noum-Shufu is found on a reversed stone in one of the tombs near the Second Pyramid, which bears in other parts the names of both these Shufus.

The measurements of the Second Pyramid are:—present base, 690 ft.; former base (according to Colonel Howard Vyse), 707 ft. 9 in.; present perpendicular height (calculating the angle 52° 20′), 446 ft. 9 in.; former height, 454 ft. 8 in.

Herodotus supposes it was 40 feet less in height than the Great Pyramid, but the real difference was only 24 ft. 6 in.

It is singular that Herodotus takes no notice of the sphinx, which was made at least as early as the 18th dynasty, as it bears the name of Thothmes IV. The Egyptians called it Hor-m-kho, or Re-m-sho, "the sun in his resting-place" (the western horizon), which was converted by the Greeks into Armachis.—[G. W.]

[2] This was red granite of Syene; and Herodotus appears to be correct in saying that the lower tier was of that stone, or at least the casing, which was all that he could see; and the numbers of fragments of granite lying about this pyramid show that it has been partly faced with it. The casing which remains on the upper part is of the limestone of the eastern hills. All the pyramids were opened by the Arab caliphs in the hopes of finding treasure. Pausanias (IV. ix. 36) points at Herodotus

hill, an elevation not far short of a hundred feet in height. The reign of Chephren lasted fifty-six years.

128. Thus the affliction of Egypt endured for the space of one hundred and six years, during the whole of which time the temples were shut up and never opened. The Egyptians so detest the memory of these kings that they do not much like even to mention their names. Hence they commonly call the pyramids after Philition,[3] a shepherd who at that time fed his flocks about the place.

129. After Chephren, Mycerinus[4] (they said) son of Cheops, ascended the throne. This prince disapproved the conduct of his father, re-opened the temples, and allowed the people, who were ground down to the lowest point of misery, to return to their occupations, and to resume the practice of sacrifice. His justice in the decision of causes was beyond that of all the former kings. The Egyptians praise him in this respect more highly than any of their other monarchs, declaring that he not only gave his judgments with fairness, but also, when any one was dissatisfied with his sentence, made compensation to him out of his own purse, and thus pacified his anger. Mycerinus had established his character for mildness, and was acting as I

---

when he says "the Greeks admire foreign wonders more than those of their own country, and some of their greatest historians have described the pyramids of Egypt with the greatest precision, though they have said nothing of the royal treasury of Minyas, nor of the walls of Tirynthus, which are not less wonderful than those pyramids." Aristotle (Polit. vii. 11) considers them merely the result of great labour, displaying the power of kings, and the misery inflicted on the people; which Pliny has re-echoed by calling them an idle and silly display of royal wealth and of vanity (xxxvi. 12). Later writers have repeated this, without even knowing the object they were built for, and it would be unjust to suppose them merely monumental.—[G. W.]

[3] This can have no connexion with the invasion, or the memory, of the Shepherd-kings, at least as founders of the pyramids, which some have conjectured; for those monuments were raised long before the rule of the Shepherd-kings in Egypt. —[G. W.]

In the mind of the Egyptians two periods of oppression may have gradually come to be confounded, and they may have ascribed to the tyranny of the Shepherd-kings what in reality belonged to a far earlier time of misrule. It should not be forgotten that the Shepherds, whether Philistines, Hittites, or other Scyths, would at any rate invade Egypt from *Palestine*, and so naturally be regarded by the Egyptians as Philistines. Hence perhaps the name of Pelusium (= Philistine-town) applied to the last city which they held in Egypt. (See Lepsius, Chron. der Egypter, i. p. 341.)

[4] He is called Mencheres by Manetho, and Mecherinus by Diodorus. In the

hieroglyphics the name is   which   reads   Men-ka-re,

Men-ku-re, or Men-ker-re.—[G. W.]

have described, when the stroke of calamity fell on him. First of all his daughter died, the only child that he possessed. Experiencing a bitter grief at this visitation, in his sorrow he conceived the wish to entomb his child in some unusual way. He therefore caused a cow to be made of wood, and after the interior had been hollowed out, he had the whole surface coated with gold ; and in this novel tomb laid the dead body of his daughter.

130. The cow was not placed underground, but continued visible to my times : it was at Saïs, in the royal palace, where it occupied a chamber richly adorned. Every day there are burnt before it aromatics of every kind ; and all night long a lamp is kept burning in the apartment.[5] In an adjoining chamber are statues which the priests at Saïs declared to represent the various concubines of Mycerinus. They are colossal figures in wood, of the number of about twenty, and are represented naked. Whose images they really are, I cannot say—I can only repeat the account which was given to me.

131. Concerning these colossal figures and the sacred cow, there is also another tale narrated, which runs thus : " Mycerinus was enamoured of his daughter, and offered her violence— the damsel for grief hanged herself, and Mycerinus entombed her in the cow. Then her mother cut off the hands of all her tiring-maids, because they had sided with the father, and betrayed the child ; and so the statues of the maids have no hands." All this is mere fable in my judgment, especially what is said about the hands of the colossal statues. I could plainly see that the figures had only lost their hands through the effect of time. They had dropped off, and were still lying on the ground about the feet of the statues.

132. As for the cow, the greater portion of it is hidden by a scarlet coverture ; the head and neck, however, which are visible, are coated very thickly with gold,[6] and between the horns there is a representation in gold of the orb of the sun. The figure is not erect, but lying down, with the limbs under the body ; the dimensions being fully those of a large animal of the kind. Every year it is taken from the apartment where it is kept, and exposed to the light of day—this is done at the season when the

---

[5] This is evidently, from what follows (see ch. 132), in honour of a deity, and not of the daughter of Mycerinus ; and the fact of the Egyptians lamenting, and beating themselves in honour of Osiris, shows that the cow represented either Athor, or Isis, in the character of a goddess of Amenti. (See Plut. de Isid. et Osir. s. 39.) Herodotus very properly doubts the story about the daughter and the concubines of Mycerinus, which he thinks a mere fable.—[G. W.]

[6] The gold used by the Egyptians for overlaying the faces of mummies, and ornamental objects, is often remarkable for its thickness.—[G. W.]

Egyptians beat themselves in honour of one of their gods, whose name I am unwilling to mention in connexion with such a matter.[7] They say that the daughter of Mycerinus requested her father in her dying moments to allow her once a year to see the sun.

133. After the death of his daughter, Mycerinus was visited with a second calamity, of which I shall now proceed to give an account. An oracle reached him from the town of Buto,[8] which said, "Six years only shalt thou live upon the earth, and in the seventh thou shalt end thy days." Mycerinus, indignant, sent an angry message to the oracle, reproaching the god with his injustice—"My father and uncle," he said, "though they shut up the temples, took no thought of the gods, and destroyed multitudes of men, nevertheless enjoyed a long life; I, who am pious, am to die so soon!" There came in reply a second message from the oracle—"For this very reason is thy life brought so quickly to a close—thou hast not done as it behoved thee. Egypt was fated to suffer affliction one hundred and fifty years—the two kings who preceded thee upon the throne understood this—thou hast not understood it." Mycerinus, when this answer reached him, perceiving that his doom was fixed, had lamps prepared, which he lighted every day at eventime, and feasted and enjoyed himself unceasingly both day and night, moving about in the marsh-country[9] and the woods, and visiting all the places that he heard were agreeable sojourns. His wish was to prove the oracle false, by turning the nights into days, and so living twelve years in the space of six.

134. He too left a pyramid, but much inferior in size to his father's.[1] It is a square, each side of which falls short of three

---

[7] This was Osiris. See notes on chs. 60, 61, 85, and 130.—[G. W.]

[8] See notes [2], [3] on ch. 155.

[9] These were the resort of the wealthy Egyptians who wished to enjoy the pleasures of the chase. They were also places of refuge in time of danger, to which Anysis, Amyrtæus, and others fled.—[G. W.]

[1] The measurements of this pyramid are—length of base 333 feet; former length, according to Col. H. Vyse, 354·6; present perpendicular height 203·7 inches; former height, according to Col. H. Vyse, 218·0; angle of the casing 51°. Herodotus says it was much smaller than that of Cheops, being 20 feet short of 3 plethra each face, or 280 feet; but this is too little, and Pliny gives it 363 Roman feet, or about 350 English feet; observing at the same time that, though smaller than the other two, it was far more beautiful, on account of the granite that coated it; which Herodotus and Strabo say reached only half-way up, or according to Diodorus to the fifteenth tier. It now extends 36 feet 9 inches from the base on the Western, and 25 feet 10 on the Northern side. The granite stones have bevelled edges, a common style of building in Egypt, Syria, and Italy, in ancient times; and round the entrance a space has been cut into the surface of the stones, as if to let in some ornament, probably of metal, which bore an inscription containing the king's name, or some funeral sculptures, similar to those in the small chambers attached to the pyramids of Gebel Berkel. In this pyramid were found the name and coffin of Mencheres.—[G. W.]

plethra by twenty feet, and is built for half its height of the
stone of Ethiopia. Some of the Greeks call it the work of Rhodôpis[2] the courtezan, but they report falsely. It seems to me
that these persons cannot have any real knowledge who Rhodôpis

[2] Her real name was Doricha, and Rhodopis, "the rosy-cheeked," was merely
an epithet. It was under this name of Doricha that she was mentioned by Sappho ;
and that Herodotus was not mistaken in calling her Rhodopis, as Athenæus supposes (Deipn. xiii. p. 596), is fully proved by Strabo. Rhodopis when liberated remained in Egypt ; where even before Greeks resorted to that country foreign women
often followed the occupations of the modern "*Almeh.*" They are figured on the
monuments dancing and playing musical instruments to divert parties of guests, and
are distinguished by their head-dress from native Egyptian women. The reason of
her having been confounded with Nitocris was owing, as Zoega suggested, to her
having been also called "the rosy-cheeked," like the Egyptian Queen, who is described by Eusebius (from Manetho) as "flaxen haired with rosy cheeks." Ælian's
story of Psammetichus being the king into whose lap the eagle dropped the sandal
of Rhodopis, and of her marriage with him (Ælian, Var. Hist. xiii. 33), shows that
he mistook the princess Neitakri of the 26th dynasty, the wife of Psammetichus III.,
for the ancient Nitocris (Neitakri). (See note [3] on ch. 100.) Strabo, from whom
Ælian borrowed it, does not mention the name of the king, but says that the pyr-

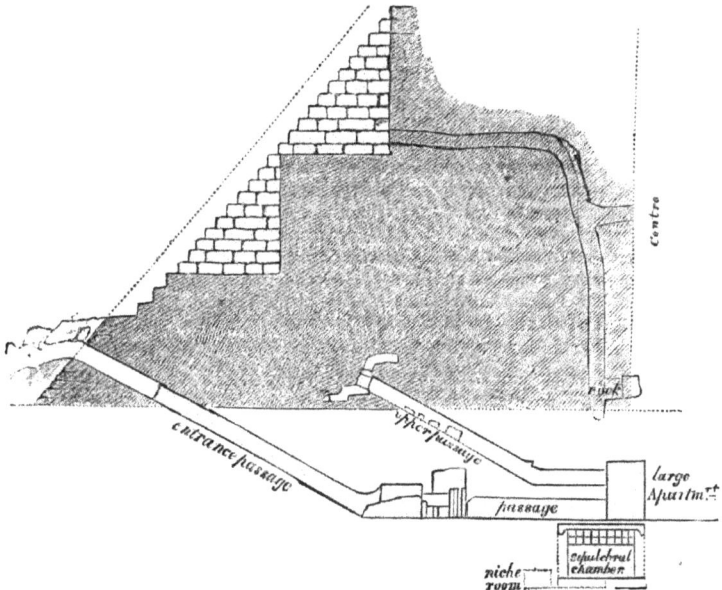

amid was erected to the memory of "Doricha, as she is called by Sappho, whom
others name Rhodopé." (Strabo, xvii. p. 1146.) Diodorus (i. 64) says "some think
the pyramid was erected as a tomb for Rhodopis by certain monarchs who had loved
her," an idea borrowed from the mention of Psammetichus and the twelve monarchs
or kings. The third pyramid was said by Eusebius and Africanus to have been
built by Nitocris, the last of the 8th dynasty ; and it is very possible that both she
and Mencheres (Mycerinus) may have a claim to that monument. We know that
the latter was buried there, not only from Herodotus, but from the coffin bearing
his name found there by Colonel Howard Vyse. There is, however, reason to believe the pyramid was originally smaller, and afterwards enlarged, when a new en-

was ; otherwise they would scarcely have ascribed to her a work on which uncounted treasures, so to speak, must have been expended. Rhodôpis also lived during the reign of Amasis, not of Mycerinus, and was thus very many years later than the time of the kings who built the pyramids. She was a Thracian by birth, and was the slave of Iadmon, son of Hephæstopolis, a Samian. Æsop, the fable-writer, was one of her fellow-slaves.' That Æsop belonged to Iadmon is proved by many facts—among others, by this. When the Delphians, in obedience to the command of the oracle, made proclamation that if any one claimed compensation for the murder of Æsop he should receive it,' the person who at last came forward was Iadmon, grandson of the former Iadmon, and he received the compensation. Æsop therefore must certainly have been the former Iadmon's slave.

135. Rhodôpis really arrived in Egypt under the conduct of Xantheus the Samian ; she was brought there to exercise her trade, but was redeemed for a vast sum by Charaxus, a Mytilenæan, the son of Scamandrônymus, and brother of Sappho the poetess.' After thus obtaining her freedom, she remained in

---

trance was made, and the old (now the upper) passage to the chamber was closed by the masonry of the larger pyramid built over its mouth. This may be better explained by the diagram, reduced from Colonel Howard Vyse's Plate. And this renders it possible, and even probable, that the third pyramid had two occupants, the last of whom may have been Nitocris. Herodotus shows the impossibility of this pyramid having been built by the Greek Rhodopis, because she lived in the reign of Amasis, very many years after the death of the founders of those monuments; but Lucan, notwithstanding this, buries Amasis himself there, "Pyramidum tumulis evulsus Amasis," and even the Ptolemies, who were not born when Herodotus wrote his history—

     "Cum Ptolemæorum manes . . . .,
     Pyramides claudant . . . ."

but neither time nor facts embarrass a poet.—[G. W.]

    ' Æsop is said to have been, like Rhodopis, a Thracian. (Heraclid. Pont. Fr. x. ; Schol. ad Arist. Av. 471.) According to Eugæon (Fr. 8), he was a native of Mesembria.

    ' Plutarch (De serâ Num. Vind. p. 556, F.) tells us that Æsop, who was on intimate terms with Crœsus (cf. Suidas), was despatched by him to Delphi, with orders to make a magnificent sacrifice, and give the Delphians four minæ a-piece. In consequence, however, of a quarrel which he had with them, Æsop after his sacrifice gave the Delphians nothing, but sent all the money back to Sardis. Hereupon the Delphians got up a charge of sacrilege against him, and killed him by throwing him down from the rock Hyampæa (infra, viii. 39). The Scholiast on Aristophanes (Vesp. 1446) adds, that the occasion of quarrel was a jest of the poet's, who rallied the Delphians on their want of landed property, and their submitting to depend on the sacrifices for their daily food. They contrived their revenge by hiding one of the sacred vessels in his baggage, and then after his departure pursuing him and discovering it. To this last fact Aristophanes alludes. (Vesp. 1440-1, ed. Bothe.)

    ' Charaxus, the brother of Sappho, traded in wine from Lesbos, which he was in

Egypt, and as she was very beautiful, amassed great wealth, for a person in her condition ; not, however, enough to enable her to erect such a work as this pyramid.   Any one who likes may go and see to what the tenth part of her wealth amounted, and he will thereby learn that her riches must not be imagined to have been very wonderfully great.   Wishing to leave a memorial of herself in Greece, she determined to have something made the like of which was not to be found in any temple, and to offer it at the shrine at Delphi.   So she set apart a tenth of her possessions, and purchased with the money a quantity of iron spits,[6] such as are fit for roasting oxen whole, whereof she made a present to the oracle.   They are still to be seen there, lying of a heap, behind the altar which the Chians dedicated, opposite the sanctuary.   Naucratis seems somehow to be the place where such women are most attractive.   First there was this Rhodôpis of whom we have been speaking, so celebrated a person that her name came to be familiar to all the Greeks ; and, afterwards, there was another, called Archidicé, notorious throughout Greece, though not so much talked of as her predecessor.   Charaxus, after ransoming Rhodôpis, returned to Mytilene, and was often lashed by Sappho in her poetry.   But enough has been said on the subject of this courtezan.

the habit of taking to Naucratis, the entrepot of all Greek merchandise. (Strabo, xvii. p. 1146.)   It is probable that both he and Rhodopis were lampooned by Sappho, since in Herodotus the word "μιν," seems to refer to the former, while Athenæus says it was Rhodopis.   According to Ovid (Her. Ep. 15) this Sappho was the same whose love for Phaon made her throw herself from the Leucadian rock into the sea (Strabo, x. p. 311): but others mention two Sapphos, one of Mytilene, the other of Eresus, in Lesbos. (Ælian. Var. Hist. xii. 9.   Athenæus, Deipn. xiii. p. 596.)—[G. W.]

[6] Similar spits, or skewers, of three or four feet long, have been found in the Etruscan tombs, arranged in the same manner as the small ones still in use in the East. (See woodcut.)—[G. W.]

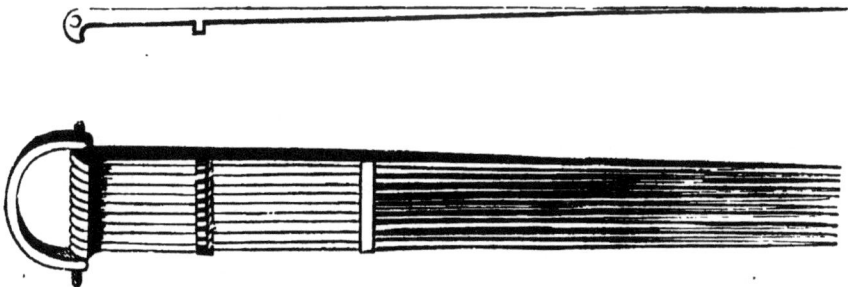

136. After Mycerinus, the priests said, Asychis [7] ascended the throne. He built the eastern gateway [8] of the temple of Vulcan, which in size and beauty far surpasses the other three. All the four gateways have figures graven on them, and a vast amount of architectural ornament, but the gateway of Asychis is by far the most richly adorned. In the reign of this king, money being scarce and commercial dealings straitened, a law was passed that the borrower might pledge his father's body [9] to raise the sum whereof he had need. A proviso was appended to this law, giving the lender authority over the entire sepulchre of the borrower, so that a man who took up money under this pledge, if he died without paying the debt, could not obtain burial either in his own ancestral tomb, or in any other, nor could he during his lifetime bury in his own tomb any member of his family. The same king, desirous of eclipsing all his predeces-

---

[7] The hieroglyphical name of this king is not known. It resembles that of the Sabacos, whose names were represented by a crocodile, *Savak*, the Greek *σοῦχος*. He could not be one of those of the 18th dynasty, since Memphis was then in the hands of the Shepherd-kings, nor is he likely to have been the Sabaco who is said by Manetho to have put Bocchoris, the Saite, to death, and whom Herodotus appears to mention in ch. 137 ; but as Diodorus (i. 94) speaks of Sasyches, a predecessor of Sesostris, who made great additions to the laws of Egypt, and who is evidently the Asychis of Herodotus, it is more probable that he was Shishak, of the 22nd dynasty (perhaps partly confounded with some other king), which is confirmed by Josephus (Bell. Jud. vi. 10) calling the Egyptian king who took Jerusalem Asochæus. —[G. W.]

[8] The lofty pyramidal towers forming the façades of the courts, or vestibules, of the temple. See notes on chs. 91 and 155.—[G. W.]

[9] The Egyptians, like other people, found the necessity of enacting new laws concerning debt at different times. This of Asychis gave the creditor the right of taking possession of the tomb of the debtor, which was the greatest pledge, since he could not be buried unless the debt had been paid. It was the right of burial he lost, not the body of the father, as fathers could not be supposed to die conveniently to stand security for their sons, and the law would have foreseen the possibility of there being many sons of one father. Usury was forbidden, as with the Jews (Ps. xx. 5 ; Levit. xxv. 36, 37), and Moslems ; and the interest was not allowed to increase beyond double the original sum. The goods really belonging to the debtor might be seized, but not his person, since every individual was looked upon as belonging to the state, which might require his services, and it was considered unjust to punish his family by depriving him of the power of supporting them. (Diodor. i. 78.) This law was introduced by Bocchoris, who also enacted that no agreement should be binding without a contract in writing ; and if any one took an oath that the money had not been lent him, the debt was not recognized, unless a written agreement could be produced. The number of witnesses, required for the execution of the most trifling contract, is shown by those discovered at Thebes, of the time of the Ptolemies ; where sixteen names are appended to the sale of the moiety of certain sums collected on account of a few tombs, and of services performed to the dead, amounting only to 400 pieces of brass. (Dr. Young's Discovs. in Eg. Lit.) So great a number also proves how necessary they thought it to guard against "false witness," which was even provided for in the Jewish covenant by a distinct commandment. See At. Eg. W. vol. ii. pp. 49, 57, 70.—[G. W.]

sors upon the throne, left as a monument of his reign a pyramid
of brick.[1] It bears an inscription, cut in stone, which runs thus :—

[1] The use of crude brick was general in Egypt, for dwelling-houses, tombs, and
ordinary buildings, the walls of towns, fortresses, and of the sacred enclosures of
temples, and for all purposes where stone was not required, which last was nearly
confined to temples, quays, and reservoirs.   Even some small ancient temples were
of crude bricks, which were merely baked in the sun, and never burnt in early

" Despise me not in comparison with the stone pyramids ;[2] for I surpass them all, as much as Jove surpasses the other gods. A pole was plunged into a lake, and the mud which clave thereto was gathered ; and bricks were made of the mud, and so I was formed." Such were the chief actions of this prince.

137. He was succeeded on the throne, they said, by a blind man, a native of Anysis,[3] whose own name also was Anysis.

Pharaonic times. A great number of people were employed in this extensive man-ufacture; it was an occupation to which many prisoners of war were condemned, who, like the Jews, worked for the king, bricks being a government monopoly. The process is represented at Thebes, and is rendered doubly interesting from its exact correspondence with that described in Exodus (v. 7–19), showing the hardness of the work, the tales of bricks, the bringing of the straw, and the Egyptian task-masters set over the foreign workmen.   Aristophanes (Birds, 1132, and Frogs, 1647) speaks of the Egyptian bricklayers and labourers as noted workmen, but without describing the manufacture of bricks.

    The Theban bricks of Thothmes III. measure 1 ft. by 0·75, and 0·55 in thickness, weighing 37 lbs. 10 ozs. ; and one of Amunoph III., in the British Museum, is 0·11·3 inches by 0·5·8 and 0·3·9 in thickness, and weighs 13 lbs.; but those of the pyramid of Howâra are 1 ft. 5 in. by 0·8·8 to 0·8·9 and 0·3·8 thick, and weigh 48 lbs. 6 ozs.

They were frequently stamped with a king's name while making, as Roman burnt bricks were with the names of a god, a place, a consul, a legion, a maker, or with some other mark.   Vitruvius thinks that crude bricks were not fit for use in Italy, till they were two years old; and the people of Utica kept them for five years.   (Vitruv. 2, 3.) Though the Jews are not distinctly mentioned on the Egyp-tian monuments, and the copyists of Manetho have confounded them with the Shepherds, it is not impossible that the name of the city of Abaris may point to that of the Hebrews, or *Abarim* עברים (Gen. xi. 15).—[G. W.]

    [2] The superiority of this over the stone pyramids has been supposed to be in the invention or adoption of the arch, forming the roof of its chambers and pas-sages.   But this would require Asychis to have lived at least before the 18th dy-nasty, arches being common in the reign of Amunoph I., the second king of that dynasty, and possibly long before his time.   Here again Herodotus appears to have confounded an earlier and a later king. (On the early use of the arch see my At. Eg. pp. 16, 18, 19, 69, 70.) Several brick pyramids still remain in Egypt ; there are several small ones at Thebes ; but the larg-est are two near the modern Dashoor, or Mensheeh, and two others at the entrance to the Fyoóm, at Illahoon, and El Hawâra.   It seems these four were originally cased with stone, and some blocks remain projecting from the crude brick mass, to which the outer covering of masonry was once attached, similar to those in some of the old tombs near Rome. That at Hawâra, which stands at the end of the labyrinth, was built upon a nucleus of rock, like the great pyramid of Geezeh, which was found by Colonel Howard Vyse to rise to about the height of 40 ft. within it.—[G. W.]

    [3] This may be Ei-ñ-esi, "city (abode) of Isis, or Iseum." It could not be the Hanes of Isaiah (xxx. 4). See note on Book iii. ch. 5.—[G. W.]

Under him Egypt was invaded by a vast army of Ethiopians,[4] led by Sabacôs,[5] their king. The blind Anysis fled away to the marsh-country, and the Ethiopian was lord of the land for fifty years, during which his mode of rule was the following :—When an Egyptian was guilty of an offence, his plan was not to punish him with death : instead of so doing, he sentenced him, according to the nature of his crime, to raise the ground to a greater or a less extent in the neighbourhood of the city to which he belonged. Thus the cities came to be elevated even more than

[4] This conquest by the Ethiopians points to the accession of the 25th dynasty, which coming immediately after Bocchoris, the sole king of the 24th, shows that the latter may have been deprived of the throne by Sabaco. He, and his successors, are given in Manetho's list :—

24th Dynasty of one Saïte.
" Bocchoris " (the Wise).

25th Dynasty of Ethiopian family.
" Sabaco," Sabakôn, Sabaco I.
" Sebechon," Sevechus, Sabaco II.
" Teraces," Tearchus, Tirhaka, (Tehrak).

It has been doubted which of the Sabacos was the So, or Sava, of 2 Kings xvii. 4; and which Sabaco, or Shebek, reigned first. Shebek I. appears, from Mr. Layard's discovery of his name at Koyunjik, to be So. A stela at Florence reckons 71 years from the 3rd of Necho to the 35th of Amasis, who died in 525, and the 44th year of Amasis is found on the monuments, and we also find that Psammetichus reigned directly after Tirhaka; so that it is possible that Necho, the father of Psammetichus, was a contemporary of Sabaco, as Herodotus states (ch. 152). Of these dates, and the supposed era of Sennacherib, see Hist. Notice in App. ch. viii. § 83. While the two Sabacos possessed the country, Stephinathis, Nechepsos, and Necho I. may have assumed a nominal regal power; though the twelve kings could only have been chiefs of nomes, or districts in the Delta.
When the Egyptians mention kings who did nothing memorable, or the rule of a priest-king like Sethos, or twelve kings ruling the country; and when the monuments show that nothing was done worthy of record, or that kings with the title of priest ruled in some part of the country, or that a priest dedicated a monument instead of a king, there appears evidence of foreign rule in Egypt. We see this at the time of the Shepherd invasion, before the accession of the 18th dynasty; again, before and after the accession of the 22nd and 23rd, both foreign dynasties, and about the 24th, as well as before the 26th, in the time of the so-called twelve kings. These twelve kings or monarchs could not have governed the whole of Egypt, nor could they have made the labyrinth, as Herodotus states (ch. 148), which had evidently been erected long before.
The discovery of the stelæ in the Apis tombs by M. Mariette now shows that Psammetichus I. was the immediate successor of Tirhaka.—[G. W.]
[5] Herodotus mentions only one Sabaco, but the monuments and Manetho notice two, the Sabakôn and Sebichôs (Sevéchos) of Manetho, called Shebek in the hieroglyphics. One of these is the same as So (Savá), the contemporary of Hosea, King of Israel, who is said (in 2 Kings xvii. 4) to have made a treaty with the King of Egypt, and to have refused the annual tribute to Shalmanezer, King of Assyria. Tirhakah, the Tarchos, or Tarachus, of Manetho, Tearchon of Strabo, and the Tehrak of the hieroglyphics, is noticed in 2 Kings xix. 9, and Isaiah xxxvii. 9, as King of Ethiopia, who had come out to fight against the King of Assyria. It has been said that Sabacon has not been found on the Egyptian monuments; if so, no other king mentioned by the Greeks is met with, since the orthography of all differs from the Greek form. A monument at Sakkára gives the name of the second Sabaco, Shebek, or Sevechon.—[G. W.]

they were before.   As early as the time of Sesostris, they had
been raised by those who dug the canals in his reign ; this
second elevation of the soil under the Ethiopian king gave them
a very lofty position.   Among the many cities which thus attained to a great elevation, none (I think) was raised so much
as the town called Bubastis, where there is a temple of the goddess Bubastis, which well deserves to be described.   Other
temples may be grander, and may have cost more in the building, but there is none so pleasant to the eye as this of Bubastis.
The Bubastis of the Egyptians is the same as the Artemis
(Diana) of the Greeks.

138. The following is a description of this edifice :*—Excepting the entrance, the whole forms an island.   Two artificial
channels from the Nile, one on either side of the temple, en-
compass the building, leaving only a narrow passage by which
it is approached.   These channels are each a hundred feet wide,
and are thickly shaded with trees.   The gateway is sixty feet
in height, and is ornamented with figures cut upon the stone,
six cubits high and well worthy of notice.   The temple stands
in the middle of the city, and is visible on all sides as one walks
round it ; for as the city has been raised up by embankment,
while the temple has been left untouched in its original condition, you look down upon it wheresoever you are.   A low wall

---

* This account of the position of the temple of Bubastis is very accurate.   The
height of the mound, the site of the temple in a low space beneath the houses, from
which you look down upon it, are the very peculiarities any one would remark on
visiting the remains at Tel Basta.   One street, which Herodotus mentions as leading to the temple of Mercury, is quite apparent, and his length of 3 stadia falls short
of its real length, which is 2250 feet.   On the way is the square he speaks of, 900
feet from the temple of Pasht (Bubastis), and apparently 200 ft. broad, though now
much reduced in size by the fallen materials of the houses that surrounded it.
Some fallen blocks mark the position of the temple of Mercury, but the remains of
that of Pasht are rather more extensive, and show that it measured about 500 feet
in length.   We may readily credit the assertion of Herodotus respecting its beauty,
since the whole was of the finest red granite, and was surrounded by a sacred enclosure about 600 feet square (agreeing with the stadium of Herodotus), beyond
which was a larger circuit, measuring 940 feet by 1200, containing the minor one
and the canal he mentions, and once planted, like the other, with a grove of trees.   In
this perhaps was the usual lake belonging to the temple.   Among the sculptures are
the names of a goddess, who may be either Bubastis or Buto (see notes on ch. 59),
and of Remeses II., of Osorkon I., and of Amyrtæus (?) ; and as the two first kings
reigned long before the visit of Herodotus, we know that the temple was the one
he saw.   (See M. Eg. W. vol. i. p. 427–430.)   The columns of the vestibule had
capitals representing the buds of water-plants, but near the old branch of the
river, the modern canal of Moëz, is another column with a palm-tree capital, said to
have been taken from this temple, which has the names of Remeses II. and Osorkon
I. ; and was when entire about 22 feet high.   Amidst the houses on the N. W. side
are the thick walls of a fort, which protected the temple below ; and to the E. of
the town is a large open space, enclosed by a wall now converted into mounds.
Osorkon is said to have been called Hercules by the Egyptians.—[G. W.]

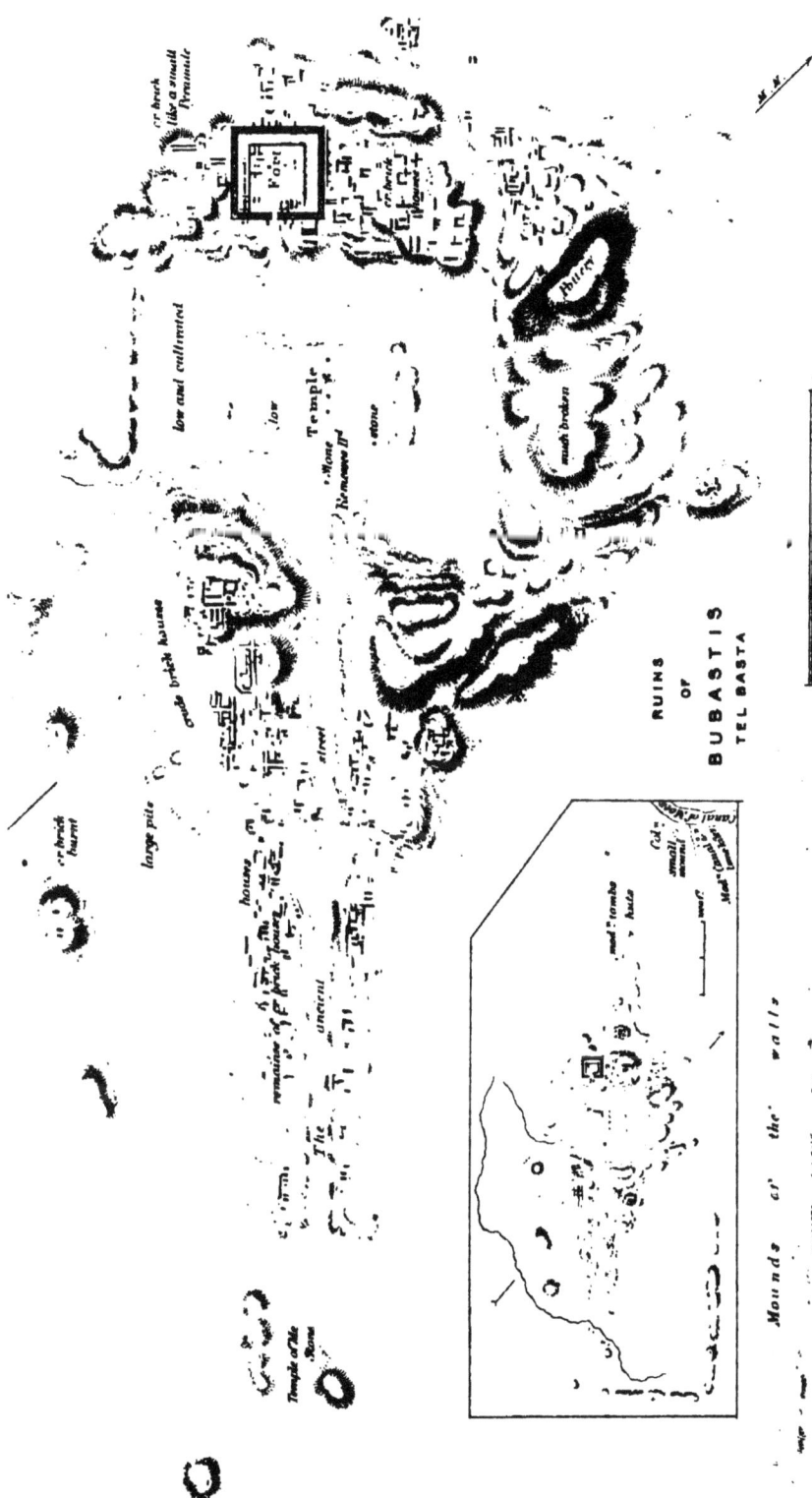

RUINS
OF
BUBASTIS
TEL BASTA

Mounds of the walls

Temple

low

low and cultivated

Some
Remains of
stone

Places

much broken

large pile

crude brick houses

house

street

ancient

The

remains of crude brick houses

of brick house

Temple of the Sun

Or brick
like a small
Peninsula

Fort

P A.Knapp Lith? N.Y.

Publ. by D.Appleton & C?N.Y.

runs round the enclosure, having figures engraved upon it, and inside there is a grove of beautiful tall trees growing round the shrine, which contains the image of the goddess. The enclosure is a furlong in length, and the same in breadth. The entrance to it is by a road paved with stone for a distance of about three furlongs, which passes straight through the market-place with an easterly direction, and is four hundred feet in width. Trees of an extraordinary height grow on each side the road, which conducts from the temple of Bubastis to that of Mercury.

139. The Ethiopian finally quitted Egypt, the priests said, by a hasty flight under the following circumstances. He saw in his sleep a vision :—a man stood by his side, and counselled him to gather together all the priests of Egypt and cut every one of them asunder. On this, according to the account which he himself gave, it came into his mind that the gods intended hereby to lead him to commit an act of sacrilege, which would be sure to draw down upon him some punishment either at the hands of gods or men. So he resolved not to do the deed suggested to him, but rather to retire from Egypt, as the time during which it was fated that he should hold the country had now (he thought) expired. For before he left Ethiopia he had been told by the oracles which are venerated there, that he was to reign fifty years over Egypt. The years were now fled, and the dream had come to trouble him ; he therefore of his own accord withdrew from the land.

140. As soon as Sabacôs was gone, the blind king left the marshes, and resumed the government. He had lived in the marsh-region the whole time, having formed for himself an island there by a mixture of earth and ashes. While he remained, the natives had orders to bring him food unbeknown to the Ethiopian, and latterly, at his request, each man had brought him, with the food, a certain quantity of ashes. Before Amyrtæus,[7] no one was able to discover the site of this island,[8] which continued unknown to the kings of Egypt who preceded him on the throne for the space of seven hundred years and more.[9] The name which it bears is Elbo. It is about ten furlongs across in each direction.

[7] See note on Book iii. ch. 17.

[8] This island appears to have stood at the S. E. corner of the lake of Buto, now Lake *Boorlos.*—[G. W.]

[9] The 700 years before Amyrtæus would bring the time of this king to about 1155 B.C., which ought to point to the flight of some king; but it does not agree with the period of the Sheshonks of the 22nd dynasty, who are supposed to have been of an Assyrian family. The interval could not be calculated from Anysis, since from the beginning of the first Sabaco's reign to the defeat of Amyrtæus was only a period of 515 years.—[G. W.]

141. The next king, I was told, was a priest of Vulcan, called Sethôs.[1] This monarch despised and neglected the warrior class of the Egyptians,[2] as though he did not need their services. Among other indignities which he offered them, he took from them the lands which they had possessed under all the previous kings, consisting of twelve acres of choice land for each warrior. Afterwards, therefore, when Sanacharib, king of the Arabians[3] and Assyrians, marched his vast army into Egypt, the warriors one and all refused to come to his aid. On this the monarch, greatly distressed, entered into the inner sanctuary, and before the image of the god, bewailed the fate which impended over him. As he wept he fell asleep, and dreamt that the god came and stood at his side, bidding him be of good cheer, and go boldly forth and meet the Arabian host, which would do him no hurt, as he himself would send those who should help him. Sethôs, then, relying on the dream, collected such of the Egyptians as were willing to follow him, who were

---

[1] No mention is made by Herodotus of Bocchoris (nor of his father Tnephachthus, the Technatis of Plutarch); and the lists of Manetho, as well as Diodorus, omit the Asychis and Anysis of Herodotus. Sethôs again, whom Herodotus calls a contemporary of Sennacherib, is unnoticed in Manetho's lists; and as Tirhaka was king of the whole country from Napata in Ethiopia to the frontier of Syria, no other Pharaoh could have ruled at that time in Egypt. We may therefore conclude that Herodotus has given to a *priest* of Pthah the title of *king*. The miraculous defeat of the Assyrian king mentioned both by the Egyptians and the Jews is remarkable. Some have attributed the destruction of his army to a plague; but plague does not destroy upwards of 185,000 men in one night. The omission of all notice of Tirhaka by the Egyptian informants of Herodotus may have been owing to jealousy of the Ethiopians. The Assyrians defeated by Tirhaka are represented at Medeenet Haboo in Thebes, and in his temple at Gebel Berkel, wearing cross-belts.—[G. W.]

[2] The same spirit of insubordination may have been growing up among the soldiers which afterwards broke out in the reign of Psammetichus; but it could not have had any effect while the Ethiopian kings of the 25th dynasty ruled the country (see note [5] on ch. 152). It is not impossible that it had already been the cause of the introduction of the Ethiopian rule; and the desertion of the troops to Ethiopia in the reign of Psammetichus may have been connected with a similar but unsuccessful attempt. There could not have been any Egyptian *king* contemporary with the 25th dynasty, since the Sabacos (neither of whom gave the throne to the Egyptians) were succeeded by Tirhaka.—[G. W.]

[3] It is curious to find Sennacherib called the "king of *the Arabians* and Assyrians"—an order of words which seems even to regard him as *rather* an Arabian than an Assyrian king. In the same spirit his army is termed afterwards "the Arabian host." It is impossible altogether to defend the view which Herodotus here discloses, but we may understand how such a mistake was possible, if we remember how Arabians were mixed up with other races in Lower Mesopotamia (see Essay x. in vol. i. § 11), and what an extensive influence a great Assyrian king would exercise over the tribes of the desert, especially those bordering on Mesopotamia. The ethnic connexion of the two great Semitic races would render union between them comparatively easy; and so we find Arabian kings at one time paramount over Assyria (Beros. Fr. 11), while now apparently the case was reversed, and an Assyrian prince bore sway over some considerable number of the Arab tribes.

none of them warriors, but traders, artisans, and market-people; and with these marched to Pelusium, which commands the entrance into Egypt, and there pitched his camp. As the two armies lay here opposite one another, there came in the night a multitude of field-mice, which devoured all the quivers and bow-strings of the enemy, and ate the thongs by which they managed their shields.[4] Next morning they commenced their flight, and great multitudes fell, as they had no arms with which to defend themselves. There stands to this day in the temple of Vulcan, a stone statue of Sethôs, with a mouse in his hand,[5] and an inscription to this effect—"Look on me, and learn to reverence the gods."

142. Thus far I have spoken on the authority of the Egyptians and their priests. They declare that from their first king to this last-mentioned monarch, the priest of Vulcan, was a period of three hundred and forty-one generations;[6] such, at least, they say, was the number both of their kings and of their high priests, during this interval. Now three hundred generations of men make ten thousand years, three generations filling up the century; and the remaining forty-one generations make thirteen hundred and forty years. Thus the whole number of years is eleven thousand, three hundred and forty; in which entire space, they said, no god had ever appeared in a human form; nothing of this kind had happened either under the former or under the later Egyptian kings. The sun, however, had within this period of time, on four several occasions, moved from his wonted course,[7] twice rising where he now sets, and

---

[4] For a representation of the "thongs" intended, see vol. i. p. 237.

[5] If any particular reverence was paid to mice at Memphis, it probably arose from some other mysterious reason. They were emblems of the generating and perhaps of the producing principle; and some thought them to be endued with prophetic power (a merit attributed now in some degree to rats on certain occasions). (See B. iv. note on ch. 192.) The people of Troas are said to have revered mice "because they gnawed the bowstrings of their enemies" (Eust. Il. i. 39), and Apollo, who was called Smintheus (from σμίνθος, a "mouse"), was represented on coins of Alexandria Troas with a mouse in his hand (Müller, Anc. Art. s. 361. 5). There was also a statue of him by Scopas with a mouse under his foot, in his temple at Chrysé (Strabo, xiii. p. 416), commemorative of their "gnawing the leathern parts of the enemy's arms," or because their "abounding near the temple made them sacred;" but Apollo Smintheus was worshipped in Greece also and other places, which argues against the story of the bow-strings being Egyptian.—[G. W.]

[6] From Menes to Sethos (or to Tirhaka his contemporary), which he reckons at 11,340 years. The exactly similar *number* of kings and high-priests is of course impossible. The era of Menes is shown by the monuments not to require a very extravagant date. The 341 generations, according to his calculation, do not make 11,340 but 11,366⅔ years. This priest Sethos appears to be mistaken for king Sethos (Sethi) of the 19th dynasty; of a very different age and character.—[G. W.]

[7] This has been very ingeniously shown by Mr. Poole (Horæ Ægyptiacæ, p. 94)

twice setting where he now rises. Egypt was in no degree affected by these changes ; the productions of the land, and of the
river, remained the same; nor was there anything unusual either
in the diseases or the deaths.

143. When Hecatæus the historian[1] was at Thebes, and,
discoursing of his genealogy, traced his descent to a god in the
person of his sixteenth ancestor, the priests of Jupiter did to
him exactly as they afterwards did to me, though I made no
boast of my family.   They led me into the inner sanctuary,
which is a spacious chamber, and showed me a multitude
of colossal statues, in wood, which they counted up, and found
to amount to the exact number they had said; the custom being
for every high priest during his lifetime to set up his statue in
the temple.   As they showed me the figures and reckoned them
up, they assured me that each was the son of the one preceding
him ; and this they repeated throughout the whole line, beginning with the representation of the priest last deceased, and
continuing till they had completed the series.   When Hecatæus, in giving his genealogy, mentioned a god as his sixteenth
ancestor, the priests opposed their genealogy to his, going
through this list, and refusing to allow that any man was ever
born of a god.   Their colossal figures were each, they said, a
Pirômis, born of a Pirômis,[2] and the number of them was three

to refer to "the solar risings of stars having fallen on those days of the vague
year on which the settings fell in the time of Sethos ; and "the historian by a natural mistake supposed they spoke of the sun itself." This is confirmed by Pomponius
Mela, who only differs in stating that the king to whose reign they calculated was
Amasis.—[G. W.]

[1] This is the first distinct mention of Hecatæus, who has been glanced at more
than once. (Vide supra, chaps. 21, 23.) He had flourished from about B.C. 520 to
B.C. 475, and had done far more than any other writer to pave the way for Herodotus. His works were of two kinds, geographical and historical. Under the former
head he wrote a description of the known world (Γῆς περίοδος), chiefly the result of
his own travels (Agathemer. I. i. p. 172), which must have been of considerable service to our author. Under the latter he wrote his genealogies, which were for the
most part mythical, but contained occasionally important history (vide infra, vi. 137).
The political influence of Hecatæus is noticed by Herodotus in two passages (v. 36,
125). He is the only prose-writer whom Herodotus mentions by name. The term
λογοποιός, which he applies to him both here and in Book v., I have translated
"historian" rather than "chronicler," because in Herodotus the word implies no
disrespect, being the term by which he would probably have designated himself.
"Prose-writer" is perhaps its most literal meaning, as it is antithetical to ἐποποιός,
"a writer of poetry."

[2] The Egyptians justly ridiculed the Greeks for deriving their origin from gods,
which were attributes of the Deity ; and nothing could appear more inconsistent
than to claim for an ancestor Hercules, the abstract idea of strength. Pirômis or
Pi-rôme was the usual Egyptian word for "man," with the definite article πι, "the,"
prefixed, and the simple and obvious meaning of the observation here recorded
was, that each of the statues represented a "man" engendered by a "man" without there being any god or hero among them. The translation which Herodotus
gives of the term, καλὸς καὶ ἀγαθός, is justified neither by the meaning of Piromi,
nor by the sense required.—[G. W.]

hundred and forty-five ; through the whole series Piromis followed Piromis, and the line did not run up either to a god or a hero.   The word *Piromis* may be rendered " gentleman."

144. Of such a nature were, they said, the beings represented by these images—they were very far indeed from being gods. However, in the times anterior to them it was otherwise ; then Egypt had gods for its rulers,[1] who dwelt upon the earth with men, one being always supreme above the rest.   The last of these was Horus, the son of Osiris, called by the Greeks Apollo. He deposed Typhon,[2] and ruled over Egypt as its last god-king. Osiris is named Dionysus (Bacchus) by the Greeks.

145. The Greeks regard Hercules, Bacchus, and Pan as the youngest of the gods.   With the Egyptians, contrariwise, Pan is exceedingly ancient,[3] and belongs to those whom they call " the eight gods," who existed before the rest.   Hercules is one of the gods of the second order, who are known as " the twelve ;" and Bacchus belongs to the gods of the third order, whom the twelve produced.   I have already mentioned how many years intervened according to the Egyptians between the birth of Hercules and the reign of Amasis.[4]   From Pan to this period they count a still longer time ; and even from Bacchus, who is the youngest of the three, they reckon fifteen thousand years to the reign of that king.   In these matters they say they cannot be mistaken, as they have always kept count of the years, and noted them in their registers.   But from the present day to the time of Bacchus, the reputed son of Semelé, daughter of Cadmus, is a period of not more than sixteen hundred years ; to that of Hercules, son of Alcmêna, is about nine hundred ; while to the time of Pan, son of Penelopé (Pan, according to the Greeks, was her child by Mercury), is a shorter space than to the Trojan war,[5] eight hundred years or thereabouts.

[1] This is in accordance with the account given by Manetho and with the Turin Papyrus, both which represent the gods as the first kings of Egypt before Menes. The last of them in the papyrus is also Horus the younger, the son of Osiris (see note [2] ch. 4, and note [5] ch. 99).   This Horus was distinct from Aroeris (Hor-oeri), the elder Horus, the brother of Osiris, and also from Hor-pocrates, the infant-son of Osiris and Isis, said by Eratosthenes to be "the god of day."   See note [9] on ch. 92.—[G. W.]

[2] Typhon, or rather Seth, the brother of Osiris, was the abstract idea of "evil," as Osiris was of "good ; " and in after times many fables (as Plutarch shows) arose out of this opposite nature of the two deities.   For both were adored until a change took place respecting Seth, brought about apparently by foreign influence.   (See note [3] on ch. 171.)   It is singular that names so like Typhon should occur in other languages.   In Arabic Tyfoon (like τυφὼς) is a whirlwind, and Tufán is the "Deluge ; " and the same word occurs in Chinese as Ty-fong.   On the different constructions put upon the fable of Osiris and Typhon, see notes [3] and [4] on ch. 171.—[G. W.]

[3] See note [20] on ch. 4, note [6] on ch. 42, and note [1] on ch. 43.   [4] Supra, ch. 43.

[5] The dates for the Trojan war vary almost two centuries.   Duris placed it as

146. It is open to all to receive whichever he may prefer of these two traditions ; my own opinion about them has been already declared.   If indeed these gods had been publicly known, and had grown old in Greece, as was the case with Hercules, son of Amphitryon, Bacchus, son of Semelé, and Pan, son of Penelopé, it might have been said that the last-mentioned personages were men who bore the names of certain previously existing deities.   But Bacchus, according to the Greek tradition, was no sooner born than he was sewn up in Jupiter's thigh, and carried off to Nysa,* above Egypt, in Ethiopia ; and as to Pan,

early as B.C. 1335 (Clem. Alex. Stromat. i. p. 337, A.).   Clemens in B.C. 1149. Isocrates, Ephorus, Democritus, and Phanias, seem to have inclined to the latter, Herodotus, Thucydides, the author of the Life of Homer, and the compiler of the Parian Marble, to the earlier period.   The date now usually received, B.C. 1183, is that of Eratosthenes, whose chronology was purely artificial, and rested on no solid basis.   The following is a list of the principal views on this subject:—

		B.C.
Duris placed the fall of Troy in	. . . .	1335
Author of the Life of Homer	. . . . .	1270
Herodotus	. . . .	1260+
Thucydides .	. . . . . .	1260+
Parian Marble	. . . . . .	1209
Eratosthenes .	. . . . . .	1183
Sosibius	. . . .	1171
Ephorus	. . . .	1169
Clemens	. . . , . . .	1149

* The story of Bacchus being taken to Nysa in Ethiopia is explained by the identity of Osiris and that god.   Nysa looks like n-isi (for éi-n-isi), Iseum ; but there were several cities, caves, and hills of this name, and some in Greece. Those of Arabia (Diodor. i. 15 ; iii. 6ł) and India (Arrian. Ind. c. v. ; Q. Curt. viii. 10) were most noted.   Diodorus (iii. 6ł) says Bacchus was nursed at Nysa, an island of the river Triton in Libya ; and the Theban Bacchus in the Nysæan cave between Phœnicia and Egypt (iv. 2).   He also mentions Nysa in Arabia (iii. 6ł) and the city of Nysa in Arabia Felix, near Egypt, where Osiris was educated, and who from his father Jove and this place was called Dionysus (i. 15 ; see Her. iii. 97 ; Virg. Æn. vi. 805 ; Ovid. Met. iv. 13).   Diodorus saying (i. 19) that Nysa in India was built by Osiris, in imitation of that of Egypt, seems to give an Egyptian origin to the name.   Pomp. Mela (iii. 7), speaking of India, says "of the cities, which are numerous, Nysa is the largest and most celebrated ;" and mentions Mount Meros sacred to Jove.   Philostratus (Vit. Apoll. Tyan. ii. 1) speaks of "the Indians calling Bacchus Nyseus, from a place in their country, called Nysa ;" and (ii. 4) of a "hill near Nysa called Meros (thigh), where Bacchus was born," and of "the hill Nysa," Hesychius says "Nysa and the Nysæan Mount are not in one place alone, but in Arabia, Ethiopia, Egypt, Babylon, Erythea, Thrace, Thessaly, Cilicia, India, Libya, Lydia, Macedonia, Naxus, and about the Pangeum, a place in Syria ;" to which may be added Eubœa, Phæacia (Schol. Apollon. Rhod. iv. 540, 983), and Phrygia, near the river Sangarius. (Eustath. in Dionys. Perieg. 940. See also Schol. Hom. Il. vi. 133 ; ii. 508 ; Eurip. Bacch. 556 ; Soph. Antig. 1131 ; Strabo, xv. 687, 701 ; Dion. Perieg. Il. 626, 940, 1159 ; Schol. Apoll. Rhod. ii. 904, 1211.)   Pliny (vi. 21) says, "Nysam urbem plerique Indiæ adscribunt, montemque Merum Libero patri sacrum, unde origo fabulæ Jovis femine (μηρῷ) editum."   Plin. v. 18 says "Scythopolis was formerly Nysa ;" and Juvenal mentions Nysa on Mt. Parnassus (vii. 63).   The Hindoos have also a sacred mountain called Meru.   The custom of having "holy hills" was of very early date, and common to the Egyptians, Jews, Greeks, and many people.   Gebel Berkel in Ethiopia is always called "the holy hill" on the monuments there (see n. ⁊ on ch. 29).   Part of Mount Sinai was so considered by the early Pharaohs, and by the Jews, Christians, and Moslems to this day ; and

they do not even profess to know what happened to him after his birth.   To me, therefore, it is quite manifest that the names of these gods became known to the Greeks after those of their other deities, and that they count their birth from the time when they first acquired a knowledge of them.   Thus far my narrative rests on the accounts given by the Egyptians.

147. In what follows I have the authority, not of the Egyptians only, but of others also who agree with them.   I shall speak likewise in part from my own observation.   When the Egyptians regained their liberty after the reign of the priest of Vulcan, unable to continue any while without a king, they divided Egypt into twelve districts, and set twelve kings[7] over them.   These twelve kings, united together by intermarriages, ruled Egypt in peace, having entered into engagements with one another not to depose any of their number, nor to aim at any aggrandisement of one above the rest, but to dwell together in perfect amity.   Now the reason why they made these stipulations, and guarded with care against their infraction, was, because at the very first establishment of the twelve kingdoms, an oracle had declared—"That he among them who should pour in Vulcan's temple a libation from a cup of bronze,[8] would become monarch of the whole land of Egypt."   Now the twelve held their meetings at all the temples.

148. To bind themselves yet more closely together, it seemed good to them to have a common monument.   In pursuance of this resolution they made the Labyrinth which lies a little above Lake Mœris,[9] in the neighbourhood of the place called the city

pilgrimages to it will readily account for those inscriptions called Sinaïtic, which are evidently not Jewish, but of a sea-faring people of that coast, since they have left similar records in the same language at the watering-places on the Egyptian side of the Red Sea as far S. as lat. 29° and 27° 50', where the Israelites could never have been (see App. CH. v. § 30).—[G. W.]

[7] The sarcastic observation that as they could not exist without a king, they elected twelve, must have been amusing to the Greeks.   They were probably only governors of the twelve principal nomes, not of all Egypt but of the Delta, to which Strabo gives ten and Ptolemy twenty-four, and which in later times contained thirty-five, including the Oasis of Ammon.   (See note [4] on ch. 137, and n. [7] ch. 164; of the Nomes of Egypt.)   Pliny speaks of sixteen nomes of all Egypt who met in the Labyrinth (xxxvi. 13); and Strabo (xvii. p. 558) states that the number of nomes corresponded to that of its chambers, when it was first built.—[G. W.]

[8] This should not have been remarkable if those cups were so commonly used in Egypt as Herodotus says.   See note [8] on ch. 37.—[G. W.] *p. 35*

[9] The position of the natural lake is well known; but M. Linant has discovered that of the artificial Mœris, near the site of Crocodilopolis, now *Medeenet-el-Fyoóm*. It has long formed part of the cultivated plain of the Fyoóm, and Pliny's using the word "*fuit*" shows it was no longer used in his time.   It was an extensive reservoir secured by dams, and from its channels conveyed the water in different directions to all parts of that inland province.   A small reservoir at the modern town, a very humble imitation of the Lake Mœris, supplies in the same manner the various

of Crocodiles.[1] I visited this place, and found it to surpass description ; for if all the walls and other great works of the Greeks could be put together in one, they would not equal, either for labour or expense, this Labyrinth ;[2] and yet the temple of Ephesus is a building worthy of note,[3] and so is the temple of

streams that irrigate the Fyoóm; and the ancient lake being a work of man accords with Pliny's "Mœridis lacus hoc est fossa grandis," as well as with the assertion of Herodotus. The other lake, now Birket-el-Korn, is formed by nature, and receives as in former times the superabundant water that ran off after the lands had been irrigated by the channels from the artificial Morris. See M. Linant's Memoir on his interesting and important discovery.—[G. W. *Je Lanien tolus a Menritram, of Coire*

[1] Afterwards called Arsinoë, from the wife and sister of Ptolemy Philadelphus, like the port on the Red Sea (now Suez). The reason of the crocodile being sacred in this inland province was to ensure the maintenance of the canals, as De Pauw observes (vol. ii. pt. iii. s. 7. p. 122).—[G. W.]

[2] The admiration expressed by Herodotus for the Labyrinth is singular, when. there were so many far more magnificent buildings at Thebes, of which he takes no notice. It was probably the beauty of the stone, the richness of its decoration, and the peculiarity of its plan that struck him so much. Remains of the white stones he mentions may still be traced even in the upper part; they are a hard silicious limestone, and the broken columns of red granite with bud capitals, are perhaps those alluded to by Pliny, who supposes them porphyry. Strabo gives the length of the Labyrinth as a stadium, which agrees very nearly with the actual measurement, and makes the pyramid at the end of it 4 plethra, or 400 feet, square, and the same in height, which Herodotus calculates at 50 orgyies, or 300 feet (see note [2] on ch. 136). The excavations made by the Prussian commission have ascertained the exact size and plan of the Labyrinth. The oldest name found there was of Amun-m-he III., who corresponds to Ameres, and whose immediate predecessor Lamaris (or Labaris) is said by Manetho to have made the Labyrinth. Perhaps μεϑ' ὃν Δάμαρις was corrupted from μεϑ' ὃν δὶ Μάρις. These resemblances of names led to numerous mistakes of Greek writers (see note [8] on ch. 13, and note [9] on ch. 100). Gliddon thinks Labyrinth was so called from Labaris (Otia Ægyptiaca). Strabo's position of the Labyrinth is well described; and his distance of 100 stadia from Arsinoë agrees very well with the 11¼ Eng. m. from the centre of its mounds to the pyramid of Hawára. Diodorus calls the founder of the Labyrinth Mendes ; and Pliny (xxxvi. 13), who erroneously places it in the Heracleopolite nome, and attributes it to king Petesucus, or Tithoës, shows that it stood near the frontier of the Crocodilopolite nome (or Fyoóm); and his expression "primus factus est" implies that it was added to by other kings. This was usual in Egyptian monuments ; and the names of more than one king at the Labyrinth prove it was the case there also. If the number of chambers was equal to that of the nomes of Egypt, it must have varied greatly at different times (see note [7] on ch. 164).—[G. W.]

[3] The original temple of Diana at Ephesus seems to have been destroyed by the Cimmerians (see the Essays appended to Book i., Essay i. § 14) in their great incursion during the reign of Ardys. The temple which Herodotus saw was then begun to be built by Chersiphron of Cnossus and his son Metagenes, contemporaries of Theodorus and Rhœcus, the builders of the Samian Herœum. (Cf. Vitruv. præf. ad lib. vii.; Strab. xiv. p. 918; Plin. H. N. xxxvi. 14.) These architects did not live to complete their work, which was finished by Demetrius and Peonius of Ephesus, the rebuilder of the temple of Apollo at Branchidæ. (Vitruv. l. s. c.) The architecture of the temple of Chersiphron was Ionic. (Vitruv. iii. 2.) It was, according to Pliny, 220 years in building. After its destruction by Eratostratus in the year of Alexander's birth (Plut. Alex. c. 1. Timæus, Fr. 137), the temple of Diana was rebuilt with greater magnificence, and probably on a larger scale, than before ; as the dimensions given by Pliny considerably exceed those which observation assigns to the Herœum of Samos, while the Herœum was in the days of Herodotus "the largest of Greek temples " (infra, iii. 60). No traces

Samos.[4] The pyramids likewise surpass description, and are severally equal to a number of the greatest works of the Greeks, but the Labyrinth surpasses the pyramids. It has twelve courts, *adjecu* all of them roofed, with gates exactly opposite to one another, *this* six looking to the north, and six to the south. A single wall surrounds the entire building. There are two different sorts of chambers throughout—half under ground, half above ground, the latter built upon the former; the whole number of these chambers is three thousand, fifteen hundred of each kind. The upper chambers I myself passed through and saw, and what I say concerning them is from my own observation; of the underground chambers I can only speak from report : for the keepers of the building could not be got to show them, since they contained (as they said) the sepulchres of the kings who built the Labyrinth, and also those of the sacred crocodiles. Thus it is from hearsay only that I can speak of the lower chambers. The upper chambers, however, I saw with my own eyes, and found them to excel all other human productions; for the passages through the houses, and the varied windings of the paths across the courts, excited in me infinite admiration, as I passed from the courts into chambers, and from the chambers into colonnades, and from the colonnades into fresh houses, and again from these into courts unseen before. The roof was throughout of stone, like the walls; and the walls were covered all over with figures ; every court was surrounded with a colonnade, which was built of white stones exquisitely fitted together. At the corner of the Labyrinth stands a pyramid, forty fathoms high, with large figures engraved on it ; which is entered by a subterranean passage.

149. Wonderful as is the Labyrinth, the work called the Lake of Mœris,[5] which is close by the Labyrinth, is yet more astonishing. The measure of its circumference is sixty schœnes, or three thousand six hundred furlongs, which is equal to the entire length of Egypt along the sea-coast. The lake stretches in its longest direction from north to south, and in its deepest parts is of the depth of fifty fathoms. It is manifestly an artificial excavation, for nearly in the centre there stand two pyramids,[6] rising to the height of fifty fathoms above the surface of

---

remain of this much-admired fabric (Chandler, vol. i. p. 153), unless the ruins noticed by Mr. Hamilton, near the western extremity of the town (Asia Minor, vol. ii. pp. 24–5), are admitted to mark its site.

[4] Vide infra, iii. 60, note.
[5] See note [7] to the preceding chapter.
[6] No traces remain of these pyramids. The ruins at Biáhmoo show from their

the water, and extending as far beneath, crowned each of them with a colossal statue sitting upon a throne. Thus these pyramids are one hundred fathoms high, which is exactly a furlong (stadium) of six hundred feet: the fathom being six feet in length, or four cubits, which is the same thing, since a cubit measures six, and a foot four, palms.[7] The water of the lake does not come out of the ground, which is here excessively dry,[8] but is introduced by a canal from the Nile. The current sets for six months into the lake from the river, and for the next six months into the river from the lake. While it runs outward it returns a talent of silver daily to the royal treasury from the fish that are taken,[9] but when the current is the other way the return sinks to one-third of that sum.

forms, and from the angle of their walls, 67°, that they were not pyramids; unless a triangular facing made up the pyramid (see ch. 125, n. [9]).—[G. W.] ✸

[7] The measures of Herodotus are almost all drawn either from portions of the human body, or from bodily actions easily performable. His smallest measure is the δάκτυλος, or "finger's breadth," four of which go to the παλαιστή ("palm" or "hand's breadth"), while three palms make the σπιθαμή ("span"), and four the πούς ("foot"). The πῆχυς ("cubit," or length from the tip of the fingers to the elbow) is a foot and a half, or two spans; the ὀργυιά ("fathom," or extent to which the arms can reach when extended) is four cubits, or six feet. The πλέθρον (a word the derivation of which is uncertain) is 100 feet; and the στάδιον (or distance to which a man could run before he required to stop) is six plethra, or 600 feet. These are the only measures used by Herodotus, besides the schœne and parasang, by which he found distances determined in Egypt and Persia respectively. The following table will exhibit his scheme of measures:—

1 δάκτυλος.							
4	1 παλαιστή.						
12	3	1 σπιθαμή.					
16	4	1¼	1 πούς.				
24	6	2	1½	1 πῆχυς.			
96	24	8	6	4	1 ὀργυιά.		
1600	400	133⅓	100	66⅔	16⅔	1 πλέθρον.	
9600	2400	800	600	400	100	6	1 στάδιον.

[8] This is the nature of the basin on which the alluvial soil has been deposited; but it resembles the whole valley of the Nile in being destitute of springs, which are only met with in two or three places. The wells are all formed by the filtration of water from the river. In the Birket-el-Korn are some springs, serving, with the annual supply from the Nile, to keep up the water of the lake, which in the deepest part has only 24 feet, and it is gradually becoming more shallow from the mud brought into it by the canals.—[G. W.]

[9] A great quantity of fish is caught even at the present day at the mouths of the canals, when they are closed, and the water is prevented from returning to the Nile. It affords a considerable revenue to the government. It is farmed by certain villages on the banks, and some idea may be formed of its value by the village of Agaleth at Thebes paying annually for its small canal 1500 piastres, equal till lately to 21l. The custom of farming the fisheries was probably derived by the Arab government from the ancient Egyptians, but El Makrisi mentions it as

150. The natives told me that there was a subterranean passage from this lake[1] to the Libyan Syrtis, running westward into the interior by the hills above Memphis. As I could not anywhere see the earth which had been taken out when the excavation was made, and I was curious to know what had become of it, I asked the Egyptians who live closest to the lake where the earth had been put. The answer that they gave me I readily accepted as true, since I had heard of the same thing being done in Nineveh of the Assyrians. There, once upon a time, certain thieves having formed a plan to get into their possession the vast treasures of Sardanapalus, the Ninevite king,[2] which were laid up in subterranean treasuries, proceeded to tunnel a passage from the house where they lived into the royal palace, calculating the distance and the direction. At nightfall they took the earth from the excavation and carried it to the river Tigris, which ran by Nineveh, continuing to get rid of it in this manner until they had accomplished their purpose. It was exactly in the same way that the Egyptians disposed of the mould from their excavation, except that they did it by day and not by night ; for as fast as the earth was dug, they carried it to the Nile, which they knew would disperse it far and wide. Such was the account which I received of the formation of this lake.

151. The twelve kings for some time dealt honourably by one another, but at length it happened that on a certain occasion, when they had met to worship in the temple of Vulcan, the high-priest on the last day of the festival, in bringing forth the golden goblets from which they were wont to pour the libations, mistook the number, and brought eleven goblets only for the twelve princes. Psammetichus was standing last, and being left without a cup, he took his helmet, which was of bronze,[3] from

---

of comparatively late introduction. (See. Silv. de Sacy's Relation de l'Egypte, par Abd-al-latif, p. 283, note.) Herodotus reckons the revenue from the fish of the Lake Mœris at a talent of silver (193*l*. 15*s*. English, or as some compute it, 225*l*., or 243*l*. 15*s*.) daily ; and when the water flowed from the Nile into the lake at 20 minæ (64*l*. 12*s*., or 81*l*. 1*s*. 8*d*.), amounting at the lowest calculation to more than 47,000*l*. a-year. According to Diodorus (i. 52) this was part of the pin-money of the queens. See n. [2] ch. 98.—[G. W.]

[1] Herodotus here evidently alludes to the natural lake, now *Birket-el-Korn*, not to the artificial Mœris. The belief in underground communications is still very prevalent in Egypt (as in other countries) to the present day ; and might very reasonably arise from what we see in limestone formations.—[G. W.]

[2] It is uncertain which Assyrian king is here intended. The Greeks recognised two monarchs of the name—one a warrior, who seems to be *Asshur-dan-pal*, the father of the Black Obelisk king ; the other the voluptuary, who closed the long series of Assyrian sovereigns.

[3] If this were so, and the other kings wore the same kind of helmet, the Egyp-

off his head, stretched it out to receive the liquor, and so made
his libation. All the kings were accustomed to wear helmets,
and all indeed wore them at this very time. Nor was there any
crafty design in the action of Psammetichus. The eleven, however, when they came to consider what had been done, and bethought them of the oracle which had declared " that he who, of
the twelve, should pour a libation from a cup of bronze, the same
would be king of the whole land of Egypt," doubted at first if
they should not put Psammetichus to death. Finding, however,
upon examination, that he had acted in the matter without any
guilty intent, they did not think it would be just to kill him ;
but determined, instead, to strip him of the chief part of his
power and to banish him to the marshes, forbidding him to leave
them, or to hold any communication with the rest of Egypt.

152. This was the second time that Psammetichus had been
driven into banishment. On a former occasion he had fled from
Sabacôs the Ethiopian,⁴ who had put his father Necôs to death ;
and had taken refuge in Syria, from whence, after the retirement
of the Ethiop in consequence of his dream, he was brought back
by the Egyptians of the Saïtic canton. Now it was his ill-for-
tune to be banished a second time by the eleven kings, on account
of the libation which he had poured from his helmet ; on this occasion he fled to the marshes. Feeling that he was an injured man,
and designing to avenge himself upon his persecutors, Psammetichus sent to the city of Buto, where there is an oracle of Latona,
the most veracious of all the oracles of the Egyptians, and having
inquired concerning means of vengeance, received for answer,
that " Vengeance would come from the sea, when brazen men
should appear." Great was his incredulity when this answer
arrived, for never, he thought, would brazen men arrive to be
his helpers. However, not long afterwards certain Carians and
Ionians, who had left their country on a voyage of plunder, were
carried by stress of weather to Egypt, where they disembarked,
all equipped in their brazen armour, and were seen by the natives, one of whom carried the tidings to Psammetichus, and, as
he had never before seen men clad in brass, he reported that

tians would not have been surprised at seeing men in similar armour coming from
the sea (ch. 152). Bronze armour was of very early date in Egypt, and was therefore no novelty in the reign of Psammetichus. It is represented in the tombs of
the kings at Thebes, and bronze plates, forming part of a corslet of scale armour,
have been found bearing the name of Sheshonk, and are in Dr. Abbott's collection.
(See note on B. vii. ch. 89.) Χάλκος is really "bronze," ὀρείχαλκος "brass." Objects have been found of brass as well as of bronze in Egypt.—[G. W.]

⁴ On the Sabacos, Tirhaka, and Psammetichus, see notes ⁴ and ⁵ on ch. 137, and
Hist. Notice in App. CH. viii. § 31–34.—[G. W.]

brazen men had come from the sea and were plundering the plain. Psammetichus, perceiving at once that the oracle was accomplished, made friendly advances to the strangers, and engaged them, by splendid promises, to enter into his service. He then, with their aid and that of the Egyptians who espoused his cause, attacked the eleven and vanquished them.[5]

[5] The improbability of a few Ionian and Carian pirates having enabled Psammetichus to obtain possession of the throne is sufficiently obvious. The Egyptians may not have been willing to inform Herodotus how long their kings had employed Greek mercenary troops before the Persian invasion; and a body of troops would not have landed opportunely to fulfil an oracle. This was in fact the first time that the Egyptian Pharaohs had recourse to Greek mercenaries, and began to find their utility; and though the ancient kings in the glorious times of Egypt's great power had foreign auxiliaries (see woodcut; and that in note, B. vii. ch. 61, where three of these people are enemies of Egypt), they were levies composing part of the army, like those of the various nations which contributed to the expeditions of Xerxes and other Persian monarchs. But the introduction of Greek paid troops into the Egyptian service excited the jealousy of the native army (who could not have been long in perceiving the superiority of those strangers); and the favour shown to them led to the defection of the Egyptian troops (see note [3] on ch. 30). The Egyptian army had lost its former military ardour; and now that Syria was so often threatened by the powerful nations of Asia, it was natural that Psammetichus should seek to employ foreigners, whose courage and fidelity he could trust. (See Hist. Notice, App. CH. viii. § 34.)   Herodotus states that these Greek troops were the first foreigners allowed to establish themselves in Egypt; that is, after the Shepherds and Israelites left it (see note [6] ch. 112). Strabo (xvii. p. 1131) speaks of the employment of mercenary troops in Egypt as an old custom. That of Psammetichus differed from the earlier system of auxiliaries; it was a sign of weakness, and was fatal to Egypt as to Carthage (see Macchiavelli, Princ. c. 13). Polyænus says that Psammetichus took the Carians into his pay hoping that the plumes they wore on their helmets pointed to the oracle, which had warned Temanthes, then king of Egypt, against cocks. (Cp. Plut. Vit. Artax. of Carian crests). With them he therefore attacked Temanthes, and having killed him, gave those soldiers a quarter in Memphis, thence called Caromemphis. The mercenary troops or "hired men," in the time of "Necho," are mentioned in Jeremiah (xlvi. 21).—[G. W.]

Foreign Auxiliaries in the time of Remeses III.

153. When Psammetichus had thus become sole monarch of Egypt, he built the southern gateway of the temple of Vulcan in Memphis, and also a court for Apis, in which Apis[6] is kept whenever he makes his appearance in Egypt. This court is opposite the gateway of Psammetichus, and is surrounded with a colonnade and adorned with a multitude of figures. Instead of pillars, the colonnade rests upon colossal statues, twelve cubits in height. The Greek name for Apis is Epaphus.

154. To the Ionians and Carians[7] who had lent him their assistance Psammetichus assigned as abodes two places opposite to each other, one on either side of the Nile, which received the name of "the Camps."[8] He also made good all the splendid promises by which he had gained their support; and further, he entrusted to their care certain Egyptian children, whom they were to teach the language of the Greeks. These children, thus instructed, became the parents of the entire class of interpreters[9] in Egypt. The Ionians and Carians occupied for many years the places assigned them by Psammetichus, which lay near the sea, a little below the city of Bubastis, on the Pelusiac mouth of the Nile.[1] King Amasis, long afterwards, removed the Greeks hence, and settled them at Memphis to guard him against the native Egyptians. From the date of the original settlement of these persons in Egypt, we Greeks, through our intercourse with them, have acquired an accurate knowledge of

---

[6] This court was surrounded by Osiride pillars, like that of Medeenet Haboo at Thebes. Attached to it were probably the two stables, "delubra," or "thalami," mentioned by Pliny (viii. 46); and Strabo (xvii. p. 555) says, "before the sêkos or chamber where Apis is kept is a vestibule, in which is another chamber for the mother of the sacred bull, and into this vestibule Apis is sometimes introduced, particularly when shown to strangers; at other times he is only seen through a window of the sêkos. . . . . The temple of Apis is close to that of Vulcan." Pliny pretends that the entry of Apis into the one or the other of the "delubra" was a good or a bad omen. On Apis, see above, ch. 38, note [9], and compare B. iii. ch. 28.—[G. W.]

[7] The Carians seem to have been fond of engaging themselves as mercenary soldiers from a very early date, and to have continued the practice so long as they were their own masters. According to some commentators, the expression in Homer (Il. ix. 378), ἐν Καρὸς αἴσῃ, is to be understood in this sense. (See the Schol. ad Platon. ed. Ruhnken, p. 322, and comp. the note of Heyne, vol. v. p. 605.) Archilochus certainly spoke of them as notorious for mercenary service, as appears from the well-known line—

καὶ δὴ 'πίκουρος, ὥστε Κὰρ, κεκλήσομαι.

The Scholiast on Plato says that they were the first to engage in the occupation, and quotes Ephorus as an authority.

[8] See note [6] on ch. 112.

[9] See end of note [8] on ch. 164.

[1] The site chosen for the Greek camps shows that they were thought necessary as a defence against foreign invasion from the eastward. (See Diodor. i. 67.) The Roman *Scenæ Veteranorum* were not very far from this.—[G. W.]

An Isolated Egyptian Temple, within its Temenos, or sacred Enclosure; with the Priests bringing in the Ark of the God. Beyond are villas, canals, and the Nile.

the several events in Egyptian history, from the reign of Psammetichus downwards; but before his time no foreigners had ever taken up their residence in that land. The docks where their vessels were laid up, and the ruins of their habitations, were still to be seen in my day at the place where they dwelt originally, before they were removed by Amasis. Such was the mode by which Psammetichus became master of Egypt.

155. I have already made mention more than once of the Egyptian oracle,[2] and as it well deserves notice, I shall now proceed to give an account of it more at length. It is a temple of Latona,[3] situated in the midst of a great city on the Sebennytic mouth of the Nile, at some distance up the river from the sea. The name of the city, as I have before observed, is Buto; and in it are two other temples also, one of Apollo and one of Diana. Latona's temple, which contains the oracle, is a spacious building with a gateway ten fathoms in height.[4] The most wonderful thing that was actually to be seen about this temple[5] was a chapel in the enclosure made of a single stone,[6] the length and

---

[2] Supra, chs. 83, 133, and 152. There were several other oracles, but that of Buto, or Latona, was held in the highest repute. (See ch. 83.)

[3] Herodotus says that this goddess was one of the great Deities (ch. 156). She appears to be a character of Maut, and may, in one of her characters, be Thriphis, the goddess of Athribis, where the Mygale or shrew-mouse, which was sacred to Buto, was said by Strabo to have been worshipped. I have seen a small figure of a hedgehog with the name of Buto upon it. Buto, as Champollion supposed, was probably primæval darkness. (See notes [3] and [4] on B. ii. ch. 59, and App. CH. iii. § 2, *Maut.*) Lucian (De Deâ Syriâ, s. 36) says there were many oracles in Egypt, as in Greece, Asia, and Libya, the responses of which were given "by priests and prophets." The principal ones in Egypt were of Buto, Hercules (Gem), Apollo (Horus), Minerva (Neith), Diana (Bubastis), Mars (Honurius, or more probably Mandoo, see note [4] on ch. 63), and Jupiter (Amun, at Thebes; see chs. 54, 57, 83, 111, 133). That of Besa was also noted, which was said by Ammianus Marcellinus to have been at Abydus, or, according to others, near the more modern Antinoöpolis; but it is uncertain who that Deity was. Heliopolis had also its oracle (Macrob. Satur. i. 30); but the most celebrated was that of "Ammon" in the Oasis. The position of the city of Latona, near the Sebennytic mouth, was on the W. bank, between that branch of the Nile and the lake, about 20 miles from the sea. The isle of Chemmis was in that lake. Herodotus is supposed to have been indebted to Hecatæus for the mention of this island. (See Müller's Fragm. Hist. Græc. vol. i.)—[G. W.]

[4] This is the height of the pyramidal towers of the propylæum, or court of entrance. The 10 orgyiæ, or 60 feet, is the full height of those towers, which seldom exceed 50. In front, on either side of the entrance, was usually a colossus of the king, before which stood two obelisks terminating an avenue, or dromos, of sphinxes. Clemens confounds the propylæum with the pronaos.' Pylon, pylôné, and propylon, are applied to the stone gateway, when standing alone before the temple; and the same kind of entrance is repeated between the two towers of the inner court or propylæum, immediately "before the door" of the actual temple, or at least of its portico. A stone pylon is also placed as a *side* entrance to the crude brick enclosure of a temenos.—[G. W.]

[5] Herodotus says, "the most wonderful thing *that was actually to be seen*," because he considers that the wonder of the floating island, which he "did not see" (ch. 156), would, if true, have been still more astonishing.

[6] According to these measurements, supposing the walls to have been only 6 feet

height of which were the same, each wall being forty cubits square, and the whole a single block! Another block of stone formed the roof, and projected at the eaves to the extent of four cubits.

156. This, as I have said, was what astonished me the most, of all the things that were actually to be seen about the temple. The next greatest marvel was the island called Chemmis. This island lies in the middle of a broad and deep lake close by the temple, and the natives declare that it floats. For my own part I did not see it float, or even move; and I wondered greatly, when they told me concerning it, whether there be really such a thing as a floating island.[7] It has a grand temple of Apollo built upon it, in which are three distinct altars. Palm-trees grow on it in great abundance, and many other trees, some of which bear fruit, while others are barren. The Egyptians tell the following story in connexion with this island, to explain the way in which it first came to float:—"In former times, when the isle was still fixed and motionless, Latona, one of the eight gods of the first order, who dwelt in the city of Buto, where now she has her oracle, received Apollo as a sacred charge from Isis,

thick, and the material granite, as in other monoliths, this monument would weigh upwards of 6738 tons, being 76,032 cubic feet, without the cornice, which was placed on the roof. The reigns of the Psammetichi and other kings of this 26th dynasty, were the period of the renaissance or revival of art in Egypt; both for the size and beauty of the monuments; and though the sculptures are not so spirited as during the 18th and 19th dynasties, they have great elegance, sharpness of execution, and beauty of finish. It is singular that though the sculptures and paintings in the tombs near the pyramids are inferior to those of the best age, and though progress is perceptible in different times, there is no really rude or archaic style in Egypt; there are no specimens of a primitive state, or early attempts in art, such as are found in other countries; and the masonry of the oldest monuments that remain, the pyramids, vies with that of any subsequent age, particularly in their exquisitely wrought granite. The art of Egypt was of native growth, and was original and characteristic; but the Egyptians, like all other people, borrowed occasionally from those with whom they had early intercourse; and as the Assyrians adopted from them the winged globe, the lotus, and many other emblems or devices, the Egyptians seem also to have taken from Assyria certain ornaments unknown in Egypt before and during the 12th dynasty. Among these may be mentioned vases with the heads of a horse, a cock, a vulture, or an eagle (such as is given to the supposed Assyrian deity Nisroch), the knot, and the feather patterns, and perhaps some of the trappings of the horse, an animal apparently introduced from Asia. Even the Typhonian monster with feathers on his head, so common under the 22nd dynasty, seems to have some connexion with Asia, as well as with Libya. Those devices first occur on monuments of the 18th and 19th dynasties, whose kings came much in contact with the Assyrians; and it was perhaps from them that the pointed arch of that time was copied, which, though not on the principle of the true arch, appears to have been cut into the stone roof, in *imitation* of what the Egyptians had seen, as the round one was in imitation of the brick arches they had themselves so long used (see n. ¹ ch. 136).—[G. W.]

[7] Hecatæus had related the marvels of this island, which he called Chembis, without any appearance of incredulity. (Fr. 284.) There is a tacit allusion to him in this passage.

and saved him by hiding him in what is now called the floating
island. Typhon meanwhile was searching everywhere in hopes
of finding the child of Osiris." (According to the Egyptians,
Apollo and Diana are the children of Bacchus and Isis ;³ while
Latona is their nurse and their preserver. They call Apollo, in
their language, Horus ; Ceres they call Isis ; Diana, Bubastis.
From this Egyptian tradition, and from no other, it must have
been that Æschylus, the son of Euphorion, took the idea, which
is found in none of the earlier poets, of making Diana the
daughter of Ceres.⁹) The island, therefore, in consequence of
this event, was first made to float. Such at least is the account
which the Egyptians give.

157. Psammetichus ruled Egypt for fifty-four years, during
twenty-nine of which he pressed the siege of Azôtus¹ without

    ⁸ Apollo was Horus, the son of Isis and Osiris (Ceres and Bacchus); but he had
no sister in Egyptian mythology, and Diana was Bubastis or Pasht, who appears to
be one of the great deities, and was the second member of the great triad of
Memphis, composed of Phtha, Pasht, and Nofre-Atmoo. The Diana of the Greeks
was daughter of Latona; and Herodotus and Plutarch say that Æschylus was the
only one who mentions her as Ceres, in imitation of the Egyptians. Aroeris and
even Hor-Hat were also supposed by the Greeks to answer to Apollo, from their
having a hawk's head like Horus. They therefore called the city of Hor-Hat
Apollinopolis Magna (*Edfoo*), and that of Aroeris Apollinopolis Parva (*Koos*).—
[G. W.]
    ⁹ Pausanias reports this also (VIII. xxxvii. § 3), but seems to be merely following
Herodotus. It is not a happy conjecture of Bähr's (not. ad loc.) that it was for revealing this secret (?) that Æschylus was accused of violating the mysteries. The
mention of Æschylus is important, as showing that Herodotus was acquainted with
his writings.
    ¹ Azotus is Ashdod or Ashdoodeh of sacred scripture. This shows how much
the Egyptian power had declined when Psammetichus was obliged to besiege a city
near the confines of Egypt for so long a time as twenty-nine years, the armies of
the Pharaohs in the glorious days of the 18th and 19th dynasties being in the constant habit of traversing the whole country from the Nile to the Euphrates. Diodorus says it was in the Syrian campaign that the Egyptian troops deserted from
Psammetichus. The capture of Azotus facilitated the advance of his son Neco when
he continued the war. The duration of the siege of Azotus was probably owing to
its having received an Assyrian garrison, being an important advanced point to
keep the Egyptians in check ; and the king of Nineveh was perhaps prevented by
circumstances at that time from sending to succour it. For Tartan had been sent
by "Sargòn, king of Assyria," and had taken Ashdod (Isaiah xx. 1). He was the
same who went from Sennacherib, the son and successor of Sargòn, to Hezekiah (2
Kings xviii. 17) four years afterwards, with Rabsaris and Rabshakeh, B. C. 710, just
before the defeat of Sennacherib. Tartan is thought not to be the name of an individual, but the title "*general*," though the two others are names. The mention
of Ethiopians and Egyptians taken prisoners by the Assyrians (Is. xx. 4) doubtless
refers to the previous capture of Azotus, when it held a mixed garrison (Egypt having then an Ethiopian dynasty) which was compelled to surrender to the Assyrians.
Ashdod was the strong city of the Philistines, where they took the ark "into the
house of Dagon" (1 Sam. v. 2); and that it was always a fortified place is shown
by the name signifying, like the Arabic, *shedeed*, "strong." In the wars between
the Egyptians and Assyrians it was at one time in the possession of one, at another
of the rival power. Psammetichus reigned according to Herodotus fifty-four years,
and his fifty-fourth year occurs on the Apis Stelæ (see Historical Notice of Egypt in
Appendix, CH. viii. § 33).—[G. W.]

intermission, till finally he took the place.   Azôtus is a great
town in Syria.   Of all the cities that we know, none ever stood
so long a siege.

158. Psammetichus left a son called Necôs, who succeeded
him upon the throne.   This prince was the first to attempt the
construction of the canal to the Red Sea,[2]—a work completed
afterwards by Darius the Persian[3]—the length of which is four
days' journey, and the width such as to admit of two triremes
being rowed along it abreast.   The water is derived from the
Nile, which the canal leaves a little above the city of Bubastis,[4]

[2] Herodotus says Neco (or Necôs) began the canal, and Strabo attributes it to
"Psammetichus his son;" but the ruins on its banks show that it already existed in
the time of Remeses II., and that the statement of Aristotle, Strabo, and Pliny, who
ascribe its commencement at least to Sesostris, is founded on fact.   That from its
sandy site it would require frequent re-excavating is very evident, and these successive operations may have given to the different kings by whom they were performed the credit of commencing the canal.   It is certainly inconsistent to suppose
that the Egyptians (who of all people had the greatest experience in making canals,
and who even to the late time of Nero were the people consulted about cutting through
the Isthmus of Corinth—Lucian) should have been obliged to wait for its completion
till the accession of the Ptolemies.   The authority of Herodotus suffices to prove that it
was completed in his time to the Red Sea; and the monuments of Remeses at a town
on its banks prove that it existed in his reign.   Neco may have discontinued the re-
opening of it; Darius may have completed it, as Herodotus states, both here and
in Book iv. ch. 39; and it may have been re-opened and improved by the Ptolemies
and again by the Arabs.   In like manner, though the Alexandrian canal is attributed entirely to Mohammed Ali, this does not prove that it was not the successor of
an older canal, which left the Nile at another point.   The trade of Egypt was very
great with other countries, to which she exported corn at a remote period; and
we find from Athenæus (ii. c. 3) that Bacchylides, who lived about the time of
Pindar, speaks of corn going to Greece in ships from Egypt, when he says, "all
men when drunk fancy they are kings, their houses are resplendent with gold and
ivory, and corn-bearing ships bring over the bright sea the abundant wealth of
Egypt."   Wheat is represented as its staple commodity, at the coronation of the
early Egyptian kings.   The trade with Arabia by sea appears to have opened as
early as the 12th dynasty, and afterwards extended to India.   But even under the
Ptolemies and Cæsars, it was confined to the western coast and the islands; and in
Strabo's time "few merchants went from Egypt to the Ganges" (xv. p. 472).   The
first Egyptian port on the Red Sea was probably Ænnum, afterwards Philotera,
from the youngest sister of Ptolemy Philadelphus (now old Kossayr), at the watering-
place near which are the monuments of Amun-m-he II. and Osirtasen II.—[G. W.]
[3] An inscription of Darius in the Persian Cuneiform character is engraved upon
the Suez stone near the embouchure of the ancient canal.   It reads: "Daryavush
naqa wazarka," "Darius the Great King."   (Behistun Memoir, vol. i. p. 313.)
[4] The commencement of the Red Sea canal was in different places at various
periods.   In the time of Herodotus it left the Pelusiac branch a little above
Bubastis; it was afterwards supplied with water by the Amnis Trajanus, which left
the Nile at Babylon (near old Cairo), and the portion of it that remains now begins
a short distance from Belbays, which is about 11 miles south of Bubastis.   Strabo
must be wrong in saying it was at Phacusa, which is too low down the stream.   The
difference of 13 feet between the levels of the Red Sea and Mediterranean is now
proved to be an error.   Pliny says that Ptolemy desisted from the work finding the
Red Sea was 3 cubits (4½ feet) higher than the land of Egypt; but, independent of
our knowing that it was already finished in Herodotus' time, it is obvious that a
people accustomed to sluices, and every contrivance necessary for water of various
levels, would not be deterred by this, or a far greater, difference in the height of

near Patûmus, the Arabian town,[5] being continued thence until
it joins the Red Sea. At first it is carried along the Arabian
side of the Egyptian plain, as far as the chain of hills opposite
Memphis, whereby the plain is bounded, and in which lie the
great stone quarries; here it skirts the base of the hills running
in a direction from west to east; after which it turns, and enters
a narrow pass, trending southwards from this point, until it
enters the Arabian Gulf. From the northern sea to that which
is called the southern or Erythræan, the shortest and quickest
passage, which is from Mount Casius, the boundary between
Egypt and Syria, to the Gulf of Arabia, is a distance of exactly
one thousand furlongs.[6] But the way by the canal is very much

the sea and the Nile, and Diodorus expressly states that sluices were constructed at
its mouth. If so these were on account of the different levels, which varied mate-
rially at high and low Nile, and at each tide, of 5 to 6 feet, in the Red Sea, and to
prevent the sea-water from tainting that of the canal. The city of the Eels, Phagroriopolis, was evidently founded on its banks to insure the maintenance of the
canal. The place of the sluices appears to be traceable near Suez, where a channel
in the rock has been cut to form the mouth of the canal. It is probable that the
merchandise was transhipped from the boats in the canal to those in the harbour,
on the other side of the quay, and that sluices were not opened except during the
inundation, when the stream ran from the Nile to the Red Sea. In the time of the
Romans it was still used, but afterwards fell into disuse, and was choked up until
the caliph Omar re-opened it, in order to send supplies to Arabia, in record of which
benefit he received the title of "Prince of the Faithful," *Emeer el Momeneen*, which
was continued to or assumed by his successors. It was closed 134 years afterwards
by El Munsoor Aboo Gáfer, the 2nd Abbaside Caliph, to prevent supplies going to
Medeeneh, then in the hands of one of the descendants of Ali; since which time it
has remained closed, though El Hakem is said to have once more rendered it navigable for boats, A. D. 1000. After that it was filled up with sand, though some water
passed during the high Nile as far as Shekh Hanáydik and the Bitter Lakes, until
Mohammed Ali closed it entirely, and the canal now only goes to Tel e' Rigabeh,
about 26 miles from Belbays. Its course was nearly due east for 35 miles from
Belbays as far as Shekh Hanáydik, when it curved to the southward and ran by the
Bitter Lakes to the sea. Its sea-mouth in early times was probably farther N.; the
land having risen about Suez.—[G. W.]

[5] Herodotus calls Patumus an Arabian town, as lying on the east side of the
Nile. Patumos was not (as I formerly supposed) near the Red Sea, but at the commencement of the canal, and was the Pithom mentioned in Exod. i. 11. It was the
Thoum (Thou) of the Itinerary of Antôninus, 54 M. P. from Babylon, whose site appears to be marked by the ruined town opposite *Tel el Wâdee*, 6 miles east of the
mouth of the canal. From Thoum to the Bitter Lakes may be about 38 miles, and
from Thoum to the sea about 80. Pliny reckons 37 M. P. from the western entrance
of the canal to the Bitter Lakes, giving it a breadth of 100 feet and a depth of 40
(6. 33). Of its length, according to Herodotus, see following note. (See M. Eg.
W. i. 310 to 316.)

Pithom פתם is related to the word Thummim תמים, which is translated in the
Septuagint "Truth," and is taken from the Egyptian *Thmei*, "Truth," or "Justice,"
whence the Greek θέμις and ἔτυμος. The *double* capacity of the Egyptian goddess
Thmei is retained in Thum*mim*.—[G. W.]

[6] This Herodotus considers less than the length of the canal; but his 1000 stadia
(about 114 Eng. m. at 600 Greek feet to the stadium) are too much; and he appears
to have included in it the whole distance by water from the Mediterranean to the
Red Sea, both by the Nile *and* the canal. The length of the canal was about 80

longer, on account of the crookedness of its course. A hundred and twenty thousand of the Egyptians, employed upon the work in the reign of Necôs, lost their lives in making the excavation.[7] He at length desisted from his undertaking, in consequence of an oracle which warned him " that he was labouring for the barbarian."[8] The Egyptians call by the name of barbarians all such as speak a language different from their own.

159. Necôs, when he gave up the construction of the canal, turned all his thoughts to war, and set to work to build a fleet of triremes,[9] some intended for service in the northern sea, and some for the navigation of the Erythræan. These last were built in the Arabian Gulf, where the dry docks in which they lay are still visible. These fleets he employed wherever he had occasion ; while he also made war by land upon the Syrians, and defeated them in a pitched battle at Magdolus,[1] after which he

miles, or, if measured from the Bubastite branch to the Red Sea, about 96. The shortest distance from the Mediterranean to the Red Sea overland is about 76 miles. The line from Mount Casius is not the shortest, being about 90 miles.—[G. W.]

[7] This calls to mind the loss of life when the Alexandrian canal was made by Mohammed Ali, but we may suppose the numbers greatly exaggerated. Mohammed Ali lost 10,000 men. The reason was that they were collected from distant parts of the country, and taken to the spot, and no food being provided for them, those whose families failed to send them provisions died of hunger, and some few from fatigue or accidents.—[G. W.]

[8] This was owing to the increasing power of the Asiatic nations. Berber was apparently an Egyptian name applied to some people of Africa, as now to the Nubians, who do not call *themselves* Berbers. It was afterwards extended to, and adopted by, other people. It was used by the Egyptians as early at least as the 18th dynasty. It is one of many instances of reduplication of the original word. Ber became Berber, as Mar Marmar, in Marmarica, a district of North Africa ; and the B and M being transmutable letters, Marmarica and Barbarica would apply equally well to the coast of Barbary.—[G. W.]

[9] Fleets had been equipped and built by Sesostris ; and Herodotus speaks of the docks, or the stocks, where the ships of Neco were made. The Egyptians had one fleet on the Red Sea, and another on the Mediterranean ; and their ships of war are represented on a temple of Remeses III.—[G. W.]

[1] The place here intended seems to be Megiddo, where Josiah lost his life, between Gilgal and Mount Carmel, on the road through Syria northwards, and not Migdol (Μαγδωλός), which was in Egypt. The similarity of the two names easily led to the mistake (2 Chron. xxxv. 22). Neco had then gone " to fight against Carchemish by Euphrates," and Josiah attacked him on his march, in the " valley of Megiddo," " as he went up against the king of Assyria to the river Euphrates" (2 Kings xxiii. 29). Neco is there called " Pharaoh (Phrah)-Nechoh."

The position of the Jews between the two great rival powers exposed them to the resentment of the one against whom they took part ; as was the case with Hoshea, king of Israel, when he sided with " So, king of Egypt," and Shalmaneser, king of Assyria, " carried Israel away into captivity" (2 Kings xvii. 4, 6).—[G. W.]

There were two cities known to the Jews by the name of Migdol (מִגְדּוֹל) ; one, mentioned in Exodus (xiv. 2) and Jeremiah (xlvi. 14), was not only on the borders of Egypt, but was actually *in* Egypt, as is apparent from both passages. This is undoubtedly the Magdôlus of classical writers, which appeared in Hecatæus as " an Egyptian city" (πόλις Αἰγύπτου, Fr. 282), and which in the itinerary of Antonine (p. 14) is placed 12 Roman miles to the *west* or *north-west* (not east, as Bähr says, vol.

made himself master of Cadytis,[2] a large city of Syria. The dress which he wore on these occasions he sent to Branchidæ in Milesia, as an offering to Apollo.[3] After having reigned in all sixteen years,[4] Necôs died, and at his death bequeathed the throne to his son Psammis.

160. In the reign of Psammis,[5] ambassadors from Elis[6] ar-

i. p. 921) of Pelusium. The other, called for distinction's sake Migdol-el (מִגְדַּל־אֵל), was in the lot of Naphtali (Josh. xix. 38) and is fairly identified with the "Magdala" of St. Matthew (xv. 39)—the birthplace of Mary *Magdalene*. This place, which retains its name almost unchanged (Stanley's Palestine, p. 375), was on the borders of the Sea of Galilee, at the south-eastern corner of the plain of Gennesareth. Herodotus probably meant this last place by his Magdôlus, rather than the Magdôlus of Egypt. But he may well have made a confusion between it and Megiddo (מְגִדּוֹ), just as " some MSS. in Matth. xv. 39 turn Magdala into Magedon" (Stanley, l. s. c.).

[2] After the defeat and death of Josiah, Neco proceeded to Carchemish, and on his return, finding that the Jews had put Jehoahaz, his son, on the throne, "he made him a prisoner at Riblah, in the land of Hamath, and after having imposed a tribute of 100 talents of silver and a talent of gold upon Jerusalem, he made his brother Eliakim (whose name he changed to Jehoiakim) king in his stead, carrying Jehoahaz captive to Egypt, where he died" (2 Kings xxiii. 29). Cadytis has generally been considered the Greek form of the name of Jerusalem, *Kadesh*, or *Kadusha*, "the holy" (given it after the building of the Temple by Solomon, and retained in its Arabic name *El Kods*), which was applied to other places, as *Kadesh-Barnea*, &c.; but as Herodotus says (iii. 5) Cadytis appeared to him to be not much smaller than Sardis, as he probably never went to Jerusalem, and as he mentions the *seaport* towns from Cadytis to Jenysus, it is thought not to be the Jewish capital, but rather to lie on the coast. Toussaint thinks it was Gaza. Herodotus calling it a city of the "Syrians of Palestine" (iii. 5) led to the conclusion that it was Jerusalem, as he seems to apply that name to the Jews (ii. 104): but Cadytis is supposed to be the Khazita taken by Shalmaneser, which was certainly Gaza, or Ghuzzeh. He could scarcely have meant by Cadytis in ii. 159, Jerusalem; and in iii. 5, Gaza; yet his taking *Gaza, after* the defeat of Josiah and his march to Carchemish, would be inconsistent; not so *Jerusalem*.—[G. W.]

[3] Neco's dedication of his corslet to Apollo was doubtless a compliment to the Greek troops in his pay, who had now become so necessary to the Egyptian kings.— [G. W.]

For an account of the temple of Apollo at Branchidæ, see note [7] on B. i. ch. 157.

[4] The reverses which soon afterwards befell the Egyptians were not mentioned to Herodotus. Neco was defeated at Carchemish by Nebuchadnezzar, in the 4th year of Jehoiakim (Jer. xlvi. 2), and lost all the territory which it had been so long the object of the Pharoahs to possess. For "the king of Babylon took, from the river of Egypt unto the river Euphrates, all that pertained to the king of Egypt" (2 Kings xxiv. 7). This river of Egypt was the small torrent-bed that formed the boundary of the country on the N.E. side by the modern El Aréesh. Jerusalem was afterwards taken by Nebuchadnezzar, and the people were led into captivity to Babylon (Jer. lii. 28, 29, 30 ; 2 Kings xxiv. and xxv.), when some Jews fled to Egypt (2 Kings xxv. 26), and settled at Tahpanhes, or Daphnæ, near Pelusium (Jer xliii. 9), a strongly fortified post (Her. s. 11), where the king of Egypt had a palace , and also at Migdol, at Noph, and in the land of Pathros (Jer. xliv. 1). This was in the reign of Hophra or Apries. See Hist. Notice in App. to Book ii.—[G. W.]

[5] Psammis is called Psammetichus (Psamatik) in the sculptures, and was succeeded by a third king of that name, whose wife was called Nitocris (Ncitacri), and whose daughter married Amasis. (See note [3] on ch. 100.) Psammis appears to be Psammetichus II. of the monuments.—[G. W.]

[6] This shows the great repute of the Egyptians for learning, even at this time, when they had greatly declined as a nation.—[G. W.]

rived in Egypt, boasting that their arrangements for the conduct of the Olympic games were the best and fairest that could be devised, and fancying that not even the Egyptians, who surpassed all other nations in wisdom, could add anything to their perfection. When these persons reached Egypt, and explained the reason of their visit, the king summoned an assembly of all the wisest of the Egyptians. They met, and the Eleans having given them a full account of all their rules and regulations with respect to the contests, said that they had come to Egypt for the express purpose of learning whether the Egyptians could improve the fairness of their regulations in any particular. The Egyptians considered awhile, and then made inquiry, "If they allowed their own citizens to enter the lists?" The Eleans answered, "That the lists were open to all Greeks, whether they belonged to Elis or to any other state." Hereupon the Egyptians observed, "That if this were so, they departed from justice very widely, since it was impossible but that they would favour their own countrymen, and deal unfairly by foreigners. If therefore they really wished to manage the games with fairness, and if this was the object of their coming to Egypt, they advised them to confine the contests to strangers, and allow no native of Elis to be a candidate." Such was the advice which the Egyptians gave to the Eleans.

161. Psammis reigned only six years. He attacked Ethiopia,[7] and died almost directly afterwards. Apries, his son,[8]

Diodorus transfers the story to the reign of Amasis, and says the answer was given by that king himself (i. 95). Plutarch (Quæst. Plat. vol. ii. p. 1000, A) assigns it to one of the wise men. The real impartiality of the Eleans was generally admitted (cf. Plut. Apophtheg. Reg. p. 190, C. Dio Chrysost. Rhod. p. 344, C), and is evidenced by the fact that in the only complete list of Olympian victors which we possess, that of the winners of the foot-race or stadium, Eleans occur but eight times between the original institution of the games B.C. 776, and the reign of Caracalla, A.D. 217, a period of 993 years, or 249 Olympiads. Of these eight victors three occur within the first five Olympiads, when the contest was probably confined to Elis and its immediate neighbourhood. (See Euseb. Chron. Can. Pars i. c. xxxiii.)

[7] The names of Psammetichus I. and II. frequently occur at Asouan, as well as that of Amasis.—[G. W.]

[8] Apries is the Pharaoh-Hophra of Jeremiah (xliv. 30), whose dethronement seems to be thus foretold: "I will give Pharaoh-Hophra, king of Egypt, into the hands of his enemies, and of them that seek his life." His reign was at first very prosperous, more so than of any other king of this dynasty, except his great-grandfather, Psammetichus I. He sent an expedition against Cyprus and Sidon, and engaged the king of Tyre by sea, and having taken Gaza (Jer. xlvii. 1) he besieged Sidon, and reduced the whole of the coast of Phœnicia (Diod. i. 68), and advancing to Jerusalem, forced the Chaldees to raise the siege (Jer. xxxvii. 5–11), thus recovering much of the territory wrested from his grandfather, Neco. But fortune then deserted him, and Nebuchadnezzar returned to the siege of Jerusalem and took it in the 11th year of Zedekiah (Jer. xxix. 1, 2). According to the account given by the Egyptians to Herodotus, it was an unsuccessful expedition he sent to Cyrene which

succeeded him upon the throne, who, excepting Psammetichus, his great-grandfather, was the most prosperous of all the kings that ever ruled over Egypt. The length of his reign was twenty-five years, and in the course of it he marched an army to attack Sidon, and fought a battle with the king of Tyre by sea. When at length the time came that was fated to bring him woe, an occasion arose which I shall describe more fully in my Libyan history,[b] only touching it very briefly here. An army despatched by Apries to attack Cyrênê having met with a terrible reverse, the Egyptians laid the blame on him, imagining that he had, of malice prepense, sent the troops into the jaws of destruction. They believed he had wished a vast number of them to be slain, in order that he himself might reign with more security over the rest of the Egyptians. Indignant therefore at this usage, the soldiers who returned and the friends of the slain broke instantly into revolt. *openly*

162. Apries, on learning these circumstances, sent Amasis to the rebels, to appease the tumult by persuasion. Upon his arrival, as he was seeking to restrain the malcontents by his exhortations, one of them, coming behind him, put a helmet on his head, saying, as he put it on, that he thereby crowned him king. Amasis was not altogether displeased at the action, as his conduct soon made manifest : for no sooner had the insurgents agreed to make him actually their king, than he prepared to march with them against Apries. That monarch, on tidings of these events reaching him, sent Patarbêmis, one of his courtiers, a man of high rank, to Amasis, with orders to bring him alive into his presence. Patarbêmis, on arriving at the place where Amasis was, called on him to come back with him to the king, whereupon Amasis broke a coarse jest, and said, "Prythee take that back to thy master." When the envoy, notwithstanding this reply, persisted in his request, exhorting Amasis to obey the summons of the king, he made answer, "that this was exactly what he had long been intending to do ; Apries

---

caused his downfall—Amasis, who was sent to recall the Egyptian troops to their duty, having taken advantage of that movement to usurp the throne, which he ascended after Apries had reigned, as Manetho says, 19, or, according to Herodotus, 25 years. The name of Hophra, or Apries (Haiphra-het), occurs on a few monuments ; but another king, Psammetichus III., intervenes between Psammetichus II. (Psammis) and Amasis, whose daughter was married to Amasis. The reign of Psammetichus III. may have been included in that of Apries. Amasis died in 525 B.C., and as Herodotus assigns him 44 years, which date is found on the monuments, his reign began at least as early as 569 B.C., and probably much earlier ; but these events, and the dates, are very uncertain. See Hist. Notice in App., and note [6], ch. 169, and note [6], ch. 177.—[G. W.]

[b] Infra, iv. 159.

* Ἐκ τῆς ἰσείης — c. iii.......ix. ??

would have no reason to complain of him on the score of delay ;
he would shortly come himself to the king, and bring others
with him." [1]   Patarbêmis, upon this, comprehending the intention of Amasis, partly from his replies, and partly from the
preparations which he saw in progress, departed hastily, wishing
to inform the king with all speed of what was going on. Apries,
however, when he saw him approaching without Amasis, fell
into a paroxysm of rage ; and not giving himself time for re-
flection, commanded the nose and ears of Patarbêmis to be cut
off. Then the rest of the Egyptians, who had hitherto espoused
the cause of Apries, when they saw a man of such note among
them so shamefully outraged, without a moment's hesitation
went over to the rebels, and put themselves at the disposal of
Amasis.

163. Apries, informed of this new calamity, armed his mercenaries, and led them against the Egyptians : this was a body
of Carians and Ionians,[2] numbering thirty thousand men, which
was now with him at Saïs,[3] where his palace stood—a vast
building, well worthy of notice. The army of Apries marched
out to attack the host of the Egyptians, while that of Amasis
went forth to fight the strangers ; and now both armies drew
near the city of Momemphis,[4] and prepared for the coming
fight.

164. The Egyptians are divided into seven distinct classes [5]

---

[1] Compare the answer of Cyrus to Astyages (i. 127), which shows that this was
a commonplace—the answer supposed to be proper for a powerful rebel.

[2] The Greek troops continued in the pay of the king. The state of Egypt, and
the dethronement of Apries, are predicted in Isa. xix. 2, and in Jer. xliv. 30. (See
Hist. Notice, in App. ch. viii. § 37.) As Amasis put himself at the head of the
Egyptian army, and Apries had the Greeks with him, it is evident that the former
was alone employed against Cyrene, either out of fear of sending Greeks there, or
from their unwillingness to fight against a Greek colony. Amasis afterwards (infra,
ch. 181) wisely courted the friendship of the Greeks of Cyrene.—[G. W.]

[3] Manetho agreed with Herodotus in representing this dynasty (his 26th) as Saite.
(Fr. 66 and 67.) That the family of Psammetichus belonged to Sais had been
already indicated, by what is related of the Saites bringing Psammetichus back from
Syria (supra, ch. 152).

[4] Momemphis was on the edge of the desert, near the mouth of the Lycus
canal, some way below the modern village of Algam.—[G. W.]

[5] These classes, rather than *castes*, were, according to Herodotus—1. The sacerdotal. 2. The military. 3. The herdmen. 4. Swineherds. 5. Shopkeepers. 6.
Interpreters. 7. Boatmen. Diodorus (i. 28) says that, like the Athenians, who
derived this institution from Egypt, they were distributed into three classes: 1. The
priests. 2. The peasants, from whom the soldiers were levied. 3. The artificers.
But in another place (i. 74) he extends the number to five, and reckons the pastors,
husbandmen and artificers, independent of the soldiers and priests. Strabo (xvii. p.
541) limits them to three—the soldiers, husbandmen, and priests ; and Plato
(Timæus) divides them into six bodies—the priests, artificers, shepherds, huntsmen,
husbandmen, and soldiers. The sailors employed in ships of war appear to have

—these are, the priests, the warriors, the cowherds, the swineherds, the tradesmen, the interpreters, and the boatmen.   Their
titles indicate their occupations.   The warriors consist of Hermotybians and Calasirians,[6] who come from different cantons,[7]
the whole of Egypt being parcelled out into districts bearing
this name.

165. The following cantons furnish the Hermotybians—the

been of the military class, as Herodotus (Book ix. ch. 82) shows them to have been
of the Calasiries and Hermotybies.

From these different statements we may conclude that the Egyptians were divided into five general classes, which were subdivided again, as is the case in India
even with the castes.   The 1st was the sacerdotal order ; the 2nd the soldiers and
sailors ; the 3rd peasants, or the agricultural class ; the 4th the tradesmen ; and the
5th the plebs, or common people.   The 1st consisted of priests of various grades,
from the pontiffs to the inferior functionaries employed in the temples ; the 2nd of
soldiers and sailors of the navy ; the 3rd was subdivided into farmers, gardeners,
huntsmen, Nile-boatmen, and others ; the 4th was composed of artificers, and
various tradesmen, notaries, musicians (not sacred), builders, sculptors, and potters ;
and the 5th of pastors, fowlers, fishermen, labourers, and poor people.   Some of
these again were subdivided, as pastors into oxherds, shepherds, goatherds, and
swineherds ; which last, according to Herodotus, were the lowest grade, even of the
whole community, since no one would establish any family tie with them, and they
could not enter a temple without a previous purification ; which resembles the
treatment of swineherds in India at this day.

Though Diodorus places the soldiers with the husbandmen, it is more probable
that they constituted a class by themselves ; not that their following agricultural
pursuits degraded them ; for even a Hindoo soldier in like manner may cultivate
land without fear of reproach.   According to Megasthenes the Indians were divided
into seven castes ; they have now four. . (See Strabo, xv. p. 1118.)   Herodotus says
each person followed the profession or occupation of his father, as with the Lacedæmonians (Book vi. ch. 60) ; but it seems that, though frequently of the same class
and occupation as his father, this was not compulsory.   Each person belonged to
one of the classes, and it is not probable that he would follow an inferior occupation,
or enter a lower class than his father, unless circumstances rendered it necessary :
for the sculptures show that sons sometimes did so, and priests, soldiers, and others
holding civil offices are found among the members of the same family.   The
Egyptians had not, therefore, real castes, but classes, as has already been shown by
Mr. Birch and M. Ampère.   Proofs of this, from the families of men in trade, and
others, are not so readily established, as few monuments remain, except of priests
and military men—the aristocracy of Egypt.

Quarters of a town were appropriated to certain trades (as now at Cairo) ; hence
"the leather-cutters of the Memnonia," at Thebes, in the papyrus of Anastasy.
(Dr. Young's Discov. in Eg. Lit., p. 66.)   The interpreters, Herodotus says (ch. 154),
were the descendants of those Egyptians who had been taught Greek by the Ionians
in the service of Psammetichus, which would certainly apply rather to a class than
to a caste, and his statement (whether true or not) respecting the low origin of
Amasis shows he had not in view castes, but classes.—[G. W.]

[6] This name (as Mr. Birch has shown) is Klashr, followed by the figure of an
archer, or the representation of an Egyptian soldier ; bowmen being the chief corps
of the army.   The Calasiries were probably all, or mostly archers.   See note on
Book ix. ch. 32.—[G. W.]

[7] The number of the nomes or cantons varied at different times.   Herodotus
mentions only 18 ; but in the time of Sesostris there were 86, and the same under
the Ptolemies and Cæsars ; 10, according to Strabo, being assigned to the Thebaid,
10 to the Delta, and 16 to the intermediate province.   This triple division varied
at another time, and consisted of Upper and Lower Egypt, with an intervening province containing 7 nomes, and hence called Heptanomis.   In after times an eighth,

cantons of Busiris, Saïs, Chemmis, Paprêmis, that of the island called Prosôpitis,[5] and half of Natho.[6] They number, when most numerous, a hundred and sixty thousand. None of them ever practises a trade, but all are given wholly to war.

166. The cantons of the Calasirians are different—they include the following :—the cantons of Thebes,[1] Bubastis,[2] Aphthis,[3] Tanis,[4] Mendes, Sebennytus, Athribis, Pharbæthus,

the Arsinoïte, was added to Heptanomis; and the divisions were, 1. Upper Egypt, to the Thebaica-phylaké (φυλακή) now *Daroot e' Shereéf.*   2. Heptanomis, to the fork of the Delta. And 3. Lower Egypt, containing the northern part to the sea. Pliny gives 44 nomes to all Egypt, some under other than the usual names. Ptolemy mentions 24 in the Delta, or Lower Egypt, which under the later Roman emperors was divided into four districts—Augustamnica prima and secunda, Ægyptus 1[a] and 2da, still containing the same nomes ; and in the time of Arcadius, the son of Theodosius the Great, Heptanomis received the name of Arcadia. The Thebaïd was made into two parts, Upper and Lower, the line of separation being Panopolis and Ptolemais-Hermii ; and the nomes were then increased to 58, of which the Delta contained 35, including the Oasis of Ammon. These nomes were as follows :—[See next page.]

Each Nome was governed by a Nomarch, to whom was entrusted the levying of taxes, and various duties connected with the administration of the province. See Mr. Harris's Standards of the Nomes and Toparchies of Egypt. His discovery cannot be too highly appreciated. He has also those of Ethiopia, which we may hope will be published.—[G. W.]

[5] Of Busiris, see note [6] on ch. 61, and preceding note. The Busirite nome was next to the Sebennytic, and to the south of it. Of Saïs, see note [9] on ch. 62, and note [9] on ch. 170. Of Chemmis, see note [4] on ch. 91 ; it was in Upper Egypt. Of Papremis, see note [4] on ch. 63. Of Prosopitis, see note [1] on ch. 41.—[G. W.]

[6] This was the tract between the Sebennytic, or Busiritic branch, and the Thermuthiac, which ran to the east of Xoïs.—[G. W.]

[1] It is singular that only two nomes of Upper Egypt are here mentioned, Thebes and Chemmis. But as Herodotus has mentioned so few of the nomes, it is more probable that he has overlooked some, than that no soldiers belonged to any in Upper Egypt but the Theban and Chemmite. The largest force was necessarily *quartered* in these northern nomes, being wanted for defence against the enemy from the eastward : but it does not follow that they were nearly all *raised* there. Besides the nome of Thebes on the east, was the Pathyritic on the opposite bank, which contained "the Libyan suburb" of Thebes, or the "Memnoneia." (See Dr. Young, Disc. Eg. Lit., p. 66.) It was called Pa-Athor, "belonging to Athor " (Venus), who presided over the West. The Theban and Chemmite may have been the two that furnished the troops of the Ethiopian frontier, and of the garrisons in Upper Egypt. According to Herodotus the whole force was 410,000 men. Diodorus (i. 54) makes it amount, in the time of Sesostris, to 600,000 foot, 24,000 horse, and 27 chariots ; but he probably included in these the auxiliaries.—[G. W.]

[2] See notes on chs. 59, 60, 138.

[3] The position of this nome is uncertain.—[G. W.]

[4] The city of Tanis is the Zoan of sacred Scripture, and the modern San or Zan, —the Gami (or Djami) or Athennes, of the Copts. It has extensive mounds, and remains of a small temple of the time of Remeses the Great, remarkable from its having at least ten, if not twelve obelisks. The name of Osirtasen III. found there (see Burton's Excerpta, pl. 38, 39, 40) shows that an older temple once stood at Tanis : and the great antiquity of Tanis is also shown by its existing in the time of Abraham, and being founded seven years after Hebron, where Sarah died (Gen. xxiii. 2 ; Num. xiii. 22). In "the field of Zoan" the miracles of Moses are said to have been performed (Ps. lxxviii. 12); and its present desolation shows how completely the prophecies against it have been fulfilled. (Ezek. xxx. 14; Isa. xix. 11; xxx. 4.)—[G. W.]

The Nomes of the Delta, or Lower Egypt, beginning from the East, were:

Province.	Nome.	Chief City.	Modern Name.
Ægyptus Secunda. Augustamnica Prima et Secunda.	1. Heliopolis	Heliopolis	Matareèh.
	2. Bubastites.	Bubastis	Tel Basta.
	3. Anthribites (with the Isle of Myecphoris,	Athribis	Benha-el-Assal.
	4. Heroöpolites	Hero	Abookesháyd (?)
	5. Phagroriopolites	Phagroriopolis	Shekh Hanáydik (?)
	6. Arabia	Phacusa	Tel Fakkoos.
	7. Sethroïtes	Sethrum, or Heracleöpolis Parva	Tel Sharóeg (?)
	8. Tanites	Tanis	San.
	9. Pharbæthites	Pharbæthus	Harbayt, or Heurbayt.
	10. Leontopolites	Leontopolis	Tanbool (?)
	11. Neont (Neut)	Panephysis	Menzaleh.
	12. Mendesius	Mendes	Ashmoon (?)
	13. Papremites	Papremis	
	14. Busirites	Busiris	Abooseer (?)
	15. Sebennytes	Sebennytus	Semenhood.
	16. Anysis	Anysis, or Iseum (?)	Bebayt.
	17. Sebennytes Inferior....	Pachnamunis..............	
Ægyptus Prima.	18. Elearchia..............	....	
	19. The Isle of Natho	Natho	Sahragt.
	20. Xoïtes..................	Xoïs	Sakha.
	21. Onuphites	Onuphis	Banoob (?)
	22. Nitrites (Nitriotis).....	Nitria	Zakeek (?)
	23. Prosopites..............	Prosopis, or Niciu........	Menoof (?) or Ibshádeh (?)
	24. Phthemphites	Tava....................	Shooni (?)
	25. Saïtes	Saïs (Ssa)	Sa-el-Hágar.
	26. Phtheneotes	Butos....................	
	27. Cabasites	Cabasa..................	Kom Shabas.
	28. Naucratites	Naucratis	
	29. Metelites	Metelis	Fooah.
	30. Alexandrinorum.......	Alexandria, Racotis	Iskenderéèh.
	31. Hermopolites..........	Hermopolis Parva	Damanhoor.
	32. Menelaïtes..............	Menelaïs	
	33. Letopolites	Letopolis Latonæ Civitas	Weseem (?)
	34. Marea, Libya	Marea....................	El Hayt (?)
	35. Hammoniacus	Hammonis	Seewah (Siwah).

(For the Delta, its towns, and branches of the Nile, see Egypt and Thebes, vol. i. p. 399 to 455.)

The Nomes of Upper Egypt, or the Thebaïd, and of Heptanomis, beginning from the North, were:

Province.	Nome.	Chief City.	Modern Name.
Heptanomis.	1. Memphites	Memphis..................	Mitrahenny.
	2. Aphroditopolites........	Aphroditopolis	Atfèèh.
	3. Arsinoïtes	Crocodilopolis, or Arsinoë	Medeénet el Fyoom.
	4. Heracleopolites........	Heracleopolis	Anásieh.
	5. Oxyrhinchites	Oxyrhinchus	Behnesa.
	6. Cynopolites	Cynopolis	El Kays.
	7. Hermopolites..........	Hermopolis Magna........	Oshmoonáyn.
	8. Antinoïtes ("in which are included the two Oases." Ptol. 4, 5.)	Antinoë..................	Shekh Abádeh, or Insiné.
Thebaïs, or Ægyptus Superior. Low. Theb. Upper Thebais.	9. Lycopolites..............	Lycopolis	Sioót.
	10. Hypselites..............	Hypselis	Shodb.
	11. Antæopolites	Antæopolis	Gow (Kow) el Kebeér.
	12. Aphroditopolites.......	Aphroditopolis	Itfoo.
	13. Panopolites............	Panopolis	Ekhmim, or Akhmeem.
	14. Thinites................	"This, near Abydus:" afterwards the capital was Ptolemaïs-Hermii,	Birbeh (?) or El Beerbeh (?
	15. Diospolites..............	Diospolis Parva	Menshéèh.
	16. Tentyrites..............	Tentyris, Tentyra	How.
	17. Coptites..............	Coptos..................	Dendera.
	18. Thebarum	Thebæ, Diospolis Magna, "Egyptian Thebes."	Koft, or Kebt. Karnak, and Luxor.
	19. Pathyrites..............	The Libyan, or Western part of Thebes	Koorna.
	20. Hermonthites	Hermonthis	Ermént.
	21. Latopolites	Latopolis..............	Esné.
	22. Apollinopolites	Apollinopolis Magna.......	Edfoo.
	23. Ombites..............	Ombos	Kôm-Ombo.

Thmuis, Onuphis, Anysis, and Myecphoris [5]—this last canton consists of an island which lies over against the town of Bubastis. The Calasirians, when at their greatest number, have amounted to two hundred and fifty thousand. Like the Hermotybians they are forbidden to pursue any trade, and devote themselves entirely to warlike exercises, the son following the father's calling.

167. Whether the Greeks borrowed from the Egyptians their notions about trade, like so many others, I cannot say for certain.[6] I have remarked that the Thracians, the Scyths, the Persians, the Lydians, and almost all other barbarians, hold the citizens who practise trades, and their children, in less repute than the rest, while they esteem as noble those who keep aloof from handicrafts, and especially honour such as are given wholly to war. These ideas prevail throughout the whole of Greece, particularly among the Lacedæmonians. Corinth is the place where mechanics are least despised.[7]

[5] See note [7] on Mendes, ch. 42. Sebennytus, the modern *Semenood*, has no remains, except a few sculptured stones, on one of which are the name and figure of the god. (See note [1] on ch. 48.) They are of the late time of Alexander, the son of Alexander the Great, in whose name Ptolemy Lagus was then Governor of Egypt. Semenood stands on the west bank of the modern Damietta branch. Athribis, now *Benha-el-Assal*, from its "honey," is marked by its mounds, still called Atreéb. The town was nearly a mile in length, E. and W., and three-fourths of a mile N. and S. It is on the E. bank of the old Sebennytic (and modern Damietta) branch. Pharbæthus, now *Harbayt* (the same as the old name without the article P.), is between 12 and 13 miles to the N. of Bubastis. It stood on the Tanitic branch. The site of Thmuis is marked by a granite monolith at Tel-Etmai, bearing the name of Amasis. Its Coptic name is *Thmoui*. It stands a short distance to the south of the Mendesian branch. Onuphis is supposed to have stood in the Sebennytic branch, a little below its union with the Phatmetic channel, and a little to the W. of Anysis, probably at the modern *Banoob*. Anysis may be Iseum, now *Bebayt* (see note [8] on ch. 61), about 6 miles below Sebennytus; and the name is probably ei-n-isi, "house (city) of Isis." Myecphoris was an island between the Tanitic and Pelusiac branches. See M. Eg. W., vol. i. pp. 399–452.—[G. W.]

[6] These notions were not necessarily borrowed by one people from another, being very general in a certain state of society.—[G. W.]

[7] It is curious to find this trait in a Dorian state. But the situation of Corinth led so naturally to extensive trade, and thence to that splendour and magnificence of living by which the useful and ornamental arts are most encouraged, that in spite of Dorian pride and exclusiveness, the mechanic's occupation came soon to be regarded with a good deal of favour. As early as the time of Cypselus elaborate works of art proceeded from the Corinthian workshops, as the golden statue of Jupiter at Olympia (Paus. v. ii. § 4), and the plane-tree in the Corinthian treasury at Delphi (Plut. Sept. Sap. 21). Afterwards, under Periander, art was still more encouraged, and the offerings of the Cypselidæ at various shrines were such as to bear a comparison with the works of Polycrates at Samos and of the Pisistratidæ at Athens. (Ar. Pol. v. 9. Comp. Eph. Fr. 106, and Theophr. ap. Phot. in Κυψελιδῶι ἀνάθημα.) A little later a Corinthian architect rebuilt the temple at Delphi. (Pausan. X. v. ad fin.) Finally, Corinth became noted for the peculiar composition of its bronze, which was regarded as better suited for works of art than any other, and which under the name of Æs Corinthiacum was celebrated throughout the world. (Plin. H. N. xxxiv. 8.)

168. The warrior class in Egypt had certain special privileges in which none of the rest of the Egyptians participated except the priests. In the first place each man had twelve *arurœ*[2] of land assigned him free from tax. (The *arura* is a square of a hundred Egyptian cubits, the Egyptian cubit being of the same length as the Samian.[2]) All the warriors enjoyed this privilege together; but there were other advantages which came to each in rotation, the same man never obtaining them twice. A thousand Calasirians, and the same number of Hermotybians, formed in alternate years the body-guard of the king; and during their year of service these persons, besides their *arurœ*, received a daily portion of meat and drink, consisting of five pounds of baked bread, two pounds of beef, and four cups of wine.[1]

169. When Apries, at the head of his mercenaries,[2] and Amasis, in command of the whole native force of the Egyptians, encountered one another near the city of Momemphis,[3] an engagement presently took place. The foreign troops fought bravely, but were overpowered by numbers, in which they fell very far short of their adversaries. It is said that Apries believed that there was not a god who could cast him down from his eminence,[4] so firmly did he think that he had established himself in his kingdom. But at this time the battle went against him, and, his army being worsted, he fell into the enemy's hands, and was brought back a prisoner to Saïs,[5] where

---

[2] The arura, according to Herodotus and Horapollo, was a square of 100 cubits, and contained 10,000 square cubits, about 22,500 square feet. It was a little more than three-fourths of an English acre; and was only a land measure. The 12 arurœ were about nine English acres. Diodorus says the land of Egypt had been divided by Sesostris into three parts, one of which was assigned to the military class, in order that they might be more ready to undergo the hazards of war, when they had property in the country for which they fought. This answered well at first, but in time the soldiers became more fond of their property than of glory, and another occupation took away the taste for war, as was the case with the Janissaries of Turkey.—[G. W.]

[2] On the Egyptian cubit, see App. ch. iv. ad fin. It seems to have been rather more than 20¼ English inches. The ordinary Greek cubit was 18½ inches.

[1] These 2000 spearmen, selected by turns from the army, as a body-guard, had daily rations of 5 minæ (6 lbs. 8 oz. 14 dwt. 6 grs.) of bread, 2 of beef (2 lbs. 8 oz. 5 dwt. 17 grs.), and 4 arusters, or a little more than 2 pints of wine, during their annual service. The mina seems to have been 16¹/₇ oz.; the talent about 80 lbs. Troy. The mina in hieroglyphics is called *men*, or *mna*; in Coptic, *emna*, or *amna*; and the talent *ginshâr*. See P. A. Eg. W., vol. ii. p. 259.—[G. W.]

[2] See note [2] on ch. 163, and note [5] on ch. 152.

[3] See note [4] on ch. 163.

[4] This was probably after having obliged the Babylonians to retire from before Jerusalem (see note [5] on ch. 161); for before the end of his reign the return of Nebuchadnezzar must have convinced him of his enemy's power. His pride is noticed in Ezek. xxix. 3, 8, 9. See note [5] on ch. 177.—[G. W.]

[5] This was the royal residence of this 26th Saïte dynasty; and the sacred temenos or enclosure, containing the temple and the lake, was surrounded by massive

he was lodged in what had been his own house, but was now the palace of Amasis. Amasis treated him with kindness,[6] and kept him in the palace for a while; but, finding his conduct blamed by the Egyptians, who charged him with acting unjustly in preserving a man who had shown himself so bitter an enemy both to them and him, he gave Apries over into the hands of his former subjects, to deal with as they chose. Then the Egyptians took him and strangled him, but having so done, they buried him in the sepulchre of his fathers. This tomb is in the temple of Minerva, very near the sanctuary, on the left hand as one enters. The Saïtes buried all the kings who belonged to their canton inside this temple; and thus it even contains the tomb of Amasis as well as that of Apries and his family. The latter is not so close to the sanctuary as the former, but still it is within the temple. It stands in the court, and is a spacious cloister, built of stone, and adorned with pillars carved so as to resemble palm-trees,[7] and with other sumptuous ornaments.

walls of crude brick. Some houses also stood within it, but the town itself was outside the walls. It was the custom of the Egyptians in the early periods to enclose their garrison towns with strong crude brick walls, generally about fifteen or twenty feet thick, and fifty feet high, crowned with battlements in the form of Egyptian shields, as a breastwork to the spacious rampart, which was ascended by broad inclined planes; and the temples had usually a separate enclosure within this general circuit. In their regular fortresses the outer walls were strengthened with square towers at intervals; and parallel to the outer walls was a lower one of circumvallation, distant about twelve to fifteen feet, the object of which was to prevent the enemy bringing his battering rams, or other engines directly against the main walls, before he had thrown down this advanced one; which, when the place was surrounded by a ditch, stood in the middle of it, and served as a tenaille and ravelin. In larger fortifications the ditch had both a scarp and counterscarp, and even a regular glacis (as at Semneh); and the low wall in the ditch was of stone, as at Contra Pselcis. There was also a wall running out at right angles from (and of equal height with) the main wall, which crossed the ditch, for the purpose of raking it, by what we should call a "flanking fire." There was one main gate, between two towers; and on the river side was a water-gate, protected by a covertway. This was a regular system of fortification; but after the accession of the 18th dynasty these fortresses appear to have been seldom built; and the lofty stone towers of the Propylæa being added to the temples became detached forts in each city, and an asylum for what was most precious, the sacred things, the persons of the king and priests, and the treasury, as well as a protection against foreign and domestic foes. (See Aristot. Polit. iv. 11.) Even Thebes had no wall of circuit; its hundred gates (a weakness in a wall) were those of the numerous courts of its temples; and though the fortresses of Pelusium, and other strongholds of the frontiers, still continued to be used, towns were seldom enclosed by a wall, except small ones on a pass, or in some commanding position. See a letter in the Transactions of the Society of Literature, vol. iv., new series, on the level of the Nile and Egyptian fortification.—[G. W.]

[6] It has been thought that Apries may have continued to be nominally king, until Amasis had sufficiently established his power and reconciled the Egyptians to his usurpation; and the latter years of his reign may have been included in "the 44 years of Amasis;" but the shortness of that period, and the Apis stelæ, disprove this.—[G. W.]

[7] They are common in Egyptian temples, particularly in the Delta, where they

Within the cloister is a chamber with folding doors, behind which lies the sepulchre of the king.

170. Here too, in this same precinct of Minerva at Saïs, is the burial-place of one whom I think it not right to mention in such a connexion.[8] It stands behind the temple, against the back-wall, which it entirely covers. There are also some large stone obelisks in the enclosure, and there is a lake[9] near them, adorned with an edging of stone. In form it is circular, and in size, as it seemed to me, about equal to the lake in Delos called " the Hoop."[1]

171. On this lake it is that the Egyptians represent by night

are often of granite, as at Bubastis, and Tanis. The date-palm was not, as Dr. Pickering thinks (p. 373), introduced into Egypt in the Hyksos period, being represented on the tombs about the Pyramids of the 4th dynasty, where rafters for rooms are shown to have been already made of it, as at the present day. The palm-branch was also the emblem of " years " in the oldest dates. Its not being indicated at periods of which no records remain is no proof of its not being known in Africa then, or long before ; negative inferences are very doubtful ; and the evidence of a plant, or an animal, being found in ancient Egypt is frequently derived from the accidental preservation of a *single* monument. See Dr. Pickering's valuable work, the Races of Man, p. 386, *seq.*—[G. W.]

[8] This was Osiris, in honour of whom many ceremonies were performed at Saïs, as in some other towns.—[G. W.]

[9] This lake still remains at Saïs, the modern *Sa-el-Hagar,* " Sa of the stone ; " the ancient name being Ssa. (See above, note [9] on ch. 62.) The stone casing, which always lined the sides of these sacred lakes, (and which may be seen at Thebes, Hermonthes, and other places,) is entirely gone ; but the extent of the main enclosure, which included within it the lake and temple, is very evident ; and the massive crude brick walls are standing to a great height. They are about seventy feet thick, and have layers of reeds and rushes at intervals, to serve as binders. The lake is still supplied by a canal from the river. Some ruined houses stand on a ground within the enclosure (at B D) near the lake, perhaps on the site of the palace, but of a much later time than Amasis. Many have been burnt. Their lofty walls in one part have obtained the name of El Kala, " the Citadel." It is difficult to ascertain the position of the temple of Minerva, as no ruins remain above ground, and you come to water a very short way below the surface, the Nile being of higher level than in former times. It stood within a " *temenos,*" or inner sacred enclosure near the lake, probably about E in the plan. At G may have been the royal tombs. Other tombs are in the mounds outside near the modern village, at P, and at Q beyond the canal to the westward, is another burial-place, of private individuals. The lake is no longer, if it ever was, " round," but oblong, measuring nearly 2000 feet by 750. (See plan opposite.)—[G. W.]

[1] The Delian lake was a famous feature of the great temple or sacred enclosure of Apollo, which was the chief glory of that island. It is celebrated by the ancient poet Theognis (B.C. 548) under the same appellation (τροχοειδής) assigned it by Herodotus (Theogn. 7) ; and is twice mentioned, once as τροχόεσσα (Hymn. ad Del. 261), and once as περιηγής (Hymn. ad Apoll. 59), by Callimachus. Apollo was supposed to have been born upon its banks. Larcher (note ad loc.) shows satisfactorily that it was situated within the sacred enclosure ; and decides with good reason in favour of its identity with the oval basin discovered by Messrs. Spon and Wheeler in 1675, of which an account is given in their Travels (vol. i. p. 85, French Tr.). The dimensions, which do not seem to have been accurately measured, are reckoned at 300 paces (1500 feet) by 200 (1000 feet). It was thus an oval, like the lake at Saïs, and not *very* different in its dimensions.

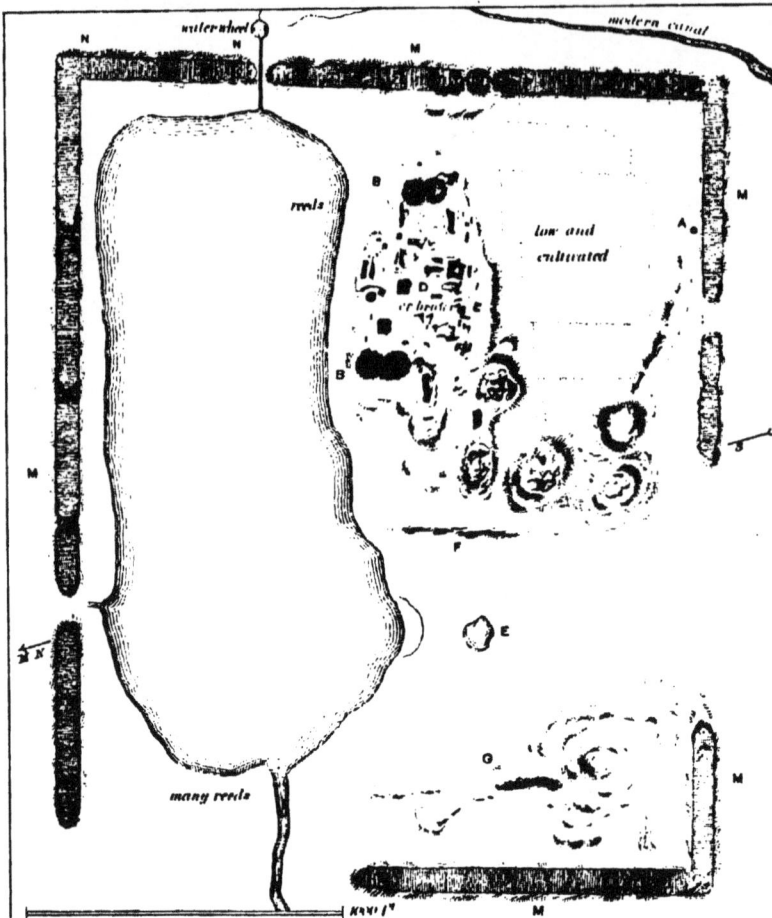

PLAN of SAÏS

A   Circular building on level with the ground of burnt brick
B B   Massive buildings of crude brick like towers
D.   Remains of er brick buildings. This part is called now el Kala the citadel C has been bared
E   Site of the Temple of Neith (Minerva)
F.G.   The walls of the Temenos or sacred enclosure surrounding the temple
     which was about 1400 feet broad by about the same in length
L   The lake, where the ceremonies were performed at the fête of Saïs
M   Walls of the town of er brick, 80 feet thick. This walled part is 1800 N &c S & 1100 E&W wide
N   Here the outer face of the wall is seen
P.P.   Remains of er brick houses. O. Mounds with granite block and sarcophagus.

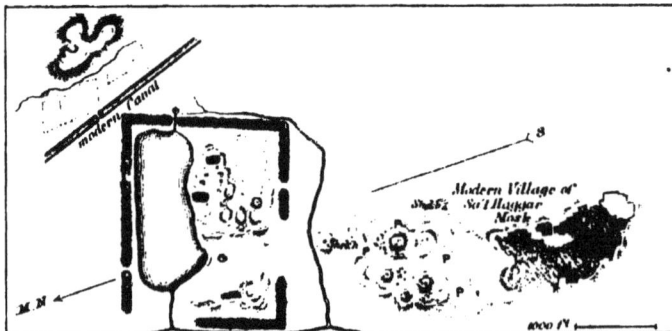

Sarony Major & Knapp Lith' N.Y.   Publ. by D. Appleton & Co. N.Y.

his sufferings [2] whose name I refrain from mentioning, and this representation they call their Mysteries. [3] I know well the

[2] The Egyptians and the Syrians had each the myth of a dying god; but they selected a different phænomenon for its basis; the former the Nile, the Syrians, the aspect of nature, or, as Macrobius shows (Saturn. i. 26), the sun; which, during one part of the year manifesting its vivifying effects on the earth's surface, seemed to die on the approach of winter; and hence the notion of a god, who was both mortal and immortal. In the religion of Greece we trace this more obscurely; but the Cretans believed that Jupiter had died, and even showed his tomb (Cic. Nat. Deor. 3), which made Callimachus, taking it literally, revile the Cretans as "liars:"

Κρῆτες ἀεὶ ψεῦσται, καὶ γὰρ τάφον, ὦ ἄνα, σεῖο
Κρῆτες ἐτεκτήσαντο, σὺ δ' οὐ θάνες, ἔσσι γὰρ αἰεί,

—an epithet quoted by St. Paul from Epimenides. (Epistle to Titus i. 12.) This belief was perhaps borrowed from Egypt, or from Syria; for the Greeks derided the notion of a god dying; whence the remark of Xenophanes, and others, to the Egyptians, "If ye believe them to be gods, why do ye weep for them; if they deserve your lamentations, why repute them to be gods?" Plut. de Is. 71.) They, on the other hand, committed the error of making men into gods, and misunderstanding the allegorical views of the Egyptians and others, ran into the grossest errors respecting those deities they adopted. In Crete again, Apollo's grief for Atymnius was commemorated "'Απόλλων δακρυχέων ἐρατεινὸν 'Ατύμνιον," as that of Venus for Adonis in Syria, where the women sitting and weeping for Tammûz (Tamooz), and the Jews weeping in the high places, when they fell off to the idolatry of their neighbours (Ezek. viii. 6, 14; Jerem. iii. 21), show the general custom of the Syrians. The wailing of the orthodox Jews, though not unusual, was of a different kind (Numb. xxv. 6), and was permitted except on festivals. (Joseph. xi. 55.) The lamentations of the Egyptians led to the remark of Apuleius: "Ægyptiorum numinum fana plena plangoribus, Græca plerumque choreis."—[G. W.]

[3] The sufferings and death of Osiris were the great mystery of the Egyptian religion; and some traces of it are perceptible among other people of antiquity. His being the divine goodness, and the abstract idea of "good," his manifestation upon earth (like an Indian god), his death, and resurrection, and his office as judge of the dead in a future state, look like the early revelation of a future manifestation of the deity converted into a mythological fable; and are not less remarkable than that notion of the Egyptians mentioned by Plutarch (in Vit. Numæ), that a woman might conceive by the approach of some divine spirit. As Osiris signified "good," Typhon (or rather Seth) was "evil," and the remarkable notion of good and evil being brothers is abundantly illustrated in the early sculptures; nor was it till a change was made, apparently by foreigners from Asia, who held the doctrine of the two principles, that evil became confounded with sin, when the brother of Osiris no longer received divine honours. (See At. Eg. W., p. 124 to 127.) Till then sin, "the great serpent," or Aphophis, "the giant," was distinct from Seth, who was a deity, and part of the divine system, which recalls those words of Isaiah (xlv. 7), "I form the light, and create darkness; I make peace, and create evil; I the Lord do these things;" and

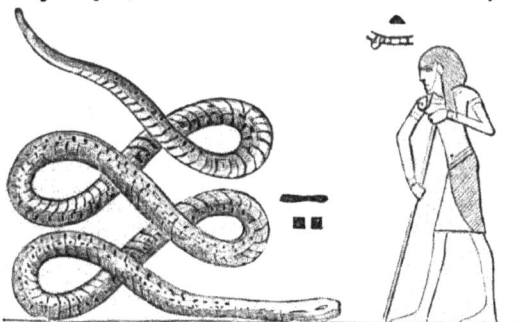

No. I.

in Amos (iii. 6), "shall there be evil in a city, and the Lord hath not done it?" In like manner the my-whole course of the proceedings in these ceremonies,[4] but they shall not pass my lips. So too, with regard to the mysteries of

thology of India admitted the creator and destroyer as characters of the divine Being. Seth was even called Baal-Seth, and made the god of their enemies also, which was from war being an evil, as peace in the above verse is equivalent to good; and in (Baal) Zephon we may perhaps trace the name of Typhon. In the same sense the Egyptians represented Seth teaching a Pharaoh the use of the bow, and other weapons of destruction, which were producers of evil. Sin, the giant Aphophis, as "the great serpent," often with a human head, being represented pierced by the spear of Horus, or of Atmoo (as Re the "Sun"), recalls the war of the gods and giants, and the fable of Apollo (or the sun) and the Python. Comp. the serpent slain by Vishnoo. (See note on Book iv. ch. 191.) Osiris may be said rather to have presided over the judgment of the dead, than to have judged them; he gave admission, to those who were found worthy, to the abode of happiness. He was not the avenging deity; he did not punish, nor could he show mercy, or subvert the judgment pronounced. It was a simple question of fact. If wicked, they were destined to suffer punishment. A man's actions were balanced in the scales against justice or truth, and if found wanting he was excluded from future happiness. Thus, though the Egyptians are said to believe the gods were capable of influencing destiny (Euseb. Pr. Ev. iii. 4) it is evident that Osiris (like the Greek Zeus) was bound by it; and the wicked were punished, not because he rejected them, but because they *were* wicked. Each man's conscience, released from the sinful body, was his own judge; and self-condemnation hereafter followed up the γνῶϑι and αἰσχύνεο σεαυτὸν enjoined on earth. Thoth, therefore (or

No. II.

that part of the divine nature called intellect and conscience), weighed and condemned; and Horus (who had been left on earth to follow out the conquests of his father Osiris after he had returned to heaven) ushered in the just to the divine presence.—[G. W.]

[4] These mysteries of Osiris, Herodotus says, were introduced into Greece by the daughters of Danaus. (See note [5] on ch. 91, note [1] on ch. 107, note [4] on ch. 182, and Book vi. n. ch. 53.) The fables of antiquity had generally several meanings; they were either historical, physical, or religious. The less instructed were led to believe Osiris represented some natural phenomenon; as the inundation of the Nile, which disappearing again, and losing its effects in the sea, was construed into the manifestation and death of the deity, destroyed by Typhon; and the story of his body having been carried to Byblus, and that of the head which went annually from Egypt to that place, swimming on the sea (Lucian de Deâ Syriâ) for seven days, were the allegory of the water of the Nile carried by the currents to the Syrian coast; though Pausanias (x. 12) says they lamented Osiris, "when the Nile began to rise." His fabulous history was also thought by the Greeks to be connected with the sun; but it was not so viewed in early times by the Egyptians; and this was rather an Asiatic notion, and an instance of the usual adaptation of deities to each other in different mythologies. Least of all was he thought to be a man deified; and as Plutarch says (de Isid. s. 11, 20), "we are not to suppose the adventures related of him were actually true, or ever happened in fact;" and the real meaning of them was confined to those initiated into the higher mysteries. (See foregoing n.) The

Ceres, which the Greeks term "the Thesmophoria,"⁵ I know them, but I shall not mention them, except so far as may be done without impiety.   The daughters of Danaus brought these rites from Egypt, and taught them to the Pelasgic women of the Peloponnese.   Afterwards when the inhabitants of the peninsula were driven from their homes by the Dorians, the rites perished.   Only in Arcadia, where the natives remained and were not compelled to migrate,⁶ their observance continued.

172. After Apries had been put to death in the way that I have described above, Amasis reigned over Egypt.   He belonged to the canton of Saïs, being a native of the town called Siouph.⁷ At first his subjects looked down on him and held him in small esteem, because he had been a mere private person, and of a house of no great distinction ; but after a time Amasis succeeded in reconciling them to his rule, not by severity, but by cleverness.   Among his other splendour he had a golden foot-pan, in which his guests and himself were wont upon occasion to wash their feet.   This vessel he caused to be broken in pieces, and made of the gold an image of one of the gods, which he set up in the most public place in the whole city ; upon which the Egyptians flocked to the image, and worshipped it with the utmost reverence.   Amasis, finding this was so, called an assem-

death of Adonis, and of Bacchus, and the story of Osiris being enticed by Typhon to get into a chest, which floated down the river, and was conveyed to " Byblus in Phœnicia," shows a close connexion between different religions ; and the rites of Adonis were performed in the temple of Venus at that place. (Lucian de Deâ Syr.)   Isis having found the chest, brought it back by sea to Egypt, and concealed it till she could meet her son Horus.   In the meantime Typhon discovered it, and having cut up the body into fourteen pieces, distributed them over different parts of the country.   She then went in a boat made of papyrus rushes, in quest of the scattered members, and having found them, buried them in various places, which accounts for the many burial-places of Osiris, as her adventures by water do for the representations on the lake of Saïs.   The portion of the mysteries imparted to strangers, as to Herodotus, Plutarch, and others, and even to Pythagoras, was limited ; and the more important secrets were not even revealed to all "the priests, but to those only who were the most approved." (Clemens. Strom. v. 7, p.

Of the resemblance of the Indian Rama, his army of Satyrs, and his conquest of India, see Sir W. Jones, vol. i. p. 262.   In the Vedas (written before the later notions about transmigration of the soul) is a deity called Yama, who bears a strong resemblance to Osiris, being the ruler of the dead, who gives a place of happiness hereafter to the souls of good men.   The analogy is made more striking by his having lived on earth with his sister and wife Yami (as Osiris with Isis) ; and they, like Adam and Eve, were the parents of the human race.   See Journ. American Orient. Soc., vol. iii. No. 2, pp. 328, 336.—[G. W.]

⁵ See note on Book vi. ch. 16.   ⁶ Compare viii. 73, and note ad loc.

⁷ This place is supposed to have stood to the north of Saïs, at *Seffeh*, on the east bank of the modern Rosetta branch.   Plato thinks Amasis was from Saïs itself (in Tim.)—Herodotus says he was of plebeian origin ; but the two facts of his having become King of Egypt, and having married the daughter of a king, argue against this assertion ; and Diodorus, with more reason, describes him as a person of consequence, which is confirmed by his rank as a general, and his being a distinguished member of the military class.—[G. W.]

bly, and opened the matter to them, explaining how the image
had been made of the foot-pan, wherein they had been wont
formerly to wash their feet and to put all manner of filth, yet
now it was greatly reverenced. "And truly," he went on to
say, "it had gone with him as with the foot-pan. If he was a
private person formerly, yet now he had come to be their king.
And so he bade them honour and reverence him." Such was
the mode in which he won over the Egyptians, and brought
them to be content to do him service.

173. The following was the general habit of his life :—From
early dawn to the time when the forum is wont to fill,[b] he sed-
ulously transacted all the business that was brought before him ;
during the remainder of the day he drank and joked with his
guests, passing the time in witty and, sometimes, scarce seemly
conversation. It grieved his friends that he should thus demean
himself, and accordingly some of them chid him on the subject,
saying to him,—"Oh ! king, thou dost but ill guard thy royal
dignity whilst thou allowest thyself in such levities. Thou
shouldest sit in state upon a stately throne, and busy thyself
with affairs the whole day long. So would the Egyptians feel
that a great man rules them, and thou wouldst be better spoken
of. But now thou conductest thyself in no kingly fashion."
Amasis answered them thus :—"Bowmen bend their bows
when they wish to shoot ; unbrace them when the shooting is
over. Were they kept always strung they would break, and
fail the archer in time of need. So it is with men. If they
give themselves constantly to serious work, and never indulge
awhile in pastime or sport, they lose their senses, and become
mad or moody. Knowing this, I divide my life between pastime
and business." Thus he answered his friends.

174. It is said that Amasis, even while he was a private
man, had the same tastes for drinking and jesting, and was
averse to engaging in any serious employment. He lived in
constant feasts and revelries, and whenever his means failed him,
he roamed about and robbed people. On such occasions the

---

[b] In early times the Greeks divided the day into three parts, as in Homer, Iliad
xxi. 111, ἠώς, δείλη, μέσον ἦμαρ. The division, according to Dio Chrysostomus (De
Gloriâ Orat. 67 ; see also Jul. Pollux Onom. i. 68) was πρωΐ, sunrise, or early morn ;
περὶ πληθουσαν ἀγοράν, market time (Xenoph. Anab. 1.), or forenoon, the third hour ;
μεσημβρία, midday ; δείλη, or περὶ δείλην, afternoon, or the ninth hour ; and ἑσπέρα,
evening, or sunset. These are very like the Arabic divisions at the present time,
for each of which they have a stated number of prayers : subh, "morning" (which
is also subdivided into el fegr, "daybreak," answering to the Greek ὄρθριον, "dawn ");
dúha, "forenoon ;" dohr, "midday ;" asser, "afternoon" (midway between noon
and sunset) ; and múghreb, "sunset ;" after which is the Esher, at one hour and a
half after sunset, when the last or fifth set of daily prayers is said.—[G. W.]

persons from whom he had stolen would bring him, if he denied the charge, before the nearest oracle ; sometimes, the oracle would pronounce him guilty of the theft, at other times it would acquit him.   When afterwards he came to be king, he neglected the temples of such gods as had declared that he was not a thief, and neither contributed to their adornment, nor frequented them for sacrifice ; since he regarded them as utterly worthless, and their oracles as wholly false : but the gods who had detected his guilt he considered to be true gods whose oracles did not deceive ; and these he honoured exceedingly.

175. First of all, therefore, he built the gateway [9] of the temple of Minerva at Saïs, which is an astonishing work, far surpassing all other buildings of the same kind both in extent and height, and built with stones of rare size and excellency. In the next place, he presented to the temple a number of large colossal statues, and several prodigious andro-sphinxes,[1] besides

---

[9] Not a "portico," as Larcher supposes, but the lofty towers of the Area, or Court of Entrance, which Herodotus properly describes of great height and size. See note [4] on ch. 155, and woodcut there.—[G. W.]

[1] The usual sphinxes of the *dromos*, or avenue, leading to the entrance of the large temples.   Sometimes kneeling rams were substituted for androsphinxes, as at Karnak, Gebel Berkel, and other places ; and sometimes lions.   The androsphinx had the head of a man and the body of a lion, symbolising the union of intellectual and physical strength, and Clemens and Plutarch say they were placed before the temples as types of the mysterious nature of the Deity. (Strom. v. 5, p. 664, and 7, p. 671, and Plut. de Is. s. 9.)   There were also the criosphinx, with the head of a ram ; the hieracosphinx, with that of a hawk ; and sometimes the paintings represented an asp, or some other snake (see woodcut below, No. VII. fig. 2), in lieu of a head, attached to the body of a lion.   Egyptian sphinxes were not composed of a woman and a lion, like those of Greece ; and if an instance occurs of this, it was a mere caprice, and probably a foreign innovation, justified by its representing a queen, the wife of King Horus, of the 18th dynasty ; and they are sometimes seen in the sculptures that portray the spoil taken from Asiatic nations.   One of them forms the cover of a vase, either of gold or silver ; rings (or ore) of which are probably contained in the sealed bags below ; and the same head is affixed to other ornaments taken from the same countries, in the immediate neighbourhood of the Naharayn, or Mesopotamia, by the arms of Sethi, the father of the great Remeses. Another foreign sphinx has the crested head of the Assyrian "*nisr.*"

One sphinx has been found of the early time of the 6th dynasty (in the possession of Mr. Larking, of Alexandria), having the name of King Merenre ; and another of the 12th dynasty (on a scarabæus of the Louvre) ; which at once decide the

No. I.   No. II.

certain stones for the repairs, of a most extraordinary size.
Some of these he got from the quarries over against Memphis,

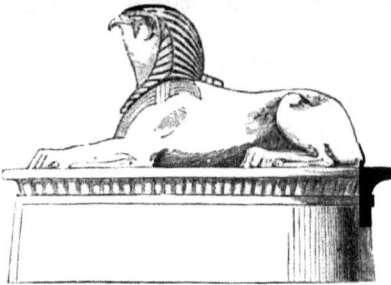

No. III.   No. IV.

priority of those of Egypt. The great sphinx at the Pyramids is of the time of a
Thothmes of the 18th dynasty (note [1] on ch. 127). Sometimes an androsphinx, instead of the lion's paws, has human hands, with a vase, or censer, between them.
The winged sphinx is rare in Egypt; but a few solitary instances occur of it on the
monuments, and on scarabæi; as well as of the hawk-headed sphinx, called *sefer*,

No. V.   No. VI.

which is winged (fig. 3). There is also a fabulous animal called *sak*, with the head of a
hawk, the body of a lion, and the tail terminating in a lotus flower (fig. 5)—a strange
combination of the bird, quadruped, and vegetable—as well as other fanciful crea-

No. VII.

but the largest were brought from Elephantiné,[2] which is twenty
days' voyage from Saïs.   Of all these wonderful masses that
which I most admire is a chamber made of a single stone,[3] which
was quarried at Elephantiné.   It took three years to convey
this block from the quarry to Saïs ; and in the conveyance were
employed no fewer than two thousand labourers, who were all
from the class of boatmen.   The length of this chamber on the
outside is twenty-one cubits, its breadth fourteen cubits, and
its height eight.   The measurements inside are the following :—
the length, eighteen cubits and five-sixths ; the breadth, twelve
cubits ; and the height, five.   It lies near the entrance of the
temple, where it was left in consequence of the following circumstance :—It happened that the architect, just as the stone
had reached the spot where it now stands, heaved a sigh, considering the length of time that the removal had taken, and
feeling wearied with the heavy toil.   The sigh was heard by
Amasis, who regarding it as an omen, would not allow the
chamber to be moved forward any further.   Some, however,
say, that one of the workmen engaged at the levers was crushed
and killed by the mass, and that this was the reason of its being
left where it now stands.

tures, one of which has the spotted body of a leopard, with a winged human head
on its back resembling a modern cherub ; and another is like a gazelle with wings
(fig. 1).   There is also the square-eared quadruped, the emblem of Seth (fig. 4).
The unicorn also occurs in the same early paintings.   To this was generally attached the idea of great " strength " (Numb. xxiii. 22, and xxiv. 8), for which the real
unicorn (the rhinoceros) was noted ; and with this view the sculptors of the Nineveh
obelisk, and of Persepolis (Ker Porter, i. Pl. 35), who had never seen it, represented
it under the form of a bull, their emblem of strength (Cp. Pausan. ix. 21): but the
Egyptian unicorn, even in the early time of the 12th dynasty, was the rhinoceros ;
and though less known then than afterwards, it had the pointed nose and small tail
of that animal, of which it is a rude representation.   Over it is " ebo," a name applied also to "ivory," and to any large beast.   The winged Greek sphinxes, so common on vases, are partly Egyptian, partly Phœnician in their character, the recurved
tips of the wings being evidently taken from those of Astarte.   (See woodcut No.
4 in App. to B. iii. Essay i.)
    The Romans sometimes gave to sphinxes the head of a man, sometimes of a
woman, with the royal asp upon the forehead, in sculptures of late time.   It is remarkable that in India a sphinx is said to represent the fourth avatar of Vishnoo,
and in Thibet it is called nara-sinhas, "man-lion," or merely sinhas, "lion," pronounced singhas, like σφιγγας.—[G. W.]
    [2] These were granite blocks.—[G. W.]
    [3] The form and dimensions of this monolith were very like that of the same king
at Tel-et-mai, Thmuis, or Leontopolis (given in Mr. Burton's Excerpta, plate 41),
which measures 21 ft. 9 high, 13 ft. broad, and 11 ft. 7 deep, and internally 19 ft.
3, 8 ft., and 8 ft. 3.   That of Saïs, according to Herodotus, was 31 ft. 6 long, 22 ft.
broad, and 12 ft. high, and, within, 28 ft. 3, 18 ft., and 7¼.   His *length* is really the
height, when standing erect.   It was not equal in weight to the granite Colossus of
Remeses at Thebes, which weighed upwards of 887 tons, and it was far inferior to
the monolith of Buto, which was taken from the same quarries.   See note [6] on ch.
155.—[G. W.]

176. To the other temples of much note Amasis also made magnificent offerings—at Memphis, for instance, he gave the recumbent colossus [4] in front of the temple of Vulcan, which is seventy-five feet long. Two other colossal statues stand on the same base, each twenty feet high, carved in the stone of Ethiopia, one on either side of the temple. There is also a stone colossus of the same size at Saïs, recumbent like that at Memphis. Amasis finally built the temple of Isis at Memphis, a vast structure, well worth seeing.

177. It is said that the reign of Amasis was the most prosperous time that Egypt ever saw,[5]—the river was more liberal

---

[4] It was an unusual position for an Egyptian statue ; and this, as well as the other at Memphis, and the monolith, many have been left on the ground, in consequence of the troubles which came upon Egypt at the time; and which the Egyptians concealed from Herodotus. Strabo speaks of a Colossus of a single stone, lying before the dromos of the temple at Memphis, in which the bull fights were held. This may be the statue of Amasis.—[G.W.]

[5] This can only relate to the internal state of the country ; and what Herodotus afterwards says shows this was his meaning. The flourishing internal condition of Egypt is certainly proved by the monuments, and the wealth of private individuals was very remarkable; but Egypt had lost all its power abroad, and had long been threatened, if not actually invaded, by the Babylonians. Indeed the civil war between Apries and Amasis had probably given Nebuchadnezzar an opportunity for interfering in Egypt; and if Amasis was forced to pay tribute to the Babylonians for quiet possession of the throne, this might account for the prophecy in Ezekiel (ch. xxix.), which is so perplexing, that Egypt should be given to Nebuchadnezzar, and be "a base kingdom," raising itself no more to "rule over the nations." Its being the basest of kingdoms, uninhabited forty years (v. 11), and its cities desolate, appears to accord badly with the prosperous time of Amasis; if all this was to happen after the year 585 B. C., when Tyre was taken, and consequently to extend into his reign (Ezek. xxix. 18). Still less could the captivity of Egypt date before the fall of Nineveh, as has been supposed from Nahum (iii. 8). The successful reign of Apries, and his obliging the Chaldeans to raise the siege of Jerusalem (Jer. xxxvii. 5), render it impossible ; and the civil war between Apries and Amasis happening after the taking of Tyre, would agree better with the statement of Ezekiel (xxix. 18) as to the time of Nebuchadnezzar's invasion of Egypt. That it took place is directly stated by Ezekiel and Jeremiah (xliii. 10, and xlvi. 13): the opportunity for interference was favourable for the Babylonians ; and the mere fact of a tribute being imposed by Nebuchadnezzar would account for the great calamities described by those prophets, which to the Egyptians would be the utmost humiliation. Many tributes too were imposed on people without absolute conquest or invasion. The reference to the pride of Apries in Ezekiel (xxix. 3) also argues that it was at his downfall; and this is again foretold in Isaiah (xix. 2). There is, however, a difficulty in the forty years, occupying as they would so great a portion of the reign of Amasis. (See Hist. Notice, App. CH. viii., end of § 37). During his reign, and before 554 B. C. (when Sardis was taken), Croesus had made a treaty of alliance with Amasis, as well as with the Babylonians, at the time that Labynetus (Nabonidus?) reigned in Babylon (supra, i. 77); from which it might be argued that the Egyptians were bound to follow the policy of the Babylonians ; and the Egyptian phalanx in the Lydian army is mentioned by Xenophon. (See Cyrop. vi. ii. 10, and vii. i. 30–45.) Again, it has been supposed that the captivity of Egypt should rather refer to the Persian invasion, which could scarcely have been overlooked in prophecy ; but these denouncements did not allude to events about to happen *long after* the fall of Jerusalem ; they were to show the hopelessness of trusting to Egypt against the power of Babylon ; and the invasion of Egypt by the Persians had no connexion with Jewish history. Nor is it certain that 40 is always to be taken as an exact

to the land, and the land brought forth more abundantly for the service of man than had ever been known before ; while the number of inhabited cities was not less than twenty thousand. It was this king Amasis who established the law that every Egyptian should appear once a year before the governor of his canton,[6] and show his means of living ; or, failing to do so, and to prove that he got an honest livelihood, should be put to death. Solon the Athenian borrowed this law from the Egyptians, and imposed it on his countrymen, who have observed it ever since. It is indeed an excellent custom.

178. Amasis was partial to the Greeks,[7] and among other favours which he granted them, gave to such as liked to settle in Egypt the city of Naucratis [8] for their residence. To those

number; its frequent occurrence in the Bible (like 7 and some others) shows this could not be ; and 4, or 40, is considered to signify "completion," or "perfection," like the square, and the number 24 in Arabic. See Hist. Notice, § 38, and note [2] on ch. 100, and on ch. 8, Book iii.—[G. W.]

[6] Each nome, or canton, was governed by a monarch. Herodotus attributes this law to Amasis; but it appears to have been much older; since we find in the sculptures of the 18th dynasty bodies of men presenting themselves before the magistrates for registration. It is possible that Amosis, the first king of that dynasty, made the law, and that the resemblance of the two names led to the mistake. Diodorus (i. 77) mentions it as an Egyptian law, and agrees with Herodotus in saying that Solon introduced it at Athens; but it was Draco who made death the punishment at Athens; which was altered by Solon (Plut. Life of Solon), "who repealed

all Draco's laws, excepting those concerning murder, because they were too severe;" "insomuch that those who were convicted of idleness were condemned to die."[1] But Solon "ordered the Areopagites to ascertain how every man got his living, and to chastise the idle."—[G. W.]

[7] Amasis had reason to be hostile to the Greeks, who had assisted Apries, but perceiving the value of their aid, he became friendly to them, and granted them many privileges, which had the effect of inducing many to settle in Egypt, and afterwards led them to assist the Egyptians in freeing their country from the Persians. —[G. W.]

[8] This was " formerly " the only commercial entrepôt for Greek merchandise, and

who only wished to trade upon the. coast, and did not want to fix their abode in the country, he granted certain lands where they might set up altars and erect temples to the gods. Of these temples the grandest and most famous, which is also the most frequented, is that called " the Hellenium." It was built conjointly by the Ionians, Dorians, and Æolians, the following cities taking part in the work,—the Ionian states of Chios, Teos, Phocæa, and Clazomenæ ; Rhodes, Cnidus, Halicarnassus, and Phasêlis [2] of the Dorians ; and Mytilêne of the Æolians. These are the states to whom the temple belongs, and they have the right of appointing the governors of the factory ; the other cities which claim a share in the building, claim what in no sense belongs to them. Three nations, however, consecrated for themselves separate temples, the Eginetans one to Jupiter, the Samians to Juno, and the Milesians to Apollo.[1]

179. In ancient times there was no factory but Naucratis in the whole of Egypt ; and if a person entered one of the other mouths of the Nile, he was obliged to swear, that he had not come there of his own free will. Having so done, he was bound to sail in his ship to the Canobic mouth, or, were that impossible owing to contrary winds, he must take his warès by boat all round the Delta, and so bring them to Naucratis, which had an exclusive privilege.

was established for the first time by Amasis. The privileges enjoyed by Naucratis were not only owing to the exclusive regulations of the Egyptians, like those of the Chinese at the present day, but were a precaution against pirates landing on the coast, under pretence of trading. (See notes [5] and [1] on chs. 112 and 154.) The exact position of Naucratis is unknown. The name is Greek, like that of Archander (supra. ch. 98). Of the Naucratis garlands, see Athen. Deip. xv.—[G. W.]

The story told by Strabo (xvii. p. 1137) of the foundation of Naucratis by the Milesians *in the time of Inarus* is entitled to no manner of credit. It may be questioned whether Naucratis was in any real sense "a Milesian colony."

[2] Phasêlis lay on the east coast of Lycia, directly at the base of Mount Solyma (*Takhtalu*). It was sometimes reckoned to Pamphylia (Plin. H. N. v. 27 ; Mela, i. 14; Steph. Byz. ad voc.), but more commonly, and by the best geographers, to Lycia (Scyl. Peripl. p. 94; Strab. xiv. p. 952; Ptolem. v. 3; Arrian. i. 24, &c.). According to tradition, it was founded by Lacius, the brother of Antiphêmus, the Lindian colonizer of Gela. (Heropyth. and Philosteph. ap. Athen. Deipn. vii. p. 297, f. and Aristænet. ap. Steph. Byz. ad voc. Γέλα.) This would place its foundation about B. C. 690. There seems to be no doubt that it was a purely Greek town.

The remains of Phasêlis are very considerable, and have been carefully described by Capt. Beaufort. (Karamania, pp. 59–70.) Its modern name is *Tekrova*. The part of the coast where it is situated abounds in woods of pine, which explains its ancient name of Pityussa. (See Steph. Byz. ad voc. Φασηλίς.)

The other places here mentioned are too well known to need comment.

[1] That is, to the gods specially worshipped in their respective countries. The great temple of Jupiter Panhellenius in Egina, briefly described by Pausanias (II. xxix. § 6), is well known to travellers. That of Apollo at Branchidæ, and that of Juno at Samos, have been already noticed. (Supra, i. 157, ii. 148.)

180. It happened in the reign of Amasis that the temple of Delphi had been accidentally burnt,[2] and the Amphictyons[3] had contracted to have it rebuilt for three hundred talents, of which sum one-fourth was to be furnished by the Delphians. Under these circumstances the Delphians went from city to city begging contributions, and among their other wanderings came to Egypt, and asked for help. From few other places did they obtain so much—Amasis gave them a thousand talents of alum,[4] and the Greek settlers, twenty minæ.[5]

181. A league was concluded by Amasis with the Cyrenæans, by which Cyrêné and Egypt became close friends and allies. He likewise took a wife from that city, either as a sign of his friendly feeling, or because he had a fancy to marry a Greek woman. However this may be, certain it is that he espoused a lady of Cyrêné, by name Ladicé,[6] daughter, some say, of Battus or Arcesilaüs, the king[7]—others, of Critobûlus, one of the chief citizens. When the time came to complete the contract, Amasis was struck with weakness. Astonished hereat —for he was not wont to be so afflicted—the king thus addressed his bride : " Woman, thou hast certainly bewitched me—now therefore be sure thou shalt perish more miserably than ever woman perished yet." Ladicé protested her innocence, but in vain; Amasis was not softened. Hereupon she made a vow internally, that if he recovered within the day (for no longer time was allowed her), she would present a statue to the temple of Venus at Cyrêné. Immediately she obtained her wish, and

---

[2] The temple at Delphi was burnt in the year B. C. 548 (Pausan. X. v. § 5), consequently in the 21st year of Amasis. According to one account (Philoch. Fr. 70), it was purposely destroyed by the Pisistratidæ. But this was probably a calumny. Its reconstruction by the Alcmæonidæ, who took the contract from the Amphictyons, is noticed in Book v. ch. 62.

[3] See note on Book vii. ch. 200.

[4] That of Egypt was celebrated: "laudatissima in Ægypto." (Plin. xxxv. 15.) Much is still obtained in the Oasis, but the best is from Sheb (which signifies " alum"), to the south of the Great Oasis, on the caravan road from Darfûr.—[G. W.]

[5] Twenty minæ would be somewhat more than eighty pounds of our money. The entire sum which the Delphians had to collect exceeded 18,000l.

[6] One wife of Amasis was a daughter of the third Psammetichus, and another is mentioned on the monuments called Tashot, which looks like a foreign (Asiatic) name. Amasis had the title of Naitsi, "son of Neith," or Minerva; and this name, Ames-Neitsi, has been changed by Pliny into Seneserteus, who (he says) reigned when Pythagoras was in Egypt.—[G. W.]

[7] Some of the MSS. give the reading " Battus, the son of Arcesilaüs," which Wesseling prefers. But the weight of authority is on the other side. The chronology of the Cyrenæan kings is so obscure, that it is difficult to say which monarch or monarchs are intended. Perhaps Battus the Happy, and Arcesilaüs II., his son, have the best claim. (See note on Book iv. ch. 163.)

the king's weakness disappeared. Amasis loved her greatly
ever after, and Ladicé performed her vow. The statue which
she caused to be made, and sent to Cyrêné, continued there to
my day, standing with its face looking outwards from the city.
Ladicé herself, when Cambyses conquered Egypt, suffered no
wrong ; for Cambyses, on learning of her who she was, sent her
back unharmed to her country.

182. Besides the marks of favour already mentioned, Amasis
also enriched with offerings many of the Greek temples. He
sent to Cyrêné a statue of Minerva covered with plates of gold,[3]
and a painted likeness[9] of himself. To the Minerva of Lindus

---

[3] Statues of this kind were not uncommon (infra, vi. 118). The most famous
was that of Minerva at Delphi, which the Athenians dedicated from the spoils of
their victory at the Eurymedon. (Pausan. X. xv. § 3 ; Clitod. Fr. 15.)

[9] The Egyptians had actual portraits of their kings at a very remote period ;
and those in the sculptures were real likenesses. That sent by Amasis to Cyrene
was on wood, like the πίνακες, or γραφαὶ (tabulæ), of the Greeks ; and similar pictures are shown to have been painted in Egypt as early as the 12th dynasty, nearly

2000 B. C. (Cp. Pliny, xxxv. 3, vii. 56, where he says, "Gyges, the Lydian, first
invented painting in Egypt.") In Greece pictures (often hung up in temples) were
works of the best artists, frescoes and others on walls being an inferior branch of
art ("nulla gloria artificum est, nisi eorum qui tabulas pinxere ; " Plin. xxxv. 10) ;
and we may conclude that in Egypt also the real artists were those who painted
pictures. The bas-reliefs and paintings on the monuments were executed more
mechanically, the figures being drawn in squares ; but in many cases the use of the
squares was for *copying* the figures from smaller original designs of the master-ar-
tist ; and some figures were drawn at once without the squares, and then corrected
by the master. When in squares, 19 parts were given to the height of a man from
the top of the head to the plant of the foot ; and so systematic was this method,
that in statues Diodorus says (i. 98) the various portions of the same figure, made
by several artists in different places, when brought together, would agree perfectly,
and make a complete whole. In his time, however, the proportions had been altered,
and he gives 21¼ parts as the height of the figure. It seems, too, that they were
somewhat different in statues and painted figures. These last also varied at times.
The above, of 19 parts, was used in the best period of art during the 18th and 19th
dynasties. The figures were then a little more elongated than during the reigns of
the Memphite kings (a greater distance being given from the plant of the
foot to the knee), and still more than under the Ptolemies, when an attempt to
bring the proportions nearer to the real figure altered its character, and gave it a
clumsiness, without any approach to greater truth. For the Egyptian style was

Mode of drawing Egyptian figures in squares, from a tomb at Thebes.

he gave two statues in stone, and a linen corslet [1] well worth inspection. To the Samian Juno he presented two statues of himself, made in wood,[2] which stood in the great temple to my

quite conventional, and could never be subjected to any other rules; and the Ptolemaic figure, as Dr. Lepsius observes, "was a bad imitation of foreign and ill-understood art." (See his Letters from Egypt, p. 117.) With the Greeks the length of the foot was "the measure whose proportion to the entire height was generally maintained" (Müller, Anct. Art. p. 392); but as in Egypt it is equal in length to 3 squares, or parts, it cannot answer for a figure of 19. And six of these feet coming only to the forehead, which varied so much as to be "$\frac{1}{2}$, or $\frac{1}{3}$, or less of another square," shows that neither the foot, nor the arbitrary and variable point to which it was measured, could be any guide. In the best period, from the ground to the knee was 6 parts, or 2 feet; but the figure was greater in breadth as compared to its height in the pyramid period than during the 18th and 19th dynasty; the distance from the ground to the knee, though 6 parts, was less than 2 feet, and the waist was nearly 3 parts (or 2$\frac{5}{8}$); while at the 18th dynasty period it was only 2 parts in breadth. In the old pyramid time the length of the foot was $\frac{1}{8}$ of the whole figure to the top of the head; in the other period much less (3 × 6 being 18); so that there must have been another standard; and the *great* difference was in the breadth, compared to the height, of the figure; a difference in the *number* of the squares is also said to have been met with. (See *Handbook of Egypt, Route* 29, *Ombos*.)

There are some portraits painted on wood and affixed to mummy cases, but these are of Greek and Roman time, and an innovation not Egyptian.—[G. W.]

[1] Some of these linen corslets were of very remarkable texture; and Herodotus (iii. 47) mentions another presented by Amasis to the Lacedæmonians, which was carried off by the Samians. It was ornamented with numerous figures of animals, worked in gold and cotton. Each thread was worthy of admiration, for though very fine, every one was composed of 360 other threads, all distinct, the quality being similar to that dedicated to Minerva at Lindus. Gold thread, it should be observed, is mentioned in Exod. xxxix. 3 for working in rich colours (see At. Eg. vol. iii. p. 128). It has been conjectured that the "tree-wool" of Herodotus was silk; but cotton is commonly used for embroidery even at the present day. (See above, ch. 86, note [6].) A similar corslet with figures of animals is represented in the tomb of Remeses III. at Thebes. Lucan (Phars. x. 142) mentions the needlework of Egypt:

"Candida Sidonio perlucent pectora filo,
Quod Nilotis acus compressum pectine
  Serum
Solvit, et extenso laxavit stamina velo."

Pliny (xix. 1) notices "the corslet of Amasis, shown in the Temple of Minerva at Rhodes," which seems to have been nearly pulled to pieces (as it would be now), to test "the 365 threads."—[G. W.]

[2] These were not uncommon; and many have been found of kings who

day, behind the doors. Samos was honoured with these gifts on account of the bond of friendship subsisting between Amasis and Polycrates, the son of Æaces :[3] Lindus, for no such reason, but because of the tradition that the daughters of Danaus[4] touched there in their flight from the sons of Ægyptus, and built the temple of Minerva. Such were the offerings of Amasis. He likewise took Cyprus, which no man had ever done before,[5] and compelled it to pay him a tribute.[6]

preceded Amasis in the same buildings where granite and other statues of the same period were placed. Pausanias (ii. 19) says "all ancient statues were of wood, especially those of the Egyptians;" and if in Egypt they were no proof of antiquity, still the oldest there also were probably of wood.—[G. W.]

[3] Vide infra, iii. 39—43.

[4] The flight of Danaus from Egypt to Greece is not only mentioned by Herodotus, but by Manetho and others, and was credited both by Greeks and Egyptians; and it is certaiuly very improbable (as Mr Kenrick observes) that the Greeks would have traced the colonisation of Argos, and the origin of certain rites, to Egypt, unless there had been some authority for the story. The foundation of the Temple of Lindus in Rhodes by the daughters of Danaus, when flying from Egypt, accords with the notion of colonisation and religious rites passing from the Egyptians to the Greeks; and the tradition of the relationship between Ægyptus, Danaus, and Belus, connects the three countries of Egypt, Greece, and Phœnicia. See note [4], ch. 101, and note [1], ch. 107.—[G. W.]

[5] Cyprus seems to have been first occupied by the Chittim, a Japhetic race (Gen. x. 4). To them must be attributed the foundation of the original capital, Citium. Before the Trojan war, however, the Phœnicians had made themselves masters of the island, which they may have named Cyprus, from the abundance of the herb cyprus (Lawsonia alba), called in the Hebrew כֹּפֶר, which is found there. (Steph. Byz. ad voc. Κύπρος. Plin. H. N. xii. 24.) According to Greek tradition, the conquest was effected by a certain Cinyras, a Syrian king (Theopomp. Fr. 111; Apollod. iii. xiv. § 3), whom Homer makes contemporary with Agamemnon. (Il. xi. 20). His capital was Paphos. If we may believe Virgil, the Cittæans soon regained their independence, for Belus, the father of Dido (more properly Matgen, Menand. ap. Joseph. c. Ap. i. 18), had again to reduce the island (Æn. i. 621–2), where, according to Alexander of Ephesus, he built (rebuilt?) the two cities of Citium and Lapéthus. (See Steph. Byz. ad voc. Λάπηθος.) A hundred and fifty years afterwards we find the Cittæans again in revolt. They had renounced their allegiance to Elulæus, king of Tyre, and were assisted in their struggle by Shalmaneser (Menand. ap. Joseph. A. J. ix. 14), or more probably Sargon, his successor, whose well-known inscription, found in Cyprus, probably commemorates this event. After the fall of the Assyrian empire, Phœnicia seems to have recovered her supremacy, and thenceforth Cyprus followed her fortunes; being now attacked by Amasis as a sequel to the Phœnician wars of his predecessor (supra, ch. 161; cp. Diod. Sic. i. 68). So, too, when Phœnicia submitted to Cambyses, Cyprus immediately followed her example (infra, iii. 19). Concerning the Greek colonies in Cyprus, see note on Book v. ch. 104.

[6] Mr. Blakesley says (note ad loc.): "It is impossible that Cyprus could have been reduced without a fleet, and Egypt did not possess one of her own." He then proceeds to speculate on the quarter whence an auxiliary naval force was at this time procured, and decides in favour of Samos. But Neco had made Egypt a naval power (supra, ch. 159), which she thenceforth continued to be. Under Apries she contended against Phœnicia (ch. 161), undoubtedly with her own ships, not with "some Hellenic auxiliary naval force," as Mr. Blakesley supposes. Her continued possession of a large navy after her conquest by the Persians is marked in vi. 6, where her vessels are engaged against the Ionians, and again in vii. 89, where she furnishes 200 triremes (the largest contingent, after that of Phœnicia) to the fleet of Xerxes.

APPENDIX TO BOOK II.

CHAPTER I.

"THE EGYPTIANS BEFORE THE REIGN OF THEIR KING PSAMMETI CHUS BELIEVED THEMSELVES TO BE THE MOST ANCIENT OF MANKIND."—Chap. 2.

The Egyptians from Asia. Egyptian and Celtic. Semitic character of Egyptian. Evidences of an older language than Zend and Sanscrit. *Ba* or *Pa*, and *Ma*, primitive cries of infants, made into father and mother. m for b. *Bek* not to be pronounced by an untutored child. Bek, name of bread in Egypt. The story told to Herodotus. Claim of the Scythians to be an early race.

IF Egypt is not the oldest civilised nation of antiquity, it may vie with any other known in history; and the *records* of its civilisation, left by the monuments, unquestionably date far before those of any other country. But the inhabitants of the valley of the Nile were not the most ancient of mankind, they evidently derived their origin from Asia; and the parent stock, from which they were a very early offset, claim a higher antiquity in the history of the human race. Their skull shows them to have been of the Caucasian stock, and distinct from the African tribes Westward of the Nile; and they are evidently related to the oldest races of Central Asia. (See note * on ch. 15.) The Egyptian language might, from its grammar, appear to claim a Semitic origin, but it is not really one of that family, like the Arabic, Hebrew, and others; nor is it one of the languages of the Sanscritic family, though it shows a primitive affinity to the Sanscrit in certain points; and this has been accounted for by the Egyptians being an offset from the early "undivided Asiatic stock;"—a conclusion consistent with the fact of their language being "much less developed than the Semitic and Sanscritic, and yet admitting the principle of those inflexions and radical formations, which we find developed, sometimes in one, sometimes in the other, of those great families." Besides certain affinities with the Sanscrit, it has others with the Celtic, and the languages of Africa; and Dr. Ch. Meyer thinks that Celtic "in all its non-Sanscritic features most strikingly corresponds with the old Egyptian." It is also the opinion of M. Müller that the Egyptian bears an affinity "both to the Arian and Semitic dialects," from its having been an offset of the original Asiatic tongue, which was their common parent before this was broken up into the Turanian, Arian, and Semitic.

In its grammatical construction, Egyptian has the greatest resemblance to the Semitic; and if it has less of this character than the

Hebrew, and other purely Semitic dialects, this is explained by the latter having been developed after the separation of the original tongue into Arian and Semitic, and by the Egyptian having retained a portion of both elements.   There is, however, a possibility that the Egyptian may have been a compound language, formed from two or more *after* the first migration of the race; and foreign elements may have been then added to it, as in the case of some other languages.

It is also interesting to observe that while the Semitic languages are confined to the south-west part of Asia, including Mesopotamia, Syria, and Arabia, the same elements are met with in the languages of Africa.

Though Zend and Sanscrit are the oldest languages of the Indo-European family, still these two are offsets of an older primitive one; and among other evidences of this may be mentioned the changes that words had already undergone in Zend and Sanscrit from the original form they had in the parent tongue; as in the number " twenty," which being in the Zend " *Visaiti*," and in Sanscrit " *Vinsati*," shows that they have thrown off the " d " of the original dva, " two," of dvisaiti, and of dvinsati (as the Latin " viginti " is a corrupted form of " dviginti ") ; and this is the more remarkable as the original form is maintained in the " dvadeset," or " dvaes," of the Slavonic; and " twice " in Sanscrit is *dvis*.   Another evidence is obtained from the Sanscrit verb *asmi*, " I am," where *santi*, " they are," is put for *asanti*, &c.

The word " Bekos " is thought to be Phrygian; and Strabo, following Hipponax, says it was the Cyprian word for bread. (vii. p. 340.)

Larcher remarks that deprived of its Greek termination, " os," and reduced to " Bek," it looks like an imitation of the bleating of the goats, which the children had been accustomed to hear; but it might rather be considered one of the two primitive sounds (ba or pa, and ma) first uttered by infants, which have been the origin of the names of father and mother in the earliest offsets from the parent language of mankind: thus matar (*Zend*) ; matar (*Sanscr.*); mater (*Lat.*), and μήτηρ (*Gr.*) ; muder (*Germ.*); mátor (*Slav.*); mam (*Welsh*); um (*Heb.* and *Arab.*); ammá (*Tamil*); eme " woman " (*Mongol*, whence the terminations of khanem and begum) ; ima " wife " (*Ostiak*); ema " mother " (*Finnish*); ema " female " (*Magyar*); hime   ℨIΜΕ   " wife," " woman," and mau (t-mau, mau-t), " mother " (*Egyptian*).

The same with ab, or *pa ;* and though it has been observed that Greek and Sanscrit have the verbs of similar meaning πάω and μάω, pa and ma ; and that πάτηρ, μήτηρ, pitar, matar, are regularly formed; the existence of the same roots in other languages claims for them a far earlier origin; and they were borrowed from the first efforts of the infant's speech.

It is remarkable that the two consonants which begin these sounds " ba," " ma," are commutable labials, " b " being frequently put for " m," in many languages; as in ancient Egypt, chnubis for chnumis ; Gemnoute changed into Sebennytus and Semenhoud; the river Bagradas converted into Magradah ; the Mandela into Bardela, and many others ; and the modern Greeks, who have no "b," are obliged to introduce an "m" before a "p," to imitate the sound,—*fabrica* being written by them *phamprika*. The natural sound, then, at the beginning of the word *bek* might have been pronounced by a child, but not the "k," unless instructed to make the necessary artificial effort ; and one untaught to speak would not have the power of uttering any but labial sounds.   The fact, therefore, of the children not being able to go beyond "be," the beginning of the word, renders the story doubtful ; and still less can we believe that the Egyptians gave precedence to the Phrygians from the use of the word *bek ;* since their own word "oik," "ak," "cake," "bread," or with the definite article *poik* (pronounced in Coptic *bayk*, like our word "*bake*") would be at once construed, by a people already convinced that they were the oldest of men, into a proof of their own claims ; for those cakes of bread were used by the Egyptians in all their offerings to the gods.   The story, then, may be considered one of the many current among the Greek *ciceroni* in Egypt, which were similar to those concocted at the present day in the "Frank quarter" of an eastern city ; and we may acquit Psammetichus of ignorance of his own, as well as of other, languages.

And though Herodotus says he learnt the story itself from the priests of Memphis, it is evident that, being ignorant of the language, he was at the mercy of an interpreter.

Justin (ii. 1) and Ammianus Marcellinus (xxii. 15) also mention a question between the Egyptians and Scythians respecting their comparative antiquity, which was considered with some show of reason to end in favour of the latter, as they inhabited those high lands of Central Asia, naturally the first freed from the water that once covered the earth, and therefore the first inhabited ; and the antiquity of the races of Central Asia is fully borne out by modern ethnological researches.—[G. W.]

CHAPTER II.

"THE EGYPTIANS WERE THE FIRST TO DISCOVER THE SOLAR YEAR."—Chap. 4.

(See note * on Chap. 51, and below, Appendix, CH. vii.)

The 12 months in Egypt. Years of 360, 365, and 365¼ days. The three seasons. Length of the year corrected. Sothic year. The year of 365 days. The dates of kings' reigns. The Square or Sothic year. The Lunar year. The Arab year. The Jewish year. Intercalation of the Egyptians and Greeks.

THOUGH Herodotus does not call the twelve portions, into which the Egyptian year was divided, months, it is certain that the original division was taken as among most other people from the moon; the hieroglyphic signifying "month" being the crescent. The Egyptians had three years: one unintercalated, of 360 days; and two intercalated, respectively of 365 and 365¼ days. They were divided into three seasons ("spring, summer, and winter," according to Diodorus, i. 11), each composed of four months of 30 days; and in the two intercalated years five days were added at the end of the twelfth month, which completed the 365 days; the quarter day in the last of them being added every fourth year, as in our leap-year.

The three seasons were thus represented with the four months belonging to each:—

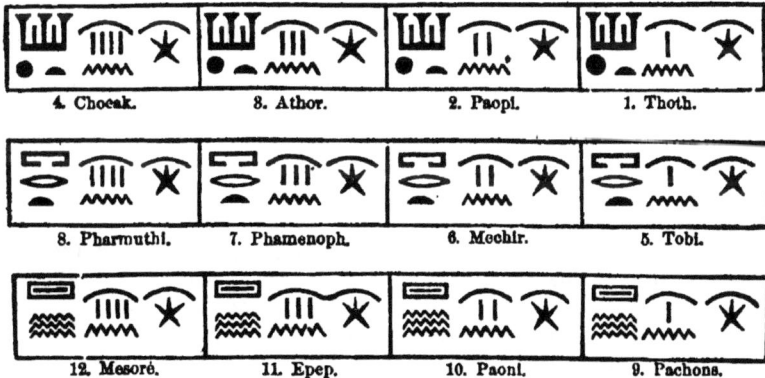

4. Choeak.   3. Athor.   2. Paopi.   1. Thoth.

8. Pharmuthi.   7. Phamenoph.   6. Mechir.   5. Tobi.

12. Mesoré.   11. Epep.   10. Paoni.   9. Pachons.

The first season began with the month Thoth (the first day of which, in the time of Augustus, B. C. 24, coincided with the 29th August, O. S.), and was composed of the four months Thoth, Paopi, Athor, Choeak; the second of Tobi, Mechir, Phamenoth, Pharmuthi;

the third of Pachons, Paoni, Epep, and Mesoré; at the end of which were added the five days of the intercalated year. The names of the seasons appear to be, 1st, of the plants; 2nd, of flowering, or harvest, and 3rd, of the waters, or inundation; which originally corresponded nearly to 1 , November, December, January and February; 2 , March, April, May and June; 3°, July, August, September and October. But as, in course of time, the seasons changed, and those of summer fell in winter, they found it necessary to make another correction; and for this purpose they resolved on ascertaining the period that elapsed between the return of a fixed star to the same place in the heavens, which they perceived would not be variable as were their conventional seasons. The heliacal rising of the dog-star, Sothis, was therefore the point fixed upon, and in 1460 Sothic (or 1461 of their vague) years, they found that it rose again heliacally, that their seasons had returned to their original places again, and that they had lost one whole year, according to the calculation of 365 days. This showed them that the difference of a quarter of a day annually required that one day every four years should be intercalated to complete the true year; and though they had already devised other means of fixing the return of a certain period of the year, this was the first nearly accurate determination of its length. The period when they first began their observations, as well as that still more remote one when the first intercalated year of 365 days came into use, must have been long before the year 1322 B. C.; and an inscription (in the Turin Museum) of the time of Amunoph I., the second king of the 18th dynasty, mentions the year of 365 days. Lepsius and M. de Rougé have also shown that the five days were already noticed in the 12th dynasty, and that the rite of Sothis was celebrated at the same period. The heliacal rising of Sothis was therefore ascertained long before the year 1322; and the reputed antiquity of the intercalary days is shown by their being ascribed, according to Strabo, to Hermes; as well as by the fable of the five sons of Seb having been born on those days; nor would the Egyptian kings have " sworn to retain the sacred year of 365 days without intercalating any day or month," unless the Sothic year had been already invented. Herodotus also says that they were indebted to the *stars* for their mode of adjusting the year and its seasons. But there is reason to believe that the still older year of 360 days was retained for the dates of kings' reigns; and that this unintercalated year of 360 days was the one used in their records and monumental stelæ: thus, an Apis was born in the 53rd year of Psammetichus I., the 19th Mechir, and died in the 16th year of Neco on the 6th Paopi, aged 16 years, 7 months, and 17 days. Now from 19 Mechir to 6 Paopi are 210 days + 11 to the end of Mechir + 6 of Paopi = 227, or 7 months 17 days over the 16 years; without any intercalary 5 days. It is, however, *possible* that the 5 days were included in the last month of the year, and that it was a year of 365 days; but there is no mention of the 31st, or any other day beyond the 30th, of Mésoré.

The Sothic year of 365¼ days was called the square year, the *annus quadratus* of Pliny (ii. 47); and the same mentioned by Diodorus (i. 50),

Macrobius (i. 16), and Horapollo. It appears to be represented in hieroglyphics by a square instead of the sun of the two vague years. The retention of the unintercalated and intercalated vague year would prevent the confusion which might have been expected from the older and later chronological memoirs having been kept in years of a different reckoning; for it was always easy to turn these last into Sothic years, when more accurate calculations were required; and this Sothic, or sidereal year, was reserved for particular occasions, as the old Coptic year is used by the modern Egyptians when they wish to fix any particular period, or to ascertain the proper season for agricultural purposes.

The Egyptians had therefore an object in retaining the vague year, in order that the festivals of the gods, in course of time, might pass through the different seasons of the year, as Geminus the Rhodian (who lived in 77 B. C.) informs us. It is also evident, that without the accuracy of the Sothic year they could not, as Herodotus supposes, have fixed the exact return of the seasons.

We may conclude, that the Egyptians had at first a lunar year which being regulated by the moon, and divided into 12 moons, or months, led to a month being ever after represented in hieroglyphics by a moon; but this would only have been at a most remote period before the establishment of the Egyptian monarchy; and some might hence derive an argument in favour of the early use of hieroglyphics, and suppose that they were invented before the introduction of the solar months. In India also the lunar year was older than the solar.

The lunar year still continues in use among the Arabs, and other Moslems, and the origin of a month has been the same in many countries; but their year is only of 354 days. The Aztecs, again, had months of 13 days, of which 1461 made their cycle of 52 years, by which the supernumerary quarter day was accurately adjusted. But though the Arabs always used lunar months, it has been ascertained by Mr. Lane, and by M. Caussin de Perceval, that their years were intercalated for about two centuries, until the 10th year of the Hégira, when the intercalation was discontinued by Mohammed's order; so that the usual mode of adjusting Arab chronology with our own is not quite correct.

It is a singular fact, that Moses in describing the abatement of the waters of the Deluge, calculates five months at 150 days (Gen. viii. 3, 4), or 30 days to a month, being the same as the unintercalated Egyptian year; the lunar however was that first used by the Hebrews; and, as in other languages, their name for the moon signified also a month. The lunar year of the Jews consisted of 12 months, which began (as with the Arabs) directly the new moon appeared; they varied in their length, and in order to rectify the loss of the 11 days, in the real length of the year, they added a thirteenth month every third, and sometimes every second year, to make up the deficiency, so that their months and festivals did not (like those of the Arabs) go through the various seasons of the year.

Herodotus considers the intercalation of the Egyptians better than that of the Greeks, who added a month at the end of every 2nd year, making them alternately of 12 and 13 months. This indeed would cause an excess, which the omission of 1 month every 8th year by the Greeks would not rectify. (See *Censorinus*, de Die Nat. c. 18.) Herodotus calculates the Greek months at 30 days each, and the 12 months at 360 days, when he says seventy years, without including intercalary months, are 25,200 days, *i. e.* 360×70, which, he adds, the 35 intercalary months will increase by 1050 days (35×30), making a total of 26,250 days for 70 years. This would be 375 days to the year. (See n.¹, ch. 32, Bk. i.) On the Greek intercalation see Macrobius, Saturn. i. 14, who says the Greeks made their year of 354 days, and perceiving that 11¼ days were wanting to the true year, they added 90 days, or 3 months, every 8 years. Strabo (xvii. p. 554) says the Greeks were ignorant (of the true length) of the year until Eudoxus was in Egypt; and this was in the late time of the 2nd Nectanebo, about B. c. 360; and Macrobius affirms that the Egyptians always possessed the true calculation of the length of the year,—"anni certus modus apud solos semper Ægyptios fuit." (Saturn. i. 7.) He then mentions the primitive year among other people—as the Arcadians, who divided it into 3 months; other Greeks making it consist of 354 days (a lunar year); and the Romans under Romulus, who divided it into 10 months, beginning with March.—[G. W.]

CHAPTER III.

"THE EGYPTIANS FIRST BROUGHT INTO. USE THE NAMES OF THE TWELVE GODS WHICH THE GREEKS ADOPTED FROM THEM."— Chap. 4.

Different orders of gods. The great gods of the first order. The second order. Place of Re, or the Sun. Classification of the gods. Sabaism not a part of the Egyptian religion. Pantheism. Name of Re, Phrah, and Pharaoh. Position of Re in the second order. Rank of Osiris. Children of Seb. The third order. The other most noted deities. Other gods. Foreign divinities. Chief god of a city and the triad. Deities multiplied to a great extent—the unity. Offices of the deity characters of Jupiter. Resemblances of gods to be traced from one original. Subdivision of the deity—local gods. Personifications—Nature gods. Sacred trees and mountains. Common origin of religious systems. Greek philosophy. Creation and early state of the earth.

IT is evident that some gods held a higher rank throughout the country than others, and that many were of minor importance, while some were merely local divinities. But it is not certain that the great gods were limited to 8, or the 2nd rank to 12; there are also proofs of some, reputed to belong to the 2nd and 3rd orders, holding a higher position than this gradation would sanction, and two of different orders are combined, or substituted for each other. It is not possible to arrange all the gods in the 3 orders as stated by Herodotus, nor can the 12 have been all born of the 8; there was however some distinction of the kind, the 8 agreeing with the 8 Cabiri (*i. e.* "great" gods) of the Phœnicians (see note * on ch. 51), and the others with the 12 gods of Olympus, and the Consentes of the Romans; though it is uncertain how this arrangement applied to them. Those who have the best claim to a place among the 8 great gods are,—1. Amun; 2. Maut; 3. Noum, or Nou (Noub, Nef, Kneph); 4. Sáté; 5. Pthah; 6. Neith; 7. Khem; 8. Pasht, who seems also to combine the character of Buto, under whose name she was worshipped at Bubastis.

1. *Amun*, the great god of Thebes, "the King of the gods," answered to Jupiter; 2. *Maut*, the "Mother" of all, or the maternal principle (probably the *môt* of Sanconiatho, see App. Book iii. Essay i. § 3, 11), appears to be sometimes a character of Buto (Latona), primæval darkness, from which sprang light; 3. *Noum*, Nu, Nou (or Noubai? called also Noub, Nef, Kneph, Cnuphis, and Chnubis, the ram-headed god), who was also considered to answer to Jupiter, as his companion (4.) *Sáté* did to Juno, was the great god of the Cataracts, of Ethiopia, and of the Oases; and in later temples, especially of Roman time, he often received the name of Amun:—the "contortis cornibus Ammon." (See notes on ch. 29, 42, Book ii., and on ch. 181, Book iv.) There is a striking resemblance between the Semitic Nef, "breath," and the

Coptic nibe, nifi, nouf, " spiritus;" and between the hieroglyphic num (with the article pnum), and the πνεῦμα, "spirit," which Diodorus says was the name of the Egyptian Jupiter. He was the " soul of the world " (comp. " mens agitat molem, et magno se corpore miscet "). The ram, his emblem, stands for *bai* " soul," and hence the Asp also received the name of Bait. The " *K* " of Kneph is evidently a corrupt addition, as Knoub for Noub; the change of *m* and *b* in Noub is easily explained (see above, in ch. i. § 6); and the name " Noub " is perhaps connected with Nubia as well as with gold. The very general introduction of the ram's head on the prow of the sacred boats, or arks, of other gods, seems to point to the early and universal worship of this god, and to connect him; as his mysterious boat does, with the spirit that moved on the waters. He is said to be Agathodemon, and the Asp being his emblem, confirms this statement of Eusebius.

5. *Pthah* was the creative power, the maker of all material things, " the father of the gods," and assimilated by the Greeks, through a gross notion of the Δημιουργός, or Opifex Mundi, to their Hephæstus (Vulcan). He was the god of Memphis. He had not so high a rank in Greece, nor in India, where Agni (*ignis* of Latin, *ogan* "fire" of Slavonic) was an inferior deity to Mahadeva, or Siva.

6. *Neith*, the goddess of Saïs, answered to Athênê or Minerva; she was self-born, and ἀρσενόθηλυς, she therefore sometimes had the sceptre given to male deities. (See note ' on ch. 62, Book ii.)

7. *Khem*, the generative-principle, and universal nature, was represented as a phallic figure. He was the god of Coptos, the " Πὰν Θηβῶν," and the Pan of Chemmis (Panopolis)—the Egyptian Pan, who, as Herodotus justly observes (ch. 145, Book ii.), was one of the 8 great gods. Of him is said in the hieroglyphic legend, " thy title is ' father of thine own father.' " (See notes ' and ' on ch. 42, and App. Book iii. Essay i. § 11.)

8. *Pasht*, Bubastis, answered to Artemis, or Diana; as at the Speos Artemidos.

It is not easy to determine the 12 gods of the 2nd order; and I only do this temporarily, as I have long since done in my Materia Hieroglyphica (p. 58); but I must not omit to state that they do not appear always to have been the same, and that the children of the 8 great gods do not *necessarily* hold a place among those of the 2nd order. (For the form of those of the other gods, whose names are mentioned below, see At. Eg. W., vol. v., Plates.)

The 12 deities of the most importance after the 8, and who may have been those of the 2nd order, are :—

1. *Re*, Ra, or Phrah, the Sun, the father of many deities, and combined with others of the 1st, 2nd, and even 3rd order.

2. *Seb*, Chronos, or Saturn. He was also the earth. Being the father of Osiris, and other deities of the 3rd order, he was called " father of the gods." The goose was his emblem. (See note ' ch. 72.)

3. *Neipe*, Rhea, wife of Seb. She was the Vault of Heaven, and was called " mother of the gods."

4. *Khons*, the 3rd member of the Great Triad of Thebes, composed

of Amun, Maut, and Khons their offspring. He is supposed to be a character of Hercules, and also of the ·Moon. In the Etymologicum Magnum, Hercules is called Chon.

5. *Anouké*, Estia, or ·Vesta, the 3rd member of the Great Triad of the Cataracts, composed of Noum (Nou), Sate, and Anouké. (See note [*] on ch. 62.) Estia is Festia with the digamma.

6. *Atmou*, *Atmoo*, *Atum*, or *Atm*, is "Darkness," the Sun after sunset (comp. Atmeh, "darkness," *Arabic*) sol· inferus, and called Re-Atum. Mr. Birch thinks him the negative principle, *tem* signifying "not."

7. *Moui*, apparently the same as Gom or Hercules, the splendour and ·light of the Sun, and therefore called a "son of Re."

8. *Tafne* (Daphne), or Tafne-t, a lion-headed goddess, perhaps the same as Thriphis, who is with Khem at Athribis and Panopolis.

9. *Thoth*, the intellect; Hermes or Mercury; the Moon (Lunus), a male god as in India; and Time in the sense of passing period. Anubis is also Time, past and future. (Plutarch de Is. s. 44.)

10. *Savak*,.the crocodile-headed god, often called Savak-Re.

11. *Eileithyia*, Ilithyia, or Lucina, Seben, Seneb, or Neben.

12. *Mandoo*, *Mandou*, or *Munt* (Mars), quite distinct from Mandulis or Malouli of Kalabshi (Talmis), where both gods are represented. From him Hermonthis received its name.

I had formerly placed Re among the 8 great gods, instead of Pasht, or Bubastis; but the position she held as second member of the Great Triad of Memphis, gives her the same claim as Maut, the consort of Amun. I am much disposed to make a separate class of deities connected with Re; who has a different name at his rising, at his meridian height, and at night. He is also the solar disc, and the shining sun or solar light (*Ubn-re*). The Sun-worshippers, or Stranger Kings of the 18th dynasty had a triad composed of *Atin-re*, *Moui* (solar splendour), and *Re*. Besides other characters, he is the soul of the world; his title Re is added to the names of other gods; and several deities are sons and daughters of the Sun. In these offices they are distinct from the deified attributes of the ideal, or primary god, which are necessarily of a different nature from the Sun-gods. There is at the same time a point of union between some of those attributes and certain characters of the Sun, or Re; who is connected with many gods of the first, second, and third orders;—Amun had the name Amun-Re; Nou (or Noum) was Noum-Re, and even Atin-Re; and the additional title of Re is also assigned to deities of the 2nd order, as to Savak, Mandou, and others.

In giving three orders I have been guided by Herodotus, though it is evident the numerous gods of Egypt were not confined to that number. If such were the sole classification, the greater part of the deities would be altogether omitted; and it is impossible to make them accord with his orders, even if we allow many of them to be repetitions of the same god under other characters. For some were characters of the deities belonging to the 1st or 2nd orders; but even then they were distinct, and members of some other group; as all the attributes of the one god became distinct deities. Nor can all those connected with the Sun be classified under one group. They may however claim a separate arrangement, like the Osiride family, which is supposed to form the third order; and this distinct classification of Sun-gods might be used to explain the nature of several important members of the Egyptian Pantheon.

Though actual Sabaism was not a part of the religion of the Egyptians, and the worship of the Sun and Moon was of a different kind, still it may have been connected with their earlier belief; which may be inferred from the idea of " prayer " being represented in hieroglyphics by a man holding up his hands, accompanied by a star. It is not impossible that when they immigrated into the Valley of the Nile they may have brought with them that Asiatic superstition, combined with some purer notions which they had of the Deity; but afterwards having endeavoured to reconcile the notion of physical and material, with ideal and incorporeal gods, they abandoned their earlier mode of worshipping the Sun and Moon. This last seems to accord with their religion as we see it on their monuments; where the Sun was chiefly looked upon as the visible representative of the generative, or vivifying, principle of Nature.

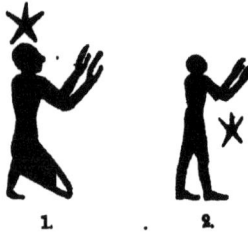

1.   2.

The disc of the Sun and the crescent of the Moon were placed as emblems on the heads of gods, and elsewhere; as the name of Re (the " Sun ") was appended to their titles; and these deities received a worship, but it was not Sabaism, and no notice was taken of the stars as objects of adoration. And when some " Stranger Kings " from Asia re-introduced the worship of the real Sun's disc, the innovation was odious to the Egyptians, and was expelled for ever with the usurpers who had forcibly established it in the country. Macrobius, indeed, endeavours to show that nearly all the gods corresponded to the Sun; and Chæremon thinks " the Egyptians had no gods but the Sun and planets; and that all related to physical operations, having no reference to incorporeal and living essences " (Eus. Pr. Evang. iii. 4). But this correspondence was distinct from Sabaism; and if many gods did " correspond to the sun," still the Sabäoth worship of the Sun and stars was not the religion of the Egyptians even in the earliest times of which any monuments remain. Many deities were characters of the Sun; and its daily course from its rising to its setting, and at different periods of the year (as well as certain phænomena—its supposed offspring), gave rise to beings who may be classed among Nature-gods; as in the mythology of India and Greece.

The Egyptians, as they advanced in religious speculation, adopted a Pantheism, according to which (while the belief in one Supreme Being was taught to the initiated) the attributes of the Deity were separated under various heads, as the " Creator," the divine wisdom, the generative, and other principles; and even created things, which were thought to partake of the divine essence, were permitted to receive divine worship.

The name of Re is remarkable for its resemblance to the *ouro*, "light" of Coptic, and the *Aor* of Hebrew (whence the *Urim*, "lights") and to Horus, and Aroeris (Hor-oeri, "Horus the chief"), to *har*, "heat," to ὥρα, *hora*, "season" or "hour," as well as to the names of the Sun in several African dialects, as Airo, ayero, eer, uiro, ghurrah, and others. It is the same as "Phrah," or Pharaoh, the Egyptian Pí-Re, "the Sun," *Memphiticè* Phra; which was first suggested by the Duke of Northumberland and Colonel Felix. Re had different characters: as the rising Sun he was a form of Horus; at midday Re; and Ubn-re, "the shining Sun;" as the solar disc Atin-re; when below the horizon Re-Atum, Atmou, or Atum, "darkness."

I have stated the reasons for placing Pasht (Bubastis) among the 8 great gods in preference to Re; and it would not only be inconsistent to place the created in the same rank as the creator, but Re has Athor as the 2nd member of his principal triad, and is himself the second of a minor triad composed of Amun, Re, and Horus. Again, though Re is the father of many deities, he has no claim on this account; since Nilus, and even Apé (Thebes), are called the "father" and "mother of the gods;" Asclepius is a son of Pthah without being one of the 12 gods; and Nepthys is called daughter of Re in the same building where she is allowed to be the sister of Isis. These and similar relationships therefore prove no more regarding the classification of the gods, than do the facts of Pthah being called "father of the gods" (while one only, Asclepius, is mentioned as his son), and of Re not being called by that title, though there are so many deities recorded in the sculptures as his children. And if Re was not one of the 8 great gods, this does not necessarily place him in an inferior position, since Osiris, who was the greatest of all, and was with Isis worshipped throughout the country, belonged to the 3rd order. For Osiris had this honour from being the god whose mysteries contained the most important secrets; his rites comprised the chief part of the Egyptian wisdom; he was the chief of Amenti, or Hades, and he was a heavenly as well as an *inferial* deity. There was also an important reason for his being of the last, or newest order of gods; he related particularly to man, the last and most perfect work of the creation; and as the Deity was at first the Monad, then the Creator, ("creation being God passing into activity,") he did not become Osiris until man was placed upon the earth. He there manifested himself also (like Booddha) for the benefit of man, who looked to him for happiness in a future state. (See notes ², ³, ⁴ on ch. 171, Book ii.)

It ought, however, to be observed, that the same god may belong to two different orders in two of his characters, and may be produced from different parents. Even Maut is once called "daughter of Re," and Re is said to be "engendered by Khem," as Khem was his own father; and Minerva at Sais proclaimed that "she proceeded from herself." But these apparent inconsistencies are readily explained by the nature of the Egyptian mythological system.

If it is necessary to confine the gods of the 3rd order to the children of Seb, a fourth and other orders might also be admitted (as I have already suggested in the "Materia Hieroglyphica"); for since those of the 2nd order are limited to twelve, it would be denying the accuracy of Herodotus, without any authority from the monuments, to class any of the numerous deities that remain together with the twelve of the 2nd order. There are, however, some lists of Deities on the monuments, in which eight, or sometimes twelve, are thus arranged: 1. Mandou, 2. Atmou, 3. Moui, 4. Tafne, 5. Seb, 6. Netpe, 7. Osiris, 8. Isis; or these eight with 9. Seth, 10. Nepthys, 11. Horus, and 12. Athor.

The 3rd order contains the children of Seb and Netpe:—1. Osiris. 2. Aroeris, or the Elder Horus, "son of Netpe." 3. Seth (Typhon). 4. Isis. 5. Nepthys (Nêb-t-êi), "lady of the house," corresponding to Vesta in one character (see note* on ch. 62); but we may perhaps include in the same order the younger Horus, the son of Osiris and Isis; as well as Harpocrates, their infant son, the emblem of childhood; and Anubis, the son of Osiris. The Younger Horus was the god of Victory and "the defender of his father;" and in like manner the Greek Apollo, to whom he corresponded, was represented as a "youthful god." (Comp. Lucian de Deâ Syr.)

Of the remaining deities the most noted were:—1. Tbmei, Mei, or Ma, in her two capacities of Truth and Justice, *Alètheia* and *Themis*, called "Daughter of the Sun," sometimes represented without a head, and who ought, perhaps, to belong to the 2nd order of Deities. 2. Athor (*èi-t-Hor*, "Horus's mundane habitation") Venus, often substituted for Isis, called "Daughter of the Sun," answering to the West, or the place where the setting Sun was received into her arms. (See note ¹ ch. 44, note* ch. 122, Book ii., and App. Book iii .Essay i. § 16.) 3. Nofr-Atmou, perhaps a variation of Atmou. 4. Hor-Hat, frequently as the winged globe, one of the characters of the Sun, generally called Agathodæmon. 5. Hacte (Hecate?), a goddess with a lion's head. 6. Selk, with a scorpion on her head. 7. Tore, a god connected with Pthah. 8. Amunta, perhaps a female Amun. 9. Tpe, "the heavens." 10. Hapi, or the god Nilus. 11. Ranno, the asp-headed goddess, perhaps a character of Agathodæmon (see Calmet, Pl. 69). 12. Hermes Trismegistus, a form of Thoth. 13. Asclepius, Mòtph, or "Imoph," called "the son of Pthah," probably the origin of the Emeph of Iamblichus. 14. Sofh, perhaps the goddess of Speech; and about 50 more, some of whom were local divinities, as "the Land of Egypt;" "the East" and "the West" (bank); *Ap, Apé,* or *Tápé,* "Thebes;" and the personifications of other cities.

There were also various forms of early gods, as frog-headed deities connected with Pthah; and the offspring of local triads, as Pneb-to, Hor-pi-re, and other forms of the infant Horus; the Apis, a form of Osiris, who was the Sarapis (*i. e.* Osir-Api) of Memphis, and other representations of well-known gods, together with minor divinities and genii: as Cerberus, the monster who guarded Amenti "the region of the dead;" the 4 genii of Amenti, with the heads of a man, a cynocephalus, a jackal, and a hawk; the 6 spirits with the heads of hawks and jackals; the 12 hours of day and night; the 42 assessors at the future judgment, each of whom presided over, or bore witness to a particular sin; and the giant Apap (Aphôphis)—"the great serpent,' and the emblem of wickedness.

Many of the 50 gods above alluded to were certainly of late introduction; but those whose names I have mentioned were of early date, as well as many of minor note; and for the figures of all the gods I must refer to my Anct. Egyptians. Some of them are called children of the Sun. There were also a few foreign deities, as Ranpo, the god of battles, and the goddess of war, Anata or Anta (see Appendix of Book iii. Essay i. § 21), Astarte, and others, who were of early introduction; but the character given to Seth, who was called Baal-Seth and the god of the Gentiles, is explained by his being the cause of evil. (See note ⁴ on ch. 171.) The introduction of foreign gods finds a parallel among other people of antiquity, whose readiness to adopt a god from another religion is one of the peculiarities of Polytheism; and the complacency of the Romans on this point is well known.

In each city of Egypt one deity was the chief object of worship; he was the guardian of the place, and he had the most conspicuous post in the adytum of its temple. The town had also its particular triad, composed of 3 members, the third proceeding from the other two; and the principal cities of Egypt, as Thebes and Memphis, had two of the great gods as the first members of their triads. They might be gods of any order, and the 2 first members not necessarily of the first rank; for one of the 1st, or of the 2nd order, might be combined even with a local deity to produce the 3d of still inferior rank in the divine scale; and these in latter times became multiplied and brought down to a very low order of beings, the divine essence being thought to pervade in a greater or less degree all the creations of the deity. It was merely the extension of the same idea; as an instance of which the great divine wisdom might combine with the *genius* of a city to produce a king. And to show how the divine and human natures of a king were thought to be distinct, he was often represented offering to himself in the Egyptian sculptures, his human doing homage to his divine character.

With such views it is not surprising that the Egyptians multiplied their deities to an endless extent; and plants, and even stones were thought to partake in some degree of the divine nature; but the notion that Egyptian gods were represented as animals and not under the human form is quite erroneous, the latter being by far the most usual. Originally, indeed, they had the Unity, worshipped under a particular character; which was the case in other countries also, each considering him their protector, and giving him a peculiar form and name, though really the same one god; and it was only when forsaken by him that they supposed their enemies were permitted to triumph over them. (Comp. also Josephus, Antiq. viii. 10. 3, of the Jews and Shishak.) But it was not long before they subdivided the one god, and made his attributes into different deities. In like manner the Hindoos have one supreme Being, Brahme (neuter), the great one, who, when he creates, becomes Brahma (masculine); when he manifests himself by the operation of his divine spirit, becomes Vishnu, the pervader, or Narayan, "moving on the waters," called also the first male; when he destroys, becomes Siva, or Mahadiva, "Great god;" and as Brahma, Vishnu, and Siva, is the Creator, Preserver, and Destroyer, which last answers to the regenerator of what only changes its form; and reproduces what he destroys. (See Sir W. Jones, vol. i. p. 249; and Asiat. Res. vol. vii. p. 280; and my note ' on ch. 123, Book ii.)

The same original belief in one god may be observed in Greek mythology; and this accordance of early traditions agrees with the Indian notion that "truth was originally deposited with men, but gradually slumbered and was forgotten; the knowledge of it however returning like a recollection." For in Greece, Zeus was also universal, and omnipotent, the one god, containing all within himself; and he was the Monad, the beginning and end of all. (Somn. Scip. c. 6; Aristot. de Mund. 7.)

Ζεὺς κεφαλή· Ζεὺς μέσσα, Διὸς δ'ἐκ πάντα τέτυκται. (line 2.)
Ἐν κράτος, εἷς Δαίμων γένετο, μέγας ἀρχὸς ἀπάντων. (line 8.)
Πάντα γὰρ ἐν μεγάλῳ Ζηνὸς τάδε σώματι κεῖται. (line 12.)
Orphic Fragm.

Ζεύς ἐστιν αἰθήρ, Ζεὺς δὲ γῆ. Ζεὺς δ' οὐρανός·
Ζεύς τοι τὰ πάντα.—Æsch. Fragm. 295.

(Comp. Clemens Strom. v. p. 603.)

At the same time each of the various offices of the Deity was known under its peculiar title. (See note A. in App. to Book i.) Jupiter was also prefixed to the names of foreign gods, as Jupiter-Ammon, Jupiter-Sarapis, Jupiter-Baal-Markôs, and many others; and though the Sun had its special Deity, altars were raised to Jupiter-the-Sun. He was also the manifestation of the Deity, like Osiris, who was the son of Seb, the Saturn of the Egyptians. Thus Osiris, Amun, and Noum, though so unlike, were each supposed by the Greeks to answer to Jupiter. Hesiod, too, calls Jupiter the youngest of the gods; as Osiris was in the third order of Deities, though the greatest of all; and the correspondence was completed by both being thought to have died. This notion, common to Egypt, Syria, and Crete, as to the Booddhists, and other people, is one of many instances of the occurrence of similar religious views in different countries (see notes ',' ch. 171); but there is also evidence of the Greeks having borrowed much from Egypt in their early mythology, as well as in later times, after their religion had long been formed; and the worship of Isis spread from Egypt to Greece and its islands, as it afterwards did to Rome. But the corrupt practices introduced at Alexandria, and more especially at Canopus, and thence carried to Europe, were no part of the Egyptian religion; they proceeded from the gross views taken, through ignorance, of certain allegorical representations, and were quite opposed, in their sensual and material character, to the simple expression of the hieroglyphical mind of Egypt.

It is easy to perceive in all the religions of antiquity why so many divinities resemble each other, why they differ in some points, and how they may be traced to one original; while others, being merely local, have a totally different character. Though they began by subdividing the one Deity, they subsequently laboured to show that all the gods were one; and this last, which was one of the great mysteries of Egypt, was much insisted upon by the philosophers of Greece. Even the names of some Deities show they came from one and the same, as Zeus-Dios, Dis, Iav, Jovi, Dius-piter, Dies-piter, Jupiter, (Iapeter?), Iacchus, and Janus, who was said to be a character of Apollo, as Jana was Diana (Macrob. Saturn. i. 5), corresponding to Phœbus and Phœbe; and Macrobius not only identifies most of the gods with the Sun, but makes Apollo and Bacchus, though so very dissimilar, the same (Saturn. i. 20). Again, the *Olympian*, or heavenly, and the *inferial* gods were essentially the same; Pluto was only a character of Jupiter; and Ceres and Bacchus belonged to both classes, in which they resembled Isis and Osiris. The same notion led to the belief in a Sol inferus—a deity particularly Egyptian, and connected with the Sun-gods.

The Deity once divided, there was no limit to the number of his attributes of various kinds and of different grades; and in Egypt everything that partook of the divine essence became a god. Emblems were added to the catalogue; and though not really deities, they called forth feelings of respect, which the ignorant would not readily distinguish from actual worship. The Greeks, too, besides the greater gods, gave a presiding spirit to almost every part of visible Nature; trees of various kinds had their dryads, hama-dryads, and other nymphs; rivers, lakes, marshes, and wells had their Naiads, as plains, mountains, caves, and the like, had their presiding spirits; and each "genius loci" of later times varied with the place. These were mere personifications,—an inferior grade of Nature-gods,—who had no mysteries, and could not be identified with the one original Deity, as the local divinities of Egyptian towns were different from those who held a rank in the first, second, and third orders of gods.

Tree-worship, and the respect for holy mountains, were African as well as Egyptian superstitions; and they extended also to Asia.

Besides the evidence of a common origin, from the analogies in the Egyptian, Indian, Greek, and other systems, we perceive that mythology had advanced to a certain point before the early migrations took place from central Asia. And if in aftertimes each introduced local changes, they often borrowed so largely from their neighbours, that a strong resemblance was maintained; and hence the religions resembled each other, partly from having a common origin, partly from direct imitation, and partly from adaptation; which last continued to a late period.

The philosophical view taken by the Greeks of the nature of the Deity was also different from their mythological system; and that followed by Thales and others was rather metaphysical than religious. Directly they began to adopt the inquiry into the nature of the Deity, they admitted that he must be One and Supreme; and he received whatever name appeared to convey the clearest notion of the First Principle. How far any of their notions, or at least the inquiry that led to them, may be traced to an acquaintance with Egyptian speculation, it is difficult to determine; Thales, and many more philosophers, studied in Egypt, and must have begun, or have sought to promote, their inquiry during their visit to the learned people of that age; and in justice to them we must admit that they went to study there for some purpose. At all events their early thoughts could not but have been greatly influenced by an intercourse with Egypt, though many a succeeding philosopher suggested some new view of the First Cause; speculation taking a varied range, and often returning under different names to a similar conclusion. Still, many early Greek philosophers admitted not only an ideal deity as a first cause, a divine intelligence, the "holy infinite spirit" of Empedocles, or other notions of the One; but, like Alcmæon of Crotona (according to some a pupil of Pythagoras, according to others of the Ionian school), "attributed a divinity to the sun and stars *as well as* to the mind" (Cic. Nat. Deor. i.). Plato, too, besides the incorporeal God, admits "the heavens, stars, and earth, the mind, and those gods handed down from our ancestors" to be the Deity; and Chrysippus, called by Cicero (Nat. Deor. i. and iii.) the most subtle of the Stoics, extended the divine catalogue still farther; which recalls the Egyptian system of a metaphysical and a mysterious view of the divine nature, and *at the same time* the admission of a worship of the Sun. (See note ' on chap. 51, and note on ch. 123, B. ii.)

. Of the Egyptian theory of the creation some notion may perhaps be obtained from the account given in Ovid (Met. i. and xxv.) borrowed from the Pythagoreans; as of their belief in the destruction of the earth by fire, adopted by the Stoics. (Ovid. Met. i. 256; Seneca, Nat. Quæst. iii. 13 and 28; Plut. de Placit. Phil iv. 7.) They even thought it had been subject to several catastrophes, "not to one deluge only, but to many;" and believed in a variety of destructions "that have been, and again will be, the greatest of those arising from fire and water" (Plat. Tim. pp. 466, 467). The idea that the world had successive creations and destructions is also expressly stated in the Indian Manu.

But though some subjects seem to point to the creation, in the tombs of the kings, perhaps also to the destruction (as well as to man's future punishment) of the world by fire, there are few direct indications of its creation beyond some mysterious allusions to the agency of Pthah (the creator), or the representation of Noum (Nef), the divine spirit passing in his boat "on the waters," or fashioning the clay on a potter's wheel. This last is also done by Pthah, which seems to correspond with the doctrine of Empedocles, as well as with the notion expressed in Genesis that the *matter* already existed "without form and void" (*tohóo oo bohóo*); and *not* that it was then for the first time called into existence. For, (as Mr. Stuart Poole has observed) the same expression, *tohóo oo bohóo*, is used in Jeremiah (iv. 23), where the land "without form and void" was only "desolate," not destroyed nor brought "to a full end" (v. 27), but depopulated and deprived of light. (Cp. Ps. civ. 30.)

They probably had a notion of the indefinite period that intervened between "the beginning" and the creation of man, which is in accordance with the Bible account, as St. Gregory Nazianzen and others have supposed, and which seems to be pointed out by the Hebrew text, where in the two first verses the past tense of the verbs ("God *created*" (*bard*) and "the earth *was* without form") is used; while in the 3rd, and some

other verses, we have *iamer* (" *says* "), and *ibra* (" *creates* "); for though
these have a past sense, that construction is not a *necessary* one, and the
verb might have been placed *after*, instead of *before*, the noun, as in the
2nd verse.   The creation of plants before animals, as in " the third day "
of Genesis, was also an ancient, perhaps an Egyptian, belief; and " Empedocles says the first of all living things were trees, that sprang from
the earth before the sun expanded itself."   (Comp. Plut. de Plac. Phil.
v. c. 26.)   The tradition among the Hebrews of the world having been
created in autumn was borrowed from Egypt, to which climate only (as
Miss F. Corbaux has shown) the idea that autumn was the period of
the world's creation, or renewal, would apply.—[G. W.]

CHAPTER IV.

"WHEN MŒRIS WAS KING," &c.—Chap. 13.

Rise of the Nile 16 cubits.   Differed in different parts of Egypt.   Oldest Nilometer.
The lowering of the Nile in Ethiopia by the giving way of the rocks at Silsilis.
Ethiopia affected by it, but not Egypt below Silsilis.   Other Nilometers and
measurements.   Length of the Egyptian cubit.

" *When Mœris was king,*" *says Herodotus,* "*the Nile overflowed all Egypt
below Memphis, as soon as it rose so little as* 8 *cubits,*" and this, he adds,
was not 900 years before his visit, when it required 15 or 16 cubits to
inundate the country.   But the 16 figures of children (or cubits, Lucian.
Rhet. Præc. sec. 6) on the statue of the Nile at Rome show that it rose
16 cubits in the time of the Roman Empire; in 1720 sixteen cubits were
still cited as the requisite height for irrigating the land about Memphis;
and the same has continued to be the rise of the river at old Cairo to
this day.   For the proportion is always kept up by the bed of the river
rising in an equal ratio with the land it irrigates, and the notion of
Savary and others that the Nile no longer floods the Delta, is proved
by experience to be quite erroneous.   This also dispels the gloomy
prognostications of Herodotus that the Nile will at some time cease to
inundate the land.

The Mekeeas pillar at old Cairo, it is true, is calculated to contain
24 cubits, but this number merely implies " completion," and it has
been ascertained by M. Coste that the 24 Cairene cubits are only equal
to about 16 or 16½ real cubits.   The height of the inundation varies of
course, as it always did, in different parts of Egypt, being about 40
feet at Asouan, 36 at Thebes, 25 at Cairo, and 4 at the Rosetta and
Damietta mouths; and Plutarch gives 28 cubits as the highest rise at
Elephantine, 15 at Memphis, and 7 at Xois and Mendes, in the Delta
(de Isid. s. 43).   The Nilometer at Elephantine is the one seen by
Strabo, and used under the Empire, as the rise of the Nile is recorded
there in the 35th year of Augustus, and in the reigns of other Emperors.
The highest remaining scale is 27 cubits; but it has no record of the
inundation at that height, though Plutarch speaks of 28; and the highest recorded there is of 26 cubits, 4 palms, and 1 digit.   This, at the
ratio stated by Plutarch, would give little more than 14 at Memphis;
but Pliny (v. 9) says the proper rise of the Nile is 16 cubits, and the
highest known was of 18 in the reign of Claudius, which was extraordinary and calamitous.   Ammianus Marcellinus (22), in the time of
Julian, also says, " no landed proprietor wishes for more than 16
cubits."   The same is stated by El Edrisi and other Arab writers.

(See Mém. de l'Acad., vol. xvi. p. 333 to 377; M. Eg. W., p. 279 to 284; and At. Eg. W., vol. iv. p. 27 to 31). The great staircase of Elephantine extends far above the highest scale, and measures 59 feet, and with the 9 steps of the lower one, the total from the base is nearly. 69 feet, while the total of the scales that remain measures only about 21 feet; but the cubits, 27 (KE) marked on the highest, answer to a height of 46 ft. 10⅜ in., which shows that this was reckoned from a lower level than the base of the lowest staircase.

From all that has been said it is evident that the change from the time of Mœris to Herodotus could not have been what he supposes; and that the full rise of the Nile about Memphis was always reckoned at 16 cubits. The 8 cubits in the time of Mœris were either calculated from a different level, or were the rise of the river at some place in the Delta far below Memphis.

The oldest Nilometer, according to Diodorus, was erected at Memphis; and on the rocks at Semneh, above the second cataract, are some curious records of the rise of the Nile during the reigns of Amun-m-he III. and other kings of the 12th dynasty, which show that the river does not now rise there within 26 feet of the height indicated in those inscriptions. But this was only a local change, confined to Ethiopia, and the small tract between the first cataract and Silsilis; and it was owing to a giving way of the rocks at Silsilis, which till then had kept up the water of the Nile to a much higher level south of that point. For though the plains of Ethiopia were left without the benefit of the annual inundation, no effect was produced by it in Egypt north of Silsilis, except the passing injury done to the land just below that place by the sudden rush of water at the moment the barrier was burst through. The channel is still very narrow there, being only 1095 feet broad, and tradition pretends that the navigation was in old times impeded by a *chain* thrown across it by a king of the country, from which the name of Silsil is thought to be derived. But though *silsili* signifies a "chain" in Arabic, the name of Silsilis was known long before the Arabs occupied Egypt; and it is not impossible that its Coptic appellation, *Golgel*, may have been borrowed from the catastrophe that occurred there, and point to an earthquake as its cause; or from a similar word, *Golgol*, alluding apparently to the many channels worn by the cataracts there, or to the breaking away of the rocks at the time of the fall of the barrier.

The change in the level of the Nile was disastrous for Ethiopia, since it left the plains of that hitherto well-irrigated country far above the reach of the annual inundation; and, as it is shown, by the position of caves in the rocks near the Nile, and by the foundation of buildings on the deposit, to have happened only a short time before the accession of the 18th dynasty, it is singular that no mention should have been made of so remarkable an occurrence either by Manetho or any other historian. The narrow strip of land in Nubia and Southern Ethiopia, as well as the broad plains of Dongola, and even some valleys at the edge of the eastern desert, are covered with this ancient deposit; I have seen water-worn rocks that prove the former extent of the annual inundation in spots often very distant from the banks; and even now this soil is capable of cultivation if watered by artificial irrigation. Though this change did not affect Egypt below Silsilis, it is not impossible that the measurements of Mœris may apply to other observations made in his reign in Egypt also; and the discovery of the name of Amun-m-he III. at the Labyrinth by Dr. Lepsius, shows that this was at least *one* of the kings to whom the name of Mœris was ascribed. (See note ° on ch. 13, B. ii.) Other measurements are mentioned at different times besides those under Mœris and in the days of Herodotus. A Nilometer stood at Eileithyias in the age of the Ptolemies; there was one at Memphis, the site of which is still pointed out by tradition; that of Elephantine remains with its scales and inscriptions recording the rise of the Nile in the reigns of the Roman Emperors; a moveable one was preserved in the temple of Sarapis at Alexandria till the time of Constantine, and was afterwards transferred to a Christian church; the Arabs in 700 A. D. erected one at Helwan, which gave place to that made, about 715, by the caliph Suleyman in the Isle of Roda, and this again was succeeded by the "Mekeeas" of Mamoon, A. D. 815, finished in 860 by Motawukkel-al-Allah, which has continued to be the government Nilometer to the present day.

The length of the ancient Egyptian cubit and its parts may be stated as follows :—

			Of the Nilometer of Elephantine.		Of Memphis, according to Jomard.
1 digit or dactylus .	= English inches	"	0·7366	.	0·73115
4 " 1 palm . .	=	"	2·9464	.	2·9247
28 " 7· " 1 cubit =		"	20·6250	.	20·47291

The lengths of different Egyptian cubits are :—

	Millimetres.		Eng. inches.
The cubit in the Turin Museum, according to my measurement	522²/₁₀	or	20·5730
The same, according to Jomard . . .	522⁷/₁₀	or	20·5786
Another	523	or	20·6180
Another	524	or	20·6584
Jomard's cubit of Memphis, mentioned above .	520	or	20·4729
Cubit of Elephantine Nilometer, according to Jomard	527	or·	20·7484
The same, according to my measurement . . .			20·6250
Part of a cubit found by me on a stone at Asouan .		about	21·0000
The cubit, according to Mr. Perring's calculation, at the Pyramids, do.			20·6280(?)
Mr. Harris' cubit from Thebes			20·6500

From all which it is evident that they are the same measure, and not two different cubits; and there is nothing to show that the Egyptians used cubits of 24, 28, and 32 digits.[1]—[G. W.]

[1] See Ancient Egyptians, W., vol. iv. p. 31.

CHAPTER V.

"THEY HAVE TWO QUITE DIFFERENT KINDS OF WRITING, ONE OF WHICH IS CALLED SACRED, THE OTHER COMMON."—Chap. 36.

Hieratic and Demotic, the two sorts of letters written from right to left. Hieroglyphics. Three kinds of writing. Hieratic. Demotic, or enchorial. The three characters. First use of demotic. Of symbolic hieroglyphics: The ikonographic. The tropical. The enigmatic. Symbolic also put with phonetic hieroglyphics. Determinatives after the word, or name of an object. Initial letters for the whole words, to be called *limited initial signs.* Distinct from other "mixed signs." Syllabic signs. Medial vowel placed at the end of a word. Earliest use of hieroglyphics. Mode of placing hieroglyphics. First letter of a word taken as a character. Determinative signs. They began with representative signs. The plural number. Abstract ideas. Phonetic system found necessary. Some parts of the verb. Negative sign. Invention of the real alphabetic writing Phœnician. Greek letters. Digamma originally written. Sinaitic inscriptions not of the Israelites. Tau used for the cross. Materials used for writing upon. The papyrus.

THESE two kinds of writing, written, as he says, from right to left, evidently apply to the hieratic and demotic (or enchorial); for though the hieratic was derived from an abbreviated mode of writing hieroglyphics, it was a different character; as the demotic was distinct from the hieroglyphic and the hieratic. The same is stated by Diodorus (i. 81), who says "the children of the priests were taught two different kinds of writing;".... "but the generality of the people learn only from their parents, or relations, what is required for the exercise of their peculiar professions, a few only being taught anything of literature, and those principally the better class of artificers." Herodotus and Diodorus consider the hieroglyphics merely monumental; but they were not confined to *monuments,* nor to sacred purposes. Clemens (Strom. v. p. 555) more correctly reckons three kinds of writing: 1, the epistolographic; 2, the hieratic, or sacerdotal; 3, the hieroglyphic, which was an ordinary written character like the other two; and originally the only one. He then divides the hieroglyphic into, 1, *kyriologic* (directly expressed by the first letter or initial of the name of the hieroglyphic object), and 2, *symbolic,* which was either directly expressed by *imitation,* or written by *tropes,* or altogether *allegorically by certain enigmas.* As an example of the kyriologic, he says they make a circle to represent the "sun," and "a crescent for the moon," "according to their direct form;" in the tropical method they substitute one thing for another which has a certain resemblance to it. It is therefore suited to express the praises of their kings in theological myths. Of the third or enigmatic an example may be given in their representing the planets from their motion by serpents, and the sun by a beetle (or more properly by a hawk). The scheme of Clemens may be thus represented :—

Egyptian writing.

Epistolographic.		Hieroglyphic.	
		Kyriologic (phonetic, by the initial letters).	Symbolic.
By direct imitation, or representation ikonographic, or ideographic.		By Tropes, or anaglyphic.	Allegoric, Enigmatic, or Emblematic.

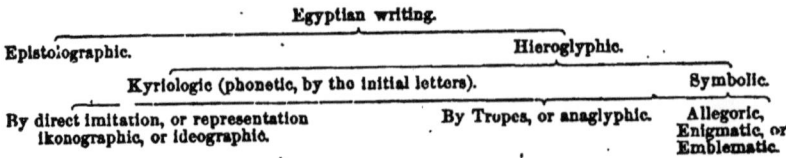

The *hieratic*, which was derived from the hieroglyphic, was invented at least as early as the 9th dynasty, and fell into disuse when the demotic had been introduced. It consisted of phonetic, and also of symbolic signs. It was written from right to left, and was the character used by the priests and sacred scribes, whence its name.

The *demotic* or *enchorial*, the epistolographic of Clemens, was a simplified form of the hieratic, and a nearer approach towards the alphabetic system; though we find in it syllabic and some ikonographic or ideographic signs, as the palm-branch and sun for "a year," with others (see the following woodcut, which reads " the year 6, the month Mesoré, the 20th day," or " the 6th year, the 20th day of the fourth month of the .waters, of King Ptolemy "); and the several characters still amounted, according to Brugsch, to 275, including ligatures, and numerals, or perhaps even exceeded that number.' Plutarch ·is therefore wrong in limiting the number of letters in the Egyptian alphabet to twenty-five (de Is. s. 56). One great peculiarity pointed out by Brugsch is that demotic was used for the vulgar dialect, and is therefore more correctly called *demotic* than *enchorial;* but it was also used in historical papyri. It was also invariably written, like the hieratic, from right to left.

The form of the hieroglyphic, the hieratic, and the demotic, differed more in some characters than in others, as may be seen in the woodcut; where the transition from the first (sometimes through the second) to the

Hierog.

Hierat.

Demot.

demotic may be perceived. It is not quite certain when the demotic first came into use, but it was at least as early as the reign of Psammetichus II., of the 26th dynasty; and it had therefore long been employed when Herodotus visited Egypt. Soon after its invention it was adopted for all ordinary purposes; it was taught as part of an Egyptian education; and after it, according to Clemens, they learnt the hieratic, and *lastly* the hieroglyphic. But this gradation, if ever observed, could only have been in later times; for in the early period, before the epistolographic, or demotic, was invented, the educated Egyptians must either have learnt the hieroglyphic, or the hieratic character, or have been left without any knowledge of reading and writing, which would have been tantamount to no education at all; whereas we know on the contrary that hieroglyphics were commonly understood by all educated persons. Many too learnt hieroglyphics to whom the hieratic was not taught; nor could the hieroglyphic have been at any time the *last* they learnt, since the invention of the hieratic was intended to enable the priests to possess a written character not generally known to the rest of the Egyptians.

In symbolic hieroglyphics, 1. The *ikonographic, representational,* or *imitative* hieroglyphics, are those that present the object itself, as the *sun's disc,* to signify the " *sun* " ● ; the *crescent* ☽ to signify the " *moon;*" a *male and female figure* apply to *man and woman* when separate, and signify *mankind* when together, as in this group 𓀀 𓀀, with or without the word " *rot* " (" *mankind* ").

2. The *tropical* hieroglyphics substitute one object for another, to which it bears an analogy, as *heaven and a star* ⵣ for " *night;*" a leg in a trap 𓃀 for " *deceit;*" *a pen and inkstand* (or writer's palette) 𓏞 for " *writing,*" " *to write,*" or a " *scribe;*" and a man *breaking his own head* with an axe, or a club, for the " *wicked,*"—suicide being considered the most wicked action of a man. Again, the sun is put for a " *day;*" and the *moon* for a " *month;*" a youth with his finger to his mouth 𓀔 for a " *child;*" a man *armed with bow and quiver,* a " *soldier* " 𓀎 ; a man *pouring out a libation from a vase,* or merely the *vase* itself 𓀾, a " *priest;*" a man with his hands bound behind his back, " *a captive* " 𓀢 ; the *ground-plan of a house,* a " *temple*" or a " *house,*" 𓉐 ; as a *valve* signified a " *door;*" the *firmament,* or the *ceiling* of a room, studded with stars, " *the heaven* " 𓇯 ; and a man *raising his hand, and calling to another,* was the exclamation " *oh,*" and the vocative " *o* " (below, p. 264). An egg ● signified a " child," or " son;" a *face* " *before,*" or a " *chief;*" and a lion's fore-part " the *beginning,*" and the hind-quarter " *the end,*" as in this sentence 𓄿𓃭𓃭𓃭 " In the beginning of the year, (and) in the end of the year."

3. The *enigmatic* put an *emblematic* figure, or object, in lieu of the one intended to be represented, as a *hawk* for the " *sun* " 𓅃 ; a *seated figure*

with a *curved beard* for a "*god.*" It is sometimes difficult to distinguish between tropical and enigmatic hieroglyphics; as when the two

water-plants are put for the "*upper* and *lower country,*" being emblems of the two districts where they principally grew, Upper and Lower Egypt. But it will be evident that the tropical is the nearest of the three to the phonetic, in compass, and power of expression, from its being able more readily to express abstract ideas and facts.

These three kinds of what Clemens calls *symbolic* (or more properly *figure-hieroglyphics*, in contradistinction to kyriologic, phonetic, or *letter-hieroglyphics*), were either used *alone*, or in *company* with the phonetically-written word they represented. Thus, 1. the word *Re*, "sun," might be written in letters *only*, or be *also* followed by the ikonograph the *solar disc* (which if alone would still have the same meaning *Re*, "sun"); and as we might write the word "horse," and place after it a figure of that animal, they did the same after their word *htr*, or *hthor* "horse"

. So too the word "moon," *Aah*, or *Ioh*, was followed by

the crescent, and *rôt* "*mankind*" by the figure of a man

and woman. Again, a man in the action of *beating* was placed either alone, or after the verb to beat "*hei*," to have that meaning. In these cases the sign so following the phonetic word has been called a *determinative*, from its serving to determine the meaning of what preceded it. 2. In the same manner the *tropical* hieroglyphics might be alone, or in company with the word written phonetically; and the expression "to write," *skhai*, might be followed, or not, by its tropical hieroglyphic, the "pen and inkstand" as its determinative sign; as the *man killing himself* might be preceded by the word *sheft*, "wicked." 3. The *emblematic* figure—a *hawk* signifying the "sun"—might also be alone, or after the name "*Re*" written phonetically, as a determinative sign; and as a general rule the determinative followed, instead of preceding the names, in which it differed from the Chinese and Assyrian systems. Determinatives are therefore of three kinds,—ikonographic, tropical, and enigmatic.

This union of both phonetic and symbolic hieroglyphics is commonly adopted, and may be considered the remains of the original pictorial writing combined with the phonetic system.

Some hieroglyphics again are used as pure ikonographs, and phonetically also; as the plan of a house, which with a line added to it answers for the letter *e*, in *ei* "house," though alone it also represented a "house," or "abode."

Some which are tropical when alone are phonetic in combination, as the sign for "gold" *noub* also stands for the letter *n*.

Some too, which are emblematic, are phonetic in words, as the crocodile's tail, the symbol of "Egypt," when combined with an owl ' m," answers to " kh " of the word khemi " Egypt," as well as of khame or hame " black."   In these cases they are the initial letters of the words they represent; so the guitar (or nabl) signifies "good," whether standing alone ▌, or as the initial of the word nofr " good " ; and the tau, or crux ansata, signifies " life " (or " living "), whether it stands alone ☥ or as the initial of the word written phonetically in full ☥〰 onkh, or ankh.   But these are only used, each for its own particular word, and do not stand for n, or o in any other.   Moreover, they cannot be called ikonographic; otherwise the guitar would some times signify what it represents—a " guitar , " nor can they be called determinatives, not being used to follow and determine the sense of the word, but forming part of it when written phonetically.   Nor can they be classed among the simple phonetic characters, as they are only used in their own words of which they are the first letter, and not in any others where the same letter occurs.   Of the same kind is the " stand," or barred emblem of stability, which with a hand signifies t t " to establish," and which is not employed for t in other words.   These may be called limited initial signs.

They may also be distinguished as specific signs, while others employed for any words are generic.   They have been called " mixed signs " together with many others, some of which, however, are of a different kind, and ought to be placed in a distinct order; as the human head with the mat and two lines reading dpé, " head," or " upon; " for this is both ikonographic and phonetic.   It stands for a " head " as well as for the letter a, and differs therefore from the guitar and others of limited force.   This remark applies also to others, that have been ranked among " mixed signs."

Besides the employment of one or more single signs for a letter, there were some which stood for words of one syllable, in this manner : a sign which was followed by one particular vowel, or consonant, forming the word, was frequently placed alone (without its complement) for the whole monosyllable : thus the hoe " M " often stood for mer (or mar), without the mouth representing the r ; and the spiked stand " M " stood for the whole or monosyllabic word men, without the zigzag "n," that sometimes follows to complete it; and in mes " born " the first sign answering to " m" was put alone for the whole word without the complementary " s."

The Egyptians had also a singular mode of placing a sign, representing a medial vowel, after the consonant it preceded in the word; thus, for Aan they wrote ana; for Khons, Khnso; Canana for Canaan.   It must, however, be observed that the exact vowel is rarely certain, as we are obliged to supply those that are unexpressed ; and in Coptic they are so changeable as to give us little help. Sometimes, too, the consonant beginning a word was doubled, as *Ssa*, for *Sa*, or *Sau*. (Perhaps also in *Seiris* for *Osiris*.)

In hieroglyphics of the earliest periods there were fewer phonetic characters than in after ages, being nearer to the original picture-writing. The number of signs also varied at different times; but they may be reckoned at from 900 to 1000.

The period when hieroglyphics, the oldest Egyptian characters, were first used, is uncertain. They are found in the Great Pyramid of the time of the 4th dynasty, and had evidently been invented long before, having already assumed a cursive style. This shows them to be far older than any other known writing; and the written documents of the ancient languages of Asia, the Sanscrit and the Zend, are of a recent time compared with those of Egypt, even if the date of the Rig Veda in the 15th century B. C. be proved. Manetho shows that the invention of writing was known in the reign of Athôthis (the son and successor of Menes), the second king of Egypt, when he ascribes to him the writing of the anatomical books; and tradition assigns to it a still earlier origin. At all events hieroglyphics, and the use of the papyrus, with the usual reed pen, are shown to have been common when the pyramids were built; and their style in the sculptures proves that they were then a very old invention.

Various new characters were added at subsequent periods, and a still greater number were introduced under the Ptolemies and Cæsars, which are not found on the early monuments; some, again, of the older times fell into disuse.

All hieroglyphics, including the linear kind, or running hand above mentioned, were written from right to left, from left to right, or in vertical columns (like Chinese), according to the space it was to fill; and the mode of reading it was towards the faces of the animals, or figures.

Thus "Phrah, the mighty," and "his son who

loves him," read from left to right; but if they faced the other way they would read from right to left, as in the previous woodcut on page 69. This is a general rule, to which there are very few exceptions.

The mode of forming the characters of phonetic signs was by taking the first letter of the name of those objects selected to be the representatives of each sound, thus: the name of an eagle, *Akhôm*, began with the sound A, and that bird was taken as the sign for that letter; an owl was chosen to represent an M, because it was the initial of *Moulag*, the name of that bird; and others in like manner; which may possibly explain the expression of Clemens, τὰ πρῶτα στοιχεῖα, "the first letters," in opposition to symbolic signs. This use of the first letters of words necessarily led to the adoption of many signs for the same character, and the hieroglyphic alphabet was consequently very large. It is not, however, to be supposed that all the signs for one letter were employed indiscriminately : the Egyptians confined themselves to particular hiero-glyphics in writing certain words ; thus Amun was written though would stand equally well for the mere letters A, M, N.   Again, ônkh, "life," and many others, are always written with the same char-acters, so that the initial alone stands for the entire word ; and if or are both used for *mai*, or *meri*, "loved," and other let-ters have their synonyms, these variations are very limited, and are adopted with great discretion, though greater latitude is allowed in the names of foreign people.   Each sign has even been thought to have its own inherent vowel.

Besides the restricted use of synonymous signs, another very impor-tant index was adopted for separating words, and for pointing out their sense.   This was the determinative sign already mentioned, which was a figure of the object itself following the phonetic word.   A particular determinative of kind was also given to objects belonging to a collective genus, as the skin and tail of an animal, " *bas*," following a word, denoted some "beast," thus , *āna*, signified an "ape."

But the skin, " *bas*," also stood for the word " *skin*," and it was there-fore a specific as well as a generic determinative ; and it was also a de-terminative of the god "*Besa*."   They also occasionally accompanied a word by another determinative sign having the same sound ; as the *goose* after the name of Apis ; or the *stone*, " *st*," that followed the name of the god *Set* or *Seth ;* &c.

A group accompanied by a sign signifying " land," pointed out some *district* or *town* of Egypt ; as another indicative of a *hilly country* stood for "*foreign land ;* " and a *line* or *tooth* was the deter-minative of a " *region*."   Several expletives were also used for various purposes ; some as tacit signs being placed after substantives, adjectives, and verbs, as the papyrus roll, , and others denoting verbs of action, &c.

In the formation of this written language the Egyptians began with what is the oldest form of writing, representational signs.   The alpha-betic system was a later invention, which grew out of picture-writing ; for, as drawing is older than writing, so picture-writing is older than al-phabetic characters, and, as Bacon justly observes, "hieroglyphics pre-ceded letters."   But the Egyptians in their representational signs, did not confine themselves to the simple delineation of the object, merely in order to signify itself; this would not have given them a written *language;* they went farther, and represented ideas also, for two legs not only signified what they represented, but implied the notion of "walking," or "motion;" and the former meaning might be pointed out by a particular mark, which showed that the object was to be taken in a

positive sense: thus ⌃ signified "walking," but ⌃ was read

"legs," which, in older times, was made by two separate legs; and a *bull* signified "strong," but when followed by a half-circle and a line, it read simply "a bull."

The plural number was marked by the same object thrice repeated,

as ⌐ "god," ⋔ "gods," or by three lines following it, ⌐ ; but

the Egyptians had no dual. (Of their mode of writing numbers, see n. on ch. 36, B. ii.) A *circle* or *sieve*, with two short lines within or be-

low, signified "*twice*," ◎. The female sign was a small half-circle ⚫

after the word (whether singular or plural): thus an *egg* or a *goose,* signifying a "*son*," when followed by a half-circle, read "*daughter.*"

By certain combinations they portrayed an abstract idea, and a verb of action was indicated by the phonetic characters that formed it being

followed by an object representing the action: as ⊜ ‖ ⋇

"*rimi*," with an *eye* and *tears* flowing from it, signified "(*to*) *weep*," as well as "*weeping*," or "*lamentation;* " the word *mounkh,* followed by a

mallet ∿∿∿ implied "(*to*) *work*" or "*build*," or any "*work;* " *ouôn,*

followed by the valve of a door, was "(*to*) *open*," , though this

hare and zigzag line without the valve would be a tense of the verb " to be."

Sometimes the phonetic word was omitted, and the determinative sign alone portrayed the idea, as a *pair of eyes* signified "*to see* " (without the word *meio*); a *cerastes snake going into a hole* signified "*to enter,*" as its reversed position meant "*to come out;*" and many others of a similar kind. It sometimes happened (as in other languages) that the same name applied to two different objects, and then the same hieroglyphic stood for both, as ▬ *neb* for "lord," and *niben,* " all;" *iri* signified an "eye " and "to make;" and, as Dr. Young says, however much Warburton's indignation might be excited by this child's system, it is, after all, only one of the simple processes through which a written language may very naturally be supposed to advance towards a more perfect development. Emblems were also extensively employed: as the asp signified a goddess;

the crowns of upper and lower Egypt the dominion of those two districts; and several of the gods were known by the peculiar emblems chosen to represent them,—the ibis or the cynocephalus being put for the god Thoth; a square-eared fabulous animal for Seth or Typhon; the hawk for Re and ·Horus; the jackal for Anubis; and others.

But however ingeniously numerous signs were introduced to complete the sense, their mode of expressing abstract ideas was very imperfect; and another step was required beyond the use of homophonous words, emblems, and positive representations of objects. This was the invention of the phonetic system already noticed (p. 260), which was evidently allied to the adoption of words of the same sound, the initial being taken instead of the whole word. Thus, when the names of objects began with a similar sound, either of them stood for the same letter: as and for M; a hoe and a tank of water for M; siou, "a star;" a goose, sen, for s, &c. Here, as already shown, is the germ of alphabetic writing; and that a similar picture-writing was the origin of the Phœnician and the Hebrew, is proved by the latter having retained the names of the objects after their form could no longer be traced; aleph, beth, and gimel, signifying the "bull" ("chief," or "head"), the "house," and the "camel." The names of these are also traced in the alpha, beta, gamma of the Greeks, who borrowed their letters from the Phœnicians.

It is not possible in so short a space to give even a summary of the grammar of hieroglyphics; for this I must refer to Champollion's Grammaire Egyptienne; and I shall merely observe that, 1st, in combining the pronouns with a verb, a sitting figure of a man (or of a woman, or of a king) for "I" (or a small vertical line, or a reed-head, before the verb), a basket with a ring for "thou," a cerastes for "he," the bolt, or broken line, ("s") for "she," and others, followed the verb, in this manner:— "I say;" or "I give;" "thou sayest;" "he says;" "she says;" "the king says;" "we say;" "you say;" "they say;" and these same signs are also put for the various cases of the personal and possessive pronouns, wherever they are required.

2nd. The perfect tense is marked by *n* after the verb, and before the pronouns: thus " he makes " becomes " he made," or " he has made; " and the mode of expressing the passive is by adding *tou*: thus *mes*,* " born," becomes *mestou-f*, or *mesout-f*, " he was born " (natus est). We also find *mesntou-f*, (natus erat, or fuerat).

3rd. The future is formed by the auxiliary verb *ao* (or *au*), " to be," followed by the *mouth* *r* " for; " as " I am for to make," or " I will make." M. de Rougé also shows that the future is formed by prefixing *tu* to the root.

4th. The imperative mood is marked by the interjection " Oh," a figure holding forth one arm in the act of calling,

or by the word " *hoi* " , or by the

word *ma*.

5th. In the subjunctive the verb immediately follows a tense of the verb " to give," as (Osiris) " give thou that I may see "

; or the verb is preceded by *n*, " for," " that," as " that thou mayst see."

---

* *Mas* is " son " in Berber; and perhaps in Numidian, as in Masinissa.

6th. In the optative the verb is preceded by the word *mai.* 7th. The infinitive is formed by prefixing *er* to the root.

8th. The participle present is generally determined by a cerastes following it, or by a bolt, or broken line (" s "), for a female; and the same is expressed by *nt,* " who : " as " who saves," of " saving " (saviour); the plural by " *u* " or instead or " *sen.*" The participle past is formed by adding " *out* " or " *tou* " : as " established."

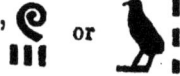

9th. The negative sign is a pair of extended arms with the palms of the hands downwards preceding the verb.

From this may also be seen how the phonetic letters were used; but even after their introduction the old representational picture-writing was not abandoned; the names of objects, though written phonetically, were often followed, as already shown, by the object itself; and though they had made the first step towards alphabetic writing, they never adopted that system which requires each letter to have only one sign to represent it; and it was not till Christianity introduced the Coptic, which was a compound of Egyptian and Greek, that *pure alphabetic* writing became practised in Egypt.

It has long been a question what people first invented alphabetic writing. Pliny says, " Ipsa gens Phœnicum in gloriâ magnâ literarum inventionis" (v. 12); and Quintus Curtius gives the honour to the Tyrians; and Diodorus to the Syrians; and Berosus, according to Polyhistor, makes Oannes teach it, with every kind of art and science, to the Babylonians (Eusebius, Chron. v. 8); all of which point to the same Phœnician origin. And if the Egyptians called themselves the inventors (Tacitus, Ann. xi. 14), and ascribed them to Menon (as Pliny says, fifteen years before Phoroneus, the oldest king of Greece, vii. 56), the claim of real *alphabetic* writing is certainly in favour of the Phœnicians, to whom also so many people are indebted for it, including the Greeks and Romans, and through them those of modern Europe. For while the Egyptians, in the hieroglyphic and hieratic, had (upwards of 2500 years before our era) the first *germ* of the alphabetic system, the Phœnicians, a highly practical people, first struck out the idea of a simple and *regular alphabet.* It was to the old Egyptian mixed plan what printing was to the previous restricted use of signets and occasional combinations of letters employed for stamping some documents; it was a new and perfect process; and if Phœnicia, under the fabled name of Cadmus (" the East "), imparted letters to Greece (Herod. v. 58), this

was long before Egypt adopted (about the 7th century B. C.) the more
perfect mode of using one character for a letter in the demotic writing.
It is singular, too, that the Greeks imitated the Phœnicians in writing
from right to left (a Semitic custom differing from the Sanscrit and
some others in Asia), and afterwards changed it to a contrary direction,
as in modern Europe; and it is possible that the Egyptians decided at
last to confine themselves to that mode of writing from right to left
from their constant intercourse with their Semitic neighbours.   The
transition from the Phœnician to the Greek may be readily perceived in
the old archaic writing. (See next page, and on Cadmus see note ¹ on
ch. 44.)

Pliny (vii. 56) says, " Cadmus brought sixteen letters from Phœnicia into Greece, to which Palamedes, in the time of the Trojan war,
added four more—Θ, Ξ, Φ, X; and Simonides afterwards introduced
four—Z, H, Ψ, Ω. Aristotle thinks there were of old eighteen—A, B,
Γ, Δ, E, Z, I, K, Λ, M, N, O, Π, P, Σ, T, Y, Φ, and that Θ, X were
added by Epicharmus rather than by Palamedes; but his Φ should rather be the Ọ or Q of ancient Greek. Anticlides states that " fifteen
years before Phoroneus, the first king of Greece, a certain Menon, in
Egypt, invented letters, ... but it appears that they were always
used.   The first who brought them into Latium were the Pelasgi."
Eusebius (Chron. i. 13) says, " Palamedes invented the first sixteen
letters—A, B, Γ, Δ, E, I, K, Λ, M, N, O, Π, P, Σ, T, Y, to which Cadmus of Miletus added three others—Θ, Φ, X; Simonides of Cos two—
H, Ω; and Epicharmus of Syracuse three more—Z, Ξ, Ψ, which completed
the twenty-four." But they all forget that the aspirate and digamma,
H and F, were among the original letters; and the double letters and
long vowels were indicated (as at Aboosimbel) long before the age of
Simonides.   The Etruscans had Z, Θ, Φ, X, and no Ξ, Ψ; and they
never added H, Ω. (See note * on ch. 30.)

It is still uncertain when the Greeks first used letters; but the absence of the written Æolic digamma in Homer is no proof that it ceased
to be employed when the Iliad was first written, since numerous inscriptions dating long after this introduce the digamma. The style
varied slightly in various parts of Greece and Asia Minor, at the same
time.   Even if letters were used so soon by the Assyrians, as Pliny
thinks (" literas semper arbitror Assyrias fuisse," vii. 56), they could
not have been the origin of those in Greece. Indeed he adds, " alii apud
Ægyptios, ... alii apud Syrios, repertas volunt;" and it was the
" Syrians " (i. e. Phœnicians) who had a *real alphabet.* * Nor is there
any evidence of the characters so much like Hebrew found in Assyria
having been used at a very remote period. Warburton (Div. Leg. vol.

* The writings of Moses date at latest in the end of the 15th century B. C., and
the Phœnician letters were probably much older; so that alphabetic characters
were used upwards of 1500 years B. C. The Arian writings are later than this; and
Sanscrit, from its letters facing to the left, while the words are written from left to
right, gives an evidence of its having borrowed letters from a Semitic source.
They are not turned, as in the later Greek, to suit the direction of the words.
In Zend the letters face to the left, as the words do; and some of them appear to
bear a resemblance to Phœnician characters.

HEBREW	PHŒNICIAN	ANÇIENT GREEK	LATER GREEK	ENGLISH.	HEBREW OF COINS.
א	✡ ✡	Λ ΛΛΛ	A A	A	✡✡
ה ב	𐤏	∧ 𐤉 C	B	B	𐤒
ג ד ר	∧∧	∧𐤉∧ C	Γ	G	ר
ר ר ד	∆ 𐤒	∆∆∇ρ	∆	D	∆
ה ה ה ת	Ⅎ	ⅎ𐤄ⅎⅇⅇ	E C	E	
ו ו ו ז	𐤍	ⅎ F		F	𐤍𐤍
ה ח ה	Ⅱ	Σ Ζ Ⅰ	Ζ	Ζ	
ה ה ג	Ⅱ	𐤇 𐤇	Η	Η	𐤇
ה ג ע ט	⊘	⊙⊗⊕◇□	Θ	Th	
י ר ו ו	∿	Ζ Ϛ ‡	Ι	Ι	∿
כ ך כ	𐤊𐤊	⅄ 𐤊 Κ	Κ	Κ	𐤊
ל ל ל	∫∟	∧∨⅃⅂	∧	L	∟∟
מ ם מ	⅏	𐤌𐤌𐤌𐤌	Μ	Μ	𐤌
נ ן נ	∫∫	𐤍𐤍𐤍𐤍	Ν	Ν	𐤍𐤍
ם ם כ	𐤎𐤎	‡ 𐤎	Ξ	Χ	
ע ע ע	Ο	⊙Ο◇□	Ο	Ο	Ο∇◇
פ ף ב ב	𝈿	𐤐 Γ	Π	Ρ	𐤐
ר ρ	∇	Ο		Q	Ρ
ר ρ	⅃𝈿𝈿	⅃𝈿𝈿ΡΡΡ	Ρ	R	𝈿ⅎ
ש ש	𐤔ⅎ ww	𐤌ⅎ𐤌𐤎Ϛ	Σ C	S	wω
ת ת	𐤕𐤕𐤕	𐤕· ✝	Τ	Τ	+Χ
ו צ	ץץ	OMITTED NOT BEING IN GREEK		𝈀	Ϡ𐤌

(See note ³ on ch. 30, and note ⁴ ch. 36, B. ii. ; and on ch. 59, B. v.)

ii. b. iv. s. 4) thinks " that Moses brought letters with the rest of his learning from Egypt ;" but the old Hebrew character was the Samaritan, which was closely allied to the Phœnician, and evidently borrowed from it ; and that too before the Egyptians had purely alphabetic-writing.

It would be *interesting* if the so-called Sinaïtic inscriptions were written by the Israelites, and were the earliest existing instance of alphabetic writing ; but we are not *on that account* justified in coming to such a conclusion ; and to show how unwarranted it is, I need only say that I have found them (beginning too with the same word so common in those at Mount Sinai) on the western, or Egyptian, side of the Red Sea, near the watering-place of Aboo-Durrag ; and they appear also at W. Umthummeràna (in the Wady Arraba), at Wady Dtháhal (in lat 28° 40'), and at the port of E'Gimsheh (near Gebel E'Zayt, opposite Ras Mohammed). They must therefore have been of a people who navigated the Red Sea, and who frequented the wells on the coast. This was long after the era of the Exodus ; and the presence of crosses, and of the Egyptian *Tau*, in some of those at Mount Sinai, argues that they were of a Christian age ; for the adoption of the *Tau* as a cross is shown, by its heading the numerous Christian inscriptions at the Great Oasis, to have been at one time very general in this part of the East.

Various materials were employed for writing upon, at different times, and in different countries. Among them were leaves, pith, and bark of trees, used at the present day (whence *liber* and *charta*), papyrus or byblus (whence *Bible*), cloth, bones, skins, leather, stones, pottery, metal, wax-tablets, and other substances.

The Greek name διφθέρα applied to skins used for writing upon, which were adopted by the Persians also (Diod. ii. 32), has been, as Major Rennell ingeniously supposes, the origin of the Persian and Arabic word " defter," applied to an " account," or " memorandum-book." Parchment was invented about 250 B. c. by Eumenes, king of Pergamus (whence its name), who, wishing to emulate the Alexandrian library, was unable to obtain papyrus paper through the jealousy of the Ptolemies. These Pergamena, the Roman membrana, were either skins of sheep, or of calves (vitulina, vellum). Pliny is wrong in supposing the papyrus was not used till the age of Alexander ; being common (together with the reed pen, palette, and other implements of later Egyptian scribes) in the time of the oldest Pharoahs, at least as early as the 3rd and 4th dynasty ; he is equally so in saying that when Homer wrote, Egypt was not all firm land ; that the papyrus was confined to the Sebennytic nome ; and that the land was afterwards raised ; making the usual mistake about Pharos (see note ' on ch. 5, Book ii.). Of old, he says, " men wrote on leaves of palms and other trees " (as now in Birmah, and other countries), " afterwards public records on lead, and private on linen and wax ;" but all this was long after the papyrus was used in Egypt. He also describes the process of making the papyrus (xiii. 11), and adds (xiii. 12), " the largest in old times was the Hieratic (for holy purposes) ; afterwards the best was called Augustan, the second Livian, the Hieratic being the third ; and the next was the Am-

phitheátric (from the place where made).   Fannius at Rome made an
improved kind, called Fannian, that not passing through his hands
being still styled Amphitheatric; and next was the Saïtic, a common
kind from inferior stalks.   The Teniotic, from the part nearest the rind,
sold for weight not for goodness; and the Emporetic of shops, for packing, not for writing upon.   The outside was only fit for ropes, and that
only if kept wet . . . . The breadth of the best is now 13 fingers (about
9⅔ inches) broad; the Hieratic two less, the Fannian 10, the Amphitheatric 9, the Saïtic less, and the Emporetic (used for business) not
above 6.   In paper, four things must be looked to, fineness, compact-
ness, whiteness, and smoothness.   Claudius Cæsar altered the Augustan,
being thin and not bearing the pen, the ink too appearing through it.
He added a second layer in thickness, and made the breadth a foot and
1½ foot, or a cubit. . . . It is made smooth or polished with a (boar's)
tooth, or a shell."   But some sheets of papyrus were much larger than
the best of Roman time; the Turin papyrus of kings was at least 14½
inches in breadth, which was of the early age of the Great Remeses;
and I have seen one of 17 and another of 18 inches, of the time of the
19th dynasty.   (See At. Eg. W., vol. iii. 61, and 146 to 151, 185; see
n. ' ch. 36, and n. ' ch. 92, Book ii.)—[G. W.]

CHAPTER VI.

"GYMNASTIC CONTESTS."—Chap. 91.

Gymnastic contests.   Game of ball.   Thimble-rig and other games.   *Mora* and draughts.
Pieces for draughts. . Dice.   Other games.

GYMNASTIC contests were not confined to the people of Chemmis, and contests of various kinds, as wrestling (No 1), single-stick, and feats of strength, were common throughout the country, at least as early as the 12th dynasty. Among their amusements was the game of ball (so much esteemed by the Greeks and Romans also), which they sometimes played by throwing up and catching several balls successively, and often mounted on the back of those who had missed the ball (the ὄνοι, "asses," as the riders were the βασιλεῖς, of the Greeks.) (No. II.) They had also the sky-ball (οὐρανία) which they sometimes caught while jumping off the ground (as in Homer, Od. Θ. 374). (No. III.) Other games were swinging each other round by the arms; two men sitting on the ground back to back striving who should rise first (No. V.); throwing knives into a block of wood, nearest to its centre, or to the edge; snatching a hoop from each other with hooked sticks (No. IV.); a man guessing a number, or which of two persons struck him on the back as he knelt, perhaps like the Greek κολλαβισμός (Jul. Poll. Onom. ix. 7); women tumbling and turning over "like a wheel," described in the Banquet of Xenophon (see At. Eg. W., vol. ii. p. 415 and to the end), for which necklaces and other rewards were given (Nos. VI., VIII.); thimble-rig (No. IX.); raising bags of sand (No. VII.) and other pastimes; among which were contests in boats; fighting with bulls; and bull-fights for prizes, which last are mentioned by Strabo at Memphis. (No. XI.) Still more common were the old game of *Mora;* comp. "micare digitis," the modern Italian *mora* (No. X. Fig. 1; No. XIII., Fig. 2); odd and even (No. X., Fig. 2); and draughts, miscalled chess, which is " *Hab*," a word now used by the Arabs for "men," or "counters." (Nos. XII., XIII.) This last was also a game in Greece; where they often threw for the move; whence Achilles and Ajax are represented on a Greek

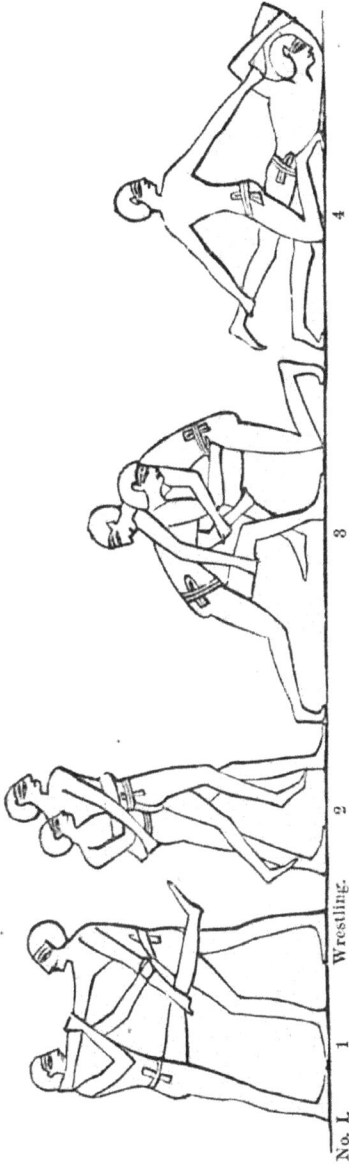

Wrestling.

No. I.　1　2　3　4

Games of Ball

No. II.　1　2　3　4　5　6

vase calling τρία, τέσσαρα, as they play. This was done by the Romans also in their *Duodecim Scripta*, and Terence says :—

> " . . . . si ludis tesseris,
> Si illud, quod maxime opus est jactu, non cadit,
> Illud quod cecidit forte, id arte ut corrigas."
>
> *Adelph.* iv. 7, 22–24.

No. III.

No. IV.   Game with a hoop.

No. V.

Plato says it was invented by Thoth, the Egyptian Mercury (Phædr., vol. iii., p. 364 tr.: T.) as well as games of hazard. In Egypt

N:. VI.   Tumblers.

No. VII.   Raising Bags of Sand.

No VIII. 1.   2.   3. Feats of Tumbling.   4.   5

draughts was a favourite among all ranks; in his palace at Medeenet
Haboo, Remeses III. amuses himself by playing it with the women of

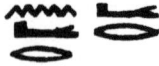

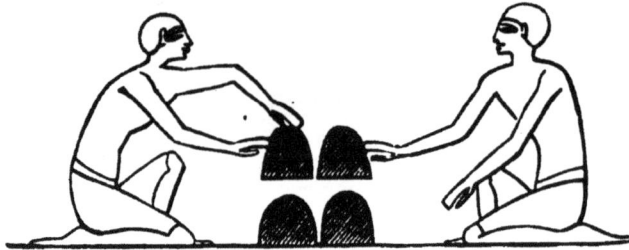

No. IX.   Thimble-rig.

No. X.   Fig. 1. Mora   and   Fig. 2. Odd and Even.

No. XI.   Bull-fight.

No. XII.   1.   Game of Draughts.   2.

his household; and its antiquity is shown by its being represented in the tombs of Beni Hassan, dating about 2000 years B.C. The pieces

No. XIII.   Fig. 1. Draughts   and   Fig. 2. Mora.

No. XIV.   Pieces for the Game of Draughts.

were nearly similar in form on the same board; one set black, the other white, of ivory, bone, or wood, and some have been found with human heads, differing for each side of the board. The largest pieces are 1¼ inch high, and 1⅛ diameter.

Dice are also met with, but of uncertain date, probably Roman.

There are two other games, of which the boards have been discovered in Egypt, with the men. The former are 11 inches long by 3¼; and one has 10 spaces in 3 rows, or 30 squares; the other 12 spaces in the upper part (or 4 spaces in 3 rows) with a long line of 8 spaces below, as an approach to it.

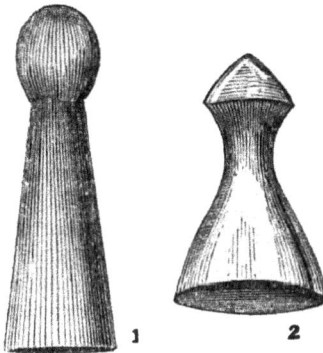

No. XV.   Pieces for Draughts.

No. XVI.   Board of an unknown Game.

resembling the arrangement of German tactics. The men, found in the drawer of the board itself, are in 2 sets, and of two different shapes

No. XVII.　　　　　　　　Another Board.

(one like our dice-boxes, the other conical, but both solid); and one set is 10, the other 9 in number; but the latter may be imperfect.

There were also other games, not easily understood; though doubtless very intelligible to the Egyptians who saw them so represented in the sculptures. (For the principal Egyptian games, see At. Eg. W., and P. A. At. Eg. W., vol. i. p. 189 to 211.)—[G. W.]

No. XVIII.　　　　　　　　An unknown Game.

No. XIX.　　1.　　　2.　　Unknown Games.　　　　3.

CHAPTER VII.

"GEOMETRY FIRST CAME TO BE KNOWN IN EGYPT, WHENCE IT PASSED INTO GREECE."—Chap. 109.

Greeks indebted to Egypt for early lessons in science. Invention of geometry. Surveying, geography. Early advancement of the Egyptians in science. Thales and others went to study in Egypt. Pythagoras borrowed much from Egypt. Heliocentric system. Revived by Copernicus. Pythagoras and Solon in Egypt. Great genius of the Greeks. Herodotus unprejudiced. The dial. The twelve hours. The division of the day by the Jews, Greeks, and Romans. The Egyptians had 10 hours of day and of night. The week of seven days in Egypt. The Aztec week of nine days. The seven-day division in Egypt. The number seven. Division by ten. Greek and Egyptian month and year of three parts.

THAT the Greeks should have been indebted to Egypt for their early lessons in science is not surprising, since it is known, in those days, to have taken the lead in all philosophical pursuits. Thales, the first Greek who arrived at any proficiency in geometry, went to study there; and his example was afterwards followed by others, who sought the best school of science and philosophy. Pliny's story of Thales (who was only born about 640 B. C.) teaching his instructors to measure the height of a pyramid by its shadow is sufficiently improbable; but that it should be repeated, and believed, at the present day is surprising; and some appear to think the Egyptians incapable of making canals until taught by the Greeks. Equally inconsistent is the story of Pythagoras' theory of musical sound; not only because he had visited countries where music had long been a profound study, but because the anvil (like a bell) gives the *same* sound when struck by different hammers, at least when struck on the same part.

If Plato ascribes the invention of geometry to Thoth; if Iamblichus says it was known in Egypt during the reign of the gods; and if Manetho attributes a knowledge of science and literature to the earliest kings; these merely argue that such pursuits were reputed to be of very remote date there; but the monuments prove the truth of the reports of ancient authors respecting the early knowledge of geometry, astronomy, and other sciences among the Egyptians. Mensuration and surveying were the first steps that led to geography; and the Egyptians were not satisfied with the bare enumeration of conquered provinces and towns; for, if we may believe Eustathius, "they recorded their march in *maps*, which were not only given to their own people, but to the Scythians also to their great astonishment."

The practical results of their knowledge had sufficiently proved the great advancement made by them ages before the Greeks were in a condition to study, or search after science. It was in Egypt that the

Israelites obtained that knowledge which enabled them to measure and "divide the land," and it was the known progress made by the Egyptians in the various branches of philosophical research that induced the Greeks to study in Egypt.   Those too who followed Thales only varied the theories he had propounded, and the subsequent visits of others, as Pythagoras, Eudoxus, and Plato, introduced fresh views, and advanced the study of Philosophy and positive science on the same grounds, but with greater knowledge, in proportion as they went deeper into the views of their teachers.   It was doubtless from Egypt that " Thales and his followers " derived the fact of " the moon receiving its light from the sun " (Plut. de Placit. Philos. ii. 28; Cic. de N. Deor. i., and Diog. Laert. 8), which Anacreon has introduced into a drinking Ode (19).

(Πίνει) ὁ δ' Ἥλιος θάλασσαν
Τὸν δ' Ἥλιον Σελήνη.

The same was the belief of Aristarchus at a later time (Vitruv. ix. 4), and Macrobius (on Cicero's Somn. Scip. i. p. 44) says "lunam, quæ luce propriâ caret, et de sole mutuatur."

No one will for a moment imagine that the wisest of the Greeks went to study in Egypt for any other reason than because it was there that the greatest discoveries were to be learnt; and that Pythagoras, or his followers (Plut. de P. Phil. iii. 11), suggested, from no previous experience, the theory (we now call Copernican) of the sun being the centre of our system (Aristot. de Cœlo, ii. 13); or the obliquity of the ecliptic (see note * on ch. 51), or the moon's borrowed light, or the proof of the milky way being a collection of stars (Plut. Pl. Phil, iii. 1) derived from the fact that the earth would otherwise intercept the light if derived from the sun, taught by Democritus and by Anaxagoras, according to Aristotle (Arist. Met. i. 8), the former of whom studied astronomy for five years in Egypt (Diodor i. 98), and mentions himself as a disciple of the priests of Egypt, and of the Magi, having also been in Persia and at Babylon (Clem. Str. i. p. 304).   The same may be said of the principle, by which the heavenly bodies were attracted to a centre, and impelled in their order (Arist. de Cœl. ii. 13), the theory of eclipses and the proofs of the earth being round (ii. 14).   These and many other notions were doubtless borrowed from Egypt, to which the Greeks chiefly resorted, or from the current opinions of the " Egyptians and Babylonians," the astronomers of those days; from whose early discoveries so much had been derived concerning the heavenly bodies (Arist. de Cœl. ii. 12).   Cicero, on the authority of Theophrastus, speaks of Hycetas of Syracuse, a Pythagorean, having the same idea respecting the earth revolving in a circle round its own axis (Acad. Quæst. ii. 39), which Diogenes Laertius says another Pythagorean, Philolaus, had propounded before him (Life of Philolaus); and Aristotle (de Cœlo, ii. 13) observes, that though the greater part of philosophers say the earth is the centre of the system, the Pythagoreans who live in Italy maintain that fire is the centre, and the earth being one of the planets rotates about the centre and makes day and night And if Plato mentions the same, as Cicero says " rather more obscurely," γῆν . . . εἰλουμένην δὲ περὶ τὸν διὰ παντὸς πόλον τεταμένον (in Tim. 80, p.

530), it is probably owing to his having heard of it while in Egypt, without giving the same attention to the subject as his predecessor Pythagoras. This heliocentric system was finally revived in Europe by Copernicus after having been for ages lost to the world; though Nicolas of Cus long before his time, and perhaps some others, were acquainted with it; and when Peru was conquered by the Spaniards it was found that the sun had there long been considered the centre of our system.

Iamblichus says Pythagoras derived his information upon different sciences from Egypt; he learned philosophy from the priests; and his theories of comets, numbers, and music, were doubtless from the same source; but the great repugnance evinced by the Egyptian priests to receive Pythagoras, will account for their withholding from him much that they knew, though his great patience and his readiness to comply with their regulations even to the rite of circumcision (Clem. Strom. i. p. 302), obtained for him more information than was imparted to any other Greek (Plut de Is. s. 10). Clemens says (Strom. i. p. 303) "Pythagoras was the disciple of Sonchês the Egyptian arch-prophet (Plutarch says of Onuphis, and Solon of Sonchis the Saïte); Plato of Sechnuphis of Heliopolis; and Eudoxus the Cnidian of Conuphis;" and he repeats the story of Plato (Tim. p. 466, tr. T.), of the Egyptian priest saying "Solon, Solon, you Greeks are always children" .... which shows what the general belief was among the Egyptians and Greeks, respecting the source of knowledge in early times. Strabo indeed (xvii. p. 554) affirms that "the Greeks did not even know the (length of the) year till Eudoxus and Plato went to Egypt" at the late period of 370 B.C. (See also Diodor. i. 28, and 81, and what is cited by Eusebius, Præp. Evang. x. p. 480, respecting the visits of several Greeks, Clem. Strom. i. 300, and Diog. Laert. Life of Thales, 15; and Cicero, Somn. Scip. who says "Plato Ægyptios omnium philosophiæ disciplinarum parentes secutus est.") The development given, in after times, by the Greek mind to what they learnt originally from Egypt, is what showed their genius, and conferred an obligation on mankind; and it is by keeping this in view, and by perceiving how the Greeks applied what they learnt, that we shall do them justice, not by erroneously attributing to them the discovery of what was already old when they were in their infancy. (See n. ⁷ ch. 35, n. * ch. 51, n. ' ch. 123.)

Herodotus, on this as on other occasions, is far above the prejudices of his countrymen; he claims no inventions borrowed from other people; and his reputation has not suffered from the injudicious accusation of Plutarch " of malevolence towards the Greeks."

" The γνώμων and the πόλος," says Herodotus, " were received by the Greeks from the Babylonians;" but they attributed the invention of the gnomon to Anaximander, and that of various dials to Eudoxus and others; some again ascribing them to Berosus (Vitruv. ix. 9). That the dial was of very early date is evident, since in the days of Hezekiah, between three and four hundred years before Eudoxus, and about one hundred years before Anaximander, it was known to the Jews, as is shown in Isaiah xxxviii. 8, and 2 Kings xx. 16, where the shadow is said to have been brought "ten degrees (mălŭth) backward, by which it had gone down on the dial (*mālûth*) of Ahaz." The Hebrew word, "step," "degree," מֲעֲלה mālh or māleh, is the same as the Arabic *dáraga*, "step" or "degree," and the Latin *gradus;* and is taken from *ālh*, "to go up." Mr. Bosanquet has explained the manner in which the sun during an annular eclipse caused the shadow to go back in what he supposes to have been really a flight of steps, and fixes the date of it in January 689. At all events the *use* of the dial was known in Judæa as early as seven centuries before our era, and it is not mentioned as a novelty. All that Anaximander could have done was to introduce it into Greece, and *adoption* should frequently be substituted for "*invention*" in the claims set up by the Greeks. Indeed they often claimed inventions centuries after they had been known to other people; and we are not surprised at the statement of Plato, that "when Solon inquired of the priests of Egypt about ancient matters, he perceived that neither he nor any one of the Greeks (as he himself declared) had any knowledge of very remote antiquity." (Plat. in Tim. p. 467.) And when Thales is shown by Laertius to have been the first who was acquainted with geometry, some notion may be had of the very modern date of science in Greece, since he was a contemporary of Crœsus (Herod. i. 75), and lived at a time when Egypt had already declined from its greatness, and more than seven centuries after astronomical calculations had been recorded on the monuments of Thebes. Clemens (Strom. i. p. 300) says Thales is thought by some to be a Phœnician, and quotes Leander and Herodotus; but the latter only says his ancestors were Phœnician (i. 170).

Vitruvius attributes the invention of the semicircular (concave) dial, or hemicyclium, to Berosus, the Chaldean historian, who was born in the reign of Alexander, which is reducing the date of it to a very recent period. This was a simple kind of πόλος (for, as before observed, the πόλος is the dial, and γνώμων merely a perpendicular rod which showed the time by the length of its shadow—see note * on ch. 109), and it was very generally used till a late period, judging from the many that have been found of Roman time. It consisted of a basin, λεκανίς, with a horizontal γνώμων in the centre of one end, and eleven converging lines in the concave part divided it into the twelve hours of the day; the older dials having been marked by degrees, probably like that of Ahaz. The Greeks marked the divisions by the first twelve letters of the alphabet, and the last four of these reading ZHΘI, "Enjoy yourself," are alluded to in this epigram, ascribed to Lucian (Epigr. 17):—

Ἐξ ὡραι μόχθοις ἱκανώταται, αἱ δὲ μετ' αὐτὰς
Γράμμασι δεικνύμεναι, ζῆθι λέγουσι βρότοις.

"Eudoxus," according to Vitruvius, "invented the Arachne (spider's web), or, as some say, Apollonius; and Aristarchus of Samos the scaphé or hemisphere, as well as the disk on a plane;" which (if he means a dial on a plane surface) was a still further improvement, and required greater knowledge for its construction. The most perfect hydraulic-clock was invented by Ctesibius, at Alexandria, in the time of Ptolemy Euergetes II.; but the more simple clepsydra was known long before, being mentioned by Aristophanes, and described by Aristotle (Probl. sec. 16, p. 933), and not being then a novelty. (See Athen.

Deipn. iv. p. 174, and xi. p. 497; Vitruv. ix. 9; Plin. vii. 87, and ii. 76, on the Horologium.)   Herodotus says the Greeks received the twelve hours from the Babylonians, and the Jews are supposed not to have adopted them till after the captivity.   The first mention of an hour is certainly in Daniel (iv. 19), where the name *sah* is the same as now used in Arabic; for though even there (as in iii. 6) the sense might require it to mean only "moment," the use of the word "time" immediately before, shows that *sah* was a division of time, which is still employed by the Arabs in the same sense of "hour" and "moment."

The Jews at first divided the day into four parts, and their night into three watches, and the mention of the dial of Ahaz proves that they had also recourse to a more minute division of time; but no hours are specified; and afterwards, when they adopted them, the numbering of their hours was irregular, as with the Arabs, being reckoned from sunrise to sunset.   The Greek word ὥρα was used long before hours were introduced into Greece.   Homer divides the day into three parts (Il. xxi. 111; see note * on ch. 173); and at Rome it consisted of two, sunrise and sunset, meridies or noon separating the two; and the twelve equal parts were adopted B. c. 291.   The natural division of the circle by its radius of 60° into six parts, and into six more by the half of those parts, or by the same radius starting from the second diameter, CD, which crosses the first, AB, at right angles, may have been the origin of this conventional division into twelve parts; as that into three parts may have been the division of the circle by the length of its diameter, of 120°.

The Egyptians had twelve hours of day and twelve of night at a very early period, but there is nothing to show whether this division was first used in Egypt or Chaldæa.   The Greeks, however, who frequented Egypt from the time of Thales, ought to have been acquainted with the twelve hours there, and their intercourse being far greater, both for study and for trade, with Egypt than with Babylon, we might suppose them more likely to receive them from the former than from that inland city; but an intercourse through Asia Minor may have brought them from the Babylonians.

It has been a question whether the Egyptians had a week of seven days.   Dio Cassius (writing in 222 A.D.) evidently shows that this was the case when he says:—τὰς ὥρας τῆς ἡμέρας καὶ νυκτὸς ἀπὸ πρώτης ἀρξάμενος ἀριθμεῖν, καὶ ἐκείνην μὲν τῷ Κρόνῳ διδούς, τὴν δὲ ἔπειτα τῷ Διΐ, καὶ τρίτην Ἄρει, τετάρτην Ἡλίῳ, πέμπτην Ἀφροδίτῃ, ἕκτην Ἑρμῇ, καὶ ἑβδόμην Σελήνῃ, κατὰ τὴν τάξιν τῶν κύκλων καθ᾿ ἣν οἱ Αἰγύπτιοι αὐτὴν νομίζουσι, καὶ τοῦτο καὶ αὖθις ποιήσας πάσας γὰρ οὕτως τὰς τέσσαρας καὶ εἴκοσιν ὥρας περιελθὼν, εὑρήσεις τὴν πρώτην τῆς ἐπιούσης ἡμέρας ὥραν ἐς τὸν Ἥλιον ἀφικομένην· καὶ τοῦτο καὶ ἐπ᾿ ἐκείνων τῶν τεσσάρων καὶ εἴκοσιν ὡρῶν κατὰ τὸν αὐτὸν τοῖς πρόσθεν λόγον πράξας, τῇ Σελήνῃ τὴν πρώτην τῆς τρίτης ἡμέρας ὥραν ἀναθήσεις, κ᾿ ἂν οὕτω καὶ διὰ τῶν λοιπῶν πορεύσῃ, τὸν προσήκοντα ἑαυτῇ θεὸν ἑκάστη ἡμέρα λήψεται.   (Hist. Rom. xxxvii. 19.)   This agrees with what Herodotus says (ch. 82) of days being consecrated to certain Deities, though the fact of the Egyptians having reckoned by ten days may argue against it.   It must, however, be observed that the division of the month into decads must date after the adoption of a solar year, and that weeks were the approximate result of the lunar division of time, which is the older of the two.   Weeks were certainly used at a very early period, as we find from Genesis and the account of the creation; and the importance of the number seven is sufficiently obvious from its frequent occurrence throughout the Bible.   It was common to all the Semitic nations and to those of India; but in China it was only used by the Buddhists, who introduced it there; and the Chinese as well as all the Mongolian races always had five-day divisions, and cycles of sixty years instead of centuries.   The Aztecs of Mexico had also weeks of five days, four of which made a month, and the year contained eighteen months of twenty days, with five days added at the end, which were unlucky; as one of them was in Egypt.   They had also their astronomical computation by months of thirteen days, 1461 of which made their cycle of fifty-two years, the same number as that of the vague years composing the Egyptian Sothic period.

That the seven-day division was known to the Egyptians seems to be proved by the seven-days fête of *Apis* (a fourth part of the number twenty-eight assigned to the years of *Osiris*' life) as well as by their seventy days' mourning for the dead, or ten weeks of seven days (Gen. l. 3); and the seven days that the head took annually to float to Byblus from Egypt (Lucian. de Deâ Syr.), the fourteen pieces into which the body of Osiris was divided, and his twenty-eight years, evidently point to the length of a week (4×7).   The time of mortification imposed on the priests lasted from seven to forty-two days (one to six weeks): οἱ μὲν δυοῖν καὶ τεσσαράκοντα, οἱ δὲ τούτων πλείους, οἱ δὲ ἐλάσσους, οὐδέποτε μέντοι τῶν ἐπτα λειπομένας (Porphyr. de Abstin. iv. 7); which shows the entire number to have been based on seven, and the same occurs again in the forty-two books of Hermes, as well as in the forty-two assessors of Amenti.   Indeed the frequent occurrence of seven shows that it was a favourite number with the Egyptians as with the Jews; and the Pythagoreans borrowed their preference for the hebdomal division from Egypt. There is no reason to conclude the Egyptians had not weeks of seven days because they divided their solar month into the very natural division of three parts of ten each; it would rather argue that the original lunar month was divided into seven-day weeks, and that the decad division was a later introduction, when the months were made to consist of thirty days.   And as the monuments are all of a time long after the thirty days were adopted, the more frequent mention of a decad instead of the hebdomal division is readily accounted for.   Moreover these months of thirty days still continued to be called "moons," as at the present day.   Dion Cassius also distinctly states that the seven days were first referred to the seven planets by the Egyptians.   (See note [1] on ch. 82, and note on ch. 8, B. iii.)

The Greeks, like the Egyptians, divided their month into three parts, and their year into three decads of months, corresponding to the three seasons of the Egyptians; and the Roman month consisted of calends, nones, and ides, the periods before each being of different lengths; but they afterwards adopted the division of weeks, giving the names of the sun, moon, and five planets to the seven days we now use. The Egyptians had both the decimal and duodecimal calculation, as the twelve hours of day and night, the twelve kings, twelve gods, twelve months: $12\times30=360$ days; and 360 cups at Osiris' tomb in Philæ; $12\times6=72$ conspirators against Osiris; and $12\times6=72$, which some fix as the number of days of the embalmed; and instances of both methods of notation are found on the oldest monuments of the 4th dynasty.—[G. W.]

CHAPTER VIII.

HISTORICAL NOTICE OF EGYPT.

Fabulous period of history—Rule of the gods—Name of Menes; supposed to be Mizraim—Believed to be a real person by the Egyptians, and to have founded Memphis.
This and Memphis—Egyptians from Asia—Memphis older than Thebes. Precedence
of Upper Egypt. Earliest notice of Thebes—Absence of early buildings. Contemporary kings—Arrangement of the early dynasties. Uncertainty of chronological
dates—Date of the Exodus. 1st, 2nd, and 3rd dynasties—Menes and his successors.
In the 2nd dynasty sacred animals worshipped; and women allowed to hold the
sceptre. 4th and 5th dynasties. The same customs in the early Pyramid period—
Mount Sinai—*Shafre* built the 2nd pyramid. 6th dynasty—The prenomen of kings.
7th, 8th, and 9th dynasties—The *Enentefs*. 11th dynasty—Contemporary kings.
12th dynasty—Osirtasen III. treated as a god. The labyrinth. The 13th dynasty
in Ethiopia. Shepherd dynasties—The Hyk-sos expelled. The 18th dynasty—The
horse from Asia. Thothmes I., II., and III., and Queen Amun-nou-het. Conquests
of Thothmes III.—His monuments. Amunoph III. and Queen Taia—The Stranger
kings—Conquests of Amunoph III. Country and features of the Stranger kings—
Related to Amunoph. Expelled from Egypt. King Horus. The 19th dynasty—
Remeses, Sethos, and Remeses the Great—Attack and defence of fortresses—Pithom
and Raamses—Canal to the Red Sea. 20th dynasty—Remeses III.—His conquests
and wealth—His sons. 21st and 22nd dynasties—Priest kings. *Sheshonk*, or Shishak—Conquers Judæa—Name of *Yudah Melchi* (kingdom of Judah). Kings' names
on the Apis stelæ. The 23rd dynasty—Assyrian names of the Sheshonk family.
The 24th dynasty—Bocchoris the Saite—Power of Assyria increasing. The 25th
dynasty of the Sabacos and Tirhaka. The 26th dynasty—Psammetichus succeeded
Tirhaka—Correction of chronology—He married an Ethiopian princess. War of
Psammetichus and desertion of his troops. Succeeded by Neco. Circumnavigation
of Africa—Defeat of Josiah. Power and fall of Apries—Probable invasion of Egypt
and substitution of Amasis for Apries by Nebuchadnezzar. Amasis—Flourishing
state of Egypt—Privileges granted to the Greeks—Treaty with Crœsus—Persian invasion. Defeat of the Egyptians—Conduct of Cambyses at first humane. Egypt
became a Persian province—27th or Persian dynasty—Revolt of the Egyptians.
28th and 29th dynasties of Egyptians. 30th dynasty of Egyptians—Nectanebo II.
defeated. Ochus recovered Egypt. Duration of the Egyptian kingdom.

THE early history of Egypt is enveloped in the same obscurity as that
of other ancient nations, and begins in like manner with its fabulous
period. The oldest dynasty therefore given by Manetho is said to have
been of the "gods and demigods," and the list of the kings in the Turin
papyrus commences also with the rule of the gods, the last of whom was
Horus the son of Isis and Osiris. And if in the seven last names that
remain of that very imperfect papyrus the order of the gods does not
exactly agree with Manetho, still there is sufficient to show that both
accounts were derived from the same source, universally acknowledged
by the Egyptian priests.

The rule of the gods has been supposed to be that of the priesthood

of those deities who governed the country before the election of a king,
like the Judges in Israel; but all accounts agree in considering Menes
the first king of Egypt. His name is mentioned in the sculptures of
the temple of Remeses II. at Thebes, and in the Turin papyrus, as well
as by Manetho and other authorities; and though the frequent occurrence of a similar name (as Manes the first king of Lydia, the Phrygian
Manis, the Minos of Crete, the Indian Menu, the Tibetan Mani, the
Siamese Manu, the German Mannus, the Welsh Menw, and others)
may seem to assign him a place among mythical beings; and though he
has been thought to be Mizraim, a personification of the " two Misrs,"
or provinces of Upper and Lower Egypt; yet he was believed to be a
real personage by the Egyptians themselves, and the events of his reign
were accepted as undoubted facts. He was represented as having
changed the course of the Nile, and founded Memphis on the site thus
artificially made for it, where he began the famous temple of Pthah
(Vulcan); and the change he made in the habits of the Egyptians was
recorded by a stella put up by Tnephachthus, the father of Bocchoris,
in the temple of Amun at Thebes; which pronounced a curse against
Menes for having induced the Egyptians to abandon their hitherto
simple mode of life.

Some might be disposed to doubt whether This, or any city in Upper
Egypt, was older than Memphis; and, as the Egyptians were a people
who immigrated from Asia into the valley of the Nile, might conclude
that they founded their first capital in Lower rather than in Upper Egypt.
The whole valley indeed was peopled from Asia; and to this day the
inhabitants bear the evident marks of an Asiatic and Caucasian origin.
Nor is it necessary to notice the long-exploded notion of civilisation
having descended, together with hieroglyphic writing, from Ethiopia—
a country always socially and intellectually inferior to Egypt, and
where hieroglyphics were only properly written when directly copied
from it.

The colour and features, as well as the conformation of their skull,
show that the immigration was one of those where a new race took
entire possession of the land, scarcely if at all amalgamating with the
aboriginal population; and in this the difference between the later invasion by the Arabs is evident; for the old Egyptian character is still
preserved, and the foreign Arab element has, after a lapse of many centuries, been mostly absorbed into that of the native race. There is
always this marked difference between immigration and conquest, that
in the latter the invaders are only a powerful minority, marrying the
native women, and leaving the whole working population in the land;
though at the same time it is evident that the foreign admixture has the
effect of changing the features, and even the colour, of the succeeding
generations, which are retained long after all the other elements are
absorbed; and this explains the resemblance of character in the ancient
and modern Egyptians, and the fact of the varied features of the latter
differing so much from those both of the ancient Egyptians and the
Arabs.

The monuments at Memphis are undoubtedly much older than those of Thebes; but the precedence always given to Upper Egypt seems to prove that some other capital there was older than Memphis; and though no monuments remain at This, still, from its being the reputed birth-place of Menes, and the chief city of the Thinite nome, as well as the royal residence of the first or Thinite dynasty, it claims the honour of having been the oldest capital of Egypt.

Both Abydus and Hermonthis, as well as other cities, were older than Thebes, which is not even mentioned on the altar of King Papi;[*] and the earliest evidences of the existence of Thebes are the tombs of the *Enentefs* of the 9th dynasty, and the vestiges of temples built by *Amun-m-he I.* and *Osirtasen.*   It is probable that Thebes succeeded to the smaller city of Hermonthis, as This gave place to Abydus; and the absence of early monuments of the 3rd and 4th dynasties in Upper Egypt may be explained by Memphis having been the royal residence of the then great ruling dynasties; while the monuments which preceded that age, from their insignificance, and the transfer of the capital of Upper Egypt to a new site, have not been preserved, or were destroyed at the period of the Shepherd invasion.   Nor can any argument be safely derived from the absence of monuments of a particular era; for at the pyramids there are no records of kings between the 5th and 26th dynasties, except the name of Remeses II. on the rock scarped to form the area half encircling the 2nd pyramid; and yet several hundred Pha-raohs ruled during that interval, many of whose names are found in Upper Egypt.   Again, no building remains of any early Memphite king, even about Memphis and the pyramids, except those monuments them-selves and the neighbouring tombs; and with the exception of these, and the Labyrinth, some fragments and small objects, some stelæ, and the obelisks of Osirtasen I. at Heliopolis and in the Fyôom, nothing is met with of old times before the 18th dynasty.   This may be reasonably ascribed to the invasion of the Shepherds, as the preservation of the early tombs may be explained by the feeling common at all times of respect for the dead.

The names of kings and the number of years given by Manetho are not all to be taken as of consecutive reigns; for not only do we know, from the authority of Manetho, that there were contemporary "kings of Thebaïs and of the other provinces of Egypt," but the monuments themselves decide this point by the mention of the years of one king's reign corresponding with those of another; and by the representation of one king meeting another, generally as his superior; as well as by vari-ous statements in papyri and other documents.   The manner in which the dynasties succeeded, and were reckoned, has been very ingeniously explained by Mr. Stuart Poole (suggested as he states by Mr. Lane); and by this scheme the difficulty of the great lapse of time required for so many consecutive Pharaohs, and the occurrence of synchronous reigns, have been reconciled.   According to it the first nineteen dynasties were thus arranged:—

---

* In the Turin Museum.

I. THINITES.	II.					
III. Memphites.	IV.	VI.	VII.	VIII.		
V. Elephantines.						
IX. Heracleopolites.		X.				
Diospolites.	XI.	XII.	XIII.	XVIII.	XIX.	
XIV. Xoïtes.						
XV, XVI. { Shepherds.						
XVII. Shepherds.						

With regard to the age of Menes and the chronology of the Egyptian kings, all is of course very uncertain. No era is given by the monuments; which merely record some events that happened under particular kings; and any calculation, based on the duration of their reigns given by Manetho, must be even more uncertain than that of genealogies. Any endeavour to make the chronology of Egypt conform to the date of the Exodus, or any other very early event mentioned in the Bible, would also lead to unsatisfactory results, since the Bible chronology is itself uncertain—the different versions of it assigning different dates to the same events. If therefore we wish to examine any portion of Egyptian chronology with a desire to ascertain the truth, we must look for facts rather than depend on what are merely *accepted* as established opinions; and be satisfied to wait for further information from such monumental records as may furnish us with astronomical data. Again, it is difficult to ascertain what periods accord exactly with those of other people; nor indeed, if we knew the very reign in which the Exodus took place, could we determine for certain its date; and even the time of Shishak who invaded Judæa cannot be fixed with precision. If therefore I abstain from assigning dates to all the reigns of the Pharaohs it is owing to the uncertainty of Egyptian chronology; though I am inclined to think that the arguments used by the Duke of Northumberland for placing the Exodus *after* the reign of Remeses II. have greater weight than my own in favour of the reign of Thothmes III.[*]

It would certainly be more agreeable to the writer, as well as to the reader, of Egyptian history, if the dates of the accession of each king and the events of his reign could be described as established facts, without the necessity of qualifying them by a doubt; but this cannot be done: and if it is necessary to break the thread of the history by conjectures, the uncertain nature of our authorities must plead an excuse. Indeed we may be well contented to have any approach towards the determination of events that happened in so remote an age.

[*First, Second, and Third Dynasties.*]—Menes having rendered his name illustrious by improving the country, and even (according to Eusebius) by conquests beyond the frontier of Egypt, was killed by a hippo-

---

[*] Mentioned in Chapter ii. of my At. Eg. vol. i. p. 77–81.

potamus, and was succeeded by his son Athôthis. The long reign of Menes, 62 years according to Africanus (or 30 according to Eusebius), and that of Kenkenes, 31 (or 39), seem to argue that even in the time of Menes, his son Athôthis ruled conjointly with him, during the last 30 years of his reign; and the sum of the two, 30 of Menes and 27 of Athôthis, accord exactly with the 57 given by Africanus to Athôthis: from which we may infer that Menes reigned 32 years alone, and 30 conjointly with his son, completing the 62 years of Africanus; and that Athôthis having ruled 27 after his father's death, his reign was calculated by Africanus at (30+27) 57 years. At the same time that Athôthis shared the Thinite throne with his father, Nekherophis (or Nekherôkhis) was probably appointed to rule the new city Memphis and the lower country, and having reigned 28 years (or two less than Athôthis with his father Menes), Athôthis then succeeded to both thrones; and the two additional years of his Memphite rule, added to the 27 of his Thinite, coincide with his computed reign of 29 at Memphis. For the 3rd dynasty ruled contemporaneously with the first, being an offset from it; and it is evident that its second king, Tosorthrus or Sesorthus, was the same as Athôthis:—the latter being " the builder of the palace at Memphis, and a physician who wrote the books on anatomy;" and Tosorthrus being " called Asclepius, from his medical knowledge, the first who built with hewn stone, and a great patron of literature." This will be more clearly understood by the following contemporaneous arrangement of the 1st and 3rd dynasties:—

1st Dynasty of Thinites.	Menes, 32 years alone, and 30 with Athôthis.	Athôthis, 27 more alone.	Kenkenes, (31 or) 39 years.		
3rd Dynasty of Memphites.	Nekherophis, 28 years contemporary with Menes.	(Athôthis) or Tosorthrus, 29 years at Memphis.	Tyreis, 7 years.	Mesokhris, 17 years.	Soyphis, 16 years.

1st Dynasty of Thinites—continued.	Venephes, 23 years.	Usaphædus, 20 years.	Miebidus, 26 years.	Semepses, 18 years.	Bienekhes, 26 years.
3rd Dynasty of Memphites—continued.	Tosertasis, 19 years.	Akhes, 42 years.		Sephuris, 30 years.	Kerpheres, 26 years.

The monuments afford us no information respecting the successors [*] of Menes in the 1st dynasty; but if the account in Manetho of the learning of Athôthis be true; if "the Libyans *revolted* in the reign of Nekherophis, and submitted again through fear on a sudden increase of the moon;" and if Menes changed the course of the Nile (as Herodotus states), their power, and the advancement already made by the Egyptians in science, must have been considerable at that period; and this is further confirmed by Manetho's account of Venephês, who lived little more than half a century after Menes, being the builder of the pyramids near Kokhômê.

According to Manetho, it was during the reign of the second king of the 2nd dynasty, Khæekhôs, or Cechôus, that "the bull Apis at Memphis, Mnevis at Heliopolis, and the Mendesian goat, were appointed to be gods;" and under his successor Binôthrus "it was decreed that women might hold the sceptre;"[†] which right led in after times to many troubles and changes of dynasties, from the claims of foreign princes, both in Asia and Ethiopia, to the throne of Egypt, through their marriage with daughters of the Pharaohs.

[*Fourth and Fifth Dynasties.*—B. c. 2450.]—The names of the kings of the 2nd Thinite dynasty are supposed by Mr. Stuart Poole to be given in the uppermost line of the Abydus tablet; and there is evidence of some of them having ruled contemporaneously with those of the 4th (Memphite) dynasty: the fourth king, *Useskef*, being found together with Soris or *Shuré*, and Menkheres of the 4th dynasty, and with *Osirkef* and *Shafre* of the 5th; while some of these, again, occur with *Shufu*, and others of the 4th and 5th dynasties. For the 5th, said to be of 9 Elephantine (or according to Eusebius of 31) kings, ruled at the same time as the 4th Memphites, and 2nd Thinites; though, from their being so frequently found mentioned with the Memphite kings, it may be questioned whether they were really from Elephantine, and the name of this island was perhaps erroneously substituted for that of some other place in Lower Egypt.

It is not till we come to the kings of the 4th dynasty that we find any important records of persons who lived under the Pharaohs; or sculptures illustrating the manners and customs of the Egyptians; and though some names of early kings occur in detached places, on scarabæi, and other objects, they do not afford any clue to their arrangement.

Shuré was the leader of the 4th dynasty; and his name, found by Mr. Perring on the blocks built into the northern pyramid of Abooseer, shows him to have been the founder of that monument. There are also other names of kings at Sakkára, of a very early date, some of whom,

---

[*] Dr. Lepsius places Senofro the third king after Menes; but he did not live till after Shufu, as the tomb where his name occurs was erected some time later than the Great Pyramid.

[†] This custom, and the influence of women, may have been derived from Africa, where they have so often held the sceptre; and in Upper Ethiopia, as in Western Africa, women still form the body guard of a king. The respect paid them, and their privileges, are shown by Pharaoh's conduct to Sarah, by the sculptures, and by Diodorus.

as the first *Tat-keré* and *Osir-n-re* (Sisires) appear to be of the 2nd and 5th dynasties; and one of them in the great pyramid of Sakkára is not unlike the Chnubus-Gneurus of Eratosthenes. Indeed it is reasonable to suppose, from their greater vicinity to Memphis, that some of the oldest pyramids would be in that spot.

This may be called the Memphite, or the Pyramid,* period. And not only does the construction of the pyramids, but the scenes depicted in the sculptured tombs of this epoch, show that the Egyptians had already the same habits and arts as in after times; and the hieroglyphics in the great pyramid, written in the cursive character on the stones before they were taken from the quarry, prove that writing had been long in use. The position too of each pyramid, corresponding as it does with the four cardinal points, and the evident object they had in view of ascertaining by the long line of one of its faces the return of a certain period of the year, prove the advancement made by the Egyptians in mathematical science; and all these evidences, being obtained from the oldest monuments that exist, introduce them to us as a people already possessing the same settled habits as in later times. We see no primitive mode of life; no barbarous customs; not even the habit, so slowly abandoned by all people, of wearing arms when not on military service; nor any archaic art. And if some clumsy figures have been found in the neighbourhood of Memphis, probably of the 3rd dynasty, their imperfections are rather attributable to the inferior skill of the workmen, than to the habitual style of the period; and rude figures were sometimes made long after the 4th dynasty.

Whatever may have been the style of construction in the pyramids of Venephes, certain it is that in the 4th dynasty, about two centuries after Menes, the blocks in the pyramids (of Geezeh), many of which were brought from the Cataracts of Syene, were put together with a precision unsurpassed by any masonry of ancient or modern times; and all these facts lead to the conclusion that the Egyptians had already made very great progress in the arts of civilization before the age of Menes, and perhaps before they immigrated into the Valley of the Nile. In the tombs of the Pyramid-period are represented the same fowling and fishing scenes; the rearing of cattle, and wild animals of the desert; the scribes using the same kind of reed, for writing on the papyrus an inventory of the estate which was to be presented to the owner; the same boats, though rigged with a double mast instead of the single one of later times; the same mode of preparing for the entertainment of guests; the same introduction of music and dancing; the same trades, as *glass-blowers*, cabinet makers, and others; as well as similar agricultural scenes, implements, and granaries. We also see the same costume of the priests; and the prophet, or *Sam*, with his leopards' skin dress; and the painted sculptures are both in relief and intaglio. And if some changes took place, they were only such as necessarily happen in all ages, and were far less marked than in other countries.

* Dr. Lepsius mentions 67 Pyramids, which necessarily represent a large number of kings; but it is unfortunate that the 67 Egyptian Pyramids cannot now be traced.

The greatest difference observable is in the form, and in some of the ornamental decorations, of the tombs; though these are not owing to any inferiority in taste, or masonic skill, but rather to a local style, which differed in certain peculiarities from that of Upper Egypt. They are sometimes attributable to the period to which they belong; for the peculiar doorways, and the round lintels, of the Memphite necropolis, are also met with in the Thebaïd, and at Raaineh, some tombs exhibit these and other features common to their contemporaries at the pyramids.

In the Pyramid-period one remarkable fact may also be noticed, that the Egyptian sculptors were not bound so rigidly to conventional forms in the human figure, as in after times; for not only do their statues then bear a closer resemblance to nature, but the delineation of the muscles, as in the arms and legs, was more decided; and the sitting figure of a scribe brought from Memphis (and now in the Louvre) shows how much more reality was given to the human form, than at a later (which was a more conventional) age. That figure, which has far greater truth and expression than any of (what is considered) the best period—the 18th and 19th dynasties—bears testimony to the skill of the early sculptors; and the style of the hieroglyphics, and the drawing of the cattle and other animals, in the tombs, are often fully equal to those in after times. Thus then no signs are found, on the earliest monuments, of a progress from infancy to the more advanced stages of art; as nothing in the customs they represent shows the social condition of the Egyptians to have been very different at that early period.

At the beginning of the 4th dynasty, the peninsula of Mount Sinai was already in the possession of the Egyptians, and its copper-mines were worked by them; and from the fact of King *Shuré* (Soris) being represented at Wády Maghára slaying an Asiatic enemy of the same race as those afterwards defeated by King *Senofro* (Senofr), we have evidence of early conquests; though they may not then have extended far beyond that peninsula. Of the Pharaohs of the 4th dynasty, the best known to us from the monuments and from ancient writers, are *Shuré* (Soris), Suphis (Cheops), and Suphis II. (or Sensuphis, a "brother of Suphis"), the *Shufu* and *Nou-Shufu* of the monuments, and Mencheres or (Mycerinus) *Men-ka-ré*. The two *Shufus* were the builders of the Great Pyramid; and that they reigned together is shown by the number of years ascribed to their reigns; by their names being both found among the quarry-marks on the blocks used in that monument; by their being on the sculptured walls of the same tomb behind the great pyramid; and by this pyramid having two funereal chambers, one for each king, rather than, as generally supposed, for the king and queen. The name of *Men-ka-ré* was found in the 3rd pyramid, as his coffin attests, which is now in the British Museum.

The ovals of the four first kings of the 5th dynasty, *Osirkef* (Usercheres), *Shafré* (Sephres), *Nofr-ir-Ke-re* (Nephercheres), and *Osir-n-ré* (Sisires), have been found with those of the 4th dynasty; and one of them, *Shafré*, called in the sculptures "of the little pyramid," appears to have been the founder of the second pyramid; but though he ought really to answer to the Cephrenes of Herodotus, the honour of founding the 2nd pyramid has been ascribed to the 2nd Suphis. His reign was long, and the names of more persons of rank, who lived under *Shafré*, are found in the vicinity of the pyramids, than of those who lived under the other Elephantine, Memphite, and Thinite kings.

The names of Pharaohs of the Pyramid-period are not found in the Thebaïd, and rarely in Central Egypt; and even where they do occur, it is not on any monuments erected by them, but only in tombs of individuals who lived in their reigns; as at Isbayda (nearly opposite Hermopolis), where *Shufu* and *Osirkef* are found together in the tomb of a man who was probably governor of the *nome* at that period.

[*Sixth Dynasty.*—b. c. 2240.]—Those of the next, or 6th, dynasty of Memphites, are more frequently met with in Central, and even in Upper, Egypt, as in the Cynopolite nome, and elsewhere; and in the tombs at Chenoboscion *Papi* (or *Mairé*) is found, together with *Meren-re* and *Nofr-ke-re;* and again with the last of these at Beni Mohammed-el-Kofóor. *Papi* also occurs at Mount Sinai and on the Kossayr road, and even at Silsilis, and with *Tati* on a rock at Eileithyias; though in the two last instances his name may have been merely inscribed by some visitor who lived at that period. *Papi* or *Mairé* has been conjectured by Chevalier Bunsen to be the Mœris of the Labyrinth; and it is not impossible that he may have been the *original* king of that name.

Other names, again, of kings of this dynasty are found at Sioôt and elsewhere, but merely on altars and small objects; and if those in the tombs, and on stelæ at Mount Sinai, the Kossayr road and Middle Egypt, show their rule to have been extensive, other monuments prove that the 11th dynasty reigned at the same time in the Thebaïd; and king *Sken-n-re* of this dynasty is stated on a papyrus (according to Brugsch) to have censured *Papi*, who ruled in Lower Egypt, for having favoured the Shepherd invaders. But there appear to have been two kings of this name; the *Papi*, however, answering to the Apappus of Eratosthenes, *Apap* * the " giant," the Phiops of Manetho's 6th dynasty, who reigned 100 years, is the one most usually mentioned on the monuments. Though no *buildings* remain south of Syene of any king before the 18th dynasty, except the ruined temples of Amun-m-he and Osirtasen at Thebes, the Labyrinth, and the pyramids and other sepulchral monuments (owing, as I have stated, to the invasion of the Shepherds); there are numerous tablets on the rocks, of that early age, which are of greater importance for history and chronology even than the temples, from their giving the dates of kings' reigns, and sometimes from their recording their victories over foreign nations; and through these we have obtained much information respecting the chronology, and the contemporaneousness of certain kings.

From these too we learn the change introduced by King *Papi*, of adding a royal prenomen to his phonetic nomen. For before his time, each Pharaoh had simply one oval (or cartouche) containing his name; and it was *Papi* who first added a royal prenomen, calling himself

---

* The Egyptian transposition of the vowel may require *Papi*, or *Popa*, to read *Apap*. Some think the other Papi to have been a Shepherd King.

Maïrê-Papi. This innovation was followed by all succeeding kings; and the prenomen was preferred for designating them, in preference to the name which often belonged to several kings. Thus the Thothmes, Amunophs, Remeses, and others, are more readily distinguished by their prenomens than by their name. Kings are also recognised by their banner, or square-title. The custom of adding the prenomen was likewise, as might be expected, adopted by the kings of the 9th and 11th dynasties, ruling as they did contemporaneously with those of the 6th; and on a coffin of one of the later *Enentefs* of the 11th dynasty, found at Thebes, this second oval was added subsequently to the inscription containing his phonetic nomen, as in the case of *Papi* at Chenoboscion. The last Pharaoh of the 6th dynasty was Queen Nitocris; whose name is given by Manetho, and by the Turin papyrus; and with her ended the rule of these Memphite kings. For at this period Lower Egypt was invaded by the Shepherds; who, about 700 years after Menes, entered the country from the north-east, and at length succeeded in depriving the Memphite princes of their throne.

[*Seventh, Eighth, Ninth, and Tenth Dynasties.*]—In the meantime " other kings " ruled in various parts of Egypt, who were contemporaries of the 6th, and of part of the 2nd and 5th dynasties; while the 7th and 8th, dispossessed by the Shepherds, merely had a nominal rule in Lower Egypt; and the 9th Heracleopolite dynasty held the Hermonthite districts at the same time that the 11th reigned at Thebes. [B. C. 2240.] Nor is it improbable that the name Heracleopolite has been substituted for Hermonthite; and the mistake may be accounted for by the names of all those kings (except the last) beginning with the characters that constitute the title of Hercules, or the god of Sebennytus; while the name of the last, *Mandotp,* or *Muntotp II.,* is the only one of them derived from Mandoo, or Munt, the god of Hermonthis. At all events it is at Hermonthis that the records of those kings, the *Enentefs* or *Nentefs,* are found; and their alliance with the kings of the 11th Theban dynasty is shown by some *Enentefs* having been buried at Thebes.

Of the 10th dynasty of Heracleopolites we know nothing, not even the names, either from Manetho or the monuments; but the ovals of several kings appear in the Turin papyrus, whose deeds not having been such as to merit a place in history are unnoticed on the temples and stelæ.

[*Eleventh Dynasty.*—B. C. 2240.]—That the kings of the 9th were contemporaries of the 11th, or the earliest Theban, dynasty is proved by the fact of the last king *Muntotp II.* being mentioned on a stela of the Kossayr road, together with the first *Amun-m-he,* whom (as Mr. Stuart Poole has shown) he established in the kingdom; and an *Enentef,* one of his predecessors, has been found by Mr. Harris in some sculptures near Silsilis with the third king of this 11th dynasty, *Muntotp I.*[*] in an inferior position to this Theban king. *Muntotp I.* reigned at least forty-five years, as a stela at Turin, erected during his life-time, contains the date of his forty-sixth year; and if not the leader of the 11th, or earliest,

* Whom I have called *Manmoph* in the Materia Hieroglyphica.

Theban dynasty, this *Muntotp I.* was evidently the great monarch whom the Diospolite Pharaohs placed at the head of their line; for the list of kings put up by Remeses II., in his temple at Thebes, has no other intervening between Menes and *Amés* the leader of the 18th, Theban, dynasty. *Amés*, again, traces from him, as in the tomb at Thebes recording the members of his family and of that of Amunoph I.; and Thothmes I. and III., Amunoph I. and III., and Horus, as well as *Sethi* and his son Remeses II., all Theban kings, mention him as if he were the founder of their line.

Several stelæ confirm the contemporaneousness of the kings of this period; and the Turin papyrus shows that *Amun-m-he I.*, the last king of the 11th dynasty, according to Manetho, was twice deposed by other kings. He was also contemporary with *Muntotp II.* of the 9th; and in the last part of his reign with *Osirtasen I.*, the leader of the 12th dynasty, whose 44th year coincided also with the 2nd year of *Amun-m-he II.*, as the 35th year of *Amun-m-he II.* corresponded with the 3rd of the second *Osirtasen*. Other synchronisms likewise occur, which it is not necessary to notice more fully; it is sufficient to show that Egypt at this period was not ruled by one sovereign, and that the mention in Manetho of Theban and " other kings " is confirmed by the monuments; and if I have already entered into certain details which may appear tedious, I plead as my excuse the importance of these synchronous reigns, and of everything relating to the succession of the early kings; which will probably receive further elucidation from the interesting papyrus in the possession of Dr. Abbott, containing as it does the names of a *Sken-n-re*, an *Enentef*, and other kings hitherto unknown to us from Manetho and the monuments.

[*Twelfth Dynasty.*—B. C. 2020.]—The *Osirtasens* and *Amun-m-hes* were powerful kings; and *Osirtasen I.* is shown by the remains of temples he founded to have ruled the whole of Egypt, from the Delta to the second cataract:—an obelisk of his still stands at Heliopolis; a fallen one is in the Fyoom; and his name appears in the oldest portion of the great temple of Karnak at Thebes, in a ruined temple opposite Eileithyias, and in another near Wady Halfeh. Sepulchral stelæ bearing his name have also been found in the Necropolis of Abydos, and historical ones in other places; and he even extended his conquests into Ethiopia. A stela of the 28th year of *Amun-m-he II.* was found at a watering-place in the desert near Kossayr, recording his conquests over the people of *Pount*, and another of *Osirtasen II.* at the same place which was probably connected with the trade of the Red Sea; and though the third *Osirtasen* has not left the same number of monuments as the first of that name, yet many of his stelæ are found at Mount Sinai, the Kossayr road, the first cataract, and other places; and it is a curious fact, that he is treated as a god by some of the kings of the 18th dynasty, as by Thothmes III. at Semneh, and by Thothmes IV. at Amada in Lower or Egyptian Ethiopia.

It is difficult to assign a reason for this unusual honour; but even though the first Osirtasen was the original Sesostris, there may have been some events connected with Ethiopia which led to the great respect paid to the memory of the third Osirtasen, and which even gave him a claim to the name of that renowned conqueror; and the peculiar sanctity he enjoyed accords with Manetho's account of Sesostris, that " he was considered by the Egyptians the first (or greatest) after Osiris." The title " good," introduced into one of the variations of his name, may also have reference to this excellence; and it is possible that his conquests in Ethiopia in his 8th year, and the establishment of the Egyptian frontier at Semneh, together with his successes over the Negroes, may have made him conspicuous as a conqueror as well as a benefactor of his country; and it is to this Sesostris that Herodotus appears really to allude, when he says he was the first king who *ruled* in Ethiopia.

The acts of the next king mentioned by Manetho accord still more correctly with what we learn from the monuments; and his Lachares, or Labaris, " who built the Labyrinth as a tomb for himself in the Arsinoïte nome," is evidently the *Amun-m-he III.* whose name has been found by Dr. Lepsius in that building. Some have thought the name Labaris to be the origin of Labyrinth; but it is more probable that the reading in Manetho, μεθ' ὃν Λάμαρις, should be μεθ' ὃν δὲ Μάρις; for he was the Mœris of the Labyrinth and doubtless of the lake also; and the observations of the annual inundations at Semneh, made by *Amun-m-he III.* confirm the belief that he was the king whose grand hydraulic works ennobled the name of Mœris.* These last also show that *Amun-m-he's* dominion extended from Ethiopia to the neighbourhood of Memphis. The governors of nomes in Central Egypt were also appointed at this period by the Pharaohs of the 12th dynasty, as we learn from the tombs of Beni Hassan and El-Bersheh; where the names of the two first Osirtasens are found. In a tomb near El-Bersheh is given the mode of drawing a colossus on a sledge, with gardening and other scenes; and the caves of Beni Hassan are well known for the numerous paintings that illustrate so fully the manners and customs of the Egyptians, and for the character of their early architecture, with its fluted columns,— the prototype of the Greek Doric.

The oldest date, on the monuments, of *Osirtasen I.*† (the Sesonchôsis of Manetho), is his 44th year; of *Amun-m-he II.* (Ammenemes) his 35th; of *Osirtasen II.*, his 3rd; of *Osirtasen III.*, his 14th; and of *Amun-m-he III.*, his 44th: showing that of Manetho's dates, which are 46, 38, 48, 8, and 8 years, the two last are far too little, and that no reliance can be placed upon them; but his order of these kings, Ammenemes, or *Amun-m-he I.* being the last of the 11th, and Sesonchôsis, or *Osirtasen I.* the first of the 12th dynasty, is confirmed by the monuments and the Turin papyrus.

[*Thirteenth Theban, and Fourteenth Xoïte, Dynasties.*—B. C. 1860.]—

---

* It was probably from the higher level of the Nile above Silsilis that the canal first led the water to the Lake Mœris (and to the general tank system of Egypt) in the time of this king; the river offering a greater fall of water before the rocks of Silsilis gave way. See n. ¹ ch. iv. and App. CH. iv. 4.

† The two signs beginning his name, and that of Osiris, may be a double s; and hence Ssiris, or Siris, would stand for s, in *Sethi.* Saïs, Siout, &c., have the double s.

The succeeding Theban dynasty, the 13th, appears to have been de
prived of its authority, even at Thebes; and the discovery of the ovals
of these kings in Ethiopia, many of whom had the Ethiopian name Sabaco, together with the evidence of the old monuments of Amun-m-he
I. and Osirtasen I. having been thrown down at Thebes, argue that
they took refuge in Ethiopia when the Shepherds advanced into Upper
Egypt, and seized its capital.   Manetho indeed relates that the Shepherd kings made long and constant attacks on the Egyptians; which
the Pharaohs of the 11th dynasty were still able to withstand; for one
of them, Amun-m-he III. (as I have just stated), retained all middle
Egypt, including the modern Fyoóm; and it was probably not till the
reign of his second successor, the Skemiophris of Manetho, the last of
the 11th dynasty, that the Thebaïd fell into their hands.   This, their
gradual conquest of the country, will account for different periods having been assigned to it, and to the duration of their rule.   And the
flight of the Egyptian kings into Ethiopia is evidently the origin of the
story told by Manetho, of a similar event; though his copyists, to suit
their own purposes, have attributed to a different cause, and to the later
period of " Amenophis," what really happened during the Shepherd invasion.   Of the 14th dynasty, of Xoïtes, no names are given either by
Manetho, or the monuments; though they appear to be mentioned in
the Turin papyrus.

[*Fifteenth, Sixteenth, and Seventeenth Dynasties—Shepherds.*—B. C.
2031.]—These invaders constituted the 15th, 16th, and 17th dynasties
of Manetho; and the statement that the 17th was composed of an equal
number of Shepherds and Theban kings is evidently erroneous.   Their
occupation of Egypt was probably owing, not to a mere love of conquest, but to the desire of maintaining a right they claimed to the
throne, through marriages with the family of the Pharaohs, or to an in-
vitation from some one of the inferior Egyptian princes who had been
dispossessed of his government; and either of these would account for
their having obtained possession of part of Lower Egypt " without a
battle," and for their having received assistance from some of the
Egyptians.   Nor was their rule like that of a people who had entered
the country for the sake of conquest; their religion was different, and
they treated that of the Egyptians with disrespect; but they were at one
time on terms of amity with some of the kings of other parts of Egypt;
and they so augmented the power of the country they governed, that on
their expulsion, Egypt, instead of having suffered under their rule, rose
immediately to that flourishing condition it enjoyed under the Pharaohs
of the 18th dynasty.   But though the power of Egypt was not diminished, the people naturally regretted their native princes; and even if all
the cruelties said to have been perpetrated by these foreigners were exaggerated, still their usurpation, and the contempt with which they
treated the religion of Egypt, made their rule odious and insupportable;
so that the name of Shepherd continued for ever to be " an abomination
unto the Egyptians."

It is not easy to determine what race of people they were; and they
have been variously pronounced to be Assyrians, Scythians, Cushites

(or Ethiopians) of Asia, Phœnicians, or Arabians.   Manetho calls them "Phœnicians," and shows them not to have been from Assyria, when he says they took precautions against "the increasing power of the Assyrians;" and the character of "Shepherds" accords far better with that of the people of Arabia.   Indeed the name *Hyk-sos* may be translated "Shepherd," or "Arab, kings;" *hyk* being the common title "king," or "ruler," given even to the Pharaohs on the monuments, and *shos*, signifying "shepherd," or answering to *Shaso*, "Arabs."   How any of the Arabians had sufficient power to invade, and obtain a footing in, Egypt, it is difficult to explain; but it is well known that a people from Arabia, called *Phœnicians*,* or the *red* race, who were originally settled on the Persian Gulf, invaded Syria, and took possession of the coast; and similar successes may have afterwards attended their invasion of Egypt, especially if aided by the alliance of some of its princes.   The statement too of Amos (ix. 7), that the Philistines of Syria came from Caphtor † (which was a name applied to Egypt), may relate to this subsequent passage of another body of Phœnicians into Syria, after their expulsion from Egypt.

Having held possession of Egypt 511 (or, according to the longest date, 625) years, the Shepherds were driven out by *Amés*, or Amosis, the first king of the 18th dynasty; and the whole of the country was then united under one king, who justly claimed the title of Lord of the "two regions," or "Upper and Lower Egypt."   From that time the events mentioned by Manetho, and his succession of kings, freed from the confusion of contemporary reigns, might have been clear and satisfactory, had it not been for the errors (often purposely) introduced by his copyists, who endeavoured to mix up the account of the sojourn of the Israelites, and their Exodus, with the history of the Shepherds; and the similarity of the names Amosis and Tethmosis (Aahmes,‡ or Amés, and Thothmes), added to the confusion.

[*Eighteenth Dynasty.*—B. c. 1520.]—With the 18th dynasty commences a more continuous monumental history of Egypt; but there is no authority from Manetho or the monuments for dividing the history of Egypt into the "old, middle, and new kingdoms:" nor was the whole of the country ruled by each king of the different dynasties in succession, during the period that elapsed from Menes to Amosis.

Egypt had long been preparing to free itself from the yoke of the Shepherds; and weakened by successive defeats, and opposed to the united forces of the Thebaïd and Ethiopia, under the energetic guidance of Amosis, these foreigners were unable to maintain their authority in the country; and an inscription of the 22nd year of Amosis, in the quarries of Másarah, saying that stones had been cut there by his order for the temple of Pthah at Memphis, as well as for that of Amun at

---

* If the Phœnicians are Hamites and Cushites, their coming from Arabia will accord with their being thought Arabians, and with the "second" invasion of Egypt by a Cushite race (infra, p. 305).

† Copthor, or Kebt Hor, was the old name of Coptos.   (See ch. 15, n. *, B. ii.)

‡ Aahmes, Iohmes, or Amés, from which were made the names of Amosis and Amasis.

Thebes, proves that Lower Egypt had already been recovered from them. In the tomb at Eileithyias, of a captain of the fleet of the same name as the king (Aahmes), that officer is said to have gone to Tanis during his reign ; so that the Shepherds must then have been expelled from the *whole* of the country; and Apion (according to Clemens) shows the Hyksos were driven from Avaris, their last stronghold, by *Amés*. This appears to be confirmed by the inscription at Eileithyias, and by Manetho's stating that Tethmosis (improperly put for Amosis) reigned 25 years after their departure.

During his reign mention is first made of the horse on the monuments; from which fact, and from its being often designated by the Semitic name *Sûs*, showing that it came from Asia, it has been supposed that it was first introduced by the Shepherd-kings. If so, they may have been in a great degree indebted for their successful invasion of Egypt to their horses and chariots; and if they conferred this boon on the Egyptians, they may be looked upon as their benefactors and the causes of their future power. Certain it is that neither at the tombs about the pyramids, nor at Beni Hassan, is there any indication of the horse,* though the animals of the country are so numerous in their paintings; and it is singular that in after times Egypt should be the country whence horses were imported into Syria by Solomon's traders; and at the time of the invasion by Sennacherib it was in Egypt that the Jews were said to put their trust "for chariots and for horsemen."

Amés apparently claimed his right to the Theban throne from *Muntotp* I. (as already stated),† as his successor Amunoph I. did from *Skenn-re*, a later king of the 11th dynasty; and Amunoph I. is frequently represented with a black queen, *Amés-nofri-aré*, who appears to have been the wife of *Amés*, and one of the holy women devoted to the service of the god of Thebes.‡ She even had the office held only by priests, of pouring out libations to Amun; and a tablet found by Mr. Harris represents Amunoph I. as the foster-child of this queen, at whose court Mr. Birch supposes that *Amés* took refuge, while preparing to expel the Shepherds. Indeed it is the marriage of *Amés* with her which is thought to have united the two families, of the 13th and 18th dynasties. There was also another queen of *Amés*, called *Aahôtp*, a white woman and an Egyptian, who is represented with the black *Amés-nofri-aré* on the same monuments, at Thebes, and in the British Museum, but in an inferior position; and this is readily explained by the greater importance of the Ethiopian princess.

B. C. 1498.—The perfect freedom of the country from all further attempts of the Shepherds enabled Amunoph I. to extend his dominions beyond the frontier, and succeeding kings of this dynasty added to his conquests both in Africa and Asia. It is also evident§ that in his reign

* See note ² on ch. 108, Book ii.   † Suprà, § 18.
‡ Queens seem to have taken this office after the death of their husbands. Amés-nofri-aré is styled "Goddess-wife of Amun."
§ From a sepulchral box from Thebes, now in the Museum at Turin, bearing his name.

the Egyptians had already adopted the five intercalary days to complete the year of 365 days;* as well as the 12 hours of day and night;† and arches of crude brick are found at Thebes bearing his name, which prove that they were in common use in tombs at that period; though all these three were doubtless of much earlier date than the era of Amunoph. He also added some new chambers to the great temple of Karnak; and his name frequently occurs at Thebes, especially in tombs belonging to individuals who lived in his reign.

The names of the kings of the 18th dynasty agree pretty well with those in Manetho; but not sufficiently to show that we can rely implicitly on him for those in other dynasties, where the monuments fail us as guides; for his second king, Chebron, is not found on the monuments, and there is some uncertainty about others even in this dynasty.

B. C. 1478.—Thothmes I., the successor of Amunoph, has left an inscription at Tombos, in Ethiopia, recording his conquests over the *Nahsi* (negroes) in his 2nd year; and the captain of the fleet already mentioned, who was in the service of the Pharaohs from Ames to Thothmes II., records his having captured 21 men, a horse, and a chariot, in the land of *Naharayn*, or Mesopotomia; so that the Egyptians must now have extended their arms far beyond their own frontier. And when we find that Thothmes I. ruled over the land of the nine bows, or Libya, we are not surprised that it should form part of his dominions, since Manetho shows that the Libyans were already under the rule of Egypt as early as the 3rd dynasty. At Thebes he made additions to the great temple of Karnak, where one of his obelisks is still standing; and other monuments at Thebes bear his name, as well as that of Thothmes II., who made some small additions to the temple at Karnak. But little notice is given of the warlike deeds of the second Thothmes, beyond his maintenance of the Egyptian rule in Ethiopia.

B. C. 1463.—His successor, Thothmes III., made himself far more conspicuous by the numerous buildings he erected in Thebes, and throughout Egypt, and by his foreign conquests. But in the early part of their reigns, both these princes (the second and third Thothmes) were associated on the throne with Queen *Amun-nou-het,* who appears to have enjoyed far greater consideration than either of them, probably owing to her having the office of regent. For not only are monuments raised in her own name, but she is represented dressed as a man, and alone presenting offerings to the gods. Such indeed was her importance, that she has been supposed to be a princess who conquered the country, perhaps even Semiramis,—who is said by Clemens (*Strom.* p. 397) to have governed Egypt; or, at least, to have had a more direct right to the throne than the Thothmes; and her title, " *Uben-t* in the foreign land,"‡ is singularly in accordance with the expression Uben-re, or Ubn-re, " the shining sun," discovered by Layard on a fragment at Nineveh, bearing that title of the sun in hieroglyphics. She was however an Egyptian princess; and prob-

---

* See Appendix to Book ii. CH. 11, on the use of the year of 365 days.
† On a mummy case at Leyden, having his name.
‡ On a scarabæus in my possession, found at Thebes. (For that of Nimroud, see the Transactions of the R. S. of Literature, 2nd series, vol. iii. p. 176.)

ably the Amensis of Manetho, who is represented to have been the sister of Amenophis, and to have reigned nearly 22 years.

Thothmes III. having attained the requisite age for mounting the throne, enjoyed a greater share of the royal power, and his name was admitted, together with that of Amun-nou-het, on some of her later monuments; still he only held an inferior position, and he never obtained the chief authority as king during her lifetime. On a statue of this period she is called "his sister;"[*] but she was probably only so by an earlier marriage of his father; and such was the hatred borne by Thothmes against her, that after her death he ordered her name to be erased from her monuments, and his own to be sculptured in its stead. But this was not always done with the care required to conceal the alterations; and sentences of this kind frequently occur: "King Thothmes, *she* has made this work for *her* father Amun." He succeeded, however, in having her name omitted from the list of Kings; and she is not mentioned even in those put up at a later time by Remeses II. at Thebes and Abydus. The most remarkable of her monuments were the great obelisks at Karnak, the largest erected at Thebes, one of which is still standing; and on the opposite side of the Nile she embellished the tomb, or rock-temple, of Thothmes I., beneath the cliffs of the Assaseéf, erecting before it a granite gateway, and making many other external additions to its courts; and numerous monuments were put up by her in other parts of Egypt. She ruled at least 15 or 16 years,[†] and alone apparently during some portion of that time; but there is a difficulty in determining the duration of these reigns, and the relationship of the two Thothmes. The Third ruled for a short time after her death; and though he commenced his reign after she had mounted the throne, he probably included the reign of Amun-nou-het in his own.

The reign of Thothmes III. is one of the most remarkable in the history of the Pharaohs. He extended his arms far into Asia, from which he received a large tribute, brought to Egypt by the chiefs of the nations he had triumphed over; and who, as was the custom of those days, often agreed to make this acknowledgment of their defeat without yielding up their country to the victorious enemy as a conquered province;[‡] and the successes obtained by Thothmes over the *Pount* § (a nation of Arabia), the *Kufa* (supposed to be the people of Cyprus), the *Rot-n-no*, and the Southern Ethiopians, are commemorated on the monuments of Thebes. The exact position of these countries cannot be easily determined, but they are evidently far from the confines of Egypt; and the elephant and bear, horses, rare woods, bitumen, and the rich gold and silver vases, brought by the *Rot-n-no;* the ebony, ivory, and precious metals, by those of *Pount;* the gold and silver vases

---

[*] Now in the British Museum, found at Thebes.

[†] Her 16th year is found on a tablet in W. Maghára, given by Laborde, and on the great obelisk at Karnak.

[‡] In some cases a *country* may have been called *conquered* (by the Egyptians, Assyrians, or others), when in fact a victory had only been gained over its *army;* perhaps even when that army was beyond its own frontier.

§ There appears to be a Pount of Southern, and another of Northern Arabia. See note ', ch. 102, and note ², ch. 108, Book ii.

of the *Kufa ;* and the cameleopards, apes, ostrich feathers, ebony, ivory, and gold in dust, ingots and rings, from Ethiopia, show the distance from which they were brought, as well as the richness of the tribute. The tight dresses, the long gloves, the red hair and blue eyes of the *Rot-n-no** also proclaim them to be of a colder climate than Syria ; though the jars of bitumen (or " *sift*," answering to the Arabic *sift*), appear to place them in the neighbourhood of the Euphrates or the Tigris.† The beauty of their silver, gold, and porcelain vases, at all events point them out as a people far advanced in luxury and taste.

Other victories are also recorded, in the great temple of Karnak, over the people of Asia ; and besides the *Rot-n-no*, the neighbouring *Nahrayn* (Mesopotamia), *Singar*, and other countries, are mentioned as having paid him tribute ; and he is represented to have " stopped at *Ninieu* (Nineveh), when he set up his stela in *Naharayn*, having enlarged the confines of Egypt."‡

Misled by the similarity of the names, *Aahmes* and *Thothmes* (and perhaps still more by Aah, "the moon," being a character of Thoth), Josephus makes Manetho say that Tethmosis, or " Thummosis, the son of Misphragmuthosis," drove out the Shepherds ; but in another quotation from the same historian, he shows that Tethmosis was no other than the first king of the 18th dynasty ; and we have already seen from the acts of Amés, and his immediate successors, that Egypt was already freed from those enemies long before the accession of Thothmes III. and his Asiatic conquests.§

The great additions he made to Karnak, and other temples in Thebes, and the remains of monuments bearing his name at Memphis, Heliopolis, Coptos, Ombos, and other cities in different parts of Egypt, show how much was done by Thothmes III. to beautify them, and to commemorate the glories of his reign ; and the style, as well as the high finish of his sculptures, were not much surpassed at any subsequent period. Indeed he seems to have taken a delight in architecture, like Adrian in later times ; and he has left more monuments than any Pharaoh except the second Remeses. And though in the reversed capitals and cornices of the columnar hall behind his granite sanctuary at Karnak,‖ he displayed a caprice consistent neither with elegance nor utility, the pure style of his other monuments shows that (like the Imperial architect), though occasionally whimsical, he was not deficient in good taste.

It was during his reign that the two obelisks were made, which at a later period were transported to Alexandria ; two others are mentioned at Thebes, dedicated to the Sun, which no longer remain ; that now standing at Constantinople was also made by him ; and the handsome one which is now at S. Giovanni Laterano, in Rome, bears his name in the central, and that of Thothmes IV. in the lateral, lines. Of his

---

* See the costumes of these and other people in woodcuts in note on ch. 61, Book vii.   † See below, p. 302.

‡ For an account of the conquests of Thothmes III. see Birch's annals of that king in the Archæologia, vol. xxxv. pp. 116–166.

§ Above, § 18.

‖ This sanctuary was rebuilt by Ptolemy, in the name of Philip Aridæus.

other monuments a very remarkable one is the chamber called "of the Kings" at Karnak, where he is represented making offerings to sixty of his predecessors; and not only do stone fragments, but the remains of crude brick enclosures, bear witness to the number of his buildings that once stood at Thebes. There are indeed more bricks bearing his name than that of any other king; and it is in the tomb, where the tribute before mentioned is recorded, that the curious process of brick-making is represented, which tallies so exactly with that described in Exodus.[*] His ovals also appear far more commonly on the smaller scarabæi than that of any other Pharaoh; and he is remarkable for the great variety in the mode of writing his name, of which I have more than thirty variations.

In Ethiopia his principal temples were those of Semneh and Amada; to the latter of which Thothmes IV. made some additions; and at both places their predecessor, Osirtasen III., of the 12th dynasty, received divine honours.[†] The two temples of Semneh were built at the beginning of his reign; and as offerings to the temple made in his 2nd year are there recorded, without the name of Amun-nou-het, Thothmes III. must have been reigning alone; which shows that his regnal years were reckoned from her death, and were not included in their joint reign; and this would be consistent with the fact of his having been very young when first associated with her on the throne. His first campaign, however, not occurring till his 22nd regnal year, would argue against it, at least on other occasions, and would require him to have reckoned also the years of his divided rule; and his conquests in Asia, mentioned in the great tablet at Karnak, date in his 29th, 30th, and 33rd years; though the first of them is styled his 5th expedition. His 6th, in his 30th year, was against the *Rot-n-no.* In his 33rd year he appears to have defeated the people of *Lemanon* also, who continued the same war; and this fact, and the name of *Ninieu* (Nineveh), occurring with that of *Naharayn*, and that of the *Takæ*, in the same neighbourhood, argue that "Lemanon" represents a country farther inland than Mount Lebanon.[‡] It is followed by the land of *Singar;* and though the mention afterwards of the *Asi*, supposed to be *Is*, bringing bitumen, appears to place these people lower down the Euphrates,[§] it is probable that most of them lived higher up to the North-west. Lemanon is also coupled with the Rot-n-no, on a monument of the first *Sethi.*[‖]

The length of the reign of Thothmes III. was far greater than is represented by Manetho, being about 47 years; and the date of his 43rd and 47th years are found on the monuments; but this difference may be attributed to his having shared the kingdom with Amun-nou-het and his brother; though the dates of Manetho are very uncertain from various causes, and from the inaccuracy of his copyists. Towards the

---

* See note [1] on ch. 136, Book ii.   † See above, § 14.

‡ See above, § 20, and below, § 25, note.

§ Herod. i. 179; Plin. xxxv. 51. Is (His, or Hit) is nearly halfway between Babylon and Carchemish.

‖ The chiefs of the Rot-n-no are said to serve the King of Egypt with their labour (bodies, or members) cutting down trees in Lemanon.

latter part of his reign he appears to have associated his son, Amunoph II., on the throne ;* but this king was not remarkable for his conquests, or the monuments he erected.   He made some additions to the great temple of Amun at Karnak ; and enlarged that of Amada in Nubia, [B.C. 1414], which was completed by his son and successor, Thothmes IV.; and here, on a stela dating in his 3rd year, Amunoph has recorded his victories over the Upper Rot-n-no, and the Ethiopians.   His name also occurs on a fallen block at the Isle of Saï, as well as that of the third Thothmes.

B. C. 1410.—Thothmes IV. has left few monuments worthy of note, except the great sphinx at the pyramids, which bears his name, and appears to have been cut out of the rock by his order ; and here again a similarity of name led Pliny to consider it the sepulchre of Amasis.

B.C. 1403.—After the two short reigns of Amunoph II. and Thothmes IV., Amunoph III. succeeded to the throne; but though he calls himself " the son of Thothmes IV., the son of Amunoph II.," there is reason to believe that he was not of pure Egyptian race, and his mother, queen *Maut-m-shoi*, was probably a foreigner.   His features differ very much from those of other Pharaohs ; and the respect paid to him by some of the " Stranger-kings," one of whom (Atin-re-Bakhan) treats him as a god in the temple founded by Amunoph at Soleb in Ethiopia, seems to confirm this, and to argue that he was partly of the same race as those kings who afterwards usurped the throne, and made their rule and name so odious to the Egyptians.   Their attachment to the memory of Amunoph is also shown by the great respect they paid to his widow, queen Taia, whose name some of their queens adopted ; and in one place a queen Taia is seated opposite Bakhan, and in another is admitted by him " to look at the flabellum of the sun."†   The worship too of the sun, with rays terminating in human hands, represented on a stela of Amunoph at Asouan, appears to indicate a connection between them;‡ for it was the very worship established by those Strangers.

It is probably to this usurpation that Manetho alludes when he speaks of the second invasion of Egypt, after the Shepherd time ; and the flight of Amunophis into Ethiopia is a mistake arising from the previous flight of a king of another name when the Shepherds advanced into the Thebaïd.   The sending of the leprous persons to the sulphur springs on the east bank of the Nile is also a misrepresentation of some real event; and that it was not a mere fable is proved by the recent discovery of those springs at Helwán.

Certain it is that the Stranger-kings did not obtain the throne till after the death of Amunoph III.; and that his power and conquests were very extensive is proved by the monuments, and by the records of victories, left by him throughout the valley of the Nile.   At Thebes he added considerably to the great temple of Karnak, and built the principal part of that of Luxor, which is remarkable for its size and beauty :

---

* A stela in the Leyden Museum.
† Lepsius, Denk. Abth. iii. Bl. 100, 101.
‡ There is, however, an instance of the Sun so represented in the time of Sethi, the father of Remeses II., on a stela on the Kossayr road.

he also erected a very elegant one on the opposite bank, rendered famous by the two large sitting Colossi of its *dromos*, or paved approach, one of which has long been known as the " vocal Memnon." It was perhaps to connect these his two temples, on the opposite sides of the river, that he made the " royal street " mentioned in the Theban papyri.   He also adorned the island of Elephantine with small but highly finished temples ; and besides that of Sedinga, he built the beautiful temple of Soleb in Ethiopia, on the columns of which he registered the names of the many nations he had vanquished in Africa and Asia ; thereby proclaiming that he not only extended his conquests still farther south, but that he had pushed the very confines of Egypt at least as far as Soleb. Among the Asiatic names are *Pount, Carchemish,* the fort of *Atesh* (or *Kadesh ?*), *Naharayn* (Mesopotamia), and many others.

From this being a complete record of his conquests, we may conclude that the temple of Soleb was erected towards the latter part of his reign ; but in one of the temples at Semneh he had previously put up a memorial of his victories over the Negroes (*Nahsi*), in which the *Abhet* and others are mentioned ; and Semneh being then the frontier fortress on that side, it was considered a suitable place for such a record.* The mode of noticing his successes is characteristic ; and we read of " living captives 150 head, children 110 head, negroes 350 head . . . . . negroes 55 head, children 265 head, total living 740 head . . . . 300 head . . . . living head 1052 . . . . "   Though he extended his arms much farther south than Soleb, and passed Napata, or Gebel Berkel, his lions which were found there were not placed by him in that city, but were originally at Soleb, as the inscription upon them shows, and were afterwards taken by Tirhaka to adorn his Ethiopian capital ; and on one of the large scarabæi, so often used by him as records, he makes " his southern frontier *Kiliee* (*Karu* or *Kalaa*),† and his northern *Naharayn* (Mesopotamia)."   In this same record‡ the name of his queen Taia is as usual introduced with his own ; and the marked respect he always paid her might have justified the notion of his having been indebted to her for his throne, had not the name of her father Ainia, and of her mother Tuia, been mentioned without any signs of royalty.   The custom of using these large scarabæi as records was much adopted by Amunoph III. ; and one of them states the number of lions he slew on a particular occasion, amounting to 102 ; and another describes a tank he made, 3700 cubits long and 700 cubits broad, for queen Taia.

Besides the remarkable fact that the features of Amunoph III. differed so much from those of the Egyptians, his tomb at Thebes is placed in a valley apart from those of the other Pharaohs, and in company with that of another of the " Stranger-kings " who has been variously called *Skhai, Eesa, Oaiee,* and *Ai,* whose wife appears also to have been a *Taia,* and who was probably the first of the seven who succeeded Amunoph III. on the throne.   For it was at his death that they ruled, mostly

---

* Brought thence by the Duke of Northumberland, as well as his lions from Gebel Berkel, and now in the British Museum.

† If this was Coloë, it was about 100 miles to the E. or E.N.E. of Axum.

‡ One in my possession, and another copied by Rosellini, mention her father.

with very short reigns; and the only ones of note were the second of
them, Amun-Toónh, and the sixth, Atin-re-Bakhan. The former has
introduced his name into the temple of Luxor, afterwards erased by
king Horus; his name and sculptures occur in a rock-tomb behind the
Red Convent near Itfoo; and he is represented in a tomb at Koorna
receiving the visit of a princess of Ethiopia, with a rich tribute from
that country. The other, who seems to have changed his name from
Amunoph IV. to Atin-re-Bakhan, shows, from the number of monuments of his time at Tel-el-Amarna, Apollinopolisparva, Thebes, and
Memphis, that his reign was long, and that he extended the arms of
Egypt into foreign lands. Tel-el-Amarna (supposed to be Psinaula)
was the capital or royal city of these princes ; but after their expulsion
its temples were utterly destroyed by the Egyptians, as was every record of them throughout the country ; and king Horus has used the
stones of their monuments, at Thebes, in the construction of the pyramidal towers he put up on the S. side of the great temple of Karnak.

The tyranny of these kings, and the change they made in the religion, rendered them odious to the Egyptians ; for they not only introduced real sun-worship, to the utter disregard of all the deities of
Egypt, but banished Amun, the great god of Thebes, from the Pantheon ; and committed those offences against the religion attributed by
Manetho to the Shepherds. But in order in some measure to reconcile
the priesthood to the change, they adopted one of the forms and names
of the sun already acknowledged by the Egyptians ; and Atin-re, the
solar disc, an ancient character of Re, was selected by them as their
god ; and this was partly from its representing the physical sun, which
they themselves worshipped, and partly perhaps from its name resembling that of their own deity. For that they were a foreign race, and
not, as Dr. Lepsius supposes, Egyptians who introduced a heresy into
the religion of their country, is sufficiently evident from their peculiar
features and strangely formed bodies; and it is not improbable that
they were Asiatic Cushites, or Ethiopians, who from intermarriage with
the Egyptian royal family claimed the throne they usurped ; and their
despotic rule is shown by the abject manner in which the soldiers and
others in their service were obliged to crouch before them. These
Cushites would accord with the Ethiopians said by Eusebius " to have
come from the river Indus and to have settled in Egypt " in the time
of Amunoph ; though we are not to suppose that they came from the
country said to belong to that race to the east of Persia, but rather from
the Ethiopia of southern Arabia, known in after times as Sheba; and if
this be true, it may account for the Thebans pointing out the statue
of Amunoph to the Greeks when they inquired after " the Ethiopian
Memnon." If Amunoph III. was related to that foreign race, he did
not become unpopular by making any of those religious changes which
rendered Bakhan* and others so hateful to the Egyptians; and Horus,

---

* Atin-re-Bakhan, or Akhen-Atin-re (" the votary of Atin-re"). The former
resembles the Apachnas of Manetho, though assigned to an earlier period; the latter
accords with Akencheres, placed at the end of the 18th dynasty.

who appears to have been a son of Amunoph, may have reconciled them
to his rule by reinstating the religion and expelling the "Strangers"
from the throne.   And the fact of the features of Horus being still unlike those of other Pharaohs will be explained by his having inherited
from his father some little of their foreign physiognomy.   Manetho's
account of their invasion, already alluded to, is evidently the same as
that mentioned by Diodorus, who states that "these foreigners being addicted to strange rites in their worship and sacrifices, the honours due
to the gods fell into disuse;" and that, "having been expelled, certain
select bodies of them passed over into Greece and other places, under
the guidance of their chiefs, the most remarkable of whom were Danaus
and Cadmus."   And the resemblance of the name Danaus to *Toonh*,
Manetho's mention of the expulsion of Armaïs or Danaus from Egypt at
this very period, and the story of Danaus introducing into Argos the
worship of Io (the name of "the moon" in the language of the Argives
and of the Egyptians), appear all to point to the same event.

   B. C. 1367–1337.—The duration of their rule is uncertain; but a
stone in their ruined city at Tel-el-Amarna, on which Thothmes IV.*
is mentioned by Atin-re-Bakhan, and the sculptures at Soleb, where
Amunoph III. is worshipped by him, prove that he ruled after both
those kings; as the destruction by Horus of the monuments of Bakhan
and the other usurpers shows they preceded that Pharaoh.

   They are not noticed in the lists of kings given by Manetho and the
monuments, all which make Horus the immediate successor of Amunoph III.; though it is possible that they may be represented by the
five kings placed, according to some versions of Manetho, between Horus
and the 19th dynasty; one of whom is the Armaïs or Danaus already
noticed.   Josephus, Africanus, and Eusebius give them as Achencherrês,
or Acherres; Rathôtis, or Rathôs; Akenchêrês, or Chebrês; Aken-
chêrrês, or Cherrês; and Armaïs, or Danaus.

   The 36th year of Amunoph III. is found in the sculptures, and he
was succeeded by his son Horus (or *Amun-men-Hor-m̀-hèb*), who on a
monument at Thebes mentions "the father of his fathers, Thothmes III."
It is at Silsilis, where he is represented nursed by a queen, that his
features bear so much resemblance to those of Amunoph;† and in the same
place mention is made of his victories over the *Cush*, or Ethiopians of
the Nile.   The selection of this spot for setting up his triumphal records
was probably connected with the opening of new quarries, as those ornamental tablets of Amunoph III. and Pthahmen at Silsilis were with
the hewing and transport of stones from that extensive bed of sandstone,
which supplied materials for so many temples in Upper and Lower
Egypt.   Horus made some additions to the great temple of Amun at
Thebes, and to other temples of Egypt; but his reign was short; and

---

   * If he was the first who married a princess of that race, this mention of him
will be explained, as well as the foreign features of his son Amunoph III., and of
his grandson Horus.
   † Traces of the customs of the Stranger-kings may here be observed in the
same abject demeanour of the soldiers before Horus, and perhaps in the many emblems of life and power depending like rays from the sun above the king.

if in the 36 to 38 years given to him by Manetho the whole period of the "Stranger-kings" is included, some idea may be formed of the duration of their rule, which was probably about 30 years. One other king, named *Resi-toti*, or *Resi-tôt*, [B. C. 1325,] is shown by a stela found by M. Mariette in the Apis tomb to have followed Horus. He is doubtless the Rathôtis or Rathôs of Manetho, according to Josephus and Africanus; but he is not noticed in the lists on the monuments. The 18th dynasty lasted about 180 years, taking the average of Manetho's lists, or more probably 210 years; from about the middle of the 16th to the middle of the 14th century B. C. It is probable that the Exodus took place in the reign of Pthahmen.

[*Nineteenth Dynasty.*—B. C. 1324.]—With Remeses I. began the 19th dynasty. His reign was of short duration, and the oldest date found on the monuments is his second year; but he is remarkable as the head of the house of Remeses, and the leader of this distinguished dynasty. He was of a different family from Horus and Amunoph III., and restored the original and pure line of the Diospolites, tracing his descent from Amunoph I. and queen Ames-nofri-aré.* He has left no records of his conquests, and few monuments, except his tomb at Thebes. This last however marks the new dynasty, by being in a different locality from that of Amunoph III., and by being the earliest one made in that valley, which was thenceforward set apart as the burial-place of the Theban kings. But the deficiency of his memorials was more than compensated for by those of his son *Sethi* I. (Sethos) and his grandson the great Remeses, [B. C. 1322,] whose long reigns were employed in extending the conquests of Egypt, and in recording them on the numerous and splendid monuments they erected in every part of the country. And their grand achievements far eclipsing those of the original Sesostris, the name and exploits of that conqueror became transferred to *Sethi* (Sethos) and his son, both of whom were confounded with him; and the resemblance of Sethos, or Sethosis, to Sesostris confirmed the error.

In the first year of his reign *Sethi* overran Syria; and in order to punish those people who had neglected to pay tribute to Egypt† during the rule of the successors of the 3rd Amunoph, he took Canaan and various strongholds in the country, and re-established friendly relations with those who had remained faithful in their allegiance to Egypt. He also extended his conquests far into Asia; and among the countries, over which he triumphed, and claimed dominion, are the Upper and Lower *Rot-n-no*, *Carmanda*, (?) *Naharayn* (Mesopotamia), and the *Khita*, supposed by Mr. Stuart Poole to be the Hittites, whose stronghold *Atesh‡* (*Ketesh*, or *Kadesh*), he believes to be Ashteroth-Karnaim. These

---

* In one place at Thebes, Remeses worships a triad composed of Amun, Ames-nofri-are, and their offspring Amunoph I.

† Among them are the people of a hilly country abounding in trees, which from its name, *Lemanon* or *Remanon*, has been supposed to be Lebanon; though, from its being mentioned with the Rot-ñ-no, it appears to be farther to the North-East, and connected with that people. See above, p. 300.

‡ In the land of *Amor*, *Amar*, or *Omar*, thought by some to be of the Amorites.

last people are also among the vanquished nations recorded in his sculptures at Karnak, as are the *Shaso*, or Arabs, *Pount, Naharayn, Singar*, and about forty others; among whom are the Cushites and other people of Africa. Later in his reign he waged war with the *Tahai*, a people whom Thothmes III. had already forced to pay tribute; and the sculptures at Karnak show he was then accompanied by his son Remeses, who after this was probably sent alone in command of an army against the Arabians and Libyans, as stated by Diodorus (i. 53).

Among the grandest monuments left by Sethi is the great hall of Karnak, on the exterior walls of which are many beautiful sculptures recording his victories, and his personal valour in killing with his own hand the enemy's chief, as well as his return to Egypt amidst the acclamations of the priests and people.

He also founded a temple on the opposite bank to his father Remeses I., which like the great hall of Karnak, and one of the largest buildings at Abydus, was completed by his son Remeses II., who appears to have shared the throne with him during the latter part of his reign. Many other grand monuments bear his name; and conspicuous among these is his tomb in the valley of the kings at Thebes,·which for the beauty of its sculptures and of its sarcophagus of oriental alabaster, as well as for the richness of its coloured details, far excels the rest of those spacious sepulchres; and if some others surpass it in extent, not even that of Remeses V., miscalled by the Greeks and Romans "of Memnon," and so highly admired by them, can be compared for beauty with the tomb of Sethi. His long reign and life appear to have ended suddenly; for after he had completed this monument, he ordered an extra chamber to be added to it, which was never finished; and the figures left in outline prove that time was wanting to complete it. He is said to have reigned 51 or 55 years, according to Manetho; but the monuments do not determine the number.

The reigns of Sethi and his son may be considered the Augustan age of Egypt, in which the arts attained to the highest degree of excellence of which they were there capable; but as in other countries their culminating point is sometimes marked by certain indications of their approaching decadence, so a little mannerism and elongated proportion began to be perceptible amidst the beauties of this period. Still the style and finish of the sculptures, the wonderful skill in engraving the granite obelisks, the hieroglyphics of which are sometimes cut to the depth of three inches, and the grace of the figures (conventional as they were) far surpass those of any other epoch; and the Remeseum, or palace-temple of Remeses II., "in the western suburb of Thebes" (called the Memnonium), is by far the best proportioned building in Egypt. It is here too that his colossal statue of red granite of Syene once stood, towering above the roof of the temple, amidst the ruins of which it now lies prostrate and broken; and this statue was remarkable as excelling all others in size and in the excellence of its sculpture. [B. C. 1311]. He was the Remeses to whom the title of "*Miamun*" was particularly applied; and though Remeses III. had the same title, it was in his prenomen, not a part of his name; and Remeses II. has therefore the best claim to the name of "Remeses-Miamun."

Distinguished as Remeses was during the lifetime of his father, he became still more remarkable after the death of Sethi, by his extensive conquests, as well as by the numerous monuments he raised throughout the country; and it is evidently by him, rather than by his father, that the great works attributed to the Great Sesostris were executed, for which Diodorus says he employed so many captives—a statement confirmed by a record on the rocks at Aboosimbel. It was to these his monuments, in particular, that the attention of Germanicus was directed by the priests during his visit to Thebes; and it was from them that his guides read to him the account of the tributes levied on foreign nations, which, in the words of Tacitus, were " haud minus magnifica quam quæ nunc vi Parthorum, aut potentia Romana jubentur."* But they were very properly shown to Germanicus as the memorials of Remeses, and not of Sesostris.

It is particularly in the great temples of Karnak and Luxor, and at the so-called Memnonium, that the victories he gained over the enemies of Egypt are recorded; the most noted of which were over the Khita, one of whose strongholds was protected by a double ditch, and by the river on which it stood. The wars waged against that people were long and obstinate; and the extent of their dominions reaching from Syria to the Euphrates, and the large force of chariots, and disciplined infantry they could bring into the field, rendered them formidable to the Egyptians in their advance into Asia. Nor have the sculptures failed to show the strength of the enemy in the attack made upon them by Remeses, or the skill with which they drew up their army to oppose him; and the tale of their defeat is graphically told by the death of their chief, drowned as he endeavoured to repass the river, and by the dispersion of their numerous chariots. This war took place in his 5th year,† as recorded at Thebes, and Aboosimbel; and he was probably satisfied in levying a tribute on that occasion, since another war broke out with the same people in his 9th year; and the treaty made with the Khita in his 21st year, recorded at Karnak, appears also to have been consequent upon another campaign.

It was during the wars with the people of Asia that Remeses inscribed the tablet on the rocks by the road-side above the Lycus, near Berytus in Syria,‡ which, like those of Sennacherib, and others of later periods, prove the usual coast road to have passed by that spot, from the age of the early Pharaohs to the time of the Romans and Arabs, as it does at the present day. The tablets of Remeses§ were dedicated,

* These records no longer exist, and the destruction of that part of the monuments that contained them will explain the reason why Thothmes III., with fewer conquests than Remeses II., has left more memorials of the tributes he levied on vanquished enemies.

† At this time he had already adopted the additional title, " approved of the Sun," in his prenomen. The idea of there being two kings called Remeses, who succeeded their father Sethi, has long been abandoned.

‡ M. de Saulcy is incredulous; but they are still there, and in his next journey he may perhaps be fortunate enough to discover them.

§ I apply stelæ to moveable records, tablets to those on rocks and walls of temples.

one to Amun the god of Thebes, another to Pthah of Memphis, the other to Re of Heliopolis; the two former the deities worshipped at the capitals of Upper and Lower Egypt, the last the god after whom he was named.

Not only do the monuments, but several papyri, record the wars he waged with the people of Asia; and it is in the Sallier papyri that mention is made of his war with the Khita in his 9th year. The enemies the Egyptians had to contend with were mostly the same in the time of Remeses II. as of Thothmes III.; and the names of the confederate people with the *Khita* are read by M. de Rougé as "*Aradus, Masou, Patasa, Kaschkasch, Oecon, Gargouatan, Chirabe, Aktan, Atesch,* and *Raka.*" Some of them were Syrian people; the *Chirabe* were probably the *Halebu*, about Haleb (or Aleppo), but not the Chalybes of Asia Minor; and *Atesch* was a strong fortress in the land of *Amar;* and the African *Berberi, Takrourir,*[*] and others he conquered, were among those previously defeated by the third Amunoph. In some of his northern wars Remeses was assisted by certain Asiatic tribes, who became allies of the Egyptians; as the *Shairetana,* a people described as living near the sea, a lake, or some large river, who continued to be in alliance with Egypt in the time of the third Remeses, when he extended the conquests of his predecessors; but our limited knowledge of the geography of those periods prevents our fixing the exact position of these and other countries, mentioned on the monuments.

Some insight is given into the mode of warfare of that age, as well as the means of attacking and defending fortified places.[†] The scaling-ladder and *testudo arietaria* had long been in use, even as early as the Osirtasens of the 12th dynasty. The latter consisted of a long pike (*terebra* or τρύπανον), and a covering of framework (*vinea*) supported on forked poles, which was sufficiently large to hold several men, and served to cover them as they mined the place, or made their preparations for an attack; and it answered both for the "*testudo ad fodiendum,*" and for that "*quæ ad congestionem fossarum paratur,*" mentioned by Vitruvius. While the miners were so engaged, the parapets were cleared by heavy showers of arrows; and the same was done when the pioneers (the *baltagis* of an eastern army) advanced to break in the gates of the place with their axes. In some of these fortified towns there was an outer, or double, or even a triple wall; the ditches being furnished with bridges, as at the fort of the Khita represented at the Memnonium; and the abutments of similar bridges are found in the ancient forts of Egypt. But these were evidently made of planks, represented in the sculptures by a flat surface, which were removed when the garrison had retired within the works before a besieging force.

It was during the repose he took between his different campaigns, and after their glorious termination, that Remeses erected the many buildings that bear his name throughout the Valley of the Nile. And the stela set up in his 35th year, in the great temple of Aboosimbel, was placed there long after its completion; and speaks no longer of

---

[*] Both are names used to this day.
[†] See note [*] on ch. 169, Book ii.

wars, but of the god, Pthah-Sokari, granting to him that the .whole world should obey him like the Khita; and alludes to his having beauti-.fied the Temple of Pthah at Memphis. Besides the temples and numerous statues he put up at Thebes and Memphis, the chief towns of each nome, and many of minor importance, were beautified with monuments erected by him, or in his honour; and if he was really the king for whom the treasure-cities Pithom and Raamses* were built by the Israelites,† the unusual splendour with which he adorned the small temple at Tanis, where numerous granite obelisks bear his name, will accord with the fact of its being one of his favourite residences in the time of Moses, when " marvellous things " were done "in the field of Zoan " (Tanis).‡ Even Ethiopia received its share of beautiful monuments; and the rock temples of Aboosimbel still excite the admiration of travellers, for the variety of their sculptures, and the grandeur of their colossi. At Napata (Gebel Berkel), the capital of Ethiopia, he also erected a temple, afterwards enlarged by Tirhaka; and notwithstanding the extent of his conquests in Asia he did not neglect to push his arms much further into Upper Ethiopia, and the Soudân, than any of his predecessors. Indeed it is with surprise that we see the evidence of the numerous monuments erected by Remeses II., even though those that remain must bear a very small proportion to the original number; more colossal and other statues remain of his time than of any other Pharaoh, and the two beautiful ones discovered at Memphis show that he adorned the temples of the northern capital with the same magnificence as those of Thebes. They prove too that the Sesostris said by Herodotus to have put up the colossi at Memphis was this Remeses.

He also undertook the grand project of opening a canal from the Nile to the Red Sea, which from the monuments on its banks was evidently finished by him; and re-opened, rather than first commenced, by Neco, or by Darius, or by Ptolemy Philadelphus. This canal began a little above Bubastis, near the town of Patumos (Pithom). It was connected with the trade of the Red Sea; and if Remeses fitted out a fleet to protect that trade, and if the same had before been done by the original Sesostris, the statement of Herodotus that Sesostris " fitted out long vessels " on that sea might apply to both these kings. Diodorus even pretends to state the number, which he reckons at 400 galleys.

Another extensive work, apparently attributable to this king, was the wall, said by Diodorus to have been built by Sesostris, on both sides of the valley, at the edge of the cultivated land, with a view to protect the peasants and their crops from the wandering Arabs; and the crude brick remains of this wall are still visible in many parts of the country, particularly where it ran over the rocky ground on the east bank. It is now called *Gisr el agóos*, " the old man's," or " old woman's dyke." By

---

* Pithom appears certainly to be taken from the name of Thmei, "Truth," the goddess who forms part of the prenomens of Remeses and his father; Raamses (Remeses) being his nomen.

† According to the Duke of Northumberland's view of the Exodus-period, mentioned above, p. 287.

‡ Psalm lxxviii. 12, 43; Isa. xix. 11, 13.

this the Arabs were prevented from coming to the valley, and obtaining corn, except at certain points where ingress and egress were permitted; and a small body of troops, or the peasants themselves, sufficed to pre- . vent any disregard of these regulations.

The partition of the lands, and the canalisation of the country, attributed to Sesostris, would apply to the earlier king rather than to Remeses II.; though land surveying and all that related to the canals and the river, were well-known in Egypt long before the age even of the Osirtasens, as is sufficiently proved by the sculptures of the pyramid-period, and, if the story is to be credited, by the change of the course of the Nile under Menes.

The length of his reign is consistent with the number of his monuments, and the extent of his conquests; and the mention of the 62nd year of Remeses in the sculptures agrees with the 61 full years ascribed to him by Manetho. According to Josephus he reigned 66 years. This accounts for his surviving so many of his twenty-three sons, and being succeeded by the 13th, *Pthahmen*.

B. C. 1245.—The reign of his successor was not remarkable for any great conquests; and if some additions were made by *Pthahmen* to the monuments of Thebes, Memphis, and other places, they were not on the same grand scale as those of his father, and of King Sethi. *Pthahmen-se-Pthah*, who succeeded Pthahmen, [B. C. 1237,] was probably indebted for the throne to his marriage with *Taosiri*, if she was really a daughter of Remeses II.; and so little was he regarded by the Egyptians, that his name is omitted from the Theban lists of kings, and even erased from his sepulchre in the valley of the Kings' tombs.

[*Twentieth Dynasty.*—B. C. 1232.]—The memory of the two following kings, Sethi II. and III., is scarcely rescued from oblivion by the chambers and the avenue of sphinxes added by the first of them to the great temple of Karnak; by their tombs; and by a few small monuments; and it remained for their successor Remeses III., [B. C. 1219,] to extend the arms of Egypt abroad, and to grace its cities with grand edifices, only surpassed by those of Sethi I. and the second Remeses.

Indeed, his temple at Medeenet Haboo is one of the most interesting monuments in Thebes, the battle-scenes most spirited, and the history of his campaigns most important; and if the style of the sculptures is not quite equal to those of Sethi I. and his son, their designs are full of spirit, and they are worthy of a king whose victories shed new lustre on the Egyptian name, and revived the days of conquest and glory. But the change he made in the mode of sculpturing the figures, and hieroglyphics, seems to have been the prelude to the decadence of art; and though gradual, its decline became evident after his reign; nor were the momentary impulse given to it by the Sheshonks, and what may be called the "revival" under the 26th dynasty, sufficient effectually to arrest its fall. The exquisite care bestowed on the sculptures at the latter period certainly did much to restore it for the time; and we admire the truth and correctness of the drawing, the sharpness and beauty of the chiselling, in the sculptures of the Psammetichi and Amasis; but it was the result of a great effort, and even if it had not been stopped by circumstances would have been insufficient to regenerate Egyptian art.

The reign of Remeses III. is a bright page in the history of Egypt. Penetrating far into Asia, he recovered the conquests that had been neglected by his immediate predecessors, and even extended them into new countries, the names of which are previously unnoticed on the monuments. But he does not appear to have attacked the Khita, though he maintained the same alliance with the *Shairetana* (or *Khairetana*), who had assisted Remeses II. in his Asiatic wars; and allied with them and two other people (one of whom was distinguished by a high cap, not unlike that of the modern Tartars) he defeated the *Rebo*, a powerful people; and afterwards inflicted severe chastisement on the *Tokari*, who, once his allies, had revolted from him. In this revolt they were joined by a portion of the maritime *Shairetana*, in whose ships they sought refuge from the conqueror, after he had chased them to the coast. But the Egyptians were as successful by water as on land; and the King, having brought round his fleet, sunk or captured their galleys and ravaged their coasts.

These *Shairetana*, or *Khairetana*, have been conjectured by Mr. Poole to be the Cheretim, or Cretans, which is not impossible; though the uncertainty of these names, and our ignorance of the geography of the countries overrun by the Egyptians, prevent our ascertaining the exact site of this and other wars recorded on the monuments; and it is prudent to abstain from any decided opinion, until further light is obtained from other documents.

The march of Remeses, on leaving Egypt for this campaign, was through several countries, some of which were at peace with him; and he is represented in one part traversing a jungle abounding in lions, before he reached the coast where his naval victory was gained. After this, he attacked several fortified towns, some surrounded by water and defended by double walls, which were speedily captured by escalade.

In one of his conflicts with the *Rebo*, the loss of the enemy is recorded by several heaps of hands, each amounting to 3,000, showing the number that had been slain in the field; and by two lines of captives, each containing 1,000 men; and these last, having been conducted into his presence when he returned home to Egypt, were presented by him, with the spoil and various trophies he had carried off, to the god of Thebes.

In the lists of countries, over which he claimed dominion, were *Naharayn* (Mesopotamia), *Rot-ǹ-no*, and other Asiatic districts; the names of many people of Africa he conquered are also mentioned in his temple at Medeenet Haboo;[*] and the wealth he amassed was preserved in the treasury there, which is probably the very one alluded to by Herodotus as belonging to Rhampsinitus. Here vases of gold and silver, bags of gold-dust, and objects made of various metals, lapis-lazuli, and other

---

[*] As the notion, long since discarded, that this name is Medeene-Thaboo, and related to *Thebes*, has been revived, it is only right to state that it is decidedly an error.

valuables were deposited; and the wealth he possessed is detailed on the sculptured walls of its several chambers.*

The longest date found on the monuments is of his 26th year; and with him closes the glorious era of Egyptian history. Eight more kings followed, bearing the name of Remeses, the four first of whom were his sons; but none of these equalled the renown of the second and third of that name. The third son of Remeses III. has been supposed to be the one in whose reign the risings of Sothis are given, which would show him to have lived in the year 1240 b. c. ;† and if this date could be positively assigned to the reign of the sixth Remeses, and another to that of Thothmes III., they would give us fixed periods of great importance for chronology. But that date for Remeses VI. presents a difficulty.

b. c. 1171.—The eighth Remeses‡ is remarkable for having main-tained the conquests of Egypt abroad. He made some additions to the Great Temple of Karnak, and has left us some historical papyri; and his marked features, conspicuous from the high bridge of his nose, have satisfactorily proved that the Egyptians represented real portraits in their sculptures. He was not a son of Remeses III., but appears to have derived his right to the throne from being a descendant of Amu-noph I. The tombs of these kings show that they did not neglect the arts; but little is to be learnt from the monuments respecting the deeds of the successors of the eighth Remeses, many of whom bore the same name; and the reigns of the last of them were probably disturbed by dissensions at home, which led to a change of dynasty.

[*Twenty-first and Twenty-second Dynasties.*—b. c. 1085.]—The sceptre appears to have passed, towards the close of the 21st dynasty, into the hands of military pontiffs; and the names of these "high priests" occur at a small lateral temple belonging to the great pile of Karnak; show-ing that their rule was not local, or confined to the Delta, but extended to Upper Egypt. They were *Amun-se-Pehor*,§ *Piönkh*, and his son *Pisham* (perhaps the Osochor, Psinaches, and Psusennes of Manetho), who had the titles and office of king, and were military chiefs also, being called "Commanders of the soldiers." They seem to have been, as Ma-netho leads us to suppose, Tanites; the high-priest of Amun, *Pisham*, being called "chief of Tanis (?) in the Delta," or "at *Hebai* (Iseum) in the Delta." Some probably ruled in right of their wives. They were succeeded by the Sheshonks, who were evidently foreigners, and, as Mr. Birch has conjectured, Assyrians;‖ whose claims to the throne may have been derived as usual from intermarriage with the royal family of Egypt, and have been put forward on the failure of the direct line. In-deed, *Sheshonk I.* seems to have married a daughter of *Pisham*; and he had the same title of "High-priest of Amun." Manetho calls the first

---

* The papyrus of Mr. Harris, so remarkable for its great size, mentions the of-ferings and buildings made by Remeses III.; but a small portion of it has as yet been opened.
† I had supposed this king to be the 9th Remeses.
‡ The 7th in my Materia Hieroglyphica.
§ I had supposed him to be Bocchoris.
‖ Tiglath-pileser I. is said to claim the conquest of Egypt, about 1120 b. c.

of the two Sheshonk dynasties Bubastites, the second, or 23d dynasty, Tanites; and the Tanite line seems to have been restored in *Pishai* of the 23d dynasty, whose name so nearly resembles the *Pisham* of the 21st. Bubastis, too, appears to have been the royal city of the kings of the 22d dynasty: and their names occur there as on other monuments, with the title " son of Pasht " (or " of Buto "), the goddess of that city.

It was at the period preceding the accession of *Sheshonk* (the Shishak of Scripture), that " Hadad, being yet a little child," having escaped from the slaughter of his countrymen, when David conquered the Edomites (1 Kings xi. 15, 17; 1 Chron. xviii. 11, 13; 2 Sam. viii. 14), " fled unto Pharaoh king of Egypt," who gave him the sister of Tahpenes [*] the queen in marriage. And as neither the queen of *Pehor*, nor of *Pisham*, had this name, we have evidence that the Pharaoh here alluded to was another king of the 21st dynasty, or some one who ruled at that time in Lower Egypt.

B. C. 000. The first Pharaoh of the 22d dynasty was *Sheshonk I.* (Shishak), the contemporary of Solomon; and it was in his reign that Jeroboam " fled into Egypt, unto Shishak king of Egypt, and was there till the death of Solomon " (1 Kings xi. 40). He was the same who in the fifth year of Rehoboam (B. C. 971) invaded Judæa, with a large Egyptian army, in which were also " the Lubims, the Sukkiims, and the Ethiopians," and a corps of 1200 chariots; and having taken the walled cities of Judah, entered Jerusalem, pillaged the temple, and " the king's house," and " carried away also the shields of gold which Solomon had made " (1 Chron. xii. 3–9). And the record of this campaign, which still remains on the outside of the great temple of Karnak, bears an additional interest from the name of " *Yuda Melchi* " (kingdom of Judah), first discovered by Champollion in the long list of captured districts and towns, put up by Sheshonk to commemorate his success.

This was the first time that Jerusalem was attacked by the Egyptians; who appear to have been friendly towards the Israelites, and to have had no motive for going out of their line of march by the sea-coast, while advancing against more distant and more powerful enemies. The Israelites, too, during the age of the great Egyptian conquerors, were not as yet fully settled " in the land; " and, having to contend with the people of Palestine, had no reason to come in contact with the Egyptians; they were, therefore, preserved from any interference of the Pharaohs; and in Solomon's time, when their power had become more extended, they were on terms of strict amity with the Egyptians, as well as with the Tyrians; and Solomon even married the daughter of a Pharaoh.

It is unfortunate that the name of this Pharaoh is not given; but it is evident that even if the priestly kings had not increased the power of Egypt, they had not allowed it to decline altogether; for knowing how acceptable the town of Gezer, belonging to the Canaanites, between Jaffa and Jerusalem, would be to his son-in-law, Pharaoh took it, and destroyed the Canaanites there, and gave it " for a present unto his daughter, Solomon's wife " (1 Kings ix. 16.)

[*] The same name as the town near Pelusium, called Daphnæ by Herodotus.

Whatever may have brought about the change of policy in Egypt, towards the Jews; whether the intrigues of Jeroboam, in order to insure his own safety by weakening the power of the King of Judah, against whom he had rebelled, or any complaint made by Rehoboam against the Egyptians for having favoured his designs; Sheshonk was satisfied with plundering the treasures " of the House of the Lord, and of the king's house :" and Jeroboam may have held these out as an inducement to the Egyptian king to undertake the expedition. "Jerusalem" itself does not appear to have been pillaged, owing to the submission of Rehoboam; but Judæa remained a conquered possession in " the hand of Shishak " (2 Chron. xii. 5, 7, 8); and was, as we have seen, catalogued in the list of the dominions of Egypt.

Though the conquests of Sheshonk were much less extensive than those of the Remeses, he has paraded them with far greater display in the long list of places, amounting to more than thirty times the number of those previously recorded by the great Egyptian conquerors. But they have not the same importance, from the mention of large districts, as the older lists; and none of those conquests, on which the older Pharaohs justly prided themselves, are here mentioned. We look in vain for Carchemish, Naharayn, or the Rot-û-no; but this campaign is most interesting, from its giving us the first and nearest approach to synchronous history; and we might fix within a few years the reign of Sheshonk, if we knew how long he lived after Solomon's death, or if the year of his reign, in which he invaded Judæa, had been recorded. He is said by Manetho to have ruled 21 years; and the date of his 21st year is found on the monuments.

The stelæ discovered by M. Mariette, in the Apis burial-place near Memphis, gives some very useful information respecting the succession of the kings of this dynasty; and even to the conquest of Egypt by Cambyses; but the deeds of the successors of Sheshonk I. seem to offer little of interest; and though their names occur at Thebes, Bubastis, and other places, nothing is found worthy of note respecting them.

The order of these kings of the 22nd, or Bubastite, dynasty, according to M. Mariette's Apis stelæ, is :—

Sheshonk I. (Shishak).

Osorkon I., his son, whose 11th year is on the monuments.

Her-sha-seb, his son, according to M. Mariette's list.

Osorkon II., his son-in-law, whose 23rd year is on an Apis stela.

Sheshonk II., his son.

Tiklat, Tiglath, or Takeloth I. (Tacelothis), whose 15th year is on the monuments. He married Keromama, granddaughter of Her-sha-seb.

Osorkon III., his son, whose 28th year is on an Apis stela, and another monument.

Sheshonk III., his son, whose 28th (and 29th?) year is on the monuments.

Tiklat, Tiglath, or Takeloth II., his son.

[*The Twenty-third Dynasty.*—B. c. 818.]—said to be of Tanites, consisting of a collateral branch of the Sheshonk family—seems, according to the Apis stelæ, to be :—

Pishai (or Pikhai).   (Psammis of Manetho ?)

Sheshonk IV., his son, who reigned at least 37 years, but who does not appear to have been succeeded by any of his sons.

Petubastes, whom Manetho places the first king of the 23rd dynasty, may have followed Sheshonk IV.; as his name has been found by M. Prisse, reading *Amun-mai-Pet-Basht* (or *Pet-Buto*), and another by Lepsius reading *Pet-se-Pasht.*   But Petubastes was not of the Sheshonk family.   The Assyrian character of the names in the families of these kings seems to confirm the opinion of Mr. Birch, that they were Assyrians : *Nimrot,* or *Nimrod,* occurs more than once ; and a prince *Takeloth* (*Tiklat* or *Tiglath*) is called chief of the *Mashoash,* a people of Asia mentioned among the enemies of Egypt in the time of the Remeses.[*]

No allusion is made on the monuments to Zerah the Cushite, or Ethiopian, who was defeated by the King of Judah (B. C. 941 ?) ; an event which should have happened about the reign of Osorkon II. (2 Chron. xiv. 9) ; and it is difficult to understand how an Ethiopian prince could have invaded Judæa, while all Egypt was in the hands of the Sheshonks ; unless, as some commentators suppose, Zerah was a King of Asiatic Ethiopia.

[*Twenty-fourth Dynasty.*—B. C. 734.]—Bocchoris the Wise, who was more famed as a legislator than a warrior, is said by Manetho to have been the sole king of the 24th dynasty.   He was the first who transferred the ruling house to Saïs, afterwards restored, and continued by the 28th dynasty until the Persian conquest.   He was the son of Tnephachthus ;[†] whose curse against Menes[‡] is consistent with the fact of his seeing the decline of Egyptian power, and with the common habit of attributing to some irrelevant cause (such as the accidental innovations of an early king) the gradual fall of a nation ; and is only worth noticing, as illustrating the declining condition of Egypt during the age of Tnephachthus and his son.

It was about this time that the foundation of Rome took place ; and great changes were beginning in Asia.   The powerful kingdom of Assyria was already preparing to supplant the rule of the Egyptians in Syria ; and a series of defeats and successes followed, until their final expulsion, under Neco, confined them to the defence of their own frontier. After a reign of six (or, according to some, of 44) years, Bocchoris is said by Diodorus to have been deposed, by Manetho to have been burnt to death, by Sabaco the Ethiopian ; though Herodotus states that the Ethiopian king came in the reign of Anysis (ii. 137), and put to death Neco the father of Psammetichus.

But besides this inconsistency, the tale of his cruelty is quite at

---

[*] Tiglath or Diglath is the old name of the Tigris according to Josephus ; the Diglit of Pliny, the Hidekel, or Digla, of Gen. ii. 14, Dan. x. 4, Eddekel of the LXX.

[†] The name of Neith may perhaps be traced in this.   [‡] Above, p. 285.

variance with what Herodotus and Diodorus (i. 60) both say of his character, and of Sabaco's retirement from the throne lest he should commit an act of injustice (Her. ii. 139), as well as with the respect paid by the kings of this Ethiopian dynasty to the customs of the Egyptians. The same character for humanity is ascribed to another Ethiopian, called by Diodorus Actisanes, whose name, however, is not mentioned either by Manetho, or the monuments; and another of them, Tirhaka, who succeeded the Sabacos, and raised the military power of the country almost to its ancient level, showed, by the numerous monuments he raised, his respect for the religion and the internal welfare of Egypt.

[*Twenty-fifth Dynasty.*—B. C. 714?]—Three or four kings, who came from Napata in Ethiopia, formed the 25th dynasty. The first was Sabaco I.; but it is uncertain which of the Sabacos, or *Shebeks*, of the monuments corresponded to the So, or Savá, of the Bible* (the Σηγωρ of the Septuagint), who made a treaty with Hosea, King of Israel: † an event which, involving the refusal of his tribute to the King of Assyria, led to the taking of Samaria and the captivity of the ten tribes.

B. C. 690.—Of the brilliant reign of . *Tehrak* their successor, the Tirhaka of the Scriptures, sufficient evidence is afforded by the monuments of Thebes and other places, as well as of his Ethiopian capital, where he enlarged and beautified the great temple beneath the " sacred mountain," now called Gebel Berkel; and the court he added to the temple of Medeenet Haboo in Thebes bears the memorials of his victories in Asia over the Assyrians. For it was during his reign that Sennacherib threatened to invade Lower Egypt, when Tirhaka advancing into Syria defeated the Assyrians; and if the Egyptians concealed this fact from Herodotus, it was doubtless from their unwillingness to acknowledge the long rule of the Ethiopians; and the priest-king Sethos he mentions may only have been the governor of Memphis and the Delta under Tirhaka. Indeed, if Sabaco was a contemporary of Neco, the father of Psammetichus, these Ethiopians may have ruled while Stephinathis, Necepsus, and Neco, placed by Manetho before Psammetichus I. in the 26th Saïte dynasty, were governors of part of Lower Egypt, and among the 12 monarchs, or chiefs of provinces, called 12 kings by Herodotus. Eusebius, however, quoting Manetho, places an Ethiopian called Ammeres ‡ before Stephinathis and his two successors.

It may be generally observed that whenever the Egyptians represented a blank, or the rule of ignoble kings, we are at liberty to conclude that a foreign dynasty was established in the country; and if any Egyptian prince exercised authority during the reign of Tirhaka, it must have been in a very secluded part of the marsh-lands of the Delta, as the monuments show his rule to have extended over all the principal

---

* The name of one of these Shebeks has been found by Mr. Layard at Kuyunjík (note ⁵ on ch. 137, Book ii. of Herodotus). The name of the second appears to be the Sebechon of Manetho.
† 2 Kings xvii. 4.
‡ Perhaps connected with *Piônkhi* and Queen *Amunatis*. (*See* following page.)

places in Egypt. Moreover, the Apis stelæ prove that Psammetichus I. was the sole and independent ruler of Egypt immediately after Tirhaka, without any intermediate king; * and an Apis, born in the 26th year of Tirhaka, died in the 21st year of Psammetichus, aged 21 years; the reign of Tirhaka having continued only ten months and four days after the death of that bull.

The discovery of these monuments by M. Mariette is most important for chronology. Like the stela of Florence they limit our dates; and they show that the hieroglyphic name of Psammetichus,† hitherto considered of the first, was really of the second of that name.

[*Twenty-sixth Dynasty.*—B. C. 664.]—The Florence stela reckons only 71 years 4 months 8 days from the 35th year of Amasis to the 3rd of Neco; if, therefore, the death of Amasis is fixed in 525 B. C., and if his reign only lasted 44 years, he must have ascended the throne 569 B. C.; but this, at the longest calculation, will only bring the accession of Psammetichus I. to 664 B. C., allowing him a reign of b4 years, as given by Herodotus and Manetho, and confirmed by one of the Apis stelæ. Another of these stelæ, in the 26th year of Tirhaka, which reckons 21 years to the 21st of Psammetichus I., shows that the beginning of Tirhaka's reign preceded the accession of Psammetichus by exactly 26 years, and therefore fell into the year 690 B. C.; and the 50 years given by Herodotus to Sabaco should probably be the whole duration of the rule of the Ethiopian, or 25th dynasty.

An important fact is also learnt from the monuments at Thebes, respecting Psammetichus I., that he married *Tapesntapes*, (?) the daughter of an Ethiopian king called *Piônkhi*, or *Peeônkh* (*c d*), and of Queen *Amunatis* (*e*), who ruled at Napata (Gebel Berkel); and this marriage resulted in the restoration of the Egyptian line of Saïte kings in the person of Psammetichus. This satisfactorily explains the retirement of the Ethiopian princes from the throne of Egypt.

One of the first measures of Psammetichus was to secure the frontiers of Egypt from foreign aggression; and his foresight was evinced by his acceptance of the services of the Greeks. But this excited the jealousy of the native troops; and the marked preference he showed the Greeks on all occasions inflamed their discontent, which was further increased by the length of the siege of Azotus; that strong place, defended by an Assyrian garrison, having only yielded to the arms of Psammetichus after a long siege; ‡ stated to have lasted to the im-

---

* This does not positively prove that no kings intervened between Tirhaka and Psammetichus I., as the latter may have included their short reigns in his own.
† Perhaps more properly Psamatik (*Psmtk*) or Psamatichus.
‡ Justifying its name, Ashdôd, or Shedéed, "the strong." (See n. ¹ ch. 157.)

probable period of 29 years. Already in an excited state of mind, they received the additional affront of being placed in the left wing, while the Greeks occupied the post of honour in the right;[*] they therefore broke out into open revolt; and quitting the camp, they united with the rest of the army in Egypt; which had become dissatisfied at a long detention, beyond the usual period of service, in the border fortresses of Marea, and Daphnæ of Pelusium; and marching up to Elephantine on the southern frontier, they were joined by that garrison also, and then withdrew into Ethiopia.[†] At first the king sent to recall them to their duty; but in vain; he therefore followed them himself as far as Elephantine, and despatched some of the Greeks to Lower Ethiopia, with his most faithful Egyptian adherents, to persuade them to return. Having overtaken them, they solemnly conjured them not to leave their country, their wives, and their families; but deaf to these entreaties, they continued their march into the Upper country; where they received the welcome they expected from the friendship subsisting between the Ethiopians and Egypt, which had been so recently ruled by their princes. Out of regard, however, for the family alliance of the Ethiopian king with Psammetichus, they were removed far from the Egyptian frontier, and settled beyond Meroë in certain lands allotted to them by the Ethiopian king; where their descendants long continued to live; retaining their distinguishing characteristics of "strangers;" as the Turks left in Ethiopia, by Soltan Selim, in later times have done, from 1517 A. D. to the present century. It was on this occasion that the inscription is supposed to have been written at Aboosimbel, mentioning the journey of Psammetichus to Elephantine.[‡]

This defection of the troops, though it did not precede the capture of Azotus, prevented Psammetichus from continuing his conquests in Syria, and recovering the influence there which the Assyrians had wrested from the Pharaohs; and obliged him, as Herodotus states (i. 164, 105), to purchase a peace from the Scythians, who having overrun all Asia, and penetrated into Syria, threatened to invade Egypt.

The services of the Ionian and Carian soldiers were rewarded by him with the gift of certain lands, called afterwards "the Camps," on the two opposite banks of the Pelusiac branch of the Nile, below Bubastis; where they remained, till Amasis, wishing to employ them, removed them to Memphis. Psammetichus also entrusted to their care several Egyptian children, to be taught Greek, from whom the interpreters, in the days of Herodotus, were descended; and this was the first time that the Egyptians relaxed their laws against foreigners, and became more favourably disposed towards them. The Greeks too then began to be better acquainted with the history, philosophy, and customs of the Egyptians; though it is surprising that they have given us little useful or reliable information, respecting a country they considered so interesting. With all their love of inquiry, and their enterprising qualities, they were not

---

[*] This appears to have been their *chief* grievance.
[†] Their reputed number of 240,000 men is evidently an exaggeration.
[‡] Mentioned in note * on ch. 30, Book ii. Herodotus says Psammetichus himself overtook them, which is not probable.

behind the secluded Egyptians in prejudice against foreigners, whom they looked upon as " barbarians ; " and though Herodotus shows they had now the opportunity of learning everything about Egypt, they have not even given us the *names* of all the kings of the 26th dynasty; nor any satisfactory account of the customs of the people.

Psammetichus next turned his attention to the internal state of Egypt, and to the embellishment of the temples. The arts were highly encouraged, and a fresh impulse being given to them during this and the subsequent reigns, a great improvement took place in the execution and high finish of the sculptures; and this period may be called the " renaissance " of Egyptian art.* To the temples Psammetichus made great additions, in Thebes and other cities; at Memphis he added the southern court, or Propylæum, of the Temple of Pthah, and opposite it a magnificent edifice for Apis, where he was kept when publicly exhibited; the roof of which was supported by colossal Osiride figures, 12 cubits high ; and it was at this period that the Apis sepulchres near Memphis began to assume more importance and extent.

B. C. 610.—Psammetichus I. was succeeded by his son Neco (or Necho), whose first care was to improve the commercial prosperity of Egypt. With this view he began to re-open the canal from the Nile to the Red Sea, till being warned by an oracle that he was working for the Barbarian, he abandoned his project—a reason more probable than the one assigned by Diodorus (i. 33) for Darius not completing it— " that the Red Sea was higher than the land of Egypt : " for the previous completion of the canal under the second Remeses, and the experience of the Egyptians in such operations,† would have shown this to be an error ; like that in modern times of supposing the Red Sea higher than the Mediterranean. Nor, even had it been so, would this have been an impediment ; as the use of sluices, so well known in Egypt, would have removed it ; and indeed they were actually adopted there to prevent the sea-water from tainting the canal, as well as to obviate the effect of the inundation, and of the high tide of from five to six feet in the Red Sea.

Neco next fitted out some ships, in order to discover if Africa was circumnavigable ; ‡ for which purpose he engaged the services of certain Phœnician mariners ; and he has the honour of having been the first to ascertain the peninsular form of that continent, about twenty-one centuries before Bartolomeo Diaz and Vasco de Gama. After this, taking advantage of the unsettled condition of Western Asia, he endeavoured to re-establish the influence of Egypt in that quarter, and to extend its conquests both by sea and land. He therefore marched a formidable army into Syria, for the purpose of capturing Carchemish on the Euphrates; when Josiah king of Judah, wishing probably to ingratiate himself with the Babylonians, and disregarding the friendly remonstrances of Neco, ventured to oppose him in the valley of Megiddo (2 Chron. xxxv. 22). The utter hopelessness of the attempt is described

* See above, p. 312.
† The inconsistency of supposing that the canal-making Egyptians were indebted to the Greeks for this canal is sufficiently obvious.
‡ Herod. iv. 42.

by the expression (in 2 Kings xxiii. 29), "Pharaoh-Nechoh . . . . . .
slew him at Megiddo, when he had seen him;" and Neco continued his
march to the Euphrates.   This is probably the same event described by
Herodotus, who says Neco met and routed the Syrians at Magdolus
(Megiddo), and afterwards took Cadytis, a large city of Syria. Returning victorious from Carchemish, he deposed Jehoahaz the son of
Josiah, who had been made king, and having "put the land to a tribute
of an hundred talents of silver and a talent of gold," he made his brother
Eliakim (whose name he changed to Jehoiakim) king in his stead, carrying away Jehoahaz captive to Egypt.   But the power of the Babylonians
had now become firmly established; and Nebuchadnezzar, king of Babylon, three years afterwards, "in the fourth year of Jehoiakim" (Jer.
xlvi. 2), took from Neco "all that pertained" to him, "from the river
(torrent) of Egypt unto the river Euphrates" (2 Kings xxiv. 7); "and
the king of Egypt came not again any more out of his land." *
      Neco reigned 16 years, according to Herodotus—a number proved
to be more correct than the six years of Manetho, by one of the Apis
stelae mentioning his 16th year; and he was succeeded by his son, Psammetichus II., the Psammis of Herodotus, [B. C. 594,] who made several
additions to the temples of Karnak at Thebes, and of Lower Egypt. The
only remarkable events of his reign were an expedition into Ethiopia, at
which time he erected, or added to, the small temple, on the east bank
opposite Philae; and the arrival of an embassy from the Eleans mentioned by Herodotus (ii. 160).   Manetho and Herodotus agree in giving him a reign of six years.   [B. C. 588.]   After him his son and successor Apries reigned according to the latter 25, according to Manetho
19 years; whose hieroglyphical name is found at Thebes, about Philae,
at Memphis, and in various places in Lower Egypt, as well as on an
obelisk afterwards removed to Rome; and one of the Apis stelae mentions a sacred bull, born in the 16th year of Neco, which was consecrated at Memphis at the end of the first year of Psammetichus II.,† and
died in the 12th of Apries, having lived nearly 18 years.   He was the
Pharaoh-Hophra of the Bible, and a contemporary of Zedekiah, king of
Judah, who had been made king by Nebuchadnezzar; and who, hoping
to throw off the yoke of Babylon, made a treaty with Egypt.
      The successes of Apries promised well; and he was considered the
most fortunate monarch, who had ruled Egypt, since his great-grandfather Psammetichus I. (Herod. ii. 161).   He also sent an expedition
against Cyprus; and besieged and took Gáza, and the city of Sidon;
defeated the king of Tyre by sea, and obliged "the Chaldæans that besieged Jerusalem" to retire (Jer. xxxvii. 5).   So elated was he by these
successes, that he thought "not even a god could overthrow him;"
which accords with the account of his arrogance in Ezekiel (xxix. 3),
where he is called "the great dragon that lieth in the midst of the
rivers, which hath said, My river is mine own, and I have made it for
myself."   But reverses followed, and the prophecy of Jeremiah—"I
will give Pharaoh-Hophra king of Egypt into the hands of his enemies,

* See n. ², ch. 159, B. ii.
† This was generally the year following its birth.

and into the hands of them that seek his life "—was fulfilled. According to Herodotus he had sent an expedition against Cyrene, and his troops being defeated, they attributed their disgrace to the king, and revolted against him; when Amasis, being sent by Apries to appease them, was induced to join the revolters.   Upon this Apries advanced to attack them, with his 30,000 Ionian and Carian auxiliaries (whom he had abstained, out of prudent motives, from sending against the Greeks of Cyrene), and with the few Egyptians who remained faithful to him; and the two armies having met at Momemphis, Apries was defeated and carried a prisoner to Saïs.   Though treated kindly by his captor, the urgent remonstrances of the Egyptians shortly afterwards obliged Amasis to put him to death; and he was buried in the royal sepulchres of Saïs.

Engaged in the war against Cyrene, Apries had not been at leisure to protect Jerusalem, from which his army had been immediately withdrawn; and the Babylonians returned, besieged it in the 9th year and 10th month of Zedekiah (Jer. xxix. 1, and 2 Kings xxv. 2), and took it in his 11th year; and having burnt it, carried away the remnant of the people into captivity, with the exception of those who were left under Gedaliah, the governor of Judæa appointed by Nebuchadnezzar, and who, on the murder of Gedaliah, fled into Egypt (Jer. xxv. 23—26).

The threat of their being overtaken in Egypt, and of the throne of Nebuchadnezzar being set on the stones at Tahpanhes,* with that of the burning and carrying away of the gods of Egypt, and the breaking of the images in Beth-Shemesh (Heliopolis), appear to point to an actual invasion of Egypt by Nebuchadnezzar during the reign of Apries (Jer. xliii. 10, xliv. 1, 30); and the wording of the sentence shows that his "enemy," and they who "seek his life," apply rather to the king of Babylon than to Amasis.   Berosus and Megasthenes also mention Nebuchadnezzar having invaded Egypt; and to this the prophecy of Isaiah (xix. 2) may refer—"I will set the Egyptians against the Egyptians, and they shall fight every one against his brother; .... city against city, and kingdom against kingdom .... The Egyptians will I give into the hand of a cruel lord, and a fierce king shall rule over them." For though it seems to relate to an earlier period, when *Assyria* was powerful (the prophecy being given soon after the time of Tirhaka), and mentions the Egyptians being captives of *Assyria,* it is more likely to allude to the state of Egypt under Apries, and to the conquest of the Babylonians.

The tale then of Amasis' rebellion seems only to have been used to conceal the truth that Apries was deposed by the Babylonians; and this accords better with the fact of Amasis being a person of rank, which is shown by the monuments, and by Diodorus, and by his marrying the daughter of Psammetichus III.; and he probably came to the throne by the intervention of Nebuchadnezzar.   The custom of Eastern nations, and the instances in the Bible at this period, of kings set up by an invader in the place of a predecessor, on condition of paying tribute, are too numerous not to render this highly probable; and thus will be

* Daphnæ of Pelusium.

explained the otherwise perplexing prophecy of the 40 years' humiliation of Egypt (Jer. xlvi. 13, 26; Ezek. xxix. 10, 11). The great desolation of Egypt, and its being *utterly waste and uninhabited* 40 years, can only be a figurative expression; intended to portray the *degradation* of Egypt, and its fall from the high position it held before the invasion by Nebuchadnezzar; since the Bible itself tells us that Hophra obliged the Babylonians to raise the siege of Jerusalem; and the reign of Amasis is shown by the monuments, and by Herodotus, to have been one of the most flourishing periods of Egyptian history.[*]

Of Psammetichus III. some monuments remain at Thebes;[†] but his reign was not noted for any event of importance, and it is not quite certain whether he followed, or preceded, Apries. His queen's name was Nitôcris (*Neith-akri*), whose father was the second Psammetichus, and his daughter became the wife of Amasis.

Amasis, *Ames*, or *Aahmes*, whose name was the same as that of the first king of the 18th dynasty (called by way of distinction Amosis), had the additional title "*Neit-se*," or " the son of Neith," the Minerva of Saïs, which was the native city of the kings of the 26th dynasty, and the royal residence until the Persian conquest. [B. C. 569.] His reign is said to have lasted 44 years; which number has been found on the monuments; though (as before observed) it may have been still longer. Herodotus, in describing the flourishing condition of Egypt at this time, states that it contained 20,000 well inhabited cities (ii. 177; Plin. v. 11), and, though this number is exaggerated, the country was prosperous; and the wealth of individuals is shown by their splendid tombs at Thebes. The immense booty, too, carried off by the Persians confirms the statement of the historian; and the reign of Amasis was remarkable for the beauty, as well as the number of the monuments he erected throughout the country, from the Cataracts to the Delta. Saïs in particular was adorned with grand monuments; and the magnificent Propylæum, or court, of the temple of Minerva far excelled any other in size and beauty, as well as in the dimensions of its stones. Before it Amasis placed several large colossi, with a *dromos* of gigantic androsphinxes, leading to the main entrance; and here was the immense monolithic edifice described by Herodotus (ii. 175), which was brought from the Cataracts, a distance of 700 miles; and which only fell short of that of Buto, in its dimensions (Herod. ii. 155). At Memphis, also, the beautiful temple of Isis he built, and the colossi he placed before the temple of Pthah, and other monuments, were highly admired; and a great monolith bearing his name still remains at Tel-E'tmai, in the Delta, similar to, though smaller than, the one of Saïs.[‡]

Amasis did not neglect the military resources of Egypt, nor allow recent events to impair its power; for he took Cyprus, and made it tributary to him (Herod. ii. 178; Diod. i. 68); and the attention he be-

---

[*] See notes on chs. 161, 177, Book ii.

[†] The inference respecting this dynasty, drawn from Herodotus not mentioning any religious edifices erected by three of its kings, is contradicted by the monuments. (Grote, Hist. Greece, vol. iii. p. 448.)

[‡] See note [9] on ch. 175, Book ii.

stowed on commerce increased the wealth of Egypt. The Greeks were particularly favoured by him, and their traders were permitted to settle at Naucratis, on the Canopic branch of the Nile; where in Herodotus' time they still had a fine temple (ii. 182). The Egyptians, with their natural caution, forbad foreign vessels to enter any other than the Canopic mouth; and affected at the same time to grant thereby a privilege to Naucratis as the Greek emporium; but while their policy, in this respect, was not unlike that of the modern Chinese towards Europeans, they really adopted a wise precaution against Greek pirates, by whom the Mediterranean has been so often infested, even to modern times.

Amasis also entered into a treaty with Crœsus * against Cyrus; and Xenophon asserts that he sent him a body of 120,000 men; which, formed into phalanxes of 10,000 men, each armed with huge shields, that covered them from head to foot, with long spears, and with swords called κοπίδες (the Egyptian *shopsh*), resisted all the attacks of the Persians in their conflict with the Lydian king, and obtained for themselves honourable terms from Cyrus; who gave them an abode in the cities of Larissa and Cyllene, near Cumæ and the sea, where their descendants remained in the time of Xenophon.† The Egyptian phalanx was doubtless the origin of those afterwards adopted in other armies, and of that which became so noted in the days of Alexander. It was of very early date in Egypt; and the large shields, and the peculiar falchions (called *shopsh*) are the same that are represented as belonging to the Egyptian heavy infantry, as early as the 6th dynasty.

The treaty made with the enemy of Persia was certainly more connected with the subsequent invasion of Egypt than the tale about Nitetis and Cambyses; and if aid was actually given, as Xenophon relates, and a large force lost, the blow thereby dealt to the power of Egypt would have been an additional inducement to the Persians to invade it.

It was during the reign of Amasis that Solon is said to have visited Egypt, as well as Thales and Pythagoras; and his friendship with Polycrates of Samos, and his subsequent abandonment of his friend, are detailed by Herodotus (iii. 41, 43); though Diodorus affirms that it was the injustice of Polycrates to his subjects which induced Amasis to desert him.

His policy in cultivating the friendship of the Greeks, though events prevented his profiting much by it, was afterwards of use to the Egyptians in their efforts to throw off the yoke of Persia; and the preparations now set on foot by the Persians to invade Egypt made him more anxious to secure it. For in fact, the son of Cyrus only carried out the designs of his father, when he made war upon Amasis. But before Cambyses reached Egypt, Amasis had died, and was succeeded by his son Psammenitus, the Psammicherites of Manetho; whose short reign of six months was cut short by the Persian conquest, B. C. 525.

The Egyptian king, with the Greek auxiliaries, had advanced to meet the invader at Pelusium; but after a severe struggle the Persians pre-

vailed, and the Egyptian army fled to Memphis. Then shutting themselves up in the fortress called "the White Wall," they awaited the
Persians; but being unable to resist the conqueror, the place was taken
by assault, and Psammenitus was made prisoner. Cambyses, however,
in accordance with Eastern custom,* and the policy of the Persians,
"who honoured the sons of kings," reinstated him on the throne as his
viceroy; and even treated the Egyptians with great indulgence, con-
firming those in office in the same employments they had hitherto held;
as is shown by the inscription on a statuette at Rome of a distinguished
personage of the priestly order, which says that in going to Saïs Cambyses presented offerings to Neith, and performed the libations and
ceremonies like those kings who had preceded him, turning out all those
who had built houses in the temple of Neith, and purifying it for the
performance of the customary rites. He also went into the holy places,
and, apparently, to the tomb of Osiris, and seems to have been initiated
like a Pharaoh; receiving also that title with the Egyptian prenomen
"*Remesot*" ("born of the sun"), added to his nomen "*Cambath;*" according to the custom of giving two ovals, or royal names, to each king.
This accords with what Herodotus says of the Egyptians treating him
as one with whom they pretended to claim relationship (iii. 2); and
Herodotus even admits that Psammenitus was pardoned, and would have
been allowed to govern Egypt as viceroy, if he had not acted deceitfully
towards the Persians;—a favour, he observes, afterwards granted by them
to Thannyras the son of Inarus, and to Pausiris the son of Amyrtæus
(iii. 15). It was only after Cambyses had failed in Ethiopia, that he
became incensed against the Egyptians; as has been shown by M. Le-
tronne and M. Ampère. It was then that the calamity happened to
Egypt, which is mentioned on the statuette (of "*Out-a-Hor-soun;*") and
from its saying that Darius afterwards ordered him to return to Egypt
while he was in Syria, it is conjectured that he was one of the medical
men taken away by Cambyses, and that the office of "doctor" is mentioned among his numerous titles.

[*Twenty-seventh Dynasty of Persians.*—B. C. 525.]—Egypt now became
a conquered province of Persia, governed by a satrap; and Cambyses
and his seven successors composed the 27th dynasty. The conduct of
Darius towards the Egyptians was mild and conciliatory; and the respect they paid him is shown by the monuments, and by the testimony
of Diodorus. Many Apis stelæ bearing his name have been found in the
sepulchres of the sacred bulls; and the principal part of the large temple in the Great Oasis was built by him,† and bears his ovals, with the
same honorary titles which (as Diodorus tells us) were granted to the
ancient sovereigns of the country. Still the Egyptians, impatient of
foreign rule, revolted from the Persians in the year before the death of
Darius, and succeeded in expelling them from the country; but in the
second year of Xerxes they were again reduced to subjection, and
Achæmenes his brother was made governor of the country.

In the fifth year of Artaxerxes (B. C. 458?) the Egyptians again re-

* As among the Turks in later times.
† Some suppose this to be Darius Nothus.

volted; and assisted by the Athenians they defied the force of 400,000 men and the fleet of 200 sail sent against them by Artaxerxes. Headed by Inarus the Libyan the son of Psammetichus, and Amyrtæus of Saïs, they routed the Persians with a loss of 100,000 men; and Achæmenes received his death wound from the hand of Inarus. But Artaxerxes resolving to subdue Egypt sent a still larger force, about four years after this, adding 200,000 men and 300 ships to the remnant of the former army, under the command of Megabyzus and Artabazus; when after an obstinate conflict, Inarus being wounded by Megabyzus, the Egyptians were routed (B. C. 452 ?). Inarus, with a body of Greeks, having fled to Byblus, which was strongly fortified, obtained for himself and his companions a promise of pardon, but was afterwards treacherously crucified by order of Artaxerxes, to satisfy Amytis and revenge the death of her son Achæmenes. Amyrtæus, more fortunate than his coadjutor, escaped to the isle of Elbo; and in the 15th year of Artaxerxes (B. C. 449–8) the Athenians having sent a fleet to the assistance of the Egyptians, hopes were once more entertained of restoring him to the throne. The project, however, was abandoned, and Egypt remained tranquil. It was probably about this time that Pausiris was made viceroy of Egypt by the Persians—his father being still concealed in the marshes —and the post being a nominal one, surrounded as he would be by the Persians, it was a favour that entailed no risk on their authority. But it failed to reconcile the conquered to the presence of their conquerors.

[*Twenty-eighth and Twenty-ninth Dynasties.*—B.C. 411.]—At length the hatred of Persian rule once more led the Egyptians to revolt; and in the 10th year of Darius Nothus (B. C. 411 ?) they succeeded in completely freeing their country from the Persians; when Amyrtæus became independent master of Egypt. His reign constituted the 28th dynasty. Amyrtæus ruled six years, and having made a treaty with the Arabians, he rendered his frontier secure from aggression in that quarter; so that the sceptre passed without interruption into the hands of his successors,[*] the four Mendesian kings of the 29th dynasty. [B. C. 405.] The first of these was Nepherites (*Nefaorot* of the hieroglyphics) who ruled six years, according to Manetho.[†] In his reign Egypt enjoyed its liberty; and Nepherites was able even to send assistance to the Lacedæmonians against the common enemy, though his fleet of 100 ships laden with corn for their army having put into Rhodes was captured by the Persians, who had lately obtained possession of that island.

Acoris, his successor, reigned 13 years (B. C. 399–386). Having made a treaty with Euagoras king of Cyprus, and secured the friendship of the Lacedæmonians, and of Gaus, the son of Tamus, an Egyptian who commanded the Persian fleet, he remained undisturbed by the Persians; and during this time he added considerably to the temples of Thebes and other places, and especially to the sculptures of one at Eileithyias left unfinished by the second Remeses.[‡] Of Psammuthis and Muthis,

---

* This does not require his age to have been so great as some have supposed; for, if born in 484 B. C., Amyrtæus would only have been 79 at his death (B. C. 405), and 18 at his first revolt.

† Diodorus mentions a Psammetichus, who preceded Nepherites, or Nephreus.

‡ I formerly supposed this temple to have been of an older king Uchoreus.

who reigned each one year, and of Nepherites II., who reigned four months, little is known either from historians, or from the monuments, and the only one of them mentioned in the sculptures is the first, whose name *Pse-maut* ("the son of Maut") is found at Thebes. The dates too at this time are very uncertain; and the accession of the next, or 30th dynasty, of three Sebennytic kings, is variously placed in 387 and 381 B. C.

[*Thirtieth Dynasty.*]—This dynasty continued 38, or according to Eusebius 20, years. The first king was Nectanebo (*Nakht-neb-f*). During his reign the Persians sent a large force under Pharnabazus and Iphicrates to recover Egypt, but owing to the dissension of the two generals, and the care taken by Nectanebo to secure the defences of the country, the Persians were unable to re-establish their authority, and entangled amidst the channels of the rising Nile they were forced to retreat. Nectanebo had therefore leisure to adorn the temples of Egypt in many of which his name may still be seen; and he was probably the last of the Pharaohs who erected an obelisk. Pliny, who calls him Nectabis, says it was without hieroglyphics.

After 13 years (or 10 according to Eusebius) B. C. 369, Nectanebo was succeeded by Teos or Tachos, who profiting by the disturbed state of the dominions of Persia, and wishing still further to weaken her power, entered into a treaty with the Lacedæmonians, and determined to attack her in Asia. The Lacedæmonians having furnished a strong force, commanded by Agesilaus in person, and assisted by a fleet under Chabrias the Athenian, Tachos advanced into Syria, taking upon himself the supreme direction of the expedition. But in the course of the campaign his nephew Nectanebo, whom he had detached from the army with a large body of Egyptian troops, made a party against him, and being assisted by his father, called also Nectanebo, who had been appointed governor of Egypt by Tachos during his absence, openly revolted. Agesilaus, already affronted at the treatment he had received from Tachos, gladly supported the pretender; and Chabrias, who had refused to join him, having been recalled by the Athenians, Tachos was unable to maintain his authority, and having fled to Sidon, and thence into Persia, his nephew Nectanebo II. was declared king (B. C. 361). There was, however, a rival competitor in a Mendesian chief, who putting himself at the head of the people, and favoured by the incapacity of Nectanebo would have succeeded in wresting the sceptre from his grasp, had he not been opposed by the talents of Agesilaus, who crushed him at once, and secured Nectanebo on the throne.

Though preparations were set on foot by Artaxerxes to recover Egypt, no expedition was sent thither by him, and dying in 363 B. C. he was succeeded by Ochus, or Artaxerxes III., in whose reign some attempts were made to reconquer the country, but without success; the consequence of which failure was a confederacy between Nectanebo and the Phœnicians, who were thus encouraged to throw off the yoke of Persia. To aid them in their revolt, and expel the Persians, Nectanebo sent them 4,000 Greeks under the orders of Mentor the Rhodian; but Ochus having soon afterwards put himself at the head of a formidable army advanced into, and overran all, Phœnicia; and Mentor having deserted to the enemy, Nectanebo was forced to take measures for the defence of his own country.   Pelusium was garrisoned by 5,000 Greeks, and his army, composed of 100,000 men, of whom 10,000 were Greeks, prepared to repel the invader.   And had it not been for the blunders of Nectanebo, the Persians might have been again foiled, as their chief attack on Pelusium was repulsed; but Nectanebo, panic-struck on seeing the Persians occupy an unguarded point, and fearing lest his retreat should be cut off, fled to Memphis.   Pelusium then surrendered, and Mentor, who had accompanied the Persians, having taken all the fortified places of Lower Egypt, Nectanebo retired into Ethiopia and Egypt once more became a Persian province.

[*Thirty-first Dynasty.*—B. c. 343.]—The reign of Ochus is represented to have been most cruel and oppressive.   Persecuting the people, and insulting their religion, he ordered the sacred bull Apis to be roasted and eaten, so that the Egyptians, according to Plutarch, "represented him in their catalogue of kings by a sword" (de Is. s. 2).   He had recovered the country in his 20th year, and reigned over it two years, and being followed by Arses and Darius, these three compose Manetho's 31st dynasty, which was terminated by Alexander's conquest of Egypt (B. c. 332), and the rule of the Macedonian kings.   These constituted the Ptolemaïc, or Lagide, dynasty; and at length in 30 B. c. Egypt became a Roman province.

Though Egypt had long ceased to be a dominant kingdom before the time of the Cæsars, the duration of its power, without reckoning its revival as a state under the Ptolemies, was far greater than generally fell to the lot of other nations; and when we compare with it the brief glory of the Persian empire to the conquest by Alexander, or that of Babylon, or even the whole period of Assyrian greatness, we find that Egypt continued to be a conquering state, and extended its arms beyond its own frontier for a far longer period than any of those countries; and calculating only its most glorious days, from the reign of Thothmes III. to that of Neco, when it lost its possessions in Asia, it may be said to have lasted as a powerful kingdom upwards of 800 years.   [For the various monuments erected by different Egyptian kings, see the Historical Chapter in my ' Manners and Customs of the Antient Egyptians,' and my ' Topography of Thebes,' and ' Modern Egyptians.']   (G. W.)

NOTE ON EGYPTIAN HISTORY.

In the summary of the history of Egypt given in the Appendix to Book II. vol. ii. p. 319, line 5, I have stated that an Apis, born in the 26th year of Tirhaka, died in the 21st year of Psammetichus 1st, "aged 21 years;" but as there is a doubt respecting the age of that bull, I think it right to state that the period between Tirhaka and Psammetichus 1st, as well as the date of Tirhaka's reign, must still be considered uncertain.   [G. W.]

THE THIRD BOOK

HISTORY OF HERODOTUS,

ENTITLED THALIA.

––––––••••––––––

1. THE above-mentioned Amasis was the Egyptian king against whom Cambyses, son of Cyrus, made his expedition ; and with him went an army composed of the many nations under his rule, among them being included both Ionic and Æolic Greeks. The reason of the invasion was the following.[1] Cambyses, by the advice of a certain Egyptian, who was angry with Amasis for having torn him from his wife and children, and given him over to the Persians, had sent a herald to Amasis to ask his daughter in marriage. His adviser was a physician, whom Amasis, when Cyrus had requested that he would send him the most skilful of all the Egyptian eye-doctors,[2] singled out as the best from the whole number. Therefore the Egyptian bore Amasis a grudge, and his reason for urging Cambyses to ask the hand of the king's daughter was, that if he complied, it might cause him

[1] Dahlmann has well remarked, that the alliance of Egypt with Lydia (vide suprà, i. 77) was quite sufficient ground of quarrel, without further personal motives. And Herodotus had already told us that the subjugation of Egypt was among the designs of Cyrus (i. 153). Indeed, two motives of a public character, each by itself enough to account for the attack, urged the Persian arms in this direction ; viz., revenge, and the lust of conquest. Mr. Grote has noticed the "impulse of aggrandisement," which formed the predominant characteristic of the Persian nation at this period (vol. iv. p. 292). And the fact that the Egyptians had dared to join in the great alliance against the growing Persian power, would render them more particularly obnoxious. But "the spirit of the time" (as Dahlmann observes), "framing its policy upon the influence of persons rather than things, required a more individual motive." (Life of Herod. ch. vii. § 3.)

[2] Vide suprà, ii. 84. The Persians have always distrusted their own skill in medicine, and depended on foreign aid. Egyptians first, and afterwards Greeks, were the court physicians of the Achæmenidæ. (Vide infra, iii. 129, and note the cases of Democedes, Appollonides of Cos, Polycritus of Mende, and Ctesias.) Frank physicians are in similar favour at the present day. On the subject of the subdivisions of the medical profession in Egypt, see Sir G. Wilkinson's note to Book ii. ch. 84.

annoyance ; if he refused, it might make Cambyses his enemy. When the message came, Amasis, who much dreaded the power of the Persians, was greatly perplexed whether to give his daughter or no ; for that Cambyses did not intend to make her his wife, but would only receive her as his concubine, he knew for certain. He therefore cast the matter in his mind, and finally resolved what he would do. There was a daughter of the late king Apries, named Nitêtis,[3] a tall and beautiful woman, the last survivor of that royal house. Amasis took this woman, and, decking her out with gold and costly garments, sent her to Persia as if she had been his own child. Some time afterwards, Cambyses, as he gave her an embrace, happened to call her by her father's name, whereupon she said to him, "I see, O king, thou knowest not how thou hast been cheated by Amasis ; who took me, and, tricking me out with gauds, sent me to thee as his own daughter. But I am in truth the child of Apries, who was his lord and master, until he rebelled against him, together with the rest of the Egyptians, and put him to death." It was this speech, and the cause of quarrel it disclosed, which roused the anger of Cambyses, son of Cyrus, and brought his arms upon Egypt. Such is the Persian story.

2. The Egyptians, however, claim Cambyses as belonging to them, declaring that he was the son of this Nitêtis. It was Cyrus, they say, and not Cambyses, who sent to Amasis for his daughter. But here they mis-state the truth. Acquainted as they are beyond all other men with the laws and customs of the Persians, they cannot but be well aware, first, that it is not the Persian wont to allow a bastard to reign when there is a legitimate heir ; and next, that Cambyses was the son of Cassandané,[4] the daughter of Pharnaspes, an Achæmenian, and not of this Egyptian. But the fact is, that they pervert history, in order to

[3] This account, which Herodotus says was that of the Persians, is utterly inadmissible, as Nitêtis would have been more than forty years of age when Cambyses came to the throne. That of the Egyptians, who pretended that Cambyses was the son of a daughter of Apries, is quite eastern, and resembles the Persian story of Alexander the Great having been born of a Persian princess. (See Malcolm's Persia, vol. i. 4, p. 70, and At. Eg. vol. i. p. 194.) The name Nitêtis is Egyptian, and answers to Athenodora, or Athenodota in Greek. The Egyptian statement that Nitêtis was sent to Cyrus, is more plausible on the score of her age ; but it is not probable. Athenæus (Deipn. xiii. p. 360) makes the demand come from Cambyses, and places this war among those caused by women. May the story have originated in a Nitocris having been married to Nebuchadnezzar ?—[G. W.]

[4] Ctesias made Cambyses the son of a certain Amytis (Persic. Excerpt. § 10), according to him the daughter of Astyages—a person not otherwise known, but whose name recalls that of the Median wife of Nebuchadnezzar (see the Essays appended to Book i. Essay iii. § 9, p. 327). Dino (Fr. 11) and Lynceas of Naucratis (Fr. 2) made him the son of Nitêtis, adopting the Egyptian story.

claim relationship with the house of Cyrus.   Such is the truth
of this matter.

3. I have also heard another account, which I do not at all
believe,—that a Persian lady came to visit the wives of Cyrus,
and seeing how tall and beautiful were the children of Cassandané, then standing by, broke out into loud praise of them, and
admired them exceedingly.   But Cassandané, wife of Cyrus, answered, "Though such the children I have borne him, yet Cyrus
slights me and gives all his regard to the new-comer from
Egypt."   Thus did she express her vexation on account of Nitêtis ; whereupon Cambyses, the eldest of her boys, exclaimed,
"Mother, when I am a man, I will turn Egypt upside down for
you."   He was but ten years old, as the tale runs, when he said
this, and astonished all the women, yet he never forgot it afterwards ; and on this account, they say, when he came to be a
man, and mounted the throne, he made his expedition against
Egypt.

4. There was another matter, quite distinct, which helped
to bring about the expedition.   One of the mercenaries of Amasis,[3] a Halicarnassian, Phanes by name, a man of good judgment, and a brave warrior, dissatisfied for some reason or other
with his master, deserted the service, and, taking ship, fled to
Cambyses, wishing to get speech with him.   As he was a person
of no small account among the mercenaries, and one who could
give very exact intelligence about Egypt, Amasis, anxious to
recover him, ordered that he should be pursued.   He gave the
matter in charge to one of the most trusty of the eunuchs, who
went in quest of the Halicarnassian in a vessel of war.   The
eunuch caught him in Lycia, but did not contrive to bring him
back to Egypt, for Phanes outwitted him by making his guards
drunk, and then escaping into Persia.   Now it happened that
Cambyses was meditating his attack on Egypt, and doubting
how he might best pass the desert, when Phanes arrived, and
not only told him all the secrets of Amasis, but advised him
also how the desert might be crossed.   He counselled him to
send an ambassador to the king of the Arabs,[4] and ask him for
safe-conduct through the region.

[3] The Carian and Ionian mercenaries mentioned repeatedly in the second Book
(chs. 152, 154, 163, &c.)   Phanes, the Halicarnassian, might have been known to
the father of Herodotus.

[4] Herodotus appears to have thought that the Arabs were united under the
government of a single king.   Sennacherib (ii. 141) is "king of the Arabians and
Assyrians ;" and here the ally of Cambyses is spoken of throughout as "*the* king of
the Arabians" (ὁ βασιλεὺς τῶν 'Αραβίων).   This cannot really have been the case ;
and the prince in question can have been no more than the most powerful *sheikh* in
those parts, whose safe-conduct was respected by all the tribes.

5. Now the only entrance into Egypt is by this desert : the country from Phœnicia to the borders of the city Cadytis[7] belongs to the people called the Palæstine Syrians ;[8] from Cadytis, which it appears to me is a city almost as large as Sardis, the marts upon the coast till you reach Jenysus' are the Arabian king's ;[10] after Jenysus the Syrians again come in, and extend to Lake Serbônis, near the place where Mount Casius juts out into the sea. At Lake Serbônis, where the tale goes that Typhon hid himself, Egypt begins. Now the whole tract between Jenysus on the one side, and Lake Serbônis and Mount Casius on the other, and this is no small space, being as much as three days' journey, is a dry desert without a drop of water.

[7] That is, Gaza (vide suprà, Book ii. ch. 159, note [5]).

[8] By the " Palæstine Syrians," or " Syrians of Palæstine " (ii. 104, vii. 89), Herodotus has been generally supposed to mean exclusively the Jews ; but there are no sufficient grounds for limiting the term to them. The Jews in the time of Herodotus must have been a very insignificant element in the population of the country known to him as Palestine Syria (iii. 91), which seems to extend from Cilicia on the north to Egypt on the south, and thus to include the entire " Syria " of Scripture and of the geographers (Scylax. Peripl. pp. 98–102; Strab. xvi. p. 1063 et seq.; Ptol. v. 15, &c.). Palestine Syria means properly " the Syria of the Philistines," who were in ancient times by far the most powerful race of southern Syria (cf. Gen. xxi. 32–4, xxvi. 14–8 ; Ex. xiii. 17, &c.), and who are thought by some to have been the Hyksos or Shepherd-invaders of Egypt (Lepsius, Chron. der Egypter, p. 341). To southern Syria the name has always attached in a peculiar way (Polemo. Fr. 13 ; Strab. xvi. p. 1103 ; Plin. H. N. v. 12 ; Pomp. Mel. i. 11 ; Ptol. l. s. c.), but Herodotus seems to extend the term to the entire country as far as the range of Amanus. (See especially iii. 91). Even in southern Syria the Jews were but one out of many tribes, and the Philistines continued powerful down to the time at which Herodotus wrote (Zech. ix. 5–6). The common notion that Herodotus by his " Syrians of Palestine " means the Jews, rests chiefly upon the statement (ii. 104) that they practised circumcision, which is thought to have been an exclusively Jewish rite. But it may be questioned whether the surrounding nations had not by the time of Herodotus adopted to some extent the practice from the Jews. Or Herodotus, who knew but little of Syria, may have regarded as a general custom what he had known practised by some Syrians, who were really Jews.

[9] Jenysus has been generally identified with the modern *Khan Yoónes*, about 15 miles S. W. of Guza (*Ghuzzeh*), about 55 eastward of the Lake Serbonis (*Subukhet Burdwól*, " the salt-marsh of Baldwin "), and 88 from Mount Casius. But this is to build on a mere accidental resemblance of name. *Khan Yoónes*, " the resting-place of Jonas," derives its appellation from the Islamitic tradition that this was the place where Jonah was thrown up by the whale. The name is therefore not older in the country than the 7th century of our era.

It may further be remarked that as Jenysus was only three days' journey from Mount Casius, its site is to be sought very much nearer to Egypt than *Khan Yoónes*. This removes some of Mr. Blakesley's objections (Excursus on Book iii. ch. 5) to the identification of Gaza with Cadytis.

[10] The ancient geographers did not usually extend Arabia to the coast of the Mediterranean. The Periplus of Scylax is imperfect at this part, but *apparently* there was no mention of Arabia. Strabo expressly says that the Syrians and Jews fill up the coast-line, and that Arabia lies *below* these nations. (Book xvi. pp. 1088–1091.) Niebuhr remarks (Vorträge über alte Geschichte, vol. i. p. 149), that the Arabians here spoken of must have been the Idumæans or Edomites, who spoke the Arabic, not the Canaanitish language. Strabo, however, seems to place the Idumæans further to the west, in the vicinity of Mount Casius (xvi. p. 1081).

6. I shall now mention a thing of which few of those who sail to Egypt are aware. Twice a year wine is brought into Egypt from every part of Greece, as well as from Phœnicia, in earthen jars ;[1] and yet in the whole country you will nowhere see, as I may say, a single jar. What then, every one will ask, becomes of the jars ? This, too, I will clear up. The burgomaster[2] of each town has to collect the wine-jars within his district, and to carry them to Memphis, where they are all filled with water by the Memphians, who then convey them to this desert tract of Syria. And so it comes to pass that all the jars which enter Egypt year by year, and are there put up to sale, find their way into Syria, whither all the old jars have gone before them.

7. This way of keeping the passage into Egypt fit for use by storing water there, was begun by the Persians so soon as they became masters of that country. As, however, at the time of which we speak the tract had not yet been so supplied, Cambyses took the advice of his Halicarnassian guest, and sent messengers to the Arabian to beg a safe-conduct through the region. The Arabian granted his prayer, and each pledged faith to the other.

8. The Arabs keep such pledges more religiously than almost any other people.[3] They plight faith with the forms following. When two men would swear a friendship, they stand on each side of a third :[4] he with a sharp stone makes a cut on the

---

[1] Besides the quantity of wine made in Egypt, a great supply was annually imported from Greece, after the trade was opened with that country. Fragments of wine jars are very commonly found in Egypt, and at the bottom of them is a pitchy or resinous sediment. This was either put in to preserve the wine, or was in consequence of its having been used in old times to prepare the inside of the skins, after they were cured (as is still done in water-skins); and afterwards continued in the jars from early habit. If they had wished to coat the inside of the porous jar, they would rather have used tasteless wax. See At. Eg. vol. ii. p. 158 to 168, and compare note [6] on Book ii. ch. 48.—[G. W.]

[2] The "demarch" in the original. The demarchs appear to have been the governors of towns, the nomarchs (ii. 177) of cantons. The latter continued even under the Romans. (Strab. xvii. p. 1132.)

[3] The fidelity of the Arabs to their engagements is noticed by all travellers. Denham says, "The Arabs have been commended by the ancients for the fidelity of their attachments, and they are still scrupulously exact to their words." (Travels, vol. i. p. 69.) Mr. Kinglake remarks, "It is not of the Bedouins that travellers are afraid, for the safe-conduct granted by the Chief of the ruling tribe is never, I believe, violated." (Eothen, p. 191.) The latter writer is speaking of the Arabs who occupy the desert crossed by Cambyses.

[4] The Arabs have still the same custom of making a third party witness to, and responsible for, their oath. When any one commits an offence against another individual, he also endeavours to find a mediator to intercede in his behalf, and the tent of that person becomes an asylum (like the refuge city of the Jews, Numb. xxxv. 11), until the compact has been settled. This was also a Greek custom (suprà, i. 35), as in the case of accidental homicide.—[G. W.]

inside of the hand of each near the middle finger, and, taking a piece from their dress, dips it in the blood of each, and moistens therewith seven stones[5] lying in the midst, calling the while on Bacchus and Urania. After this, the man who makes the pledge commends the stranger (or the citizen, if citizen he be) to all his friends, and they deem themselves bound to stand to the engagement. They have but these two gods, to wit, Bacchus and Urania ;' and they say that in their mode of cutting the hair, they follow Bacchus. Now their practice is to cut it in a ring, away from the temples. Bacchus they call in their language Orotal, and Urania, Alilat.[7]

[5] Events were often recorded in the East by stones. (Comp. the 12 stones placed in the bed of the Jordan.) The number 7 had an important meaning (as in the Bible frequently), as well as 4. The former was the fortunate number. (Of the week of 7 days, see note on Bk. ii. ch. 82.) It was also a sacred number with the Persians. Four implied "completion," or "perfection" (like the double 12, or 24, with the modern Arabs). The square, or four-sided figure had the same signification; whence Simonides calls a man "square as to his feet, his hands, and his mind;" and the "τετράγωνον" of Aristotle (Rhet. III. xi. 2, "οἶον τὸν ἀγαθὸν ἄνδρα φάναι εἶναι τετράγωνον μεταφορά") is revived in a modern metaphor. (See Clemens Strom. v. p. 562; of the Pythagorean notions (Plut. de Isid. s. 30; and of various meanings attached to numbers At. Eg. vol. iv. p. 190 to 199.)
Seven may have derived its importance from being the natural division of the old lunar month into weeks of 7 days, or 4 quarters of 7 days each; and from 4 being the number of weeks that composed it, came the idea of "completion." The 12 months led to the very conventional duodecimal division; the division by 10 being of later time, when the months were made to consist of 30 days; and from their division by 3 (3 × 10=30) came the idea of the three seasons of the year, 3 × 4 =12 months. Man may have begun counting by 10, from the fingers of the two hands (comp. πεμπάζεσθαι, Plut. de Is. s. 56), but duodecimal seems to have preceded decimal division of time, which alone was capable of giving such important meanings to numbers. The Jews made the number 10 an important division at a very early time, as the ten commandments, the tenth or tithe was given by Jacob, Gen. xxviii. 22 ; comp. Exod. xviii. 21; and twelve also, as the 12 tribes, &c. See CH. vii. App. of Bk. ii.—[G. W.]
[6] There can be little doubt that the religion of the Arabians in the time of Herodotus was astral—"the worship of the host of heaven." It may perhaps be questioned whether this form of worship is so peculiarly Arabian as to entitle it to the distinctive name, which it usually bears, of Sabæanism. But the astral character of the old Arabian idolatry is indubitable. The Bacchus and Urania of Herodotus are therefore with reason taken to represent the Sun and the Moon. (Wesseling ad loc.) The derivation of the word Orotal is very doubtful. Possibly it may be connected, as Wesseling thought, with the Hebrew אּוֹר, "light." Alilat seems to be only a variant of Alitta (i. 131), which has been already explained (note ad loc.).
[7] Urotal has been supposed to be "Allah-taal," the same name as now used by the Arabs for the Deity, signifying "God the exalted." Alilat may be merely "Goddesses," as in the beginning of the speech of Hanno, in the Pœnulus of Plautus, alonim v'alonuth, "gods and goddesses," or it may be the same as Alitta, the goddess of childbirth. (See Essay i. in the Appendix to this Book). "The idols" of Egypt, in Isaiah xix. 3, are called A'lilím, אּלילים "gods," in Genesis iii. 5, A'lehím (Elohim, or Alhim) אּלהים, which is the same as applied to "God" in the same verse and elsewhere. Al (אּל) is "God," or the "mighty." In Arabic, Allah is "God," and illâh, "deity," as la illah il' allah, "there is no deity but God." Alehí or Alhi, is a "God," as Alhi Ekrôn, "the God of Ekron (2 Kings i. 2); Awel, "first," is also related to it. Scaliger and Selden suppose Alilat to be the same as the moon, or

9. When, therefore, the Arabian had pledged his faith to the messengers of Cambyses, he straightway contrived as follows :—he filled a number of camels' skins with water, and loading therewith all the live camels that he possessed, drove them into the desert, and awaited the coming of the army. This is the more likely of the two tales that are told. The other is an improbable story, but, as it is related, I think that I ought not to pass it by. There is a great river in Arabia, called the Corys,[3] which empties itself into the Erythræan sea. The Arabian king, they say, made a pipe of the skins of oxen and. other beasts, reaching from this river all the way to the desert, and so brought the water to certain cisterns which he had had .dug in the desert to receive it. It is a twelve days' journey from the river to this desert tract. And the water, they say, was brought through three different pipes to three separate places.[4]

10. Psammenitus,[1] son of Amasis, lay encamped at the mouth of the Nile, called the Pelusiac, awaiting Cambyses. For Cambyses, when he went up against Egypt, found Amasis no longer in life : he had died after ruling Egypt forty and four years,[2] during all which time no great misfortune had befallen him. When he died, his body was embalmed, and buried in the tomb which he had himself caused to be made in the temple. After his son Psammenitus had mounted the throne, a strange prodigy occurred in Egypt :—Rain fell at Egyptian Thebes, a thing which never happened before,[4] and which, to the present

night, the lêleh (layleh) of Hebrew and Arabic. If so, Urotal should be referred to the day, or the sun, the *Aor* "light" of Hebrew.—[G. W.]

[3] The Corys is supposed to be the small torrent of Coré, mentioned by Abulfeda. Its supplying the army of Cambyses, and the channel of skins for conveying the water are a fable. A supply of water in skins carried by camels might be the origin of the story.—[G. W.]

[4] It would perhaps be wrong to reject this narrative altogether. Subterraneous aqueducts or water-courses, known by the name of *kanât* or *kahreez*, have been in use from a high antiquity throughout the East, and often convey the water of springs to a vast distance. (See Polyb. x. xxviii. § 2 ; Malcolm's Hist. of Persia, vol. i. p. 14 ; Col. Chesney's Euphrates Expedition, vol. ii. p. 657.) Cambyses may have taken the precaution of supplying his army in two ways.

[1] The name of this king has not been found. Like his father's, it contains the name of Neith, the goddess Minerva of Sais, the royal residence of the 26th Saïte dynasty.—[G. W.]

[2] Manetho, according to Africanus, assigned to Amasis 44 years (according to Eusebius 42) ; and the date of the 44th year of Aahmes, Ames, or Amasis, has been found on the monuments. Other persons were called Amasis ; and one has recorded his name in the inscription at Aboosimbel. (See note on Book ii. ch. 30.) The first king of the 18th dynasty had the same name, though generally written Amosis.—[G. W.]

[3] The temple of Minerva at Sais.(Vide suprà, ii. 169).

[4] Very heavy rain at Thebes is unusual, and happens only about once in ten years, when the valleys run with water to the Nile. Four or five showers fall there every

time, has never happened again, as the Thebans themselves
testify. In Upper Egypt it does not usually rain at all; but
on this occasion, rain fell at Thebes in small drops.

11. The Persians crossed the desert, and, pitching their
camp close to the Egyptians, made ready for battle. Hereupon
the mercenaries in the pay of Psammenitus, who were Greeks
and Carians, full of anger against Phanes for having brought a
foreign army upon Egypt, bethought themselves of a mode
whereby they might be revenged on him. Phanes had left sons
in Egypt. The mercenaries took these, and leading them to
the camp, displayed them before the eyes of their father; after
which they brought out a bowl, and, placing it in the space
between the two hosts, they led the sons of Phanes, one by one,·
to the vessel, and slew them over it.[5] When the last was dead,
water and wine were poured into the bowl, and all the soldiers
tasted of the blood, and so they went to the battle. Stubborn
was the fight which followed, and it was not till vast numbers
had been slain upon both sides, that the Egyptians turned and
fled.

12. On the field where this battle was fought I saw a very
wonderful thing which the natives pointed out to me. The
bones of the slain lie scattered upon the field in two lots, those
of the Persians in one place by themselves, as the bodies lay at
the first—those of the Egyptians in another place apart from
them : if, then, you strike the Persian skulls, even with a
pebble, they are so weak, that you break a hole in them; but
the Egyptian skulls[6] are so strong, that you may smite them
with a stone and you will scarcely break them in. They gave
me the following reason for this difference, which seemed to me
likely enough :—The Egyptians (they said) from early childhood
have the head shaved, and so by the action of the sun the skull
becomes thick and hard. The same cause prevents baldness in
Egypt, where you see fewer bald men than in any other land.
Such, then, is the reason why the skulls of the Egyptians are so

.year, after long intervals. And that heavy rain occasionally fell in ancient times is
proved by the depth of the ravines in the Valley of the Kings' tombs, which were
deeply furrowed into the earth long before the tombs were made, and consequently
long before the reign of Amasis. The same is also shown by the precautions taken
in the oldest temples at Thebes to guard the roofs against rain, and by the lions'
mouths, or gutters, for letting off the water from them. Herodotus was misinformed
respecting its "never having rained before in Upper Egypt."—[G. W.]

⁵ This was a mode of making an oath binding. See note on Book ii. ch. 119.—
[G. W.]

⁶ The thickness of the Egyptian skull is observable in the mummies; and those
of the modern Egyptians fortunately possess the same property of hardness, to
judge from the blows they bear from the Turks, and in their combats among them
selves.—[G. W.]

strong. The Persians, on the other hand, have feeble skulls, because they keep themselves shaded from the first,[7] wearing turbans upon their heads.   What I have here mentioned I saw with my own eyes, and I observed also the like at Paprêmis,[8] in the case of the Persians who were killed with Achæmenes, the son of Darius, by Inarus the Libyan.[9]

13. The Egyptians who fought in the battle, no sooner turned their backs upon the enemy, than they fled away in complete disorder to Memphis, where they shut themselves up within the walls.   Hereupon Cambyses sent a Mytilenæan vessel, with a Persian herald on board, who was to sail up the Nile to Memphis, and invite the Egyptians to a surrender. They, however, when they saw the vessel entering the town, poured forth in crowds from the castle,[1] destroyed the ship, and, tearing the crew limb from limb, so bore them into the fortress.   After this Memphis was besieged, and in due time surrendered.   Hereon the Libyans who bordered upon Egypt, fearing the fate of that country, gave themselves up to Cambyses without a battle, made an agreement to pay tribute to him, and forthwith sent him gifts.[2]   The Cyrenæans too, and the Barcæans, having the same fear as the Libyans, immediately did the like.   Cambyses received the Libyan presents very graciously, but not so the gifts of the Cyrenæans.   They had sent no more than five hundred *minæ*[3] of silver, which Cambyses, I imagine, thought too little.   He therefore snatched the money from them, and with his own hands scattered it among his soldiers.

[7] Bähr (ad loc.) understands Herodotus to allude to the seclusion of the children within the harem till the age of five years (vide suprà, i. 142).   But probably the shading by the turban is alone meant. The clause, πίλους τιάρας φορέοντες, is *exegetical* of σκιητροφέουσι.

[8] Suprà, Book ii. ch. 63, note [4].

[9] Vide infrà, vii. 7.   The revolt of Inarus is fixed by Clinton (F. H. vol. ii. p. 46) to the year B. C. 460, the fifth year of Artaxerxes.   Achæmenes had then been satrap of Egypt twenty-four years (Herod. vii. 7).   He seems to have been slain at the first outbreak of the insurrection. For the subsequent course of the revolt see Thucyd. i. 104, 109.   Compare also infrà, ch. 15.

[1] The citadel of Memphis is called by Herodotus "the white wall" (infrà, ch. 91). Memphis, according to Thucydides (i. 104), consisted of three parts, the innermost of which was strongly fortified, and was called "the white wall."   It is remarkable that Memphis is called in hieroglyphics the "white building."   There is every reason to believe that, like Thebes, the city itself was not surrounded by a wall. Memphis was also called Manouf, or "Mennofre" ("good building"), and "the land of the pyramid;" and Pthah-êi, "the abode of Pthah" (see note [7] on Book ii. ch. 99). —[G. W.]

[2] Vide infrà, iv. 165. Arcesilaüs III. was king of Cyrene at this time.

[3] If Attic minæ are intended, as is probable, the value of the Cyrenæan contribution would be little more than 2000*l*. of our money.

14. Ten days after the fort had fallen, Cambyses resolved
to try the spirit of Psammenitus, the Egyptian king, whose
whole reign had been but six months. He therefore had him
set in one of the suburbs, and many other Egyptians with him,
and there subjected him to insult. First of all he sent his
daughter out from the city, clothed in the garb of a slave, with
a pitcher to draw water. Many virgins, the daughters of the
chief nobles, accompanied her, wearing the same dress. When
the damsels came opposite the place where their fathers sate,
shedding tears and uttering cries of woe, the fathers, all but
Psammenitus, wept and wailed in return, grieving to see their
children in so sad a plight; but he, when he had looked and
seen, bent his head towards the ground. In this way passed by
the water-carriers. Next to them came Psammenitus' son, and
two thousand Egyptians of the same age with him—all of them
having ropes round their necks and bridles in their mouths—
and they too passed by on their way to suffer death for the
murder of the Mytilenæans who were destroyed, with their
vessel, in Memphis. For so had the royal judges given their
sentence—"for each Mytilenæan ten of the noblest Egyptians
must forfeit life." King Psammenitus saw the train pass on,
and knew his son was being led to death, but, while the other
Egyptians who sate around him wept and were sorely troubled,
he showed no further sign than when he saw his daughter. And
now, when they too were gone, it chanced that one of his former
boon-companions, a man advanced in years, who had been stripped of all that he had and was a beggar, came where Psammenitus, son of Amasis, and the rest of the Egyptians were,
asking alms from the soldiers. At this sight the king burst
into tears, and, weeping out aloud, called his friend by his
name, and smote himself on the head. Now there were some
who had been set to watch Psammenitus and see what he would
do as each train went by; so these persons went and told Cambyses of his behaviour. Then he, astonished at what was done,
sent a messenger to Psammenitus, and questioned him, saying,
"Psammenitus, thy lord Cambyses asketh thee why, when thou
sawest thy daughter brought to shame, and thy son on his way
to death, thou didst neither utter cry nor shed tear, while to a
beggar, who is, he hears, a stranger to thy race, thou gavest
those marks of honour." To this question Psammenitus made
answer, "O son of Cyrus, my own misfortunes were too great
for tears; but the woe of my friend deserved them. When a
man falls from splendour and plenty into beggary at the thresh-
old of old age, one may well weep for him." When the mes-

senger brought back this answer, Cambyses owned it was just;
Crœsus, likewise, the Egyptians say, burst into tears—for he
too had come into Egypt with Cambyses—and the Persians who
were present wept.   Even Cambyses himself was touched with
pity, and he forthwith gave an order, that the son of Psammenitus should be spared from the number of those appointed
to die, and Psammenitus himself brought from the suburb into
his presence.

15. The messengers were too late to save the life of Psammenitus' son, who had been cut in pieces the first of all; but
they took Psammenitus himself and brought him before the
king.   Cambyses allowed him to live with him, and gave him
no more harsh treatment; nay, could he have kept from inter-
meddling with affairs, he might have recovered Egypt, and
ruled it as governor.   For the Persian wont is to treat the sons
of kings with honour, and even to give their fathers' kingdoms
to the children of such as revolt from them.[4]   There are many
cases from which one may collect that this is the Persian rule,
and especially those of Pausiris and Thannyras.   Thannyras
was son of Inarus the Libyan, and was allowed to succeed his
father,[5] as was also Pausiris, son of Amyrtæus;[6] yet certainly

[4] It appears from the Jewish history that this was a general Oriental practice in
ancient times.   When Pharaoh-Necho deposed Jehoahaz, he made Eliakim (Jehoiakim), his brother, king over Judah (2 Kings xxiii. 34).   And when Nebuchadnezzar
deposed Jehoiachin (2 Kings xxiv. 17), he set Mattaniah (Zedekiah), his uncle, upon
the throne.   Chardin states (tom. iii. p. 310) that the same custom obtains among
the modern Persians.   [The custom of the Persians is confirmed, not only by what
Herodotus says of Thannyras, the son of Inarus, and Pausiris, the son of Amyrtæus;
but by the sculptures, which seem to show that some of the royal family of Egypt
were made governors of the country by the Persians.   The names of Thannyras and
Pausiris (Pa-osiri) are not found on the monuments.   That Cambyses was not guilty
of cruelty to the Egyptians, on his first conquest of the country, is proved by a
monument, now in the Vatican at Rome; from which we learn that he confirmed
the different Egyptian dignitaries in their offices, and even so far flattered the prejudices of the people as to conform to their religious customs, "like the kings who
ruled before him," making offerings "to the divine mother of the gods at Saïs, and
performing the usual libations in her temple to the Lord of ages."   He also took,
or received, a prænomen like the old Egyptian kings, being called (as on that monument) Kambath (Cambyses), Remesot (or Remesto), "Lord of Upper and Lower
Egypt;" and it was therefore only in consequence of the Egyptians rebelling against
him, as Herodotus plainly shows by the connivance, or at the instigation of Psammenitus, that he was induced to depart from his previous humane line of conduct
towards the Egyptians, and to disregard the Persian custom of treating the sons of
kings with indulgence.   In Book iv. ch. 166, Herodotus says that Cambyses made
Aryandês governor of Egypt.—[G. W.]
[5] Inarus fell into the hands of the Persians, and was crucified, probably in the
year B. C. 455.   (See Thucyd. i. 110; cf. Clinton's F. H. vol. ii. p. 50.)   Of Thannyras, his son, nothing further is known.   Ctesias's account of the war of Inarus and
Amyrtæus (Excerpt. § 32) seems tainted by his usual dishonesty.   It is utterly irre-
concilable with Thucydides.
[6] From this passage it has been concluded (Dahlmann's Life of Herodotus, ch.

no two persons ever did the Persians more damage than Amyrtæus and Inarus.[7] In this case Psammenitus plotted evil, and
received his reward accordingly. He was discovered to be stirring up revolt in Egypt, wherefore Cambyses, when his guilt
clearly appeared, compelled him to drink bull's blood,[8] which
presently caused his death. Such was the end of Psammenitus.

iii.; Clinton's F. H. vol. ii. p. 87; Ol. 92. 4; Mure's Lit. of Greece, vol. iv. pp. 536–
7) that Herodotus continued to write as late as B. C. 408, since in that year (according to the Chronicle of Eusebius) Amyrtæus died, after reigning over the Egyptians
for six years. It is supposed that Pausiris was appointed viceroy by the Persians
at the death of his father, and, that event being assigned to the year B. C. 408, it is
concluded that Herodotus was still adding touches to his history as late as that or
the following year. Various reasons have been adduced in an earlier portion of this
work (see the Introductory Essay, ch. i. pp. 32–4) which make it probable that
Herodotus did not really much outlive B. C. 430. The objection to this view arising
from the present chapter may be met in two ways. In the first place, it is not at
all certain that Manetho, from whom Eusebius professes to· copy, intended to place
the reign of Amyrtæus immediately before that of Nepheritis. Eusebius does not
appear to have had Manetho's work under his eyes, else, why should he in one place
(Pars I. ch. xxi.) quote him second-hand from Josephus? He probably had only
an abridgment or summary of his dynasties, in which the reign of Amyrtæus appeared
as constituting the 28th dynasty, and so as intervening between that of Darius
Nothus and Nepheritis. It is not unlikely that the summary misrepresented Manetho
here, as in other places (see Bunsen's Egypt, vol. i. p. 86, E. T.), and made dynasties
seem to be consecutive which Manetho knew and confessed to be contemporary.
Manetho's six years of Amyrtæus the Saïte are probably the very six years (from
B. C. 460 to B. C. 455) in the reign of Artaxerxes Longimanus during which Egypt is
known to have been independent of Persia, through the exertions of Inarus and Amyrtæus. (See Thucyd. i. 104, and 109–110; Ctes. Exc. Pers. 32; Diod. Sic. xi. 74;
and compare the comments of Wesseling and Larcher ad loc., and Dodwell, Ann.
Thuc. p. 99.) The authority of Syncellus is of no importance, since he merely
copies from Eusebius and Africanus, neither of whom possessed more than an abstract of Manetho.
  Secondly, if we follow Eusebius, and suppose (with Mr. Clinton) that Amyrtæus
had two reigns, each of six years, one from B. C. 460 to B. C. 455, and another (40
years later) from B. C. 414 to B. C. 408, the appointment of Pausiris must be placed
at the close of the first, not of the second reign. If Amyrtæus reigned a second
time, he was certainly not then conquered by the Persians, nor had they at that
time his kingdom to dispose of, for it passed, in the year B. C. 408, to Nepheritis,
and Egypt was not again reduced by the Persians till about B. C. 340. Pausiris
therefore must have been made viceroy when his father lost his dominion the *first*
time, which was when he fled into the marshes and concealed himself, in B. C. 455.
It is to be remarked that Herodotus says nothing, either directly or indirectly, of
the *death* of Amyrtæus, and thus makes no allusion in this passage to any event of
a later date than B. C. 455.
  [7] It appears from Herod. iii. 12 that at the commencement of the revolt of Inarus a great battle was fought near Papremis, in which Achæmenes, the brother of
Xerxes, and a vast number of the Persians, were slain. The remnant of the Persian
forces, as we learn from Thucyd. i. 104 (compare Diod. Sic. xi. 74), fled to Memphis,
and were there besieged by Inarus and the Athenians. They appear to have surrendered after a time (Thucyd. i. 109). The share which Amyrtæus had in the revolt is not very clear. His name does not occur till the year of the death of Inarus
(Thucyd. i. 110), when he appears as king of the marsh-district (ὁ ἐν τοῖς ἕλεσι
βασιλεύς; compare Herod. ii. 140). He maintained himself in this region at least
six years (Thucyd. i. 112). The particulars of the losses sustained by the Persians
at his hands are unknown to us.
  [8] There seems to have been a wide-spread belief among the ancients that bull's

16. After this Cambyses left Memphis, and went to Saïs, wishing to do that which he actually did on his arrival there. He entered the palace of Amasis, and straightway commanded that the body of the king should be brought forth from the sepulchre.   When the attendants did according to his commandment, he further bade them scourge the body, and prick it with goads, and pluck the hair from it,² and heap upon it all manner of insults.   The body, however, having been embalmed, resisted, and refused to come apart, do what they would to it ; so the attendants grew weary of their work ; whereupon Cambyses bade them take the corpse and burn it.   This was truly an impious command to give, for the Persians hold fire to be a god,¹ and never by any chance burn their dead.   Indeed this practice is unlawful, both with them and with the Egyptians—with them for the reason above-mentioned, since they deem it wrong to give the corpse of a man to a god ; and with the Egyptians, because they believe fire to be a live animal² which eats whatever it can seize, and then, glutted with the food, dies with the matter which it feeds upon.   Now to give a man's body to be devoured by beasts is in no wise agreeable to their customs, and indeed this is the very reason why they embalm their dead ; namely, to prevent them from being eaten in the grave by worms. Thus Cambyses commanded what both nations accounted unlawful.³   According to the Egyptians it was not Amasis who was thus treated,⁴ but another of their nation who was of about

blood was poisonous. According to Eusebius (Chron. Can. II. p. 324), Midas, King of Phrygia, killed himself by drinking bull's blood B. C. 694. Themistocles is said to have died in the same way (Arist Eq. 84). Also Smerdis (Ctesias. Pers. Excerpt. § 10).   According to Ctesias, Psammenitus was carried prisoner to Susa.

² This is evidently a Greek statement, and not derived from the Egyptian priests. There was no hair to pluck out, the "head and all the body" of the kings and priests being shaved. The whole story may be doubted.—[G. W.]

¹ On this point see above, i. 131; and compare the Essay "On the Religion of the Ancient Persians," vol. i. App. Essay v.

² The *rationale* of this view is given by Plutarch (Sympos. vii. p. 703) in the following words :—οὐδὲν γὰρ ἄλλο μᾶλλον ἐμψύχῳ προσέοικεν ἢ πῦρ κινούμενόν τε καὶ τρεφόμενον δι' αὑτοῦ, καὶ τῇ λαμπρότητι δηλοῦν ὥσπερ ἡ ψυχὴ καὶ σαφηνίζον ἅπαντα. "There is nothing that so resembles a live animal as fire, which moves and nourishes itself, and which moreover, like the soul, enlightens and displays all things by its brilliancy."

³ The Egyptians were averse to burning a body, not only because burning was considered the punishment of the wicked, but because it was opposed to all their prejudices in favour of its preservation. If they really believed in the return of the soul to the body this would be an additional reason. This last, however, may only have signified that man after death never lost his identity, or individuality The modern Persians and all Moslems have a great prejudice against burning the dead. The custom was very ancient in India.—[G. W.]

⁴ The body of the queen of Amasis, found at Thebes by the French officers of the Luxor, in the sarcophagus now in the British Museum, is said to have been burnt, and replaced in the tomb; but the remains of gilding upon it suffice to disprove

the same height. The Persians, believing this man's body to
be the king's, abused it in the fashion described above. Amasis,
they say, was warned by an oracle of what would happen to
him after his death : in order, therefore, to prevent the impending fate, he buried the body, which afterwards received the
blows, inside his own tomb near the entrance, commanding his
son to bury him, when he died, in the farthest recess of the same
sepulchre. For my own part I do not believe that these orders
were ever given by Amasis ; the Egyptians, as it seems to me,
falsely assert it, to save their own dignity.

17. After this Cambyses took counsel with himself, and
planned three expeditions. One was against the Carthaginians,
another against the Ammonians, and a third against the long-
lived Ethiopians, who dwelt in that part of Libya which borders
upon the southern sea.[5] He judged it best to despatch his
fleet against Carthage and to send some portion of his land
army to act against the Ammonians, while his spies went into
Ethiopia, under the pretence of carrying presents to the king,
but in reality to take note of all they saw, and especially to
observe whether there was really what is called "the table of
the sun" in Ethiopia.

18. Now the table of the sun, according to the accounts
given of it, may be thus described :—It is a meadow in the
skirts of their city full of the boiled flesh[6] of all manner of beasts,
which the magistrates are careful to store with meat every night,
and where whoever likes may come and eat during the day.

this. The appearance of burning was probably owing to the strong preparations
used in embalming the body, and is not unusual.—[G. W.]

[5] The seat of these long-lived Ethiopians is very uncertain. Larcher places
them east of Meroë, on the coast of the Red Sea (Tab. Geograp. p. 151). Bruce
imagined that he met with their descendants in the country of the Shangallas (vol.
ii. p. 554, et seq.). But Heeren (African Nations, vol. i. p. 325) correctly observes
that the Macrobii of Herodotus must be placed very much further to the south.
Not only in this passage, but again, infrà, ch. 114, they are said to dwell towards
the south, *at the farthest limits of Africa.* Their country must have lain, therefore,
beyond the Straits of Babelmandel. Heeren places them near Cape *Guardafui.* He
recognises their customs in the stories told by Cosmas (Topog. Christ. p. 138–9) of
the people of Sasu, and their descendants in the modern Somaulies. The descriptions of Homer (Il. i. 443 ; Od. i. 23, &c.) possibly referred to this people, whom
Ephorus (Fr. 38) also regarded as the remotest of mankind towards the south. It
is quite a distinct question whether the embassy of Cambyses, if a real event, was
to them, or whether he had any particular designs against their liberty. His Ethiopian expedition was undoubtedly a fact, but it had probably no more definite object
than the conquest of the Ethiopians generally.

[6] This was less common in early times, and as Athenæus says, the heroes in
Homer seldom "boil their meat, or dress it with sauces;" but in Egypt as well as
in Ethiopia boiled meat was eaten, though the Egyptians more frequently roasted
it, and boiled their fish. With the Arabs the custom of boiling meat seems to be
very ancient.—[G. W.]

The people of the land say that the earth itself brings forth the food.   Such is the description which is given of this table.[7]

19. When Cambyses had made up his mind that the spies should go, he forthwith sent to Elephantiné for certain of the Ichthyophagi [8] who were acquainted with the Ethiopian tongue ; and, while they were being fetched, issued orders to his fleet to sail against Carthage.   But the Phœnicians said they would not go, since they were bound to the Carthaginians by solemn oaths, and since besides it would be wicked in them to make war on their own children.   Now when the Phœnicians refused, the rest of the fleet was unequal to the undertaking ; and thus it was that the Carthaginians escaped, and were not enslaved by the Persians.   Cambyses thought it not right to force the war

[7] Pomponius Mela is the first writer, after Herodotus, who mentions the table of the sun. It may be doubted whether he does more than follow our author. His words are : "Est locus apparatis epulis semper refertus : et quia, ut libet, vesci volentibus licet, ἡλίου τράπεζαν appellant ; et quæ passim apposita sunt, affirmant innasci subinde divinitus" (III. 15).   The account in Solinus, whose work is an extract from the writings of the elder Pliny, is apparently formed on that of Mela (Polyhist. xxx.).   Pausanias, writing about A. D. 174, treats the whole story as a fable. Heeren (African Nations, vol. i. p. 333) explains it by the dumb trading common in Africa. (Vide infra, iv. 196, and note ad loc.) He thinks that merchants supplied the meat, that the magistrates presided, and that the natives left gold in exchange for what they took.

[8] Eratosthenes (ap. Strabon. xvi. p. 1093) and Artemidorus (ap. eund.) placed the African Ichthyophagi, or Fisheaters, on the coast of the Arabian Gulf, at its entrance, near Cape Dire (the modern *Ras-el-Bir*).   Pausanias also mentions their being the last inhabitants of the shores of the Red Sea (I. xxxiii. § 4).   Their name marks them for a maritime people, and I cannot conceive that any could have dwelt so far inland as Elephantiné. (Heeren supposes this. Afric. Nat. I. p. 337.) Perhaps Herodotus only means that some of them *happened at this time* to be at Elephantiné, and were made use of as guides. If Herodotus regarded them as natives of the country about Cape Dire, their knowledge of the language of the Macrobian Ethiopians, their neighbours, would be natural.   (See above, ch. 17, note [9].)

upon the Phœnicians, because they had yielded themselves to the Persians,⁹ and because upon the Phœnicians all his sea-service depended. The Cyprians had also joined the Persians of their own accord,¹ and took part with them in the expedition against Egypt.

20. As soon as the Ichthyophagi arrived from Elephantiné, Cambyses, having told them what they were to say, forthwith despatched them into Ethiopia with these following gifts : to wit, a purple robe,² a gold chain for the neck, armlets, an alabaster box ³ of myrrh, and a cask of palm wine. The Ethiopians to whom this embassy was sent, are said to be the tallest ⁴ and

⁹ It has been usual to ascribe the conquest of Phœnicia to Cyrus. Even Mr. Grote does so (vol. iv. p. 289). But the sole authority for this is Xenophon (Cyrop. i. i. 4), who also ascribes to Cyrus the conquest of Egypt! Dahlmann has shown (Life of Herod. ch. vii.) that, *according to Herodotus*, the acquisition belongs to the reign of Cambyses. Not only are the Phœnicians first mentioned among the Persian tributaries under this king, but it is expressly said that he, and not Cyrus, "made himself master of the sea" (προσεκτῆσθαι τὴν δάλασσαν; Herod. iii. 34), which could only be by the conquest or submission of the Phœnicians. (Compare Herod. i. 143.) Mr. Grote appears to consider that the conquest of Babylon involved the submission of Phœnicia to the Persian yoke. But even if it be allowed that Phœnicia had latterly been subject to Babylon, which is not absolutely certain, still the reduction of Babylon would not necessarily carry with it the submission of Phœnicia. The Asiatic Greeks did not submit when the Lydian kingdom fell, and the outlying province of Phœnicia would be very apt to reassert its independence on such an occasion. It is unnecessary, however, to reckon probabilities. The authority of Herodotus must be regarded as conclusive on such a matter.

It may be added, that, as the invasion of Egypt designed by Cyrus (Herod. i. 153) did not take place till the fifth year of Cambyses (vide suprà, ii. 1, note ¹, and see Clinton's F. H. vol. ii. p. 378), something must have occupied this monarch during the first four years of his reign. If Phœnicia was still independent at his accession, the delay would be accounted for.

¹ The dependency of Cyprus on Phœnicia has been already shown (note ⁸ on Book ii. ch. 182). Its surrender would be likely to follow close upon the submission of the Phœnicians.

² Various opinions have been held about the origin of the Tyrian purple. The murex is generally supposed to have given it; and some consider the "murex trunculus" to have been much used at Tyre (Spratt, vol. ii. p. 109). A shell-fish (Helix Ianthina) is found on the coast, about Tyre and Beyroot, which is remarkable for its throwing out a quantity of purple liquid when approached, in order (like the sepia) to conceal itself. The water becomes completely coloured all around it, though so very small, being only the size of a small snail, ¼ of an inch in diameter, and very delicate and fragile. Pliny, however, distinctly says, the Tyrian purple came from the buccinum and the murex (book ix. c. 36). Julius Pollux (Onom. i. 4), after mentioning the story of the porphyra shell-fish discovered by the dog of a Tyrian nymph loved by Hercules, describes the small baskets woven of rushes and rope (similar to our eel-baskets) fastened like bells along a rope, used in that fishery. Their wide mouths were so constructed with the ends of the rushes projecting, that the shell-fish easily crept in, but could not get back again; and

handsomest men in the whole world. In their customs they
differ greatly from the rest of mankind, and particularly in the

this, as well as the shell in the hand
of a statue of a Phœnician goddess,
found by Mr. Moore in Syria, would
seem to agree better with the buccinum than the murex. Pliny (ix.
36) evidently considers the (modern) tubular-mouthed murex to be
the porphyra, though he allows
they extracted the dye from both
those shells (ix. 38.) He tells a
story (ix. 25) of the murex, and its
being sacred to Venus at Gnidus.
The buccinum was the κῆρυξ of the
Greeks ; yet it seems that the murex was originally so called ; since,
Athenæus says Stratonicus pretended to be walking on tiptoe from
fear of treading on the prickly
κῆρυξ, in order to ridicule the people
of Abdera for having so many κήρυκες, "heralds" (Athen. vi. p. 349 ; see also iii. p.
85). He describes the porphyra as between a pinna and a buccinum (iii. p. 91).
Of the porphyra shell-fish, see Aristotle, Hist. An. iv. 8 ; v. 15 ; vi. 13 ; viii. 20. He
speaks of many kinds (iv. 15), some very large. Athen. iii. p. 85 to 91, and xii.
p. 528 ; Vitruv. vii. 13. Pliny (ix. 36 to 40) gives three sorts of dye from two fish
(duo sunt genera. Buccinum . . . . altera purpura vocatur). 1. The best was of
amethyst, or violet colour, made by mixing 200 parts of buccinum with 111 of purpura (ix. 38). 2. The Tyrian purple was made by dipping the wool first in the purpura or pelagia, and afterwards in the buccinum ; "it was of the colour of blood,
black to look upon, and bright in the light, whence Homer calls blood purple " (ix.
38). 3. The conchyliata, which had no buccinum dye (ix. 39), and was of a pale
hue, apparently more blue. Seneca (Nat. Quæst. i. 3) says purple does not always
come out alike out of the same shell. Homer also applies porphyreus to the sea ;
but it signified any bright colour, and Horace speaks of the swan, 4 Od. i. 10, "pur-
pureis ales coloribus." Athenæus mentions it applied to the cheeks and mouth
(xiii. p. 604), and the "purpureus late qui splendeat . . . . pannus" of Horace (de
Art. Poet.) may signify either "bright," or "scarlet." This last in Greek was
πυρρός, or κόκκινος. The robe put upon the Saviour is called by St. Matthew "scarlet," κοκκίνην, by St. Mark and St. John "purple," πορφύραν, by St. Luke "gorgeous,"
λαμπράν. Strabo says (iii. p. 100) the porphyra and buccinum were both found at
Carteia, in Spain. Purple seems also to have been imported from Greece by the
Tyrians ; the best in Europe being from Laconia (Plin. ix. 36) ; and Ezekiel (xxvii.
7) says it went to Tyre from "the Isles of *Elishah*," i. e. *Hellas*, or Greece (see
Athen. Deipn. iii. p. 88). Purple was used at a very early time ; and purple and
blue are mentioned in Exodus (xxv. 4). Blue was the ὑάκινθος of the Greeks. It
was extracted from indigo, which was an Egyptian and a Persian dye. Ancient
paintings show the imperial purple was of a violet colour.—[G. W.]

³ Vases of this stone were commonly used for holding ointment. They had not
always the long shape of that class of Etruscan vases, called "Alabastron," which
even had this name when of a different material. The alabaster vases of Egypt
were of various forms and sizes. The stone was the crystallised carbonate of lime,
of a yellowish colour, generally marked with waving lines, which we call oriental
alabaster and stalagmitic arragonite ; very different from the white soft sulphate of
lime, so much used in Italy.—[G. W.]

⁴ Vide infrà, iii. 114 ; and compare Isaiah xlv. 14. "The labour of Egypt, and
the merchandise of *Ethiopia*, and of the *Sabœans, men of stature*, shall come over
to thee." Strabo says that the Ethiopians generally were of small stature (xvi. p.
1162).

way they choose their kings ; for they find out the man who is the tallest of all the citizens, and of strength equal to his height, and appoint him to rule over them.[5]

21. The Ichthyophagi, on reaching this people, delivered the gifts to the king of the country, and spoke as follows :—" Cambyses, king of the Persians, anxious to become thy ally and sworn friend, has sent us to hold converse with thee, and to bear thee the gifts thou seest, which are the things wherein he himself delights the most." Hereon the Ethiopian, who knew they came as spies, made answer :—" The king of the Persians sent you not with these gifts, because he much desired to become my sworn friend—nor is the account which ye give of yourselves true, for ye are come to search out my kingdom. Also your king is not a just man—for were he so, he had not coveted a land which is not his own, nor brought slavery on a people who never did him any wrong. Bear him this bow,[6] and say,—' The king of the Ethiops thus advises the king of the Persians—when the Persians can pull a bow of this strength thus easily, then let them come with an army of superior strength against the long-lived Ethiopians—till then, let them thank the gods[6a] that they have not put it into the heart of the sons of the Ethiops to covet countries which do not belong to them.' "

22. So speaking, he unstrung the bow, and gave it into the hands of the messengers. Then, taking the purple robe, he asked them what it was, and how it had been made. They answered truly, telling him concerning the purple, and the art of the dyer—whereat he observed, " that the men were deceitful, and their garments also." Next he took the neck-chain and the armlets, and asked about them. So the Ichthyophagi explained their use as ornaments. Then the king laughed, and

---

[5] Compare Strabo, xvi. p. 1163, and Arist. Pol. iv. iii. § 7. Bion, in his *Æthiopica*, says that the king was chosen for his beauty. (Fr. 4.)

[6] It is remarkable that the unstrung bow was the emblem of Ethiopia, or at least of that part which corresponded to the modern Nubia, and which was called in hieroglyphics " Tosh," evidently the Ethaush or Ethosh of the Coptic. Thôsh in Coptic signified a " frontier " and a " province ; " but it is differently written in hieroglyphics from Tosh, " Ethiopia." Cush (Kûsh or Kish) is the ancient, and Ethaush the Coptic name of " Ethiopia ; " and the modern Kish, or Gerf Hossayn, in Nubia, being called in Coptic papyri " Thôsh," Ethôsh, and Ethaush (whence the Latin name of that place, " Tutzis "), shows a striking connexion between them. Mr. Harris suggests that the unstrung bow, sent by the King of Ethiopia, accords with the emblem of his country—a symbol of peace, and at the same time a defiance, when accompanied by the message to the Persians to string it as easily as he did. (See notes on Book ii. chs. 29 and 106.) The name of Cush had already been given to Ethiopia on the monuments before the invasion of the Shepherds, at the beginning of the 12th dynasty. May Cush be related to Kôs " the bow ? "—[G. W.]

[6a] For another use of this commonplace, see Book i. ch. 71 ; sub fin.

fancying they were fetters, said, "the Ethiopians had much stronger ones." Thirdly, he inquired about the myrrh, and when they told him how it was made and rubbed upon the limbs, he said the same concerning it that he had said of the robe. Last of all he came to the wine, and having learnt their way of making it, he drank a draught, which greatly delighted him; whereupon he asked what the Persian king was wont to eat, and to what age the longest-lived of the Persians had been known to attain. They told him that the king ate bread, and described the nature of wheat—adding that eighty years was the longest term of man's life among the Persians. Hereat he remarked, "It did not surprise him if they fed on dirt, that they died so soon; indeed he was sure they never would have lived so long as eighty years, except for the refreshment they got from that drink (meaning the wine), wherein he confessed that the Persians surpassed the Ethiopians."

23. The Ichthyophagi then in their turn questioned the king concerning the term of life and diet of his people, and were told that most of them lived to be a hundred and twenty years old, while some even went beyond that age—they ate boiled flesh,[7] and had for their drink nothing but milk. When the Ichthyophagi showed wonder at the number of the years, he led them to a fountain, wherein, when they had washed, they found their flesh all glossy and sleek, as if they had bathed in oil—and a scent came from the spring like that of violets. The water was so weak, they said, that nothing would float in it, neither wood, nor any lighter substance, but all went to the bottom. If their account of this fountain be true, it would be their constant use of the water from it which makes them so long-lived. When they quitted the fountain the king led them to a prison, where the prisoners were all bound with fetters of gold.[8] Among these Ethiopians copper is of all metals the most scarce and valuable.[9] After they had seen the prison, they were likewise shown what is called "the table of the Sun."

[7] Supra, ch. 18, note [6].

[8] Gold abounded in Ethiopia; it is found on the frontiers of Abyssinia, and even in the Bishâree desert, which is called by Edreesee and Aboolfeda, "the land of Bega," a name the Bishareeh Arabs still give themselves. The Bishâree mines are mentioned by Agatharcides, and are the same mentioned by later writers at Ollagee, which were worked by the Arab Caliphs. They lie about seventeen or eighteen days' journey to the south-east of Derow, a village a little above Kom Ombo; but the quantity of gold, even in the time of the Caliphs, barely covered the expense of obtaining it, and when examined by order of Mohammed Ali it was not found worth while to re-open them. The matrix is quartz, and the same to which Diodorus alludes (iii. 11) under the name of φλέβας μαρμάρου τῇ λευκότητι διαφερούσας, and ἀποστιλβούσης πέτρας. See At. Eg., vol. iii. p. 221 to 234.—[G. W.]

[9] Copper is found in various places in the Eastern desert of Egypt, between the

24. Also, last of all, they were allowed to behold the coffins of the Ethiopians, which are made (according to report) of crystal,[1] after the following fashion :—When the dead body has been dried, either in the Egyptian, or in some other manner, they cover the whole with gypsum, and adorn it with painting until it is as like the living man as possible. Then they place the body in a crystal pillar which has been hollowed out to receive it, crystal being dug up in great abundance in their country, and of a kind very easy to work. You may see the corpse through the pillar within which it lies ; and it neither gives out any unpleasant odour, nor is it in any respect unseemly ; yet there is no part that is not as plainly visible as if the body was bare. The next of kin keep the crystal pillar in their houses a full year from the time of the death, and give it the first fruits continually, and honour it with sacrifice. After the year is out they bear the pillar forth, and set it up near the town.[2]

25. When the spies had now seen everything, they returned back to Egypt, and made report to Cambyses, who was stirred to anger by their words. Forthwith he set out on his march against the Ethiopians without having made any provision for the sustenance of his army, or reflected that he was about to wage war in the uttermost parts of the earth. Like a senseless madman as he was,[3] no sooner did he receive the report of the Ichthyophagi than he began his march, bidding the Greeks who were with his army remain where they were, and taking his land force with him. At Thebes, which he passed through on

Nile and the Red Sea, between latitude 24° and 33°, and specular iron at Hammami in the desert N. W. of Kossayr. The copper mines of Mount Sinai were worked by Osirtasen I., and doubtless long before, as the names of kings of the 4th dynasty occur at Wady Maghára ; and the copper mines of the Egyptian desert were evidently worked in ancient times. In Northern Ethiopia copper is perhaps rare, not so in the upper part of the White Nile ; and the numerous spears of Ethiopia and the Soudán show how abundant iron is in those countries. The iron money of Kordofan has been described by Dr. Holroyd ; and it is found in other parts of Africa. —[G. W.]

[1] This, he says below, was dug out of the earth. It should therefore be rock crystal ; but no piece of this substance could be found large enough to hold a body. It may have been some vitreous composition, coating the stone coffins in the form of a mummy, some of which are found in Egypt. This seems to be confirmed by Ctesias's account mentioned in Diodorus (ii. 15). The sacrifices made to the mummy are the usual liturgies, or services, performed to the dead, by the Egyptians also. Of glass, see note [2] on Book ii. ch. 44.—[G. W.]

[2] Much ingenuity has been expended by Heeren and others in explaining and rationalizing the marvels of this narrative. I cannot but think, with Niebuhr (Vorträge über alte Geschichte, vol. i., p. 151), that both the embassy itself, and the account given of the Macrobians, are fabúlous.

[3] Concerning the pretended madness of Cambyses, vide infrà, ch. 30, note [2].

his way, he detached from his main body some fifty thousand men, and sent them against the Ammonians with orders to carry the people into captivity, and burn the oracle of Jupiter. Mean while he himself went on with the rest of his forces against the Ethiopians. Before, however, he had accomplished one-fifth part of the distance, all that the army had in the way of provisions failed ; whereupon the men began to eat the sumpter-beasts, which shortly failed also. If then, at this time, Cambyses, seeing what was happening, had confessed himself in the wrong, and led his army back, he would have done the wisest thing that he could after the mistake made at the outset ; but as it was, he took no manner of heed, but continued to march forwards. So long as the earth gave them anything, the soldiers sustained life by eating the grass and herbs ; but when they came to the bare sand, a portion of them were guilty of a horrid deed : by tens they cast lots for a man, who was slain to be the food of the others. When Cambyses heard of these doings, alarmed at such cannibalism, he gave up his attack on Ethiopia, and retreating by the way he had come, reached Thebes, after he had lost vast numbers of his soldiers. From Thebes he marched down to Memphis, where he dismissed the Greeks, allowing them to sail home. And so ended the expedition against Ethiopia.[4]

26. The men sent to attack the Ammonians,[5] started from Thebes, having guides with them, and may be clearly traced

---

[4] The writer above quoted, while dismissing the embassy to the Macrobians, and the tales told concerning them, as fabulous, warns us against considering the expedition itself to be a fable. The communication between Egypt and Ethiopia, he remarks, was such as to render the expedition easy. Its chief object would be the conquest of Meroë. Two roads would conduct to this city—one, the road followed in part by Burckhardt in 1813 (Travels in Nubia, Part I., Journey along the banks of the Nile), along the valley of the Nile, by Old and New Dongola, a very circuitous route; the other, across the desert from *Korosko*, in Upper Egypt, to *Aboo Hamed*, the line taken by Bruce, in 1772, and Burckhardt in 1814, which is nearly direct, and is the ordinary route of the caravans. The latter was apparently preferred by Cambyses, who may have reached as far as *Wady Omgat* (lat. 22°), where the sands become quite barren (Burckhardt, p. 171). Niebuhr (l. s. c.) ascribes the failure of the expedition to the "deadly winds and sandstorms," which prevail here no less than in the Sahara; but I do not see any sufficient reason for departing on this point from our author. Burckhardt denies that the winds are *deadly*, and doubts there being any real danger to life from sandstorms in the Nubian desert (pp. 189-191); and it is very conceivable that Cambyses, without being mad, may have provisioned his army insufficiently.

Diodorus's assertion (i. 33), that Cambyses reached as far as Meroë, is as little worthy of belief as the statement with which it is connected, that he built that city. The high antiquity of Meroë has been shown (supra, Book ii. ch. 29, note [9]).

The expedition of Cambyses was not without fruit. He reduced the Ethiopians bordering upon Egypt, and made them tributary (infrà, iii. 97).

[5] For the seats of this people, vide suprà, Book ii. ch. 32, note [9].

as far as the city Oasis,[6] which is inhabited by Samians,[7] said to be of the tribe Æschrionia. The place is distant from Thebes seven days' journey across the sand, and is called in our tongue "the Island of the Blessed."[8] Thus far the army is known to have made its way ; but thenceforth nothing is to be heard of them, except what the Ammonians, and those who get their knowledge from them, report. It is certain they neither reached the Ammonians, nor ever came back to Egypt. Further than this, the Ammonians relate as follows :—That the Persians set forth from Oasis across the sand, and had reached about half way between that place and themselves, when, as they were at their midday meal, a wind arose from the south, strong and deadly, bringing with it vast columns of whirling sand, which entirely covered up the troops, and caused them wholly to disappear.[9] Thus, according to the Ammonians, did it fare with this army.

[6] The city Oasis is taken (Heeren's African Nations, vol. i. p. 212, and Bähr ad loc.), with much reason, for the modern *El Khargeh*, the chief town of what is called the great Oasis. This is distant, by one road 42, by another 52 hours (6 and 7¼ days' journey respectively), from ancient Thebes. The Egyptians in the time of Herodotus may have given the name Oasis to the city, as well as to the tract surrounding it. Oasis, the Auasis of Strabo, seems to be identical with the Coptic ⲞⲨⲀⳉⲈ, and the Arabic *El Wah*. It was applied, according to Strabo, to all inhabited places lying in the midsts of deserts (Strabo, xvii. p. 1123). Perhaps the common word *Wady*, applied by the Arabs to torrent-courses, is of kindred origin. (See Burton's Pilgrimage to Mecca, vol. i. p. 219.)

[There are the remains of a temple at El Khargeh, having the name of Darius and of some later kings. The Egyptian name of the town was

Hebi, the " plough,"

sometimes represented by the plough itself,

which was converted by the Greeks into Ibis, the Hebi of the Copts. (See note [9] on Book ii. ch. 32.) On the Oasis of Ammon, or Siwah (Seewah), see "Modern Egypt and Thebes," vol. ii. p. 374 to 379. The custom there mentioned of the "Shekh of the News" receiving all information from strangers resembles that of the Gauls, mentioned by Cæsar de Bell. Gall. i. 18.—G. W.]

[7] Dahlmann (Life of Herod. vii. § 4) observes upon this, with equal truth and humour,—"One would quite as much have expected Samos as Samians here." He regards Herodotus as deceived by an accidental similarity of names, like that which led the Greeks of the Euxine to call the national deity of the Getæ (Zamolxis) a Samian (vide infrà, iv. 95). Bähr (ad loc.) thinks the Samians might have had a settlement here for trading purposes, but when did Greeks ever settle 400 *miles from the sea-shore* for such an object?

[8] Exaggerated notions of the beauty and fertility of the Oases, derived from the contrast they presented to the barren wilderness around them, prevailed in very early times. They are grassy tracts, covered with palm-trees, and somewhat scantily supplied with water. In the 2nd and 3rd centuries A. C. they were used by the Romans as places of banishment.

[9] It is not probable that the Persian army was destroyed, as Herodotus supposes,

27. About the time when Cambyses arrived at Memphis, Apis appeared to the Egyptians. Now Apis is the god whom the Greeks call Epaphus.[1] As soon as he appeared, straightway all the Egyptians arrayed themselves in their gayest garments, and fell to feasting and jollity : which when Cambyses saw, making sure that these rejoicings were on account of his own ill success, he called before him the officers, who had charge of Memphis, and demanded of them,—" Why, when he was in Memphis before, the Egyptians had done nothing of this kind, but waited until now, when he had returned with the loss of so many of his troops ? " The officers made answer, " That one of their gods had appeared to them, a god who at long intervals of time had been accustomed to show himself in Egypt—and that always on his appearance, the whole of Egypt feasted and kept jubilee." When Cambyses heard this, he told them that they lied, and as liars he condemned them all to suffer death.

28. When they were dead, he called the priests to his presence, and questioning them received the same answer; whereupon he observed, " That he would soon know whether a tame god had really come to dwell in Egypt "—and straightway, without another word, he bade them bring Apis to him. So they went out from his presence to fetch the god. Now this Apis, or Epaphus, is the calf of a cow which is never afterwards able to bear young. The Egyptians say that fire comes down from heaven upon the cow, which thereupon conceives Apis. The calf which is so called, has the following marks :—He is black, with a square spot of white upon his forehead, and on his back the figure of an eagle ; the hairs in his tail are double, and there is a beetle upon his tongue.[2]

29. When the priests returned bringing Apis with them, Cambyses, like the harebrained person that he was, drew his dagger, and aimed at the belly of the animal, but missed his

by being overwhelmed with sand. The sandstorms of the Sahara are unpleasant, possibly even dangerous (Burckhardt, p. 191), but quite unequal to the task of suddenly overwhelming and destroying a host. If the Persian army perished in the desert from want of water, or the baleful effects of the Simoon, the shifting sands would speedily accumulate round the bodies and cover them up. [An army might lose its way during one of those dense fogs of the sand storms and die of thirst ; but not from being overwhelmed and buried by the sand. I have been in some of the worst storms of sand in that desert, and of unusual duration, for they seldom last more than one day ; but nothing of any size was " buried" in the sand.— G. W.]

[1] Vide suprà, ii. 153. [The word Epaphus looks like a misapplication of the name Apophis, the giant serpent, and the emblem of sin ; but is more probably that of Apis with a reduplication. The story of Epaphus and his mother Io show an Egyptian origin.—G. W.]

[2] Apis was supposed to be the image of the soul of Osiris (Plut. de Is. 20, 29),

mark, and stabbed him in the thigh. Then he laughed, and
said to the priests :—" Oh ! blockheads, and think ye that gods

and he was the sacred emblem of that god; but he is sometimes figured as a man
with a bull's head (probably the origin of the Minotaur), and is called Apis-Osiris,
which justifies the assertion of Strabo that " Apis was the same
as Osiris." He is usually called Apis or " Hapi, the living bull."
I have shown (Book ii. ch. 19, note), how closely his name resembles that of the god Nilus " Hapi," or " Hapi of the waters;"
and the genius of the dead, with the head of a Cynocephalus, is
also Hapi. The inundation was called "the rise of Hapi." The bull-Apis is variously described by ancient authors. Herodotus gives an account of the peculiar
marks by which he was known, which agree very well with the figures of him found
in bronze, except that the bird on his back was a vulture. Herodotus and others
suppose him to have been black, though Ovid calls him " variis coloribus Apis," and

Strabo describes him with the forehead, and some parts of the body, of a white
colour, the rest being black. Plutarch says that the fact of his more bright
and shining parts being obscured by those that were of a dark hue agrees
with the resemblance between Osiris and the moon, but this connexion between Osiris and the moon is an error; nor was a spot on his right side in
the form of a crescent, as Ammianus Marcellinus supposes, the principal sign by
which he was known. Plutarch (de Isid. 39) mentions " a gilded ox," with a pall
of the finest black linen, representing the grief of Isis for Osiris, which was Apis.
A black bull with a white crescent, or spot on his shoulder, is found in the tombs
carrying a corpse, which was a form of Apis, in the character of Osiris, as god of
the dead. Ælian pretends that Apis had twenty-nine marks, each referable to some
mystic meaning, and that the Egyptians did not allow those given by Herodotus
and Aristagoras. Ammianus says that " Apis was sacred to the moon, and Mnevis
to the sun." According to Plutarch (s. 33) Mnevis, the sacred bull of Heliopolis,
was also dedicated to Osiris, "and honoured with a reverence next to that paid to

become like this, of flesh and blood, and sensible to steel ?   A
fit god indeed for Egyptians, such an one !   But it shall cost
you dear that you have made me your laughing-stock."   When
he had so spoken, he ordered those whose business it was ' to
scourge the priests, and if they found any of the Egyptians
keeping festival to put them to death.   Thus was the feast
stopped throughout the land of Egypt, and the priests suffered
punishment.   Apis, wounded in the thigh, lay some time pining
in the temple ; at last he died of his wound, and the priests
buried him⁴ secretly without the knowledge of Cambyses.

Apis, whose sire some suppose him to be ; " and Diodorus thinks that "both Apis and
Mnevis were sacred to Osiris, and worshipped as gods throughout Egypt."   Mnevis
is described by most writers of a dark colour.   Plutarch suggests that the people of
Elis and Argos derived the notion of Bacchus with a bull's head from the figures of
Osiris (Apis-Osiris).   When Ælian (Al. 10) says they "compare Apis to Horus, being
the cause of fertility," he evidently means Osiris.   The festival of Apis lasted seven
days, when he was led in solemn procession by the priests through Memphis ; and
Pliny and Solinus pretend that children who smelt his breath were thought to be
gifted with prophecy.   This agrees with the remark of Ælian "that Apis does not
employ virgins and old women sitting on a tripod, nor does he require them to be
intoxicated with the sacred portion, but inspires boys who play round his
stable with a divine impulse, enabling them to pour forth predictions in perfect
rhythm." (See At. Eg., vol. iv. p. 347 to 359.)   Pausanias, vii. 22, says, after
stopping their ears with their hands, they took the oracular omen from the first
word they heard uttered by passers by.   On the festival lasting seven days, see note
on Book ii. ch. 109.   On Apis, see notes on Book ii. chs. 38, 60, and 153 ; and below, 29.—[G. W.]
³ Like the modern Turks, and other orientals, the Persians had certain persons
whose duty it was to inflict the bastinado and other punishments ; and it is curious
to find in the sculptures of Nineveh that the Assyrians practised the same tortures,
for which the Persians and the Turks were afterwards so noted.   We find in Mr.
Layard's drawings men pinned down to the ground and flayed alive ; some are impaled ; and other punishments are inflicted with the same systematic cruelty.   The
conduct of the Egyptians to their enemies contrasts favourably with that of the
Eastern people of antiquity ; for they only cut off the hands of the *dead*, and laid
them in " heaps " before the king (cp. 2 Kings x. 8, and 1 Sam. xviii. 27), as returns
of the enemy's killed ; and if their captives were obliged to work, this was only the
condition on which life was preserved in early times ; and we see no systematic tortures inflicted, and no cruelties beyond accidental harsh treatment by some ignorant
soldier, not unknown in the wars of Christian Europe.   The opinions of Polybius
(xv. 5) and late writers, do not apply to the ancient Egyptians, and their humanity
to slaves is shown by their conduct towards Joseph, and by the evidence of the
monuments ; indeed the murder of a slave was punishable by Egyptian law.—
[G. W.]
⁴ Plutarch says Cambyses killed the Apis, and gave it to the dogs.   It is true,
as Larcher observes, that Herodotus lived nearer the time than Plutarch ; but it is
not impossible that the Egyptians may have concealed the truth so disagreeable to
them ; and it would be more likely that Cambyses should kill, than be satisfied with
merely wounding, the sacred bull.   The burial-place of the Apis has been lately
discovered by M. Mariette close to the pyramids of Abooseer, near Memphis.   It is
an arched gallery, 2000 feet in length in one direction, and about 20 feet in height
and breadth, on each side of which is a series of chambers or recesses, every one
containing an immense granite or basalt sarcophagus, 15 feet by 8, in which the
body of the sacred bull was deposited.   Several stelæ have been found, placed
against the walls ; one of the time of Amasis, another of Nectanebo, another of a

30. And now Cambyses, who even before had not been quite in his right mind, was forthwith, as the Egyptians say, smitten with madness[5] for this crime. The first of his outrages was the slaying of Smerdis,[6] his full brother,[7] whom he had sent back to Persia from Egypt out of envy, because he drew the bow brought from the Ethiopians by the Ichthyophagi (which none of the other Persians were able to bend) the distance of two fingers' breadth.[8] When Smerdis was departed into Persia, Cambyses had a vision in his sleep—he thought a messenger from Persia came to him with tidings, that Smerdis sat upon the royal throne, and with his head touched the heavens. Fearing therefore for himself, and thinking it likely that his brother would kill him, and rule in his stead, Cambyses sent into Persia Prexaspes, whom he trusted beyond all the other Persians, bidding him put Smerdis to death. So this Prexaspes went up to Susa[9]

Ptolemy, which mention the time when the bulls were born, when enthroned, and when they died, and were buried, showing that they mostly lived from seventeen to twenty-three years. Two, however, lived 26 years, showing that the tale of Apis being allowed to live only 25 is erroneous; and, indeed, unless the others could be made to complete 25 the number would have no meaning.—[G. W.]

[5] The madness of Cambyses has been generally accepted by our writers. Bp. Thirlwall, indeed (vol. ii. ch. xiii.), observes that "the actions ascribed to him are not more extravagant than those recorded of other despots." But he accepts the actions themselves as true, and considers his tyranny to have been "wild and capricious." Mr. Grote (vol. iv. p. 296) declares that, after killing Apis, he "lost every spark of reason." But, as Heeren long ago observed, "we ought to be particularly on our guard against the evil that is related of Cambyses, inasmuch as our information is derived entirely from his enemies, the Egyptian priests" (Manual, book ii. p. 94, Engl. Tr.). The stories told of him are likely to have been either invented or exaggerated, and, so far as they are true, may be explained without implying madness. Certainly there is no appearance in the great inscription of Darius that he looked upon Cambyses as a madman, or even as wild and extravagant. The evidence is indeed merely negative, but, coupling it with the silence of Ctesias, we must conclude, I think, that *the Persians* knew nothing of the pretended madness of this king.

It may be added that the epithet (Δεσπότης) by which his subjects are said to have described his character (Herod. iii. 89), does not imply more than a strict and severe rule.

[6] The true name of this prince, which Ctesias, with his usual infelicity, gives as Tanyoxarces (Excerpt. Pers. § 8), was *Bardiya*, "Bardes," or "Bardis." The Greek form most nearly resembling this is the Mardus of Æschylus (Pers. 780, Bl.) Next in order may be placed the Merdis of Nicolaüs Damascenus and Justin (i. 4). Hence the Smerdis of Herodotus, in which the initial S is due to the same laws of euphony that produced σμάραγδος, σμάω, σμῆριγξ, σμικρός, σμῖλαξ, σμυγερός, σμύραινα, σμύρνα, κτλ. The Persian B, for which the Greeks had no real equivalent, their own B having the sound of V, was replaced, naturally enough, by the labial most akin to it, M. (Compare the Greek Megabyzus, Megabignes, &c., where the Persian prefix is Baga — Θεός.)

[7] In the original "both of the same father and of the same mother." This was true, and is expressed *in the same words* in the Behistun inscription (Col. I. par. 10): "Hamátá hampitá Kabujiyahyá" (ὁμομήτριος, ὁμοπάτριος Καμβύσει).

[8] This is contradicted by the inscription, which records that Smerdis was put to death *before Cambyses started for Egypt* (Beh. Ins. Col. I. par. 10).

[9] From this passage, as well as from several others (chs. 65, 70, &c.,) it would

and slew Smerdis.   Some say he killed him as they hunted together, others, that he took him down to the Erythræan Sea,
and there drowned him.[10]

appear that Susa had become the chief residence of the Persian court as early as
the time of Cambyses. (See also Ctes. Pers. § 9.)   This point, however, is involved
in great obscurity.   It is not even quite clear at what time Susiana became subject
to Persia.   Apparently it remained a province of Babylon to the time of Cyrus's
conquest (cf. Dan. viii. 2), when it passed with the Babylonian empire into the hands
of the Persians.   Was it at once made the capital?   According to Strabo and
Xenophon it would seem so, for both distinctly refer the settling of the court at
Susa to Cyrus (Strab. xv. p. 1031; Xen. Cyrop. viii. vi. § 22).   But more trustworthy writers give Cyrus only Ecbatana and Pasargadæ as his capitals. (Herod.
i. 153; Ctes. Pers. § 2–4; Nic. Damasc. Fr. 67; compare Arrian. Exp. Alex. vi. 29;
Anaxim. ap. Steph. Byz. ad voc. Πασσαργδαι.)   Ctesias and Herodotus (l. s. c.)
both make Susa the chief city of Cambyses and the later kings; and it may be supposed that the son of Cyrus, before invading Egypt, effected the change.   But
Herodotus in one place (iii. 64) speaks as if Ecbatana was the capital of Cambyses,
and the inscriptions of Darius render it extremely doubtful whether Susa was made
the capital till some time after he came to the throne.   The frequent revolts of
Susiana (Beh. Ins. Col. I. Par. 16, Col. II. Par. 3, and Col. V. Par. 1), the fact that
Darius, on a revolt, always sends, or goes, to Susiana, and the want of any indication
of his ever even resting at Susa, are arguments against the supposed residence of
the court there at the beginning of his reign.   It is probable, however, that the
change was made in the course of his reign.   The honourable position of Susiana in
one of his Inscriptions at Persepolis (Behist. Memoir, vol. i. p. 280), at the head of
the satrapies, before even Media, is significant.   And the Greeks can scarcely have
been mistaken on the point, so soon as the Persian court became a refuge for
their malcontents.   It must be borne in mind also that the ruins of the great palace
at Susa show Darius to have been its original founder (see Loftus's Chaldæa, p.
372).   Accordingly, Pliny appears to have followed a sound tradition when he made
Darius the founder (i. e. the restorer) of the Susian capital (H. N. vi. 27), which
from his time, or, at latest, from that of his successor, clearly became the chief
residence of the Persian monarchs.   See, besides Herodotus, Æschyl. Pers. 16, 124,
&c.; Neh. i. 1; Esth. i. 2, &c.
    The reasons for making Susa the capital are scarcely less obscure.   Strabo
says that the change was made on three grounds: 1. the convenient position of the
city between Persia and Babylonia; 2. its ancient dignity; and 3. the fact of its long
quiet subjection to foreign yokes.   The last of these reasons contrasts curiously with
the evident fact of its impatience under Persian rule.   The second would have applied with far greater force to Babylon.   No doubt the position of the city at the
edge of the great mountain-range, thereby easily communicating both with the upper
country east and north of Zagros, and with the great Mesopotamian plain at its
base, was an important determining cause; but other reasons may have helped to
produce the decision.   The delightful situation of Susa, the beauty of the herbage,
the excellence of the water (Geograph. Journal, vol. ix. part i. p. 70–1; compare
Athenæus, xii. p. 513 F.); and, again, the comparative retiredness of the place,
which was less a city than a palace (Dan. viii. 2; Neh. i. 1; Esther, i. 2; Plin. l. s.
c.), may have constituted attractions to a luxurious court such as that of Darius
seems to have become.
    [10] The inscription expressly confirms the fact of the putting to death of Smerdis
by his brother, and also states that the death was not generally known (Col. I. Par.
10, § 7.)   Indeed, this is sufficiently apparent from the coming forward within a
few years of two pretenders, who personated the dead prince (Col. I. Par. 11, and Col.
III. Par. 5).   Such personations can only occur when the death has been concealed.
(Compare the cases of Perkin Warbeck, and the individual who lately claimed to
be Louis XVII.)   Ctesias, differing in almost all the particulars, agrees with Herodotus and the inscriptions as to the main facts—that Cambyses suspected the fidelity
of his brother, and had him put to death secretly (Excerpt. § 10).

31. This, it is said, was the first outrage which Cambyses committed. The second was the slaying of his sister, who had accompanied him into Egypt, and lived with him as his wife, though she was his full sister,[1] the daughter both of his father and his mother. The way wherein he had made her his wife was the following:—It was not the custom of the Persians, before his time, to marry their sisters—but Cambyses, happening to fall in love with one of his, and wishing to take her to wife, as he knew that it was an uncommon thing, called together the royal judges, and put it to them, "whether there was any law which allowed a brother, if he wished, to marry his sister?" Now the royal judges are certain picked men among the Persians, who hold their office for life, or until they are found guilty of some misconduct. By them justice is administered in Persia, and they are the interpreters of the old laws, all disputes being referred to their decision. When Cambyses, therefore, put his question to these judges, they gave him an answer which was at once true and safe—"they did not find any law," they said, "allowing a brother to take his sister to wife, but they found a law, that the king of the Persians might do whatever he pleased." And so they neither warped the law through fear of Cambyses, nor ruined themselves by over stiffly maintaining the law ; but they brought another quite distinct law to the king's help, which allowed him to have his wish.[2] Cambyses, therefore, married the object of his love,[3] and no long time afterwards he took to wife another sister. It was the younger of these who went with him into Egypt, and there suffered death at his hands.

32. Concerning the manner of her death, as concerning that of Smerdis,[4] two different accounts are given. The story which the Greeks tell, is, that Cambyses had set a young dog to fight the cub of a lioness—his wife looking on at the time. Now the dog was getting the worse, when a pup of the same litter

In later times, the practice of removing, or incapacitating, all the brothers of the reigning sovereign, as persons whose pretensions might be dangerous, has prevailed almost universally both in Turkey and Persia.

[1] The Egyptians were permitted to marry their sisters by the same father and mother. Both were forbidden by the Levitical law ; but in Patriarchal times a man was permitted to marry a sister, the daughter of his father only (Gen. xx. 12). The Egyptian custom is one of those pointed at in Levit. xviii. 3.—[G. W.]

[2] It is scarcely necessary to point out the agreement between the view of Persian law here disclosed, and that furnished by Dan. ch. vi.—"The law of the Medes and Persians alters not."

[3] This was Atossa, the mother of Xerxes (vide infrà, iii. 88), who was the wife successively of Cambyses, the Pseudo-Smerdis, and Darius Hystaspes. In later times still worse incest was permitted to the kings. Artaxerxes Mnemon married two of his own daughters (Plut. Vit. Artax. Op. vol. i. p. 1870).

[4] Vide suprà, ch. 30, sub fin.

broke his chain, and came to his brother's aid—then the two dogs together fought the lion, and conquered him. The thing greatly pleased Cambyses, but his sister who was sitting by shed tears. When Cambyses saw this, he asked her why she wept : whereon she told him, that seeing the young dog come to his brother's aid made her think of Smerdis, whom there was none to help. For this speech, the Greeks say, Cambyses put her to death. But the Egyptians tell the story thus :—The two were sitting at table, when the sister took a lettuce, and stripping the leaves off, asked her brother " when he thought the lettuce looked the prettiest—when it had all its leaves on, or now that it was stripped ?" He answered, " When the leaves were on." " But thou," she rejoined, " hast done as I did to the lettuce, and made bare the house of Cyrus." Then Cambyses was wroth, and sprang fiercely upon her, though she was with child at the time. And so it came to pass that she miscarried and died.[5]

33. Thus mad was Cambyses upon his own kindred, and this either from his usage of Apis, or from some other among the many causes from which calamities are wont to arise. They say that from his birth he was afflicted with a dreadful disease, the disorder which some call " the sacred sickness."[6] It would be by no means strange, therefore, if his mind were affected in some degree, seeing that his body laboured under so sore a malady.

34. He was mad also upon others besides his kindred ; among the rest, upon Prexaspes, the man whom he esteemed beyond all the rest of the Persians, who carried his messages, and whose son held the office—an honour of no small account in Persia—of his cupbearer. Him Cambyses is said to have once addressed as follows :—" What sort of man, Prexaspes, do the Persians think me ? What do they say of me ?" Prexaspes answered, " Oh ! sire, they praise thee greatly in all things but one—they say thou art too much given to love of wine."[7]

---

[5] This story may have had no other foundation than the fact of the miscarriage, and the bitter feeling of the Egyptian priests.

[6] That the disease known under this name was epilepsy appears from the book of Hippocrates, " On the Sacred Sickness" ($\pi\epsilon\rho\grave{\iota}\ \tau\hat{\eta}s\ \iota\rho\hat{\eta}s\ \nu o\acute{\nu}\sigma o\nu$). The Tuscans still call it " mal benedetto." Its sudden and terrible character caused it to be regarded as a divine visitation. Whether Cambyses was really subject to it, or not, we have no means of deciding.

[7] The drinking propensities of the Persians generally have been already noticed by Herodotus (i. 133). Niebuhr (Vorträge, vol. i. p. 153) remarks that Cambyses was not the only one of the Persian kings who had a passion for wine. He notices the permanency of the national character in this respect, on which point see Col. Rawlinson's note upon Herod. i. 133 (suprà, vol. i. p. 211, note [9]). Plutarch relates

Such Prexaspes told him was the judgment of the Persians; whereupon Cambyses, full of rage, made answer, " What ? they say now that I drink too much wine, and so have lost my senses, and am gone out of my mind ! Then their former speeches about me were untrue." For once, when the Persians were sitting with him, and Crœsus was by, he had asked them, " What sort of man they thought him compared to his father Cyrus ?" Hereon they had answered, "That he surpassed his father, for he was lord of all that his father ever ruled, and further had made himself master of Egypt, and the sea." Then Crœsus, who was standing near, and misliked the comparison, spoke thus to Cambyses : "In my judgment, O ! son of Cyrus, thou art not equal to thy father, for thou hast not yet left behind thee such a son as he." Cambyses was delighted when he heard this reply, and praised the judgment of Crœsus.

35. Recollecting these answers, Cambyses spoke fiercely to Prexaspes, saying, " Judge now thyself, Prexaspes, whether the Persians tell the truth, or whether it is not they who are mad for speaking as they do. Look there now at thy son standing in the vestibule—if I shoot and hit him right in the middle of the heart, it will be plain the Persians have no grounds for what they say : if I miss him, then I allow that the Persians are right, and that I am out of my mind." So speaking he drew the bow to the full, and struck the boy, who straightway fell down dead. Then Cambyses ordered the body to be opened, and the wound examined ; and when the arrow was found to have entered the heart, the king was quite overjoyed, and said to the father with a laugh, " Now thou seest plainly, Prexaspes, that it is not I who am mad, but the Persians who have lost their senses. I pray thee tell me, sawest thou ever mortal man send an arrow with a better aim ?" Prexaspes, seeing that the king was not in his right mind, and fearing for himself, replied, " Oh ! my lord, I do not think that god himself could shoot so dexterously." Such was the outrage which Cambyses committed at this time : at another, he took twelve of the noblest Persians, and, without bringing any charge worthy of death against them, buried them all up to the neck.⁵

of the younger Cyrus, that he boasted of being able to drink more wine, and carry it better, than his brother (οἶνον πλείονα πίνειν καὶ φέρειν. Op. vol. i. p. 1854.)
⁵ This mode of punishment is still in use at the present day, and goes by the name of " Tree-planting." Feti-Ali-Shah once sent for Astra-chan, one of his courtiers, and with an appearance of great friendliness took him round his garden, showing him all its beauties. When he had finished the circuit, he appealed to Astra-chan to know " what his garden still lacked ?" " Nothing," said the courtier ; " it is quite perfect." " I think differently," replied the king ; " I must decidedly

36. Hereupon Crœsus the Lydian thought it right to admonish Cambyses, which he did in these words following :—"Oh! king, allow not thyself to give way entirely to thy youth, and the heat of thy temper, but check and control thyself. It is well to look to consequences, and in forethought is true wisdom. Thou layest hold of men, who are thy fellow-citizens, and without cause of complaint, slayest them—thou even puttest children to death—bethink thee now, if thou shalt often do things like these, will not the Persians rise in revolt against thee ? It is by thy father's wish that I offer thee advice ; he charged me strictly to give thee such counsel as I might see to be most for thy good." In thus advising Cambyses, Crœsus meant nothing but what was friendly. But Cambyses answered him, "Dost thou presume to offer me advice ? Right well thou ruledst thy own country when thou wert a king, and right sage advice thou gavest my father Cyrus, bidding him cross the Araxes and fight the Massagetæ in their own land, when they were willing to have passed over into ours. By thy misdirection of thine own affairs thou broughtest ruin upon thyself, and by thy bad counsel, which he followed, thou broughtest ruin upon Cyrus, my father. But thou shalt not escape punishment now, for I have long been seeking to find some occasion against thee." As he thus spoke, Cambyses took up his bow to shoot at Crœsus ; but Crœsus ran hastily out, and escaped. So when Cambyses found that he could not kill him with his bow, he bade his servants seize him, and put him to death. The servants, however, who knew their master's humour, thought it best to hide Crœsus ; that so, if Cambyses relented, and asked for him, they might bring him out, and get a reward for having saved his life—if, on the other hand, he did not relent, or regret the loss, they might then despatch him. Not long afterwards, Cambyses did in fact regret the loss of Crœsus, and the servants, perceiving it, let him know that he was still alive. "I am glad," said he, "that Crœsus lives, but as for you who saved him, ye shall not escape my vengeance, but shall all of you be put to death." And he did even as he had said.

37. Many other wild outrages of this sort did Cambyses commit, both upon the Persians and the allies, while he still stayed at Memphis ; among the rest he opened the ancient sepulchres, and examined the bodies that were buried in them.

plant a tree in it." Astra-chan, who knew the king's meaning only too well, fell at his feet, and begged his life ; which he obtained at the price of surrendering to the king the lady to whom he was betrothed. (See Niebuhr's Vorträge, vol. i. p. 155.)

He likewise went into the temple of Vulcan, and made great sport of the image.   For the image of Vulcan* is very like the Patæci[1] of the Phœnicians, wherewith they ornament the prows of their ships of war.   If persons have not seen these, I will explain in a different way—it is a figure resembling that of a pigmy.   He went also into the temple of the Cabiri,[2] which it

* The pigmy figures of Pthah-Sokari are often found in Egypt, principally, as might be supposed, about Memphis. He usually had a scarabæus on his head. He was also figured as a man with a hawk's head; and the prow of his ark or sacred boat was ornamented with the head of an oryx. This was carried in procession by sixteen or more priests, in the same manner as the arks of the other gods (see note * on Bk. ii. ch. 58); and that it was looked upon with particular respect throughout Egypt is shown by its being attended by the king in person at Thebes, as well as by a high-priest or prophet, clad in the leopard-skin dress, and by another who may answer to the δαδοῦχος, or torch-bearer. (Cp. the Hierophant or Prophet, the Daduchus, the Priest dressed like the moon, the Herald who recited the ritual, and the Epimeletæ, and other priests, at the Eleusinian Mysteries.) It is preceded by the banner and the sacred sceptre of the god, borne also by eighteen priests, and attended by another pontiff in the leopard-skin robes. Pthah-Sokari, or Pthah-Sokar-Osiris, seems to be the union of the great god Pthah, the creative power, and the mysterious Osiris; and it is not impossible that those three may combine the three orders of gods, being the Creator, the vivifying Deity, and the god of a future state; but the ceremony of carrying the boat or ark of Sokari appears really to refer to the mysterious death of Osiris (see At. Eg. W., vol. iv. p. 255, 359). The deformed figure of the Pthah of Memphis doubtless gave rise to the fable of the lameness of the Greek Hephæstus or Vulcan, and perhaps to the Gnostic notion of the Demiurgus being of an imperfect nature. Some of the pigmy figures, of late time, have the lion's skin of Hercules, which seems to connect them with the god of Tyre.—[G. W.]

[1] The Patæci of the Phœnicians have been learnedly discussed by Bochart (Phaleg. ii. iii.) and Selden (de Dîs Syris, ii. 16). They were dwarf figures of gods, apparently of *any* gods, placed, according to Herodotus, at the prow, according to Hesychius and Suidas, at the poop of a galley. They were probably intended to protect the ship from harm. The word is variously derived. Scaliger and Selden connect it with the Hebrew פתח "insculpere," and פתוחים "sculpturæ;" Bochart with בטח "confidere, securum esse;" Mowers (Phönizier, vol. i. p. 653) with the Greek πατάσσω.   Bunsen (Egypt. vol. i. p. 383) approves of the derivation of Scaliger and Selden, but takes פתח in the sense which it bears in Kal, of "aperire, retegere." With this root he identifies etymologically the Pthah of the Egyptians, who is "the great revealer," and whose name has no Egyptian derivation.   Perhaps it is simplest to regard Πάταικοι as פתוחים "images." [From πάταικος has come the French word "fétiche."—G. W.]

[2] The Cabiri were properly Phœnician gods. (See note on Book ii. ch. 51.)

[Pthah-Sokari-Osiris may possibly represent the Cabiri of Egypt, though the Phœnician Cabiri being eight in number would argue that they were the eight great gods of Egypt. The Cabiri of Samothrace were thought to be the same as the Corybantes and Curetes; and these being so much connected with the Mysteries of

is unlawful for any one to enter except the priests, and not only made sport of the images, but even burnt them.[2a]   They are made like the statue of Vulcan, who is said to have been their father.

38. Thus it appears certain to me, by a great variety of proofs, that Cambyses was raving mad ; he would not else have set himself to make a mock of holy rites and long-established usages.   For if one were to offer men to choose out of all the customs in the world such as seemed to them the best, they would examine the whole number, and end by preferring their own ;[3] so convinced are they that their own usages far surpass those of all others.   Unless, therefore, a man was mad, it is not likely that he would make sport of such matters.   That people have this feeling about their laws may be seen by very many proofs : among others, by the following.   Darius, after he had got the kingdom, called into his presence certain Greeks who were at hand, and asked—"What he should pay them to eat the bodies of their fathers when they died ?"   To which they answered, that there was no sum that would tempt them to do such a thing.   He then sent for certain Indians, of the race called Callatians,[4] men who eat their fathers,[5] and asked

Ceres seems to point to the office of Pthah-Sokari-Osiris (see At. Eg., vol. v. p. 54; vol. iv. p. 184).   Herodotus calls them sons of Vulcan, but we have no son of Pthah mentioned on the monuments, except Aimothph, or Asclepius, and he is not figured like the pigmy god of Memphis.   Damascius, in his life of Isidorus, says, "the Asclepius of Berytus is neither Greek nor Egyptian, but of Phœnician origin; for (seven) sons were born to Sadyk, called Dioscuri and Cabiri, and the eighth of them was Esmun, who is interpreted Asclepius."   Esmun signifies in fact "eight," whence the name of Hermopolis Shmoun B̄, "the two eights;" and Esmun is evidently related to the Hebrew Shemeneh and the Arabic Themánieh or Tseman. But neither this nor the mention of Asclepius will explain the character of the Cabiri, though the number eight seems to point to the eight great gods, among whom Asclepius cannot be admitted.   The name Cabiri, "great," is certainly Phœnician and not Egyptian.   But whether the eight great gods, or Pthah-Sokar-Osiris, the Cabiri could not be *sons* of Pthah.   (See schol. on Apollon. Rhod.) There is a valuable note on the Cabiri in Kenrick's Herodotus, p. 264.—[G. W.]

[2a] Later authors assert that Cambyses broke the vocal statue of Memnon (Syncellus, p. 151, C; Paschal Chron. p. 144), and some that he utterly destroyed Thebes (John of Antioch, Fr. 27).   The former tradition, which rests on the authority of a certain Polyænus of Athens, seems worthy of attention.

[3] This just remark of Herodotus is one of many tending to show how unprejudiced and sensible his opinions were ; and we may readily absolve him from the folly of believing many of the strange stories he relates, against which indeed he guards himself by saying he merely reports what he hears without giving credit to all himself, or expecting others to do so.—[G. W.]

[4] Probably the same as the Calantians of ch. 97, and the Calatians of Hecatæus (Fr. 177).

[5] Vide infrà, iii. 99, and compare the custom of the Issedonians, iv. 26.   Instances of this strange barbarism have been collected by Fabricius (ad Sext. Empir. Hypotyp. iii. 24).   Marco Polo notes the practice as existing in Sumatra in his day.   (See note [1] to ch. 99.)

them, while the Greeks stood by, and knew by the help of an interpreter all that was said—"What he should give them to burn the bodies of their fathers at their decease?" The Indians exclaimed aloud, and bade him forbear such language. Such is men's wont herein; and Pindar was right, in my judgment, when he said, "Law is the king o'er all."[a]

39. While Cambyses was carrying on this war in Egypt, the Lacedæmonians likewise sent a force to Samos against Polycrates, the son of Æaces, who had by insurrection made himself master of that island.[7] At the outset he divided the state into three parts,[8] and shared the kingdom with his brothers, Pantagnôtus and Syloson; but later, having killed the former and banished the latter, who was the younger of the two, he held the whole island. Hereupon he made a contract of friendship with Amasis the Egyptian king, sending him gifts, and receiving from him others in return. In a little while his power so greatly increased, that the fame of it went abroad throughout Ionia and the rest of Greece.[9] Wherever he turned his arms, success waited on him. He had a fleet of a hundred penteconters, and

---

[a] This passage, which is not contained in the extant works of Pindar, is given more at length by Plato in the Gorgias (p. 484, B.). It ran thus:—

νόμος, ὁ πάντων βασιλεὺς
θνατῶν τε καὶ ἀθανάτων,
ἄγει δικαιῶν τὸ βιαιότατον
ὑπερτάτᾳ χερί· τεκμαίρομαι
ἔργοισιν Ἡρακλέος, ἐπεὶ ἀπριάτας—

Su Pind. fry.151(48)—Schl. Aristides—Ed. Dind. vol.9. p.408

The poet appears to be speaking of that law or necessity which the Greeks believed to rule alike over gods and men. Herodotus, forgetful of the context, quotes the words of the poet in quite a different sense from that which they were intended to bear. (On the reading δικαιῶν τὸ βιαιότατον, compare Leg. iii. p. 714 E.)

[7] See below, ch. 120.

[8] Some writers have seen in this passage a division of the Samian people into three tribes (Panofka. Res Samiorum, p. 81; Bähr ad Herod. iii. 26), of which the names are thought to be preserved in Herodotus and the Etymologicum Magnum. The Etymologicum Magnum gives the tribes Astypalæa and Schesia, while Herod. (iii. 26) mentions the tribe Æschrionia. But it is, at the least, doubtful whether anything more is meant here than a division of power among the brothers.

[9] The great power and prosperity of Samos under Polycrates were celebrated by the native historian Alexis, and by Clytus, the disciple of Aristotle. The details which they furnish show an enlightened policy. Polycrates not only raised magnificent works (infrà, ch. 60, note [19]), but enriched Samos with the best products of other lands. He introduced there the Attic and Milesian breeds of sheep, the Scyrian and Naxian goats, the Sicilian pigs, and the Molossian and Laconian hounds *iii.54* (Alex. Fr. 2; Clyt. Fr. 2). He likewise attracted thither the best artisans from all quarters by the offer of high wages. (See below concerning Democedes, ch. 131, which is an instance of this policy.) Among the measures whereby he attained the popularity which enabled him to make himself king, it is mentioned that he was in the habit of lending his rich hangings and valuable plate to any one who wanted it for a wedding-feast or other banquet of more than common importance (Alex. l. s. c.).

bowmen to the number of a thousand.[10]   Herewith he plundered all, without distinction of friend or foe ; for he argued that a friend was better pleased if you gave him back what you had taken from him, than if you spared him at the first.   He captured many of the islands and several towns upon the mainland.   Among his other doings he overcame the Lesbians in a sea-fight, when they came with all their forces to the help of Miletus, and made a number of them prisoners.   These persons, laden with fetters, dug the moat which surrounds the castle at Samos.[11]

40. The exceeding good fortune of Polycrates did not escape the notice of Amasis, who was much disturbed thereat.   When therefore his successes continued increasing, Amasis wrote him the following letter, and sent it to Samos.   "Amasis to Polycrates thus sayeth : It is a pleasure to hear of a friend and ally prospering, but thy exceeding prosperity does not cause me joy, for as much as I know that the gods are envious.   My wish for myself, and for those whom I love, is, to be now successful, and now to meet with a check ; thus passing through life amid alternate good and ill, rather than with perpetual good fortune.   For never yet did I hear tell of any one succeeding in all his undertakings, who did not meet with calamity at last, and come to utter ruin.   Now, therefore, give ear to my words, and meet thy good luck in this way.   Bethink thee which of all thy treasures thou valuest most and canst least bear to part with ; take it, whatsoever it be, and throw it away, so that it may be sure. never to come any more into the sight of man.   Then, if thy good fortune be not thenceforth chequered with ill, save thyself from harm by again doing as I have counselled."

41. When Polycrates read this letter, and perceived that the advice of Amasis was good, he considered carefully with himself which of the treasures that he had in store it would grieve him most to lose.   After much thought he made up his mind that it was a signet-ring which he was wont to wear, an emerald set in gold,[1] the workmanship of Theodore, son of

---

[10] These bowmen were Samians.   Polycrates maintained also a large body of foreign mercenaries. (Vide infrà, iii. 45, where the ἐπίκουροι μισθωτοί are contrasted with the τοξόται οἰκήϊοι.)   On the difference between triremes and penteconters see Book I. ch. 152, note [1].

[11] The town Samos, not the island, is of course here meant.   The islands of the Egean almost all derived their name from their chief city.

[1] Pliny and Solinus say that the stone of Polycrates' ring was a sardonyx ; and the former that in his time one was shown in the Temple of Concord at Rome, given by Augustus, which was "believed" to be his (Plin. xxxvii. 2, 4 ; xxxiii. 6).   Clemens (Pædag. iii. p. 1247A) supposes that a lyre was engraved on it ; and Pausanias (viii. 14) says, "that fine emerald, the seal of Polycrates, was engraved by

Telecles, a Samian.[2] So he determined to throw this away ; and, manning a penteconter, he went on board, and bade the sailors put out into the open sea. When he was now a long way from the island, he took the ring from his finger, and, in the sight of all those who were on board, flung it into the deep. This done, he returned home, and gave vent to his sorrow.

42. Now it happened five or six days afterwards that a fisherman caught a fish so large and beautiful, that he thought it well deserved to be made a present of to the king.[3] So he took it with him to the gate of the palace, and said that he wanted to see Polycrates. Then Polycrates allowed him to come in, and the fisherman gave him the fish with these words following— " Sir king, when I took this prize, I thought I would not carry it to market, though I am a poor man who live by my trade. I said to myself, it is worthy of Polycrates and his greatness ; and so I brought it here to give it to you." The speech pleased the king, who thus spoke in reply :— " Thou didst right well, friend, and I am doubly indebted, both for the gift and for the speech. Come now, and sup with me." So the fisherman went home, esteeming it a high honour that he had been asked to sup with the king. Meanwhile the servants, on cutting open the fish, found the signet of their master in its belly. No sooner did they see it than they seized upon it, and, hastening to Polycrates with great joy, restored it to him, and told him in what way it had been found. The king, who saw something providential in the matter, forthwith wrote a letter to Amasis, telling him all that had happened, what he had himself done, and what had been the upshot—and despatched the letter to Egypt.

43. When Amasis had read the letter of Polycrates, he perceived that it does not belong to man to save his fellow-man from the fate which is in store for him ; likewise he felt certain that Polycrates would end ill, as he prospered in everything, even finding what he had thrown away. So he sent a herald

Theodorus." The story of the fisherman and the ring has been adopted by the Arabs with variations.—[G. W.]

[2] Concerning this artist, see above, Book i. ch. 51, note [6]. The early eminence of the Samians in the arts is evidenced by many other facts recorded by Herodotus. Mandrocles, who constructed the bridge of boats across the Bosphorus, was a Samian (infrà, iv. 88). He was also a patron of the arts, as appears in the same passage. Rhœcus, a native artist, built the great temple of Juno at Samos (infrà, ch. 60). That temple itself, with its beautiful ornaments (see iv. 152), and the other great Samian works mentioned below (iii. 60), were among the most wonderful sights that our author had anywhere beheld. Aristotle compares the constructions of Polycrates (ἔργα Πολυκράτεια) with the pyramids of Egypt, and the magnificent erections of Pisistratus (Polit. v, ix. 4).

[3] Compare with this the narrative in the Fourth Satire of Juvenal (34-69).

to Samos, and dissolved the contract of friendship.[4] This he
did, that when the great and heavy misfortune came, he might
escape the grief which he would have felt if the sufferer had
been his bond-friend.

44. It was with this Polycrates, so fortunate in every undertaking, that the Lacedæmonians now went to war.   Certain
Samians, the same who afterwards founded the city of Cydonia
in Crete,[5] had earnestly intreated their help.   For Polycrates,
at the time when Cambyses, son of Cyrus, was gathering together an armament against Egypt, had sent to beg him not to
omit to ask aid from Samos ; whereupon Cambyses with much
readiness despatched a messenger to the island, and made request that Polycrates would give some ships to the naval force
which he was collecting against Egypt.   Polycrates straightway
picked out from among the citizens such as he thought most
likely to stir revolt against him, and manned with them forty
triremes,[6] which he sent to Cambyses, bidding him keep the
men safe, and never allow them to return home.

45. Now some accounts say that these Samians did not
reach Egypt ; for that when they were off Carpathus,[7] they took
counsel together and resolved to sail no further.   But others
maintain that they did go to Egypt, and, finding themselves
watched, deserted, and sailed back to Samos.   There Polycrates
went out against them with his fleet, and a battle was fought
and gained by the exiles ; after which they disembarked upon
the island and engaged the land forces of Polycrates, but were
defeated, and so sailed off to Lacedæmon.   Some relate that
the Samians from Egypt overcame Polycrates, but it seems to
me untruly ; for had the Samians been strong enough to conquer

---

[4] Mr. Grote (Hist. of Greece, vol. iv. p. 323) suspects, with reason, that "it was
Polycrates who, with characteristic faithlessness, broke off his friendship with
Amasis, finding it suitable to his policy to cultivate the alliance of Cambyses." (Vide
infrà, iii. 44.)   [5] Infrà, ch. 59.

[6] The naval force of Polycrates was said (suprà, ch. 39) to have consisted of
penteconters, that is, vessels propelled by fifty rowers sitting on a level, as in
modern row-boats.   His ships are now called triremes, or vessels having three
banks of oars, and three tiers of rowers.   Both statements cannot be true.   I
conceive the former to be the more correct.   For although Ameinocles the Corinthian had made the Samians acquainted with the trireme as early as B. C. 700, as we
learn from Thucydides (i. 13), yet the Ionian navies continued till after the time of
Polcyrates, according to the testimony of the same author, to be almost entirely
composed of penteconters.   The navy of Polycrates is expressly mentioned among
those of which it is said—φαίνεται τριήρεσι μὲν ὀλίγαις χρώμενα, πεντηκοντέροις
δὲ καὶ πλοίοις μακροῖς ἐξηρτυμένα (Thucyd. i. 14).   Polycrates probably had a fleet of
a hundred vessels, some few of which—certainly not forty—were triremes, the rest
chiefly penteconters.

[7] Carpathus, the modern *Scarpanto*, half-way between Rhodes and Crete, would
lie directly in the passage from Samos to Egypt.

Polycrates by themselves, they would not have needed to call in the aid of the Lacedæmonians. And moreover, it is not likely that a king who had in his pay so large a body of foreign mercenaries, and maintained likewise such a force of native bowmen, would have been worsted by an army so small as that of the returned Samians. As for his own subjects, to hinder them from betraying him and joining the exiles, Polycrates shut up their wives and children in the sheds built to shelter his ships,[8] and was ready to burn sheds and all in case of need.

46. When the banished Samians reached Sparta, they had audience of the magistrates, before whom they made a long speech, as was natural with persons greatly in want of aid. Accordingly at this first sitting the Spartans answered them, that they had forgotten the first half of their speech, and could make nothing of the remainder. Afterwards the Samians had another audience, whereat they simply said, showing a bag which they had brought with them, "The bag wants flour." The Spartans answered that they did not need to have said "the bag;"[9] however, they resolved to give them aid.

47. Then the Lacedæmonians made ready and set forth to the attack of Samos, from a motive of gratitude, if we may believe the Samians, because the Samians had once sent ships to their aid against the Messenians,[10] but as the Spartans themselves say, not so much from any wish to assist the Samians who begged their help, as from a desire to punish the people who had seized the bowl which they sent to Crœsus,[1] and the corselet which Amasis, king of Egypt, sent as a present to them. The Samians made prize of this corselet the year before they took the bowl—it was of linen, and had a vast number of figures of animals inwoven into its fabric, and was likewise embroidered with gold and tree-wool.[2] What is most worthy of admiration in it is, that each of the twists, although of fine texture, contains within it three hundred and sixty threads, all of them clearly visible. The corselet which Amasis gave to the temple of Minerva in Lindus is just such another.[3]

---

[8] Beloe calls these dry-docks or ship-sheds (νεώσοικοι) "harbours," and informs us that Polycrates intended to burn the women and children, "*and the harbours along with them,*" if a revolt broke out!

[9] Τῷ ϑυλάκῳ is the *word* bag, not the bag itself, as Mr. Grote (vol. iii. p. 325) explains it. (Cf. Schweighæuser's Lat. version, and Bähr ad loc.)

[10] Probably in the second Messenian war, which took place after Ameinocles had made triremes for the Samians; lasting from B. C. 685 to B. C. 668, according to Pausanias (iv. 15-23).   [1] Vide suprà, i. 70.

[2] This is the name by which Herodotus designates "cotton," as is plain from ch. 106 of this Book, and from Book vii. ch. 65. Concerning the cotton manufactures of Egypt, vide suprà, Book ii. ch. 86, note [6].

[3] Vide suprà, ii. 182.

48. The Corinthians likewise right willingly lent a helping hand towards the expedition against Samos ; for a generation earlier, about the time of the seizure of the wine-bowl,[4] they too had suffered insult at the hands of the Samians. It happened that Periander, son of Cypselus, had taken three hundred boys, children of the chief nobles among the Corcyræans, and sent them to Alyattes for eunuchs ; the men who had them in charge touched at Samos on their way to Sardis ; whereupon the Samians, having found out what was to become of the boys when they reached that city, first prompted them to take sanctuary at the temple of Diana ; and after this, when the Corinthians, as they were forbidden to tear the suppliants from the holy place, sought to cut off from them all supplies of food,[5] invented a festival in their behoof, which they celebrate to this day with the self-same rites. Each evening, as night closed in, during the whole time that the boys continued there, choirs of youths and virgins were placed about the temple, carrying in their hands cakes made of sesame and honey, in order that the Corcyræan boys might snatch the cakes, and so get enough to live upon.

49. And this went on for so long, that at last the Corinthians who had charge of the boys gave them up, and took their departure, upon which the Samians conveyed them back to Corcyra.[5a] If, now, after the death of Periander, the Corinthians

[4] This passage involves chronological difficulties of no ordinary character. As the expedition of the Spartans belongs (at the earliest) to the year B. C. 525, the rescue of the 300 boys, being a generation (30 years) earlier, should bear date B. C. 555, and this is about the time of the taking of the wine-bowl. But, 1. Alyattes had been many years (12 probably, 5 at any rate) dead then; and, 2. Periander, according to all the chronologists (Sosicrates, Diog. Laertius, Eusebius, Syncellus, &c.), had been dead a still longer time (30 years). Two considerations will in some degree lessen these difficulties. First, Herodotus must be regarded as speaking *loosely*. He cannot mean that the rescue of the boys and the capture of the bowl exactly synchronised, for the boys were sent to *Alyattes*, the bowl to *Crœsus* near the close of his reign, 14 years after the death of his father. Thus these two events were at least 14 years apart. The same looseness of expression may extend to the phrase "a generation earlier," which may mean 40 or 45 years before. Secondly, the chronologers are not to be depended on. They may all resolve themselves into the single not very trustworthy authority of Sosicrates ; and there are many reasons (see Larcher's Notes on Herod. iii. 48) for thinking that Periander lived later than the date assigned to him. I should be inclined to place the single authority of Herodotus above that of all the professed chronologers; and on the strength of this passage and another (v. 94), I should think it probable that Periander's reign came down at least as low as B. C. 567.

[5] Compare the similar cases of Cylon and his adherents (Thucyd. i. 126), and of Pausanias (ib. i. 134). See also the Hercules Furens of Euripides (l. 52):

πάντων δὲ χρεῖος τάσδ' ἕδρας φυλάσσομεν
σίτων, ποτῶν, ἐσθῆτος——

[5a] The Pseudo-Plutarch declares this to be untrue. According to him the

and Corcyræans had been good friends, it is not to be imagined that the former would ever have taken part in the expedition against Samos for such a reason as this; but as, in fact, the two people have always, ever since the first settlement of the island, been enemies to one another,⁶ this outrage was remembered, and the Corinthians bore the Samians a grudge for it. Periander had chosen the youths from among the first families in Corcyra, and sent them a present to Alyattes, to revenge a wrong which he had received. For it was the Corcyræans who began the quarrel and injured Periander by an outrage of a horrid nature.

50. After Periander had put to death his wife Melissa, it chanced that on this first affliction a second followed of a different kind. His wife had borne him two sons, and one of them had now reached the age of seventeen, the other of eighteen years, when their mother's father, Procles, tyrant of Epidaurus,⁷ asked them to his court. They went, and Procles treated them with much kindness, as was natural, considering they were his own daughter's children. At length, when the time for parting came, Procles, as he was sending them on their way, said, "Know you now, my children, who it was that caused your mother's death?" The elder son took no account of this speech, but the younger, whose name was Lycophron,⁷ᵃ was sorely troubled at it—so much so, that when he got back to Corinth, looking upon his father as his mother's murderer, he would neither speak to him, nor answer when spoken to, nor utter a word in reply to all his questionings. So Periander at last growing furious at such behaviour, banished him from his house.

Samians wished to preserve the boys, but could not have succeeded unless the Cnidians had come to their assistance. The Cnidians, he says, drove off the Corinthian guard, rescued the boys, and took them back to Corcyra. He quotes Antenor and Dionysius the Chalcidian as his authorities (Plut. ii. p. 859 E). Pliny also gives the same account (H. N. ix. 25).

⁶ See Thucyd. i. 25, where some reasons for the enmity are given. Corcyra never treated Corinth with the respect due (according to Greek ideas) from a colony to the parent state.

⁷ According to Heraclides Ponticus, a pupil of Plato's (ap. Diog. Laert. i. 94), the name of Periander's wife was Lysidé. She was daughter of Procles and Eristheneia. Pythænetus, however, called her Melissa, and related that Periander fell in love with her from seeing her in the simple Dorian dress dispensing wine to her father's labourers (Fr. 6). Eristheneia was daughter of Aristocrates II., king of Arcadia. The tomb of Melissa too was shown at Epidaurus in Pausanias's time (Pausan. II. xxviii. 4).

⁷ᵃ Nicolaüs Damascenus made the name of this prince, Nicolaüs, in other respects following the story of Herodotus. Lycophron, according to him, was a different son of Periander, who was put to death in consequence of his tyranny over the Periœci. He also gave Periander two other sons, Evagoras and Gorgus (Fr. 60). This last is clearly the Gordias of Aristotle (Pol. v. 9, p. 193).

51. The younger son gone, he turned to the elder and asked him, " what it was that their grandfather had said to them ?" Then he related in how kind and friendly a fashion he had received them ; but, not having taken any notice of the speech which Procles had uttered at parting, he quite forgot to mention it. Periander insisted that it was not possible this should be all—their grandfather must have given them some hint or other—and he went on pressing him, till at last the lad remembered the parting speech and told it. Periander, after he had turned the whole matter over in his thoughts, and felt unwilling to give way at all, sent a messenger to the persons who had opened their houses to his outcast son, and forbade them to harbour him. Then the boy, when he was chased from one friend, sought refuge with another, but was driven from shelter to shelter by the threats of his father, who menaced all those that took him in, and commanded them to shut their doors against him. Still, as fast as he was forced to leave one house he went to another, and was received by the inmates ; for his acquaintance, although in no small alarm, yet gave him shelter, as he was Periander's son.

52. At last Periander made proclamation that whoever harboured his son or even spoke to him,[8] should forfeit a certain sum of money to Apollo. On hearing this no one any longer liked to take him in, or even to hold converse with him, and he himself did not think it right to seek to do what was forbidden ; so, abiding by his resolve, he made his lodging in the public porticos. When four days had passed in this way, Periander, seeing how wretched his son was, that he neither washed nor took any food, felt moved with compassion towards him ; wherefore, foregoing his anger, he approached him, and said, " Which is better, oh ! my son, to fare as now thou farest, or to receive my crown and all the good things that I possess, on the one condition of submitting thyself to thy father ? See, now, though my own child, and lord of this wealthy Corinth, thou hast brought thyself to a beggar's life, because thou must resist and

---

[8] Compare the proclamation which Sophocles puts in the mouth of Œdipus (Tyrann. 236):

τὸν ἄνδρ' ἀπαυδῶ τοῦτον, ὅστις ἐστί, γῆς
τῆσδ', ἧς ἐγὼ κράτη τε καὶ θρόνους νέμω,
μήτ' εἰσδέχεσθαι, μήτε προσφωνεῖν τινά,
μήτ' ἐν θεῶν εὐχαῖσι κ. τ. λ.—
ὠθεῖν δ' ἀπ' οἴκων πάντας, κ. τ. λ.

There is a close resemblance in the thought, but no such similarity of expression as to indicate plagiarism on either side. See, however, the arguments of Dr. Donaldson (Transactions of London Philolog. Soc. i. p. 164.)

treat with anger him whom it least behoves thee to oppose.
If there has been a calamity, and thou bearest me ill will on
that account, bethink thee that I too feel it, and am the greatest sufferer, in as much as it was by me that the deed was done.
For thyself, now that thou knowest how much better a thing it
is to be envied than pitied, and how dangerous it is to indulge
anger against parents and superiors, come back with me to thy
home." With such words as these did Periander chide his son;
but the son made no reply except to remind his father that he
was indebted to the god in the penalty for coming and holding
converse with him. Then Periander knew that there was no
cure for the youth's malady, nor means of overcoming it; so he
prepared a ship and sent him away out of his sight to Corcyra,
which island at that time belonged to him. As for Procles,
Periander, regarding him as the true author of all his present
troubles, went to war with him as soon as his son was gone,
and not only made himself master of his kingdom Epidaurus,
but also took Procles himself, and carried him into captivity.

53. As time went on, and Periander came to be old, he found
himself no longer equal to the oversight and management of affairs. Seeing, therefore, in his eldest son no manner of ability,
but knowing him to be dull and blockish, he sent to Corcyra and
recalled Lycophron to take the kingdom. Lycophron, however,
did not even deign to ask the bearer of this message a question.
But Periander's heart was set upon the youth, so he sent again
to him, this time by his own daughter, the sister of Lycophron,
who would, he thought, have more power to persuade him than
any other person. Then she, when she reached Corcyra, spoke
thus with her brother :—"Dost thou wish the kingdom, brother,
to pass into strange hands, and our father's wealth to be made a
prey, rather than thyself return to enjoy it? Come back home
with me, and cease to punish thyself. It is scant gain, this obsti-
nacy. Why seek to cure evil by evil? Mercy, remember, is by
many set above justice. Many, also, while pushing their mother's claims have forfeited their father's fortune. Power is a slip-
pery thing—it has many suitors; and he is old and stricken in
years—let not thy own inheritance go to another." Thus did
the sister, who had been tutored by Periander what to say, urge
all the arguments most likely to have weight with her brother.
He however made answer, " That so long as he knew his father
to be still alive, he would never go back to Corinth." When
the sister brought Periander this reply, he sent to his son a third
time by a herald, and said he would come himself to Corcyra,

and let his son take his place at Corinth as heir to his kingdom. To these terms Lycophron agreed ; and Periander was making ready to pass into Corcyra and his son to return to Corinth, when the Corcyræans, being informed of what was taking place, to keep Periander away, put the young man to death.[9] For this reason it was that Periander took vengeance on the Corcy-ræans.

54. The Lacedæmonians arrived before Samos with a mighty armament, and forthwith laid siege to the place. In one of the assaults upon the walls, they forced their way to the top of the tower which stands by the sea on the side where the suburb is, but Polycrates came in person to the rescue with a strong force, and beat them back. Meanwhile at the upper tower, which stood on the ridge of the hill,[1] the besieged, both mercenaries and Samians, made a sally ; but after they had withstood the Lacedæmonians a short time, they fled backwards, and the La-cedæmonians, pressing upon them, slew numbers.

55. If now all who were present had behaved that day like Archias and Lycôpas, two of the Lacedæmonians, Samos might have been taken. For these two heroes, following hard upon the flying Samians, entered the city along with them, and, be-ing all alone, and their retreat cut off, were slain within the walls of the place. I myself once fell in with the grandson of this Archias, a man named Archias like his grandsire, and the son of Samius, whom I met at Pitana,[2] to which canton he be-longed. He respected the Samians beyond all other foreigners, and he told me that his father was called Samius, because his grandfather Archias died in Samos so gloriously, and that the reason why he respected the Samians so greatly was, that his grandsire was buried with public honours by the Samian people.

[9] The Scholiast on Thucyd. i. 13, states that the naval battle there spoken of as the earliest upon record, took place in a war between Corinth and Corcyra arising out of this murder. And Bouhier (Dissert. xv. p. 167), to make this possible, proposes to read ἑξήκοντα καὶ ἕ κ α τ ο ν for ἑξήκοντα καὶ διακόσια in the passage of Thucydides. But there seem to be no sufficient grounds for this alteration. Cf. Bähr ad loc., and Larcher's Notes, vol. iii. p. 307.

[1] The town of Samos was situated mainly to the south of a long hog-backed hill called Ampelus. (Strab. x. p. 713.) The fortifications extended to the top of this hill, which is more than 700 feet above the sea level, and were then carried along its northern edge. (See plan on next page.) The wall had towers throughout its whole extent. The tower intended by Herodotus is probably one of those at the western extremity of Ampelus.

[2] Pitana, which is placed by Pausanias (III. xvi. 6) on a par with Mesoa, Cyno-sura, and Limnæ, all portions of Sparta, seems to have been one of those villages which, according to Thucydides (i. 10), made up the town. Its exact position can perhaps scarcely be determined. See, however, Col. Leake's Morea, vol. i. p. 176. That Heyse (Quæst. Herodot. i. p. 89) should suppose the Æolic Pitana (v. s. i. 149) to be here intended, is most extraordinary.

56. The Lacedæmonians besieged Samos during forty days, but not making any progress before the place, they raised the siege at the end of that time, and returned home to the Peloponnese. There is a silly tale told, that Polycrates struck a quantity of the coin of his country in lead, and, coating it with gold,

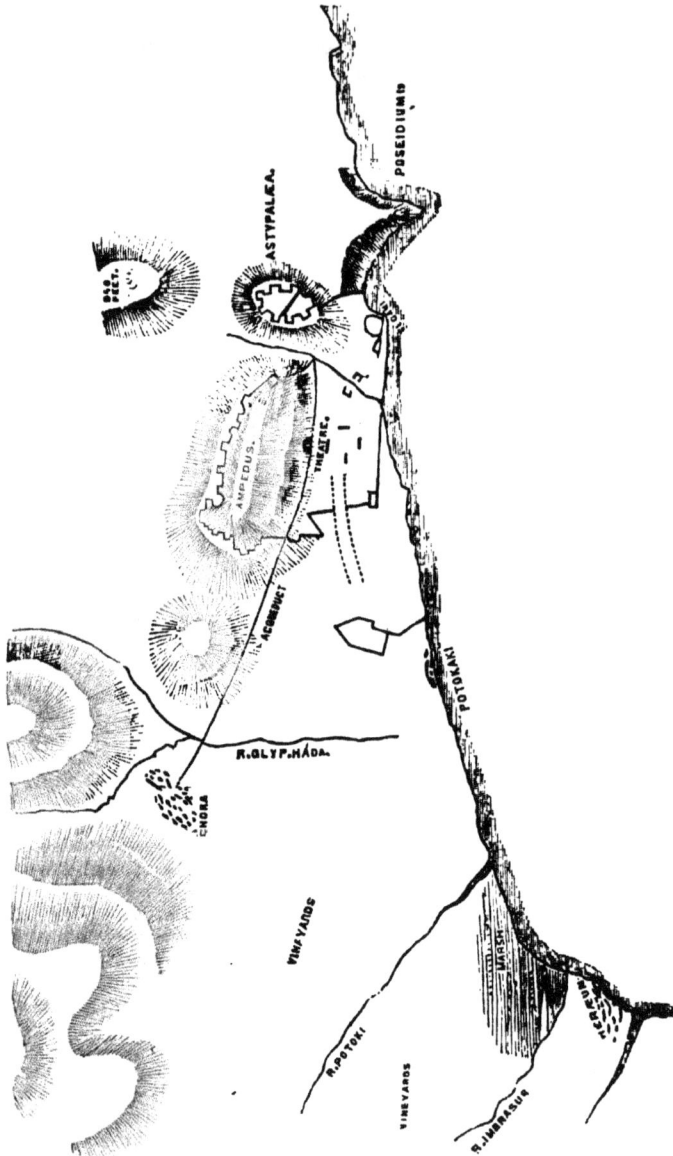

Plan of Samos.

gave it to the Lacedæmonians, who on receiving it took their departure.[3]

This was the first expedition into Asia of the Lacedæmonian Dorians.[4]

57. The Samians who had fought against Polycrates, when they knew that the Lacedæmonians were about to forsake them, left Samos themselves, and sailed to Siphnos.[5] They happened to be in want of money ; and the Siphnians at that time were at the height of their greatness, no islanders having so much wealth as they.   There were mines of gold and silver in their country, and of so rich a yield, that from a tithe of the ores the Siphnians furnished out a treasury at Delphi which was on a par with the grandest there.[6]   What the mines yielded was divided year by year among the citizens.   At the time when they formed the treasury, the Siphnians consulted the oracle, and

[3] This tale may have been false, yet it is not without its value. It shows the general opinion of the corruptibility of the Spartans. The peculiar attractions possessed by the *vetitum nefas* may account for the greater openness of the Spartans to bribery than the other Greeks. Traces of this national characteristic appear in other parts of Herodotus's history; for instance, in the story of Mæandrius (iii. 148), in that of Cleomenes (v. 51) and in that of Leotychidas (vi. 72). It becomes more marked in Thucydides, where we find that Plistoanax was banished for receiving bribes from Pericles (v. 16); that Pausanias made sure that he would be able to obtain an acquittal by bribing his judges (i. 131); and that all the commanders on the Spartan side took bribes from Tissaphernes, except Hermocrates of Syracuse (viii. 45). Other writers add similar traits—as Plutarch (Lysand. c. 16), who tells us that Gylippus was accused of embezzlement, and Aristotle (Polit. ii. vi.), who mentions that certain Ephors in his own time, in return for a bribe, were willing to have ruined the city. Finally, it seems to have been generally recognised through Greece that avarice and corruptibility were among the chief failings of the Spartan character. (See Plat. Alc. i. p. 122 ; Aristoph. Pax. 600–625 ; Aristot. Pol. ii. vi.)

[4] These words are emphatic. They mark the place which this expedition occupies in the mind of Herodotus. It is an aggression of the Greeks upon ASIA, and therefore a passage in the history of the great quarrel between Persia and Greece, for all Asia is the King's (i. 4). Indeed, it is probable that Polycrates, though really independent, was in *nominal* subjection to Persia. This is implied both in the statement (i. 169), that "*the Ionians of the islands* gave themselves up to Cyrus," and in the request of Polycrates (iii. 44) that Cambyses "would not omit to ask aid from Samos." Cambyses was only collecting troops from his subjects.

[5] Siphnos (the modern *Sifanto*) is one of the western Cyclades. It is situated in the 37th parallel of latitude, a little south of the direct course from Samos to Hermione. Lead was still abundant in the island in the time of Tournefort (Voyage du Levant, tom. i. p. 174), but the gold and silver mines had failed before the time of Pausanias (x. xi. § 2). Ross found traces of copper and iron about the galleries leading to the old mines which are in the neighbourhood of the chapel of St. Sostis (Inselreise, vol. i. p. 141). He also noticed a hard lead-like metal—"ein schweres bleiähnliches metall" (ib. 140). Bochart derives the name Siphnos from the Hebrew צָפַן, "recondere, thesaurizare" (Phaleg. i. xiv. p. 413). He considers that the first settlers were Phœnicians.

[6] Pausanias, in the second century A. C., saw this treasury (l. s. c.). He relates that the mines were submerged because the Siphnians, from avarice, ceased to pay the tithe of the ores to Delphi. The same account is given by Suidas (v. Σίφνιοι). Ross thinks the fact of the submersion highly probable (vol. i. p. 141).

asked whether their good things would remain to them many years. The Pytheness made answer as follows:—

> "When the Prytanies' seat shines white[1] in the island of Siphnos,
> White-browed all the forum—need then of a true seer's wisdom—
> Danger will threat from a wooden host, and a herald in scarlet."

Now about this time the forum of the Siphnians and their townhall or prytaneum had been adorned with Parian marble.[8]

58. The Siphnians, however, were unable to understand the oracle, either at the time when it was given, or afterwards on the arrival of the Samians. For these last no sooner came to anchor off the island than they sent one of their vessels, with an ambassage on board, to the city. All ships in these early times were painted with vermilion;[9] and this was what the Pytheness had meant when she told them to beware of danger "from a wooden host, and a herald in scarlet." So the ambassadors came ashore and besought the Siphnians to lend them ten talents, but the Siphnians refused, whereupon the Samians began to plunder their lands. Tidings of this reached the Siphnians, who straightway sallied forth to save their crops; then a battle was fought, in which the Siphnians suffered defeat, and many of their number were cut off from the city by the Samians, after which these latter forced the Siphnians to give them a hundred talents.

59. With this money they bought of the Hermionians the island of Hydrea,[1] off the coast of the Peloponnese, and this

---

[1] The mention of whiteness here, and the expression "*then*," show that the attack was to be made before the Siphnians had had time to colour their buildings. In Herodotus's time they were evidently painted, but "*then*" they had merely the natural hue of the white marble. The Greek custom of painting their monuments was common from the earliest to the latest times, and traces of colour are found on the Parthenon and other buildings. At first they were covered with painted stucco; and when marble took its place it received the same coloured ornaments for which it was as well suited as its less durable predecessor.—[G. W.]

[8] This is the first known instance of the use of Parian marble in ornamental building. It was later, though perhaps not by many years, that the Alcmæonidæ, having undertaken the contract for rebuilding the temple of Delphi, faced the whole with Parian marble instead of common stone (vide infra, v. 62). The vicinity of Paros to Siphnos (about 20 miles) may account for its earlier use there than elsewhere.

[9] Yet Homer almost invariably speaks of "black ships" (νῆες μέλαιναι). Perhaps, however, there is no contradiction here. For Homer's ships are φοινικοπάρηοι (Od. xi. 124, xxiii. 272) or μιλτοπάρηοι (Il. ii. 637, Od. ix. 125), "crimson-cheeked," or "*vermilion*-cheeked." It would seem that while the hull of the vessel was in the main black, being probably covered with pitch or some similar substance, the sides above the water, which Homer called the "cheeks" of the ship, were red. Herodotus may not mean more than this.

[1] Hydrea retains its name almost unchanged in the modern "Hydra," an island about twelve miles long, and only two or three broad, off the coast of the Argolic peninsula. As it is bare and produces nothing, it could only be of value to a nautical people. At present its inhabitants, the Hydriots, are accounted the best sailors in the Levant

they gave in trust to the Trœzenians,[2] to keep for them, while they themselves went on to Crete, and founded the city of Cydonia. They had not meant, when they sat sail, to settle there, but only to drive out the Zacynthians from the island. However they rested at Cydonia,[3] where they flourished greatly for five years. It was they who built the various temples that may still be seen at that place, and among them the fane of Dictyna.[4] But in the sixth year they were attacked by the Eginetans, who beat them in a sea-fight, and, with the help of the Cretans, reduced them all to slavery. The beaks of their ships, which carried the figure of a wild boar, they sawed off and laid them up in the temple of Minerva in Egina. The Eginetans took part against the Samians on account of an ancient grudge, since the Samians had first, when Amphicrates was king of Samos,[5] made war on them and done great harm to their island, suffering, however, much damage also themselves. Such was the reason which moved the Eginetans to make this attack.[6]

60. I have dwelt the longer on the affairs of the Samians, because three of the greatest works in all Greece were made by them. One is a tunnel, under a hill one hundred and fifty fathoms high, carried entirely through the base of the hill, with a mouth at either end.[7] The length of the cutting is seven furlongs

---

[2] Trœzen and Hermione, though contained within the district commonly called Argolis, yet appear always as independent states. Trœzen is mentioned among the confederated Greeks at Artemisium (Herod. viii. 1), and again at Salamis, where Hermione likewise appears (ib. 43). Both occur among the allies of the Corinthians in their war with Corcyra, B. C. 436 (Thucyd. i. 27); and both seem, although not expressly named, to have been allies of Sparta in the Poloponnesian war. Hence the ravaging of their territory by Pericles in the second year (ib. ii. 56). Hermione is probably the modern "Kastri." (See Col. Leake's Morea, vol. ii. p. 461.) The ruins of Trœzen are near *Dhamalá*, opposite Calauria (ibid. p. 446).

[3] Cydonia lay on the northern coast of Crete, towards the western end of the island (long. 24° East). The modern town of *Khania* is near the site.

[4] Dictyna, or Dictynna, was the same as Britomartis, an ancient goddess of the Cretans. The Greeks usually regarded her as identical with their Artemis (Diana). See Callimach. Hymn. ad Dian. 190; Diod. Sic. v. 76; Pausanias, II. xxx.; Solinus. Polyhist. xi. p. 21, &c. Britomartis is said to have meant "dulcis virgo" (Solin. l. s. c.). No satisfactory account has been given of the name Dictynna.

[5] It is impossible to fix the date of the reign of Amphicrates. Panofka (Sam. Res, p. 26) supposes that it could scarcely be earlier than the 25th Olympiad, B. C. 670.

[6] If we may believe Strabo (viii. p. 545), the Eginetans themselves colonized Cydonia, so that their attack would seem to have been caused by commercial jealousy.

[7] One of the mouths of this tunnel, that to the N. W. of the present harbour, had been already discovered, but it remained little known till M. Guerin a short time ago rediscovered it, and cleared out the sand and stones to the distance of about 540 paces. M. Guerin also commenced some excavations in search of the site of the temple of Juno, but was stopped by the proprietor of the land. Excavations of Greek remains are difficult, whether belonging to Turks or Greeks, and at Delphi every opposition was made even to my copying the inscriptions there.—[G. W.]

—the height and width are each eight feet. Along the whole course there is a second cutting, twenty cubits deep and three feet broad, whereby water is brought, through pipes, from an abundant source into the city. The architect of this tunnel was Eupalinus, son of Naustrophus, a Megarian. Such is the first of their great works : the second is a mole in the sea, which goes all round the harbour, near twenty fathoms deep, and in length above two furlongs. The third is a temple ; the largest of all the temples known to us,[8] whereof Rhœcus,[9] son of Phileus, a Samian, was first architect. Because of these works I have dwelt the longer on the affairs of Samos.[10]

61. While Cambyses, son of Cyrus, after losing his senses, still lingered in Egypt, two Magi,[1] brothers, revolted against him. One of them had been left in Persia by Cambyses as comptroller of his household ; and it was he who began the revolt. Aware that Smerdis was dead, and that his death was hid, and known to few of the Persians, while most believed that he was still alive, he laid his plan, and made a bold stroke for the crown. He had a brother—the same of whom I spoke before as his partner in the revolt—who happened greatly to resemble Smerdis

[8] Herodotus means no doubt "the largest *Greek* temple," since the Egyptian temples were of much greater size. Though so little of it remains, only one column now standing, the plan of the Heræum has been ascertained, and shows a length of 346, and a breadth of 189 feet. (See the next page.) This greatly exceeds all the other temples of Asia Minor whose dimensions are known, except that of Ephesus, which was of later date (suprà, ii. 148, note [9]). The Olympium at Athens, and the Doric temples at Agrigentum and Selinus, are longer than the Samian Heræum, but their area is not so great. (See Leake's Asia Minor, Additional Notes, pp. 346–352.) The architecture of the Heræum is Ionic.

[9] According to Pausanias (VIII. xiv. §5), and Pliny (Hist. Nat. xxxv. xii. §43), this Rhœcus was joint-inventor with Theodore the Samian of the art of casting statues in bronze. He also built, in conjunction with Theodore and Smilis, the great labyrinth at Lemnos (Plin. H. N. xxxvi. 13, and compare xxxiv. 8.)

[10] It is probable that these are the ἔργα Πολυκράτεια of Aristotle (Polit. v. . xi); for even if Rhœcus be rightly assigned to the 8th century B. C., which is uncertain, yet the temple, which he planned and commenced, may not have been completed till the time of Polycrates. Aristotle looks upon these works as marks of the grinding tyranny under which the Samians groaned at this period, but it may be questioned whether they were really of an oppressive character. The policy of Polycrates, like that of Pisistratus, seems to have been to conciliate the masses. Duris related that when any of his common soldiers fell in battle, he assigned the care of their bereaved mothers to some of the richer citizens, telling them to regard them as their own mothers (Fr. 49). And his works were doubtless in great part to give employment to the poorer classes. (Compare the cases of Pisistratus, Pericles, Appius Claudius Cæcus, and both Napoleons.)

[1] The Behistun Inscription mentions but a single Magus, and Ctesias (Persic. Exc. § 10) knows of only one. Still it would be rash here to reject the story of Herodotus, which is quite compatible with the brief narrative of the inscription. Dionysius of Miletus appears to have mentioned both brothers; at least we are told by a Scholiast that he called Patizeithes by the name of Panzuthes. He was an older writer than Herodotus. See the Introductory Essay, ch. ii. p. 37.

the son of Cyrus,[2] whom Cambyses his brother had put to death. And not only was this brother of his like Smerdis in person, but he also bore the selfsame name, to wit Smerdis.[3] Patizeithes, the other magus, having persuaded him that he would carry the whole business through, took him and made him sit ·upon the royal throne.[4] Having so done, he sent heralds through all the land, to Egypt and elsewhere, to make proclamation to the

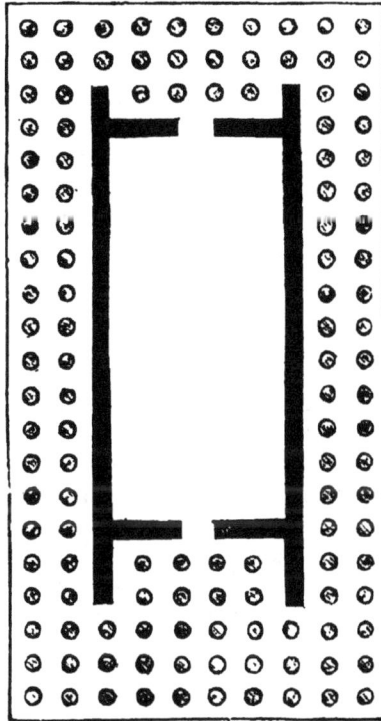

[2] So Ctesias (l. s. c.), and the personation, which is placed beyond a doubt by the inscriptions, would imply a certain amount of likeness. But the subsequent concealment (ch. 68), if true, would show that the likeness was not very close.

[3] Here Herodotus was, most certainly, mistaken. The pretender's name was Gomates (Gaumâta; see Behist. Inscript. Col. i. par. 11, § 2, et seqq.), a trace of which (the *only* trace in all antiquity) may be found in the *Cometes* of Trogus Pompeius (ap. Justin. i. ix.) This author, however, assigns the name to the wrong brother. The Sphendadates of Ctesias is not a name but a Zend title, *Spĕñtadâta*, "given to the Holy One." (See Col. Rawlinson's Memoir on the Beh. Ins. vol. ii. p. 136; and compare Mithradates, "given to Mithra.")

[4] That the seizure of the supreme power by the Pseudo-Smerdis met with no opposition at the time, is confirmed by the Behistun inscription, which tells us that Gomates no sooner came forward and declared himself to be Smerdis (Bardius), son of Cyrus, than "the whole state became rebellious—from Cambyses it went over to that Bardius, both Persia and Media, and the other provinces" (Col. i. par. 11, §§ 6, 7; cf. also the 12th and 13th paragraphs).

troops that henceforth they were to obey Smerdis the son of Cyrus, and not Cambyses.

62. The other heralds therefore made proclamation as they were ordered, and likewise the herald whose place it was to proceed into Egypt. He, when he reached Agbatana in Syria,[5] finding Cambyses and his army there, went straight into the middle of the host, and standing forth before them all, made the proclamation which Patizeithes the Magus·had commanded. Cambyses no sooner heard him, than believing that what the herald said was true, and imagining that he had been betrayed by Prexaspes (who, he supposed, had not put Smerdis to death when sent into Persia for that purpose), he turned his eyes full upon Prexaspes, and said, "Is this the way, Prexaspes, that thou didst my errand?" "Oh! my liege," answered the other, "there is no truth in the tidings that Smerdis thy brother has revolted against thee, nor hast thou to fear in time to come any quarrel, great or small, with that man. With my own hands I wrought thy will on him, and with my own hands I buried him. If of a truth the dead can leave their graves, expect Astyages the Mede to rise and fight against thee ; but if the course of nature be the same as formerly, then be sure no ill will ever come upon thee from this quarter. Now therefore my counsel is, that we send in pursuit of the herald, and strictly question him who it was that charged him to bid us obey king Smerdis."

63. When Prexaspes had so spoken, and Cambyses had approved his words, the herald was forthwith pursued, and brought back to the king. Then Prexaspes said to him, "Sirrah, thou bear'st us a message, sayst thou, from Smerdis, son of Cyrus. Now answer truly, and go thy way scathless. Did Smerdis have thee to his presence and give thee thy orders, or hadst

---

[5] The existence of a Syrian Agbatana is very questionable. Stephen of Byzantium (ad voc.) quotes Demetrius as mentioning that there were two Agbatanas, a Median, and a Syrian; and Pliny (Hist. Nat. v. 19) says that the town Carmel was anciently called Ecbatana. But no writer except Herodotus knows of an actually existing Agbatana in Syria. There was indeed a town in Syria called by the Greeks Batansea (Joseph. Ant. ii. ix.), or Betana (Judith i. 9), the Basan of the Jews, which gave name to the whole district east and south-east of Galilee. This is the Βαταγέαι of Steph. Byz. It was the ancient capital of the kingdom of Og (Num. xxi. 88). Hyde (Relig. Vet. Pers. App. p. 416) regards the notion of a Syrian Ecbatana as arising out of this name. He supposes the prefix Ec- or Ag- to represent the Arabian article El or Al. Ecbatana and Agbatana are, he says, corruptions of El-Batana and Al-Batana.

Mr. Blakesley's identification of the Syrian Agbatana with Hamath or Hamah—based on the statement of Stephen that it was called Epiphania, which was a name of Hamath—is very uncertain. Many towns may have been called Epiphania.

The name Batansea still remains in the modern appellation of the district, which is El-Bataniyeh. Here Mr. Graham has recently discovered a vast number of ancient cities, the houses in which are almost perfect.

thou them from one of his officers ? " The herald answered,
" Truly I have not set eyes on Smerdis son of Cyrus, since the
day when king Cambyses led the Persians into Egypt. The
man who gave me my orders was the Magus that Cambyses left
in charge of the household ; but he said that Smerdis son of
Cyrus sent you the message." In all this the herald spoke
nothing but the strict truth. Then Cambyses said thus to
Prexaspes :—" Thou art free from all blame, Prexaspes, since, as
a right good man, thou hast not failed to do the thing which
I commanded. But tell me now, which of the Persians can have
taken the name of Smerdis, and revolted from me ? " " I think,
my liege," he answered, " that I apprehend the whole business.
The men who have risen in revolt against thee are the two
Magi, Patizeithes, who was left comptroller of thy household,
and his brother, who is named Smerdis."

64. Cambyses no sooner heard the name of Smerdis than he
was struck with the truth of Prexaspes' words, and the fulfil-
ment of his own dream—the dream, I mean, which he had in
former days, when one appeared to him in his sleep and told
him that Smerdis sat upon the royal throne, and with his head
touched the heavens.[6] So when he saw that he had needlessly
slain his brother Smerdis, he wept and bewailed his loss : after
which, smarting with vexation as he thought of all his ill luck,
he sprang hastily upon his steed, meaning to march his army
with all haste to Susa against the Magus. As he made his
spring, the button of his sword-sheath fell off, and the bared
point entered his thigh, wounding him exactly where he had
himself once wounded the Egyptian god Apis.[7] Then Cambyses, feeling that he had got his death-wound, inquired the
name of the place where he was, and was answered ' Agbatana.'
Now before this it had been told him by the oracle at Buto that
he should end his days at Agbatana. He, however, had understood the Median Agbatana, where all his treasures were, and
had thought that he should die there at a good old age, but the
oracle meant Agbatana in Syria.[8] So when Cambyses heard

[6] Suprà, ch. 30.
[7] The details here are suspicious, since they evidently come from the Egyptian
priests, who wish to represent the death of Cambyses as a judgment upon him for
his impiety. Ctesias related that Cambyses wounded himself with a knife, with
which he was carving a piece of wood for his amusement (Excerpt. Persic. § 10).
Both writers represent the wound as accidental, and both agree as to its situation.
The words of the Behistun Inscription cause a suspicion that the death may have
been a suicide. Cambyses, it is said, after the whole empire had revolted, " self-
wishing to die, died" (uvâmarshiyush amariyata, Col. par. i. 11, § 10).
[8] Beloe (vol. ii. p. 227) compares with this tale the tradition of our own Henry
IV., who had been warned prophetically that he was to die at Jerusalem, and who

the name of the place, the double shock that he had received, from the revolt of the Magus and from his wound, brought him back to his senses. And he understood now the true meaning of the oracle, and said, " Here then Cambyses, son of Cyrus, is doomed to die."

65. At this time he said no more ; but twenty days afterwards he called to his presence all the chief Persians who were with the army, and addressed them as follows :—" Persians, needs must I tell you now what hitherto I have striven with the greatest care to keep concealed. When I was in Egypt I saw in my sleep a vision, which would that I had never beheld ! I thought a messenger came to me from my home, and said that Smerdis sate upon the royal throne, and with his head touched the heavens. Then I feared to be cast from my throne by Smerdis my brother, and I did what was more hasty than wise. Ah ! truly, do what they may, it is impossible for men to turn aside the coming fate. I, in my folly, sent Prexaspes to Susa to put my brother to death. So this great woe was accomplished, and I then lived without fear, never imagining that, after Smerdis was dead, I need dread revolt from any other. But herein I had quite mistaken what was about to happen, and so I slew my brother without any need,[9] and nevertheless have lost my crown. For it was Smerdis the Magus, and not Smerdis my brother, of whose rebellion God forewarned me by the vision. The deed is done, however, and Smerdis, son of Cyrus, be sure is lost to you. The Magi have the royal power—Patizeithes, whom I left at Susa to overlook my household, and Smerdis his brother. There was one who would have been bound beyond all others to avenge the wrongs I have suffered from these Magians, but he, alas ! has perished by a horrid fate, deprived of life by those nearest and dearest to him. In his default, nothing now remains for me but to tell you, O Persians, what I would wish to have done after I have breathed my last. Therefore, in the name of the gods that watch over our royal house, I charge you all, and especially such of you as are Achæmenids, that ye do not tamely allow the kingdom to go back to the Medes.[10] Recover it one way or another, by

---

died in the Jerusalem chamber at Westminster. Shakspeare notices this story (2nd Part of Henry IV. Act iv. Sc. iv.

[9] Here for once Schweighæuser has, I think, mistaken the sense. He renders οὐδὲν δέον, "præter jus et fas ; " but surely it is equivalent to the μάτην of ch. 64. What vexes Cambyses is not that he killed his brother unjustly, but that he did it without any need.

[10] Heeren (Asiatic Nations, vol. i. p. 346) and Mr. Grote (Hist. of Greece, vol. iv. pp. 298–302) accept the representation of Herodotus, that this was a transfer of

force or fraud ; by fraud, if it is by fraud that they have seized on it ; by force, if force has helped them in their enterprise. Do this, and then may your land bring you forth fruit abundantly, and your wives bear children, and your herds increase, and freedom be your portion for ever : but do it not—make no brave struggle to regain the kingdom—and then my curse be on you, and may the opposite of all these things happen to you —and not only so, but may you, one and all, perish at the last by such a fate as mine ! " Then Cambyses, when he left speaking, bewailed his whole misfortune from beginning to end.

66. Whereupon the Persians, seeing their king weep, rent the garments that they had on, and uttered lamentable cries ;[11] after which, as the bone presently grew carious, and the limb gangrened, Cambyses, son of Cyrus, died. He had reigned in all seven years and five months,[1] and left no issue behind him, male or female. The Persians who had heard his words, put no faith in anything that he said concerning the Magi having the royal power ; but believed that he spoke out of hatred towards Smerdis, and had invented the tale of his death to cause the whole Persian race to rise up in arms against him. Thus they were convinced that it was Smerdis the son of Cyrus who had rebelled and now sate on the throne. For Prexaspes stoutly denied that he had slain Smerdis, since it was not safe for him, after Cambyses was dead, to allow that a son of Cyrus had met death at his hands.

67. Thus then Cambyses died, and the Magus now reigned in security, and passed himself off for Smerdis the son of Cyrus. And so went by the seven months which were wanting to complete the eighth year of Cambyses.[2] His subjects, while his

sovereignty from the Persians to the Medes. The Behistun Inscription proves that it was not so. Gomates the Magian arose from Pissiachada, a town which it is almost certain was in Persia proper. His cause was first adopted in Persia. And Darius expresses his surprise that "neither Persian, *nor Median*, nor any one of his own family dispossessed him" (Col. i. par. 13, § 2). See Appendix, Essay ii., "On the Magian Revolution and the Reign of the Pseudo-Smerdis."

[11] Mr. Blakesley (not. ad loc.) well compares the picture in the Persæ of Æschylus, lines 1017–1055.

[1] Vide infra, ch. 67. That the reigns of Cambyses and the Pseudo-Smerdis occupied eight years, more than seven of which belonged to Cambyses, is certain from the Canon of Ptolemy, which gives exactly eight years between the death of Cyrus and the accession of Darius. The reign of the Pseudo-Smerdis is omitted from the Canon, because no reign is given which occupied only a fraction of a year. Nineteen years are assigned to Cambyses by Clemens Alex. (Strom. i. p. 895); and 18 by Ctesias (Excerpt. Persic. § 12), unless this is a wrong reading (IH for H). Manetho probably gave the true time, eight years. (Compare Euseb. Chron. Can. I. xx., and Euseb. ap. Sync. p. 76, with Africanus ap. Syncell. p. 75.)

[2] Eusebius is clearly in error when he reckons the reign of the Magi as additional to the eight years of Cambyses (Chron. Can. ii. p. 835). His authority, Manetho, did not do so.

reign lasted, received great benefits from him, insomuch that, when he died, all the dwellers in Asia mourned his loss exceedingly, except only the Persians. For no sooner did he come to the throne than forthwith he sent round to every nation under his rule, and granted them freedom from war-service and from taxes for the space of three years.

68. In the eighth month, however, it was discovered who he was in the mode following. There was a man called Otanes, the son of Pharnaspes,[3] who for rank and wealth was equal to the greatest of the Persians.[4] This Otanes was the first to suspect that the Magus was not Smerdis the son of Cyrus, and to surmise moreover who he really was. He was led to guess the truth by the king never quitting the citadel,[5] and never calling before him any of the Persian noblemen. As soon therefore as his suspicions were aroused, he adopted the following measures: —One of his daughters, who was called Phædima, had been married to Cambyses, and was taken to wife, together with the rest of Cambyses' wives, by the Magus. To this daughter Otanes sent a message, and inquired of her, " who it was whose bed she shared,—was it Smerdis the son of Cyrus, or was it some

---

[3] Called in the Behistun Inscription *Utána*, son of *Thukhra*, i. e. Otanes, son of *Socris* (Col. iv. par. 18, § 5).

[4] Herodotus probably regarded Otanes as brother of Cassandané (supra, ch. 2), and therefore uncle of Cambyses and Smerdis. This appears to have been a mistake. But there is reason to believe that Otanes was really descended from Pharnaces, king of Cappadocia, who married Atossa, sister of Cambyses, the great-grandfather of Cyrus the Great. The genealogy is thus given by Diodorus:—

Pharnaces m. Atossa, sister of Cambyses the Persian.
|
Gallus
|
Smerdis
|
Artamnes
|
Anaphas (i. e. Otanes), one of the seven conspirators.

There is no doubt that the Anaphas of Diodorus is the Otanes of Herodotus. He is plainly identical with the Onaphas of Ctesias, placed by him *at the head* of his list. And Anaphas or Onophas was a family-name in the house of Otanes, as appears from Book vii. ch. 62. The two names are indeed perpetually confounded. See Col. Rawlinson's note on the Persian inscription at Behistun (Journal of Asiatic Society, vol. xii. part ii. p. xiii.).

[5] By the citadel (ἀκρόπολις) it is uncertain whether Herodotus means the citadel proper, or only the royal palace at *Susa* (v. infr. ch. 70), called by the Greeks "the Memnonium," which he speaks of below (v. 54) as τὰ βασιλήϊα τὰ Μεμνόνια (cf. Strab. xv. p. 1031, ἡ δὲ ἀκρόπολις ἐκαλεῖτο Μεμνόνειον), and which was no doubt strongly fortified. As this occupied a portion of the modern mound of Sus (see note on Book v. ch. 49), it might be considered as included in the acropolis. Col. Rawlinson thus describes the great mound:—"As I approached the ruins I was particularly struck with the extraordinary height of this mound, which *appears to have constituted the fort of the city*. By a rough calculation with the sextant, I found the height of the lower platform to be between 80 and 90 feet, and that of

other man ? "   Phædima in reply declared "she did not know—Smerdis the son of Cyrus she had never seen, and so she could not tell whose bed she shared."   Upon this Otanes sent a second time, and said, "If thou dost not know Smerdis son of Cyrus thyself, ask queen Atossa who it is with whom ye both live—she cannot fail to know her own brother."   To this the daughter made answer, "I can neither get speech with Atossa, nor with any of the women who lodge in the palace.   For no sooner did this man, be he who he may, obtain the kingdom, than he parted us from one another, and gave us all separate chambers."

69. This made the matter seem still more plain to Otanes. Nevertheless he sent a third message to his daughter in these words following :—"Daughter, thou art of noble blood—thou wilt not shrink from a risk which thy father bids thee encounter. If this fellow be not Smerdis the son of Cyrus, but the man whom I think him to be, his boldness in taking thee to be his wife, and lording it over the Persians, must not be allowed to pass unpunished.   Now therefore do as I command—when next he passes the night with thee, wait till thou art sure he is fast

the great mound to be about 165 feet.   The platform, which is square, I estimated to measure two miles and a half; the mound, which I paced, measured 1100 yards round the base, and 850 round the summit.   The slope is very steep—so steep, indeed, as only to admit of ascent by two pathways."   (Notes on a March from Zohab to Khuzistan, Journal of Geograph. Society, vol. ix. part i. p. 68.)   Lieut. Glascott

found the height of the great mound or true acropolis to be 119 feet, and the circumference of the summit 2850 feet.   (Loftus's Chaldæa, p. 343).   The subjoined representation of the mound is taken from the work of Col. Chesney (Euphrat. Exped. vol. ii. p. 356).   The great strength of the Susian acropolis appears from Polybius (v. 48, § 14).

asleep, and then feel for his ears.   If thou findest him to have
ears, then believe him to be Smerdis the son of Cyrus, but if he
has none, know him for Smerdis the Magian."   Phædima returned for answer, "It would be a great risk.   If he was without ears, and caught her feeling for them, she well knew he
would make away with her—nevertheless she would venture."
So Otanes got his daughter's promise that she would do as he
desired.   Now Smerdis the Magian had had his ears cut off in
the lifetime of Cyrus son of Cambyses, as a punishment for a
crime of no slight heinousness.⁶   Phædima therefore, Otanes'
daughter, bent on accomplishing what she had promised her
father, when her turn came, and she was taken to the bed of
the Magus (in Persia a man's wives sleep with him in their
turns⁷), waited till he was sound asleep, and then felt for his
ears.   She quickly perceived that he had no ears ; and of this,
as soon as day dawned, she sent word to her father.

70.   Then Otanes took to him two of the chief Persians, As-
pathines⁸ and Gobryas,⁹ men whom it was most advisable to
trust in such a matter, and told them everything.   Now they
had already of themselves suspected how the matter stood.
When Otanes therefore laid his reasons before them they at once
came into his views ; and it was agreed that each of the three
should take as companion in the work the Persian in whom he
placed the greatest confidence.   Then Otanes chose ¹ Inta-

---

⁶ See, below, the story of Zopyrus, which implies that such mutilation was an
ordinary punishment (infra, ch. 154–158).   Brisson (de Regn. Pers. ii. pp. 334–5)
has collected a number of instances, extending from the age of Cyrus to that of
Julian, which sufficiently prove this.   A more important testimony than any of his
is that of the Behistun Inscription (Col. ii. par. 13, § 4), which shows us that this
punishment was inflicted by Darius on the great Median rebel Phraortes.   It is
still practised at the present day both in Turkey and Persia.

⁷ Compare Esther ii. 12.   "Now when every maid's *turn was come* to go in to
king Ahasuerus, after she had been twelve months, according to the manner of the
women," &c.

⁸ Aspathines seems to represent the *Aspachaná* of the Nakhsh-i-Rustam inscription, who was not one of the seven conspirators, but was the quiver-bearer of Darius.
The name given by the inscription in the place of Aspathines is Ardomanes (*Ardumanish*).   This is the only name out of the seven in which Herodotus was wrong.
Ctesias was wrong in every name but two (Hydarnes and Darius).

⁹ Gobryas, the *Gaubaruwa* of the monuments, appears to have been the bow-
bearer of Darius.   At least a person of the name is represented in that capacity at
Nakhsh-i-Rustam.   Such an office might, I think, have been held by a Persian of
very exalted rank.   He is joined on the monument, as here, with Aspathines (*Aspachaná*) the quiver-bearer.   His father's name (like his son's) was Mardonius
(*Marduniya*).

¹ Herodotus is here more exact than either Ctesias or Æschylus.   Ctesias calls
this conspirator Artaphernes (Excerpt. Persic. § 14) ; Æschylus, Artaphrenes (Pers.
782, Blomf.).   The inscription gives the name as *Vidafrand*, or (in the Scythian
copy) *Vindaparna*, which would be very sufficiently rendered by the Greek
Ἰνταφέρνης.   It is worthy of notice that in the Behistun Inscription Intaphernes is

phernes, Gobryas Megabyzus,[2] and Aspathines Hydarnes.[3] Aftei the number had thus become six, Darius, the son of Hystaspes, arrived at Susa from Persia, whereof his father was governor.[4] On his coming it seemed good to the six to take him likewise into their counsels.[5]

71. After this, the men, being now seven in all,[6] met together to exchange oaths, and hold discourse with one another. And when it came to the turn of Darius to speak his mind, he

placed *at the head* of the list of conspirators. He may therefore be regarded as probably the chief, next to Darius. Hence we may understand why Æschylus ascribes the killing of the pseudo-Smerdis to him—

$$\tau\grave{o}\nu\ \delta\grave{e}\ \sigma\grave{v}\nu\ \delta\acute{o}\lambda\varphi$$
$$\text{'Α}ρταφρένης\ ἔκτεινεν\ ἐσθλὸς\ ἐν\ δόμοις,$$
$$ξύν\ ἀνδράσιν\ φίλοισιν,\ οἷς\ τόδ'\ ἦν\ χρέος.$$

(Pers. 781-2.)

We may also suspect a deeper meaning in the narrative of his death (infra, ch. 118) than appears upon the surface. (See note ad loc.)

[2] In the Persian, *Bagabuksha*.

[3] *Vidarna* in the inscription; in Ctesias, Idernes; Indarnes in Plutarch. He was employed by Darius on occasion of the Median revolt, and gained a great victory over the Medes in their own country (Behist. Ins., Col. ii. par. 6, §§ 4-11). He was afterwards appointed by Xerxes to the command of the Asiatic coast (infra, vii. 135). One of his sons, named (like his father) Hydarnes, commanded the Immortals in the army of Xerxes (ib. 83). Another, Sisamnes, led the Arian contingent (ib. 66). According to Strabo, "the descendants of Hydarnes became kings of Armenia, and reigned there from the time of Darius to that of Antiochus the Great" (xi. p. 771).

[4] The curious fact, that Darius became king in his father's lifetime, is confirmed by the great inscription, where we find Hystaspes employed as one of his son's generals in subduing the rebellious Parthians (Col. ii. par. 16). He appears, however, rather as satrap of Parthia than Persia.

[5] Darius represents the matter somewhat differently. According to him, "No one dared to say anything concerning Gomates the Magian, *till he arrived*" (Beh. Inscr., Col. i. par. 13, § 6). But Darius would be apt to exaggerate in his own favour.

[6] Writers of great eminence (Niebuhr, Vorträge, vol. i. p. 158; Heeren, As. Nat. vol. i. p. 348) have seen in this conspiracy of the Seven Persians a movement of the nation (National-bewegung) under the leadership of the seven great heads of tribes or families, and not a mere casual junction of individuals. Niebuhr maintains that throughout the whole Persian history there were seven families who had a rank greatly beyond all the rest (l. s. c.). And certainly there is a passage in the book of Ezra (vii. 14), and another in the book of Esther (i. 14), which favour the notion of seven princes or councillors who stood in some very special relation to the king. But if the royal house of the Achæmenidæ was one of the seven great families, as the king would be the head of that house, we should have expected *six* princes or councillors. And after the disgrace of Intaphernes (infra, 118-9) we should have looked to find but five. It may be questioned, therefore, whether the passages in Ezra and Esther lend any countenance to the theory of Niebuhr. The Behistun Inscription is thoroughly confirmatory of the view of the matter taken by Herodotus. Not only is no mention made of the families of the six conspirators, but they are distinctly spoken of as lending their *individual* aid to Darius. "On the 10th day of the month Bagayadish, then it was, with *my faithful men*, I slew that Gomates" (Col. i. par. 13, § 9). "These are *the men who alone were there* when I slew Gomates—these men *alone laboured* in my service" (Col. iv. par. 18, §§ 2, 3.)

said as follows :—"Methought no one but I knew that Smerdis, the son of Cyrus, was not now alive, and that Smerdis the Magian ruled over us ; on this account I came hither with speed, to compass the death of the Magian.   But as it seems the matter is known to you all, and not to me only, my judgment is that we should act at once, and not any longer delay.   For to do so were not well."   Otanes spoke upon this :—" Son of Hystaspes," said he, " thou art the child of a brave father, and seemest likely to show thyself as bold a gallant as he.   Beware, however, of rash haste in this matter ; do not hurry so, but proceed with soberness.   We must add to our number ere we adventure to strike the blow."   " Not so," Darius rejoined—" for let all present be well assured, that if the advice of Otanes guide our acts, we shall perish most miserably.   Some one will betray our plot to the Magians for lucre's sake.   Ye ought to have kept the matter to yourselves, and so made the venture ; but as ye have chosen to take others into your secret, and have opened the matter to me, take my advice and make the attempt to-day —or if not, if a single day be suffered to pass by, be sure that I will let no one betray me to the Magian.   I myself will go to him, and plainly denounce you all."

72. Otanes, when he saw Darius so hot, replied, " But if thou wilt force us to action, and not allow a day's delay, tell us, I pray thee, how we shall get entrance into the palace, so as to set upon them.   Guards are placed every where as thou thyself well knowest—for if thou hast not seen, at least thou hast heard tell of them.   How are we to pass these guards, I ask thee ? " " Otanes," answered Darius, " there are many things easy enough in act, which by speech it is hard to explain.   There are also things concerning which speech is easy, but no noble action follows when the speech is done.   As for these guards, ye know well that we shall not find it hard to make our way through them.   Our rank alone would cause them to allow us to enter, —shame and fear alike forbidding them to say us nay.   But besides, I have the fairest plea that can be conceived for gaining admission.   I can say that I have just come from Persia, and have a message to deliver to the king from my father.   An untruth must be spoken, where need requires.   For whether men lie, or say true, it is with one and the same object.   Men lie, because they think to gain by deceiving others ; and speak the truth, because they expect to get something by their true speaking, and to be trusted afterwards in more important matters. Thus, though their conduct is so opposite, the end of both is alike.   If there were no gain to be got, your true-speaking man

would tell untruths as much as your liar, and your liar would tell the truth as much as your true-speaking man.[7]   The door-keeper, who lets us in readily, shall have his guerdon some day or other ; but woe to the man who resists us, he must forthwith be declared an enemy.   Forcing our way past him, we will press in and go straight to our work."

73. After Darius had thus said, Gobryas spoke as follows : —"Dear friends, when will a fitter occasion offer for us to recover the kingdom, or, if we are not strong enough, at least die in the attempt ?   Consider that we Persians are governed by a Median Magus, and one, too, who has had his ears cut off ! Some of you were present when Cambyses lay upon his death-bed—such, doubtless, remember what curses he called down upon the Persians if they made no effort to recover the kingdom. Then, indeed, we paid but little heed to what he said, because we thought he spoke out of hatred to set us against his brother. Now, however, my vote is, that we do as Darius has counselled —march straight in a body to the palace from the place where we now are, and forthwith set upon the Magian."   So Gobryas spake, and the others all approved.

74. While the seven were thus taking counsel together, it so chanced that the following events were happening :—The Magi had been thinking what they had best do, and had resolved for many reasons to make a friend of Prexaspes.   They knew how cruelly he had been outraged by Cambyses, who slew his son with an arrow ;[8] they were also aware that it was by his hand that Smerdis the son of Cyrus fell, and that he was the only person privy to that prince's death ; and they further found him to be held in the highest esteem by all the Persians.   So they called him to them, made him their friend, and bound him by a promise and by oaths to keep silence about the fraud which they were practising upon the Persians, and not discover it to any one ; and they pledged themselves that in this case they would give him thousands of gifts of every sort and kind.[9]   So Prexaspes

---

[7] This elaborate apology for a most justifiable untruth, instead of showing (as Larcher thinks) that veracity was not much regarded in Persia, is strongly indicative of the contrary.   No justification would have been thought necessary, unless in a country where there was almost a superstitious regard for verbal truth.   The speech is of course not to be looked upon as historical, but it is in character—being thoroughly Persian in its sentiment.   The arguments used seem, however, to have come from the mint of the Sophists.   (Compare Plat. Rep. ii. § 3, pp. 359-60; Arist. Eth. v. 9, § 16.)

[8] Vide suprà, ch. 35.

[9] Literally, "ten thousand of every thing;" that is, of every thing which it was customary to give.   Similar expressions occur elsewhere in their strict proper sense (see i. 50, iv. 88, ix. 81, &c.), but here the phrase can only be a strong hyperbole.

agreed ; and the Magi, when they found that they had persuaded him so far, went on to another proposal, and said they would assemble the Persians at the foot of the palace wall, and he should mount one of the towers and harangue them from it, assuring them that Smerdis the son of Cyrus, and none but he, ruled the land.   This they bade him do, because Prexaspes was a man of great weight with his countrymen, and had often declared in public that Smerdis the son of Cyrus was still alive, and denied being his murderer.

75. Prexaspes said he was quite ready to do their will in the matter ; so the Magi assembled the people, and placed Prexaspes upon the top of the tower, and told him to make his speech. Then this man, forgetting of set purpose all that the Magi had entreated him to say, began with Achæmenes, and traced down the descent of Cyrus ; after which, when he came to that king, he recounted all the services that had been rendered by him to the Persians, from whence he went on to declare the truth, which hitherto he had concealed, he said, because it would not have been safe for him to make it known, but now necessity was laid on him to disclose the whole.   Then he told how, forced to it by Cambyses, he had himself taken the life of Smerdis, son of Cyrus, and how that Persia was now ruled by the Magi.   Last of all, with many curses upon the Persians if they did not recover the kingdom, and wreak vengeance on the Magi, he threw himself headlong from the tower into the abyss below.   Such was the end of Prexaspes, a man all his life of high repute among the Persians.[10]

76. And now the seven Persians, having resolved that they would attack the Magi without more delay, first offered prayers to the gods and then set off for the palace, quite unacquainted with what had been done by Prexaspes.   The news of his doings reached them upon their way, when they had accomplished about half the distance.   Hereupon they turned aside out of the road, and consulted together.   Otanes and his party said they must certainly put off the business, and not make the attack when affairs were in such a ferment.   Darius, on the other hand, and his friends, were against any change of plan, and wished to go straight on, and not lose a moment.   Now, as they strove together,

[10] Ctesias transfers this story, with some variations in the details, to a certain Ixabates, one of the chief eunuchs.   Ixabates, according to him, was not the person who killed Smerdis, but being high in the confidence of Cambyses, knew for certain that he had been killed.   After publicly proclaiming the deception, he took refuge in one of the temples, from which he was dragged by the order of the Magus, and beheaded for his temerity.

suddenly there came in sight two pairs of vultures, and seven pairs of hawks, pursuing them, and the hawks tore the vultures both with their claws and bills.   At this sight the seven with one accord came in to the opinion of Darius, and encouraged by the omen hastened on towards the palace.

77. At the gate they were received as Darius had foretold. The guards, who had no suspicion that they came for any ill purpose, and held the chief Persians in much reverence, let them pass without difficulty—it seemed as if they were under the special protection of the gods—none even asked them any question.   When they were now in the great court they fell in with certain of the eunuchs, whose business it was to carry the king's messages, who stopped them and asked what they wanted, while at the same time they threatened the doorkeepers for having let them in.   The seven sought to press on, but the eunuchs would not suffer them.   Then these men, with cheers encouraging one another, drew their daggers, and stabbing those who strove to withstand them, rushed forward to the apartment of the males.

78. Now both the Magi were at this time within, holding counsel upon the matter of Prexaspes.   So when they heard the stir among the eunuchs, and their loud cries, they ran out themselves, to see what was happening.   Instantly perceiving their danger, they both flew to arms ; one had just time to seize his bow, the other got hold of his lance ; when straightway the fight began.   The one whose weapon was the bow found it of no service at all, the foe was too near, and the combat too close to allow of his using it.   But the other made a stout defence with his lance, wounding two of the seven, Aspathines in the leg, and Intaphernes in the eye.   This wound did not kill Intaphernes, but it cost him his sight.   The other Magus, when he found his bow of no avail, fled into a chamber which opened out into the apartment of the males, intending to shut to the doors.   But two of the seven entered the room with him, Darius and Gobryas. Gobryas seized the Magus and grappled with him, while Darius stood over them, not knowing what to do, for it was dark,[11] and

[11] The Persian, like the Assyrian palaces, consisted of one or more central halls or courts, probably open to the sky, on which adjoined a number of ceiled chambers of small size, without windows, and only lighted through the doorway, which opened into the court.   (See the Essays appended to vol. i. ; Essay vii. § 12, and compare Loftus's Chaldæa, pp. 373-6, and Layard's Nineveh and Babylon, pp. 646-8.) Modern houses in Persia are often on the same plan—there being a central hall or *Iwan* rising to the top of the building, and round it small rooms in two or three separate stories, opening by windows into it, whilst "the inner chamber, *having no windows at all,* have no more light than that which reaches them through the door." (Layard, p. 649.)

he was afraid that if he struck a blow he might kill Gobryas. Then Gobryas, when he perceived that Darius stood doing nothing, asked him, "why his hand was idle?" "I fear to hurt thee," he answered. "Fear not," said Gobryas, "strike, though it be through both." Darius did as he desired, drove his dagger home, and by good hap killed the Magus.[1]

79. Thus were the Magi slain, and the seven, cutting off both the heads, and leaving their own wounded in the palace, partly because they were disabled, and partly to guard the citadel, went forth from the gates with the heads in their hands, shouting and making an uproar. They called out to all the Persians that they met, and told them what had happened, showing them the heads of the Magi, while at the same time they slew every Magus who fell in their way. Then the Persians, when they knew what the seven had done, and understood the fraud of the Magi, thought it but just to follow the example set them, and, drawing their daggers, they killed the Magi wherever they could find any. Such was their fury, that, unless night had closed in, not a single Magus would have been left alive. The Persians observe this day with one accord, and keep it more strictly than any other in the whole year. It is then that they hold the great festival, which they call the Magophonia.[2]   No Magus

---

[1] The death of the Magus is somewhat differently related by Ctesias. He says: "The seven got admission into the palace through Bagapates (Megabates), who kept the keys. On their entrance they found the Magus sleeping with one of his concubines, a Babylonian. When he saw them, he sprang from his couch, and not finding any weapon of war at hand (for Bagapates had conveyed them all secretly away), he brake in pieces a chair, made of gold, and seizing one of the legs, therewith defended himself. At last the stabs of the seven killed him; and he died after a reign of seven months." (Excerpt. Pers. § 14.)

The Behistun Inscription throws but little light on the circumstances of the death. It contributes, however, one fact, which is incompatible with the narratives alike of Ctesias and of Herodotus. Gomates is represented by both historians as slain at Susa, in the royal palace. Æschylus has the same tradition (τὸν δὲ σὺν δόλῳ Ἀρταφρένης ἔκτεινεν ἐσθλὸς ἐν δόμοις· Pers. l. s. c.). But the inscription states that he was killed "at the fort named Sictachotes, in the district of Media called Nisæa" (Col. i. par. 13, § 10). It is probable that he had fled thither for greater security.

That the six nobles did really assist Darius in the final attack is evident, both from the passage, "On the 10th day of the month Bagayadish, then it was, with my faithful men, I thus slew that Gomates" (Col. i. par. 13, § 9), and from the formal inscription of their names in the 18th paragraph of the 4th column.

It is remarkable that, no less than three times, Darius distinctly affirms that "he slew Gomates" (Col. i. par. 13, §§ 9 and 10; and Col. iv. par. 18, § 2).

[2] Here for once Ctesias and our author are of accord. Both speak of the festival as continuing in their own day. Ctesias says: "The feast of the Magophonia is celebrated (ἄγεται) by the Persians on the day upon which Sphendadates the Magus was put to death" (Excerpt. Pers. § 15). It is certainly strange that, after the Magian religion was combined with the Persian, and while the Magi constituted as they certainly did by the time of Ctesias) the priest-caste of the Persian nation,

may show himself abroad during the whole time that the feast lasts ; but all must remain at home the entire day.

80. And now when five days were gone, and the hubbub had settled down, the conspirators met together to consult about the situation of affairs. At this meeting speeches were made, to which many of the Greeks give no credence, but they were made nevertheless.[2] Otanes recommended that the management of public affairs should be entrusted to the whole nation. "To me," he said, "it seems advisable, that we should no longer have a single man to rule over us—the rule of one is neither good nor pleasant. Ye cannot have forgotten to what lengths Cambyses went in his haughty tyranny, and the haughtiness of the Magi ye have yourselves experienced. How indeed is it possible that monarchy should be a well-adjusted thing, when it allows a man to do as he likes without being answerable ? Such licence is enough to stir strange and unwonted thoughts in the heart of the worthiest of men. Give a person this power, and straightway his manifold good things puff him up with pride, while envy is so natural to human kind that it cannot but arise in him. But pride and envy together include all wickedness ; both leading on to deeds of savage violence. True it is that kings, possessing as they do all that heart can desire, ought to be void of envy, but the contrary is seen in their conduct towards the citizens. They are jealous of the most virtuous among their subjects, and wish their death ; while they take delight in the meanest and basest, being ever ready to listen to the tales of slanderers. A king, besides, is beyond all other men inconsistent with himself. Pay him court in moderation, and he is angry because you do not show him more profound respect—show him profound respect, and he is offended again, because (as he says) you fawn on him. But the worst of all is,

---

this custom should have been maintained. If, however, we remember that the reign of the Pseudo-Smerdis in Persia was not only the triumph of a religion, but also the domination for a time of the priests over the warriors, we may conceive the possibility of such a custom being still retained. It would be a perpetual warning to the priests against going beyond the line of their own functions, and trenching on the civil power.

[2] The incredulity of the Greeks is again alluded to (infra, vi. 43). Moderns have generally seen the unhistorical character of the narrative. (Heeren, As. Nat. I. ii. p. 347 ; Thirlwall, vol. ii. ch. xiii. ; Grote, vol. iv. p. 300 ; Bähr, ad loc., &c.) No doubt Herodotus had Persian authority for his tale ; but it is so utterly at variance with Oriental notions as to be absolutely incredible. It is not likely that even any debate took place as to who should be king. That point would be settled before the attack upon the usurper ; and it is probable that Darius succeeded to the throne by right of birth. (See below, ch. 86, note [9].) It is almost unnecessary to add that the Behistun Inscription lends no support to this part of the narrative of Herodotus.

that he sets aside the laws of the land, puts men to death without trial, and subjects women to violence. The rule of the many, on the other hand, has, in the first place, the fairest of names, to wit, *isonomy* ;[4] and further it is free from all those outrages which a king is wont to commit. There, places are given by lot, the magistrate is answerable for what he does, and measures rest with the commonalty. I vote, therefore, that we do away with monarchy, and raise the people to power. For the people are all in all."

81. Such were the sentiments of Otanes. Megabyzus spoke next, and advised the setting up of an oligarchy :—"In all that Otanes has said to persuade you to put down monarchy," he observed, "I fully concur ; but his recommendation that we should call the people to power seems to me not the best advice. For there is nothing so void of understanding, nothing so full of wantonness as the unwieldy rabble. It were folly not to be borne for men, while seeking to escape the wantonness of a tyrant, to give themselves up to the wantonness of a rude unbridled mob. The tyrant, in all his doings, at least knows what he is about, but a mob is altogether devoid of knowledge ; for how should there be any knowledge in a rabble, untaught, and with no natural sense of what is right and fit ? It rushes wildly into state affairs with all the fury of a stream swollen in the winter, and confuses everything. Let the enemies of the Persians be ruled by democracies ; but let us choose out from the citizens a certain number of the worthiest, and put the government into their hands. For thus both we ourselves shall be among the governors, and power being entrusted to the best men, it is likely that the best counsels will prevail in the state."

82. This was the advice which Megabyzus gave, and after him Darius came forward, and spoke as follows :—"All that Megabyzus said against democracy was well said, I think ; but about oligarchy he did not speak advisedly ; for take these three forms of government, democracy, oligarchy, and monarchy, and let them each be at their best, I maintain that monarchy far surpasses the other two. What government can possibly be better than that of the very best man in the whole state ? The counsels of such a man are like himself, and so he governs

---

[4] Modern languages have no single word to express the Greek ἰσονομία, which signified that perfect equality of all civil and political rights which was the fundamental notion of the Greek democracy. (Cf. Hermann's Manual, § 66.) Lange expresses the meaning tolerably in his "Freiheit und Gleichheit;" but that is a phrase, and not a name. Beloe gives "equality" only, and thereby loses the chief force of the original word. Larcher's "isonomie" seems to me better than either of these.

the mass of the people to their heart's content ; while at the same time his measures against evil-doers are kept more secret than in other states.   Contrariwise, in oligarchies, where men vie with each other in the service of the commonwealth, fierce enmities are apt to arise between man and man, each wishing to be leader, and to carry his own measures ; whence violent quarrels come, which lead to open strife, often ending in blood-shed.   Then monarchy is sure to follow ; and this too shows how far that rule surpasses all others.   Again, in a democracy, it is impossible but that there will be malpractices : these malpractices, however, do not lead to enmities, but to close friend-ships, which are formed among those engaged in them, who must hold well together to carry on their villanies.   And so things go on until a man stands forth as champion of the commonalty, and puts down the evil-doers.   Straightway the author of so great a service is admired by all, and from being admired soon comes to be appointed king ; so that here too it is plain that monarchy is the best government.   Lastly, to sum up all in a word, whence, I ask, was it that we got the freedom which we enjoy ?—did democracy give it us, or oligarchy, or a monarch ?   As a single man recovered our freedom for us, my sentence is that we keep to the rule of one.   Even apart from this, we ought not to change the laws of our forefathers when they work fairly ; for to do so, is not well."

83. Such were the three opinions brought forward at this meeting ; the four other Persians voted in favour of the last. Otanes, who wished to give his countrymen a democracy, when he found the decision against him, arose a second time, and spoke thus before the assembly :—" Brother conspirators, it is plain that the king who is to be chosen will be one of ourselves, whether we make the choice by casting lots for the prize, or by letting the people decide which of us they will have to rule over them, or in any other way.   Now, as I have neither a mind to rule nor to be ruled, I shall not enter the lists with you in this matter.   I withdraw, however, on one condition—none of you shall claim to exercise rule over me or my seed for ever."   The six agreed to these terms, and Otanes withdrew and stood aloof from the contest.   And still to this day the family of Otanes continues to be the only free family in Persia ; those who belong to it submit to the rule of the king only so far as they themselves choose ; they are bound, however, to observe the laws of the land like the other Persians.[5]

* This statement of Herodotus can scarcely have been without a groundwork of

84. After this the six took counsel together, as to the fairest way of setting up a king : and first, with respect to Otanes, they resolved, that if any of their own number got the kingdom, Otanes and his seed after him should receive year by year, as a mark of special honour, a Median robe,[6] and all such other gifts as are accounted the most honourable in Persia. And these they resolved to give him, because he was the man who first planned the outbreak, and who brought the seven together. These privileges, therefore, were assigned specially to Otanes. The following were made common to them all :—It was to be free to each, whenever he pleased, to enter the palace unannounced, unless the king were in the company of one of his wives ; and the king was to be bound to marry into no family excepting those of the conspirators.[7] Concerning the appointment of a king, the resolve to which they came was the following :—They would ride out together next morning into the skirts of the city, and he whose steed first neighed after the sun was up should have the kingdom.

85. Now Darius had a groom, a sharp-witted knave, called Œbares. After the meeting had broken up, Darius sent for him, and said, " Œbares, this is the way in which the king is to

truth. The family of Otanes must have stood in his time upon a higher footing than any other family in Persia. If, however, the whole story of the debate be, as seems certain, a fiction, we must look for some other origin of this house's privileges. It may be found, perhaps, in its superior rank, and *old* connexion with the royal house of the Achæmenidæ. Otanes, as has been already shown (v. s. ch. 68, n. [6]), was descended from Pharnaces, king of Cappadocia, and Atossa, daughter of Cambyses, great-grandfather of Cyrus the Great. His daughter Phædima (Fatima ?) was married to Cambyses (supra, ch. 68), and became successively the wife of the Pseudo-Smerdis, and of Darius (infra, ch. 88). No other noble family in Persia is found so early connected with the reigning branch of the family of the Achæmenidæ. Thus the greatness of this house dates from *before* the conspiracy ; and though undoubtedly a very prominent part was taken by Otanes in the struggle (evidenced by the place his name occupies in the lists of Herodotus, Ctesias, and the Behistun Inscription), yet it may be doubted whether any new rank devolved upon his family in consequence. The continued greatness of his house is indicated by the fact that Xerxes married his granddaughter, Amestris. (Ctesias, Exc. Pers. § 20.)

[6] The Median robe has been already described (v. s. i. 135, note [6]). Herodotus gives another instance of the practice of presenting this robe as a gift of honour (infra, vii. 116). Xenophon makes Cyrus present Median garments to his chief friends (Cyrop. viii. i. 40). The Median garment was so usually given by the Persian kings, that in later times it got the name of δωροφορική. (See Ælian. V. H. i. xxii. and Hesych. ad. voc.)

Garments have at all times been gifts of honour in the East. (Gen. xlv. 22 ; 2 Kings v. 5 ; 2 Chron. ix. 24, &c.) The practice continues in the *kaftan* of the present day.

[7] So far as can be traced this rule was always observed. Darius, besides his wives from the family of the Alcmæonidæ, married Phædima, daughter of Otanes, and a daughter of Gobryas (infra, vii. 2). Xerxes took to wife Amestris, daughter of Onophas, the son of Otanes. (Ctes. Exc. Pers. § 20.)

be chosen—we are to mount our horses, and the man whose horse first neighs after the sun is up is to have the kingdom. If then you have any cleverness, contrive a plan whereby the prize may fall to us, and not go to another." "Truly, master," Œbares answered, "if it depends on this whether thou shalt be king or no, set thine heart at ease, and fear nothing : I have a charm which is sure not to fail." "If thou hast really aught of the kind," said Darius, "hasten to get it ready. The matter does not brook delay, for the trial is to be to-morrow." So Œbares when he heard that, did as follows :—When night came, he took one of the mares, the chief favourite of the horse which Darius rode, and tethering it in the suburb, brought his master's horse to the place ; then, after leading him round and round the mare several times, nearer and nearer at each circuit, he ended by letting them come together.

86. And now, when the morning broke, the six Persians, according to agreement, met together on horseback, and rode out to the suburb. As they went along they neared the spot where the mare was tethered the night before, whereupon the horse of Darius sprang forward and neighed. Just at the same time, though the sky was clear and bright, there was a flash of lightning, followed by a thunder-clap. It seemed as if the heavens conspired with Darius, and hereby inaugurated him king : so the five other nobles leaped with one accord from their steeds, and bowed down before him and owned him for their king.[8]

87. This is the account which some of the Persians gave of the contrivance of Œbares ; but there are others who relate the matter differently. They say that in the morning he stroked the mare with his hand, which he then hid in his trousers until the sun rose and the horses were about to start, when he suddenly drew his hand forth and put it to the nostrils of his master's horse, which immediately snorted and neighed.

88. Thus was Darius, son of Hystaspes, appointed king ; and, except the Arabians, all they of Asia were subject to him ; for Cyrus, and after him Cambyses,[9] had brought them all under.

---

[8] It has been already observed that Darius probably succeeded to the throne by right of birth. Failing the line of Cyrus, which (it is plain) was now extinct, the line of Darius (so far as we can tell) was next in succession. See the genealogical tree of the Achæmenids (Book vii. ch. 11, note). Of course, if this view be correct, Hystaspes was the rightful heir ; but, as his years prevented him from undertaking the post of leader in the conspiracy, he would naturally cede his rights to his son.

[9] The Phœnicians and Cyprians would be here alluded to—perhaps also the Cilicians. There is no direct evidence at what time Cilicia became subject to Persia. It was a free state in the time of Crœsus (i. 28) ; it appears next as a satrapy under Darius (infra, ch. 90).

The Arabians were never subject as slaves to the Persians, but had a league of friendship with them from the time when they brought Cambyses on his way as he went into Egypt ; for had they been unfriendly the Persians could never have made their invasion.

Darius married, first of all,[1] the following women, who were all of them Persians, namely, two daughters of Cyrus, Atossa and Artystône ; of these, Atossa had been twice married before, once to Cambyses, her brother, and once to the Magus ; the other, Artystône, was a virgin. He married also Parmys, daughter of Smerdis, son of Cyrus ; and he likewise took to wife the daughter of Otanes, who had made the discovery about the Magus. And now when his power was established firmly throughout all the kingdoms, the first thing that he did was to set up a carving in stone, which showed a man mounted upon a horse, with an inscription in these words following :—
"Darius, son of Hystaspes, by aid of his good horse " (here followed the horse's name), " and of his good groom Œbares, got himself the kingdom of the Persians."[2]

89. This he set up in Persia, and afterwards he proceeded to establish twenty governments of the kind which the Persians call satrapies,[3] assigning to each its governor, and fixing the trib-

[1] Darius had married a daughter of Gobryas before his accession (vii. 2). He also took to wife his niece, Phratagûne, the daughter of his brother Artanes (vii. 224). Still the idea of De Hammer, that Mahomet's institution of four wives was derived from an ancient custom of the Oriental nations (Hist. Osman. i. p. 565), may be correct. And this may be an instance of the practice. For the daughter of Gobryas may have been dead before the accession of Darius, and he may not have married Phratagûne till after the death of one of the four wives mentioned in the text.

[2] Herodotus had probably not seen this figure, but received the account of it which he transmits, and the explanation of the inscription, from others. Perhaps his informants had no means of reading the writing, for the sculpture, like those at Behistun, may have been placed at an inaccessible height. The story of Œbares, which must be regarded as a genuine Persian legend, probably arose out of the work of art. Dr. Donaldson in a very ingenious paper (Journ. of As. Soc. vol. xvi. part i. pp. 1-7) has endeavoured to restore the actual inscription from the account of Herodotus. He regards the supposed groom as Ormuzd, and the name Œbares as arising from the Persian word *frdbara* (— dedit), which is common in the sculptures (Behist. Ins., Col. i. Par. 9, § 2, &c.). But it may be doubted whether he has sufficient data for the conclusions which he draws.

Curiously enough, another Persian legend, found in Nicholas of Damascus (Fragm. Hist. Gr. vol. iii. p. 400, et seqq.), assigns a prominent part in the original elevation of the Achæmenidæ, by the successes of Cyrus, to an Œbares. Here too we find the etymology of the name correctly given, as ἀγαθάγγελος, "the bearer of good tidings." This latter is probably the Œbares of Ctesias (§ 2-5).

[3] The word "satrap" is found twice in the great inscription at Behistun (Col. iii. par. 8, § 4, and par. 9, § 2). It is spelt "*khshatrapá*." The derivation is un doubtedly *khshatram*, "crown" or "empire," and *pa* (Sans. पा Pers. پاس or پان (یان‎), "keeper, preserver." The satraps are the great "upholders of the crown," and

ute which was to be paid him by the several nations.   And
generally he joined together in one satrapy the nations that were
neighbours, but sometimes he passed over the nearer tribes, and
put in their stead those which were more remote.[4]   The following is an account of these governments, and of the yearly tribute
which they paid to the king :—Such as brought their tribute in
silver were ordered to pay according to the Babylonian talent ;
while the Euboic was the standard measure for such as brought
gold.   Now the Babylonian talent contains seventy Euboic
minæ.[5]   During all the reign of Cyrus, and afterwards when
Cambyses ruled, there were no fixed tributes, but the nations
severally brought gifts to the king.   On account of this and
other like doings, the Persians say that Darius was a huckster,
Cambyses a master, and Cyrus a father ; for Darius looked to
making a gain in everything ; Cambyses was harsh and reckless ;
while Cyrus was gentle, and procured them all manner of goods.

90.   The Ionians, the Magnesians of Asia,[6] the Æolians, the

the provinces take their name of satrapy from them. (See Col. Rawlinson's Vocabulary of the Ancient Persian Language, p. 116.)
  [4] See Appendix, Essay iii. "On the Persian System of Administration and Government," p. 435.
  [5] Standards of weight probably passed into Greece from Asia, whence the word
mina (μνᾶ, comp. Heb. מָנֶה) seems certainly to have been derived. That the standard known to the Greeks as the Euboic was an Asiatic one, is plain from this passage. The old Attic, which bore so remarkable a proportion to it, must have had
the same origin. We may trace the existence of three standards in early times,
proportioned to each other as 8, 7, and 6. The first is the original Attic, which is
identical with the Eginetan ; the second is the Babylonian; and the third the Euboic.
If the ancient Attic is reckoned as 100, the Babylonian will be 87·5, and the Euboic
75. Hence it will be true to say, with Herodotus, that the Babylonian talent contains 70 Euboic minæ instead of 60, or is to the Euboic as 7 to 6 (for 87·5 : 75 exactly as 7 : 6); and with Ælian (V. H. i. 22), that the Babylonian talent contains
72 Attic minæ, or is to the later Attic talent as 6 : 5. For the later Attic talent
stood to the older as 78 to 100 (Plut. Sol. c. 15), and 87·5 : 78 almost exactly as
6 : 5. Böckh has shown (Econ. of Athens, i. p. 193) how this awkward proportion
of the later to the earlier Attic talent arose from an accident, Solon having intended
to assimilate the Attic standard to the Euboic. Properly there were but two distinct
standards in Greece—the original Attic (which continued as the commercial standard at Athens), and was also known as the Eginetan, and the Euboic, or Asiatic
gold standard, from which the later Attic was an accidental deviation.
  The Babylonian weights discovered by Mr. Layard (Nineveh and Babylon, p.
601) agree fairly with this estimate. They furnish a mina of somewhat more than
16 oz. Troy, or nearly 18 oz. avoirdupois, which stands to the Attic mina of 15¹/₈
oz., nearly in the proportion required. There is a slight deficiency on the Babylonian side, which may be accounted for by the greater waste of the more ancient metal.
  If the (later) Attic talent was worth 243l. 15s. of our money, the Euboic (silver)
talent would be 250l. 8s. 5d., and the Babylonian 292l. 3s. 3d.
  [6] There were two towns of the name of Magnesia in Asia Minor, Magnesia under
Sipylus and Magnesia on the Mæander. (See note ² on Book i. ch. 161.) Both
were situated inland, and had the character of Pelasgic cities. They were built
probably by that indigenous Pelasgic population to which the Mæonians also be-

Carians, the Lycians, the Milyans,[7] and the Pamphylians, paid their tribute in a single sum, which was fixed at four hundred talents of silver. These formed together the first satrapy.

The Mysians, Lydians, Lasonians,[8] Cabalians, and Hygennians[9] paid the sum of five hundred talents. This was the second satrapy.

The Hellespontians, of the right coast as one enters the straits, the Phrygians, the Asiatic Thracians, the Paphlagonians, the Mariandynians, and the Syrians[10] paid a tribute of three hundred and sixty talents. This was the third satrapy.

The Cilicians gave three hundred and sixty white horses, one for each day in the year,[1] and five hundred talents of silver. Of this sum one hundred and forty talents went to pay the cavalry which guarded the country, while the remaining three hundred and sixty were received by Darius. This was the fourth satrapy.

91. The country reaching from the city of Posideïum[2] (built by Amphilocus, son of Amphiaraüs, on the confines of Syria and Cilicia) to the borders of Egypt, excluding therefrom a district which belonged to Arabia, and was free from tax,[3] paid a tribute of three hundred and fifty talents. All Phœnicia, Palæstine Syria, and Cyprus, were herein contained. This was the fifth satrapy.

From Egypt, and the neighbouring parts of Libya, together

---

longed. They would therefore be earlier than any of the Greek colonies upon the coast. Herodotus here distinguishes them from the Magnesians of Europe (infrà, vii. 132, &c.), a Thessalian people, who were possibly of the same race.

[7] Vide suprà, i. 173. The Milyans are reckoned as a separate people also by Ephorus. (Fragm. Hist. Gr. vol. i. p. 258.)

[8] In the seventh Book (ch. 77) Herodotus identifies the Cabalians and the Lasonians. According to that passage, both Cabalians and Lasonians would appear to have been Mæonians, remnants of the ancient people expelled by the conquering Lydians. Probably they occupied the high tract between Lydia and Lycia, which is ascribed commonly to Phrygia. The Cabalians appear to have extended into Lycia, occupying there the high plain between Milyas and the valley of the Xanthus. (See Appendix to Book i. Essay ii. § 8, v.)

[9] The Hygennians are not mentioned by any other author, whence Valckenaer proposed, instead of Λασονίων, καὶ Καβαλίων, καὶ Ὑγεννέων, to read Λασονίων τῶν καὶ Καβαλίων καλευμένων. It is possible that the reading ought to be Ὑγεννέων (Τ having become Γ), and that the people of Etenna, a town in Pisidia (Polyb. v. 73), are intended. (See the Museum Philolog. vol. i. p. 634.)

[10] That is, the Cappadocians. (Vide suprà, i. 72.)

[1] Compare i. 32, and ii. 4.

[2] Posideïum lay about 12 miles south of the embouchure of the Orontes. It is mentioned by Strabo (xvi. p. 1103, and p. 1127). The modern town of Bosyt preserves the name. Syria was usually considered to begin at the southern extremity of the gulf of Issus, nearly half a degree north of Posideïum.

[3] The district here spoken of is that between Gaza (Cadytis) and Jenysus (vide suprà, ch. 5), which Cambyses traversed on his road to Egypt. Concerning the exemption of the Arabs from tribute, vide infrà, ch. 97.

with the towns of Cyrêné and Barca, which belonged to the Egyptian satrapy, the tribute which came in was seven hundred talents.   These seven hundred talents did not include the profits of the fisheries of Lake Mœris,[4] nor the corn furnished to the troops at Memphis.   Corn was supplied to 120,000 Persians, who dwelt at Memphis in the quarter called the White Castle,[5] and to a number of auxiliaries.   This was the sixth satrapy.

The Sattagydians,[6] the Gandarians, the Dadicæ, and the Aparytæ, who were all reckoned together, paid a tribute of a hundred and seventy talents.   This was the seventh satrapy.

Susa, and the other parts of Cissia, paid three hundred talents.   This was the eighth satrapy.

92. From Babylonia, and the rest of Assyria, were drawn a thousand talents of silver, and five hundred boy-eunuchs.   This was the ninth satrapy.

Agbatana, and the other parts of Media, together with the Paricanians,[7] and Orthocorybantes,[8] paid in all four hundred and fifty talents.   This was the tenth satrapy.

The Caspians, Pausicæ,[9] Pantimathi, and Daritæ, were joined in one government, and paid the sum of two hundred talents.   This was the eleventh satrapy.

From the Bactrian tribes as far as the Ægli,[1] the tribute received was three hundred and sixty talents.   This was the twelfth satrapy.

93. From Pactyïca,[2] Armenia, and the countries reaching thence to the Euxine, the sum drawn was four hundred talents. This was the thirteenth satrapy.

[4] See n. B. ii. ch. 149.
[5] Vide suprà, ch. 13, note.
[6] This is the only mention of the Sattagydians in any classical writer. They appear, however, in the inscriptions of Darius as *Thatagush* (Beh. Ins. Col. i. par. 6, § 4; Persep. Ins. No. 4, line 17; Nakhsh-i-Rustam Ins. line 24), and evidently lie towards the extreme east.   The Gandarians and Dadicæ are mentioned again (vii. 66). The Aparytæ are unknown.
[7] The Parætaceni are perhaps meant here. They were often regarded as distinct from the Medes. (See App. to Book i. Essay x. § 10, iv.) Or the Paricanians may, as Mr. C. Müller thinks, be the Hyrcanians. (See the Map of the Satrapies in Vol. III.)
[8] No writer but Herodotus mentions the Orthocorybantes.
[9] The Pausicæ are perhaps the Pœsiani of Strabo (xi. p. 744) and the Pæsicæ of Pliny (H. N. vi. 17). The Pantimathi and Daritæ are unknown.
[1] The Ægli are probably the Αὐγαλοὶ of Ptolemy (vi. 12), whom he places on the Jaxartes, and perhaps the Αἴγηλοι mentioned by Stephen as "a Median nation." I am indebted to Mr. C. Müller for the further conjecture that they are the Αἰγαῖοι (which he would read Αἰγλοί) of the Paschal Chronicle (p. 321). This passage is thought to fix their position to the site of Alexandria eschata.
[2] This Pactyïca must be distinguished from the region of the same name on the Upper Indus (infra, ch. 102, and iv. 44). It undoubtedly adjoined Armenia.

The Sagartians, Sarangians, Thamanæans,[3] Utians,[4] and Mycians,[5] together with the inhabitants of the islands in the Erythræan sea, where the king sends those whom he banishes, furnished altogether a tribute of six hundred talents. This was the fourteenth satrapy.

The Sacans and Caspians gave two hundred and fifty talents. This was the fifteenth satrapy.

The Parthians, Chorasmians, Sogdians, and Arians, gave three hundred. This was the sixteenth satrapy.

94. The Paricanians and Ethiopians of Asia furnished a tribute of four hundred talents. This was the seventeenth satrapy.

The Matienians, Saspeires, and Alarodians were rated to pay two hundred talents. This was the eighteenth satrapy.

---

[3] Agathias has a Κώμη Θαμανῶν in the Kurdish mountains (iv. 29). Otherwise no writer but Herodotus mentions the Thamanæans. Their name seems to linger in that of the modern *Taymounees*, whom the maps place in the vicinity of Herat. Herodotus again refers to them (infra, ch. 117).

[4] The Utians are perhaps the Uxians of Strabo (xi. p. 1032) and Arrian (Exp. Alex. iii. 17), who dwelt in the *Bakhtiyari* mountains.

[5] No other writer, if we except Stephen, mentions the Mycians or Mecians. They appear, however, in the Inscriptions as *Maka*, and their name is, perhaps, to be recognised in the modern *Mekran*.

[6] It is interesting to compare with this enumeration the three authentic lists of the Persian provinces which are contained in the Inscriptions of Darius. They are as follows :—

At Behistun.	At Persepolis.	At Nakhsh-i-Rustam.
Persia	Susiana	Media
Susiana	Media	Susiana
Babylonia	Babylonia	Parthia
Assyria	Arabia	Aria
Arabia	Assyria	Bactria
Egypt	Egypt	Sogdiana
Saparda	Armenia	Chorasmia
Ionia	Cappadocia	Zarangia
Media	Saparda	Arachosia
Armenia	Ionia	Sattagydia
Cappadocia	*Sagartia	Gandaria
Parthia	Parthia	India
Zarangia	Zarangia	Sacia (?)
Aria	Aria	Babylonia
Chorasmia	Bactria	Assyria
Bactria	Sogdiana	Arabia
Sogdiana	Chorasmia	Egypt
Gandaria	Sattagydia	Armenia
Sacia	Arachosia	Cappadocia
Sattagydia	*India	Saparda
Arachosia	Gandaria	Ionia
Mecia	Sacia	*Sacia
	Mecia	*The Islands (Cyclades ?)
		*The Scodræ (?)
		*Ionia
		*The Tacabri (?)
		*The Budians
		*The Ethiopians
		*The Mardians (?)
		*The Carchians

N. B. The provinces marked with an asterisk are not included in the earlier lists.

The Moschi, Tibareni, Macrones, Mosynœci, and Mares had to pay three hundred talents. This was the nineteenth satrapy.

The Indians, who are more numerous than any other nation with which we are acquainted, paid a tribute exceeding that of every other people, to wit, three hundred and sixty talents of gold-dust. This was the twentieth satrapy.[6]

95. If the Babylonian money here spoken of be reduced to the Euboic scale, it will make nine thousand five hundred and forty such talents ; and if the gold be reckoned at thirteen times the worth of silver,[7] the Indian gold-dust will come to four thousand six hundred and eighty talents. Add these two amounts together, and the whole revenue which came in to Darius year by year will be found to be in Euboic money fourteen thousand five hundred and sixty talents, not to mention parts of a talent.[8]

96. Such was the revenue which Darius derived from Asia and a small part of Libya. Later in his reign the sum was increased by the tribute of the islands, and of the nations of Europe as far as Thessaly. The great king stores away the tribute which he receives[9] after this fashion—he melts it down, and while it is in a liquid state runs it into earthen vessels, which

[7] In Greece the relative value of gold varied at different times. Herodotus says gold was to silver as 13 to 1, afterwards in Plato and Xenophon's time (and more than 100 years after the death of Alexander) it was 10 to 1, owing to the quantity of gold brought in through the Persian war. It long continued at 10 to 1 (Liv. xxxviii. 11) except when an accident altered the proportion of those metals. In the time of Theodosius II. it was as 18 to 1 ; and in the middle ages and 16th century 11 and 12 to 1. Before the discovery of America 11 and 10 to 1 in England ; and after great fluctuations, it was in Newton's time 16 to 1, becoming at length 14¼ to 1 in our own days, before the discoveries in California and Australia.—[G. W.]

[8] It is impossible to reconcile Herodotus's numbers, and equally impossible to say where the mistake lies. According to the items of his account the sum total of the silver amounts to 7740 Babylonian talents. This would equal 9030 Euboic talents ; instead of which he gives, in his present text, 9540 ; being an excess over the items of 510 E. talents. Again, having stated the silver to amount to 9540 E. talents, and the gold-dust to be equal to 4680 E. talents (a correct estimate on his premises), he gives the whole amount as 14,560 instead of 14,220 E. talents ; so that again he is in excess, this time, by 340 talents. Thus we seem to have a double error, which it is quite impossible to remedy.

Taking the lowest estimate which his numbers allow (13,710 E. talents), the annual revenue of Persia was about three millions and a half of our money. The higher estimate would raise it to about 3,646,000l. The present revenue of the Persian empire is estimated at something more than 3,000,000l. (Kinneir's Persia, p. 47). But it must be remembered in any comparison between the resources of Ancient Persia and of modern countries, that the ancient money revenue corresponds to the modern Civil List, since it simply served to defray the expenses of the Court.

[9] Arrian relates that Alexander found 50,000 talents of silver laid up in store at Susa, when he took that city. (Exped. Alex. III. xvi.) There were further stores in Persepolis and Pasargadæ (ibid. xviii.). On the Persian coinage, see notes on Book iv. ch. 166, and Book vii. ch. 28.

are afterwards removed, leaving the metal in a solid mass. When money is wanted, he coins as much of this bullion as the occasion requires.

97. Such then were the governments, and such the amounts of tribute at which they were assessed respectively. Persia alone has not been reckoned among the tributaries—and for this reason, because the country of the Persians is altogether exempt from tax. The following peoples paid no settled tribute, but brought gifts to the king : first, the Ethiopians bordering upon Egypt,[10] who were reduced by Cambyses when he made war on the long-lived Ethiopians, and who dwell about the sacred city of Nysa,[1] and have festivals in honour of Bacchus. The grain on which they and their next neighbours feed is the same as that used by the Calantian Indians.[2] Their dwelling houses are underground.[3] Every third year these two nations brought—and they still bring to my day—two chœnices of virgin gold, two hundred logs of ebony,[4] five Ethiopian boys, and twenty elephant tusks. The

[10] These were the inhabitants of Lower Ethiopia and Nubia. Ebony (*habni*, Eg. ; *ebnoos*, Arab.) and ivory ("*ab*," "*ebo*," Eg.) had always been brought as a tribute to the Egyptian monarchs of the 18th and other dynasties, as well as rings and ingots of gold and silver, with various productions of the country and of the interior of Africa, apes, giraffes, skins of leopards, and even cattle and hounds.—[G. W.]

[1] Vide suprà, ii. 146, note [6].

[2] Vide suprà, ch. 38, note [4]. As nothing has been said about the grain eaten by the Calantians, various emendations have been proposed. Valckenaer would read σήματι for σπέρματι, Wesseling ἔργματι. Hence Larcher's "coutumes à l'égard des morts," and Lange's "*Todtenbräuche*." But there seems to be no sufficient reason for departing from the reading of the MSS. The grain intended is probably rice.

[3] This notion probably arose from their having mud huts, so common in central Africa, and was the origin of the story and name of the Troglodytæ, who lived between Nubia and the Red Sea.—[G. W.]

[4] They not only brought logs of ebony, with other ornamental woods and elephants' teeth, as tribute to the Pharaohs, but used ebony clubs in battle (No. II.)

No. I.

No. II.

Colchians, and the neighbouring tribes who dwell between them and the Caucasus—for so far the Persian rule reaches, while north of the Caucasus no one fears them any longer—undertook to furnish a gift, which in my day was still brought every fifth year, consisting of a hundred boys, and the same number of maidens.[5]   The Arabs brought every year a thousand talents of frankincense.   Such were the gifts which the king received over and above the tribute-money.

98. The way in which the Indians get the plentiful supply of gold, which enables them to furnish year by year so vast an amount of gold-dust to the king is the following :—Eastward of India lies a tract which is entirely sand.   Indeed of all the inhabitants of Asia, concerning whom anything certain is known, the Indians dwell the nearest to the east, and the rising of the sun. Beyond them the whole country is desert on account of the sand.[6] The tribes of Indians are numerous, and do not all speak the same language[7]—some are wandering tribes, others not.   They

which exactly resemble those they have at the present day, 1 ft. 6 in. long (No III. 1 & 2).   Besides the modern club called *lissán* (mentioned in n. B. vii. ch. 69, wood-cut No. II.) is one of a lighter kind used by the modern Ethiopians in dromedary-riding.   This is also seen in the hands of royal attendants in the old sculptures. Some Ethiopian dandies have this light *lissán* covered with alternate bands of red, blue, and green cloth, and a net-work of brass wire.—[G. W.]

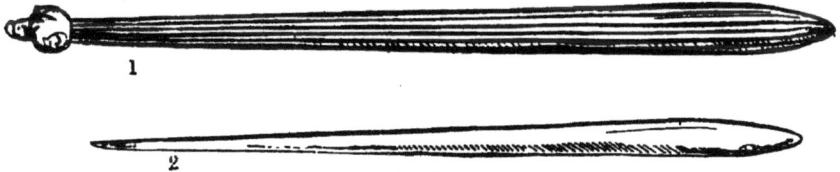

No. III.

[5] It is curious to find the practice of exporting their children so ancient in these regions.   Circassia still supplies wives to almost all the wealthy Turks, and the Mamelukes are said to have been composed entirely of those who had been brought when young from the same country. (See Rennell's Geography of Herodotus, p. 525, note.)

[6] The India of Herodotus is the true *ancient* India (the *Hapta Hendu* of the Vendidad), the region about the Upper Indus, best known to us at present under the name of the Punj-aub.   Herodotus knows nothing of the great southern penin-sula.   Probably, therefore, the desert of which he speaks as extending indefinitely eastward, is the vast elevated sandy tract lying north of the Himalaya, between that range and the Tchien Chan chain, which stretches in a direction a little north of east, from Cashmere to the longitude of Pekin, a distance of above 2000 miles.   This tract includes the great desert of Cobi or Shamoo. (See Humboldt's Aspects of Nature, vol. i. pp. 74–5, E. T.)

[7] The Hindoo races are supposed to have been settled in India as early as 1200 B. C. ; which is the date assigned to the Vedas, though these appear not to be all of one period.   Some limit their date to 880 B. C.   Having advanced from Central Asia through Cabul, the Hindoos established themselves on the Indus (Sindhu, "the river ") and throughout the Penj-ab ("five waters" or "streams "), whence they

who dwell in the marshes along the river,[8] live on raw fish, which they take in boats made of reeds, each formed out of a single joint.[9] These Indians wear a dress of sedge, which they cut in the river and bruise ; afterwards they weave it into mats, and wear it as we wear a breast-plate.

99. Eastward of these Indians are another tribe, called Padæans,[10] who are wanderers, and live on raw flesh. This tribe is said to have the following customs :—If one of their number be ill, man or woman, they take the sick person, and if he be a man, the men of his acquaintance proceed to put him to death, because, they say, his flesh would be spoilt for them if he pined and wasted away with sickness. The man protests he is not ill in the least ; but his friends will not accept his denial—in spite of all he can say, they kill him, and feast themselves on his body. So also if a woman be sick, the women, who are her friends, take her and do with her exactly the same as the men. If one of them reaches to old age, about which there is seldom any question, as commonly before that time they have had some disease or other, and so have been put to death—but if a man, notwith-

gradually extended their conquests southward; and they had already conquered most of the aboriginal tribes before the time of Herodotus.

The language of the Hindoos differs entirely from those of the aborigines; and the relationship of the Sanscrit to the Zend of ancient Persia, and to the Greek, Teutonic, and other European languages, accords well with their common origin from Central Asia. The Vedas are written in a dialect of an older type than the Sanscrit, and still nearer to the Zend of the Avesta.

The aborigines are still found in Ceylon and in Southern India as well as in the hill-country in other parts; and their customs differ as much as their languages from those of the Hindoos. They are supposed to be of Scythian origin; and if, as some think, there is an analogy between their languages (as the Tamul and others) and the Semitic dialects, this may be explained by their relationship to the parent tongue before its separation into Arian and Semitic, as in the case of the Egyptian (see n. ch. 2, Bk. ii. in Ap. ch. i.) They have no castes ; but this institution is even thought to have been unknown to the Hindoos when they first settled in India; and is the result of conquest. They are first mentioned by Megasthenes B. C. 302.— [G. W.]

[8] By the "river" is meant the Indus. It does not appear that Herodotus was aware of the existence of the Ganges, which only became known to the Greeks by the expedition of Alexander. (Cf. Strabo, book xv.)

[9] So Pliny : " Arundini quidem Indicæ arborea altitudo ; navigiorumque etiam vicem præstant, si credimus, singula internodia." (Hist. Nat. xvi. 36.) Cuvier says that one species of the bamboo, the *Bambus arundinacea*, grows to the height of 60 feet.

[10] The only certain mention of the Padæans by any other ancient writer is that in the well-known lines of Tibullus :

"Impia nec sævis celebrans convivia mensis
Ultima vicinus Phœbo tenet arva Padæus."—IV. i. 144.

A fragment of Nicolaüs Damascenus is conjecturally applied to them. (See Valckenaer ad Herod. iii. 99, and comp. Müller's Fr. Hist. Gr. iii. p. 464). According to this, among the Padæans not the sacrificer but the wisest of those present began the ceremonies, and the only thing for which men prayed was justice.

standing, comes to be old, then they offer him in sacrifice to their gods, and afterwards eat his flesh.[1]

100. There is another set of Indians whose customs are very different. They refuse to put any live animal to death,[2] they sow no corn, and have no dwelling-houses. Vegetables are their only food. There is a plant which grows wild in their country, bearing seed about the size of millet-seed in a calyx : their wont is to gather this seed and having boiled it, calyx and all, to use it for food. If one of them is attacked with sickness, he goes forth into the wilderness, and lies down to die ; no one has the least concern either for the sick or for the dead.

101. All the tribes which I have mentioned live together like the brute beasts :[3] they have also all the same tint of skin, which approaches that of the Ethiopians.[4] Their country is a long way from Persia towards the south : nor had king Darius ever any authority over them.

102. Besides these, there are Indians of another tribe, who border on the city Caspatyrus,[5] and the country of Pactyïca ;[6]

---

[1] Vide suprà, ch. 38. The same custom is said to have prevailed among the Massagetæ (i. 216) and the Issedonians (iv. 26); and a similiar one is mentioned by Strabo as existing among the Caspians (xi. p. 753), and the Derbices (ibid. p. 756). Marco Polo found the practice in Sumatra in his own day. "The people of Dragoian," he says, "observe this horrible custom in cases where any member of their family is afflicted with a disease. The relations of the sick person send for the magicians, whom they require, on examination of the symptoms, to declare whether he will recover or not. . . . If the decision be that he cannot, the relations then call in certain men whose peculiar duty it is, and who perform their business with dexterity, to close the mouth of the patient until he is suffocated. This being done, they cut the body in pieces in order to prepare it as victuals, and when it has been so dressed the relations assemble, and in a convivial manner eat the whole of it, not leaving so much as the marrow in the bones." (Travels, p. 610, E. T.) According to some modern writers (Elphinstone's Cabul, vol. i. p. 45, 2nd ed.), cannibalism continues in the countries bordering on the Indus to the present day.

[2] The repugnance of true Brahmins to take away life is well known. The Mahrattas are said to have the same prejudice. Heeren (As. Nat. vol. i. p. 303), thinks that the latter are intended in this place. But his arguments are not very convincing.

[3] "Concubitus corum, more pecorum, in aperto est." In Book i. ch. 216, nearly the same is related of the Massagetæ. Herodotus adds, "Semen eorundem genitale, non, sicut aliorum hominum, album, sed nigrum, pro colore corporis: cujusmodi semen et Æthiopes edere solent." Aristotle denies these statements of Herodotus. (Hist. An. iii. 22 ; Gener. An. ii. 2.)

[4] If the Ethiopians and Indians had the same colour, which is not black as that of the Negro, it is evident that the Egyptians could not be "black," as Herodotus states in B. ii. ch. 104. (See n. [4] on that chapter.)—[G. W.]

[5] Heeren (As. Nat. vol. i. p. 293) regards the city of Caspatyrus (the Caspapyrus of Hecatæus, Fr. 179) as the modern Cabul; but his data are very insufficient. De Hammer (Ann. Vien. vol. li. p. 86) and Schlegel (Berlin. Taschenb. 1829, p. 17), suggests Cashmere. But neither of these towns is really on the main stream of the Indus, on which Caspatyrus seems to be placed. Infra, iv. 44.

[6] Herodotus appears to recognise two districts of this name, one on the confines of Armenia (suprà, ch. 93), the other upon the Indus.

these people dwell northward of all the rest of the Indians, and follow nearly the same mode of life as the Bactrians. They are more warlike than any of the other tribes, and from them the men are sent forth who go to procure the gold. For it is in this part of India that the sandy desert lies. Here, in this desert, there lived amid the sand great ants, in size somewhat less than dogs, but bigger than foxes. The Persian king has a number of them, which have been caught by the hunters in the land whereof we are speaking. These ants make their dwellings underground, and like the Greek ants, which they very much resemble in shape, throw up sand-heaps as they burrow. Now the sand which they throw up is full of gold.[7] The Indians, when they go into the desert to collect this sand, take three camels and harness them together, a female in the middle and a male on either side, in a leading-rein. The rider sits on the female, and they are particular to choose for the purpose one that has but just dropped her young; for their female camels can run as fast as horses, while they bear burthens very much better.

103. As the Greeks are well acquainted with the shape of the camel, I shall not trouble to describe it; but I shall mention what seems to have escaped their notice. The camel has in its hind legs four thigh-bones and four knee-joints.[8]

---

[7] It is curious to find the same narrative, told gravely, not only by Megasthenes (Fr. 39), Dio. (Or. xxxv. p. 436), Pliny (Hist. Nat. xi. 36), Mela (iii. vii. 2), and Ælian (H. An. iii. 4), but also by Prester John (Ungkhan) in the 12th century. His words, as reported by Bähr (note ad loc.), are these:—

"In quâdam provinciâ nostrâ sunt formicæ in magnitudine catulorum, habentes septem pedes, et alas quatuor—istæ formicæ ab occasu solis ad ortum morantur sub terrâ et fodiunt purissimum aurum totâ nocte—quærunt victum suum totâ die —in nocte autem veniunt homines de cunctis civitatibus ad colligendum ipsum aurum et imponunt elephantibus—quando formicæ sunt suprâ terram, nullus ibi audet accedere, propter crudelitatem et ferocitatem ipsarum." According to Tzschuck (ad Pomp. Mel. iii. vii. § 2) some of the Arabian writers have the same tale. Nearchus declared that he had seen the skins of these ants. (Arrian. Indic. 15.) And so late as the year 1559 one was (it is said) sent as a present from the Shah of Persia to Solyman II. This is described by De Thou in the "History of his Time" as "formica Indica, canis mediocris magnitudine, animal mordax et sævum." (xxiv. p. 809.)

Modern research has not discovered anything very satisfactory either with respect to the animal intended, or the habits ascribed to it. Perhaps the most plausible conjecture is that which identifies it with the Pengolin, or Ant-eater (*Manis Pentedactyla* of Linnæus), which burrows on the sandy plains of northern India. (See Blakesley ad loc.)

Professor Wilson suggests that the entire story arose from the fact that the gold collected in the plains of Little Thibet is commonly called *Pippilika*, or "ant-gold" —the name being given to it from a belief that colonies of ants, by clearing away the sand or soil, leave the ore exposed. (Journal of As. Soc. vol. xiii. pp. 137 and 143.)

[8] This is of course untrue, and it is difficult to understand how Herodotus could entertain such a notion. There is no real difference, as regards the anatomy of the

104. When the Indians therefore have thus equipped themselves they set off in quest of the gold, calculating the time so that they may be engaged in seizing it during the most sultry part of the day, when the ants hide themselves to escape the heat. The sun in those parts shines fiercest in the morning, not, as elsewhere, at noonday ; the greatest heat is from the time when he has reached a certain height, until the hour at which the market closes. During this space he burns much more furiously than at midday in Greece, so that the men there are said at that time to drench themselves with water. At noon his heat is much the same in India as in other countries, after which, as the day declines, the warmth is only equal to that of the morning sun elsewhere. Towards evening the coolness increases, till about sunset it becomes very cold.[9]

105. When the Indians reach the place where the gold is, they fill their bags with the sand, and ride away at their best speed : the ants, however, scenting them, as the Persians say, rush forth in pursuit. Now these animals are so swift, they declare, that there is nothing in the world like them : if it were not, therefore, that the Indians get a start while the ants are

---

leg, between the horse and the camel. In each the leg is composed of four bones which are united by three joints, but of these two only—the real knee, which is more apparent in the camel than in other quadrupeds owing to the length of the thigh-bone, and the hough—have at all the look of knee-joints. Even if the fetlock joint be counted, there can be but three *knees* ; for it is impossible to extend that character to the hip-joint, which is wholly concealed.

[9] Bredow (Geograph. et Uranolog. Herod. viii.) and Niebuhr (Geography of Herodotus, p. 10, E. T.) explain this from Herodotus's notion of the earth as a flat plain, on the whole of which the sun rose (and again set) at the same moment. The east therefore, which was close to the sun in the morning, was hottest at that time ; the west was then coldest. In the evening the case was exactly reversed. Thus Herodotus would not be describing any fact, but only his own conceptions of what must be the case. It may, however, be questioned whether this is a full account of the matter. Herodotus is apparently narrating *what he had heard*, and it belongs to his simplicity not to mix up his own speculations with the relations which he had received from others. Probably his own anticipations had been confirmed by the accounts which had reached him of the actual climate of the gold region. The following statement is made by Moorcroft with regard to the temperature of the region north of the Himalaya :—" At *eight in the morning* the sun overtops the hills which surround the little valley of Niti, and blazes with a fierceness of which we were the more sensible from the cold of the morning. *About three the heat falls off most rapidly.* I have never before experienced so sudden a transition from heat to cold, and contrariwise. At night I am only comfortably warm with all the bedclothes that I can muster. At sunrise a thick coarse woollen wrapping-gown, over-shirt, cotton waistcoat, and double cotton coat, is only just sufficient to keep out the cold. At nine the outer coat must be thrown off ; at ten it is desirable to get quit of the other ; and at noon the rest of the garments are at least incommodious from the heat. The reverse of this process becomes necessary from half-past three till night " (As. Res. vol. xii. p. 399, note). It must be remembered that in Greece, as with ourselves, the afternoon was the warmest part of the day (see Buttmann's Lexilogus, p. 225, and especially note [7]).

mustering, not a single gold-gatherer could escape. During the flight the male camels, which are not so fleet as the females, grow tired, and begin to drag, first one, and then the other ; but the females recollect the young which they have left behind, and never give way or flag.[1] Such, according to the Persians, is the manner in which the Indians get the greater part of their gold , some is dug out of the earth, but of this the supply is more scanty.[2]

106. It seems as if the extreme regions of the earth were blessed by nature with the most excellent productions, just in the same way that Greece enjoys a climate more excellently tempered than any other country.[3] In India, which, as I observed lately, is the furthest region of the inhabited world towards the east, all the four-footed beasts and the birds are very much bigger than those found elsewhere, except only the horses, which are surpassed by the Median breed called the Nisæan.[4] Gold too is produced there in vast abundance, some dug from the earth, some washed down by the rivers, some carried off in the mode which I have but now described. And further, there are trees which grow wild there, the fruit whereof is a wool exceeding in beauty and goodness that of sheep. The natives make their clothes of this tree-wool.[5]

107. Arabia is the last of inhabited lands towards the south, and it is the only country which produces frankincense, myrrh, cassia, cinnamon, and ladanum.[6] The Arabians[7] do not get any

[1] Marko Polo relates that when the Tatars make incursions into the country lying to the north of them, they adopt the same device of riding mares which have foals, and which are therefore anxious to get back to their young. (Travels, p. 745.)

[2] The whole of this region of Central Asia is in the highest degree auriferous. The ranges of the Hindoo-Koosh, Belur Tagh, Mus Tagh, and Altai, especially abound with this precious metal. In the Altai mountains, rude traces of ancient mining have been found. (Heeren's As. Nat. i. p. 47.) Bokhara and Thibet are especially renowned for their productiveness. On the gold of Thibet, see As. Res. vol. xii., pp. 437-9, &c.

[3] Herodotus seems to ascribe the excellence of the climate of Greece to its central situation, equally remote from all the extremities of the earth. He does not see that this centrality is only relative, each nation being the centre of the world known to it. Aristotle (Polit. vii. 6) goes beyond Herodotus, and attributes the well-attempered disposition of the Greeks to the same cause. (τὸ τῶν Ἑλλήνων γένος, ὥσπερ μεσεύει κατὰ τοὺς τόπους, οὕτως ἀμφοῖν μετέχει, καὶ γὰρ ἔνθυμον καὶ διανοητικόν ἐστι.)

[4] Nisæa (Nisáya) is mentioned as a district of Media in the Behistun Inscription (Col. i. par. 18, § 11). Concerning its locality and the excellency of its horses, see note on Book vii. ch. 40.

[5] Vide supra, ch. 47. "Tree-wool" is exactly the German name for cotton (Baumwolle).

[6] Lédanon or ladanon, a resin or gum, answering to the ládin of the Arabs, was produced by the shrub lédon, the Cistus Creticus of Dioscorides, or Cistus ladani-

of these, except the myrrh,[8] without trouble.   The frankincense they procure by means of the gum styrax,[9] which the Greeks obtain from the Phœnicians ; this they burn, and thereby obtain the spice.   For the trees which bear the frankincense are guarded by winged serpents, small in size, and of varied colours, whereof vast numbers hang about every tree.   They are of the same kind as the serpents that invade Egypt ;[10] and there is nothing but the smoke of the styrax which will drive them from the trees.

108. The Arabians say that the whole world would swarm with these serpents, if they were not kept in check in the way in which I know that vipers are.   Of a truth Divine Providence does appear to be, as indeed one might expect beforehand, a wise contriver.   For timid animals which are a prey to others are all made to produce young abundantly, that so the species may not be entirely eaten up and lost ; while savage and noxious creatures are made very unfruitful.   The hare, for instance, which is hunted alike by beasts, birds, and men, breeds so abun-

ferus, a native of Cyprus and Candia. (Cp. Plin. xii. 17 ; see below, n. ch. 112.)   It is now brought from Constantinople and the Greek islands.   It differed from the libanôtus or frankincense, which was produced by the libanus-tree, the *Juniperus Lycia*, or the *Boswellia Thurifera*, a native of Arabia, whence Virgil says, " Solis est thurea virga Sabæis." (G. ii. 117).   This last was used for sacrifices (Her. i. 183 ; ii. 40), and not for embalming (Her. ii. 86).   It is the libán of the Arabs, and the same as the Hebrew libaneh or liboneh, "incense," which came from Sheba or southern Arabia (Is. lx. 6 ; Jer. vi. 20).   The libán, which is explained in Arabic by the word "kondor," answers to the χόνδρος λιβανωτοῦ of the Greek, the "granum thuris."   The bokhôor-el-burr, so common in Syria and Egypt, the coarse particles of frankincense, made into a cake and used for incense, as in some Christian churches, seems to be an inferior kind of " granum," or "mica thuris."   The libán or libanôtus is still a production of Arabia, particularly of Hadramaut.   Herodotus extends the epithet "libanótophoros," or thuriferus, to all Arabia (B. ii. ch. 8.)   The name libán would seem to be taken from its whiteness, lubn, lebn, of the Hebrew, whence lubn, "milk," and Mount Lebanon (or Mont Blanc), so called from its snow.   Pliny (xii. 17), citing Herodotus, says the Arabs brought yearly a talent-weight of "thus" to the kings of Persia, and he erroneously thinks it went to Persia at an earlier time than to Syria or Egypt.—[G. W.]

[7] The Arabs supplied Egypt with various spices and gums which were required for embalming and other purposes.   In Genesis xxxvii. 25, the Ishmaelites or Arabs were going to Egypt from "Gilead with their camels bearing spicery, and balm, and myrrh." (See n. B. ii. ch. 86.)   The names are nukáth, נכאת styrax (the Arabic nukah, ﻛﺞ), gum tragacanth, tziri צרי opobalsam, and lot לט laden.—[G. W.]

[8] Smyrna, the Greek name of *myrrh*, is the same as that of the city.   " Mir " (Exod. xxx. 23), the Hebrew word, is said to be from its "dropping."   It either gave its name to, or received it from, " bitterness," mir or mor signifying "bitter," both in Hebrew and Arabic.   The tree which produces it is a native of Arabia and of the Somauli country S. of Abyssinia (called by Ehrenberg Balsamodendron myrrha), (Strabo, xvi. p. 535 ; Diodor. ii. 49).   Plutarch (de Isid. s. 80) says the Egyptians called it " bal," but in Coptic it had the name "shal," which to a Greek would have been unpronounceable and unwritable.—[G. W.]

[9] This is the "gum storax" of modern commerce.

[10] Vide supra, ii. 75.   If serpents, they should be oviparous.—[G. W.]

dantly as even to superfetate,[1] a thing which is true of no other animal. You find in a hare's belly, at one and the same time, some of the young all covered with fur, others quite naked, others again just fully formed in the womb, while the hare perhaps has lately conceived afresh. The lioness, on the other hand, which is one of the strongest and boldest[2] of brutes, brings forth young but once in her lifetime,[3] and then a single cub;[4] she cannot possibly conceive again, since she loses her womb at the same time that she drops her young.[5] The reason of this is, that as soon as the cub begins to stir inside the dam, his claws, which are sharper than those of any other animal, scratch the womb; as time goes on, and he grows bigger, he tears it ever more and more; so that at last, when the birth comes, there is not a morsel in the whole womb that is sound.

109. Now with respect to the vipers and the winged snakes of Arabia, if they increased as fast as their nature would allow, impossible were it for man to maintain himself upon the earth. Accordingly it is found that when the male and female come together, at the very moment of impregnation, the female seizes the male by the neck, and having once fastened, cannot be brought to leave go till she has bit the neck entirely through. And so the male perishes; but after a while he is revenged upon the female by means of the young, which, while still unborn, gnaw a passage through the womb, and then through the belly of their mother, and so make their entrance into the world. Contrariwise, other snakes, which are harmless, lay eggs, and hatch a vast number of young. Vipers are found in all parts of the world, but the winged serpents are nowhere seen except in Arabia, where they are all congregated together. This makes them appear so numerous.

110. Such, then, is the way in which the Arabians obtain their frankincense; their manner of collecting the cassia[5] is the

[1] This fact has been often questioned; but (as Bähr shows) it has in its favour Linnæus, and the author of the Allgemeine Historie der Natur (Hamb. and Leips. 1757). The former says: "Lepus immensus parturitione per totam æstatem, superfetatione haud rarâ" (i. p. 161).
[2] The courage of the lion has been recently called in question by Mr. Gordon Cumming and Dr. Livingstone, whose experience certainly tends to lower the character of the king of brutes. Still, under the pressure of hunger, or where he has cubs to defend, the boldness of the lion is remarkable. (See Mr. Gordon Cumming's Lion-Hunter, pp. 119, 316, &c.)
[3] The fabulous character of the whole of this account was known to Aristotle, who truly observes that the lioness brings forth young in the spring of the year for many years in succession, and more usually lays up two cubs than one. (Hist. An. vi. 31.)
[4] According to Mr. Gordon Cumming, it is not uncommon for the lioness to have three or four cubs at a birth. (Lion-Hunter, pp. 116, 326, &c.)
[5] Cassia and cinnamon, according to Larcher (note ad loc.), are from the same

following :—They cover all their body and their face with the hides of oxen and other skins, leaving only holes for the eyes, and thus protected go in search of the cassia, which grows in a lake of no great depth. All round the shores and in the lake itself there dwell a number of winged animals, much resembling bats, which screech horribly, and are very valiant. These creatures they must keep from their eyes all the while that they gather the cassia.[6]

111. Still more wonderful is the mode in which they collect the cinnamon.[7] Where the wood grows, and what country produces it, they cannot tell—only some, following probability, relate that it comes from the country in which Bacchus was

tree, the only difference being that cinnamon is properly the branch with the bark on ; cassia is the bark without the branch. Since the former ceased to be an article of commerce, the latter has usurped its name. Thus our cinnamon is not the cinnamon of the ancients, but their cassia. The word cassia is derived from a Hebrew root (קצע), which means "to cut or scrape off the surface;" whence also מַקְצֻעָה, "a plane."

[6] The cassia is supposed to be the Laurus cassia, or, according to some, the Cassia fistula. In Hebrew (Exod. xxx. 24) it is called kedh (קדה) or ketziâh (קציעה), signifying " split " or " peeled off," which would apply to the Laurus cassia, or to our modern cinnamon. But Herodotus says they "gathered" the cassia, it should not therefore be cinnamon; and the Laurus cassia and Laurus cinnamomum are too much alike to be considered in those days two distinct trees. If a fruit, was this the nutmeg, the Myristica moschata? But it is of the Laurus tribe also, and does not grow in shallow water, nor does the cinnamon, which requires a dry sandy soil, as Pliny states (xii. 19). Cassia is supposed to be the Malay word *kashu*, " wood; " but this and cinnamon were perhaps both Arab or Phœnician names. Pliny's description of the "casia" (xii. 19) certainly agrees very well with the real cinnamon.—[G.W.]

[7] The modern cinnamon is the rind of the Laurus cinnamomum of Ceylon, the Arabic Kirfeh. The name cinnamomum has been applied to different plants. That of Herodotus, taken by birds to build their nests, could not have been a cinnamon-branch; and, if not altogether a fable, should rather be the calamus, or aromatic reed, mentioned in Exodus xxx. 23, and by Diodorus, ii. 49; Dionysius, Perieg. 937; Plin. xii. 22; and other writers. Pliny, though he speaks of a bird building its nest of "cinnamum" in Arabia (x. 33), denies that the real cinnamon (cinnamomum) grows in that country (xii. 18); and (in c. 19) treats "Herodotus as a great dealer in fables for the story of birds building their nests of cinnamon and cassia," which he makes the production of Ethiopia. The cinnamon was kept cut like a coppice, and the twigs were thought the best. The cinnamomum or cinnamon was of *two kinds* (Plin. xii. 19), and the cinnamum which grew in Syria and Arabia, according to Pliny, was a *distinct plant* (xii. 18, and xvi. 32). A coarse grass still grows in the deserts between Nubia and the Red Sea, which has the same aromatic scent as cinnamon. Strabo (xvi. p. 535, ed. Cas.) mentions cinnamomum, thus or libanus, and myrrh, as productions of Arabia; but this cinnamon was either a different plant, or merely imported through that country. Again, in b. ii. p. 65, and b. xvii. (beg[s]. p. 540) he makes it a production of the country above Meroë, and in b. xvii. p. 543, he says Sesostris went into Ethiopia, even to the " cinnamomiferous" region. Others also place this region to the S. of Abyssinia. Dionys. Perieg., who mentions it in Southern Arabia, says (944):—

'Ορνιθες δ' ἑτέρωθεν ἀοικήτων ἀπὸ νήσων
'Ηλθον φύλλα φέροντες ἀκηρασίων κιναμώμων.

And this should be Pliny's " cinnamum."—[G. W.] *See ... ... m. xviii, p. 32.*

brought up.[8] Great birds, they say, bring the sticks which we Greeks, taking the word from the Phœnicians,[9] call cinnamon, and carry them up into the air to make their nests. These are fastened with a sort of mud to a sheer face of rock, where no foot of man is able to climb. So the Arabians, to get the cinnamon, use the following artifice. They cut all the oxen and asses and beasts of burthen that die in their land into large pieces, which they carry with them into those regions, and place near the nests : then they withdraw to a distance, and the old birds, swooping down, seize the pieces of meat and fly with them up to their nests ; which, not being able to support the weight, break off and fall to the ground.[1] Hereupon the Arabians return and collect the cinnamon, which is afterwards carried from Arabia into other countries.

112. Ledanum, which the Arabs call *ladanum*, is procured in a yet stranger fashion. Found in a most inodorous place, it is the sweetest-scented of all substances. It is gathered from the beards of he-goats,[2] where it is found sticking like gum, having come from the bushes on which they browse. It is used in many sorts of unguents, and is what the Arabs burn chiefly as incense.

113. Concerning the spices of Arabia let no more be said. The whole country is scented with them, and exhales an odour marvellously sweet. There are also in Arabia two kinds of sheep worthy of admiration, the like of which is nowhere else to be

---

[8] Ethiopia probably, v. s. ii. 146.

[9] The Phœnician word was probably identical with the Hebrew, which is קִנָּמוֹן, *cinnamon* (Exod. xxx. 23 ; Cant. iv. 14). Hence the Greek κιννάμωμον, and the Latin "*cinnamum.*" Bochart (Phaleg. ii. iii.) observes that *all* the Greek names of spices are of Semitic origin. Cassia is the קְצִיעָה of Ps. xlv. 9. Myrrh (σμύρνα) is מוֹר (Cant. iii. 6). Frankincense (λιβανωτός) is לְבוֹנָה (Cant. iv. 14). In the same way he identifies galbanum, bdellium, nard, aloes, &c., with Hebrew words. Ledanum is omitted from his list, but perhaps it may be connected with the Hebrew לֹט (Gen. xxxvii. 25 ; cf. Buxtorf ad voc.). As the Phœnicians imported all these spices into Greece, they would naturally be known to the Greeks by Phœnician names.

[1] Bochart (l. s. c.) suggests an etymological foundation to this story. He remarks that in Hebrew the word קִנִּים, *kinnim*, means "nests," and קִנֵּן, *kinnen*, "to build a nest." Hence, he says, an occasion for the fable. The story, however, evidently belongs to a whole class of Eastern tales, wherein an important part is played by great birds. Compare the *rocs* in the story of Sinbad the Sailor in the Arabian Nights, and the tale related by Marco Polo (Travels, p. 658) of the mines of Golconda.

[2] Pliny (xii. 17) says the ladanum adhered to the hair of goats, as they browsed upon the mastic shrub, and this fact evidently led to the statement of Herodotus (see n. [8] on ch. 107). The mastic is another resin from the *Pistaccia Orientalis*, so common still in Greece, where it is called, as of old, σχῖνος, a name given also to the *P. Lentiscus.*—[G. W.]

seen ;[2] the one kind has long tails, not less than three cubits in length, which, if they were allowed to trail on the ground, would be bruised and fall into sores. As it is, all the shepherds know enough of carpentering to make little trucks for their sheep's tails. The trucks are placed under the tails, each sheep having one to himself, and the tails are then tied down upon them. The other kind has a broad tail, which is a cubit across sometimes.[4]

114. Where the south declines towards the setting sun lies the country called Ethiopia, the last inhabited land in that direction. There gold is obtained in great plenty,[5] huge elephants abound, with wild trees of all sorts, and ebony ; and the men are taller, handsomer, and longer lived than anywhere else.

115. Now these are the furthest regions of the world in Asia and Libya. Of the extreme tracts of Europe towards the west I cannot speak with any certainty ; for I do not allow that there is any river, to which the barbarians give the name of Eridanus, emptying itself into the northern sea, whence (as the tale goes) amber is procured ;[6] nor do I know of any islands called

---

[2] Sheep of this character have acquired among our writers the name of Cape Sheep, from the fact that they are the species chiefly affected by our settlers at the Cape of Good Hope. They are common in Africa and throughout the East, being found not only in Arabia, but in Persia, Syria, Affghanistan, Egypt, Barbary, and even Asia Minor. A recent traveller, writing from Smyrna, says:—"The sheep of the country are the Cape sheep, having a kind of apron tail, entirely of rich marrowy fat, extending to the width of their hind quarters, and frequently trailing on the ground; the weight of the tail is often more than six or eight pounds." (Fellows's Asia Minor, p. 10.)

Leo Africanus, writing in the 15th century, regards the broad tail as the great difference between the sheep of Africa and that of Europe. He declares that one which *he had seen* in Egypt weighed 80 lbs. He also mentions the use of trucks (ix. p. 293 A), which is still common in North Africa:—"Vervecibus," he says, "adeo crassescit cauda ut seipsos dimovere non possint; verum qui eorum curam gerunt, caudam exiguis vehiculis alligantes gradum promovere faciunt."

[4] Perhaps a variety, rather than a distinct species. (Cf. Heeren's As. Nat. vol. ii. p. 119.)

[5] Vide supra, ch. 22. With regard to the ebony, see ch. 97, note [4]. For the size of the men, see ch. 20, note [4].

[6] Here Herodotus is over-cautious, and rejects as fable what we can see to be truth. The amber district upon the northern sea is the coast of the Baltic about the gulf of Dantzig, and the mouths of the Vistula and Niemen (the Frische Nehrung and Kurische Nehrung of our maps), which is still one of the best amber regions in the world. The very name, Eridanus, lingers there in the Rhodaune, the small stream which washes the west side of the town of Dantzig. It is possible that in early times the name attached rather to the Vistula than the Rhodaune. For the word Eridanus (= Rhodanus) seems to have been applied by the early inhabitants of Europe, especially to great and strong-running rivers. The Italian Eridanus (the Po), the Transalpine Rhodanus (the Rhône), and the still more northern Rhenus (the Rhine), a name in which we may recognise a similar contraction to that which has now changed Rhodanus into Rhône, are all streams of this character. The main root of the word appears in the Sanscrit *sru-*, the Greek ῥε- ῥυ- (hre-, hru-, or rhe-, rhu-), the Latin *ri-*vus, our *ri*-ver, the German *rinnen*, &c. This root appears

the Cassiterides [7] (Tin Islands), whence the tin comes which we use. For in the first place the name Eridanus is manifestly not

to have been common to all the Indo-Germanic nations. In Eridanus, Rhodanus, &c., it is joined with a root dan (= "stream," or "water"), which is also very widely spread, appearing in the words *Danube, Dane, Dniester, Dnieper, Don, Donau, Donetz, Tanais, Tana,* and perhaps in Jor-*dan*.

[7] This name was applied to the Selinæ, or Scilly Isles; and the imperfect information respecting the site of the mines of tin led to the belief that they were there, instead of on the mainland (of Cornwall). Strabo thought they were in the open sea between Spain and Britain (iii. 125), and that they produced tin, though he allows this was exported from Britain to Gaul. Polybius was aware that it came from Britain; and Diodorus (v. 21, 22) mentions its being found and smelted near Belerium (the Land's End), and being run into pigs (εἰς ἀστραγάλων ῥυθμούς) it was carried to an island off Britain called Ictis, in carts, at low tide, when the channel is dry. It was there bought by traders, who took it on horses through Gaul to the mouth of the Rhone. He afterwards speaks of "tin-mines of the Cassiterides Islands, lying off Iberia, in the ocean," and of the quantity sent from Britain through Gaul to Massalia and Narbóna. Ictis is the Vectis of Pliny and Ptolemy, Vecta of Antoninus' Itinerary, now the Isle of Wight, but the Ictis mentioned by Diodorus was evidently St. Michael's Mount in Cornwall. Timæus speaks of Mictis, 6 days' sail from Britain (Plin. iv. 30). Pliny and Solinus also thought the Cassiterides were out at sea over against Spain (iv. 36; vii. 57). Strabo says, "they are 10 in number, one only inhabited, near to each other, and lying northward from the port of the Artabri (Finisterre or Corunna). The people live by their cattle, and having mines of tin and lead, they exchange these and skins for pottery, salt, and bronze manufactures." Ptolemy thought they were 10, and P. Mela (iii. 6) says they were called Cassiterides from the tin that abounded there. He does not mention them in Britain, but "in Celticis." All these accounts show how confused an idea they had of them, and how well the Phœnicians kept the secret of the tin-mines, which is further proved by the well-known story of the Phœnician captain, who, when chased by a Roman, steered upon a shoal, and caused the wreck of his own and his pursuer's ship, rather than betray it; for which he was rewarded from the public treasury (Strabo, iii. at the end). The bronze swords, daggers, and spear-heads of beautiful workmanship, found in England, which have neither a Greek nor a Roman type, were probably *first* introduced by this trade.

The Greek name Κασσίτερος is the same as the Arabic *Kasdeer;* but the notion that it was a British word is at once disproved by *Kastíra,* signifying "tin" in Sanscrit. Its Hebrew name *Bedeel,* בדיל, "separated," a "substitute" (*perhaps* an "alloy"), may refer to its principal use in making bronze, or to its being found with silver in the ore. Pliny calls it "lead," or "white lead" (iv. 30; vii. 57); Pomponius Mela (iii. 6) merely "lead." A blue metal in the Egyptian sculptures is called *Khasd,* or *Khusbt,* and in another place mention is made of *Khasit;* but this has been thought to be lapis lazzuli. In Coptic tin is *Thram,* or *Thran,* and *Basensh,* ⲃⲁⲥⲛⲟ. According to Mr. Crawfurd it is called in India *Kalahi,* and by the Malays *Timah.*

The Arabs call tin *safèëh.* Their *téneka,* "tin-plate," bears a resemblance to the German *zinn,* the Swedish *tenn,* the Icelandic *din,* and our *tin.* Pliny (iv. 34) mentions it in the North of Spain; and a small quantity is still found in Lugo, and another district of Gallicia; but it was principally obtained by the Phœnicians from Britain. It is, however, probable, from its being known by the Sanscrit name *kastira,* that it went at a very remote period from the Malay Islands to India and Central Asia; and Ezekiel mentions tin, with silver, iron, and lead, coming to Tyre from Tarshish (xxvii. 12), which was the same Tarshish, on the Indian Ocean, whence Solomon received "gold, silver, ivory, apes, and peacocks," once every three years (2 Chron. ix. 21), and to which the ships built by Jehoshaphat and Ahaziah were to go from Eziongeber "on the Red Sea in the land of Edom" (1 Kings xxii. 48; 2 Chron. xx. 36, 37). The first mention of tin in the Bible is in Num. xxxi. 22; and

a barbarian word at all, but a Greek name, invented by some poet or other ; and secondly, though I have taken vast pains, I have never been able to get an assurance from an eye-witness that there is any sea on the further side of Europe.   Nevertheless, tin and amber [8] do certainly come to us from the ends of the earth.

116. The northern parts of Europe are very much richer in gold than any other region : [9] but how it is procured I have no

in Isaiah i. 25, and Ezek. xxii. 18, it is mentioned as an alloy. It is not possible to decide when it was first brought from Britain, but probably at a very early time. Tin is mentioned in the Periplus among the imports *from* Egypt to the Indian coast, and it was brought long before that from Britain by the Phœnicians. Tin was not discovered in Germany till 1240 A. D.

The quantity used of old for making bronze was very great, and the remote period when that mixed metal was made shows how early the mines of one or the other of these countries were known. An Egyptian bronze, apparently cast, has been found bearing the name of Papi of the 6th dynasty, more than 2000 years B. C.; and bronze knives appear from the sculptures to have been used before that time.   Bronze was first merely hammered into shape, then cast, then cast hollow on a core or inner mould. In Egypt, Assyria, Greece, and Rome, it had generally 10 or 20 parts of tin to 90 or 80 of copper, but for ornamental purposes the alloys varied, and silver was sometimes introduced.

One pig of tin has been found in England, which, as it differs from those made by the Romans, Normans, and others, is supposed to be Phœnician. It is remarkable from its shape, and from a particular mark upon it, evidently taken from the usual form of the trough into which the metal was run. It is in the *Truro* Museum, and a cast of it is in the Museum of Practical Geology in London. It is about 2 ft. 11 in. long, 11 in. broad, and 3 in. high.

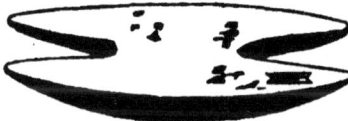

The Carthaginians also went to Britain for tin, as the Tyrians had before. See the Poem of Festus Avienus on Himilco's exploring the N.W. coasts of Europe, between 362 and 350 B. C.   The islands of the Albioni and Hiberni are both mentioned, and the tin islands Œstrymnides near Albion. (Of Carthage and early Greek colonies, see Vell. Paterculus, and n. 4 on Book ii. ch. 32.)—[G. W.]

[8] Herodotus is quite correct in his information respecting amber being found at the extremity of Europe, though not at the West. Sotacus (according to Pliny, xxxvii. 11) thought in Britain.   Pliny mentions the insects in amber, and speaks of its coming from North Germany, where it was called "glesum" (glass?). Compare Tacit. Germ. 45.   Diodorus (v. 22) says it is found at an island above Gaul, over against Scythia, called Basilea, thrown up by the sea, and nowhere else. It still comes mainly from the south coast of the Baltic, between Königsberg and Memel, but is not quite unknown in other parts of Europe. It is remarkable that the amber of Catania contains insects of Europe, that of the Baltic has insects of Asia.— [G. W.]

[9] It appears, by the mention of the Arimaspi, that the European gold region of which Herodotus here speaks, is the district east of the Ural Mountains, which modern geography would assign to Asia. (Vide infrà, iv. 27.) Herodotus, it must be remembered, regards Europe as extending the whole length of both Africa and Asia, since he makes the Phasis, the Caspian, and the Araxes (Jaxartes) the boundaries between Asia and Europe (infrà, iv. 45). He would therefore assign the whole of Siberia, including the Ural and Altai chains, to Europe. The Russian gold-mines in these mountain-ranges, which were not very productive up to a recent period (Heeren's As. Nat. i. p. 45), have yielded enormously of late years. The annual production at the present time is said to be from four to five million pounds sterling.

certain knowledge. The story runs, that the one-eyed Arimaspi purloin it from the griffins ; but here too I am incredulous, and cannot persuade myself that there is a race of men born with one eye, who in all else resemble the rest of mankind. Nevertheless it seems to be true that the extreme regions of the earth, which surround and shut up within themselves all other countries, produce the things which are the rarest, and which men reckon the most beautiful.

117. There is a plain in Asia which is shut in on all sides by a mountain-range, and in this mountain-range are five openings. The plain lies on the confines of the Chorasmians, Hyrcanians, Parthians, Sarangians, and Thaminæans, and belonged formerly to the first-mentioned of those peoples. Ever since the Persians, however, obtained the mastery of Asia, it has been the property of the Great King. A mighty river, called the Aces,[10] flows from the hills inclosing the plain ; and this stream, formerly, splitting into five channels, ran through the five openings in the hills, and watered the lands of the five nations which dwell around. The Persian came, however, and conquered the region, and then it went ill with the people of these lands. The Great King blocked up all the passages between the hills with dykes and flood-gates, and so prevented the water from flowing out. Then the plain within the hills became a sea, for the river kept rising, and the water could find no outlet. From that time the five nations which were wont formerly to have the use of the stream, losing their accustomed supply of water, have been in great distress. In winter, indeed, they have rain from heaven like the rest of the world, but in summer, after sowing their millet and their sesame, they always stood in need of water from the river. When, therefore, they suffer from this want, hastening to Persia, men and women alike, they take their station at

[10] The Aces has been taken for the Oxus (*Jyhun*), the Ochus (*Tejend?*) the Margus (*Murgab*), the Acesines (*Chenab*), and the Etymander (*Helmend*). See Bähr ad loc. It should undoubtedly be a stream in the vicinity of the Elburz range, near Meshed or Herat, where alone the territories of the five nations named could approach one another. But no river can be found which at all answers the description. The plain and the five openings are probably a fable ; but the origin of the tale may be found in the distribution by the Persian Government of the waters (most likely) of the Heri-rud, which is capable of being led through the hills into the low country north of the range, or of being prolonged westward along the range, or finally of being turned southward into the desert. (See Ferrier's Caravan Journeys, pp. 139 et. seqq.) The wild tribes now quarrel for this stream, and not unfrequently turn its course. In such quarrels blood is often shed, and sometimes they are even the occasion of actual wars (ibid. pp. 276, 305, &c.). Under a strong government, the water supply would of course have been regulated, and so good an opportunity of raising a revenue was no doubt seized with alacrity. For the modern Persian custom see the next note.

the gate of the king's palace, and wail aloud.   Then the king orders the flood-gates to be opened towards the country whose need is greatest, and lets the soil drink until it has had enough ; after which the gates on this side are shut, and others are un-closed for the nation which, of the remainder, needs it most. It has been told me that the king never gives the order to open the gates till the suppliants have paid him a large sum of money over and above the tribute.[11]

118. Of the seven Persians who rose up against the Magus, one, Intaphernes, lost his life very shortly after the outbreak,[1] for an act of insolence.   He wished to enter the palace and transact a certain business with the king.   Now the law was that all those who had taken part in the rising against the Magus might enter unannounced into the king's presence, unless he happened to be in private with his wife.[2]   So Intaphernes would not have any one announce him, but, as he belonged to the seven, claimed it as his right to go in.   The doorkeeper, however, and chief usher forbade his entrance, since the king, they said, was with his wife.   But Intaphernes thought they told lies ; so, drawing his scymitar, he cut off their noses and their ears,[3] and, hanging them on the bridle of his horse, put the bridle round their necks, and so let them go.

119. Then these two men went and showed themselves to the king, and told him how it had come to pass that they were thus treated.   Darius trembled lest it was by the common con-

[11] The sale of water is now practised throughout the whole of Persia, and the money thus raised forms a considerable item in the revenue.   Each province has its Mirab, or Water-Lord, who superintends the distribution of the water within his district, and collects the payments due on this account from the inhabitants.   Chardin says : " Chaque province a un officier établi sur les eaux de la province, qu'on appelle Mirab, c'est-à-dire *Prince de l'Eau*, qui règle la distribution de l'eau partout, avec grande exactitude, ayant toujours ses gens aux courans des ruisseaux pour les faire aller de canton en canton, et de champ en champ, selon ses ordres. . . Les terres et les jardins d'Ispahan, et des environs, payent vingt sols l'année au Roi par *girib*, qui est leur mesure de terre ordinaire, laquelle est moindre qu'un arpent " (tom. iii. p. 100.   Compare Chesney's Euphrat. Exp. vol. ii. p. 660).

[1] It seems probable that Herodotus places this event too early in the history. It can scarcely have occurred before the revolt of Babylon (infrà, 150-9), or Intaphernes would not have occupied the post of honour which he fills in the Behistun Inscription (Col. iv. par. 18, § 4), which was set up subsequently to that event.   (See Col. Rawlinson's Additional Note on the Beh. Insc. p. xii.)

[2] Supra, ch. 84.   It may be suspected that the revolt of Intaphernes was a more serious matter than Herodotus imagined.   Æschylus, who made Intaphernes (his Artaphrenes) the actual slayer of the Pseudo-Smerdis, regarded him as king of Persia before Darius.   (Pers. l. 774, Scholef.   Compare, however, Bloomfield's note ad loc.)

[3] This mode of punishment has always been common in the East.   With regard to its frequency in ancient Persia see note [6] to ch. 69.   Chardin notices its continuance to his day (tom. iii. p. 293).   Its infliction by the revolted Sepoys on our own countrymen and countrywomen in 1857 will occur to all readers.

sent of the six that the deed had been done ; he therefore sent
for them all in turn, and sounded them to know if they approved the conduct of Intaphernes. When he found by their
answers that there had been no concert between him and them,
he laid hands on Intaphernes, his children, and all his near kindred ; strongly suspecting that he and his friends were about to
raise a revolt. When all had been seized and put in chains, as
malefactors condemned to death, the wife of Intaphernes came
and stood continually at the palace-gates, weeping and wailing
sore. So Darius after a while, seeing that she never ceased to
stand and weep, was touched with pity for her, and bade a messenger go to her and say, "Lady, king Darius gives thee as a
boon the life of one of thy kinsmen—choose which thou wilt of
the prisoners." Then she pondered awhile before she answered,
"If the king grants me the life of one alone, I make choice of
my brother." Darius when he heard the reply, was astonished,
and sent again, saying, " Lady, the king bids thee tell him why
it is that thou passest by thy husband and thy children, and
preferrest to have the life of thy brother spared. He is not so
near to thee as thy children, nor so dear as thy husband." She
answered, "Oh ! king, if the gods will, I may have another
husband and other children when these are gone. But as my
father and my mother are no more, it is impossible that I should
have another brother.⁴ This was my thought when I asked to
have my brother spared." Then it seemed to Darius that the
lady spoke well, and he gave her, besides the life that she had
asked, the life also of her eldest son, because he was greatly
pleased with her. But he slew all the rest. Thus one of the
seven died, in the way I have described, very shortly after the
insurrection.

120. About the time of Cambyses' last sickness, the following events happened. There was a certain Orœtes,⁵ a Persian,
whom Cyrus had made governor of Sardis. This man conceived
a most unholy wish. He had never suffered wrong⁶ or had an

---

⁴ The resemblance of this to Antigone's speech is very striking :—

πόσις μὲν ἄν μοι, κατθανόντος, ἄλλος ἦν,
καὶ παῖς ἀπ' ἄλλου φωτός, εἰ τοῦδ' ἠμπλακον·
μητρὸς δ' ἐν Ἅιδου καὶ πατρὸς κεκευθότοιν,
οὐκ ἔστ' ἀδελφὸς ὅστις ἂν βλαστοῖ ποτε.
                                        Soph. Antig. 909-912.

But the internal evidence would show Sophocles rather than Herodotus to have
been the plagiarist. (See Blakesley's note ad loc.)
    ⁵ Orontes, according to other writers. (Diod. Sic. xxi. ; Lucian. Contempl. 14.)
    ⁶ Diodorus (l. s. c.) mentions an outrage committed by Polycrates, which he
regards as a ground of quarrel between him and Orœtes. Certain Lydians, he says,

ill word from Polycrates the Samian—nay, he had not so much
as seen him in all his life ; yet, notwithstanding, he conceived
the wish to seize him and put him to death. This wish, according to the account which the most part give, arose from what
happened one day as he was sitting with another Persian in the
gate of the king's palace. The man's name was Mitrobates,
and he was ruler of the satrapy of Dascyleium.[7] He and Orœtes had been talking together, and from talking they fell to
quarrelling and comparing their merits ; whereupon Mitrobates
said to Orœtes reproachfully, "Art thou worthy to be called a
man, when, near as Samos lies to thy government, and easy as
it is to conquer, thou hast omitted to bring it under the dominion of the king? Easy to conquer, said I? Why, a mere

had fled from the oppressive government of the Sardian Satrap, and taken refuge at
Samos. Polycrates received them courteously, but afterwards murdered them for
the sake of their wealth. But it is not easy to see how this would anger Orœtes,
who could have had no particular interest in the welfare of the fugitives.

[7] Dascyleium was the capital city of the great northern satrapy, which at this
time (according to Herodotus, suprà, ch. 90) included the whole of Phrygia. In
later times central Phrygia certainly formed a distinct satrapy, and the satrapy of
which Dascyleium was the capital was called the satrapy of Mysia, of Phrygia on
the Hellespont, or sometimes of Æolis. (Cf. Arrian. i. 12, and Xen. Hell. III. i. 10
and ii. 1.) Xenophon describes the city as a most luxurious residence. "Here,"
he says, "was the palace of the satrap, Pharnabazus ; and in the neighbourhood were
many great villages abounding with all the necessaries of life. There were vast
numbers of animals of the chase, some in enclosed parks, others in the open country. A river flowed by full of all kinds of fish : and there were also in the region
round about a multitude of birds for such as were skilled in fowling." (Hellen. IV.
i. § 15.)
    The beauty of the scenery and the richness of the soil in this part of Bithynia
are noticed by modern travellers. (Hamilton's Asia Minor, ii. p. 85.) The exact
site of Dascyleium is doubtful. The modern Turkish village of *Diaskilli*, which
certainly retains the name, is supposed to mark the place where the city stood.
(Rennell, W. Asia, i. p. 104.) If that village, however, be correctly given in the
maps, which place it upon the coast, I cannot think that it occupies the site of
the ancient Dascyleium. That city must, I think, like all the other Asiatic capitals
(Sardis, Celænæ, Xanthus, Tarsus, &c.) have lain at some distance from the shore.
This is evidenced by the silence of Xenophon and Strabo, and the omission of Das-
cyleium from Scylax's Periplus. From the two passages in Strabo (xii. p. 797 and
830) where Dascyleium is mentioned, it may be collected that it lay upon the modern
Lufer Sú, the Nilofer of Rennell, where that stream formed a lake, Strabo's lake
Dascylitis, before its junction with the Rhyndacus. The maps mostly make the Lufer
Sú run into the sea, a little to the east of the Rhyndacus. This is incorrect. The
naval surveys have shown that no river of importance enters the sea between the
Ascanias, at the head of the gulf of Moudaniah and the mouth of the Rhyndacus.
There seems to be no doubt, therefore, although this part of the interior has not
been fully explored, that the Lufer Sú joins the Rhyndacus some way from its
mouth. It would, therefore, be the Rhymus of Hecatæus (Fragm. 202), and the
whole statement of that writer would (with one correction) express the truth. Ἐπὶ
δ' Ἀλαζίᾳ πόλει ποταμὸς ὁ Ῥῦμος ῥέων διὰ Μυγδόνης πεδίον ἀπὸ (l. ἐπ l) δύσιος ἐκ τῆς
λίμνης τῆς Δασκυλιτίδος ἐς Ῥυνδακὸν ἐσβάλλει.
    According to Stephen (ad voc.) Dascyleium was founded by a certain Dascylus,
whom he calls "the son of Periaudus." It is uncertain whether he means the father
of Gyges.

common citizen, with the help of fifteen men-at-arms, mastered the island, and is still king of it." Orœtes, they say, took this reproach greatly to heart; but, instead of seeking to revenge himself on the man by whom it was uttered, he conceived the desire of destroying Polycrates, since it was on Polycrates' account that the reproach had fallen on him.

121. Another less common version of the story is that Orœtes sent a herald to Samos to make a request, the nature of which is not stated; Polycrates was at the time reclining in the apartment of the males, and Anacreon the Teian was with him; when therefore the herald came forward to converse, Polycrates, either out of studied contempt for the power of Orœtes, or it may be merely by chance, was lying with his face turned away towards the wall; and so he lay all the time that the herald spake, and when he ended, did not even vouchsafe him a word.

122. Such are the two reasons alleged for the death of Polycrates; it is open to all to believe which they please. What is certain is, that Orœtes, while residing at Magnesia on the Mæander, sent a Lydian, by name Myrsus, the son of Gyges,[8] with a message to Polycrates at Samos, well knowing what that monarch designed. For Polycrates entertained a design which no other Greek, so far as we know, ever formed before him, unless it were Minos the Cnossian,[9] and those (if there were any such) who had the mastery of the Ægean at an earlier time—Polycrates, I say, was the first of mere human birth who conceived the design of gaining the empire of the sea, and aspired to rule over Ionia and the islands.[1] Knowing then that Polycrates was thus minded, Orœtes sent his message, which ran as follows :—

"Orœtes to Polycrates thus sayeth : I hear thou raisest thy thoughts high, but thy means are not equal to thy ambition. Listen then to my words, and learn how thou mayest at once serve thyself and preserve me. King Cambyses is bent on my destruction—of this I have warning from a sure hand. Come thou, therefore, and fetch me away, me and all my wealth—share my wealth with me, and then, so far as money can aid,

---

[8] Vide infrà, v. 121.

[9] Concerning the Θαλασσοκρατία of Minos, cf. Thucyd. i. 4 and 8. The clear line which Herodotus here draws between the heroic and the historic period is very remarkable. Thucydides makes no such distinction. (See i. 9–10; ii. 15, &c.)

[1] The Samians are generally said to have obtained the Θαλασσοκρατία under Polycrates (cf. Thucyd. i. 13; Euseb. Chron. Can. ii. p. 334; Ol. 62, 4), whose authority over the islands is shown by his taking Rhenéa and giving it to the Delians. (Thuc. l. s. c.) According to Eusebius this was the *thirteenth* Θαλασσοκρατία after that of Minos; none of the intermediate Θαλασσοκρατίαι, however, are associated with the name of a *person*.

thou mayest make thyself master of the whole of Greece. But if thou doubtest of my wealth, send the trustiest of thy followers, and I will show my treasures to him."

123. Polycrates, when he heard this message, was full of joy, and straightway approved the terms ; but, as money was what he chiefly desired, before stirring in the business he sent his secretary, Mæandrius, son of Mæandrius,[2] a Samian, to look into the matter. This was the man who, not very long afterwards, made an offering at the temple of Juno of all the furniture which had adorned the male apartments in the palace of Polycrates, an offering well worth seeing. Orœtes learning that one was coming to view his treasures, contrived as follows :—he filled eight great chests almost brimful of stones, and then covering over the stones with gold, corded the chests, and so held them in readiness.[3] When Mæandrius arrived, he was shown this as Orœtes' treasure, and having seen it returned to Samos.

124. On hearing his account, Polycrates, notwithstanding many warnings given him by the soothsayers, and much dissuasion of his friends, made ready to go in person. Even the dream which visited his daughter failed to check him. She had dreamed that she saw her father hanging high in air, washed by Jove, and anointed by the sun. Having therefore thus dreamed, she used every effort to prevent her father from going ; even as he went on board his penteconter crying after him with words of evil omen. Then Polycrates threatened her that, if he returned in safety, he would keep her unmarried many years. She answered, "Oh ! that he might perform his threat ; far better for her to remain long unmarried than to be bereft of her father !"

125. Polycrates, however, making light of all the counsel offered him, set sail and went to Orœtes. Many friends accompanied him ; among the rest, Democêdes, the son of Calliphon, a native of Crotona, who was a physician, and the best skilled in his art of all men then living. Polycrates, on his arrival at Magnesia, perished miserably, in a way unworthy of his rank and of his lofty schemes. For, if we except the Syracusans,[4]

[2] This is the only instance in Herodotus of a Greek bearing the name of his father. Two cases occur of Persians—Artaphernes, son of Artaphernes (vi. 94), and Hydarnes, son of Hydarnes (vii. 83). By the time of Demosthenes, the practice had become common in Greece. (Cf. Valck. ad loc.)

[3] Compare the similar artifice by which Hannibal deceived the Gortynians (Corn. Nep. Vit. Hannibal. § 9): "Amphoras complures complet plumbo ; summas operit auro et argento."

[4] Gelo, Hiero, and Thrasybulus, three brothers, who successively ruled over Syracuse from B. C. 485 to B. C. 466. (Vide infra, vii. 153, et seqq.). For the magnificence of Hiero, see Pindar. Pyth. i.-iii.

there has never been one of the Greek tyrants who was to be compared with Polycrates for magnificence.   Orœtes, however, slew him in a mode which is not fit to be described,[5] and then hung his dead body upon a cross.   His Samian followers Orœtes let go free, bidding them thank him that they were allowed their liberty ; the rest, who were in part slaves, in part free foreigners, he alike treated as his slaves by conquest.   Then was the dream of the daughter of Polycrates fulfilled ; for Polycrates, as he hung upon the cross, and rain fell on him, was washed by Jupiter ; and he was anointed by the sun, when his own moisture overspread his body.   And so the vast good fortune of Polycrates came at last to the end which Amasis the Egyptian king had prophesied in days gone by.

126. It was not long before retribution for the murder of Polycrates overtook Orœtes.   After the death of Cambyses, and during all the time that the Magus sat upon the throne, Orœtes remained in Sardis, and brought no help to the Persians, whom the Medes had robbed of the sovereignty.   On the contrary, amid the troubles of this season,[6] he slew Mitrobates, the

[5] It is conjectured that he was flayed alive. (Wesseling, Bähr, Larcher, ad loc.) I should be inclined to suspect some more horrible and unusual mode of death, such as that mentioned by Plutarch in his life of Artaxerxes, under the name of σκάφευσις, and described by him at great length (§ 16).

[6] The "troubles of this season" form the main subject-matter of the Behistun Inscription.   They may be summed up as follows :—

1. A revolt in Susiana, under Atrines, son of Opadarmes, which was put down easily.

2. A revolt of Babylonia, under a pretender claiming to be the son of the last king, Labynetus (Nabunit), which was of the most serious character, requiring the presence of Darius himself to quell it.   Two great battles were fought between the king's forces and the insurgents, in both of which Darius was victorious.   Babylon then submitted, without standing a siege.

3. A combined revolt of the three most important provinces of Assyria, Media, and Armenia.   A descendant, real or supposed, of the ancient line of Median kings ("Xathrites, of the race of Cyaxares") was placed upon the throne.   Six actions were fought between the rebels and the king's generals, of whom Hydarnes was one ; and at last Darius took the field in person.   Xathrites was then defeated, taken prisoner, and put to death at Agbatana.   This is the Median revolt of Herodotus (i. 130).

4. An unimportant revolt in Sagartia.

5. A rebellion in the Eastern provinces of Parthia, Hyrcania, and Margiana, a district of Bactria, which was suppressed by Hystaspes, the father of Darius, aided by Dadarses, satrap of Bactria.

6. An insurrection in Persia, where another pretender came forward to personate Smerdis, and assumed the title of king of Persia.

7. A rebellion in Arachosia, fomented by this Pseudo-Smerdis.

8. A second revolt of Babylon, probably the one which Herodotus intended to describe, which was put down by one of Darius's generals, named Intaphres.

9. A rebellion of the Sacæ or Scythians.

These troubles appear to have occupied the first six years of the reign of Darius.   It is impossible to say at what point of time within this period the proceedings against Orœtes took place.   They certainly preceded the second revolt of Babylon, but perhaps not by more than a year or two.

satrap of Dascyleium, who had cast the reproach upon him in the matter of Polycrates ; and he slew also Mitrobates' son, Cranaspes,—both men of high repute among the Persians.   He was likewise guilty of many other acts of insolence ; among the rest, of the following :—There was a courier sent to him by Darius whose message was not to his mind—Orœtes had him waylaid and murdered on his road back to the king ; the man and his horse both disappeared, and no traces were left of either.

127. Darius therefore was no sooner settled upon the throne than he longed to take vengeance upon Orœtes for all his misdoings, and especially for the murder of Mitrobates and his son. To send an armed force openly against him, however, he did not think advisable, as the whole kingdom was still unsettled, and he too was but lately come to the throne, while Orœtes, as he understood, had a great power. In truth a thousand Persians attended on him as a body-guard, and he held the satrapies of Phrygia, Lydia, and Ionia.[7]   Darius therefore proceeded by artifice.   He called together a meeting of all the chief of the Persians, and thus addressed them :—" Who among you, oh ! Persians, will undertake to accomplish me a matter by skill without force or tumult ?   Force is misplaced where the work wants skilful management.   Who, then, will undertake to bring me Orœtes alive, or else to kill him ?   He never did the Persians any good in his life, and he has wrought us abundant injury.   Two of our number, Mitrobates and his son, he has slain ; and when messengers go to recall him, even though they have their mandate from me, with an insolence which is not to be endured, he puts them to death.[8]   We must kill this man, therefore, before he does the Persians any greater hurt."

128. Thus spoke Darius ; and straightway thirty of those present came forward and offered themselves for the work. As they strove together, Darius interfered, and bade them have recourse to the lot.   Accordingly lots were cast, and the task fell to Bagæus, son of Artontes.   Then Bagæus caused many letters to be written on divers matters, and sealed them all with the king's signet ; after which he took the letters with him, and

---

[7] The first, second, and third satrapies of our author (v. s. ch. 90), being the whole of Asia Minor except Cilicia.   But it may be questioned whether the satrapial system *was* yet introduced.

[8] Turkish pachas and Persian governors have often had recourse to similar stratagems.   Chardin says (tom. iii. p. 310: " Il y a des exemples de gouverneurs qui ont ou retardé, ou empêché de ses exécutions.   Ils avoient eu avis qu'on avoit résolu de les perdre de cette manière, et ils avoient *mis des gens en embuscade pour enlever le courier*, ou pour lüi prendre l'ordre du Roi, en le volant."   Ali Pacha is said to have done this repeatedly.

departed for Sardis. On his arrival he was shown into the presence of Orœtes, when he uncovered the letters one by one, and giving them to the king's secretary—every satrap has with him a king's secretary [*]—commanded him to read their contents. Herein his design was to try the fidelity of the body-guard, and to see if they would be likely to fall away from Orœtes. When therefore he saw that they showed the letters all due respect, and even more highly reverenced their contents, he gave the secretary a paper in which was written, "Persians, king Darius forbids you to guard Orœtes." The soldiers at these words laid aside their spears. So Bagæus, finding that they obeyed this mandate, took courage, and gave into the secretary's hands the last letter, wherein it was written, "King Darius commands the Persians who are in Sardis to kill Orœtes." Then the guards drew their swords and slew him upon the spot. Thus did retribution for the murder of Polycrates the Samian overtake Orœtes the Persian.

129. Soon after the treasures of Orœtes had been conveyed to Sardis [10] it happened that king Darius, as he leaped from his horse during the chase, sprained his foot. The sprain was one of no common severity, for the ancle-bone was forced quite out of the socket. Now Darius already had at his court certain Egyptians whom he reckoned the best-skilled physicians in all the world ;[1] to their aid, therefore, he had recourse ; but they twisted the foot so clumsily, and used such violence, that they only made the mischief greater. For seven days and seven nights the king lay without sleep, so grievous was the pain he suffered. On the eighth day of his indisposition, one who had heard before leaving Sardis of the skill of Democêdes the Crotoniat, told Darius, who commanded that he should be brought with all speed into his presence. When, therefore, they had found him among the slaves of Orœtes, quite uncared for by any one, they brought him just as he was, clanking his fetters, and all clothed in rags, before the king.

[*] In modern Persia the court attaches *three* officers to every governor of a province, one of whom is even now called secretary. His business is to keep the king informed of all that passes at the court of the governor. (See Chardin, tom. iii. p. 302.)

[10] In the East the disgrace of a governor, or other great man, has always involved the forfeiture of his property to the crown. Chardin says : "Toute disgrace en Perse emporte infailliblement avec soi la confiscation des biens" (tom. iii. p. 310). So we find in the decrees of Cyrus, reported by Josephus (Antiq. xii. 1), that transgressors were to be crucified, and their goods forfeited to the king (τὰς οὐσίας αὐτῶν εἶναι βασιλικάς); compare also Antiq. xii. ch. 4.

[1] On the celebrity of the Egyptians as physicians see Book ii. ch. 84, note [4], and supra, ch. i. note [2].

130. As soon as he was entered into the presence, Darius asked him if he knew medicine—to which he answered " No," for he feared that if he made himself known he would lose all chance of ever again beholding Greece. Darius, however, perceiving that he dealt deceitfully, and really understood the art, bade those who had brought him to the presence, go fetch the scourges and the pricking-irons.[2] Upon this Democêdes made confession, but at the same time said, that he had no thorough knowledge of medicine—he had but lived some time with a physician, and in this way had gained a slight smattering of the art. However, Darius put himself under his care, and Democêdes, by using the remedies customary among the Greeks, and exchanging the violent treatment of the Egyptians for milder means, first enabled him to get some sleep, and then in a very little time restored him altogether, after he had quite lost the hope of ever having the use of his foot. Hereupon the king presented Democêdes with two sets of fetters wrought in gold ; so Democêdes asked if he meant to double his sufferings, because he had brought him back to health ? Darius was pleased at the speech, and bade the eunuchs take Democêdes to see his wives, which they did accordingly, telling them all that this was the man who had saved the king's life. Then each of the wives dipped with a saucer into the chest of gold, and gave so bountifully to Democêdes, that a slave named Sciton, who followed him, and picked up the staters[3] which fell from the saucers, gathered together a great heap of gold.

131. This Democêdes left his country and became attached to Polycrates in the following way :—His father, who dwelt at Crotona, was a man of a savage temper, and treated him cruelly. When, therefore, he could no longer bear such constant ill-usage, Democêdes left his home, and sailed away to Ægina. There he set up in business, and succeeded the first year in surpassing all the best-skilled physicians of the place, notwithstanding that he was without instruments, and had with him none of the appliances needful for the practice of his art. In the second year the state of Ægina hired his services at the price of a talent ; in

---

[2] Perhaps the *blinding*-irons, the τερόναι σιδηραῖ of Procopius (De Bell. Pers. i. 7, § 6). In ancient, as in modern times, putting out the eyes has been a Persian punishment. (Cf. Xen. Anab. i. ix. 13.)

[3] By staters we must here understand Darics, the earliest gold-coin of Persia. Herodotus in another place calls them Daric staters (vii. 28). These were of very nearly the same value as the staters principally current in Greece. The stater of Cyzicus weighed, probably, about 140 grains ; that of Athens 132¼ ; that of Lampsacus 129 ; that of Phocæa 127. The Daric is found, from the specimens which remain, to weigh 128¼ grains. (See Hussey's Ancient Weights and Measures, ch. vii. ; and vide infrà, vii. 28.)

the third the Athenians engaged him at a hundred minæ ; and in the fourth Polycrates at two talents.⁴ So he went to Samos, and there took up his abode. It was in no small measure from his success that the Crotoniats came to be reckoned such good physicians ; for about this period the physicians of Crotona had the name of being the best, and those of Cyrênê the second best, in all Greece. The Argives, about the same time, were thought to be the first musicians in Greece.

132. After Democêdes had cured Darius at Susa, he dwelt there in a large house, and feasted daily at the king's table, nor did he lack anything that his heart desired, excepting liberty to return to his country. By interceding for them with Darius, he saved the lives of the Egyptian physicians who had had the care of the king before he came, when they were about to be impaled, because they had been surpassed by a Greek : and further, he succeeded in rescuing an Elean soothsayer,⁵ who had followed the fortunes of Polycrates, and was lying in utter neglect among his slaves. In short there was no one who stood so high as Democêdes in the favour of the king.

133. Moreover, within a little while it happened that Atossa, the daughter of Cyrus, who was married to Darius, had a boil form upon her breast, which, after it burst, began to spread and increase. Now so long as the sore was of no great size, she hid it through shame and made no mention of it to any one ; but when it became worse, she sent at last for Democêdes, and showed it to him. Democêdes said that he would make her well, but she must first promise him with an oath that if he cured ·her she would grant him whatever request he might prefer ; assuring her at the same time that it should be nothing which she could blush to hear.

134. On these terms Democêdes applied his art, and soon cured the abscess ; and Atossa, when she had heard his request, spake thus one night to Darius :—

⁴ Herodotus, where he mentions no standard, must be regarded as intending the Attic, which was in general use throughout Greece in his own day. The salary of Democedes will therefore be :—1st year, 60 *minæ*, or 243*l.* 15*s.* ; 2nd year, 100 *minæ*, or 406*l.* 5*s.* ; 3rd year, 120 *minæ*, or 487*l.* 10*s.* Valckenaer thinks that neither Athens nor Ægina could have afforded such large sums (note ad loc.). But it must be remembered that Athens was at this time under the tyranny of Pisistratus. Perhaps, however, the descendants of Democedes, from whom Herodotus, it is likely, received the tale, magnified the amount, to enhance the glory of their ancestor. The employment of state-physicians in Greece is noticed by Xenophon (Mem. iv. ii. § 5) and Plato (Gorg. pp. 21–4 ; Leg. iv. p. 193.)

⁵ Elis about this time appears to have furnished soothsayers to all Greece. The Phocians (viii. 36) had an Elean soothsayer, named Tellias. And at Platæa the soothsayers on both sides were of the same nation (ix. 33, and 37). The gift was hereditary in certain families (vide infrà, ix. 33).

"It seemeth to me strange, my lord, that, with the mighty power which is thine, thou sittest idle, and neither makest any conquest, nor advancest the power of the Persians. Methinks that one who is so young, and so richly endowed with wealth, should perform some noble achievement to prove to the Persians that it is a man who governs them. Another reason, too, should urge thee to attempt some enterprise. Not only does it befit thee to show the Persians that a man rules them, but for thy own peace thou shouldest waste their strength in wars lest idleness breed revolt against thy authority. Now, too, whilst thou art still young, thou mayest well accomplish some exploit ; for as the body grows in strength the mind too ripens, and as the body ages, the mind's powers decay, till at last it becomes dulled to everything."

So spake Atossa, as Democêdes had instructed her. Darius answered :—" Dear lady, thou hast uttered the very thoughts that occupy my brain. I am minded to construct a bridge which shall join our continent with the other, and so carry war into Scythia. Yet a brief space and all will be accomplished as thou desirest."

But Atossa rejoined :—" Look now, this war with Scythia were best reserved awhile—for the Scythians may be conquered at any time. Prithee, lead me thy host first into Greece. I long to be served by some of those Lacedæmonian maids of whom I have heard so much. I want also Argive, and Athenian, and Corinthian women.[*] There is now at the court a man who can tell thee better than any one else in the whole world whatever thou wouldst know concerning Greece, and who might serve thee right well as guide : I mean him who performed the cure on thy foot."

" Dear lady," Darius answered, " since it is thy wish that we try first the valour of the Greeks, it were best, methinks, before marching against them, to send some Persians to spy out the land ; they may go in company with the man thou mentionest, and when they have seen and learnt all, they can bring us back a full report. Then, having a more perfect knowledge of them, I will begin the war."

---

[*] It has been remarked (Mure's Lit. of Greece, vol. iv. p. 406) that this anecdote is at variance with others in Herodotus, which represent the Persians as profoundly ignorant of the leading Greek states at a date long subsequent to the present. (See below, v. 73, and especially v. 105, where utter ignorance of the Athenians is ascribed to *Darius*.) The contradiction is certainly glaring, and no doubt the anecdotes came from different sources. That in the text is in all probability derived from the descendants of Democedes at Crotona, and thus has some claim to attention. (See however note [*] on ch. 138.)

135. Darius, having so spoke, put no long distance between the word and the deed, but as soon as day broke he summoned to his presence fifteen Persians of note, and bade them take Democêdes for their guide, and explore the sea-coasts of Greece. Above all, they were to be sure to bring Democêdes back with them, and not suffer him to run away and escape. After he had given these orders, Darius sent for Democêdes, and besought him to serve as guide to the Persians, and when he had shown them the whole of Greece to come back to Persia. He should take, he said, all the valuables he possessed as presents to his father and his brothers, and he should receive on his return a far more abundant store. Moreover, the king added, he would give him, as his contribution towards the presents, a merchant-ship[7] laden with all manner of precious things, which should accompany him on his voyage. Now I do not believe that Darius, when he made these promises, had any guile in his heart : Democêdes, however, who suspected that the king spoke to try him, took care not to snatch at the offers with any haste ; but said, "he would leave his own goods behind to enjoy upon his return—the merchant-ship which the king proposed to grant him to carry gifts to his brothers, that he would accept at the king's hands." So when Darius had laid his orders upon Democêdes, he sent him and the Persians away to the coast.

136. The men went down to Phœnicia, to Sidon, the Phœnician town, where straightway they fitted out two triremes and a trading vessel, which they loaded with all manner of precious merchandise ; and, everything being now ready, they set sail for Greece. When they had made the land, they kept along the shore and examined it, taking notes of all that they saw ;[8] and

---

[7] Literally, "a round-built vessel." The word γαυλός (γαῦλος) is clearly of Semitic origin, and connects with the Hebrew גֹּל "volvo," and גַּלְגַּל "orbis, sphæra." All manner of round objects are named from this root: as, גֻּלְגֹּלֶת "a skull" (comp. Golgotha); מְגִלָּה "a scroll;" גִּלָּיוֹן "a mirror;" גָּלָל "dung" (of horses); גֻּלָּה "a cup, a bowl." This last word seems to be the original of the Greek γαῦλος, which is used for a bowl or bucket (infra, vi. 119), as well as for a round-built vessel. It may be remarked that the Greek writers use γαῦλος specially, if not solely, for a Phœnician merchant-ship. See below, viii. 97, γαυλούς Φοινικητους. And Callimachus, Κυπρόδε Σιδόνιός με κατήγαγεν ἐνθάδε γαῦλος. Epicharmus (ap. Athen. Deip. vii. p. 320, C.), γαυλοῖσιν ἐν Φοινικικοῖς. And the Scholiast (ad Aristoph. Av. 572), γαῦλος, Φοινικικόν. And Hesychius, γαῦλοι, τὰ ποιμενικὰ τοῦ γάλακτος ἀγγεῖα, καὶ τὰ Φοινικὰ (l. Φοινικικὰ) πλοῖα. (See Bochart's Phaleg. ii. xi.)

[8] Larcher renders "ils levèrent le plan," and Lange "zeichneten sie auf." But ἀπογράφειν never bears this meaning in Greek; it is always "to take notes" or "register." (See ii. 145, v. 29, vii. 100, and compare Scott and Liddell in voc.) The map exhibited by Aristagoras at Athens (infrà, v. 49) appears to have been the earliest of which Herodotus had any knowledge.

in this way they explored the greater portion of the country, and all the most famous regions, until at last they reached Tarentum in Italy. There Aristophilides, king of the Tarentines,[9] out of kindness to Democêdes, took the rudders off the Median ships, and detained their crews as spies. Meanwhile Democêdes escaped to Crotona, his native city,[10] whereupon Aristophilides released the Persians from prison, and gave their rudders back to them.

137. The Persians now quitted Tarentum, and sailed to Crotona in pursuit of Democêdes ; they found him in the market-place, where they straightway laid violent hands on him. Some of the Crotoniats, who greatly feared the power of the Persians, were willing to give him up ; but others resisted, held Democêdes fast, and even struck the Persians with their walking-sticks. They, on their part, kept crying out, " Men of Crotona, beware what you do. It is the king's runaway slave that you are rescuing. Think you Darius will tamely submit to such an insult ? Think you, that if you carry off the man from us, it will hereafter go well with you ? Will you not rather be the first persons on whom we shall make war ? Will not your city be the first we shall seek to lead away captive ? " Thus they spake, but the Crotoniats did not heed them : they rescued Democêdes,[11] and seized also the trading-ship which the Persians had brought with them from Phœnicia. Thus robbed, and bereft of their guide, the Persians gave up all hope of exploring the rest of Greece, and set sail for Asia. As they were departing, Democêdes sent to them and begged they would inform Darius that the daughter of Milo was affianced to him as his bride. For the name of Milo the wrestler was in high repute with the king.[1] My belief is, that Democêdes hastened

[9] Aristophilides is king ($\beta \alpha \sigma \iota \lambda \epsilon \grave{\upsilon} s$), not tyrant ($\tau \acute{\upsilon} \rho \alpha \nu \nu o s$), of Tarentum. As Tarentum was founded from Sparta (Ephor. Frag. 53; Antioch. Frag. 14), it is probable that it had constitutional kings from the first.

[10] Crotona (the modern town of *Crotone*, a bishop's see, and a place of some trade) was distant about 150 miles along shore from Tarentum (*Taranto*).

[11] The reality of this rescue receives a certain degree of confirmation from a story told by Athenæus (Deipn. xii. p. 522, A.). It was a custom at Crotona, he says, for the attendant of the chief magistrate to wear, on the 7th of each month, a Persian garment—the tradition being that this was done to commemorate the rescue of Democêdes, because the Crotoniats at that time stripped his dress off the Persian who laid hands upon their fellow-citizens, and to mark their contempt, put it on this officer. Mr. Blakesley inaccurately assigns this story to Timæus (not. ad loc.).

[1] Milo is said to have carried off the prize for wrestling, six times at the Olympic, and seven times at the Pythian, games (Paus. VI. xiv. 2 ; Aul. Gell. N. Att. xv. 16). On his great strength, see Athenæus, x. p. 412, E ; and compare Schol. ad Theocrit. iv. 6. Mr. Grote remarks with justice that " gigantic muscular force " would be appreciated in Persia much more than intellectual ability (iv. p. 327).

his marriage by the payment of a large sum of money for the purpose of showing Darius that he was a man of mark in his own country.

138. The Persians weighed anchor and left Crotona, but being wrecked on the coast of Iapygia,[2] were made slaves by the inhabitants. From this condition they were rescued by Gillus,[3] a banished Tarentine, who ransomed them at his own cost, and took them back to Darius. Darius offered to repay this service by granting Gillus whatever boon he chose to ask; whereupon Gillus told the king of his misfortune, and begged to be restored to his country. Fearing, however, that he might bring trouble on Greece if a vast armament were sent to Italy on his account, he added that it would content him if the Cnidians undertook to obtain his recall. Now the Cnidians were close friends of the Tarentines,[4] which made him think there was no likelier means of procuring his return. Darius promised, and performed his part; for he sent a messenger to Cnidus, and commanded the Cnidians to restore Gillus. The Cnidians did as he wished, but found themselves unable to persuade the Tarentines, and were too weak to attempt force. Such, then, was the course which this matter took. These were the first Persians who ever came from Asia to Greece;[5] and they were sent to spy out the land for the reason which I have before mentioned.

139. After this, king Darius besieged and took Samos, which was the first city, Greek or Barbarian, that he conquered. The cause of his making war upon Samos was the following:— At the time when Cambyses, son of Cyrus, marched against Egypt, vast numbers of Greeks flocked thither, some, as might

---

[2] The Iapygian promontory (*Capo di Leuca*) was always difficult to double. (See Plutarch. vit. Pyrrh. § 15.

[3] Was this the Gillus, ruler of Crotona, who ransomed Pythagoras from Cambyses, according to Apuleius? (Florid. ii. 15, p. 59). Wesseling thinks so (note ad loc.).

[4] Their common Dorian origin may in some degree account for this.

[5] Compare the conclusion of ch. 56. In the mind of Herodotus this voyage is of the greatest importance. It is the first step towards the invasion of Greece, and so a chief link in the chain of his history. Whether Darius attached much importance to it is a different matter. We must bear in mind that the details have evidently come from the descendants of Democedes, with whom Herodotus would have been brought into contact in Magna Græcia. The whole colouring of the story, therefore, would be what Democedes, plainly a vain-glorious man (ch. 137), chose to make it. I attach less credit to the details than Mr. Grote, who accepts not only the incidents, but much of the colouring (vol. iv. pp. 347–351). Dahlmann's remarks appear to me very sensible: "That after the conclusion of the Babylonian rebellion," he says, "Darius should have marched, not against Greece, but against Scythia, shows perhaps that we must not estimate the influence of the physician too highly. *Everybody wishes to be thought to have had a share in the political events of his day*" (Life of Herod. vii. § 4, end).

have been looked for, to push their trade ; others, to serve in his army ; others again, merely to see the land : among these last was Syloson, son of Æaces, and brother of Polycrates, at that time an exile from Samos.[6] This Syloson, during his stay in Egypt, met with a singular piece of good fortune. He happened one day to put on a scarlet cloak, and thus attired to go into the market-place at Memphis, when Darius, who was one of Cambyses' body-guard, and not at that time a man of any account,[7] saw him, and taking a strong liking to the dress, went up and offered to purchase it. Syloson perceived how anxious he was, and by a lucky inspiration answered : " There is no price at which I would sell my cloak, but I will give it thee for nothing, if it must needs be thine." Darius thanked him, and accepted the garment.

140. Poor Syloson felt at the time that he had fooled away his cloak in a very simple manner ; but afterwards, when in the course of years Cambyses died, and the seven Persians rose in revolt against the Magus, and Darius was the man chosen out of the seven to have the kingdom, Syloson learnt that the person to whom the crown had come was the very man who had coveted his cloak in Egypt, and to whom he had freely given it. So he made his way to Susa, and seating himself at the portal of the royal palace, gave out that he was a benefactor of the king.[8] Then the doorkeeper went and told Darius. Amazed at what he heard, the king said thus within himself :—" What Greek can have been my benefactor, or to which of them do I owe anything, so lately as I have got the kingdom ? Scarcely a man of them all has been here, not more than one or two certainly, since I came to the throne. Nor do I remember that I am in the debt of any Greek. However, bring him in, and

---

[6] Vide suprà, ch. 39.

[7] This could not be true, yet it is a necessary feature in the story, which supposes Syloson to have had no interested motive in making Darius the present. Darius, the Achæmenian, of the blood royal, failing the issue of Cyrus the Great, heir-presumptive (as is likely) to the throne, could not be a mere guardsman in the service of Cambyses, or a personage of small account. The whole story of the cloak is suspicious: it seems to be one of those amusing pieces of provincial gossip which were current among the lively Greeks (compare the dramatic stories of Phanes, Democedes, &c.), and which exactly pleased the fancy of the Halicarnassian. Both from the Behistun Inscription and from the previous narrative of Herodotus (suprà, ch. 70), it may be gathered that Darius was never in Egypt at all, but remained at home when Cambyses made his expedition. Syloson was a refugee at his court, as Demaratus was afterwards (vii. 3); and obtained his request, because Darius was glad of so good an opportunity of destroying the quasi-independence of Samos, which had long been galling to the Persians (v. s. ch. 120).

[8] The king's benefactors (*Orosangæ*) were a body of persons whose names were formally enregistered in the royal archives (vide infra, viii. 85). Syloson makes a claim to be put on this list.

let me hear what he means by his boast." So the doorkeeper
ushered Syloson into the presence, and the interpreters asked
him who he was, and what he had done that he should call himself a benefactor of the king. Then Syloson told the whole
story of the cloak, and said that it was he who had made
Darius the present. Hereupon Darius exclaimed, " Oh ! thou
most generous of men, art thou indeed he who, when I had no
power at all, gavest me something, albeit little ? Truly the
favour is as great as a very grand present would be nowadays.
I will therefore give thee in return gold and silver without stint,
that thou mayst never repent of having rendered a service to
Darius, son of Hystaspes." "Give me not, O king," replied
Syloson, " either silver or gold, but recover me Samos, my
native land, and let that be thy gift to me. It belongs now to
a slave of ours, who, when Orœtes put my brother Polycrates
to death, became its master. Give me Samos, I beg ; but give
it unharmed, with no bloodshed—no leading into captivity."

141. When he heard this, Darius sent off an army, under
Otanes, one of the seven, with orders to accomplish all that Syloson had desired. And Otanes went down to the coast and
made ready to cross over.

142. The government of Samos was held at this time by
Mæandrius, son of Mæandrius,[*] whom Polycrates had appointed
as his deputy. This person conceived the wish to act like the
justest of men, but it was not allowed him to do so. On receiving tidings of the death of Polycrates, he forthwith raised
an altar to Jove the Protector of Freedom, and assigned it the
piece of ground which may still be seen in the suburb. This
done, he assembled all the citizens, and spoke to them as follows :—

" Ye know, friends, that the sceptre of Polycrates, and all
his power, has passed into my hands, and if I choose I may
rule over you. But what I condemn in another I will, if I may,
avoid myself. I never approved the ambition of Polycrates to
lord it over men as good as himself, nor looked with favour on
any of those who have done the like. Now therefore, since he
has fulfilled his destiny, I lay down my office, and proclaim
equal rights. All that I claim in return is six talents from the
treasures of Polycrates, and the priesthood of Jove the Protector of Freedom, for myself and my descendants for ever.
Allow me this, as the man by whom his temple has been built,
and by whom ye yourselves are now restored to liberty." As

[*] Vide supra, ch. 123.

soon as Mæandrius had ended, one of the Samians rose up and said, "As if thou wert fit to rule us, base-born[10] and rascal as thou art ! Think rather of accounting for the moneys which thou hast fingered."

143. The man who thus spoke was a certain Telesarchus, one of the leading citizens. Mæandrius, therefore, feeling sure that if he laid down the sovereign power some one else would become tyrant in his room, gave up the thought of relinquishing it. Withdrawing to the citadel, he sent for the chief men one by one, under pretence of showing them his accounts, and as fast as they came arrested them and put them in irons. So these men were bound; and Mæandrius within a short time fell sick: whereupon Lycarêtus,[11] one of his brothers, thinking that he was going to die, and wishing to make his own accession to the throne the easier, slew all the prisoners. It seemed that the Samians did not choose to be a free people.

144. When the Persians whose business it was to restore Syloson reached Samos, not a man was found to lift up his hand against them. Mæandrius and his partisans expressed themselves willing to quit the island upon certain terms, and these terms were agreed to by Otanes. After the treaty was made, the most distinguished of the Persians had their thrones[1] brought, and seated themselves over against the citadel.

145. Now the king Mæandrius had a lightheaded brother—Charilaüs by name—whom for some offence or other he had shut up in prison: this man heard what was going on, and peering through his bars, saw the Persians sitting peacefully upon their seats, whereupon he exclaimed aloud, and said he must speak with Mæandrius. When this was reported to him, Mæandrius gave orders that Charilaüs should be released from prison and brought into his presence. No sooner did he arrive than he began reviling and abusing his brother, and strove to persuade him to attack the Persians. "Thou meanest-spirited of men," he said, "thou canst keep me, thy brother, chained in a dungeon, notwithstanding that I have done nothing worthy of bonds; but when the Persians come and drive thee forth a houseless wanderer from thy native land, thou lookest on, and

---

[10] Mæandrius had been the secretary (γραμματιστὴς) of Polycrates (v. s. ch. 123), which would indicate a humble origin.

[11] For the ultimate fate of Lycaretus, see below, Book v. ch. 27.

[1] For a representation of the Persian throne, see note on Book vii. ch. 15. Darius is mentioned as sitting upon a throne at the siege of Babylon (infrà, ch. 155), and Xerxes at Thermopylæ (vii. 211, ad fin.) and Salamis (viii. 90). So Sennacherib is represented in the Assyrian sculptures. (Layard's Nin. aud Babylon, p. 150).

hast not the heart to seek revenge, though they might so easily be subdued. If thou, however, art afraid, lend me thy soldiers, and I will make them pay dearly for their coming here. I engage too to send thee first safe out of the island."

146. So spake Charilaüs, and Mæandrius gave consent ; not (I believe) that he was so void of sense as to imagine that his own forces could overcome those of the king, but because he was jealous of Syloson, and did not wish him to get so quietly an unharmed city. He desired therefore to rouse the anger of the Persians against Samos, that so he might deliver it up to Syloson with its power at the lowest possible ebb ; for he knew well that if the Persians met with a disaster they would be furious against the Samians, while he himself felt secure of a retreat at any time that he liked, since he had a secret passage underground[2] leading from the citadel to the sea. Mæandrius accordingly took ship and sailed away from Samos ; and Charilaüs, having armed all the mercenaries, threw open the gates, and fell upon the Persians, who looked for nothing less, since they supposed that the whole matter had been arranged by treaty. At the first onslaught therefore all the Persians of most note, men who were in the habit of using litters,[3] were slain by the mercenaries ; the rest of the army, however, came to the rescue, defeated the mercenaries, and drove them back into the citadel.

147. Then Otanes, the general, when he saw the great calamity which had befallen the Persians, made up his mind to forget the orders which Darius had given him, "not to kill or enslave a single Samian, but to deliver up the island unharmed to Syloson," and gave the word to his army that they should slay the Samians, both men and boys, wherever they could find them. Upon this some of his troops laid siege to the citadel, while others began the massacre, killing all they met, some outside, some inside the temples.

148. Mæandrius fled from Samos to Lacedæmon,[4] and con-

---

[2] That the art of tunnelling was known at Samos is evident from what is said above (ch. 60), and from the remains which have been found in the island. (See note [7] on ch. 60.)

[3] This seems to me the best explanation of the expression τοὺς διφροφορευμένους. The reference is not to the seats on which they were sitting (which are called θρόνοι, not δίφροι), but to the palanquins in which they were ordinarily carried. (See the Etymolog. Magn. and compare Hesychius and Suidas ad voc.) Mr. Blakesley regards the δίφρος as a footstool, and understands τοὺς διφροφορευμένους as those who were attended by footstool-bearers (διφροφόροι—comp. Athen. Deipn. xii. p. 514, A.), but this appears to be a later sense.

[4] As the Samian exiles a little earlier (ch. 45), so Mæandrius now seeks aid from Sparta, the only Greek state that was thought likely to undertake such an expedition

veyed thither all the riches which he had brought away from the island, after which he acted as follows. Having placed upon his board all the gold and silver vessels that he had, and bade his servants employ themselves in cleaning them, he himself went and entered into conversation with Cleomenes, son of Anaxandrides, king of Sparta, and as they talked brought him along to his house. There Cleomenes, seeing the plate, was filled with wonder and astonishment ; whereon the other begged that he would carry home with him any of the vessels that he liked. Mæandrius said this two or three times ; but Cleomenes here displayed surpassing honesty.[5] He refused the gift, and thinking that if Mæandrius made the same offers to others he would get the aid he sought, the Spartan king went straight to the ephors and told them "it would be best for Sparta that the Samian stranger should be sent away from the Peloponnese ; for otherwise he might perchance persuade himself or some other Spartan to be base." The ephors took his advice, and let Mæandrius know by a herald that he must leave the city.

149. Meanwhile the Persians netted[6] Samos, and delivered it up to Syloson, stripped of all its men. After some time, however, this same general Otanes was induced to repeople it by a dream which he had, and a loathsome disease that seized on him.

150. After the armament of Otanes had set sail for Samos, the Babylonians revolted,[7] having made every preparation for

---

Crœsus before (i. 69), and Aristagoras afterwards (v. 38), followed the same course. It was not until refused by Sparta that even the latter applied to Athens.

[5] It was rarely that the Spartan kings, or indeed their other leaders, could resist a bribe. Cleomenes himself almost yielded (infra, v. 51). Leotychides was bribed (vi. 72). Pausanias was corrupted by offers from the Persians (Thucyd. i. 129). Eurybiades was bribed by Themistocles (infra, viii. 5); Plistoanax and Cleandrides by Pericles (Thucyd. ii. 21, Plut. Pericl. c. 22) ; Astyochus by Tissaphernes (Thucyd. viii. 50). Pausanias returned home readily when summoned, because he expected to secure his acquittal by bribery (ib. i. 131). Gylippus was accused of embezzlement (Plut. Lysandr. c. 16). The difficulties which the Lycurgean regulations threw in the way of amassing treasure seem to have whetted the appetite for gain, and to have made the Spartans more venal than the other Greeks. (Cf. Arist. Pol. ii. 6, pp. 57–8, ed. Tauch.)

[6] For the description of this process see below, Book vi. ch. 31. Strabo (xiv. p. 915) ascribes the depopulation of Samos to the harshness of Syloson's government ; and quotes in illustration the proverb, ἕκητι Συλοσῶντος εὐρυχωρίη. But this proverb is quite compatible with the account of Herodotus.

Samos does not appear to have suffered very greatly by these transactions, since in the Ionian revolt, not twenty years afterwards, she was able to furnish sixty ships (vi. 8). The severities exercised by the Persians are probably exaggerated.

[7] It has been already mentioned that Babylon revolted twice from Darius, once in the first, and a second time in the fourth year of his reign. It cannot be determined which of these two revolts Herodotus intended to describe. Of the former, which was quelled by Darius in person, the details are given in the Behistun Inscription (Col. i. par. 16–19, Col. ii. par. 1). The latter is briefly described in Col.

defence. During all the time that the Magus was king, and while the seven were conspiring, they had profited by the troubles, and had made themselves ready against a siege. And it happened somehow or other that no one perceived what they were doing. At last when the time came for rebelling openly, they did as follows :—having first set apart their mothers, each man chose besides out of his whole household one woman, whomsoever he pleased ; these alone were allowed to live, while all the rest were brought to one place and strangled. The women chosen were kept to make bread for the men ;[8] the others were strangled that they might not consume the stores.

151. When tidings reached Darius of what had happened, he drew together all his power, and began the war by marching straight upon Babylon, and laying siege to the place. The Babylonians, however, cared not a whit for his siege.[9] Mounting upon the battlements that crowned their walls, they insulted and jeered at Darius and his mighty host. One even shouted to them and said, "Why sit ye there, Persians ? why do ye not go back to your homes ? Till mules foal ye will not take our city." This was said by a Babylonian who thought that a mule would never foal.

152. Now when a year and seven months had passed, Darius and his army were quite wearied out, finding that they could not anyhow take the city. All stratagems and all arts had been used, and yet the king could not prevail—not even when he tried the means by which Cyrus made himself master of the place. The Babylonians were ever upon the watch, and he found no way of conquering them.

153. At last, in the twentieth month, a marvellous thing happened to Zopyrus, son of the Megabyzus who was among the seven men that overthrew the Magus. One of his sumpter-mules gave birth to a foal.[10] Zopyrus, when they told him,

iii. par. 13, 14. Neither of these two accounts agrees in any point with the narrative of Herodotus.

Ctesias (Exc. Pers. § 22) asserted that the details given by Herodotus belonged, not to any siege under Darius, but to one which took place in the reign of Xerxes. Zopyrus, according to him, was governor of Babylon at the time, and was killed by the rebels. It was Megabyzus, his son, who, to avenge his father, mutilated himself. Traces of this siege of Babylon by Xerxes, and the severities consequent upon it, appear in Herodotus (i. 183, end), Arrian (Exped. Alex. vii. 17), and Plutarch (Apophthegm. p. 173, C.).

[8] Compare Thucyd. ii. 78. Mr. Blakesley well remarks on the large place which bread-making would occupy in the duties of the ancient domestic. The "bread-maker" had not merely to mix and bake the bread, but to grind the flour. (Cf. Exodus xi. 5; Matt. xxiv. 41; Hom. Od. xx. 105–111, &c.)

[9] Compare their confidence when besieged by Cyrus (supra, i. 190).

[10] Ctesias appears to have denied this part of the story altogether (Exc. Pers. L

not thinking that it could be true, went and saw the colt with his own eyes ; after which he commanded his servants to tell no one what had come to pass, while he himself pondered the matter.   Calling to mind then the words of the Babylonian at the beginning of the siege, "Till mules foal ye shall not take our city"—he thought, as he reflected on this speech, that Babylon might now be taken.   For it seemed to him that there was a divine providence in the man having used the phrase, and then his mule having foaled.

154. As soon therefore as he felt within himself that Babylon was fated to be taken, he went to Darius and asked him if he set a very high value on its conquest.   When he found that Darius did indeed value it highly, he considered further with himself how he might make the deed his own, and be the man to take Babylon.   Noble exploits in Persia are ever highly honoured and bring their authors to greatness.   He therefore reviewed all ways of bringing the city under, but found none by which he could hope to prevail, unless he maimed himself and then went over to the enemy.   To do this seeming to him a light matter, he mutilated himself in a way that was utterly without remedy.   For he cut off his own nose and ears, and then, clipping his hair close and flogging himself with a scourge, he came in this plight before Darius.

155. Wrath stirred within the king at the sight of a man of his lofty rank in such a condition ; leaping down from his throne, he exclaimed aloud, and asked Zopyrus who it was that had disfigured him, and what he had done to be so treated. Zopyrus answered, "There is not a man in the world, but thou, oh ! king, that could reduce me to such a plight—no stranger's hands have wrought this work on me but my own only.   I maimed myself because I could not endure that the Assyrians should laugh at the Persians."   "Wretched man," said Darius, "thou coverest the foulest deed with the fairest possible name, when thou sayest thy maiming is to help our siege forward. How will thy disfigurement, thou simpleton, induce the enemy to yield one day the sooner ?   Surely thou hadst gone out of thy mind when thou didst so misuse thyself."   "Had I told thee," rejoined the other, "what I was bent on doing, thou wouldest not have suffered it ; as it is, I kept my own counsel, and so accomplished my plans.   Now, therefore, if there be no failure on thy part, we shall take Babylon.   I will desert to the enemy as I am, and when I get into their city I will tell them

s. c.) On the possibility of the occurrence, see Arist. Hist. An. vi. 24; Plin. H. N. viii. 44; and compare Beckmann ad Arist. Ausc. Mirab. c. 70.

that it is by thee I have been thus treated. I think they will
believe my words, and entrust me with a command of troops.
Thou, on thy part, must wait till the tenth day after I am entered within the town, and then place near to the gates of Semiramis a detachment of thy army, troops for whose loss thou wilt
care little, a thousand men. Wait, after that, seven days, and
post me another detachment, two thousand strong, at the Nineveh gates ; then let twenty days pass, and at the end of that
time station near the Chaldæan gates a body of four thousand.
Let neither these nor the former troops be armed with any
weapons but their swords—those thou mayest leave them.
After the twenty days are over, bid thy whole army attack the
city on every side, and put me two bodies of Persians, one at
the Belian, the other at the Cissian gates ; for I expect, that,
on account of my successes, the Babylonians will entrust everything, even the keys of their gates,[11] to me. Then it will be for
me and my Persians to do the rest." [1]

156. Having left these instructions, Zopyrus fled towards
the gates of the town, often looking back, to give himself the
air of a deserter. The men upon the towers, whose business it
was to keep a look-out, observing him, hastened down, and
setting one of the gates slightly ajar, questioned him who he
was, and on what errand he had come. He replied that he was
Zopyrus, and had deserted to them from the Persians. Then
the doorkeepers, when they heard this, carried him at once
before the magistrates. Introduced into the assembly, he
began to bewail his misfortunes, telling them that Darius had

[11] Properly "bolt-drawers," which were very like those now used in the East—a
straight piece of wood, with upright pins, corresponding with those that fall down
into the bolt, and which are pushed up by this key so as to enable the bolt to be
drawn back. Iron keys were also used at an early period for smaller fastenings.—
[G. W.] *Jut see Arnyson n. AThie.ii.4,*
[1] The stratagem of Zopyrus has small claims to be considered a historic fact.
It seems impossible that either Zopyrus, who (according to both Herodotus and
Ctesias) was for many years satrap of Babylonia, or Megabyzus his son, who was
one of the six great generals of Xerxes' army (infra, vii. 82), and afterwards commanded the Persians in Egypt (infra, ch. 160), could have been the sufferer of such
a terrible mutilation. For the Orientals will not serve under a mutilated man (vide
suprà, ch. 73, ἀρχόμεθα ὑπὸ Μήδου ἀνδρὸς Μάγου, καὶ τούτου ὦτα οὐκ ἔχον-
τος). And the statement of Polyænus (vii. 11, § 8), that the stratagem was copied
from an attempt made by a certain Sacan beyond the Oxus to destroy the army
of Darius, seems to throw the whole narrative into the region of romance. For "the
story told by Polyænus is, in its minutest features, identical with a certain standard
Oriental tale, applied in different ages, by the Persian bards and traditionists to
Firuz and the Hiyathelah, by Abu Rihan to Kanishka and the Indians, and by the
historians of Cashmeer to their famous king, Lalitaditya " (Col. Rawlinson, Note to
Behist. Inscr. p. xvi.).
    It is curious to find the Latin writers stealing the same tale to adorn their own
history (Livy, i. 54; Ovid, Fast. ii. 691, &c.).

maltreated him in the way they could see, only because he had given advice that the siege should be raised, since there seemed no hope of taking the city. "And now," he went on to say, "my coming to you, Babylonians, will prove the greatest gain that you could possibly receive, while to Darius and the Persians it will be the severest loss. Verily he by whom I have been so mutilated, shall not escape unpunished. And truly all the paths of his counsels are known to me." Thus did Zopyrus speak.

157. The Babylonians, seeing a Persian of such exalted rank in so grievous a plight, his nose and ears cut off, his body red with marks of scourging and with blood, had no suspicion but that he spoke the truth, and was really come to be their friend and helper. They were ready, therefore, to grant him anything that he asked ; and on his suing for a command, they entrusted to him a body of troops, with the help of which he proceeded to do as he had arranged with Darius. On the tenth day after his flight he led out his detachment, and surrounding the thousand men, whom Darius according to agreement had sent first, he fell upon them and slew them all. Then the Babylonians, seeing that his deeds were as brave as his words, were beyond measure pleased, and set no bounds to their trust. He waited, however, and when the next period agreed on had elapsed, again with a band of picked men he sallied forth, and slaughtered the two thousand. After this second exploit, his praise was in all mouths. Once more, however, he waited till the interval appointed had gone by, and then leading the troops to the place where the four thousand were, he put them also to the sword. This last victory gave the finishing stroke to his power, and made him all in all with the Babylonians : accordingly they committed to him the command of their whole army, and put the keys of their city into his hands.

158. Darius now, still keeping to the plan agreed upon, attacked the walls on every side, whereupon Zopyrus played out the remainder of his stratagem. While the Babylonians, crowding to the walls, did their best to resist the Persian assault, he threw open the Cissian and the Belian gates,[2] and admitted the enemy. Such of the Babylonians as witnessed the treachery,

---

[2] The situation of the gates which are mentioned in this and a previous chapter (ch. 155) cannot be exactly determined, owing to the complete disappearance of the ancient wall of Babylon. (See Essay iv. at the end of the volume.) No doubt, however, the Belian and the Cissian gates were to the S.E., the former probably deriving its name from the fact that it led to *Niffer*, the city of Bel-Nimrod. (See vol. i. Essay x. p. 485). The "Ninevite gate" would lie to the north. That of Semiramis is altogether uncertain.

took refuge in the temple of Jupiter Belus ; the rest, who did not see it, kept at their posts, till at last they too learnt that they were betrayed.

159. Thus was Babylon taken for the second time. Darius, having become master of the place, destroyed the wall,[3] and tore down all the gates ; for Cyrus had done neither the one nor the other when he took Babylon.[4] He then chose out near three thousand[5] of the leading citizens, and caused them to be crucified, while he allowed the remainder still to inhabit the city. Further, wishing to prevent the race of the Babylonians from becoming extinct, he provided wives for them in the room of those whom (as I explained before) they strangled, to save their stores. These he levied from the nations bordering on Babylonia, who were each required to send so large a number to Babylon, that in all there were collected no fewer than fifty thousand. It is from these women that the Babylonians of our times are sprung.

160. As for Zopyrus, he was considered by Darius to have surpassed, in the greatness of his achievements, all other Persians, whether of former or of later times, except only Cyrus— with whom no Persian ever yet thought himself worthy to compare. Darius, as the story goes, would often say "that he had rather Zopyrus were unmaimed, than be master of twenty more Babylons."[6] And he honoured Zopyrus greatly ; year by year he

---

[3] It is probable that Darius contented himself with breaking breaches in the great wall, instead of undertaking the enormous and useless labour of levelling the immense mounds which begirt Babylon. The walls must have been tolerably complete when Babylon stood a siege against the forces of Xerxes. Even in the time of Herodotus, so much was left that he could speak of the wall as still *encircling* the city (περιθέει, i. 178). Ctesias saw portions of it. (Diod. Sic. ii. 7.) See the Essays appended to Book i. Essay viii. § 26, note [6].

[4] Berosus, on the contrary, declared that the outer walls were entirely destroyed by the orders of Cyrus (ap. Joseph. c. Apion. i. 20). Here again we may understand that breaches were made, which the inhabitants repaired when they determined upon revolt.

[5] Mr. Grote (Hist. of Greece, vol. iv. p. 311) compares with this the wholesale executions of revolted Strelitzes sanctioned by Peter the Great, which took place at Moscow in the year 1698. *Two thousand* are said to have been hung round the walls of the town, and otherwise killed, on that occasion. The Inscriptions of Darius give no indication of his having ever countenanced a massacre of the extent here mentioned. Such bloody measures accord rather with the temper of Xerxes, who, it is evident, treated the Babylonians with far greater severity than Darius (suprà, i. 183, and Arrian, Exp. Alex. vii. 17). That monarch, to judge by the Behistun Inscription, contented himself, on the first occasion of the revolt of Babylon, with putting to death the pretender who headed the rebellion (Beh. Inscr. Col. ii. par. 1, § 5), while on the second occasion he punished with death both the rebel chief and a certain number, which could not have been very large, of his *principal* followers (Beh. Inscr. Col. iii. par. 13, Babyl. Tr.). The impaling of captives had been practised at an earlier date by the Assyrians (Layard's Nineveh and Babylon, p. 355).

[6] Plutarch tells of this Zopyrus the story which Herodotus relates (iv. 143) of

presented him with all the gifts which are held in most esteem among the Persians ;[7] he gave him likewise the government of Babylon for his life, free from tribute ; and he also granted him many other favours. Megabyzus, who held the command in Egypt against the Athenians and their allies,[8] was a son of this Zopyrus. And Zopyrus, who fled from Persia to Athens,[9] was a son of this Megabyzus.

Megabazus, the conqueror of Thrace: that Darius being asked of what he would like to have as many as there were grains in the pomegranate which he was eating, replied "Zopyruses" (Apophthegm. p. 173, A.).

[7] Ctesias mentioned as the chief of these presents a golden hand-mill (μύλην χρυσῆν), weighing six talents, and worth somewhat more than 3000*l.* This, according to him, was the most honourable gift that a Persian subject could receive (Exc. Pers. § 22).

[8] Cf. Thucyd. i. 109. And Ctesias, Exc. Pers. 32–3. Megabyzus married Amytis, daughter of Xerxes, was one of the six superior generals of the Persian army in the Greek campaign, drove the Athenians out of Egypt, and put down the Egyptian revolt; revolted himself against Artaxerxes for not observing the terms granted to Inarus, was reconciled with him, and died in Persia at an advanced age.

[9] This is probably the latest event recorded by Herodotus. It is mentioned by Ctesias almost immediately before the death of Artaxerxes, and so belongs most likely to the year b. c. 426 or 425. There are, however, no means of exactly fixing its date. Zopyrus led the Athenians against Caunus, which he hoped to be able to bring over; but the Caunians resisted, and Zopyrus lost his life in the attempt (Ctesias, Exc. Pers. § 43.)

APPENDIX TO BOOK III.

ESSAY I.

ON THE WORSHIP OF VENUS-URANIA THROUGHOUT THE EAST.—[G. W.]

1. Alilat.—Mylitta or Alitta, from *weled*, "to bear children." 2. Had different names in different countries. 3. A Nature-Goddess. 4. The Syrian Goddess. 5. The Paphian Venus, or Urania, identified with Astarte and Anaitis. 6. Tanat, or Anata. 7. Diana of Ephesus. 8. The mother and child. 9. Alitta and Elissa. 10. Gods of the Khonds. 11. Maut the mother. 12. Juno-Lucina, Diana, and Astarte. 13. Europa and Cadmus. 14. Semiramis the dove. 15. Derceto or Atargatis. 16. Athara and Athor. 17. Inscription at Caervorran, and names of the Syrian Goddess. 18. Figure of Astarte. 19. Baal, Moloch, and other deities of Syria. 20. Arcles, Melicertes, or Hercules. 21. Rimmon and other Syrian deities—Some introduced into Egypt.

1. SOME suppose *Alilat* to mean simply the "Goddesses;" but she is generally thought to be Venus *Urania*, and the same whose worship Herodotus tells us (i. 131) was borrowed by the Persians from the Assyrians and *Arabians*. In ch. 131, Book i. Herodotus says, "the Arabians call Venus *Alitta*, and the Assyrians call Venus *Mylitta*;" and this he confirms in ch. 199. Like the *Alitta* of the Arabs, *Mylitta* corresponded to Lucina, who presided over child-birth. Both these names are Semitic, and are derived from *weled, walada*, "to bear children." (Mulatto is from the past participle of the same verb.) Indeed, Sargon (according to M. Oppert, on the Khorsabad bulls) says "Nisroch directs the marriages of men, and the Queen of the Gods (Mylitta) presides at their birth: I have inscribed on the great northern gates the names of Nisroch and Mylitta." She was the same Deity worshipped

2. in many countries under various denominations; and nowhere perhaps do we see more clearly how the same one from some slight variation of attribute or office was made into several different Deities, and how many may be brought back to the original one. In reality she represented the Productive Principle, Nature, or the Earth, as the generative or vivifying principle was typified by the Sun. She was Astarte in Phœnicia and in other countries (Cic. Nat. Deor. 3); who is even said by Sanconiatho to have had a cow's head (like Athor, the Venus of Egypt), whence called Ashteroth-Karnaim or Astaroth-Kornim, *i. e.* "of the horns" (Gen. xiv. 5). She was the Venus Urania, said by Pausanias (i. 14) to have been chiefly honoured by the Assyrians. She was Anaitis in Persia and Armenia, and even in Assyria, who also answered to Venus; and the Venus of Assyria held a child in her arms

3. (see Layard's Nineveh and Babylon, p. 477), like Athor and Isis in Egypt. She was Ceres, δημήτηρ or γημήτηρ, as the Mother Earth, or

prolific Nature (see Macrob. Saturn. i. 26, and Note on B. ii. ch. 9). She was the " Queen of Heaven," the Moon (who in India is also a form of the god of Nature); she was Rhea or Cybele, the Angidistis or Cybele of Phrygia (Strabo, xii. p. 390); she answered to the Greek Eileithyiæ, who at first were several Goddesses, as well as to Juno, Diana, and Lucina, which three had at different times the same office; she corresponded to Minerva; and in Greece to the original Aphroditê, who became at last the mere personation of beauty and voluptuousness. In Egypt Isis and Athor and also Seben (or Seneb) the Goddess of Eileithyia, answer to her in different capacities; and a Goddess is found there standing on a lion, like "Mother Earth," mentioned by Macrobius (Saturn. i. 26; see At. Eg. pl. lxix.), and again on Assyrian monuments; both which are probably of similar origin.

From the necessity of making a distinction between her charac- 4. ters in the same country, she was called Venus-Urania, who was the great Syrian Goddess. Berosus says Anaitis was first introduced into Persia, into Babylon, Susa, Ecbatana, and Damascus about the time of Arta xerxes II., the son of Darius; but she was doubtless known long before in the latter city. (See notes on B. iii. chs. 131 and 70). The 5. temple of the Paphian Venus or Venus-Urania is represented on the coins of Sardis, identifying Astarte and Anaitis. Strabo mentions Anaitis (xi. p. 352; xv. p. 594) with Omanus, as Persian Deities, as Herodotus does Venus-Urania. In Egypt even Anaitis was worshipped at an early time as Anat or Anta, the Goddess of War, armed with a spear and shield, and raising a pole-axe in the act of striking. (See At. Eg. pl. lxx. pt. i.) She appears to have been a foreign Goddess adopted by the Egyptians. Neith, the Minerva of Egypt, who often carries a bow and arrows, may have been related to Anata. The Phœnician 6. Tanith or Tanat, who answered to Artemis (Diana), as shown by an inscription at Athens, where Abd-Tanat is translated "Artemidorus" in lieu of "slave," or "votary, of Tanat," was the same Goddess; and Plutarch (Vit. Artaxerx.) says "Diana of Ecbatana is there called Anitis." She was called Tanata by Plutarch, who says she was worshipped in the time of Artaxerxes Mnemon; and Berosus, in saying that Artaxerxes Ochus first introduced the worship of Ἀφροδίτης Ταναΐδος, proves her to be the Goddess Venus. This identification of Anata and Venus is further shown by a papyrus (published by Champollion), where Venus is said to be "Neith in the East country, and Sme in the lotus and waters of the West;" and the Venus of Sparta and Cythera wore the dress and arms of Minerva.

Tanat or Thanith was also the name of a place in Cyprus, where Astarte was worshipped. (See the Duc de Luyne's Kings of Citium; cp. Citium and Chittim, (Kitium and Kitim) the Hebrew name of Cyprus.) Tanath is thought to be Mylitta, which agrees with the 7. office of Diana in early times. Diana of Ephesus had the attributes of prolific Nature, and on some coins she stands between figures of the Sun and Moon. She is also as a huntress with the stag (see below). Lanzi thinks Anata the origin of the Greek θάνατος. In a Persian inscription the name is written Anahid or Anahata, in Babylonian Anakhitu, in Greek Τάναις; and it is a curious fact that the planet Venus is still called in Persian Anahid, اناهید. The T is only the feminine sign prefixed to Anaïd.

8.
Mylitta was properly "*the mother of the child*," and not Lucina; but they easily became confounded. And not only do Mylitta and

No. 1.   From Idalium.   No. 2.   Isis and Horus of Egypt.

Alitta signify "the child-bearing" (deity), but the idea of a mother-goddess is found in many mythological systems. In India Devaki nurses her child Crishna, who is an Avatar, or incarnation of Vishnoo; and who, like his mother and some other Deities, has a glory of rays round his head. (See Kreuzer, Rel. de l'Antiq. par Guigniaut, pl. xiii.; and Sir W. Jones, vol. i. p. 266.) The mother and child are also found among the idols of Mexico. Even Juno nursed Hercules (see Winckelmann, Mon. Ined. No. xiv.), and several small statuettes have been discovered at Idalium in Cyprus, where, as at Paphos, Venus was particularly worshipped, which represent a Goddess nursing an infant, bearing a marked resemblance to the Egyptian Isis with Horus. From the same origin was the Greek fable of Venus and Cupid. On the Etruscan mirrors is another figure, having a glory of rays on her head, holding a dead child, said to represent Aurora with Memnon.

9.
Alitta occurs in the Carthaginian name Elissa, given to Dido, whose story was perhaps derived from, and connected with, the introduction of the worship of Venus into Italy, where, as in Greece, she rose from the sea; and Astarte, the Phœnician Venus, was one of the Deities of Etruria. Some have thought Elissa to be the name of El (Ἥλιος), with the feminine termination.

As Mylitta or Alitta was the producing principle, the Deity in that character was, according to human notions, a female. The Earth was chosen to represent that principle; and we even find in the religion of an aboriginal race in India, the Khonds (according to Capt. Charters Macpherson), that their two great Deities were Bella or Boora Pennu, the "Sun" or "god of light," and his wife Tari, "the Earth;" the latter opposed to Boora, as evil to good, but still worshipped. 10.

Some shades of difference next led to various subdivisions of this primary Goddess (as in the case of the primary god), and she who presided over childbirth was made distinct from the "mother." But the relationship was still traceable; and the Egyptians ascribed the Vulture, the emblem of maternity, to the two Goddesses *Maut* ("Mother"), and *Seben* (Lucina). Buto (Latona) too, being primæval darkness or "night, the genesis of all things," had the attributes of Maut. Again, Maut was without any child, merely the abstract idea of mother; while Isis was represented with the infant Horus, as a direct personification of the maternal office. All was the result of their mode of reasoning; and nothing, as Plutarch says, was set down by chance. Existence implied and required a beginning, and all living beings a birth. Without therefore really believing that one Deity was born of another, they made each part of the general system; and one Goddess was said to be born of herself, as another, Khem, the god of Generation, was styled "the father of his own father," and consequently "the husband of his mother," since production could only be an effect of the generative principle. Maut was in like manner her own mother, "proceeding from herself," as was said of Neith (Minerva) in her legend at Saïs. These were supposed to be the necessary operations of the divine power after creation had begun; and the abstract ideas, that were embodied and became gods, were subjected to the same rules as all other beings which proceeded or were endowed with life. Such Deities were not thought to be physical realities, nor could they even always be represented, as in the case of the "mother of herself;" they were principles and abstract notions, and it was a necessary consequence that each (like this of maternity, for instance) should be subject to its own laws; showing that the Egyptian system was not regulated by, or made to accord with, an after-thought, as some have supposed, but devised according to a consistent and set theory. 11.

12. A similar idea is also found in Indian mythology, where Bhavani, the wife of Mahadeva, or Siva, answers to Juno-Lucina, or Diana-Solvizona of the Romans, as well as to Venus-Urania, who presided over gestation; and Lucretius very properly invokes Venus at the beginning of his Hymn on Nature, where he says, lib. i. v. 5 :—

"Per te quoniam genus omne animantium
Concipitur, visitque exortum lumina solis;"

and v. 22 :—

. . . "Quæ quoniam rerum naturam sola gubernas."

(See Sir W. Jones, vol. i. p. 260.) Again, the original identity of

Diana of Ephesus and the most noted of
Goddesses, Venus-Urania, is shown by the
assertion of Demetrius that "all Asia and
the world" worshipped the great Goddess
Diana (Acts xix. 29); and Venus being
called "Mylitta by the Assyrians," shows
the latter to be really the same as, or a
character of, the great Astarte or Ashtor-
eth of Syria. Lucian thinks Astarte was
the Moon, which was one of the characters
of this universal Goddess, and his opinion
is confirmed by the Assyrian name of the
moon being Ishtar. Even the word ἀστήρ
(star) is thought to be related to Astarte.
Lucian says she was supposed to be Europa,
13. the sister of Cadmus (de Deâ. Syr.);
but this is a misconception, except as
far as Europe, or the West, was sister to Kadm, or the East.

No. 8.   Found in Malta.

Plutarch (de Isid. s. 15) seems to identify Astarte even with Minerva
(see note on ch. 44, B. ii.). The dove was sacred to her, which she
carries on her hand; and two are often seen as her emblems; sometimes
on her breast, as in a statue at Citta Vecchia, in Malta, and on the Roman
coins of Paphos, Askalon, and other places. Even the doves of Dodona
appear to be connected with her widely-spread worship (Strabo, vii. p.
277; Herod. ii. 55). Herodotus (i. 105) pronounces the temple of
Venus-Urania at Askalon to be the oldest of this Goddess, who, like
Aphrodite, was related to the sea, and is represented standing in a boat
on the coins of Askalon and Tripolis; and Pausanias pretends that the
worship went to Askalon from Assyria (i. 14). The Egyptian Athor
(Venus) is also figured on coins of the Empire with doves near her,
unless indeed they are intended for hawks (see Zoega). The bull was
also said to belong to Astarte, as a type of sovereignty, which accords
14. with her reputed identity with Europa.
Lucian thinks Semiramis was the dove, which the Syrians
abstained from eating, out of respect to her; as from the fish, which was
sacred to the half-fish, half-woman Goddess Derceto, her mother (see
note on B. ii. ch. 109); and Diodorus (ii. 4 and 20) says she was called
Semiramis, the Syrian name for a dove, from having been fed by doves
when abandoned by Derceto. (Cp. Ovid. Met. iv. 45.) Derceto or
15. Dercetus was the same as Atergatis or Atargatis, the A being omitted
in the "Greek name Derceto," as Pliny calls it (v. 23); and
Derceto is said by Lucian and Diodorus to be a woman in the upper
part, who from the thighs downward terminated in a fish's tail. This
cetaceous monster was the "fabulosa Ceto," said by Pliny (v. 14) to be
worshipped at Joppa. According to Athenæus (Deipn. viii. p. 84E)
Atergatis was suffocated in a lake near Askalon with her son *Ichthys*, by
king Mopsus, and devoured by fish; and he relates another reason for
fish of gold and silver being dedicated to the Deity (viii. p. 346D).
Jonah signifies a "dove," and the connexion with the "fish" and Joppa

is remarkable.   Atargatis was the same as Athara (Strabo, vi. p. 540.)
She was worshipped at Hierapolis, Bambyce (near Aleppo) or "Magog
of the Syrians" (Plin. v. 23; Strabo, xvi. p. 515), and was called a
Syrian or Assyrian Goddess.   It is not impossible that the name
Κυθήρη was derived from Athara; and the island of Cythera was 16.
called after the Venus of the Phœnicians who colonised it.   The
resemblance of Athar or Athra, "fire" (in the Zend), to the beginning
of her name, recalls the Babylonian Adar, "fire," but it is not necessarily connected with Atargatis, nor with Athor, the Venus of Egypt;
and Athor claims hers as a native appellation, being Ei-t-hor, "the
abode of Horus," which shows her to be closely allied to Isis.   But
still Athor may have been originally a foreign Deity transferred to Egypt,
and the name Athara may easily have been made to accord with an
Egyptian one of similar sound; which, being thought to connect her
with Isis, obtained for her the emblems of the mother of Horus.

Besides the authority of Lucian (de Deâ Syriâ), who shows that the
Juno of Hierapolis resembled "Minerva, Venus, the Moon, Rhea,
Diana, Nemesis, and the Parcæ,"
we have evidence from other
sources of the various characters
of the same Goddess; and an
inscription, found at Caervorran
(now in the Museum of New-
castle), thus identifies the Syrian
Goddess with Cybele, "the mother of the gods," with "Ceres,"
and others: "Imminet leoni
Virgo cœlesti situ, spicifera, justi
inventrix, urbium conditrix, ex
quis muneribus nossi contigit
Deos.   Ergo eadem mater Di-
vum, Pax, Virtus, Ceres, DEA
SYRIA, lance vitam et jura pensi-
tans, in cœlo visum Syria sidus
edidit, Libyæ colendum; inde
cuncti didicimus; ita intellexit
numine inductus tuo Marcus
Cæcilius Donatianus militaris
tribunus in præfecto, dono Prin-
cipis."   Astarte is identified with
Atargatis again, by the mention
of the latter with the temple[1]
that was in Carnaim (Ashteroth-
Kornim) or Carnion, a strong
city of Gilead (see 1 Maccab. v.
26, 43; and 2 Mac. xii. 21–26);
and with the Syrian Goddess,
by Lucian, as well as Xenophon,

No. 4.   Figure of Astarte, found in Etruria.

[1] Called in the Septuagint version the "*Atargateion.*"

mentioning the sanctity of fish and pigeons (or doves) among the Syrians (cp. Xenoph. Anab. i.).

Macrobius (Saturn i. 30) says, "to the great god Adad 'the one' is added the Goddess Atargatis; these being the Sun and *Earth;* and her statue stands on lions, as the Phrygians represent the Mother-Goddess Earth." (See below, p. 452.) (From this Adad or Hadad is derived the Syrian name of Ben-Hadad (1 Kings xv. 18). On the Goddess *Earth* and the bearded Apollo (Baal, or the Sun) at Hierapolis, see Macrobius (Saturn. i. 19). Both the Syrians and Assyrians "considered the dove a Goddess " (Diodor. ii. 4, 20; Athenag. Legat.); and the fable of the Egg that fell from heaven into the Euphrates, and was hatched by two doves, appears to be a variation of that of Semiramis, and relates also to Astarte.

18.

The usual form of Astarte was a Goddess with four wings, having a pointed cap, and holding a dove on her hand (woodcut No. 4). Beneath her feet was the peculiar volute ornament found on Phœnician monuments; which being sculptured on the walls of Crendi, in Malta, argues that those singular Druidical-shaped ruins (the Hagar Keem, "upright stones ") are of a people whose religion bore some relationship to that of Phœnicia; though they are not Phœnician, for the Phœnicians would not have made such rude monuments. Diodorus (v. 12) confirms what we know from other sources, that Malta "was colonised by the Phœnicians, on their way to the West, as well as Gaulus (Gozo), which was first frequented by them," and where similar ruins are found, and on a grander scale (called the Torre dei Giganti).

Some coins of Malta have a figure of Osiris with four similar wings, on the reverse.

The Great Goddess of the East, Astarte, is found in all the colonies of the Phœnicians; in Cyprus, Sardinia, Malta, and Spain; and she also occurs among the deities of the Etruscans. (See note on Book vii. ch. 166.) Her cap is the same as on many. of the small heads found in Cyprus. (See Herod. i. 106.) It was sometimes turreted (like that of Cybele) as on the coins of Sidon, Gaza, Aradus, and

No. 5.   Found at Idalium, in Cyprus.

others, where she is frequently seen standing on the prow of a boat, being the protectress of mariners, as well as of sea-ports. In Paphos, as in Syria, she was worshipped under the form of a conical stone, instead of a statue, which is figured on the coins of Cyprus (Tacit. His. ii. 3) with the area before the temple mentioned by Pliny. Astarte was even admitted into the Egyptian Pantheon, and she was "Venus the stranger," mentioned by Herodotus at Memphis. (See note on Bk. ii. ch. 112.) The name of Astarte is in Hebrew עשתרת Ashtarth or Astart, or, as we write it, Ashteroth, Ashtaroth, or Astaroth (Gen. xiv. 5; Judg. ii. 13; Deut. i. 4). Ashtaróth (1 Sam. vii. 4) is a plural form. like Baalim; and Baalim and Ashtaroth answered to "gods and goddesses." The Venus of Persia, Anaïtis, was worshipped also in Assyria and Armenia (Strabo, xi. p. 352; xii. p. 385; xv. p. 504), as some think as early as the time of Cyrus, but more probably much later. (See above in this note, p. 455.) Macrobius (Saturn. iii. 7) speaks of a bearded Venus in Cyprus, and says she is called by Aristophanes "Aphroditos" (comp. Hesychius and Serv. on Virg. Æn. ii. v. 632), apparently according with the notion of Jupiter being of two sexes as well as of many characters, and with the Egyptian notion of a self-producing and self-engendering deity. (See Orphic Fragm., and Appendix to Bk. ii. ch. 3, pp. 289–290.) This union of the two sexes is found also in Hindoo mythology, and is similarly emblematic of the generative and productive principles.

19.

There were other deities in Syria (Judg. x. 6); as the Great Baal, Belus, the "Lord," "master" (Hercules, or the sun); and Moloch, or Moloch (Melek) the "king," the Milcom "of the Ammonites," perhaps "the High King," or "their king." (Amos v. 26; 1 Kings, xi. 5, 7.) Some have thought Baal and Bel (Isaiah xlvi. 1) different gods. Baal and Molech (like Adonai) were really *titles* of the god (see note on ch. 32, Bk. ii.) which are found united in the name of Malach-Bêlus, mentioned with Agli-bôlus, as a Deity of the country in an inscription at Palmyra; and as the former was the Sun, the latter was the god Moon (Lunus), whose name was derived from agl, "to rotate." (Cp. the Arabic agl, "a wheel.") Melek is from the same root as *Amlak*, "take hold of," "possess," or "rule," and Memlook (p. p.) "ruled," "slave;" but Amalek (Amlek עמלק), and Amalekite (Amleki) are not related to Melek, or Moloch, מלך.

There were also Chemosh (Kemôsh) of the Moabites (1 Kings xi. 7) thought to be the Khem of Egypt; Nebo "his Lord" supposed to be Mercury; Muth or "death" answering to Pluto; and others noticed in sacred and profane history. Baaltis, or Dionê of Byblus, mentioned by Sanconiatho, was probably a female Baal, and a character of Astarte, and the Cypress (still retained in the East as an ornamental device and as a funereal tree) was sacred to her as the Persia was to Athor. Baal had various characters, as Baal-Berith (Judg. viii. 33) of Shechem; Baal-Markôs, to whom a temple was dedicated near Berytus (Beiroot), with altars to "Jovi Baal-Markôdi, perhaps the same as Merodach (Jerem. l. 2) or Merdok (whence Mardokempalus, the fourth successor of Nabonassar in the Canon of Ptolemy). Pul, Phul, and Pal, were Baal, or Belus. Baal, as well as Ἥλιος, is connected with the Semitic *Al* "God," and from him Baalbek (Heliopolis) received its name. *Comp.* the Welsh Haul "sun," the Mœso-Gothic *Uil* "sun," and the Gothic *Ell* "fire." The sun-god Bella, or Boora-Pennu, "god of light" of the Khonds also recalls the Epirotic name Pieli; though this is perhaps only similar to the Slavonic *bielo* "white," to which a Slavonian author pretends Baal to be related. Some derive Baal from Ba, "father" and aJ, "god;" as Babel (Babylon) was from Bab-el (or Ilu) "gate of god." Damascius says the Phœnicians and Syrians call Chronos ʼHλ, Βῆλ, and Βολαϑὴν, and Sanconiatho, quoted by Eusebius, makes ἰλὺς the same as Chronos. (See note ʼ on Bk. ii. ch. 44.)

20. Among the Syrian gods, Selden (de Diis Syr.) mentions Ourchol (*comp.* Our, "light") the same as Arcles, whence Hercules, the Etruscan Hercle, or Ercle; Nonnus makes Hercules the Babylonian sun; he was the Phœnician Baal, and the Hercules of Egypt was also connected with Re. (See note on ch. 43, Bk. ii., and ch. 8, Bk. iii.) It is singular that Africanus calls one of the Shepherd-kings Arcles, or Archles; and Dr. Cumberland thinks Certes to be Melicertes, or Melkarthus, the name of the Hercules of Tyre. (See note on Bk. ii. ch. 104.) Melkarthus means "Lord of the city;" and Molech "of the Ammonites," is probably this name of Hercules; Kartha "the city" being omitted. (See note on Bk. ii. ch. 44.)

21. The Syrian god Rimmon (2 Kings v. 18) appears from his name Rimôn, "pomegranate," to be related to the Jupiter of Mount Casius, whose statue held that fruit in its hand (Achilles Tatius, iii.); and Remphan, whose star the Israelites worshipped (Acts vii. 43) at the same time with Moloch and Chiun (Amos v. 26), is thought to be the same as the Egyptian god of War Ranpo—a foreign deity, who is found in Egypt with a goddess standing on a lion, apparently also of foreign introduction, answering to the Phrygian Cybele, or "Mother Earth." (See At. Eg., plate 69.) The mention of the star with Remphan (in Acts) and with Chiun (in Amos) has made some suppose these to be the same deity; but the name of the Egyptian goddess on the lion is Chen or Ken; and it is remarkable that she occurs on the same stela with Ranpo and Anata (evidently Anaïtis) the Egyptian Bellona. Some think Chiun to be the Chons (Hercules) of Egypt, and the Saturn of the Syrians. The resemblance of Ken to Chiun, Ranpo to Remphan, Anata to Anaïtis in Egypt, are singular; the appearance of those deities proclaims a foreign origin; and the names of the children of Ammon, as well as of "Chemosh their god," are too near to the Khem and Ammon (Amun) of Egypt to be accidental. Some may connect Seth with the same name in Syria. (Astarte is mentioned in note ʼ on Bk. i. ch. 105.) For another view of the Assyrian Mylitta, see Sir Henry Rawlinson's "Essay on the Religion of the Assyrians and Babylonians" in the Appendix to Book I.—[G. W.]

ESSAY II.

ON THE MAGIAN REVOLUTION, AND THE REIGN OF THE PSEUDO-SMERDIS.

1. Ordinary theory on the subject—the revolution a Median outbreak. 2. Proofs to the contrary—(i.) from the inscriptions—(ii.) from the general tenor of ancient history. 3. Unsound basis of the theory—the Magi not Medes. 4. The revolution really religious. 5. Proof of this from the inscriptions. 6. Religious ideas connected with the name of Darius.

1. The character of the revolution which placed Gomates [1] the Magian upon the throne of Cyrus has been represented by most modern writers in a light which is at once inconsistent with the recently discovered Persian monuments, and with the view of the event which the general outline of the history, as presented by the ancient writers, would most naturally suggest to us.   Heeren,[2] Niebuhr,[3] and Grote [4] unite in regarding the accession of the Pseudo-Smerdis as a *national* revolution, whereby the Medes regained their ancient supremacy over the Persians.   This view rests upon certain incidental expressions in Herodotus[5] which find an echo in later Greek writers of no weight or authority.[6]   The expressions are, undoubtedly, strong, and it must be confessed that in the mind of Herodotus the idea existed which has been put so prominently forward

---

[1] I give him the name which he bears in the native monuments—a trace of which remains in the Cometes of Trogus Pompeius (ap. Justin. i. 9), who however misapplies the appellation, giving it to the other brother, the Patizeithes of Herodotus.

[2] Asiatic Nations, vol. i. p. 346, E. T.   His words are: "it is usual to consider this revolution as an attempt of the Magians to get possession of the sovereign authority, because the principal conspirators belonged to that caste; but by the express evidence of the most credible authorities" (he refers in a note to Plato [!] and Herodotus), "the conspiracy had a higher object, the re-establishment of the monarchy of the Medes.   The Magians, as we have observed, were a Median race; and it was natural for the Medes, when the true stock of Cyrus had ended in Cambyses, to aim at a resumption of their ancient sway."

[3] Vorträge über alte Geschichte, vol. i. 157.   He says: "Es muss sein, dass es eine wahre politische Revolution war, nicht bloss in der Dynastie, sondern in Regiment, wodurch die Herrschaft von den Persern an die Meder, und unter diesen wieder an die Mager gekommen war."

[4] History of Greece, vol. iv. p. 301.   "Smerdis represents preponderance to the Medes over the Persians, and comparative degradation to the latter.   The Medes and the Magians are in this case identical: for the Magians, though indispensable in the capacity of priests to the Persians, were essentially one of the seven (!) Median tribes.   It thus appears that though Smerdis ruled as a son of the great Cyrus, yet he ruled by means of Medes and Magians, depriving the Persians of that supreme privilege and predominance to which they had become accustomed."

[5] There are three passages where a *Median* character is ascribed to the revolt by Herodotus, viz., iii. 65, iii. 73, and iii. 126.

[6] Especially Plato in the famous passage of his Laws (iii. 12. v. 695, p. 99, Tauchn.).

by the above-mentioned writers. Still it is worthy of remark, that even in Herodotus, the direct narrative does not convey the idea with any distinctness, and it has to be drawn out from notices dropped incidentally. The advocates of the Median theory themselves admit this. Mr. Grote says : " When we put together all the incidental notices which he (Herodotus) lets drop, it will be found that the change of sceptre from Smerdis to Darius was a far larger political event than his direct narrative would seem to announce."[1] Niebuhr goes yet further, and professes openly to depart from Herodotus, who represents the change (he says) as merely one of dynasty, and does not give it its true political importance, as a transfer of empire from the Persian to the Median nation.[8] Thus it appears that even in Herodotus himself, the idea that the struggle was one of nationalities, and that Media triumphed in the person of the Pseudo-Smerdis, is not consistently maintained or asserted with that clearness and distinctness which was to have been expected if the usurpation had really possessed the character attributed to it.[9]

2. That the oppressed nationality of the Medes did not triumph by the accession of Gomates to the throne, is apparent, first from the inscriptions of Darius, and secondly from the general tenor of ancient history.

(i.) The evidence of the inscriptions is, of necessity, chiefly negative. Gomates is never said to have been a Mede, nor is there any mention of the Medes as particularly connected with the revolution.[1] The idea of a national struggle is manifestly absent from the mind of Darius, who, if he had really wrested the sovereignty from the Medes, and restored it to the Persians, would undoubtedly have set forth such an exploit with sufficient clearness. The national character of the various revolts which occurred after he ascended the throne, *is* distinctly stated.

But further, there is some positive evidence that the usurpation of Gomates was not a Median triumph. For, 1. Gomates is represented as a native of a region which it is almost certain was in Persia Proper.

---

[7] Hist. of Greece, l. s. c.

[8] "Nach Herodots Erzählung müsste man nun glauben, es wäre bloss dies verändert worden, dass ein Mager unter dem Namen des Persers an der Spitze gestanden, und es wäre dabei geblieben, dass die Perser geherrscht hätten, nur unter einem Könige, der ein Medischer Mager gewesen wäre . . . . . . *Es muss aber hier anders gewesen sein*."—Vorträge, l. s. c.

[9] If the Medes at this time regained their supremacy over the Persians, the alteration of relation should have been noticed in Book i. ch. 130. Not only is there no mention of the reign of the Pseudo-Smerdis in that place, but we are plainly given to understand that the subjection of the Medes to the Persians continued uninterruptedly until the revolt from Darius, which happened (we know) in the third year of his reign. Even in the third Book the Median character of the revolt is not put prominently forward. This is what Mr. Grote, in the passage above quoted, confesses.

[1] Media indeed is mentioned, but it is only in connexion with Persia and the other provinces. Col. i. par. 10, § 10: "Then the lie became abounding in the land, both in Persia and in Media, and in the other provinces." Col. i. par. 11, § 7: "From Cambyses the state went over to him (Gomates), both Persia and Media, and the other provinces." Col. i. par. 12, § 3: "After Gomates the Magian had dispossessed Cambyses both of Persia and Media, and the dependent provinces, he did according to his desire."

"He arose from Pissiachádá, the mountain's name Aracadres, from thence."[2]   Pissiachádá, it appears from another passage,[3] was towards the extreme east of Persia, not far from Parga, the modern *Fahraj*, which lies between *Shiras* and *Kermán*.   He was therefore, at least by birth, if not by descent, a Persian.   2. Persia, not Media, is represented as taking the most prominent part in the revolt.   "The whole state went over to Gomates," we are told, *both Persia* and Media, and 'the other provinces."   And again, "Gomates the Magian dispossessed Cambyses *both of Persia*, and Media, and the dependent provinces."   3. Equal surprise is expressed that the Medes did not rise against the usurper, as that the Persians submitted to him.   "There was not a man," says Darius, "neither Persian, *nor Median*, nor any one of our family, who would dispossess that Gomates the Magian of the crown."[4]

(ii.)   The general tenor of ancient history leads to the same result. 1. The *facts* related by Herodotus, as distinguished from his *opinion* of the national character of the revolution.   There is nothing in the course of events, setting aside the speeches supposed to be made, which would indicate that the Medes have any particular interest in the struggle. No special favour is shown to the Medes by the Pseudo-Smerdis;[5] there is no transfer of the seat of empire from Susa to Ecbatana[6]—no removal of Persian governors[7]—no resistance is offered by the Medes to the counter-revolution[8]—no brand of disgrace set upon the Medes by way of punishment.[9]   Everything, as will be shown hereafter, concurs to indicate that the revolution was social, not national—Magian not Median—the ascendancy of a religion, not the revolt of a people.   2. The authority of other writers of weight, whose testimony is independent of Herodotus.   Among these the first place is due to Æschylus, who wrote within 50 years of the event (20 years earlier than Herodotus), and whose play of the Persæ indicates very exact acquaintance with Persian history.[1]   Æschylus, enumerating the sovereign lords of Asia, when he comes to the Pseudo-Smerdis, says: "The fifth was Mardus, *a disgrace to his country*, unworthy occupant of the ancient throne;"[2] an

---

[2] Behistun Inscription, Col. i. par. 11, § 3.

[3] Ibid., Col. iii. par. 7, § 2.   [4] Ib., Col. i. par. 13, § 2.

[5] He exempts from taxation and military service for three years, not Media specially, but the whole empire (Herod. iii. 67).

[6] Susa is mentioned as still the capital (Herod. iii. 70).

[7] Orœtes certainly retained his command during the Magian usurpation (Herod. iii. 126). He was a Persian (ἀνὴρ Πέρσης, iii. 120). Hystaspes is represented as continuing to be satrap of Persia (iii. 70). Aryandes, whom Cambyses had made satrap of Egypt, remained undisturbed in his office (iv. 166).

[8] The revolt of Media, *three years afterwards*, in conjunction with Armenia and Assyria (Beh. Ins., Col. ii. pars. 5–13 ; Herod. i, 130), cannot with any fairness be connected with the downfall of the Magus.

[9] The success of the conspiracy leads to a general massacre, not of the Medes, but of the Magi; and is commemorated by an annual festival—the Magophonia, not Medophonia.

[1] Æschylus, who fought at Marathon (Marm. Par. 63, Müller), would have his information from the prisoners taken at that battle, who might many of them have been grown up at the time of the Magian revolution, thirty-one years earlier.

[2]   πέμπτος δὲ Μάρδος ἦρξεν, αἰσχύνη πάτρᾳ,
          θρόνοισί τ' ἀρχαίοισιν.—Pers. 780–1.

expression which has no meaning if the Magus was a Mede, and his usurpation raised his country, Media, from the condition of a subject to that of a sovereign state,—but which has a very pregnant meaning if he was a Persian of inferior rank and position, who, to effect a religious revolution, established himself on the throne. To the authority of Æschylus may be added that of Ctesias, by whom the Magus is never said to have been a Mede.[*] Ctesias here is not (so far as appears) designedly opposing Herodotus, which makes his testimony the more valuable.

3. It may be observed further, that the whole notion of the Magian revolution being a transfer of empire from the Persians to the Medes, both in the mind of Herodotus and in that of the recent authors who have so prominently put it forward, rests upon the assumption that the Magi at this time were exclusively a Median race. "The Magians," says Mr. Grote, "though indispensable in the capacity of priests to the Persians, were essentially one of the seven Median tribes."[4] And Heeren more briefly lays it down:—"The Magians, as we have observed, were a Median race."[*] But was this really so? Is it true that at any time the Magi were exclusively Median? Herodotus certainly enumerates the Magi among the six (not seven) tribes of Media,[*] and does not mention them among the ten tribes of Persia.[7] And this proves no doubt that Magism had been received into greater favour in the one country than in the other. But Magism itself was, as has been already shown,[*] the old Scythic religion, and was professed wherever there was a Scythic population, which was certainly the case in Persia as much as in Media.[*] If the success of the Pseudo-Smerdis was a national triumph at all, it was the triumph of the Scyths over their conquerors, not of one Arian people over another. But in fact there was nothing national, scarcely anything even political in the change, which was a religious revolution, not a revolt or a transfer of empire.

4. The truth seems to be that the Arians who overran Asia from the Hindoo Koosh to the shores of the Persian Gulf, were everywhere but a small element in the population of the countries subdued by them; and thus, although in the first flush of conquest they succeeded in imposing their religion, which was Dualism, upon the vanquished nations, very shortly, in every country which they occupied, a reaction set in. The religion of the mass refused to be crushed or stifled, and gradually rose from its depression and made head against the invading worship. Such reactions are common whenever sudden conquests are made, and may be traced in the language and manners, as well as in the religion of the conquered countries. In some places, as in Media, the period of struggle was short, and the victors readily yielded, and became the disciples of the vanquished in religious matters.[1] In Persia the

---

[*] Excerpt. Persic. §§ 10–14.   [4] Hist. of Greece, l. s. c.
[*] Asiatic Nations, l. s. c.   [*] Herod. i. 101.   [7] Ibid. i. 125.
[*] See Appendix to Book i. Essay v., "On the Religion of the Ancient Persians."
[*] The inscriptions of Cyrus at Pasargadæ, as well as those of Darius at Persepolis and Nakhsh-i-Rustam, have a Scythic transcript.
[1] See Appendix to Book i. Essay v., § 6, and note [*].

case was different. The Achæmenian monarchs were staunch upholders of their ancestral creed,[2] and showed no favour towards a belief which was that of the great mass of their subjects. Yet despite the frowns of the court, Magism made progress. The Arian Persians, a simple and impressionable people, gradually inclined towards it.[3] The Magi grew in power and influence. At last all seemed ripe for a change, and the priests of the old religion, taking advantage of the prolonged absence of the Great King in Egypt, resolved to strike the final blow, and to substitute for the existing State religion, which was Arian Dualism, the old Magian belief and worship, to which the bulk even of the dominant Persians were well-disposed. A professor of the Magian religion, himself (according to all accounts) a Magus, was placed upon the throne of Cyrus. Perhaps the Magi feared to trust any but a member of their own body—perhaps they looked further, and designed a transference of the supreme power from the warrior to the priest caste of the nation.[4] In any case they seem to have surpassed the limits of discretion, and to have over-reached themselves on the occasion. The Persians, indifferent, or, it may be, well-inclined to a religious change, could not tolerate the political novelty of a Priest-King. As soon as it became known that the successor of Cambyses was not his brother Smerdis, but a Magus, the nobles conspired. Darius, the young head of the house of the Achæmenidæ, by right of his birth, took the lead. Gomates was slain, and a general massacre, like that which the Jews were allowed by Ahasuerus,[5] struck terror into the Magi and their adherents. The Arian religion was restored; the temples were rebuilt; and the annual festival of the Magophonia was instituted,[6] to deter the Magian priests from ever again repeating their bold adventure. Magism remained under a cloud, from which it only gradually emerged, as the Arian faith, which it had not been able to displace, became corrupted by intermixture with it.

5. The religious character of the revolution is clearly marked in the great inscription of Darius. The origin of the troubles is ascribed to the fact, that "when Cambyses had proceeded to Egypt, then the state became wicked. Then *the lie* became abounding in the land, both in Persia and in Media, and in the other provinces." "The god Ormazd," as it is expressed in another place,[7] "created lies, that they should deceive the people." The acts recorded of Gomates—and it

---

[2] See the Inscriptions *passim*. And note the absence from the Persepolitan sculptures of any representation of *sacrificial* worship.

[3] This is apparent from the statement of Darius : "When Cambyses had gone to Egypt, *then* the state became heretical: then the lie became abounding in the land, both in Persia and in Media, and in the other provinces. *Afterwards* there was a certain man, a Magian, named Gomates" (Beh. Ins., Col. i. pars 10, 11).

[4] The Magi, it is probable, were an actual *caste*. The pastoral, agricultural, and warrior tribes of Persia, were not perhaps strictly castes, since all were soldiers upon occasion, but the *profession* of arms was limited to the warriors.

[5] Esther, ch. ix. Niebuhr makes this comparison (Vorträge, vol. i. p. 158), but without regarding the narrative in the book of Esther as historical.

[6] Ctesias agrees with Herodotus both as to the origin and the continuance of this strange observance (Exc. Pers. § 15).   [7] Beh. Ins., Col. iv. par. 4. ·

must be borne in mind that they are the only acts which Darius records of him—are religious changes. They are the destruction of temples, and the abolition of the existing worship, consisting principally, it would appear, of sacred chantings. The acts of Darius, immediately upon his accession, are the exact counterpart of these. His first care is to "re-build the temples which Gomates had destroyed, and to restore to the people the sacred chants and worship, of which Gomates had deprived them."* To this zeal he ascribes the protection which he has received from Ormazd. "For this reason Ormazd brought help to me, and the other gods which are, because I was not *wicked*, nor was I a *liar*, nor was I a tyrant."* And he commends his example herein to the imitation of his successors on the throne, who are exhorted to " keep themselves from *lies*," and " destroy utterly the man who may be a *liar*." ¹

6. And hence we find in general history that Darius enjoys the repu-tation of having been a great religious reformer. This is the true meaning of that oft-repeated statement,* so violently absurd in the letter, that Darius was contemporary with Zoroaster. The later Persian religion, after Magism had corrupted it, was still regarded as the system established by Darius. Hence the introduction of the name *Gustasp* into the Zendavesta, and hence the respect paid even by the modern Zoroas-trians to the memory of the son of Hystaspes. The very efforts which he made against Magism, or the religion of Zoroaster, have served to connect him in men's minds with the system which he opposed. As the last known reformer of the Persian religion, he was identified in the popular judgment with the religion such as it eventually became. Doctrines long associated with the name of Zoroaster came thus to be regarded as deriving their origin from Darius; and as the most conve-nient mode of reconciling the contending claims of the two, a synchronism was supposed, and Zoroaster became a prophet, under whose inspired advice King Darius reformed and purified the religion of his people.

* Beh. Ins., Col. i. par. 14.   * Ibid., Col. iv. par. 18.
¹ Ibid., Col. iv. par. 5.
* Plin. H. N. xxx. 1 ; Amm. Marcell. xxiii. 6 ; Agathias, ii. 24.

ESSAY III.

ON THE PERSIAN SYSTEM OF ADMINISTRATION AND GOVERNMENT.

1. Uniformity of Oriental Governments. 2. Satrapial system of Persia. 3. Danger of revolt—safeguards. 4. Power and wealth of the Satraps. 5. Institution of Royal Judges. 6. Fixity of the royal revenue. 7. The border Satraps. 8. Extra-satrapial dependencies. 9. Satrapies not always geographically continuous. 10. Modes by which the subjection of the conquered races was maintained—(i.) Disarming—(ii.) Transplantation—(iii.) Maintenance of a standing army. 11. Position and power of the monarch. 12. Privileges of the Persians. 13. Gradations of rank among them.

1. THE ancient Persian monarchy, both in its origin and in its internal administration, closely resembled the modern Persian and Turkish Governments. Since the fall of the Assyrian and Babylonian kingdoms, the empires of the East have uniformly arisen from the sudden triumph of conquering nomadic hordes over more settled and civilised communities. A Cyrus, a Genghis Khan, a Timour, an Othman, a Nadir Shah, has led the hardy inhabitants of the steppes or of the mountain tracts, against effete races, long established in softer regions, and abandoned to sloth and sensuality. Slow conquests, long struggles of race against race, amalgamations, insensible growth and development of political systems, to which we are habituated in the records of the West, are unknown to the countries lying eastward of the Hellespont. In every case a conqueror rapidly overruns an enormous tract of territory, inhabited by many and diverse nations, overpowers their resistance or receives their submission, and imposes on them a system of government, rude and inartificial indeed, but sufficient ordinarily to maintain their subjection, till the time comes when a fresh irruption and a fresh conqueror repeat the process, which seems to be the only renovation whereof Oriental realms are capable. The imposed system itself is, in its general features, for the most part, one and the same. The rapid conquest causes no assimilation. The nations retain their languages, habits, manners, religions, laws, and sometimes even their native princes. The empire is thus of necessity broken up into provinces. In each province a royal officer representing the monarch—a Satrap, a Khan, or a Pasha—bears absolute sway, responsible to the crown for the tranquillity of his district, and bound to furnish periodically, or at call, the supplies of men and money, which constitute the chief value of their conquests to the conquerors. Through these officers the unity of the whole kingdom is maintained, and in their connexion with the persons under their charge, and with the central government the entire character of the system, and its special aspect in the kingdom under consideration, may for the most part be traced.

2. In the Persian empire, as in other Asiatic governments, the

monarch was all in all. Regarded as the absolute proprietor, not only
of the entire territory, but of the persons and properties of its inhabitants, all power necessarily emanated from him, and was only exercised
by others as his substitutes, and so long as he chose to delegate to them
a portion of his authority. The satraps were nominated by the king at
his pleasure, from any class of his subjects;[1] they held office while the
king chose, and were liable to deprivation or death at any moment, without other formality than the presentation of the royal *firman*.[2] Originally
they were charged with the civil administration only of their provinces,
their special business being to collect the tribute (a fixed sum, at least
from the time of Darius[3]) from the inhabitants, and remit it to the
treasury. They had besides to pay the troops maintained in their
satrapy, to see to the administration of justice, and to exercise a general
supervision, alike over the external safety and the internal tranquillity
of the district under them.[4] Their office was distinct from that of the
commanders of the troops, who like them received their appointment
from the monarch, and were answerable for the defence of the territory
from foreign or domestic foes;[5] and distinct likewise from that of the
commandants of the garrisons,[6] who were charged with the maintenance
of the strongholds. It sometimes happened that the office of commander
of the troops was united with that of satrap, more especially in the
frontier provinces, where a divided command would have been dangerous.[7]

[1] No doubt they were ordinarily Persians, and Persians of the tribe of the Pasargadæ; but this was not necessary. The king's favour could make up for all de-
ficiencies. We may see by the examples of Daniel under Cyrus (Dan. vi. 28), and
Mordecai under Xerxes (Esth. ix. 4), the power and dignity to which even members
of the subject nations might attain. Compare the cases of Tabalus, the *Lydian*
(Herod. i. 153), and Xenagoras the Halicarnassian *Greek* (ibid. ix. 107).

[2] Difficulties would occur in the execution of the king's orders, in ancient as in
modern times. Chardin speaks of several instances of governors in Persia who
maintained themselves in their governments for a long time against the will of the
Shah, by robbing the messenger of his despatches, or murdering him (vol. ii. p. 310).
And the famous Ali Pasha is known to have baffled in this way for several years the
designs of the Porte against him. That such cases were not unknown in ancient
Persia, we may gather from the history of Orœtes (Herod. iii. 126).

[3] Herod. iii. 89.

[4] Xen. Cyrop. VIII. vi. § 3. Although the Cyropædia is a romance, we may
learn from it a good deal concerning the internal administration of the Persian empire in Xenophon's time.

[5] These commanders are constantly distinguished from the satraps by Herodotus.
See v. 25, and 123; also i. 162, iv. 143, vi. 43, &c. Their independence of the
satrap is especially evident in the history of the Ionian insurrection. See v. 109,
116; vi. 6, &c.

[6] The special passage which marks this distinction is Xen. Cyrop. VIII. vi. § 1.
Heeren (As. Nat. p. 338, note [2], E. T.) thinks that it may be traced in the arrangements made by Cyrus in Lydia, Tabalus being the commandant of Sardis, Mazares
the leader of the forces, and Pactyas the satrap or governor. Certainly in modern
Persia it is the fact, that the commandants of fortresses are independent both of
the civil governor and the officer in command of the troops of the province, and receive their appointments and orders from the Shah (Chardin, iii p. 802).

[7] This was evidently the case with Tissaphernes and Pharnabazus (Thucyd. viii.;
Xen. Hell. i.–iv.), with Aryandes (Herod. iv. 166–7), and with the younger Cyrus
(Xen. Anab. i. i. § 2). Latterly it became almost universal (Arrian, Exp. Alex. iii.
8; Xen. Œcon. iv. § 11).

Two or three distinct satrapies were also occasionally accumulated in the hands of a single person, who thus became a sort of petty king, and was tempted to shake off his allegiance.   Hence revolts frequently occurred,[8] and long before the time of Alexander, whole provinces had detached themselves from the central government, and maintained only a nominal dependence.[9]

3.   To guard against this danger, the principal one to which empires of such a character are exposed, was one of the chief aims of the Persian political system.   With this view, brothers, or other near kinsmen of the monarch, were usually selected for the more important satrapies,[1] while in other cases, it was sought to attach the dangerous functionary to the interests of the crown by giving him a wife from among the princesses of the royal house.[2]   Nor was security expected from this plan without further safeguards.   The powers of the satraps were checked, and their ambitious longings controlled in various ways.   Some of these have already come under notice.   The independent authority of the military commanders and of the governors of fortresses was the most important of all, and made rebellion in ordinary cases hopeless. It was only where such distinctions had ceased to be maintained, where for one reason or another the civil and military administrations had been placed in the same hands, that a successful revolt could be contemplated.   Even, however, where this had been done, the monarch's interests were not left uncared for.   The governor of a province in ancient as in modern Persia, was attended by a royal Secretary, receiving his appointment from the Crown, and bound continually to keep watch upon the satrap, and report his proceedings to the sovereign.[3]   A practice is also said to have obtained, to which the jealousy of modern

---

[8] Orœtes was satrap of Phrygia, Lydia, and Ionia, at the time of his revolt (Herod. iii. 127).   Cyrus the younger, of Lydia, Phrygia, and Cappadocia (Xen. Anab. i. ix. § 7).   Tissaphernes after the death of Cyrus received all his governments, and held them together with his own (Xen. Hell. iii. i. § 3).

[9] Pontus was certainly in this condition, likewise Paphlagonia, and most probably Cappadocia. (See Heeren, ut suprà, p. 426, and compare his Manual of Ancient History, p. 294–7).   The Uxians of the Kurdish mountains were absolutely independent (Arr. Exp. Al. iii. 17).

[1] Hystaspes, of the blood-royal, was satrap of Persia under Cambyses (Herod. iii. 70), of Parthia under his own son Darius (Beh. Inscr., Col. iii. par. 16).   Arta-phernes, a half-brother of Darius, was made by him satrap of Lydia (Herod. v. 25).   Achæmenes, a son of Darius, was made by Xerxes satrap of Egypt (ib. vii. 7).   Masistes, another son of Darius, was about the same time satrap of Bactria (ib. ix. 113).   Pissuthnes, satrap of Lydia in the early part of the Peloponnesian war, was most likely a cousin of Artaxerxes (Thucyd. i. 115, Herod. vii. 64).   Cyrus received his extensive governments from his father (Xen. An. i. ix. § 7).   Was Tritan-tæchmes, satrap of Babylon in the time of Herodotus (i. 192) cousin to Artaxerxes? (See Herod. vii. 82, where he is called the son of Artabanus.)

[2] Pharnabazus married a daughter of Artaxerxes Mnemon (Xen. Hell. v. i. § 28).   Pausanias, when he aspired to be satrap of Greece under Xerxes, himself proposed a similar connexion (Thucyd. i. 128).   The commanders of the troops were perhaps even more often attached to the monarch in this way than the satraps.   (Cf. Herod. v. 116, vi. 43, vii. 73 : Arrian, i. 16, &c.)

[3] See Herod. iii. 128.   Chardin, Voyage en Perse, ii. p. 302 : "Il y a en chaque province avec le gouverneur . . . un *Vakannviez*, ou *Secrétaire*, mis de la main du roi, dont l'office consiste principalement à rendre compte à la cour de tout ce qui se passe."

times fails to present a parallel, whereby it was thought to secure still more completely the obedience of the provincial governors.   Royal Commissaries were sent year by year from the court to the several satrapies, to make inquiries upon the spot, and bring the king back an exact account of their condition.[4]   This usage, however, must have been gradually discontinued, or have degenerated into a formality.

4. Despite these checks the power of the satraps was at all times great, and little short of regal. As they represented the monarch, their courts were framed upon the royal model ; they had their palaces,[5] sur-rounded by magnificent parks and hunting grounds—their numerous train of eunuchs and attendants, and their own household troops or body-guard.[6]   They assessed the tribute on the several towns and villages within their jurisdiction at their pleasure, and appointed depu-ties, called sometimes like themselves satraps,[7] over cities or districts within their province, whose office was regarded as one of great dignity. So long as they were in favour at court, they ruled their satrapies with an absolute sway, involving no little tyranny and oppression.   Besides the fixed tribute which each satrap was bound to remit to the king, and the amount that he had to collect for the payment of the troops of his province, he might exact for his own personal expenses and the sup-port of his court, whatever sum he considered his province able to furnish.[8]   All persons who had any favour, or even justice to ask, approached him with gifts,[9] without which success was not to be looked for ; and hence enormous fortunes were accumulated.[1]   The sole limit upon the rapacity of the satrap was the fear of removal, in case the voice of complaint became so loud as to reach the ears of the monarch.

---

[4] See Xen. Cyrop. viii. § 16, where Xenophon expressly states that the practice continued to his day. And compare Œcon. iv. § 8.

[5] Βασίλεια. Xen. Anab. i. ii. § 7 ; Hell. iv. i. § 15. Compare Cyrop. viii. vi. §§ 11–13.

[6] Cyrop. loc. cit. § 10. The body-guard of Orœtes consisted of a thousand Per-sians (Herod. iii. 127).

[7] See the history of Zénis and Mania (Xen. Hellen. iii. i. §§ 10–12). The tribute seems to have been raised by a land-tax (Herod. vi. 42), payable partly in money and partly in kind (Herod. i. 192). Herodotus, in his account of the satrapies (iii. 90–4), gives only the money portion, or rather that part of it which went into the royal treasury. The entire amount drawn from the people was probably three or four times as much.

[8] How large this amount in some cases was is evident from what Herodotus tells us of Tritantæchmes, satrap of Babylon, whose daily revenue was an *artaba* of silver, or more than 250*l*. (See Herod. i. 192, and compare Heeren's As. Nat. i. p. 410, E. T.) Heeren has misconceived in one point the positions occupied res-pectively by the satrap and the monarch with regard to the revenue. He speaks of the satrap as paying over the balance of what he had collected to the king, after providing for his own expenditure (p. 423) ; whereas in point of fact the payment to the king was a fixed sum, and the fluctuating balance was the satrap's.

[9] See Xen. Hell. iii. i. § 10, and § 12, where what is said of Mania sufficiently indicates the usual practice. (Compare Anab. i. ix. § 22.)

[1] Tritantæchmes, besides his war-horses, owned 800 stallions, and 16,000 mares! His Indian dogs were quartered on four large villages, which he exempted from any other payment (Herod. i. 192). Tithraustes, the successor of Tissaphernes, in one year disbursed eighty talents (near 20,000*l*.), to purchase peace for his province (Xen. Hell. iii. iv. § 26, and v. § 1).

Nor did the populations suffer only in purse from the tyranny of their governors. Instances are found which show that they were without any security against the grossest affronts and indignities to their persons.[2] Such cases seem certainly to have been infrequent, and the general condition of the conquered races under the Achæmenian kings, contrasts favourably with their present state under the Turkish and Persian governments.[3]

5. One cause of this superiority may be found in the fact already alluded to, that throughout the Persian Empire the native local authorities were for the most part left standing, the satrap dealing with them, and not directly with the common people.[4] Another lay in the comparative purity of the administration of justice in ancient Persia. The institution of *royal* judges, *i. e.* judges deriving their authority directly from the king, involving as it did the separation of the judicial from the administrative office,[5] tended in this direction; and a still greater effect was probably produced by the tremendous punishments with which corruption, when proved, was visited.[6] On the whole, it would seem that while the caprice and cruelty of the kings rendered the condition of the satraps and other great men as bad as it has ever been under the worst of the Oriental despotisms,[7] the oppression of the masses was lighter than at almost any other period in Eastern history.

6. The levy on the part of the crown of *fixed* contributions from the provinces helped to protect the commons; for as the monarch gained nothing by the rapacity of his officers, but rather lost, since the provinces became exhausted, it was his interest to punish greedy, and advance just and good satraps.[8] The beneficial effect of this provision more

[2] If even Persians of the highest rank, such as Spithridates (Xen. Hell. iv. i. § 6), were in the provinces liable to have the honour of a daughter assailed (Ages. iii. § 3), what regard is likely to have been paid to the feelings of the conquered races?

[3] The remark of Mr. Grote is just, that "the empire of the Great King, while it resembled in its main political features the Turkish and Persian empires of the present day, apparently did not reach the same extreme of rapacity, corruption, and cruelty in detail" (Hist. of Greece, iv. p. 315).

[4] This was evidently the case with the Greek towns (Herod. v. 37, vi. 43); and was most likely universal, or nearly so. Native princes appear in Caria (vii. 98–9), Cyprus (v. 104, 113; and Arrian, ii. 20), Phœnicia (Herod. vii. 98; Arrian, loc. cit.), Lycia (Herod. vii. 98), Cilicia (ibid., comp. Xen. Anab. i. ii. § 12), and Paphlagonia (Xen. Hell. iv. i. § 2). The general practice of the Persians to retain them is witnessed by Herodotus (iii. 15).

[5] See Herod. iii. 31. The separation is professedly made in modern Persia and in Turkey, but it is seldom that the cadi dares to resist the khan or pasha.

[6] Cambyses slew Sisamnes on this account, flayed him from head to foot, and made his skin a covering for the judgment-seat (Herod. v. 25). Darius was on the point of crucifying Sandöces for the same reason, but spared him on account of his signal services (ib. vii. 194).

[7] The cruelties of Cambyses (Herod. iii. 35) are ascribed to madness, but they are not greater than those sanctioned by Xerxes towards his brother's wife (ib. ix. 110–112), and by Artaxerxes Mnemon towards those who disputed with him the honour of having slain Cyrus (Plut. Artax. pp. 1862–3).

[8] On the other hand, in modern Persia, where it is the business of the provincial governors or viziers to send to the treasury as much revenue as the province can possibly furnish, the oppression is extreme. The monarch is interested in the ex-

than counterbalanced the evil arising from insecurity of tenure, and from the absence, generally, of the hereditary principle from offices and employments.[*]

7. The more remote the satrapy was from the seat of government, and the more it had to fear from foreign enemies, the greater the power of its ruler, and the more nearly he approached to the condition of an independent sovereign. The satraps of Asia Minor and of Egypt received and despatched embassies, and even engaged in foreign wars without communication with the Court.[1] Besides their Persian body-guard, they maintained large bands of mercenaries, chiefly Greeks,[2] by whose aid they carried on their contests with foreign states, or with one another.[3] It was in such provinces too that the practice chiefly obtained of uniting the military with the civil administration, as well as that of entrusting to the same hands two or more satrapies. The temptation to revolt in such cases was great; for on the one hand, the jealousy of the central government was continually threatening the life or fortune of the too-powerful officer,[4] while on the other success might reasonably be anticipated, and in several instances[5] was achieved. The expedient of appointing to such posts the near relations of the monarch did not always succeed. More than one province detached itself from the empire under an Achæmenian prince, who probably found his birth and rank helped forward his ambitious projects.[6] In other cases the native princes, whom it was the liberal policy of the conqueror to uphold, took advantage of their position to re-establish complete or partial independence.[7] When Alexander invaded Asia, the Persian Empire was by

actions of his officers, and the harshest viziers rarely receive any adequate punishment. The evils of this system are seen by the Persians themselves. (See Chardin, ii., pp. 300 and 308–9.)

[*] Exceptions are found, as that of Otanes (Herod. v. 25), but the rule was as stated in the text. On the contrary, in modern Persia, the contrary rule prevails widely. (Chardin, ii. pp. 301 and 325.)

[1] As Aryandes (Herod. iv. 165–7), Pissuthnes (Thucyd. i. 115), Tissaphernes (Thucyd. viii. 5, &c.), Pharnabazus (ib. viii. 6, &c.), Tithraustes (Xen. Hell. iii. v. § 1), &c. In modern Persia the khans of the frontier provinces send and receive embassies (Chardin, ii. p. 311), but under special instructions on each occasion from the court. In ancient Persia the king seems only to have been consulted in cases of peculiar importance. (See Herod. v. 31).

[2] The younger Cyrus appears to have begun this practice (Xen. Anab. i. i. § 6). It afterwards prevailed generally through Asia Minor. (See Arrian, Exp. Alex. i.–ii. passim.) The 20,000 mercenaries who fought on the Persian side at the Granicus seem to have been all Greeks. (Arrian, i. 14, p. 30. Compare i. 12, p. 27, and i. 16, pp. 34–5.)

[3] Cyrus was for some time at open war with Tissaphernes. (Xen. Anab. i. i. Compare Hellen. iii. i. § 3.)

[4] How narrowly Cyrus escaped, when accused by Tissaphernes, we know from Xenophon (Anab. i. i. § 3). Tissaphernes himself was not so fortunate (Xen. Hell. iii. iv. § 25). Aryandes (Herod. iv. 166) and Masistes (ib. ix. 113) were both put to death on suspicion. Orœtes (ib. iii. 128) on something more. Megabates (Thucyd. i. 129) was deprived of his satrapy, for no cause that we can see.

[5] As Cappadocia and Pontus. See the next note.

[6] The case of Cyrus shows the good chance that there was of success in such a rebellion. In Cappadocia and Pontus, where branches of the Achæmenian house are found, it seems probable that royal satraps founded the dynasties.

[7] As Evagoras I. in Cyprus (Diod. Sic. xv. 2–4 and 8–9), and king Otys in

these means considerably reduced from the limits which it had reached in the days of Darius, or even of Xerxes.[*]

8. Besides the satrapies, there existed at all times on the borders of Persia, a number of countries owning the supremacy of the Great King, and contributing to the resources of the empire, but internally independent.   Such, under Cambyses, were the Ethiopians bordering upon Egypt, the Colchians and their neighbours towards the Caucasus, and the Arabs of the tract between Egypt and Palestine.[*] A similar condition was accepted by the Macedonian kings in the reign of Darius.[1] Satrapies sometimes seem to have reverted to it, making it their first step on the road to independence.   This was the case, towards the close of the monarchy, with Sacia and Cappadocia.[2] The position of such countries resembled that of Servia, Wallachia, and Moldavia under Turkey, of Thrace and Armenia under the early Cæsars.   Internal independence was allowed on the payment of a tribute, not indeed definitively fixed, but still expected to reach a certain amount.[*] A contingent of troops was also looked for in the case of a great expedition,[*] but could not, we may be sure, be demanded.   Still the strength of the empire was increased, in war as well as in peace, by these semi-independent tribes, whose communications with the court may perhaps have taken place through the satrap on whose province they bordered.[*]

9. A peculiarity in the arrangement of the satrapies, arising out of the special circumstances of the empire, deserves a few words of notice. Herodotus tells us that in some instances a satrapy was not continuous, but was made up of detached tracts of territory.[*] This was owing to the satrapial divisions being (as Heeren observes[7]) " ethnical rather than geographical," and to the local intermixture of distinct races common throughout the East.   As in modern Turkey, Greeks, Turks, Slaves, Wallacks, and Albanians live interspersed among one another,[*] so within the limits of the ancient Persia, the different nationalities lay

Paphlagonia (Xen. Hell. IV. i. §§ 3–15).   The Egyptian revolts likewise come under this head.
    [*] Heeren (Manual of Ancient History, p. 110, E. T.) asserts the contrary.   But the enumeration by Arrian of the nations which fought at Arbéla gives only twenty names in lieu of the six-and-forty of Herodotus.   Alexander's conquests account for about ten only of those which are missing.   Besides Paphlagonia, Pontus, and Sacia (Arrian, Exped. Alex. iii. 8), which were certainly lost to the empire, there seems to have been a large defection towards the south-eastern frontier.
    [*] Herod. iii. 97.   [1] Ibid. v. 18.
    [2] The Sacans and Cappadocians both sent troops to Arbéla (Arrian, loc. cit.), but the former, it is expressly said, as allies only (κατὰ συμμαχίαν).
    [*] See the story of Cambyses and the Cyrenæans, when the latter first made their submission (Herod. iii. 13, and compare iii. 97).
    [*] The Colchians, the African Ethiopians, and the Arabians, all served in the army of Xerxes (Herod. vii. 69 and 79).   The Sacans and Cappadocians, as before observed, fought at Arbela.
    [*] In this sense only can the statement made in Herod. i. 134, be accepted. (See note ad loc.)
    [*] Herod. iii. 89.   The passage is a difficult one, but seems only capable of this meaning.
    [7] Asiatic Nations, vol. i. p. 350, E. T.
    [*] A glance at the map in Professor Müller's " Languages of the Seat of War " will show this.

scattered and separated.   Certainly this was the case with the Sacans,[*] and with the Matieni,[1] and it may have been more widely prevalent.   In such cases the jurisdiction of the satrap extended over the various fragments of the race or races under his government, and was not confined to a single locality.   With the wandering tribes, which abounded in the southern and eastern regions of the empire, the arrangement must have been especially convenient.   Without it they would have been liable to be claimed as subjects by several satraps, and to have suffered a multiplied oppression; or they might perhaps, by skilful management, have escaped assessment altogether.

10. The division of the empire into satrapies was, as has been already observed, originally and primarily, for financial purposes.[2]   The collection and transmission of the tribute, in money and in kind,[3] was the satrap's first and chief duty.   He helped to maintain the supremacy of the dominant race over the conquered tribes, which to so great an extent composed the empire; but that important object was in the main secured by practices, and by an organization distinct from the satrapial authority.   A few remarks on these points will properly conclude this portion of the subject.

(i.) The conquered nations were in some instances disarmed;[4] in all, or nearly all, debarred from the profession of arms, which they could only follow when summoned from their peaceful avocations on occasion of some grand expedition.   This tended to produce among them an unwarlike temper, and so to keep them inferior to their masters, with whom the possession and profession of arms was almost universal.

(ii.) Tribes whose conquest had been very difficult, or which had revolted after subjection, were not unfrequently removed from their own country to a distant part of the empire.[5]   The close connexion of

[*] See the great inscription at Nakhsh-i-Rustam, and compare the note to Book vii. ch. 64.

[1] The Matieni on the Halys (Herod. i. 72) are geographically distinct from those who inhabited the Kurdish mountains (i. 189, v. 49, &c.).

[2] Suprà, § 2.   Compare Herod. iii. 89; Xen. Cyrop. VIII. vi. § 3.

[3] Besides the money tribute of which Herodotus gives so exact an account (iii. 90–5), a vast amount of produce was contributed by the conquered nations to the support of the army and of the court.   Babylonia supplied one-third of the latter expense (Herod. i. 192); to which we know that Media contributed annually 100,-000 sheep, and Cappadocia half that number (Strab. xi. p. 764), while other countries gave in proportion.   Egypt, besides her share of this expense, supplied corn for 120,000 soldiers, which was the number of her garrison (Herod. iii. 91).   Cilicia furnished annually 360 white horses (ib. ch. 90): Babylon, besides her corn, 500 boy-eunuchs (ibid. ch. 92).   From these instances conclusions may be drawn as to the rest of the provinces.

[4] See Herod. i. 155–7, which may be accepted thus far.   Heeren injudiciously adopts the entire narrative (As. Nat. i. p. 409, E. T.)

[5] The following are the chief known instances of this practice : I. The transportation of a large body of Egyptians to Susa by Cambyses (Ctes. § 9), of the Barcæans into Bactria (Herod. iv. 204), of the Pæonians into Asia Minor (ib. v. 17), of the Milesians to Ampé (ib. vi. 20), of the Eretrians to the Susianian Ardericca (ib. vi. 119), and of the Carians and Sitacenians into Babylonia (Arrian, Exp. Alex. iii. 48).   It is possible, as Heeren supposes (As. Nat. i. p. 340), that the Colchians may have been transported Egyptians.   Again, it is not improbable that the popu-

patriotism, and the love of liberty with local attachments, was sufficiently understood, and experience seems to have shown that by this means the most refractory could be made submissive and peaceable.

(iii.) Where extreme measures such as these were not resorted to, the subjection of the conquered nations was maintained by the more. simple and natural expedient of keeping on foot large standing armies, originally consisting entirely of native Persians,[6] and distributing them throughout the provinces. These troops occupied all the strongholds,[7] and were quartered in great numbers throughout the principal towns,[8] while a system of posts,[9] or government couriers, was so organised that rapid intelligence of a rising in any quarter could be communicated from city to city, and even from province to province. Large bodies of troops on which entire dependance could be placed, were thus within a short time concentrated wherever danger threatened, and movements of revolt on the part of the conquered, unless in countries peculiarly situated, were (while the empire retained its vigour) speedily put down.[1] In later times, when the Persian race had degenerated, and the standing army consisted in great part of mercenaries,[2] such revolts were sometimes crowned with success; but the instances are rare even at this period.[3]

11. From the condition of the conquered races, and of their immediate rulers, the satraps of the several provinces, it is time to pass to that of the dominant nation, and of the sovereign.

The Persian monarch was an irresponsible despot. Whatever limi-

---

lation of the "Egyptian villages" in Asia Minor, of which Xenophon speaks (Cyrop. vii. 1, § 45; Hell. iii. 1, § 7), settled according to him by Cyrus after his defeat of Crœsus, may really have consisted of Egyptians transported for rebellion. How recognised a feature of Persian policy such transplantation was, is indicated by the ready acceptance given to the fiction of Histiæus (Herod. vi. 3). The practice has been at all times common in the East. With regard to its use by the Assyrians, see the Essays appended to Book i. Essay vii. § 89. With regard to modern times, Chardin tells us that Shah Abbas transported several colonies of from 20,000 to 30,-000 families a distance of 200 or 300 leagues (Voyage en Perse, vol. iii. p. 292); and Ferrier speaks of the "wholesale removal of populations" as "common through Central Asia" (Caravan Journeys, p. 395.)

[6] Or perhaps of Persians *and Medes.* (See Thucyd. i. 104.)

[7] See Xen. Cyrop. viii. vi. § 1, which is confirmed historically by many passages. (Cf. Herod. ii. 30; Xen. Anab. i. iv. § 4; Arrian, Exp. Alex. i. 17, &c.)

[8] The garrison of Memphis in the time of Herodotus consisted of 120,000 Persians (Herod. iii. 91). In the time of Alexander 20,000 Persians and 20,000 mercenaries garrisoned the north-western corner of Asia Minor (Arrian, Exp. Alex. i. 14). From these numbers the enormous amount of the entire standing army may be conjectured.

[9] Ἄγγαροι, or ἀγγαρήιοι (vide infrà, viii. 98, and compare Xen. Cyrop. viii. vi. § 17).

[1] For a proof of the speed with which forces could be collected on an emergency, see Herod. v. 102. Compare v. 108. Xen. Anab. i. iv. § 5, and vii. §§ 11-12. Arrian, ut suprà. The successful revolts of conquered nations were uniformly upon the outskirts of the empire, and generally in detached districts, such as Egypt.

[2] In the latter times they seem in some satrapies to have equalled or exceeded the number of the native troops. (Arrian, l. s. c.; compare iii._7.)

[3] That of Egypt from Darius Nothus is the most remarkable. Cyprus and Paphlagonia are perhaps the only other instances. In the former success was only temporary.

tation may have been placed upon the authority of a weak and timid king by the grandees of his court, pleading the inviolability of Persian law,[4] it is certain that a sovereign of any energy of character could set himself up above all legal restraints, and follow to the fullest extent the dictates of his own caprice.   The answer of the royal judges to Cambyses sets this matter in its true light, and shows clearly that the power of the kings was absolutely without limit.   The judges "found a law that the Persian king might do whatever he pleased."[5]   Such a principle would cover any and every transgression of all rules, religious or other, which might be supposed to have a universal obligation.   Accordingly we find the Achæmenian monarchs not only tyrannising at will over the persons of their subjects, but trampling whenever it pleases them upon the most sacred religious ordinances.[6]   No class is secure from their oppression, no privilege beyond their control, no law safe from their infraction.[7]   Like other despots they are liable to the last resort of the oppressed—assassination;[8] but so long as they live, their word is law, and their will without check or hindrance.

There does not appear to have been in ancient, any more than in modern[9] Persia, a regularly established council.   The king occasionally referred matters to the decision of the royal judges,[10] and convened assemblies of the grandees for deliberation on affairs of particular importance;[1] but nothing seems to have bound him either to call such councils, or, if he called them, to abide by their sentence.[2]   When a council was summoned at the court, certain nobles, it is probable, had the right of attendance, but the monarch might invite to his council-table any persons whose judgment he valued.[3]

In default of a legitimate control the Persian kings were apt to fall under the influence, either of a favourite,[4] or more commonly of the

---

[4] See Dan. vi. 14–15 ; Herod. ix. 111.

[5] Herod. iii. 31: τῷ βασιλεύοντι Περσέων ἐξεῖναι ποιεῖν τὸ ἂν βούληται.

[6] Marriage with a sister was clearly considered as incestuous in Persia, yet Cambyses married two of his (Herod. loc. cit.).

[7] The law that the king should only marry from the families of the six conspirators (Herod. iii. 84) was one which, if any, might have seemed likely to be observed.   Yet it was broken by Ahasuerus (Xerxes?) when he espoused Esther (Esth. ii. 17).

[8] Of the nine kings who succeeded Darius, three (Xerxes I., Xerxes II., and Artaxerxes III.) were murdered.

[9] See Chardin, vol. ii. p. 296.

[10] See Herod. iii. 31.   There is no reason to suppose that these judges were, as Heeren supposes (As. Nat. i. p. 390), necessarily Magi.

[1] See Herod. vii. 8, viii. 67 ; Esth. i. 13–15.

[2] This is evident from the words and conduct of Xerxes (Herod. vii. 8, 11–18).

[3] The "seven princes of Persia" may have had the right of attendance, and so have been called par excellence the king's counsellors (Esth. i. 14 ; Ezra vii. 14), but the monarch summoned besides "all that knew law and judgment" (Esth. i. 13). Those who attended the great council of war before the invasion of Greece seem to have been the satraps and commanders of the troops throughout the provinces (Herod. vii. 8, §§ 4 and 19.)

[4] Generally a eunuch, as Spamitres (Ctes. § 29), the favourite of Xerxes in his later years ; Artoxares (ib. § 49), the favourite of Darius Nothus ; Bagoas (Diod. Sic. xvi. 50, end), the favourite of Artaxerxes Ochus, &c. ; but sometimes a noble, as Mardonius, who governed Xerxes in the beginning of his reign.

queen-mother, or of one of their wives.[*] Bred up in the seraglio, under the tutelage of eunuchs and women, and often with no definite expectation of the crown,[*] they found themselves at their accession in a state of vassalage, which they mostly lacked strength to throw off. The real ruler of Persia was in general a Bagoas, or a Parysatis, in whose hands the monarch was but a puppet, and who, from the interior of the gynæceum or harem, directed the counsels and bestowed the honours of the empire. These disorders however belong to the later period of the monarchy. They first appear at the close of the reign of Darius,[*] and only come into full play after the return of Xerxes from the Greek expedition.

12. The native Persians themselves, though equally destitute with the conquered races of any real personal freedom,[*] were permitted, by the favour or policy of their rulers, certain special privileges. The province of Persia Proper was exempt from tribute.[*] Persians had universally precedence over the other nations which composed the empire.[1] Offices and employments of importance, though not absolutely confined to them, were yet, with rare exceptions, conferred upon the dominant race.[*] They alone appear to have formed the household of the monarch.[*] Many of them received assignments upon the conquered countries, of houses, lands, and vassals,[*] from which they drew large

---

[*] See Herod. vii. 3, end; ix. 111; Plut. Artaxerx. p. 1861–6; Xen. Anab. i. i. §§ 3–4.

[*] The law of succession was very ill determined (Herod. vii. 2), and left the monarch a power within certain limits of determining his successor. This power he would rarely exercise till towards the close of his life (see Herod. i. 208; Ctes. Persic. § 8), when the character of the youth was formed.

[*] Herod. vii. 3, end: Ἡ γὰρ Ἄτοσσα εἶχε τὸ πᾶν κράτος. The accounts given by Ctesias (Persic. §§ 8, 9), which would extend to the reigns of Cambyses, and even of Cyrus, the manners of his own day, appear to me little worthy of credit.

[*] Acts of tyrannical cruelty have most commonly Persians for their objects. It is sufficient to mention the cases of Prexaspes (Herod. iii. 35), Œobazus (ib. iv. 84), Masistes (ib. ix. 111–3), Mithridates (Plutarch, ii. p. 1861), and the twelve nobles buried to the head by order of Cambyses (Herod. iii. 35, end). The higher position of the Persians brought them into contact with the sovereign more frequently than others. (See Heeren, As. Nat. i. p. 362.)

[*] Herod. iii. 97. Of course it supported its satrap and garrisons, but it paid nothing to the central government.

[1] In war (Herod. vii. 55, viii. 113, ix. 31). In processions, where the right hand, the post of honour, was assigned to them (Xen. Cyrop. viii. iii. § 10). In games (ibid. § 25). In approaching the king (ibid. § 14).

[*] It is not very uncommon to find high office entrusted to a Mede (see Herod. i. 156, 162; vi. 94; vii. 88; Beh. Inscr. ii. xiv. 6, and iii. xiv. 3), but wonderfully few instances occur of high office held by a native of any other conquered country. Profane history furnishes, I believe, but two examples, that of Tabalus (Herod. i 153), and that of Xenagoras (ibid. ix. 107). Even the Median appointments are rare compared with the Persian. Of course the cases must be excepted of tributary princes, and native rulers allowed to maintain a certain authority over their people, but forming no part of the recognised staff of the government.

[*] Heeren's arguments (As. Nat. i p. 395) scarcely prove that the household was composed entirely of Pasargadæ, but there seems no reason to doubt that it was, at least as a general rule, made up of Persians.

[*] Xen. Cyrop. viii. vi. § 5. The statement is confirmed by the known practice of conferring occasionally such gifts upon foreigners, as upon Themistocles (Thucyd. i. 138) and Demaratus (Herod. vi. 70).

470 GRADATIONS OF RANK AMONG THE PERSIANS. App. Book III.

revenues. Others accompanied the satraps to their provinces as body-
guards,[5] and lived at the expense of the inhabitants. None engaged in
trade,[6] or in any menial employ. All Persians of the tribes which were
neither agricultural or pastoral, seem, unless attached to the court, to
have followed the profession of arms. They formed a martial caste,
which held itself distinctly above the rest of the population.

13. Besides the difference here indicated between the three leading
Persian tribes and the other six, some further gradations of rank and
dignity are found to have prevailed. The tribe of the Pasargadæ, to
which the royal family of the Achæmenidæ belonged, had a decided
pre-eminence over both the Maraphians and the Maspians.[7] Among
the Pasargadæ, the royal family, which owing to the prevalence of poly-
gamy was very numerous, held the first place. Next in order seem to
have followed the families of the six conspirators, which had the privilege
of furnishing wives to the king.[8] Among these the descendants of
Otanes possessed special rights, though of what nature we have no distinct information.[9] Perhaps the representatives of these six families,
and of the royal house,[1] formed the "seven princes of Persia, which saw
the king's face, and sat the first in the kingdom."[2] Further than this
there was no order of nobility, unless we consider the possession of the
crown grants mentioned above, which were handed down from father to
son,[3] to have constituted a noble class.

Such seem to have been the chief outlines of a system, which, simple
and inartificial as it was, sufficed to maintain one of the largest empires
that the world has ever seen during a space of more than two centuries.

---

[5] Orœtes was guarded by a thousand Persians (Herod. iii. 127). The only peculiarity in his case was the number.

[6] Hence the contempt which Cyrus is said to have expressed for the Lacedæmonians (Herod. i. 153).

[7] Heeren (As. Nat. i. ch. ii.) carries this pre-eminence beyond its just bounds,
and says nothing of the rank of the Maraphians and Maspians. Yet Herodotus distinctly states it (i. 125, compare iv. 167).

[8] Herod. iii. 84 (cf. note ad loc.).

[9] We know indeed that the head of the family of Otanes received an annual
kaftan of the most splendid description. But the family must have had other rights
unknown to us, to justify the expression of Herodotus (iii. 83, διατελέει μούνη ἐλευ-
θέρη ἐοῦσα Περσέων, καὶ ἄρχεται τοσαῦτα ὅσα αὐτὴ θέλει).

[1] There is some difficulty in supposing this (see note [8] on Book iii. ch. 71); but
perhaps the royal house was represented by the head of the branch next in order
of succession to that upon the throne, which was the position of Darius at the time
of the conspiracy.

[2] Esth. i. 14.

[3] Xen. Cyrop. l. s. c. The estates of Demaratus were, we know, transmitted to
his descendants (Xen. Hell. iii. i. § 6.)

ESSAY IV.

ON THE TOPOGRAPHY OF BABYLON.

1. Want of an accurate survey.　2. Great extent of Babylon according to ancient writers.　3. No traces of the original *enceinte*.　4. General plan of the existing ruins.　5. Their position on the left bank of the Euphrates a difficulty—modes of meeting it.　6. Canal between the northern and the central ruins.　7. Mound of *Babil*, the temple of Belus—its present state.　8. Proofs of the identity.　9. Mounds of the *Kasr* and *Amrám*, the ancient palace.　10. Site of the great reservoir.　11. Palace of Neriglissar, and embankment of *Nabunit*.　12. Triangular enclosure, of the Parthian age.　13. The *Birs-Nimrud*—its present appearance.　14. Original plan of the *Birs*.　15. Its ornamentation.　16. The *Birs* rebuilt by Nebuchadnezzar—his account of the restoration.

1. THE topography of ancient Babylon is a subject which is still involved in so much doubt and difficulty that only a very slight sketch of it will be attempted in the present Essay. Accurate surveys on a large scale have recently been made by thoroughly competent persons[1] under the direction of the Indian Government; but the results have not yet reached England, and it is uncertain whether months or years may elapse before they become accessible to the public. In default of these materials it is necessary to have recourse to the very incomplete and inexact charts which have been published by the late Mr. Rich[2] and Sir R. Ker Porter[3]—charts which can only be viewed as giving a general notion of the extent of the ruins, and roughly determining a few main positions. It is clearly undesirable, when the data are so insufficient, and when they are likely to be in a year or two superseded by materials of a vastly superior character, to enter into an elaborate discussion of the various intricate questions involved in the wide subject here proposed for consideration. Certain main points may, however, be regarded as sufficiently determined, even by means of the rough surveys already published, and certain principal buildings and other features of the ancient city may be considered as identified by the inscriptions on their

[1] The chief superintendant of the surveys has been Captain Jones, already so well known from his similar labours in Upper Mesopotamia. (See As. Soc. Journ. vol. xv. Part 2, Art. v.)

[2] In his "Memoir on Babylon," first published in the *Mines de l'Orient*, and since frequently reprinted. The last and best edition is that edited by his widow in 1839.

[3] Travels, vol. ii. opp. page 349. Mr. Layard is not a separate authority. He derived the plan given in his Nineveh and Babylon (p. 490) from Sir R. K. Porter. See his acknowledgment, p. 492, note.

remains and by the descriptive documents of the Babylonian kings. To these leading features of the topography, and to these only, it is proposed at present to direct the reader's attention.

2. The most remarkable fact recorded of Babylon by the ancient writers is its extraordinary extent. According to Herodotus [4] it was a square, 120 stades or nearly 14 miles each way, covering thus an area of nearly 200 square miles! This estimate is somewhat diminished by the historians of Alexander,[5] who reduce the side to about 11 miles, and the area to something less than 130 square miles. Even this space is (according to modern notions) enormous, being five or six times the size of London. The authority, however, upon which it rests is of great weight and importance; for one cannot but suppose that accurate measurements would be made by the Greeks upon their conquest of the city.[6] It seems, therefore, necessary to accept the statement, and to suppose that a wall of great height [7] surrounded an area of the size indicated, and that the name Babylon attached in popular parlance to the entire space within the rampart. Of course, however, if the wall was of this extent, only a small proportion of the ground within it can have been covered with buildings. The Babylon thus described was not a town, but a great fortified district very partially built upon, and containing within it not only gardens and parks, but numerous fields and orchards.[8]

3. Of the great wall enclosing this space, it is agreed by almost all travellers that not a vestige remains.[9] It has been destroyed by quarrying, or has sunk into the ditch from which it arose;[10] and there is no possibility of even determining its position, unless by the merest conjecture. The earliest of the Mesopotamian explorers[1] imagined that it included within it the *Birs-Nimrud*, which is six miles from the Euphrates; but the inscriptions of Nebuchadnezzar make it certain that this vast ruin marks the site of a distinct town.[2]

[4] Book i. ch. 178.

[5] For the details see note [5] on the above-named chapter.

[6] The only argument that can be urged with any effect against this, is that the walls had perished before Alexander's conquest, and therefore that his historians only reported a tradition. But it is very unlikely that they could have altogether disappeared so early. And Abydenus expressly states that the wall of Nebuchadnezzar continued to Alexander's time. (See vol. i. Essay viii. p. 412, note [1].)

[7] On the height of the wall see note [6] on Book i. ch. 178.

[8] This is declared to have been the case by Q. Curtius (v. i. § 27). It has been generally allowed by modern writers. (See Rich's Second Memoir, p. 14; Ker Porter, vol. ii. p. 386; Layard, Nineveh and Babylon, p. 494; Niebuhr, Lectures on Ancient History, vol. i. p. 24, note [16], E. T.)

[9] M. Oppert alone, I believe, disputes this. He is of opinion that he has found traces of the walls, or rather of their towers and gates, in certain of the mounds or *Tels* which cover the flat country on either side of the Euphrates. These views will no doubt be developed in his forthcoming work on Mesopotamia. See Note B at the end of this Essay.

[10] See vol. i. Essay viii. p. 427.

[1] Rich, Second Memoir, pp. 31-2; Ker Porter, vol. ii. p. 382.

[2] M. Oppert admits that the *Birs-Nimrud* marks the site of the ancient Borsippa, but he supposes this place to have been a sort of second citadel (Acropolis minor) to Babylon, and to have lain between the outer and the inner walls.

4. The only ruins which can be confidently assigned to the ancient Babylon are the group of mounds upon the Euphrates, a little above *Hillah*, which cover a space about three miles long and from one to two miles broad, and are almost entirely inclosed within an irregular triangle, formed by two long lines of rampart (ɢɢ in the plan) and the river. These ruins are generally said to consist of three great masses of brickwork, the northernmost of which (Rich's *Mujellibeh*) is known to the Arabs as Babil (ᴀ in the plan), the central as the *Kasr* or palace (ʙ), and the southernmost (ᴄ) as the mound of *Amrám*. Besides these principal buildings there are various lesser ruins, among which the most remarkable are two long parallel lines of rampart (ғғ) having a direction nearly north and south, which shut in the central and southern ruins on the east, and a similar single line

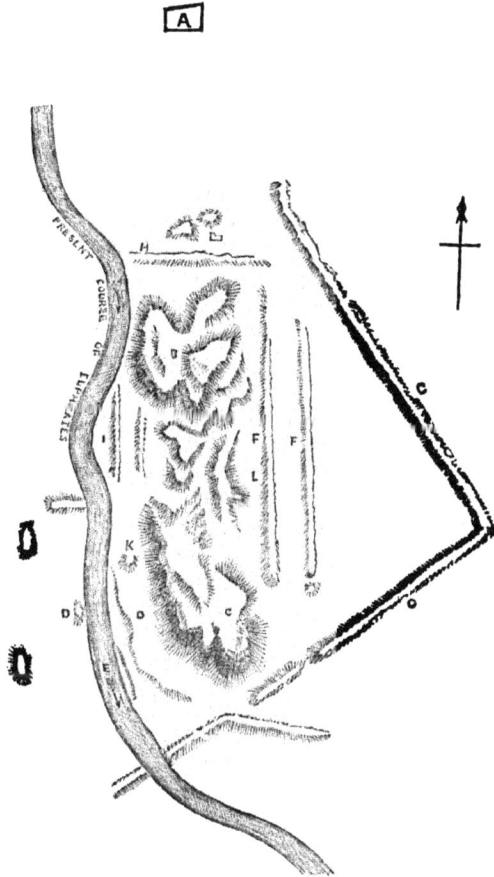

Present state of the Ruins of Babylon.

A Babil, or Temple of Belus.
B Kasr, or Palace.   } Parts of Nebuchadnezzar's
C Mound of Amrám.   }   Palace.
D Palace of Neriglissar.
E Embankment of Nabonit (the eastern faintly marked).
F Ancient Embankments of Reservoir.
G Parthian Earthwork.
L Homeira.

(ʜ), running from east to west, which bounds the central mass of ruins (the *Kasr*) towards the north. Less noticeable, but still of some visible importance, are some ruins on each side of the Euphrates (ᴅᴅ in the plan) parallel with the mound of Amrám, and an embankment along the river (ᴇ) nearly in the same locality. There are also two shorter lines of low mounds (ɪɪ) to the west of the principal ruins, with a space between them, from which extends both northwards and southwards a depression of the soil which looks like an ancient river-bed, and which is only interrupted seriously at one point (ᴋ) by an irregular mass of rubbish nearly filling up the channel. Beyond the ruins thus described, towards Hillah on the south and towards *Mohawill* on the north, are low heaps and embankments scattered irregularly over the plain. On the western side of the river, besides the ruin already mentioned (D), there are a number of lesser mounds; and both here and towards the east the ground is everywhere covered with fragments of brick and with nitre, the sure marks of former buildings.[3]

5. The difficulty which immediately strikes the observer, who, acquainted with the descriptions of Babylon given by the ancient writers,[4] casts his eye over the mass of ruins above described, is their position, almost without exception, on the left bank of the river. The ancients unanimously declare that the Euphrates flowed *through* Babylon; and that the most important buildings were placed on the opposite sides of the stream.[5] The Temple of Belus and the Royal Palace—the two chief edifices—are said to have been separated by the river, each forming a stronghold or fortress in its own division of the town. Now although it must be granted that the Euphrates, having a general tendency to run off to the westward,[6] has done much to obliterate the ruins which originally stood upon the right bank, yet it can scarcely be thought that this cause is sufficient to account for the entire disappearance of a building so vast as both these are said to have been. We *ought* to find traces both of the palace and of the temple, and they ought to be separated either by the main stream of the Euphrates or at least by a branch from it—which is certainly not the case at present with any of the important ruins. The suggestion that the *Birs-Nimrud* represented the old temple of Belus, though it is distant eight or nine miles from the true Babylon, originated in the supposed necessity of finding one or other of the two great buildings among the ruins still existing to the west of the stream. The *Birs* is the only ruin of any magnitude on the right bank at present, and the vast dimensions ascribed to Babylon by the ancients would allow of its being included within the ancient enceinte.[7] The identification, however, of the *Birs* with Borsippa—a town quite distinct from Babylon,[8] which is rendered certain by the monuments[9]—

---

[3] The particulars of this account are chiefly taken from Rich (First Memoir), Ker Porter (vol. ii. pp. 337–380), and Layard (Nineveh and Babylon, pp. 490–2), corrected from the personal recollections of Sir H. Rawlinson and Dr. Hyslop, the latter of whom was engaged with Captain Jones in the recent surveys. Reference has also been made to the letters of M. Fresnel in the *Journal Asiatique* for June and July, 1853, and to the general description of Mr. Loftus (Chaldæa, ch. ii.).

[4] Besides the description of our author (l. 178–183), the most important are those of Diodorus (ii. 7, et seqq.), which is probably derived from Ctesias, and of Berosus, as reported by Josephus (Ant. Jud. x. 11). This last seems to have been derived by Berosus directly from Nebuchadnezzar's monuments, and, if it were less corrupt, would be invaluable.

[5] Herod. i. 181. Diod. Sic. ii. 8. Strab. xvi. § 5, p. 1049. Plin. H. N. vi. 26, &c.

[6] Layard, Nin. and Bab. p. 493.

[7] This was strongly urged by Rich (Second Memoir, p. 32) and Ker Porter (vol. ii. p. 383), who were the first to propose the identification of the *Birs* with the Temple of Belus. It is echoed by Niebuhr (l. s. c.), and Fresnel (Journ. Asiatique, Juillet, 1853, p. 24).

[8] See Beros. Fr. 14, p. 508; Strab. xvi. p. 1050; Steph. Byz. ad voc., &c.

[9] See the inscription upon the Birs Cylinder, infra, p. 484, and compare the abstract of the Standard Inscription in note A at the end of this Essay.

entirely disposes of this theory ; and we are left to the alternative of supposing that one or other of the two buildings has perished, or of finding the remains of both in the ruins on the east or left bank. It is the opinion of those best qualified to judge that in the great northern mound, which the Arabs call *Babil*, may be recognised the ancient temple of Belus [10] or Bel-Merodach; while the central and northern mounds, known as the *Kasr* and the mound of *Amrám*, mark together the site of the royal residence,[1] including both the old palace (*Amrám*) and that more modern erection (the *Kasr*), which was not improperly called by Nebuchadnezzar *Taprati-nisi*, " the Wonder of Mankind." [2]

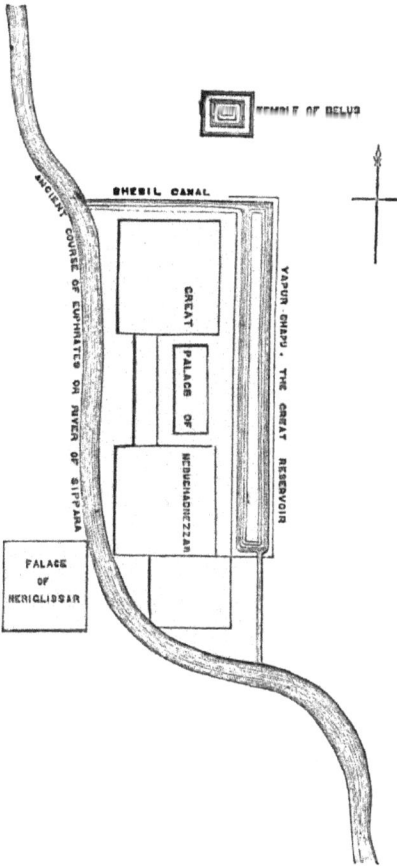

6. With respect to the difficulty which arises from the position of both these two ruins on the left bank, it may be observed that a large canal, called by Nebuchadnezzar " the *Shebil*," is said by him to have bounded his palace on the north; and that this canal, which may either have run east in the line assigned it in the accompanying plan, or have left the Euphrates higher up and have been carried in a south-east direction to the head of the great reservoir, must most certainly have intervened between the palace and the temple, and may therefore be the water-course which Herodotus regarded as the true river. It was not, however, the only or even the main watercourse which intersected Babylon. Nebuchadnezzar speaks of the " River of Sippara " [3] as the western boundary of his palace, intending by this the natural course of the Euphrates; which seems to have passed through the ruins a little to the east of the present channel, and to have again united with it about half way between the ruins and Hillah. The present course of

Portions of Ancient Babylon distinguishable in the present Ruins.

[10] Supra, vol. i. p. 249, note [c].
[1] See note [1] to Book i. ch. 181.   [2] In the Standard Inscription, infra, p. 485.
[3] Standard Inscription, l. s. c.   Sippara was situated on both sides of the river

the stream is of comparatively recent date; it passes through the palace of Neriglissar, which was built entirely upon the right bank, and has washed into an embankment by which Nabonidus appears to have checked its tendency to run off to the west.

7. The mound of *Babil*, which it is proposed to identify with the temple of Belus, is an oblong mass composed chiefly of unbaked brick, rising from the plain to the height of 140 feet,[4] and having at the top a broad flat space, broken with heaps of rubbish, and otherwise very uneven. The northern and southern faces of the mound are about

View of Babil from the West.

200 yards in length,[5] the eastern and western are respectively 182 and 136 yards.[6] All the faces, and especially that which looks to the west, present at intervals some appearance of brickwork, the bricks being sun-dried, and cemented, not with bitumen, but with mud, a thin layer of reeds occurring between each course of the

(whence the dual form Sepharvaim) about the site of the modern *Mosaib*. The Euphrates below this point was known to the Babylonians as the "river of Sippara;" just as in Arabian times, when Sippara had become *Sura*, it was known as the *Nahr-Sura*.

[4] This is Mr. Rich's estimate (First Memoir, p. 28), but as he over-estimates the height of the *Birs* by nearly one-third, no great dependence can be placed upon it.

[5] The exact measurements given by Mr. Rich are, for the north face 200 yards, and for the south 219 (First Memoir, p. 28). Sir R. Ker Porter makes them respectively 551 and 552 feet (ii. p. 340).

[6] Sir R. K. Porter makes these two sides of equal length, and gives them only 230 feet (l. s. c.)

brick.[7] Tunnels driven into the base of the mound on a level with the plain, show that the structure was formerly coated with a wall of burnt-brick masonry, supported by numerous piers and buttresses of the same material.[8] These baked bricks, as well as most of those which are found loose among the rubbish wherever it is dug into, bear the name of Nebuchadnezzar, and were laid in a fine white mortar.

8. The general character of this building, its square shape, its solid construction, its isolated grandeur, mark it as the *ziggurat* or tower of a Babylonian temple. It closely resembles in general appearance the many striking piles which break the dead level of Babylonia, in some of which inscriptions have been found proving them to be temples, as at the *Birs-i-Nimrud* and at *Mugheir*.[9] To the latter of these two edifices it bears a striking resemblance. The *Mugheir* temple is not square but oblong, and its proportions are almost the same as those of the *Babil* mound.[1] It is also, like that, cased with kiln-baked bricks, and supported by a number of shallow buttresses. The only remarkable differences between the buildings are the greater size of the Babylon temple, and the absence from it of any indication of a second stage, which is a marked feature of the Mugheir ruin. It would be rash, however, to conclude from the non-appearance of any second stage at present, that no upper stage or stages ever existed. It is to the accidental use of an imperishable material—blue slag—at the summit of the *Birs*, that the solitary preservation of that one Babylonian building in almost its pristine perfection is owing. In the absence of such a protecting cap, the upper stages of a temple would rapidly decay and disappear; and hence we find in all Babylonia but a single temple preserving the pyramidal shape, which (it is probable) was common to all or almost all of them originally.

On the whole we may conclude, with tolerable confidence, that in the great northern mound of Babylon we have the remains of that famous temple, which Herodotus describes so graphically, and which ancient writers generally declare to have been one of the chief marvels of the Eastern world. Its bricks bear the name of Nebuchadnezzar,[2] who relates that he thoroughly repaired the building;[3] and it is the only

[7] Rich, First Memoir, p. 29. Sir H. Rawlinson regards this brick-work as Parthian. (See note [8] on Book i. ch. 179.)

[8] Mr. Layard drove these tunnels, and has related the results in his "Nineveh and Babylon," pp. 503-5.

[9] See Mr. Loftus's "Chaldæa and Susiana," pp. 28-30, and 130-2.

[1] Mr. Loftus (p. 128) gives the length of the Mugheir Temple as 198 feet, and the breadth as 133 feet, which is within a fraction of 3 to 2. If we take Mr. Rich's measurement of the *west* face as the true one, we have almost exactly the same proportion (200 to 136). The chief difference is in the superior size of the Babel mound, which is measured by *yards* instead of feet.

M. Oppert believes the original shape of the *Babil* mound to have been an exact square. He seems to make the south side at present nearly 200 metres, the west 170, the east 155, and the north 120 metres. The south side he represents as almost perfect, while the north and west are greatly worn away.

[2] Layard, p. 505.

[3] In the Standard Inscription (see note A. at the end of this Essay). Compare Berosus as quoted in vol. i. (Essay viii. p. 414, note [9]).

ruin which seems to be that of a temple, among all the remains of
ancient Babylon.

9. In the vast and irregular labyrinth of mounds, which, commencing about a mile south of the *Babil* ruin, extends thence with little
interruption for nearly two miles parallel with the river, having an
average width—between a line of rampart on the east and the old course
of the Euphrates on the west—of twelve or thirteen hundred yards, it
is probable that we have merely the remains of that group of royal residences, towers, hanging gardens, &c., which formed what was called
" the palace," [4] and which are commemorated in the fragments of Berosus, [5] and the standard inscription of Nebuchadnezzar. [6] In the great
southern ruin, known as the mound of *Amrám* (c), which is 1100 yards

View of the Kasr.

in length and 800 in its greatest breadth, [7] we may recognise the remains
of the ancient palace, coeval probably with Babylon itself, which continued to be the royal residence to the time of Nabopolassar. This is
the only part of the ruins in which inscriptions belonging to early kings
have been found ; a fact which, coupled with the comparative poorness

---

[4] Herod. i. 181.   [5] Fr. 14.   See vol. i. p. 412, note [7].
[6] See note A. at the end of the Essay.
[7] Rich, First Memoir, p. 21.   Ker Porter describes the mound of Amrám as a
triangle, the sides of which are respectively 1400, 1100, and 850 feet (ii. p. 371).
M. Oppert agrees nearly with this view.   He represents the mound as triangular
and the sides as proportioned thus—the western 630 metres, the eastern 540, and the
northern 420 metres.

of the materials employed, and the entire absence from the structure (so far as appears) of all fine masonry,[a] sufficiently indicates the superior antiquity of its erection. The more northern mound (B), now called *Mujellibeh*, and crowned by the building named the *Kasr*, is undoubtedly a construction of Nebuchadnezzar, and may be almost certainly identified with the " new palace adjoining his father's," which is ascribed to him, and which he claims to have erected in *fifteen days*.[b] This mound is smaller than that of *Amrám*, being an irregular square of about 700 yards each way;[1] but it appears to have been "composed of buildings far superior to all the rest which have left traces in this quarter,"[2] and it has furnished the only sculptures and *bas-reliefs* which have as yet been discovered among the ruins.[3] The remarkable fragment on its summit, called the *Kasr*, is a solid mass of masonry, composed of pale yellow bricks of excellent quality, bound together by fine lime cement, and stamped in almost every instance with the name and titles of Nebuchadnezzar[4] Slabs inscribed by this king, and containing an

[a] Layard, p. 509.   Ker Porter, ii. pp. 371-2.   M. Oppert sees in the mound of Amrám the remains of the famous "hanging gardens" of Nebuchadnezzar.

[b] See the Standard Inscription, and compare Beros. Fr. 14 : προσκατεσκεύασε τοῖς πατρικοῖς βασιλείοις ἕτερα βασίλεια ἐχόμενα αὐτῶν, ὧν τὸ μὲν ἀνάστημα καὶ τὴν λοιπὴν πολυτέλειαν περισσὸν ἴσως ἂν εἴη λέγειν, πλὴν ὡς ὄντα μεγάλα καὶ ὑπερήφανα συνετελέσθη ἡμέραις πεντεκαίδεκα. Many slabs brought by Sir H. Rawlinson from the *Kasr*, bear the inscription, " the palace of Nebuchadnezzar." One of these is in the British Museum.

[1] Rich, First Memoir, p. 22. Ker Porter calls the length of the mound 800, and the breadth 600 feet (ii. p. 355). M. Oppert believes it to have been a square, but makes the length of the present mound from N. to S. 420 metres, the greatest breadth 380 metres, and the average breadth 300 metres.

[2] Rich, l. s. c.

[3] The most remarkable of these are a "block of basalt, roughly cut to represent a lion standing over a prostrate human figure," which is still lying *in situ* (Loftus, p. 19), and a fragment of slab or frieze, composed of figures nearly alike, representing a Babylonian deity (Layard, p. 508).

[4] Layard, p. 506. Fragments of enamelled bricks, brightly coloured, are abundant in the mound of the *Mujellibeh*. "The principal colours are a brilliant blue, red, a deep yellow, white, and black." (Layard, p. 507.) Portions of the figures of men and animals are traceable on the fragments. It is probable that these bricks formed the adornment of the interior, where hunting scenes were represented. (See the Letter of M. Fresnel in the *Journal Asiatique* for June, 1853, pp. 486-490, and comp. Diod. Sic. ii. 8.)

account of the building of the palace, have also been brought from the mound, and serve still further to identify it.

10. The two long parallel lines of rampart (ꜰ ꜰ), a mile in length, and somewhat more than 100 yards apart,[4] which shut in this entire mass of ruins upon the east, are (like the great bulk of the remains) of ancient Babylonian construction, and may either represent the "outer and inner walls" of the palace,[5] or (more probably) the embankments along "the *Yapur-Shapu*, the great reservoir of Babylon," which some one of the early kings seems to have built, but which Nebuchadnezzar greatly strengthened and enlarged.[7] The single line of rampart (ʜ) which closes in the mound of the *Kasr* upon the north, is perhaps a construction of Neriglissar, who affirms that he "made a new bed for the eastern canal (or *Shebil*), and *with brick and mortar built up its sides.*"

11. Parallel with the mound of *Amrám*, on either side of the present bed of the Euphrates, are remains (ᴅ ᴅ), which appear to have belonged to a second palace, situated on the right bank of the stream.[8] On the bricks of that portion of the building which is now on the left bank, the name and titles of Neriglissar have been found; from which it appears that he either originally constructed, or at least repaired the edifice. Near to this palace, a little more to the south, the Euphrates has washed into an embankment (ᴇ), the bricks of which are stamped with the name and titles of *Nabunit*, who is stated by Berosus[9] to have built quays along the stream.

12. The triangular boundary (ɢ ɢ), which forms the extreme eastern limit of the great mass of the ruins, does not appear to be a Babylonian, but a Parthian work; and it may therefore be omitted altogether from the present discussion. As has been already observed, no traces of the ancient *enceinte* exist; or at least, among the innumerable embankments which fret the country both to the east and to the west of the Euphrates, none has been as yet discovered with claims superior to the remainder.

13. Before concluding this Essay, it seems proper that some account should be given of the great ruin which has long disputed with *Babil* the honour of representing the Temple of Belus, and which a few years back was very completely explored by Sir H. Rawlinson.

At the distance of about six miles from Hillah, in a southwest direction, and eight or nine miles from the nearest point of the ruins above described, stands the huge pyramidical mound, to which the Arabs give the name of *Birs-Nimrud*, a solitary pile rising suddenly from the vast expanse of the desert. This mound, like that of *Babil*, is an oblong square. Its angles face the four cardinal points.[1] The north-western

---

[4] Rich, First Memoir, p. 19. Sir H. Rawlinson estimated the distance at about 70 yards.

[5] See note A., sub fin. [7] Ibid.

[8] Diodorus, it may be remarked, spoke of two palaces, one on either side of the river, and connected by a bridge (ii. 8). I have already observed that the river flowed formerly down the long valley which skirts the *Mujellibeh* and *Amrám* mounds on the west. Can the curious heap (K on the plan) be a remnant of the ancient bridge?

[9] Fr. 14. The passage is given in the first volume, p. 421, note [1].

[1] Curiously enough both Rich and Porter speak of the *sides* as facing the cardi-

and south-eastern faces, which are the largest, have been estimated to measure 643 feet; the north-eastern 420, and the south-western 376 feet.[2] The height above the plain is about 153 feet.[3] The ruin consists of two parts—a huge pyramidical mass towards the south-west, and a comparatively low projection towards the opposite quarter. The length of this latter is said to be 240 feet.[4] Thus apart from this projection, which clearly marks the vestibule or approach to the temple, the main building may be described as a pyramid 153 feet high, and 400 feet square at the base.

To the ordinary observer the mound presents the appearance rather of a natural hill, crowned by a ruin,[5] than that of a structure built entirely by the hand of man. Thirty-seven feet of solid brickwork, looking almost like a tower, stand exposed at the top, while below this the original building is almost entirely concealed beneath the masses of rubbish which have crumbled down from the upper portion. The whole structure, however, is deeply channelled by the weather, and in places the original brickwork appears, sufficiently revealing to a critical eye the true character and plan of the building. Accordingly many travellers, on a mere superficial view of the structure, came to the conclusion that it was originally built in stages,[6] and that—whether it were the remains of the Temple of Belus or no—at any rate it closely resembled that building as described by Herodotus. Sir R. Ker Porter[7] and Mr. Layard[8] even ventured on restorations of the original design, which, although not entirely in accordance with the reality, went near to anticipate the conclusions which have now been established by a close examination of the edifice.

14. It appears from the researches carried on by Sir H. Rawlinson, in

nal points, instead of the angles (see Rich's First Memoir, p. 28; Ker Porter, ii. p. 310, &c.). It was probably a fixed architectural law in Babylonia to give temples this aspect. They have it, not only at the Birs, but at *Warka* and *Mugheir*, and (I believe) wherever their position has been carefully examined (see Loftus, p. 171). Is the mound of *Babil* really an exception to the ordinary rule?

[2] Ker Porter, ii. p. 321. Rich makes the circumference 200 feet less than Porter (p. 36). He gives 762 yards (2286 feet), instead of Porter's 2082 feet.

[3] The exact measurement of Captain Jones with the theodolite is 153 ft. 6 in.

[4] Ker Porter, l. s. c.   [5] See the representation in vol. i. p. 186.

[6] Rich, First Memoir, p. 54; Ker Porter, ii. pp. 310, 322, &c.; Layard, p. 497.

[7] Vol. ii. plate 71. Sir R. K. Porter gave the building eight stages, the basement stage being a square of 500 feet. He supposed that only portions of four stages remained, and that the original height was also 500 feet.

[8] Mr. Layard gave the building six stages, and suggested that while the stages

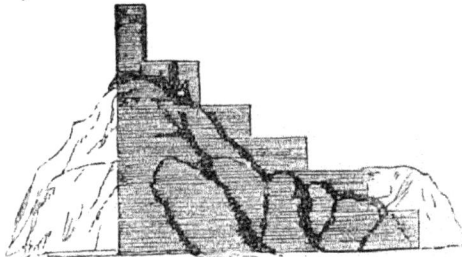

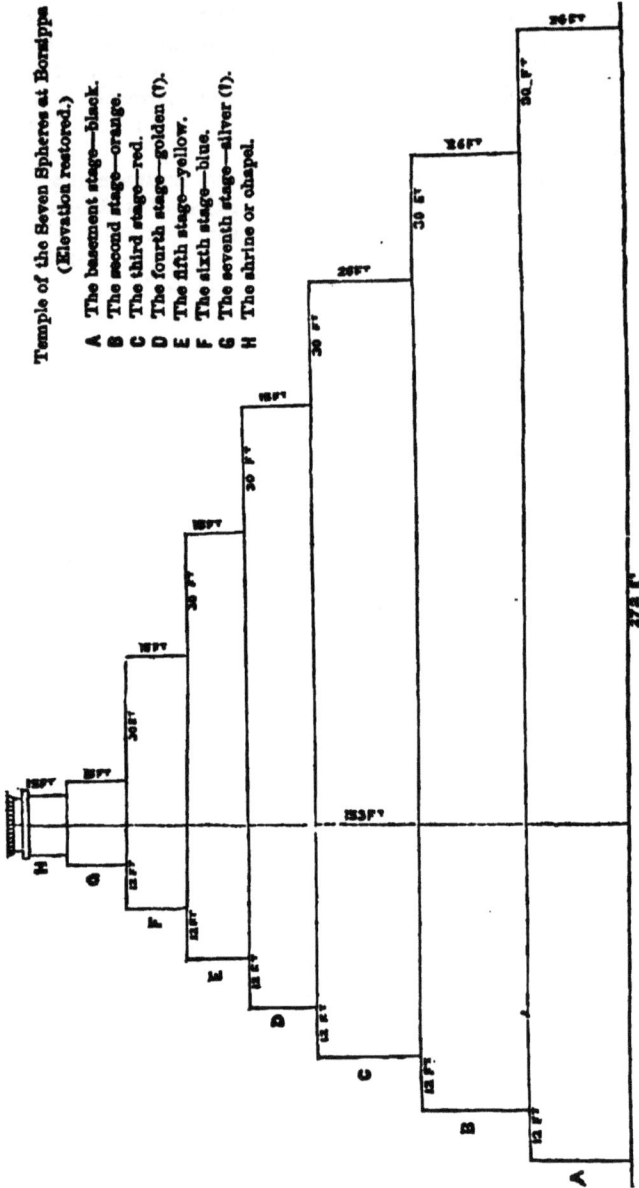

Temple of the Seven Spheres at Borsippa
(Elevation restored.)

A   The basement stage—black.
B   The second stage—orange.
C   The third stage—red.
D   The fourth stage—golden (?).
E   The fifth stage—yellow.
F   The sixth stage—blue.
G   The seventh stage—silver (?).
H   The shrine or chapel.

the year 1854, that the *Birs-Nimrud*, like the temple of Belus described by our author, was a building in seven receding stages.[1] Upon a platform of crude brick, raised a few feet above the level of the alluvial plain, was built of burnt brick, the first or basement stage—an exact square, 272 feet each way, and 26 feet in perpendicular height. Upon this stage was erected a second, 230 feet each way, and likewise 26 feet high; which, however, was not placed exactly in the middle of the first, but considerably nearer to the south-western end, which constituted the back of the building. The other stages were arranged similarly—the third being 188 feet, and again 26 feet high; the fourth 146 feet square, and 15 feet high; the fifth 104 feet square, and the same height as the fourth; the sixth 62 feet square, and again the same height; and the seventh 20 feet square and once more the same height. On the seventh stage there was probably placed the ark or tabernacle, which seems to have been again 15 feet high, and must have nearly, if not entirely, covered the top of the seventh story. The entire original height, allowing three feet for the platform, would thus have been 156 feet, or, without the platform, 153 feet. The whole formed a sort of oblique pyramid, the gentler slope facing the N.E., and the steeper incline the S.W. On the N.E. side was the grand entrance, and here stood the vestibule, a separate building, the debris from which having joined those from the temple itself, fill up the intermediate space, and very remarkably prolong the mound in this direction.

15. The ornamentation of the building was almost solely by colour. The seven stages were coloured so as to represent the seven planetary spheres,[2] according to the tints regarded by the Sabæans as appropriate to the seven luminaries—the basement stage being black, the hue assigned to Saturn; the next an orange, or raw-sienna tint,[3] the hue of Jupiter; the third a bright red, the hue of Mars; the fourth golden, the hue of the Sun; the fifth a pale yellow, the hue of Venus; the sixth dark blue, the hue of Mercury; and the seventh silver, the hue of the Moon. The tint in the first instance was given by a coating of bitumen over the face of burnt bricks; in the second and fifth, by the natural hue of the burnt bricks themselves; in the third, by the use of half-burnt bricks of a bright red clay; in the sixth by vitrifaction, after the stage was erected, of the bricks composing it, through the force of an intense heat, whereby they were converted into a mass of blue slag; and in the fourth and seventh, probably by plates of the precious metals

rose like steps on the eastern or south-eastern (north-eastern?) side, they terminated on the western or north-western (south-western?) in a "solid *perpendicular* wall" (Nin. and Bab. p. 498). The reality is half-way between Sir R. Porter's and Mr. Layard's conceptions.

[1] The accompanying restoration (see opposite) will illustrate this paragraph. Its proportions are derived from the measurements of Col. Rawlinson.

[2] See note [4] to Book i. ch. 98.

[3] Herodotus expresses this tint by the word σανδαράκινον, which is generally explained as the colour of the red sulphuret of arsenic, called by the Greeks σανδαράκη; but is thought by some to be really the colour of "sandal-wood," *Sandali* (which has that meaning) being the term commonly applied to the sphere in the astrology of the East.

forming an external casing to the brickwork.[4] Along the third stage which was of a weaker material than the rest, the flatness of the wall was broken by a row of buttresses, not placed there however for the purpose of ornamentation, but merely to give additional strength. This stage too was not, like the rest, entirely perpendicular, but had an abutment at the base, and a species of plinth formed by three rows of bricks laid on their edges between single horizontal rows. The entire mass of brickwork was also pierced throughout by a rhomboidal series of small square holes, which served to keep the structure dry, by admitting air, and also by carrying off any moisture that might penetrate into it.

16. Such were the most striking features of the great Temple of Borsippa, which was designed and named after the "Seven Spheres," but was especially dedicated to Nebo or Mercury, whose tabernacle probably occupied its summit. It was not perhaps originally superior to hundreds of temples in Babylonia; but it has escaped, far more than any other, the ravages of time, and thus is the ruin to which we are chiefly indebted for our knowledge of the plan and character of the Babylonian sacred buildings. The date of the original structure is uncertain, but is probably very ancient. In its present form the *Birs* is chiefly the work of Nebuchadnezzar, whose name appears exclusively upon the bricks composing it, and the cylinders deposited at its angles.[5] The following is the account which the royal restorer gives of his careful renovation of the edifice:—

"Behold now the building named ' the Stages of the Seven Spheres,' which was the wonder of Borsippa, had been built by a former king. He had completed forty-two *ammas* (of the height), but he did not finish its head. From the lapse of time it had become ruined; they had not taken care of the exits of the waters, so the rain and wet had penetrated into the brickwork; the casing of burnt bricks had bulged out, and the terraces of crude brick lay scattered in heaps; (then) Merodach, my great lord, inclined my heart to repair the building. I did not change its site, nor did I destroy its foundation platform; but in a fortunate month, and on an auspicious day, I undertook the rebuilding of the crude brick terraces, and the burnt brick casing (of the temple). I strengthened its foundation, and I placed a titular record in the part that I had rebuilt. I set my hand to build it up and to finish its summit. As it had been in ancient times, so I built up its structure; as it had been in former days, thus I exalted its head. Nebo, the strength-

---

[4] This, it must be remembered, is the account given by Herodotus of the manner in which the spheres of the sun and moon were represented at Agbatana (i. 98, ad fin.). It has already been shown (note ad loc.) that such a lavish display of the precious metals was in accordance with Eastern habits. At the *Birs* the fourth or golden stage presents an appearance as if the face of the wall had been entirely broken away by blows from a pickaxe. Nebuchadnezzar, in describing his temples and palaces, often speaks of them as "clothed with gold."

[5] Sir H. Rawlinson discovered two of these at the eastern and southern angles of the third stage. They were duplicates. He also found a few small fragments of another, the inscription upon which was different. There are probably many cylinders still in the building.

cner of his children, he who ministers to the gods (?), and Merodach, the supporter of sovereignty, may they cause my work to be established for ever! May it last through the seven ages! May the stability of my throne and the antiquity of my empire, secure against strangers and triumphant over many foes, continue to the end of time!"

NOTE A.

STANDARD INSCRIPTION OF NEBUCHADNEZZAR. *See B. i. ch. 178, 2.*

The Inscription begins with the various titles of Nebuchadnezzar. It then contains prayers and invocations to the gods, Merodach and Nebo. The extent of N.'s power is spoken of—it reaches from one sea to the other.

An account is then given of the wonders of Babylon, viz :—

1. The great temple of Merodach. (The mound of *Babil* is the tower or *ziggurat* of this.)
2. The Borsippa temple (or *Birs*).
3. Various other temples in Babylon and Borsippa.

The subjoined description of the city follows :—

"The double enclosure which Nabopolassar my father had made but not completed, I finished. Nabopolassar made its ditch. With two long embankments of brick and mortar he bound its bed. He made the embankment of the *Arakha*. He lined the other side of the Euphrates with brick. He made a bridge (?) over the Euphrates, but did not finish its buttresses (?). From * * * (the name of a place) he made with bricks burnt as hard as stones, by the help of the great Lord Merodach, a way (for) a branch of the *Shimat* to the waters of the *Yapur-Shapu*, the great reservoir of Babylon, opposite to the gate of *Nin*.

"The *Ingur-Bel* and the *Nimiti-Bel*—the great double wall of Babylon— I finished. With two long embankments of brick and mortar I built the sides of its ditch. I joined it on with that which my father had made. I strengthened the city. Across the river to the west I built the wall of Babylon with brick. The *Yapur-Shapu*—the reservoir of Babylon—by the grace of Merodach, I filled completely full of water. With bricks burnt as hard as stones, and with bricks in huge masses like mountains (?), the *Yapur-Shapu*, from the gate of *Mula* as far as *Nana*, who is the protectress of her votaries, by the grace of his godship (i. e. Merodach), I strengthened. With that which my father had made I joined it. I made the way of *Nana*, the protectress of her votaries. The great gates of the *Ingur-Bel* and the *Nimiti-Bel* —the reservoir of Babylon, at the time of the flood (lit. of fulness), inundated them. These gates I raised. Against the waters their foundations with brick and mortar I built. [Here follows a description of the gates, with various architectural details, and an account of the decorations, hangings, &c.] For the delight of mankind I filled the reservoir. Behold! besides the *Ingur-Bel*, the impregnable fortification of Babylon, I constructed inside Babylon on the eastern side of the river a fortification such as no king had ever made before me, viz. a long rampart, 4000 *ammas* square, as an extra defence. I excavated the ditch: with brick and mortar I bound its bed; a long rampart at its head (?) I strongly built. I adorned its gates. The folding-doors and the pillars I plated with copper. Against presumptuous enemies, who were hostile to the men of Babylon, great waters, like the waters of the ocean, I made use of abundantly. Their depths were like the depths of the vast ocean. I did not allow the waters to overflow, but the fulness of their floods I caused to flow on, restraining them with a brick embankment. . . . Thus I completely made strong the defences of Babylon. May it last for ever!

[Here follows a similar account of works at Borsippa.]

"In Babylon—the city which is the delight of my eyes, and which I have glorified—when the waters were in flood, they inundated the foundations of the great palace called *Taprati-nisi*, or "the Wonder of Mankind;" (a palace) with many chambers and lofty towers; the high-place of Royalty; (situated) in the land of Babylon, and in the middle of Babylon; stretching from the *Ingur-Bel* to the bed of the *Shebil*, the eastern canal, (and) from the bank of the Sippara river to the water of the *Yapur-Shapu;* which Nabopolassar my father built with brick and raised up; when the reservoir of Babylon was full, the gates of this palace were flooded. I raised the mound of brick on which it was built, and made smooth its platform. I cut off the floods of the water, and the foundations (of the palace) I protected against the water with bricks and mortar; and I finished it completely. Long beams I set up to support it: with pillars and beams plated with copper and strengthened with iron I built up its gates. Silver and gold, and precious stones whose names were almost unknown [Here follow several unknown names of objects, treasures of the palace], I stored up inside, and placed there the treasure-house of my kingdom. Four years (?), the seat of my kingdom in the city . . . ., which . . . . . did not rejoice (my) heart. In all my dominions I did not build a high place of power; the precious treasures of my kingdom I did not lay up. In Babylon, buildings for myself and the honour of my kingdom I did not lay out. In the worship of Merodach my lord, the joy of my heart (?), in Babylon, the city of his sovereignty and the seat of my empire, I did not sing his praises (?), and I did not furnish his altars (*i. e.* with victims), nor did I clear out the canals. [Here follow further negative clauses.]

"As a further defence in war, at the *Ingur-Bel*, the impregnable outer wall, the rampart of the Babylonians—with two strong lines of brick and mortar · I made a strong fort, 400 ammas square, inside the *Nimiti-Bel*, the inner defence of the Babylonians. Masonry of brick within them (the lines) I constructed. With the palace of my father I connected it. In a happy month and on an auspicious day its foundations I laid in the earth like * * * I completely finished its top. In fifteen days I completed it, and made it the high place of my kingdom. [Here follows a description of the ornamentation of the palace.] A strong fort of brick and mortar in strength I constructed. Inside the brick fortification another great fortification of long stones, of the size of great mountains, I made. Like *Shedim* I raised up its head. And this building I raised for a wonder; for the defence of the people I constructed it."

NOTE B.

BABYLONIAN RESEARCHES OF M. OPPERT.

Since this Essay was in type I have enjoyed the advantage of examining three *livraisons* of Plates belonging to the magnificent work which will shortly be published by M. Oppert, on the subject of the French expedition into Mesopotamia. As these plates are unaccompanied by any letter-press it is impossible at present to be sure how far they are based upon accurate measurements or observations. In some respects the views taken coincide remarkably with those expressed in the foregoing Essay. This is especially the case as regards the ancient course of the Euphrates, and the position of the lesser

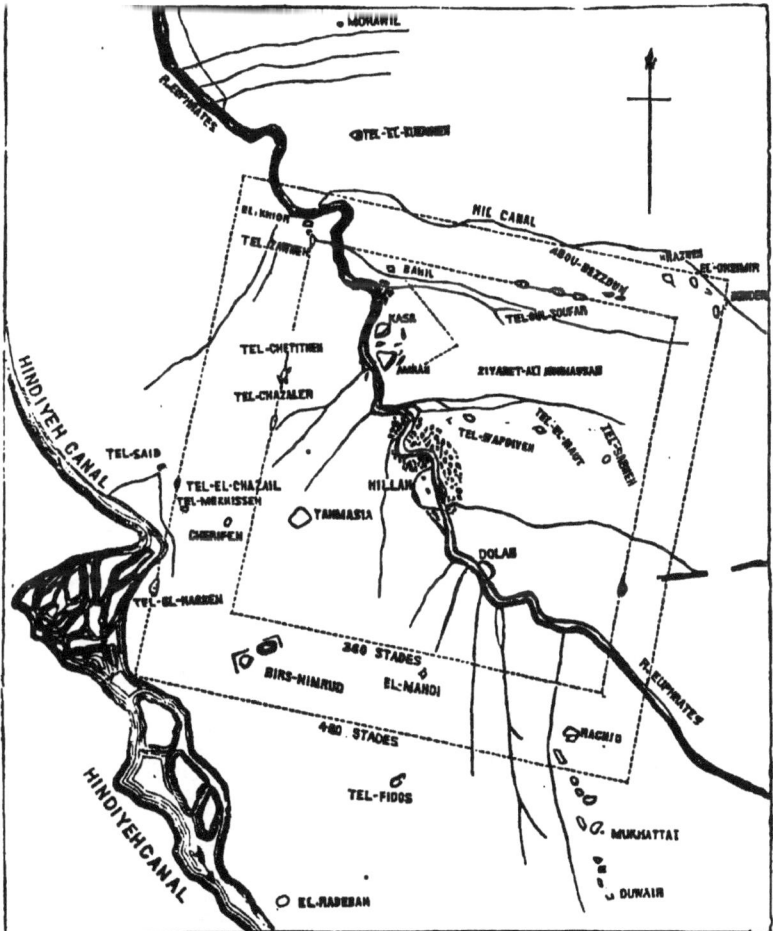

Chart of the Country round Babylon, with the limits of the ancient City, according to Oppert.

palace (that of Neriglissar) upon the right bank of the stream. In other points M. Oppert differs from all former observers, and is not confirmed by the notes and recollections of recent visitants; as in his omission of the two long parallel embankments (FF in the plan, supra, page 473), which close in the chief ruins on the east; of the single embankment (H) towards the north; and of the mound (K) on the west, which interrupts what seems to be the ancient bed of the river; and, again, in the extent and position which he assigns to the curious heap called *Homeira*. Capt. Jones's surveys will decide whether these changes are in accordance with the real features of the locality; at present the judgment is necessarily held in suspense between rival observers, whose accounts of the ruins are in many respects so different. With regard to M. Oppert's restorations of the ancient city the most remarkable points have been already noticed in the foot-notes. He believes that he has found traces of the ancient walls in certain lines of *Tels* which exist on both sides of the Euphrates. If the positions of these mounds are accurately laid down on his map, which is fairly represented by the subjoined chart, there would appear to be some

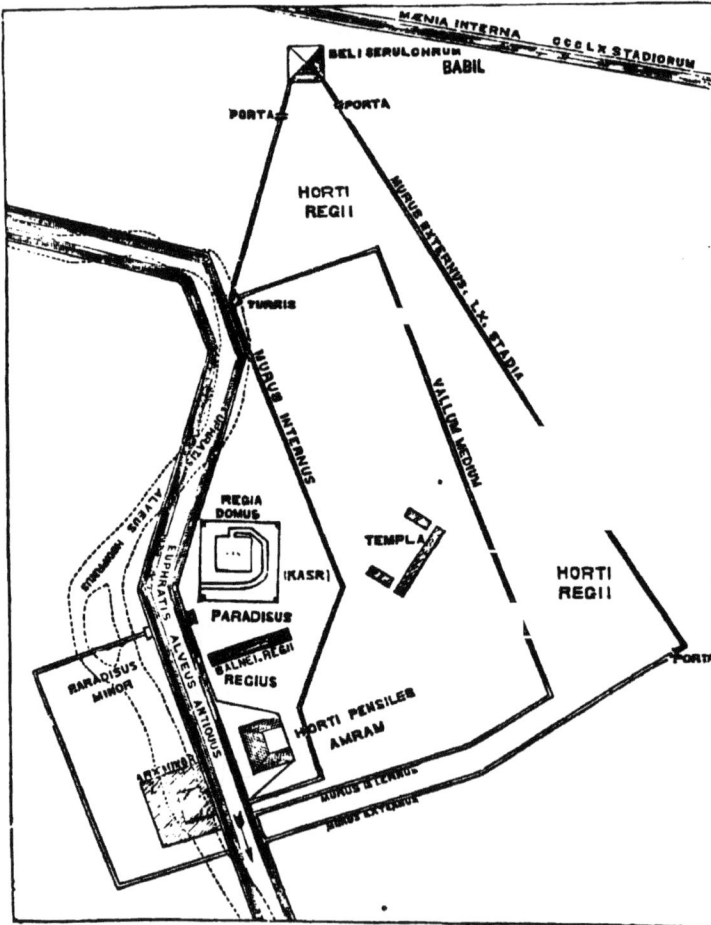

The Royal Residence at Babylon restored (after Oppert).

grounds for regarding the lesser circuit of 360 stades as really indicated by the remains in question, though, upon the showing of the map itself, the larger circuit is almost entirely unsupported.　It is an additional objection to this circuit, as placed by M. Oppert, that it includes Borsippa, which the inscriptions, the native writer Berosus, and the classical geographers, all regard as a city quite distinct from Babylon.　The inclusion of Cutha in the opposite corner of the square, marked (as M. Oppert supposes) by the ruins of *Hymar*, or *Oheimir*, is still more impossible; for Cutha was at least 15 miles from *Hymar* in a north-easterly direction, being marked, not by the *Hymar* group, but by the ruins at *Ibrahim*.　In his restoration of the royal residence—which has at least the merit of boldness—M. Oppert appears to have discarded alike the guidance of the inscriptions and that of the ancient writers.　He takes no notice of Nebuchadnezzar's "Great Reservoir," of his "*Shebil*," or "Eastern Canal," nor of the "palace of his father," which adjoined his own; he places the lesser palace opposite, not to the greater one, as Ctesias did, but to the hanging-gardens; and he regards the hanging-gardens as represented by the mound of *Amrám*, though the latter has an area at least four times as great as that ascribed by Diodorus to the former.　He also fails to give in his restoration at all a close representation of the present ruins, introducing main walls, as that between the river and *Babil*, of which he does not profess to have found a trace; placing the quay of Nabonidus above a mile higher up the stream than the place where that monarch's bricks are found; and turning into a "middle wall," what clearly appears, by the traces of water-action outside it, to have been the embankment of a canal or reservoir.　He also, in assuming the outer triangular rampart to be a Babylonian work restored by the Parthians, goes beyond the existing data, since no Babylonian remains have (it is believed) been found in that structure.　On the other hand, M. Oppert's surveys of particular ruins, as of the *Kasr*, *Babil*, and the *Birs-Nimrud*, are (apparently) much in advance of any hitherto published; while his "Views" are alike striking and original, greatly increasing the attractiveness of his work.

NOTE C.

THE GREAT INSCRIPTION OF DARIUS AT BEHISTUN.

[NOTE.—Behistun is situated on the western frontier of the ancient Media, upon the road from Babylon to the southern Ecbatana, the great thoroughfare between the eastern and the western provinces of the ancient Persia. The precipitous rock, 1700 feet high, on which the writing is inscribed, forms a portion of the great chain of Zagros, which separates the high plateau of Iran from the vast plain watered by the two streams of the Tigris and Euphrates. The inscription is engraved at the height of 300 feet from the base of the rock, and can only be reached with much exertion and difficulty. It is trilingual: one transcript is in the ancient Persian, one in Babylonian, the other in a Scythic or Tatar dialect. Col. Rawlinson gathers from the monument itself that it was executed in the fifth year of the reign of Darius, B.C. 516. The subjoined is the Persian transcript, as deciphered by Col. Rawlinson, Roman letters being substituted for the original cuneiform. Col. Rawlinson's translation is also given. The numbers are added for convenience of reference.]

See Smith's Dict. of Ane. Geog. Vol. 1, p. 369.

COLUMN I.

Par. 1. (1) Adam Dárayavush, (2) khsháyathiya vazarka, (3) khshá-yathiya ¹ *khsháy*athiyánám, (4) khsháyathiya Pársiya, (5) khshá-yathiya dahya*undm*, (6) Vishtáspahyá putra, (7) Arshámahyá napá, (8) Hakhúmani*shiyd*.²

(1) I (am) Darius, (2) the great king, (3) the king of kings, (4) the king of Persia, (5) the king of the (dependent) provinces, (6) the son of Hystaspes, (7) the grandson of Arsames, (8) the Achæmenian.

Par. 2. (1) *Thá*tiya Dárayavush khsháyathiya; (2) Maná pitá Vish-táspa; (3) Vishtáspahyá *pitá* Arsháma; (4) Arshámahyá pitá Ariyárámana; (5) Ariyáráman*ahyá pitá* Chishpáish; (6) ³ pitá Hakhámanish.

(1) Says Darius the king—(2) My father (was) Hystaspes; (3) the father of Hystaspes (was) Arsames; (4) the father of Arsames (was) Ariaramnes; (5) the father of Ariaramnes (was) Teispes; (6) the father (of Teispes) was Achæmenes.

---

¹ The italics indicate that the original is in such places illegible, and restored conjecturally.

² The accented A (á) is expressed in the original; the unaccented A (a), unless at the beginning of words, is the supplied vowel of the Sanskrit and its kindred languages.

³ Chishpáishahyá is here omitted by a mistake of the artist employed to engrave the inscription. Cf. Detached Inscriptions. No. 1, and Norris's Behist. Inscr. p. 95

Par. 3. (1) Thátiya Dárayavush khsháyath*iya*; (2) *Ava*hyarádiya va-yam Hakhámanishiyá thahyáymahya; (3) Hachá pr*uviyata amdtá* amahya; (4) Hachá pruviyata hyá amákham tauma khsh*áyathiyá* *áha*.

(1) Says Darius the king—(2) On that account we have been called Achæmenians; (3) from antiquity we have descended (?); (4) from antiquity our family have been kings.

Par. 4. (1) Thátiya Dárayavush khsháyathiya—(2) VIII.[4] maná tau-*máyá tyiya* pruwama khsháyathiyá áha; (3) adam navam; (4) IX. duvitátaranam *vayam khshá*yathiyá ámahya.

(1) Says Darius the king—(2) (There are) eight of my race who have been kings before (me); (3) I (am) the ninth; nine of us have been kings in a double line (?).

Par. 5. (1) Thátiya Dárayavush khsháyathiya—(2) *Vashná* Auramaz-dáha adam khsháyathiya amiya; (3) Auramazdá khshatram ma*ná* *frábara*.

(1) Says Darius the king—(2) By the grace of Ormazd I am king; (3) Ormazd has granted me the empire.

Par. 6. (1) Thátiya Dárayavush khsháyathiya—(2) Imá dahyáva tyá ma*ná pati*yáisha; (3) vashná Auramazdáha adamshám khsháyathiya áham; (4) Púrsa, 'Uv*aja*, *Bábi*rush, Athurá, Arabáya, Mudráya; tyiya darayahyá; Saparda, Yu*ná*, *Máda*,[b] *Arm*ina, Katapatuka, Parthva, Zaraka, Hariva, 'Uvárazmiya, Bakhtari*sh*, *Su*guda, Gadára, Saka, Thatagush, Hara'uvatish, Maka; (5) fraharvam dahyáva XXIII.

(1) Says Darius the king—(2) These are the countries which have come to me; (3) by the grace of Ormazd I have become king of them; (4) Persia, Susiana, Babylonia, Assyria, Arabia, Egypt, those which are of the sea (*i. e.* the islands), Saparda, Ionia, Media, Armenia, Cappadocia, Parthia, Zarangia, Aria, Chorasmia, Bactria, Sogdiana, Gandaria, the Sacæ, Sattagydia, Arachotia, and Mecia; (5) in all 23 provinces.

Par. 7. (1) *Thá*tiya Dárayavush khsháyathiya— (2) Imá dahyáva tyá maná patiy*disha*; (3) vashná Auramazdáha maná badaká áhatá; (4) maná bájim abaratá. (5) *Tya*shám hacháma athahya khshapaví, rauchapativá, ava akunavayatá.

[4] Numbers in the Persian inscriptions are marked thus:—1. From one to ten, a single perpendicular wedge for each unit: these wedges are placed in two rows, one above the other, the final unit (where the number is odd) being made double the length of the others.   2. Ten is marked by an arrow-head, thus, <.
[b] This is conjectural. There is room for Mada (Media) between Ionia and Armenia; but the passage is illegible both in the Persian and the Babylonian tran-script. Media (*Mata-pa*) appears in the Scythic version (Norris, p. 97).

(1) Says Darius the king—(2) These (are) the provinces which have come to me; (3) by the grace of Ormazd they have become subject to me; (4) they have brought tribute to me. (5) That which has been said to them by me, both by night and by day, it has been done (by them).

Par. 8. (1) *Thátiya* Dárayavush khsháyathiya—(2) Atara imá dahyáva, martiya hya agatá* áha, avam 'ubartam abaram. (3) Hya arika* áha, avam 'ufrastam aparasam. (4) *Vashná* Auramazdáha imá dahyáva tyaná maná dátá apriyáya. (5) Yatháshám hacháma athabya, awathá akunavayatá.

(1) Says Darius the king—(2) Within these countries the man who was good, him I have right well cherished. (3) Whoever was evil, him have I utterly rooted out. (4) By the grace of Ormazd, these are the countries by whom my laws have been observed. (5) As it has been said to them by me, so (by them) it has been done.

Par. 9. (1) Thátiya Dárayavush khsháyath*iya*—(2) *Auramazdá* maná khshatram frábara. (3) Auramazdámaiya upastám abara, yátá ima khshatram *adáraya*. (4) Vashná Auramazdáha ima khshatram dárayámiya.

(1) Says Darius the king—(2) Ormazd granted me the empire. (3) Ormazd brought help to me, so that I gained this empire. (4) By the grace of Ormazd I hold this empire.

Par. 10. (1) Thá*tiya* Dárayavush khsháyathiya—(2) Ima tya maná, kartam pasáva yathá khsh*dyathi*ya abavam. (3) Kabujiya náma, Kuraush putra, amákham taumáyd, *hauva* p*r*uvama idá khsháyathiya áha. (4) Avahyá Kabujiyahyá brátá Bardiya náma áha; (5) hamátá hampitá Kabujiyahyá. (6) Pasáva Ka*bu*j*i*ya avam Bardiyam avája. (7) Yathá Kabujiya Bardiyam awája, kárahy*a niya* azadá abava tya Bardiya avajata. (8) Pasáva Kabujiya Mudráyam *ashiya*va. (9) Yathá Kabujiya Mudráyam ashiyava, pasáva kara arika abava. (10) Pasáva darauga dahyauvá vasiya abava, utá Pársaiya, utá Mádaiya, utá *aniyá*uvá dahyaushuvá.

(1) Says Darius the king—(2) This (is) what (was) done by me after that I became king. (3) (A man) named Cambyses, son of Cyrus, of our race, he was here king before me. (4) Of that Cambyses (there was) a brother, Bardes was his name; (5) of the same mother, (and) of the same father with Cambyses. (6) Afterwards Cambyses slew that Bardes. (7) When Cambyses had slain

---

* There is a good deal of doubt as to the meaning of the two opposed words, *agata* and *arika*. Col. Rawlinson was originally inclined to translate them by "faithful" and "heretical." (See Vocabulary). The Babylonian transcript, however, gives as equivalents *pitkut* and *bisu*, and as the latter word answers to the Hebrew באשׁ, the most correct translation would seem to be simply *good* and *bad*.

Bardes, it was not known to the people that Bardes had been slain.
(8) Afterwards Cambyses proceeded to Egypt. (9) When Cambyses
had proceeded to Egypt, then the state became wicked. (10) Then
the lie became abounding in the land, both in Persia, and in Media,
and in the other provinces.

Par. 11. (1) Thátiya Dárayavush khsháyathiya—(2) Pa*sáva* martiya
Magush áha, Gaumáta náma. (3) Hauva udapatatá hachá Pishiyá'-
uvádáyá, Arakadrish náma kaufa, hachá avadasha. (4) Viyakhnahya mah*yá* XIV. rauchabish, thakatá áha, yadiya udapatatá, hauva
kárahyá avathá *a*durujiya : (5) Adam Bardiya amiya, hya Kuraush
putra, Kabujiyahyá brátá. (6) Pasáva kára haruva hamatriya
abava. (7) Hachá Kabujiyá abiya avam *a*shiyava, utá Pársa utá
Máda, utá aniyá dahyáva. (8) Khshatram hauva agarbáyatá.
(9) Garmapadahya máhyá IX. rauchabish, thakátá áha, avathá khsha-
·tram agarbáyatá. (10) Pasáva Kabujiya 'nvámarshiyush ama·
riyatá.

(1) Says Darius the king—(2) Afterwards there was a certain
man, a Magian, named Gomates. (3) He arose from Pissiachada,
the mountain named Aracadres, from thence. (4) On the 14th day
of the month Vayakhna, then it was that he arose. He thus lied to
the state :—(5) "I am Bardes, the son of Cyrus, the brother of
Cambyses." (6) Then the whole state became rebellious. (7) From
Cambyses it went over to him, both Persia, and Media, and the
other provinces. (8) He seized the empire. (9) On the 9th day
of the month Garmapada, then it was he so seized the empire.
(10) Afterwards Cambyses, unable to endure, (?) died.

Par. 12. (1) Thátiya Dárayavush khshayathiya—(2) Aita khshatram,
tya Gaumáta hya Magush ádiná Kabujiyam, aita khshatram hachá
pruviyata amákham taumáyá áha. (3) Pasáva Gaumata hya Magush
ádiná Kabujiyam utá Pársam, utá Mádam, utá aniyá ' dahyáva ;
hauva ayastá 'uváipashiyam akutá; (4) hauva khsháyathiya
abava.

(1) Says Darius the king—(2) The empire of which Gomates,
the Magian, dispossessed Cambyses, that empire from the olden
time had been in our family. (3) After Gomates the Magian had
dispossessed Cambyses both of Persia and Media and the dependent
provinces, he did according to his desire : (4) he became king.

Par. 13. (1) Thátiya Dárayavush khsháyathiya—(2) Niyasha martiya,
niya Pársa, niya Máda, niya amákham taumáyá kashchiya, hya avam
Gaumátam tyam Magum khshatram ditam chakhriya. (3) Kárashim
hachá darshama atarsa. (4) Káram vasiya avájaniyá hya paranam
Bardiyam adáná, avahyarádiya káram avájaniyá, (5) "Mátyamám
khshanásátiya tya adam niya Bardiya amiya, hya Kuraush putra."
(6) Kashchiya niya adarshanaush chischiya thastaniya pariya Gau-

mátam tyam Magum, yátá adam arasam. (7) Passáva adam Auramazdám patiyávahya; (8) Auramazdámaiya upastám abara. (9)
Bágayádaish máhyá x. rauchabish, thakatá áha avathá adam hadá
kamanaibish martiyaibish avam Gaumátam tyam Magum avájanam,
utá tyishiya fratamá martiyá anushiyá áhatá. (10) Siktha'uvatish
námá didá, Nisáya námá dahyáush Mádaiya, avadashim avájanam:
(11) khshatramshim adam ádinam. (12) Vashná Auramazdáha
adam khsháyathiya abavam; (13) Auramazdá khshatram maná
frábara.

(1) Says Darius the king—(2) There was not a man, neither
Persian, nor Median, nor any one of our family, who would dispossess that Gomates the Magian of the crown. (3) The state feared
him exceedingly. (4) He slew many people, who had known the
old Bardes; for that reason he slew them. (5) "lest they should
recognise me that I am not Bardes, the son of Cyrus." (6) No one
dared to say anything concerning Gomates the Magian, until I
arrived. (7) Then I prayed to Ormazd; (8) Ormazd brought help
to me. (9) On the 10th day of the month Bagayadish, then it was,
with my faithful men, I slew that Gomates the Magian, and those
who were his chief followers. (10) The fort named Sictachotes in
the district of Media called Nisæa, there I slew him. (11) I dispossessed him of the empire. (12) By the grace of Ormazd I became king: (13) Ormazd granted me the sceptre.

Par. 14. (1) Thátiya Dárayavush khsháyathiya—(2) Khshatram tya
hachá amákham taumíyá parábartam áha, ava adam patipadam
akunavam. (3) Adamshim gáthvá avástáyam. (4) Yathá pruvamachiya, avathá adam akunavam. (5) Ayadaná tyá Gaumáta hya
Magush viyaka, adam niyatrárayam. (6) Kárahyá abácharish
gaithámchá mániyamchá, vithabishchá tyádish Gaumáta hya Magush
adiná. (7) Adam káram gáthvá avástáyam, Pársamchá, Mádamchá,
utá aniyá dahyáva. (8) Yathá pruvamachiya avathá adam tya parábartam patiyábaram. (9) Vashná Auramazdáha ima adam akunavam.
(10) Adam hamatakhshiya yátá vitham tyám amákham gáthvá avástáyam. (11) Yathá pruvamachiya avathá adam hamatakhshiya,
vashná Auramazdáha, yathá Gaumáta hya Magush vitham tyám
amákham niya parábara.

(1) Says Darius the king—(2) The empire which had been
taken away from our family, that I recovered. (3) I established it
in its place. (4) As (it was) before, so I made (it). (5) The
temples which Gomates the Magian had destroyed, I rebuilt. (6)
The sacred offices of the state, both the religious chaunts and the
worship, (I restored) to the people, which Gomates the Magian had
deprived them of. (7) I established the state in its place, both
Persia, and Media, and the other provinces. (8) As (it was) before,
so I restored what (had been) taken away. (9) By the grace of
Ormazd I did (this). (10) I arranged so that I established our
family in its place. (11) As (it was) before, so I arranged (it), by

the grace of Ormazd, so that Gomates the Magian should not super-
sede our family.

Par. 15. (1) Thátiya Dárayavush *khshdyath*iya—(2) Ima tya adam
akunavam, pasáva yathá khsháyathiya abavam.

(1) Says Darius the king—(2) This (is) what I did, after that
I became king.

Par. 16. (1) Thátiya Dárayavush khsháyathiya—(2) Yathá adam Gaumátam tyam Magum av*ájanam*, *pas*áva I. martiya, Atrina náma,
Upadarmahyá putra, hauva udapata*tá*. (3) '*Uvaja*iya kárahyá avatha
athaha—(4) 'Adam 'U*vaja*iya khsháyathiya amiya.' (5) Pa*sáva*
'U*va*jiyá hamitriyá abava ; (6) abiya avam Atrinam ashiyava ;
(7) hauva kh*shdyathiya* abava 'Uvajaiya. (8) Uta I. martiya Bábiruviya, Naditabira náma, A*inarahyá putra*, hauva udapatatá. (0)
Bábirauva káram avathá adurujiya—(10) 'Adam Nabukudrachara
amiya, hya Nabunitahyá putra. (11) Pasáva kára hya Bábiruviya
haruva abiya avam Naditabiram ashiyava. (12) Bábirush hamatriya
a*b*ava. (13) Khshatram tya Bábirauva hauva agarbáyatá.

(1) Says Darius the king—(2) When I had slain Gomates the
Magian, then a man named Atrines, the son of Opadarmes, he
arose ; (3) to the state of Susiana thus he said ; (4) 'I am king of
Susiana.' (5) Then the Susianians became rebellious ; (6) they went
over to that Atrines ; (7) he became king of Susiana. (8) And a
man, a Babylonian, Nidintabelus by name, the son of Anires, he
arose. (9) To the state of Babylonia he thus falsely declared—
(10) 'I am Nabochodrossor, the son of Nabonidus.' (11) Afterwards the whole state of Babylon went over to that Nidintabelus.
(12) Babylon became rebellious. (13) He seized the kingdom of
Babylonia.

Par. 17. (1) Thátiya Dárayavush khsháyathiya—(2) Pasáva adam fráishayam 'Uvajam ; (3) hauva Atrina *basta* ánayatá *abiya mdm.* (4)
Adamshim avájanam.

(1) Says Darius the king—(2) Then I sent to Susiana ; (3) That
Atrines was brought to me a prisoner. (4) I slew him.

Par. 18. (1) Thátiya Dárayavush khsháyathiya—(2) Pasáva *adam Bá-*
birum ashiyavam abiya avam Naditabiram, hya Nabukudrachara
aga*u*b*atá*. (3) Kára hya Naditabirahyá Tigrám adáraya ; (4) avadá
aishatatá, utá abish náviyá áha. (5) Pasáva adam káram ma . .
káuva avákanam. (6) Aniyam dashabárim akunavam. (7) Aniyahyá
asm . . ánayám. (8) Auramazdámaiya upas*tám* abara. (9) Vashná
Auramazdáha Tigrám viyatarayám. (10) Avadá káram tyam Naditabirahyá adam ajanam vasiya. (11) Atriyátiya*hya* mábyá xxvi.
rauchabish, thakatá áha avathá hamaranam akumá.

(1) Says Darius the king—(2) Then I went to Babylon against that Nidintabelus, who was called Nabochodrossor. (3) The people of Nidintabelus held the Tigris; (4) there they were posted, and they had boats. (5) There I approached a detachment (lit. troops, people) in rafts. (6) I brought the enemy into difficulty. (7) (I) carried the enemy's position. (8) Ormazd brought help to me. (9) By the grace of Ormazd I crossed the Tigris. (10) There I slew many of the troops of that Nidintabelus. (11) On the 26th day of the month Atriyata, then it was we so fought.'

Par. 19. (1) Thátiya Dáray*avush* khsháyathiya—(2) Pasáva a*dam* Bábirum ashiyavam. (3) A*t*hiya Bábirum ya*thá* . . . áyam, Zázána náma, vardanam anuva Ufrátauvá, avadá *hauva* Nadi*ta*bira, hya Nabukudrachara agaubatú, aisha hadá kárá patish *mám, hamaran*am chartaniya. (4) Pasáwa hamaranam akumá. (5) Auramazdámaiya upastám abara. (6) *Vashná Aura*mazdáha káram tyam Naditabirahyá adam ajanam vasiya. (7) Aniya ápiyá . h . á; (8) ápishim parábara; (9) Ánámakahya máhyá II. rauchabish, thakatá áha a*vathá hamaranam akumá.*

(1) Says Darius the king—(2) Then I went to Babylon. (3) When I arrived near Babylon, at the city named Zazana, on the Euphrates, there that Nidintabelus, who was called Nabochodrossor, came with his forces against me, to do battle. (4) Then we fought a battle. (5) Ormazd brought help to me. (6) By the grace of Ormazd I slew many of the troops of that Nidintabelus—(7) the enemy was driven (?) into the water—(8) the water destroyed them. (9) On the 2nd day of the month Anamaka, then it was we so fought.

COLUMN II.

Par. 1. (1) Thátiya Dárayavush khshá*yathiya*—(2) *Pasáva Nadi*tabira hadá kama*na*ibish asbáraibish a*biya Bábi*rum ashiyava. (3) Pasáva adam Bábirum ashi*yavam*. (4) . . . . . .* áha utá Bábirum agarbá*yam, utá avam Naditabir*am agarbáyam*. (5) Pasáva avam Naditabiram adam Bábirauva awájanam.

(1) Says Darius the king—(2) Then Nidintabelus with the horsemen (that were) faithful (to him) fled to Babylon. (3) Then I went to Babylon. (4) *By the grace of Ormazd* I both took Babylon, and seized that Nidintabelus. (5) Then I slew that Nidintabelus at Babylon.

Par. 2. (1) *Thát*iya Dárayavush khsháyathiya—(2) Yátá adam Bábirauwa áham, i*má dahydwa tyá* hacháma hamitriyá abava: Pársa, 'Uvaja, Máda, Athurá, *Armina, Part*hvá, Margush, Thatagush, Saka.

' The Scythic transcript adds, "There I slew him" (Norris's Beh. Inscr. p. 105).
* The blank here may be supplied with the words "Vashná Auramazdáha" from the Scythic version (Norris, p. 106).

(1) Says Darius the king—(2) Whilst I was at Babylon, these (are) the countries which revolted against me: Persia, Susiana, Media, Assyria, Armenia, Parthia, Margiana, Sattagydia, Sacia.

Par. 3. (1) Thátiya Dárayavush khsháya*thiya*—(2) I. *mart*iya Martya náma, Chichikhraish putra, Kuganaká náma var*danam Pársiya*, avadá adáraya. (3) Hauva udapatatá· (4) 'Uvajaiya kárahyá avathá *athaha*: (5) 'Adam Imanish amiya, 'Uvajaiya khsháyathiya.'

(1) Says Darius the king—(2) A man, named Martes, the son of Sisicres, (in) the city of Persia named Cyganaca, there he dwelt. (3) He arose: (4) to the state of Susiana thus he said: (5) 'I am Imanes, king of Susiana.'

Par. 4. (1) Thátiya Dárayavush khsháya*thiya*—(2) Adakiya adam aahaniya áham abiya 'Uvajam. (3) Pasáva Lacháma . . . . 'Uva*j*iyá avam Martiyam agarbáya: (4) hyashám mathishta áha . . . . na.

(1) Says Darius the king—(2) I was moving a little way (?) in the direction of Susiana. (3) Then the Susianians, fearing (?) from me, seized that Martius. (4) He who was their chief slew him.[9]

Par. 5. (1) Thátiya Dárayavush khsháyathiya—(2) I. martiya Fravar-*tish náma, Máda,* hauva udapatatá. (3) Mádaiya kárahyá avathá athaha: (4) '*Adam Khshathrita*[10] amiya, 'Uvakhshatarahyá tau-máyá.' (5) Pasáva kára Máda hya *vithápatiya áha, hacháma* hami-triya abava. (6) Abiya avam Fravartim ashiyava: (7) *hauva khshá-yathiya a*bava Mádaiya.

(1) Says Darius the king—(2) A man, named Phraortes, a Mede, he rose up. (3) To the state of Media thus he said: (4) I am Xathrites, of the race of Cyaxares. (5) Then the Median troops who were at home revolted from me. (6) They went over to that Phraortes: (7) he became king of Media.

Par. 6. (1) Thátiya Dárayavush khsháyathiya—(2) Kára *Pársa udd Máda* hya upá mám áha, hauva kamanama áha. (3) Pasáva adam káram *fraishayam.* (4) *Vidarna* náma Pársa, maná badaka, avamshám mathishtam akunavam. (5) *Avathdshám athaham*—(6) 'Pritá avam káram tyam Mádam jatá, hya maná ni*ya gaubatiya.*' (7) *Pasáva* hauva Vidarna hadá kárá ashiyava. (8) Yathá Mádam parárasa, Ma . . .[11] *náma*, vardanam Madaiya, avadá hamaranam akunaush

---

[9] The sense of this passage, which is illegible in the Persian, is fixed by the Babylonian transcript.

[10] Restored from the detached inscription.

[11] In the Babylonian the name of this town appears as *Marua*, in the Scythic it is *Marus.*

hadá Mádaíbish.   (9) *Hya* Mádaishuvá mathishta áha, hauva adakiya
niya . . . . . . dá . . . . . (10) Auramazdámaiya upastám abara : (11)
vashná Auramazdáha kára hya *Vidarnahyá* avam káram tyam hamitriyam aja vasiya.   (12) Anámakahya *múhyá* VI. (?) rauchabish,
thakatá áha avatháshám hamaranam kartam.   (13) Pasáva *hauva
kára* hya maná Kapada námá, dahyáush Mádaiya, avadá mám *amá
naya, ydtá* adam arasam Mádam.

    (1) Says Darius the king—(2) The army of Persians and
Medes that was with me, that was faithful to me.   (3) Then I sent
forth troops.   (4) Hydarnes by name, a Persian, one of my subjects,'
him I appointed their leader.   (5) Thus I addressed them : (6) 'Go
forth (and) smite that Median state, which does not acknowledge
me.'²   (7) Then that Hydarnes marched with his army.   (8) When
he reached Media, a city of Media, named Marus (?), there he
fought a battle with the Medes.   (9) He who was the leader of the
Medes could not at all resist him (?)   (10) Ormazd · brought help to
me ; (11) by the grace of Ormazd, the troops of Hydarnes entirely
defeated that rebel army.   (12) On the 6th (?) day of the month
Anamaka, then it was the battle was thus fought by them.   (13)
Then that army of mine at (a place) called Capada, a district of
Media, waited for me until I arrived in Media.

Par. 7. (1) Thátiya Dárayavush khsháyathiya—(2) *Pasdva Dádarshish
námα*, Arminiya, maná badaka, avam adam fráishayam Arminam.
(3) *Avathshiya athaham*—(4) '*Pridiya*, kára hya hamitriya, maná
niya gaubatiya, avam *jadiya*.   (5) *Pasdva* Dádarshish ashiyava.
(6) Yathá Arminam parárasa, pasáva *hamitriyá* hagamatá paraitá
patish Dádarshim hamaranam chartaniya.   (7) . . . . náma, avaha-
nam Armaniyiya, avadá hamaranam akunava.   (8) A*uramazdámaiya*
upastám abara ; (9) vashná Auramazdáha, kára hya ma*ná avam káram*
tyam hamitriyam aja vasiya.   (10) Thuraváharahya máhyá VIII.
rauchabish, *thakatá* áha avatháshám hamaranam kartam.

    (1) Says Darius the king—(2) Then (a man), Dadarses by
name, an Armenian, one of my subjects, him I sent to Armenia.
(3) Thus I said to him—(4) 'Go forth, the rebel state, which does
not acknowledge me, smite it.'   (5) Then Dadarses marched.   (6)
When he reached Armenia, then the rebels, having collected, came
again before Dadarses, to do battle.   (7) Zoza' (?) by name, a village of Armenia, there they fought a battle.   (8) Ormazd brought
help to me ; (9) by the grace of Ormazd, my forces entirely defeated the rebel army.   (10) On the 8th day of the month Thuravahara, then it was a battle was thus fought by them.

Par. 8. (1) Thátiya D*árayavush khshdyathiya*—(2) Patiya duvitiyam
hamitriyá hagamatá paraitá pati*sh Dádarshim hamar*anam chartaniya.

---

¹ Literally, " one bound to me."   ² Literally, " which is not called mine."
This name is recovered from the Babylonian transcript.

(3) Tigra námá didá Armaniyaiya *avadá hamaranam* akunava. (4) Auramazdámaiya upastám abara; (5) vashná *Auramazdáha kára hya* maná avam káram tyam hamitryam aja vasiya. (6) *Thuravdharahya máhyá* xviii. rauchabish, thakatá áha avatháshám hama-*ranam kartam*.

(1) Says Darius the king—(2) For the second time the rebels, having collected, returned before Dadarses, to do battle. (3) The fort of Armenia named Tigra, there they fought a battle. (4) Ormazd brought help to me; (5) by the grace of Ormazd, my troops entirely defeated that rebel army. (6) On the 18th day of the month Thuravahara, then it was the battle was thus fought by them.[*]

Par. 9. (1) *Thátiya* Dárayavush khsháyathiya—(2) Patiya tritiyam ham*itryá hagamatá* paraitá patish Dádarshim hamaranam chartaniya. (3) U*hyáma náma* didá Armaniyaiya, avadá hamaranam akunava. (4) Auramazdámaiya *upastám abara ;* (5) vashná Auramazdáha kára hya maná avam káram ty*am hamitryam aja vasiya.* (6) Tháigar-chaish máhyá ix. rauchabish, thakatá áha *avatháshám hamaranam* kartam. (7) Pasáva Dádarshish chitá mám amánaya a . . . *yátá* adam arasam Mádam.

(1) Says Darius the king—(2) For the third time the rebels, having collected, returned before Dadarses, to do battle. (3) The fort of Armenia named Uhyama, there they fought a battle. (4) Ormazd brought help to me; (5) by the grace of Ormazd, my forces entirely defeated the rebel army. (6) On the ninth day of the month Thaigarchish, then it was the battle was thus fought by them. (7) Afterwards Dadarses waited for me there until I reached Media.

Par. 10. (1) Thátiya Dárayavush khsháyath*iya—*(2) *Pasáva Vumisa* náma Pársa, maná badaka, avam adam fráishayam Arminam. (3) *Avatháshiya athaham—*(4) 'Pridiya, kára hya hamitriya maná niya gaubatiya, *avam jadiya.*' (5) *Pasáva* Vumisa ashiyava. (6) Yathá Arminam parárasa, pas*áva hamitriya* hagamatá paraitá patish Vumisam hamaranam chartaniya. (7) . . . . . . *námá dahy*áush Athu-ráyá, avadá hamaranam akunava. (8) Aura*mazdámaiya upastám* abara; (9) vashná Auramazdáha, kára hya maná avam *kdram tyam* hamitriyam aja vasiya. (10) Anámakahya máhyá xv. rauchabish, *thakatá dha avathásh*ám hamaranam kartam.

(1) Says Darius the king—(2) Then (a man) named Vomises, a Persian, one of my subjects, him I sent to Armenia. (3) Thus I said to him—(4) 'Go forth, the rebel state which does not acknowledge me, smite it.' (5) Then Vomises went forth. (6) When he reached Armenia, then the rebels, having collected, came again

[*] The Babylonian transcript adds, "He slew 546 of them, and took 520 of them prisoners."

before Vomises, to do battle. (7) A district of Assyria, named
Achidus,[a] there they fought a battle. (8) Ormazd brought help to
me ; (9) by the grace of Ormazd my troops entirely defeated that
rebel army. (10) On the 15th day of the month Anamaka, then it
was the battle was thus fought by them.[b]

Par. 11. (1) Thátiya Dárayavush *khsháyathiya*—(2) *Patiya* d*uvitiyam*
hamitriyá hagamatá paraitá pa*tish Vumisam hamaranam* chartaniya.
(3) Autiyára námá, dahyáush Arminai*ya, avadá hamaranam* akunava.
(4) Auramazdámaiya upastám abara ; (5) *vashná Auramazdáha* kára
hya maná avam káram tyam hamitriyam *aja vasiya.* (6) *Thuravá-*
harahya máhyá . . iyamanam patiya avatháshám *hamaranam kartam.*
(7) Pasáva Vumisa chitá mám amánaya Arminai*ya, ydtá adam*
arasam Mádam.

(1) Says Darius the king—(2) For the second time the rebels,
having collected, came before Vomises, to do battle. (3) A district of
Armenia, named Otiara, there they fought a battle. (4) Ormazd
brought help to me; (5) by the grace of Ormazd my troops entirely defeated that rebel army. (6) In the month of Thuravahara,
upon the festival (?), the battle was thus fought by them.' (7)
Afterwards Vomises waited for me in Armenia, until I reached
Media.

Par. 12. (1) Thátiya Dárayavush khsháyathiya—(2) *Pasdva adam*
nijáyam hachá Bábiraush. (3) Ashiyavam Mádam. (4) Yathá
M*ádam parárasam,* Kudrush náma, vardanam Mádaiya, avadá hauva
Fra*vartish, hya M*ádaiya khsháyathiya agaubatá, *aisha hadá kárá*
patish mám *hamaranam charta*niya. (5) Pasáva hamaranam akumá.
(6) *Auramaz*dámaiya upastám *abara ;* (7) *vashná A*uramazdáha káram
tyam Fravartaish adam ajanam vasiya. (8) Adukanaish máhyá
xxvi. rauchabish, thakatá *áha* avathá hamaranam ak*umá.*

(1) Says Darius the king—(2) Then I went out from Babylon.
(3) I proceeded to Media. (4) When I reached Media, a city of
Media named Kudrusia, there that Phraortes, who (was) called king
of Media, came with an army against me, to do battle. (5) Then
we fought a battle. (6) Ormazd brought help to me; (7) by the
grace of Ormazd, I entirely defeated the army of Phraortes. (8)
On the 26th day of the month Adukanish, then it was we thus fought
the battle.

Par. 13. (1) *Thátiya* Dárayavush khsháyathiya—(2) Pasáva *hauva*
Fravartish hadá k*amanaibish asbd*raibish amutha, Ragá námá dahyáus*h*
M*ádaiya, avadá ashiyava.* (3) *Pasd*va adam káram frá*ishayam,* tyi-

---

[a] This name is recovered from the Scythic version, which gives *Atchitu.*
[b] The Babylonian has, "They slew of the enemy 2024."
[c] Again we have in the Babylonian the number killed in the battle, and taken
prisoners: "They slew of the enemy 2045, and took 1559 of them prisoners."

patiya Fravartish agarbatá anayatá abiya mám.   (4) Adam*shiya uta*
náham utá gaushá u*tá* .... áram frájanam, utáshiya ..... m
awajam.   (5) Duvarayámaiy*a* basta adáriya; (6) haruvashim kára
ava*ina*.   (7) Pasáva adam Hagamatánaiya uzamayápatiya akunavam.
(8) Ut*á martiyá* tyishiya fratam*d anushiyá* ahatá ava*iya* Hagamatánaiya ata*ra* didám fráhajam.

(1) Says Darius the king—(2) Then that Phraortes, with his
faithful horsemen, fled from thence to a district of Media, called
Rhages.   (3) Then I sent an army, by which Phraortes was taken
(and) brought before me.   (4) I cut off both his nose, and his ears,
and his tongue (?), and I led him away (captive ?).   (5) He was
kept chained at my door; (6) all the kingdom beheld him.   (7)
Afterwards I crucified him at Agbatana.   (8) And the men, who
were his chief followers, I slew within the citadel at Agbatana.

Par. 14. (1) *Thátiya* Dárayavush khsháyathiya—(2) I. *marti*ya, Chitratakhma náma, *Asagarti*ya, *h*auvamaiya hamatriya abava.   (3) Kárahy*á a*vathá athaha—(4) ' Adam *khsháyathi*ya amiya *Asaga*rtaiyá,
Uvakh*shatara*hyá taumáyá.'   (5) Pasáva adam káram Pú*rsam* utá
Mádam *frais*hayam.   (6) Takhamas ádá náma, Máda, maná ba*daka,
a*vamshám mathi*shtam* akunavam.   (7) *Avathá*shám athaham.   (8)
' Pritá, káram tyam *h*amitriyam hya maná niya gaubátiya, avam jatá.'
(9) Pasáva Takhama*s*páda hadá kárá a*sh*iyava.   (10) Hamaranam
akunaush hadá Chitra*takh*má.   (11) Auramazd*ámaiya* upastám abara;
(12) vashná Auramazdáha kár*a* hya maná avam kára*m tyam* hamitriyam aja, ut*á* Chitratakhmam agarbáya, *utá* ánaya abiya mám.
(13) *Pasá*vashiya adam utá náham utá gaushá frájanam, utáshiya
.... sham avajam.   (14) Duvarayámaiya basta adáriya.   (15)
Haruvashim kára a*vaina*.   (16) *Pasá*vashim Arbiráyá uzamayápatiya
akunavam.

(1) Says Darius the king—(2) A man, named Sitrantachmes,
a Sagartian, he rebelled against me.   (3) To the state thus he said—
(4) ' I am the king of Sagartia, of the race of Cyaxares.'   (5) Then
I sent forth an army of Persians and Medes.   (6) (A man) named
Tachamaspates, a Mede, one of my subjects, him I made their leader.
(7) Thus I said to them—(8) ' Go forth, (and) smite that rebel state
which does not acknowledge me.'   (9) Then Tachamaspates set
forth with his army.   (10) He fought a battle with Sitrantachmes.
(11) Ormazd brought help to me; (12) by the grace of Ormazd,
my troops defeated the rebel army, and took Sitrantachmes, and
brought (him) before me.   (13) Then I cut off both his nose and
his ears, and I led him away (captive ?).   (14) He was kept chained
at my door.   (15) All the kingdom beheld l'm.   (16) Afterwards I
crucified him at Arbela.

Par. 15. (1) Thátiya D*á*rayav*u*sh khsháyathiya—(2) Ima tya maná
kartam *Mádai*ya.

(1) Says Darius the king—(2) This is what (was) done by me in Media.

Par. 16. (1) Thátiya Dárayavush khsháyathiya—(2) Parthva utá Varkána . . . . va. (3) . . . . . . Fravartaish agaubatá; (4) Vishtáspa, maná pitá, h . . . . kára avahar . . . . átara. (5) Pasáva Vishtáspa ab . . . . anushiyá . . . . áya. (6) Vishpauztish náma, vardanam *Parthvaiya*, *aradá* hamaranam akunava. (7) *Auramaxdiyámaa upastám abara;* (8) *Vashná Auramaxdáha Vishtáspa avam káram tyam hamitriyam aja vasiya.* (9) *Viyakhnahya máhyá* XXII. *rauchabish, thakatá áha* avatháshám hamaranam kartam.*

(1) Says Darius the king—(2) Parthia and Hyrcania revolted against me. (3) They declared for Phraortes. (4) Hystaspes, my father,* . . . . (5) Afterwards Hystaspes, with the troops under his orders (?), set forth. (6) (At a place) called Hyspaostes, a town of Media, there he fought a battle. (7) Ormazd brought help to me; (8) by the grace of Ormazd, Hystaspes entirely defeated that rebel army. (9) On the 22d day of the month Viyakhna, then it was the battle (was) thus fought by them.

Column III.

Par. 1. (1) Thátiya Dárayavush khsháyathiya—(2) Pasáva adam káram Pársam fráishayam abiya Vishtáspam hachá Ragáyá. (3) Yathá hauva kára parárasa abiya Vishtáspam, pasáva Vishtáspa ayastá avam káram ashiyava. (4) Patigrabaná náma, vardanam Parthvaiya, avadá hamaranam akunaush hadá hamitriyaibish. (5) Auramazdámaiya upastám abara; (6) vashná Auramazdáha Vishtáspa avam káram tyam hamitryam aja vasiya. (7) Garmapadahya máhyá L raucha, thakatá áha avatháshám hamaranam kartam.

(1) Says Darius the king—(2) Then I sent a Persian army to Hystaspes from Rhages. (3) When that army reached Hystaspes, then Hystaspes marched forth with those troops. (4) (At a place) called Patigrabana, a city of Parthia, there he fought a battle with the rebels. (5) Ormazd brought help to me; (6) by the grace of Ormazd, Hystaspes entirely defeated that rebel army. (7) On the 1st day of the month Garmapada, then it was the battle was thus fought by them.[10]

This paragraph, which is almost entirely illegible in the Persian, can be restored in most clauses with certainty from the Babylonian and Scythic transcripts.

* The sense is recovered from the Scythic transcript, which says, "Hystaspes, my father, was in Parthia; the people revolted and forsook him; then Hystaspes," &c. (Norris, p. 115).

[10] The Babylonian adds: "He slew of their number 6560, and took 4182 of them prisoners."

Par. 2. (1) Thátiya Dárayavush khsháyathiya—(2) Pasáva dahyáush maná abava. (3) Ima tya maná kartam Parthvaiya.

(1) Says Darius the king—(2) Then the province submitted to me (became mine). (3) This is what (was) done by me in Parthia.

Par. 3. (1) Thátiya Dárayavush khsháyathiya—(2) Margush námá, dahyáush hauvamaiya hashitiyá abava. (3) I. martiya, Frúda náma, Márgava, avam mathishtam akunavatá. (4) Pasáva adam fráishayam Dádarshish náma, Parsá, maná badaka, Bákhtariyá khshatrapává, abiya avam. (5) Avatháshiya athaham—(6) 'Pridiya, avam káram jadiya, hya maná niya gaubatiya.' (7) Pasáva Dádarshish hadá kárá ashiyava. (8) Hamaranam akunaush hadá Márgayaibish. (9) Auramazdámaiya upastám abara; (10) vashná Auramazdáha kára hya maná avam káram tyam hamitriyam aja vasiya. (11) Atriyá-diyahya máhyá xxiii. rauchabish, thakatá áha, avatháshám hamara-nam kartam.

(1) Says Darius the king—(2) The province called Margiana, that revolted against me. (3) A man, named Phraortes, a Margian, him they made their leader. (4) Then I sent to him (who was) named Dadarses, (who was) my subject, and satrap of Bactria. (5) Thus I said to him—(6) 'Go forth, (and) smite that people which does not acknowledge me.' (7) Then Dadarses set forth with his forces. (8) He fought a battle with the Margians. (9) Ormazd brought help to me; (10) by the grace of Ormazd my troops entirely defeated that rebel army. (11) On the 23rd day of the month Atriyadiya, then it was the battle was thus fought by them.[1]

Par. 4. (1) Thátiya Dárayavush khsháyathiya—(2) Pasáva dahyáush maná abava. (3) Ima tya maná kartam Bákhtariyá.

(1) Says Darius the king—(2) Then the province submitted to me. (3) This is what (was) done by me in Bactria.

Par. 5. (1) Thátiya Dárayavush khsháyathiya—(2) I. martiya, Va-hyazdáta náma, Túrvá náma vardanam, Yutiyá námá dahyáush Pár-saiya, avadá adáraya. (3) Hauva duvitiyam udapatatá. (4) Pár-saiya kárahyá avathá athaha—(5) 'Adam Bardiya amiya, hya Kuraush putra.' (6) Pasáva kára Pársa, hya vitháyatiya hachá yadáyá fratarta, hauva hacháma hamitriya abava. (7) Abiya avam Vahyazdátam ashiyava. (8) Hauva khsháyathiya abava Pársaiya.

(1) Says Darius the king—(2) A man, named Veïsdates, (in) a city named Tarba, in the district of Persia called Yutiya, there he dwelt. (3) He rose up a second time. (4) To the state of Persia he thus said—(5) 'I am Bardes, the son of Cyrus.' (6) Then the

---

[1] Again the Babylonian has the additional clause: "Dadarses slew 4203 of them, and took 6562 of them prisoners."

Persian people, who were at home, being at a distance (from me) (?), revolted from me. (7) They went over to that Veïsdates. (8) He became king of Persia.

Par. 6. (1) Thátiya Dárayavush khsháyathiya—(2) Pasáva adam káram Pársam utá Mádam fráishayam hya upá mám áha. (3) Artavardiya náma, Pársa, maná badaka, avamshám mathishtam akunavam. (4) Hya aniya kára Pársa pasá maná ashiyava Mádam. (5) Pasáva Artavardiya hadá kárá ashiyava Pársam. (6) Yathá Pársam parárasa, Rakhá náma, vardanam Pársaiya, avadá hauva Vahyazdáta hya Bardiya agaubatá aisha hadá kárá patish Artavardiyam hamaranam chartaniya. (7) Pasáva hamaranam akunava. (8) Auramazdámaiya upastám abara; (9) vashná Auramazdáha kára hya maná avam káram tyam Vahyazdátahya aja vasiya. (10) Thuraváharahya máhyá xII. rauchabish, thakatá áha avatháshám hamaranam kartam.

(1) Says Darius the king—(2) Then I sent forth the Persian and Median forces which were with me. (3) (A man) named Artabardes, a Persian, one of my subjects, him I made their leader. (4) The other Persian forces accompanied me to Media. (5) Then Artabardes went with his army to Persia. (6) When he reached Persia, (at) a city of Persia called Racha, there that Veïsdates, who was called Bardes, came with an army against Artabardes, to do battle. (7) Then they fought a battle. (8) Ormazd brought help to me; (9) by the grace of Ormazd my forces entirely defeated the army of Veïsdates. (10) On the 12th day of the month Thuravahara, then it was the battle (was) thus fought by them.

Par. 7. (1) Thátiya Dárayavush khsháyathiya—(2) Pasáva hauva Vahyazdáta hadá kamanaibish asbáraibish amutha ashiyava Pishiyá-'uvádám. (3) Hachá avadasha káram ayastá hyáparam aisha patish Artavardiyam, hamaranam chartaniya. (4) Parga náma kaufa avadá hamaranam akunava. (5) Auramazdámaiya upastám abara; (6) vashná Auramazdáha kára hya maná avam káram tyam Vahyazdátahya aja vasiya. (7) Garmapadahya máhyá vi. rauchabish, thakatá áha avatháshám hamaranam kartam. (8) Utá avam Vahyazdátam agarbáya, utá martiyá tyishiya fratamá anushiyá áhata agarbáya.

(1) Says Darius the king—(2) Then that Veïsdates, with his faithful horsemen, fled thence to Pissiachada. (3) From that place he came back again with an army against Artabardes, to do battle. (4) (At) the mountain named Parga, there they fought a battle. (5) Ormazd brought help to me; (6) by the grace of Ormazd my troops entirely defeated the army of Veïsdates. (7) On the 6th day of the month Garmapada, then it was the battle (was) so fought by them. (8) They both took that Veïsdates, and they took the men who were his chief adherents.

Par. 8. (1) Thátiya Dárayavush khsháyathiya—(2) Pasáva adam avam Vahyazdátam utá martiyá tyishiya fratamá anushiyá áhata, 'Uvádaidaya náma vardanam Pársaiya, avadashish uzamayápatiya akunavam.

(1) Says Darius the king—(2) Then that Veïsdates, and the men who were his chief adherents, (at) a city of Persia, named Chodedia, there I crucified them.[1]

Par. 9. (1) Thátiya Dárayavush khsháyathiya—(2) Hauva Vahyazdáta hya Bardiya agaubatá, hauva káram fráishaya Hara'uvatim, Vivána náma, Pársa, maná badaka, Hara'uvatiyá khshatrapává, abiya avam. (3) Utásham I. martiya mathishtam akunaush, (4) Avatháshám áthaha—(5) ' Pritá, Vivánam játá, utá avam káram hya Dárayavahush khsháyathiyahyá gaubatiya.' (6) Pasáva hauva kára ashiyava, tyam Vahyazdáta fráishaya abiya Vivánam, hamaranam chartaniya. (7) Kápishkánish námá dida, avadá hamaranam akunava. (8) Auramazdámaiya upastám abara; (9) vashná Auramazdáha kára hya maná avam káram tyam hamitriyam aja vasiya. (10) Anámakahya máhyá xiii. rauchabish, thakatá áha avatháshám hamaranam kartam.

(1) Says Darius the king—(2) That Veïsdates, who was called Bardes, he sent an army to Arachotia, against (a man) named Vibanus, one of my subjects, and the satrap of Arachotia. (3) And he made a certain man their leader. (4) Thus he said to them—(5) ' Go forth, (and) smite Vibanus, and the state which acknowledges king Darius.' (6) Then the army went forth, which Veïsdates had sent against Vibanus, to do battle. (7) (At) a fort named Capiscanes,[2] there they fought a battle. (8) Ormazd brought help to me; (9) by the grace of Ormazd my troops entirely defeated the rebel army. (10) On the 13th day of the month Ánamaka, then it was the battle was thus fought by them.

Par. 10. (1) Thátiya Dárayavush khsháyathiya--(2) Patiya hyáparam hamitriyá hagamatá paraitá patish Vivánam, hamaranam chartaniya. (3) Gadutava námá dahyáush, avadá hamaranam akunava. (4) Auramazdámaiya upastám abara; (5) vashná Auramazdáha kára hya maná avam káram tyam hamitryam aja vasiya. (6) Viya*khna*hya máhyá vii. rauchabish, thakatá áha avatháshám hamaranam kartam.

(1) Says Darius the king—(2) Again the rebels, having collected, returned before Vibanus, to do battle. (3) (In) a district, named Gadytia, there they fought a battle. (4) Ormazd brought help to me; (5) by the grace of Ormazd my troops entirely defeated the rebel army. (6) On the 7th day of the month Viyakhna, then it was the battle (was) thus fought by them.

---

[1] The Babylonian and Scythian versions add—" This is what was done by me in Persia."

[2] The Scythic adds—" in Arachotia " (Norris, p. 121).

Par. 11. (1) Thátiya Dárayavush khsháyathiya—(2) Pasáva hauva martiya, hya avahyá kárahyá *mathishta dha* tyam Vahyazdáta fráishaya abiya Vivánam, hauva math*ishta hadá* kamanaibish asbáraibish ash*iyava.* (3) Arsháda námá, did*á Hara'u*vatiyá avapará atiyá*isha.* (4) *Pasáva* Vivána hadá kárá nipadiya tyiya ashiya. (5) Avadáshim agarbá*ya* utá martiyá tyishiya fratamá *a*nushiya áhata awája.

     (1) Says Darius the king—(2) Then that man, who was the leader of those troops which Veïsdates had sent against Vibanus, that leader, with the horsemen (who were) faithful (to him), fled away. (3) (At) a fort of Arachotia, named Arshada,' in that he took refuge (?) (4) Then Vibanus with his army set out in pursuit (?) (5) There he took him, and slew the men who were his chief adherents.

     ❏ ❏

Par. 12. (1) Thátiya Dárayavush khsháyathiya—(2) Pasáva dahyáush maná abava. (3) Ima tya maná kartam Hara'uvatiyá.

     (1) Says Darius the king—(2) Then the province submitted to me. (3) This is what (was) done by me in Arachotia.

Par. 13. (1) Thátiya Dárayav*ush* khsháyathiya—(2) Yátá adam Pársai*ya utá* Mádaiya áham, patiya duvitiyam Bábiruviyá hamatriyá abava hacháma. (3) I. martiya, Arakha náma, Arminiya, Hañditahya putra, hauva udapatatá. (4) Bábirauva, Dubáña náma, dahyáush hachá avadasha hauva udapatatá. (5) Avathá adurujiya—(6) ' Adam Nabukudrachara amiya, hya Nabunitahyá putra.' (7) Pasáva kára Bábiruviya hacháma hamitriya abava. (8) Abiya avam Arakham ashiyava. (9) Bábirum hauva agarbáyatá. (10) Hauva khsháyathiya abava Bábirauva.

     (1) Says Darius the king—(2) Whilst I was in Persia and Media, for the second time the Babylonians revolted from me. (3) A man, named Aracus, an Armenian, the son of Handitis, he arose. (4) A district of Babylon, named Dobana, from thence he arose. (5) Thus he falsely declared—(6) ' I am Nabochodrossor, the son of Nabonidus.' (7) Then the state of Babylon revolted from me. (8) It went over to that Aracus. (9) He seized on Babylon. (10) He became king of Babylonia.

Par. 14. (1) Thátiya Dúrayavush khsháyathiya—(2) Pasáva adam káram fráishayam Bábirum. (3) Vidafrá náma, Máda, maná badaka, avam mathishtam akunavam. (4) Avatháshám athaham ; (5) ' Prita, avam káram tyam Bábirauva jatá, hya maná niya gaubatiya.' (6) Pasáva *Vidafrá* hadá kárá ashiyava abiya Bábirum. (7) Auramazdámaiya upastám abara ; (8) vashná Auramazdáha Vidafrá Bábirum agarbáya . . . . . . (9) . . . . . . máhyá II. rauchabish, thakatá áha

     ' The Scythic adds a clause which seems to mean " the dwelling-place of Vibanus " (Norris, p. 123).

avathá avam kdram tyam hamitriyam aja vasiya. (10) . . . .
. . . . *patiya asariyatá.*

(1) Says Darius the king—(2) Then I sent an army to Baby·
lon. (3) (A man) named Intaphres, a Mede, one of my subjects,
him I made (their) leader. (4) Thus I said to them—(5) ' Go
forth, (and) smite that Babylonian state, which does not acknowledge me.' (6) Then Intaphres, with his army, marched to Babylon.
(7) Ormazd brought help to me; (8) by the grace of Ormazd Intaphres took Babylon. (9) On the 2nd * day of the month . . . . . . ,
then it was he entirely defeated that rebel people.* (10) . . . .
. . . . was slain.

COLUMN IV.

Par. 1. (1) Thátiya Dárayavush khsháyathiya—(2) Ima tya maná kartam Bábirauva.

(1) Says Darius the king—(2) This is what (was) done by me
in Babylonia.

Par. 2. (1) Thátiya Dárayavush khsháyathiya—(2) *I*ma tya adam
akunavam. (3) Vashná Au*r*amazdáha dha hamahyáyá thrada. (4)
Pasáva yathá khsháyathiyá hamitriyá abava, adam XIX. hamaraná
akunavam. (5) Vashná *Au*ramazdáha adamshám ajanam, utá IX.
khsháyathiyá agarbáyam. (6) I. Gaumáta námá, Magush, aha.
(7) *Hauva a*durujiya. (8) Avathá athaha—(9) ' Adam Bardiya
amiya, hya *Kuraush* putra.' (10) Hauva Pársam hamitriyam akuna-
ush. (11) I. *Atrina* náma, 'Uvajaiya, hauva adurujiya. (12) Avathá
athaha—(13) ' *Adam* khsháyathiya amiya 'Uvajaiya.' (14) Hauva
'Uvajam ham*itr*iyam *aku*naush maná. (15) I. Naditabira náma,
Bábiruviya, *hauva a*durujiya. (16) Avathá athaha—(17) ' Adam
Nabukudra*chara* amiya, hya Nabunitahya putra.' (18) Hauva
Bábiru*m hamitriyam* akunaush. (19) I. Martiya náma, Pársa, hauva
*aduru*jiya. (20) Avathá athaha—(21) ' Adam Imanish amiya,
'Uvajai*ya khsháyath*iya.' (22) Hauva 'Uvajam hamitriyam akunaush.
(23) I. Fravartish náma, Máda, hauva adurujiya. (24) Avathá
athaha—(25) ' *Adam Khshath*rita amiya, 'Uvakshatarahya taumáyá.'
(26) Hauva Mádam *hamitriyam* akunaush. (27) I. Chitratakhma
náma, Asagartiya, hauva *adu*rujiya. (28) Avathá athaha—(29)
' Adam khsháyathiya amiya Asagar*taiya,* '*U*vakshatarahya taumáyá.'
(30) Hauva Asagartam ha*mitriyam* akunaush. (31) I. Fráda náma,

* The Scythic gives "the XXIIᵈ day."
* This is restored from the Scythic, which gives the following as the sense of
§ 10 : "He made the army (of Aracus) prisoners, and also their leader. Then that
Aracus, and the chief men who were with him, were taken and brought before me.
Then I gave orders that they should crucify both Aracus and the chief men who
were with him."

Márgava, hauva *adu*rujiya.   (32) Avathá athaha—(33) 'Adam khsháyathiya a*miya Márgauva.'*   (34) Hauva Margum hamitriyam akunaush.   (35) I. *Vahyazd*áta náma, Pársa, hauva adurujiya.   (36) *Avathá athaha*—(37) 'Adam Bardiya amiya, hya Kuraush putra.' (38) Hau*va Pár*sam hamitriyam akunaush.   (39) I. Arakha náma, Armin*iya, hauva a*durujiya.   (40) Avathá athaha—(41) 'Adam Na-bukudrachara amiya, *hya Nabu*nitahya putra.'   (42) Hauva Bábirum hamatriyam akunau*sh*.

     (1) Says Darius the king—(2) This is what I have done.   (3) By the grace of Ormazd I have accomplished the whole.'—(4) After that the kings rebelled against me, I fought 19 battles.   (5) By the grace of Ormazd I smote them, and took 9 kings (prisoners).   (6) One was named Gomates, a Magian.   (7) He spake lies.   (8) Thus he said—(9) 'I am Bardes, the son of Cyrus.'   (10) He caused Persia to revolt.   (11) Another (was) named Atrines, a Susianian; he spake lies.   (12) Thus he said—(13) 'I am the king of Susiana.'   (14) He caused Susiana to revolt from me.   (15) Another (was) named Nidintabelus, a Babylonian; he spake lies.   (16) Thus he said—(17) 'I am Nabochodrossor, the son of Nabonidus.'   (18) He caused Babylon to revolt.   (19) Another (was) named Martes, a Persian; he spake lies.   (20) Thus he said—(21) 'I am Imanes, the king of Susiana.'   (22) He caused Susiana to revolt.   (23) Another (was) named Phrortes, a Mede; he spake lies.   (24) Thus he said—(25) 'I am Xathrites, of the race of Cyaxares.'   (26) He caused Media to revolt.   (27) Another (was) named Sitrantachmes, a Sagartian; he spake lies.   (28) Thus he said—(29) 'I am the king of Sagartia, of the race of Cyaxares.'   (30) He caused Sagartia to revolt.   (31) Another (was) named Phraates, a Margian; he spake lies.   (32) Thus he said—(33) 'I am king of Margiana.'   (34) He caused Margiana to revolt.   (35) Another (was) named Veïsdates, a Persian; he spake lies.   (36) Thus he said—(37) 'I am Bardes, the son of Cyrus.'   (38) He caused Persia to revolt.   (39) Another (was) named Aracus, an Armenian; he spake lies.   (40) Thus he said—(41) 'I am Nabochodrossor, the son of Nabonidus.'   (42) He caused Babylon to revolt.

Par. 3. (1) *Thá*tiya Dárayavush khsháyathiya—(2) Imaiya ix. khsháya-thiy*á adam ag*arbayam atara imá hamaraná.

     (1) Says Darius the king—(2) These 9 kings have I taken in these battles.

Par. 4. (1) Thátiya Dárayava*ush khshá*yathiya—(2) Dahyáva imá tya hamitriyá abava.   (3) Darauga di*va* . . . . . á akunaush, tya imaiya káram adurujiyasha.   (4) Pasáva Di . . . . á manú dastayá akunaush.   (5) Yathá mám káma, awathá Di . . . .

' The phrase *hamakydyá thrada* has been variously translated. Oppert suggests "all my life;" Benfey "altogether."

(1) Says Darius the king—(2) These are the provinces which rebelled. (3) The god Ormazd created lies that they should deceive the people.[*] (4) Afterwards the god Ormazd gave the people into my hand. (5) As I desired, so the god Ormazd did (?).[*]

Par. 5. (1) Thátiya Dárayavush khsháyathiya—(2) Tuvam ká khsháyathiya hya aparam ahya, hachá daraugá darsham patipayuvá. (3) Mar*tiya hya daraujana* ahatiya, avam ufrastam parasá. (4) Yadiya avathá *maniydhya*, dahyáushmaiya durusá ahatiya.

(1) Says Darius the king—(2) Thou who mayest be king hereafter, keep thyself entirely from lies. (3) The man who may be a liar, him destroy utterly. (4) If thou shalt thus observe, my country shall remain in its integrity.

Par. 6. (1) Thátiya *Dárayavush* khsháyathiya—(2) Ima tya adam akunavam. (3) Vashná Aurama*sddha hama*hyáyá thrada akunavam. (4) Tuvam ká hya aparam imám *dipim pati*parasáhya, tya maná kartam varnavartám thuvám mat*ya duru*jiyáhya.

(1) Says Darius the king—(2) This is what I have done. (3) By the grace of Ormazd have I achieved the performance of the whole. (4) Thou who mayest hereafter peruse this tablet, let that which has been done by me be a warning (to thee), that thou lie not.

Par. 7. (1) Thátiya Dárayavush khsháyathiya—(2) Auramazdá . . . iyiya yathá ima hashiyam niya durukhtam adam akuna*vam hamah*yáyá thrada.

(1) Says Darius the king—(2) Ormazd is my witness (?) that I have truly (not falsely) made this record of my deeds throughout.

Par. 8. (1) Thátiya Dárayavush khsháyathiya—(2) Vashná Aurama*z-ddha* . . ámaiya aniyashchiya vasiya astiya kartam, ava ahyáy*d dipiyá* niya nipishtam. (3) Avahyarádiya niya nipishtam, má*tya hya aparam* imám dipim patiparasátiya, avahyá paruva thá . . . . *tya* maná kartam nishida (?), varnavátiya durukhtam maniy*dhya*.

(1) Says Darius the king—(2) By the grace of Ormazd, that which has besides been done by me, (which is) much, I have not inscribed on this tablet. (3) On that account I have not inscribed it, lest he who hereafter might peruse this tablet, to him the many deeds (?) that have been done by me elsewhere, might seem (?) to be falsely recorded.

---

[*] Mr. Norris considers the Scythic here to mean—"The god of lies made them rebel, that they should subvert the empire" (Beh. Inscr. p. 127).

[*] It is doubtful if the Persian text uses the name of Ormazd in this paragraph, or if it merely employs the term *Diva*, "the God." The Babylonian version however proves beyond dispute, that the allusion is to Oromazdes as usual.

Par. 9. (1) Thátiya Dárayavush khsháyathiya—(2) Tyaiya pruvá khsháyathiyá . . . . . . á úha avaishám avá niya astiya kartam, yathá maná vashná *Auramazdáha* hamahyáyá duvartam.

    (1) Says Darius the king—(2) They who were kings before me, by them it has not been done as by me entirely by the grace of Ormazd.[1]

Par. 10. (1) Thátiya Dárayavush khsháyathiya—(2) . . . nuram thuvám varnavatám tya maná kartam avathá . . . . *avahyarádiya* má apagaudaya. (3) Yadiya imám hadugám niya apagaudiyáhya, kárahyá tháhya, Auramazdá thuvám daushtá biyá, ut*átaiya taumá* vasiya biyá, utá daragam jivá.

    (1) Says Darius the king—(2) Beware, my successor (?), that what has been thus *publicly* (?) done by me, on that account thou conceal not. (3) If thou conceal not this edict, (but) tell it to the country, may Ormazd be a friend to thee, and may thy off-spring be numerous, and mayest thou live long.

Par. 11. (1) Thátiya *Dárayavush khshdyathiya*—(2) Yadiya imám ha*du*-gám apagaudayáhya, niya tháhya *kárahyá*, *Auramazd*átaya jatá biyá, utatáiya taumá má biyá.

    (1) Says Darius the king—(2) If thou conceal this edict, (and) tell (it) not to the country, may Ormazd be thy enemy, and mayst thou have no offspring (lit. may there be no offspring to thee).

Par. 12. (1) *Thátiya Dárayavush* khsháyathiya—(2) Ima tya adam akunavam. Hamahyáyá thra*da vashná Auramazdáha* akunavam. (4) Auramazdámaiya upastám abara, utá *aniyá Bagáha* tyaiya hatiya.

    (1) Says Darius the king—(2) This is what I have done. (3) By the grace of Ormazd I have accomplished everything. (4) Or-mazd [2] brought help to me, and the other gods which are.

Par. 13. (1) Thátiya Dárayavush khsháyathiya—(2) *Avahyarádiya* Auramazdá upastám abara, utá aniyá Bagáha *tyaiya hatiya*, *yathá* niya arika áham, niya daraujhana áham, niya zurakara áham, ... imaiya taumá upariya abashtám upariya mám niya shakurim . . . . huvatam zura akunavam. (3) *Tyamiya* hya hamatakshatá maná vithiyá, avam ubartam abaram, hya . iyani . . . . avam upastam aparasam.

---

    [1] The mutilation of this paragraph makes the sense very doubtful. Perhaps the second and third clauses should be read entirely together, as a single sentence. See Col. Rawlinson's Babylonian Memoir, Transcript, line 101.

    [2] The Scythic version here explains the term Ormazd by adding—" Annap Ar-riyanám," "The God of the Arians" (Norris, p. 130).

(1) Says Darius the king—(2) For this reason Ormazd brought help to me, and the other gods which are, (because) that I was not wicked (heretical?), nor was I a liar, nor was I a tyrant[*] . . . . . .
. . . . (3) He who has laboured for my family, him I have cherished and protected (lit. well-cherished I have cherished) ; he who has been *hostile* (?) to me him I have utterly rooted out (well-destroyed I have destroyed).

Par. 14. (1) *Thátiya Dárayavush* khsháyathiya—(2) Tuvam *ka khshá-yathiya* hya aparam ahya, *martiya hya* daraujhana ahatiya, hyavá . . . tar . . . ahatiya, avaiya má daushtá biyá. (3) Avaiya ahifrashtádiya parasá.

(1) Says Darius the king—(2) Thou who mayest be king here-after, the man who may be a liar, and who may be an *evil-doer* (?), do not befriend them. (3) Destroy them with the edge of the sword (lit. with the destruction of the sword).

Par. 15. (1) Thátiya Dárayavush khsháyathiya—(2) Tuvam ká hya aparam imám dipim vaináhya tyám adam niyapisham, imaivá pati-kará, mátya visanáhya. (3) Yává jiváhya (?), ává *avaiya* parikará.

(1) Says Darius the king—(2) Thou who mayest hereafter be-hold this tablet, which I have engraved, and these figures, (beware) lest thou injure (them). (3) As long as thou livest, so long pre-serve them.

Par. 16. (1) Thátiya Dárayavush khsháyathiya—(2) Yadiya imám dipim vaináhya imaivá patikará, niyadish visanáhya, utámaiya yává taumá ahatiya parikaráhadish, Auramazdá thuvám daushtá biyá, *utá*taiya taumá *vasiya biyá*, utá daragam jivá, utá tya kunaváhya avatiya Auramazdá m . . . . m jadanautuva.

(1) Says Darius the king—(2) If thou shalt behold this tablet and these figures, (and) not injure them, and shalt preserve them as long as my seed endures, (then) may Ormazd be thy friend, and may thy seed be numerous, and mayest thou live long; and what-ever thou doest, may Ormazd bless it for thee in after times.

Par. 17. (1) Thátiya Dárayavush khsháyath*iya*—(2) Yadiya imám dipim, imaivá patikará vaináhya visanáhadish, utámaiya yává taumá ahatiya niyadish parikaráhya, Auramazdátaiya jatá biyá, utátai*ya taumá má biyá*, utá tya kunaváhya avataiya Auramazdá *nikatuva* (?)[1]

(1) Says Darius the king—(2) If seeing this tablet, and these

---

[*] The Babylonian version continues, "neither I nor any of my family . . . . , I obeyed the laws . . . . ."

images, thou injurest them, and preservest them not as long as my
seed endures, (then) may Ormazd be thy enemy, and mayest thou
have no offspring, and whatever thou doest, may Ormazd curse (?) it
for thee.   . . . . . .

Par. 18. (1) *Thátiya* Dárayavush khsháyathiya—(2) Imaiya martiyá
tyaiya adakiya avadá ahatá yátá adam Gaumátam tyam Magum
avájanam hya Bardiya agaubatá.   (3) Adakiya imaiya martiyá
hamatakshatá anushiyá maná; (4) Vidafraná náma, Vayaspárahyá
putra, Pársa; (5) Utána náma, Thukhrahyá putra, Pársa; (6)
Gaubaruva náma, Marduniyahyá putra, Pársa; (7) Vidarna náma,
Bagábignahyá putra, Pársa; (8) Bagabukhsha náma, Dáduhyahyá
putra, Pársa; (9) Ardumanish náma, Vahukahyá putra, Pársa.

(1) Says Darius the king—(2) These are the men who alone
were there, when I slew Gomates the Magian, who was called
Bardes. (3) These men alone laboured in my service; (4) (One)
named Intaphernes, the son of Veïspares, a Persian; (5) (One)
named Otanes, the son of Socris, a Persian; (6) (One) named Gobryas, the son of Mardonius, a Persian; (7) (One) named Hydarnes,
the son of Megabignes, a Persian; (8) (One) named Megabyzus,
the son of Dadoïs, a Persian; (9) (One) named Ardomanes, the son
of Basuces, a Persian.

Par. 19. (1) Thátiya Dárayavush khsháyathiya—(2) Tuvam ká khsháyathiya hya aparam ahya, tyámá vidám tastiyáná . . . .
. . . . tya Dárayavush . . . .
. . . . akunavam . . . .
. . . .

(1) Says Darius the king—(2) Thou who mayest be king here-
after. . . . .
. . . .

COLUMN V.[4]

Par. 1. (1) Thátiya *Dárayavush khsháyathiya*—(2) Ima *tya adam*
akunava*m; vashná Auramazdáha hamahyáyá* thrada *akunavam* . . . . .
thá khsháyathiya . . . . vajanam . . . . (3) *Dahyáush*
hauva ha*chamá hamitriyá* abava. (4) I. *martiya* . . . imima náma,
'Uvajiyá *awam mathishtam* akunava. (5) Pasáva adam káram fráishayam 'Uvajam. (6) I. *martiya* Gaubaruva náma, *Pársa, maná badaka,*

---

[4] This column has not had the benefit of Col. Rawlinson's later corrections, having been found by him on his last visit inaccessible. The Babylonian and Scythian
transcripts also here fail entirely.

avamshám *ma*tbishtam akunavam.   (7) Pa*sdva haura Gaubaruva hadá
kárá* ashiyava 'Uvajam.   (8) *Hamaranam akunaush hadá hamitriyai-*
bish   (9) *Pasáva* . . . . utáshiya marada utá . . . .
agarbáya utá ániya abiya má*m* . . . . dahyáush
. . . . janam awadá-
shim . . . .

(1) Says Darius the king—(2) This is what I have done; by
the grace of Ormazd, I have accomplished all of it . . . .
. . king . . . . (8) This province revolted against me.   (4)
A man, named . . . . imimus, him the Susianians made their chief.
(5) Then I sent troops to Susiana.   (6) A man, named Gobryas, a
Persian, one of my subjects, him I appointed (to be) their leader.
(7) Then that Gobryas with (his) troops went to Susiana.   (8) He
fought a battle with the rebels.   (9) Then . . . .
and his . . . . and . . . . seized and brought to me . . .
. . . . province . . . . there I
slew him . . . .

Par. 2. (1) *Thátiya Dára*yavush khsháyathiya—(2) . . . .
. utá dah . . . . Auramazdá . . . . áya . . . . vashná
Auramazdáha . . . . thádish akunavam.

(1) Says Darius the king—(2) . . . . and . . . .
Ormazd . . . . by the grace of Ormazd . . . .
. . . . I have done.

Par. 3. (1) *Thátiya Dárayavush khshdyath*iya—(2) Hya aparam imam
y . . . . hatiya utá jivahyá . . . .

(1) Says Darius the king—(2) Whoever may hereafter . . . . . .
. . . this . . . . and of life . . . .

Par. 4. (1) *Thátiya* Dárayavush khsháyath*iya*—(2) . . . .
ashiyavam abiya Sakám . . . . Tigram barataya
. . . . iya abiya darayam, avam . . . . ájanam ;
aniyam ay*arbáyam* . . . . abiya mám, utá . . . .
Sakuka náma, avam ag*arbáyam* . . . . avadá aniyam
math*ishtam* . . . . ám ába ; pasáva da . . . .

(1) Says Darius the king—(2) . . . . I went to Sacia
. . . . the Tigris . . . . towards the sea,
him . . . . I passed over (?) . . . . I slew ;
the enemy I seized . . . . to me, and . . . .
Sacuces by name, him I made prisoner . . . . there the
other leader (?) . . . . it was ; then . . . .

Par. 5. (1) *Thátiya* Dárayavush khsháyath*iya*—(2) . . . . má

niya Auramazdá . . . . yadiya vashná Auramazdáha
. . . . akunavam.

    (1) Says Darius the king—(2) . . . . not Ormazd . . . . .
. . . . by the grace of Ormazd . . . . I have done (it).

Par. 6. (1) Thátiya *Dárayavush khsháyathiya*—(2) . . . . . . Auramazdám
yadáta . . . . utá jivahyá utá . . . .

    (1) Says Darius the king—(2) . . . . Ormazd . . . .
and of life and . . . .

END OF VOL. II.

February, A. D. 1861. By L. E. Chittenden, one of the Delegates. Large
8vo. 626 pp. Cloth. Price, $5.00.

"The only authentic account of its proceedings."—*Indianapolis Journal.*

"It sheds floods of light upon the real causes and impulses of secession and rebellion."—*Christian Times.*

"Will be found an invaluable authority."—*New York Tribune.*

RECENT—PUBLICATIONS

OF

D. APPLETON & COMPANY,

443 and 445 Broadway, New York.

Mercantile Dictionary. A complete

vocabulary of the technicalities of Commercial Correspondence, names of Articles of Trade, and Marine Terms, in English, Spanish, and French ; with Geographical Names, Business Letters, and Tables of the Abbreviations in common use in the three languages. By I. DE VEITELLE. Square 12mo. Half morocco. Price, $3.00.

"A book of most decided necessity to all merchants, filling up a want long felt."—*Journal of Commerce.*
"It is undoubtedly a very important and serviceable work."—*Indianapolis Journal.*

The Mystical Rose; or, Mary of Naza-

reth, the Lily of the House of David. "I am the Rose of Sharon and the Lily of the Valley."—*Canticles.* "Many daughters have done virtuously, but thou excellest them all."—*Solomon.* "Blessed art thou among women."—*Gabriel.* By MARIE JOSEPHENE. 12mo. Cloth extra. Price, $2.00.;

"This elegant and charming book has just appeared ; it is worthy of a place in every family."—*Bellows Falls Times.*
"Its strong devotional character will commend it to many readers."—*Illinois State Journal.*

Cousin Alice: A Memoir of Alice B.

HAVEN. 12mo, pp. 392; with portrait. Cloth. Price, $1.75.

"This is a record of deep interest, compiled with taste, skill, and judgment."—*Christian Times.*
"Exceedingly interesting,"—*Eastern Argus.*
"Written with great vigor and simplicity."—*Boston Post.*

A Report of the Debates and Proceed-

ings in the Secret Sessions of the Conference Convention for Proposing Amendments to the Constitution of the United States, held at Washington, D. C., in February, A. D. 1861. By L. E. CHITTENDEN, one of the Delegates. Large 8vo. 626 pp. Cloth. Price, $5.00.

"The only authentic account of its proceedings."—*Indianapolis Journal.*
"It sheds floods of light upon the real causes and impulses of secession and rebellion."—*Christian Times.*
"Will be found an invaluable authority."—*New York Tribune.*

The Conflict and the Victory of Life.

Memoir of MRS. CAROLINE P. KEITH, Missionary of the Protestant Episcopal Church to India. Edited by her brother, WILLIAM C. TENNEY. "This is the victory that overcometh the world, even our faith."—*St. John*. "Thanks be to God, who giveth us the victory through our Lord Jesus Christ."—*St. Paul*. With portrait. 12mo. Price, $2.00.

"A work of real interest and instruction."—*Buffalo Courier*.

"Books like this are valuable as incentives to good, as monuments of Christian zeal, and as contributions to the practical history of the Church."—*Congregationalist*.

Sermons Preached at the Church of St.

Paul the Apostle, New York, during the year 1864. Second Edition. 18mo. 406 pp. Cloth. Price, $1.50.

"They are all stirring and vigorous, and possess more than usual merit."—*Methodist Protestant*.

"These sermons are short and practical, and admirably calculated to improve and instruct those who read them."—*Commercial Advertiser*.

The Management of Steel, including

Forging, Hardening, Tempering, Annealing, Shrinking, and Expansion, also the Case-Hardening of Iron. By GEORGE EDE, employed at the Royal Gun Factories' Department, Woolwich Arsenal. First American from Second London Edition. 12mo. Cloth. Price, 50 cents.

"This work must be valuable to machinists and workers of Iron and Steel."—*Portland Courier*.

"An instructive essay; it imparts a great deal of valuable information connected with the making of metal."—*Hartford Courant*.

Chateau Frissac; or, Home Scenes in

France. By OLIVE LOGAN, Authoress of "Photographs of Paris Life," etc., etc. Large 12mo. Cloth. Price, $2.00.

"The vivacity and ease of her style are rarely attained in works of this kind and its scenes and incidents are skilfully wrought."—*Chicago Journal*.

"The story is lively and entertaining."—*Springfield Republican*.

The Clever Woman of the Family. By

the Author of "The Heir of Redclyffe," "Heartsease," "The Young Stepmother," etc., etc. With twelve illustrations. 8vo. Paper, $1.50; cloth, $2.00.

"A charming story; fresh, vigorous, and lifelike as the works of this author always are. We are inclined to think that most readers will agree with us in pronouncing it the best which the author has yet produced."—*Portland Press*.

"A new story by this popular writer is always welcome. The 'Clever Woman of the Family,' is one of her best; bright, sharp, and piquant."—*Hartford Courant*.

"One of the cleverest, most genial novels of the times. It is written with great force and fervor. The characters are sketched with great skill."—*Troy Times*.

The Trial. More Links of the Daisy

Chain. By the Author of "The Heir of Redclyffe." Two volumes in one. Large 12mo. 390 pp. Cloth, price $1.75.

"The plot is well developed; the characters are finely sketched; it is a capital novel."—*Providence Journal.*

"It is the best novel we have seen for many months."—*Montreal Gazette.*

"It is marked by all the fascinating qualities of the works that preceded it. * * * Equal to any of her former novels."—*Commercial.*

Too Strange Not to be True. A Tale.

By Lady GEORGIANA FULLERTON, Authoress of "Ellen Middleton," "Ladybird," etc. Three volumes in one. With Illustrations. 8vo. Paper, $1.50; cloth, $2.00.

"This work, which is by far the best of the fair and gifted Authoress, is the most interesting book of fiction that has appeared for years."—*Cairo News*

'It is a strange, exciting, and extremely interesting tale, well and beautifully written. It is likely to become one of the most popular novels of the present day."—*Indianapolis Gazette.*

"A story in which truth and fiction are skilfully blended. It has quite an air of truth, and lovers of the marvellous will find in it much that is interesting."—*Boston Recorder.*

What I Saw on the West Coast of South

and North America, and at the Hawaiian Islands. By H. WILLIS BAXLEY, M.D. With numerous Illustrations. 8vo. 682 pp. Cloth. Price, $4.00.

"With great power of observation, much information, a rapid and graphic style, the author presents a vivid and instructive picture. He is free in his strictures, sweeping in his judgments, but his facts are unquestionable, and his motives and his standard of judgment just."—*Albany Argus.*

"His work will be found to contain a great deal of valuable information, many suggestive reflections, and much graphic and interesting descriptions."—*Portland Express.*

The Conversion of the Roman Empire.

The Boyle Lectures for the year 1864. Delivered at the Chapel Royal, Whitehall, by CHARLES MERIVALE, B.D., Rector of Lawford, Chaplain to the Speaker of the House of Commons, author of "A History of the Romans under the Empire." 8vo. 267 pp. Price, $2.00.

"No man living is better qualified to discuss the subject of this volume, and he has done it with marked ability. He has done it, moreover, in the interest of Christian truth, and manifests thorough appreciation of the spiritual nature and elements of Christianity."—*Evangelist.*

"The author is admirably qualified from his historical studies to connect theology with facts. The subject is a great one, and it is treated with candor, vigor, and abundant command of materials to bring out its salient points."—*Boston Transcript.*

Speeches and Occasional Addresses.

By JOHN A. DIX. 2 vols., 8vo. With portrait. Cloth. Price, $7.00.

"This collection is designed chiefly to make those who are to come after us acquainted with the part I have borne in the national movement during a quarter of a century of extraordinary activity and excitement:"—*Extract from Dedication.*

"General Dix has done a good service to American statesmanship and literature by publishing in a collected form the fruits of his ripe experience and manly sagacity."—*New York Tribune.*

Christian Ballads. By the Right Rev.

A. CLEVELAND COXE, D.D., Bishop of Western New York. Illustrated by John A. Hows. 1 vol., 8vo. 14 full page engravings, and nearly 60 head and tail pieces. Price, cloth extra, $6.00; mor. ant. or extra, $9.00; crushed levant mor., $10.00.

"These ballads have gained for the author an enviable distinction; this work stands almost without a rival."—*Christian Times.*

"Not alone do they breathe a beautiful religious and Christianlike spirit, there is much real and true poetry in them."—*Home Journal.*

Mount Vernon, and other Poems. By

HARVEY RICE. 12mo. Cloth, $1.25; half calf, extra, $3.00; full calf, extra, $4.00.

"Fresh and original in style and in thought. * * * Will be read with much satisfaction."—*Cleveland Leader.*

The Internal Revenue Laws. Act ap-

proved June 30, 1864, as amended, and the Act amendatory thereof approved March 3, 1865. With copious marginal references, a complete Analytical Index, and Tables of Taxation. Compiled by HORACE DRESSER. 8vo. Paper, 60c.; cloth, $1.00.

"An indispensable book for every citizen."

"An accurate and certainly a very complete and convenient manual."—*Congregationalist.*

The Classification of the Sciences. To

which are added Reasons for Dissenting from the Philosophy of M. COMTE. By HERBERT SPENCER, Author of "Illustrations of Universal Progress," "Education," "First Principles," "Essays: Moral, Political, and Æsthetic," and the "Principles of Psychology." 12mo. Paper. Price, 25 cents.

"In a brief, but clear manner, elaborates a plan of classification."—*Hartford Courant.*

"One of the most original and deep thinkers of the age. * * * Will greatly assist all who desire to study Mental Philosophy."—*Philadelphia Press.*

Lyrical Recreations. By Samuel Ward.

Large 12mo. Cloth. Price, $2.00.

"There is a wealth of beauty which discovers itself the more we linger over the book."—*Journal of Commerce.*

"Its pages bear abundant evidence of taste and culture."—*Springfield Republican.*

Orlean Lamar, and Other Poems, by

SARAH E. KNOWLES. 12mo. Cloth. Price, $1.25.

"Not only lively and attractive with fancy, but it has the excellence of being pure, moral, and Christian."—*Religious Herald.*

Lyra Anglicana; or, A Hymnal of Sacred

Poetry. Selected from the best English writers, and arranged after the order of the Apostles' Creed. By the Rev. GEORGE T. RIDER, M.A. 12mo. Cloth, extra, price, $2.00; morocco, or calf antique, price, $5.00.

"As beautiful and valuable a collection of Sacred Poetry as has ever appeared."—*St. Louis Press.*

"Will be found very attractive from the warm devotional tone that pervades it."—*New York Times.*

"Much of the poetry is not found in American reprints."—*Gospel Messenger.*

Lyra Americana; or, Verses of Praise

and Faith, from American Poets. Selected and arranged by the Rev. GEORGE T. RIDER, M.A. 12mo. Cloth, extra price, $2,00; morocco or calf antique, price, $5.00.

"They are selections of the most beautiful and touching poetic expressions of devotion."—*The Chronicle.*

"The collection is purely American; the lyrics are all full of devotion and praise. Unusual taste has been evinced in the selection of the poetry."—*Troy Times.*

On Radiation. The "Rede" Lecture,

delivered in the Senate House before the University of Cambridge, on Tuesday, May 16, 1865, by JOHN TYNDALL, F.R.S., Professor of Natural Philosophy in the Royal Institute and in the Royal School of Mines. Author of "Heat considered as a Mode of Motion." 12mo. Cloth. Price 50 cents.

Contributions to the Geology and the

Physical Geography of Mexico, including a Geological and Topographical Map, with profiles of some of the principal mining districts. Together with a graphic description of an ascent of the volcano Popocatepetl. Edited by Baron F. W. VON EGLOFFSTEIN. Large 8vo. Illustrated. Cloth. Price, $4.

"The general interest excited on this continent as well as in Europe by late political events in Mexico, where a wide field for mining and land speculation is about to be opened again to foreign industry and foreign capital, has induced me to submit to the public two interesting publications of this highly favored region."—*Extract from Introduction.*

Histoire de Jules Cesar.

Par S. M. I. NAPOLEON III. Tome Premier. 8vo. With Maps and Portrait. Cloth. Price, $2.50. Without maps, paper, $1.

"No work has excited as much attention as the Life of Julius Cæsar, by the Emperor Napoleon, which has been so many years in preparation, involving the expenditure of large sums of money in procuring material and examining localities."—*Miss. Republican.*

"We are glad to see it in this form, because we get a clearer insight into the illustrious author through his own vernacular. The original gives the best spirit of a book, and it is always to be preferred."—*Boston Gazette.*

The Handbook of Dining, or Corpulency.

and Leanness Scientifically Considered; comprising the Art of Dining on Correct Principles, Consistent with Easy Digestion, the Avoidance of Corpulency, and the Cure of Leanness. Together with special remarks on the subjects. By BRILLAT-SAVARIN, author of the "Physiologie du Gout." Translated by L. F. SIMPSON. 12mo. Cloth. Price, $1.25.

"This is a book that almost everybody will wish to read, as almost every one is either too fleshy or too lean, and consequently will desire to see what directions so eminent a writer as Savarin gives to prevent one and cure the other. The volume contains curious facts and suggestions, and some very valuable ones."—*Eastern Argus.*

Freedom of Mind in Willing, or Every

Being that Wills a Creative First Cause. By ROWLAND G. HAZARD. 12mo, pp. 455. Cloth. Price, $2.

"It is a very admirable work; a book for thinkers."—*Boston Gazette.*

"A valuable addition to the literature of the subject; its style is clear and its arguments both strong and well put."—*The Methodist.*

Beatrice. By Julia Kavanagh, author

of "Nathalie," "Adele," "Queen Mab," etc., etc. Three volumes in one. 12mo. Cloth. Price, $2.

"This is one of the best novels published in a long time. The authoress has achieved a reputation second to none in the literary world as a romance writer. This is her last great effort, and it is a remarkably interesting one. The plot is a candid embodiment of great ideas and action."—*Troy Times.*

"The scene is laid in one of the suburbs of London. The insight into certain phases of social life which it gives is curious. The heroine 'Beatrice' is a striking character. The plotting Frenchman 'Gervoise' is also drawn with consummate art. In a word, there is more real sturdy stuff in Beatrice than in a score of the current novels of the day."—*Albany Evening Journal.*

Report of the Council of Hygiene and

Public Health of the Citizens' Association of New York upon the Sanitary Condition of the City. Published with an introductory statement, by order of the Council of the Citizens' Association. Large 8vo, 360 pp. Illustrated with numerous maps, plans, and sketches. Cloth. Price, $5.

"Is devoted to a minute account of the causes of disease, death, and misery, and of the sanitary reforms needful to arrest those evils."—*New York Express.*

"No volume of intenser interest has ever seen the light in this city than this record of the state of things now existing. The investigations have been most thorough."—*New York Paper.*

"The result is no mere collection of statistics, but interesting, deeply interesting rehearsals of facts."—*New York Commercial Advertiser.*

At Anchor: A Story of our Civil War,

by an American. 12mo. Cloth. Price, $1.50.

"This is a story of the war, well written and interesting from the beginning to the close. Those who commence will be sure to read it through."—*Boston Journal.*

"A graceful and readable story of flirting and fighting, and love and loyalty."—*Congregationalist.*

Lightning Source UK Ltd.
Milton Keynes UK
UKHW050300261118
332756UK00028B/764/P

9 780265 757345